Building English Skills

Orange Level

Building English Skills

Purple Level

Yellow Level

Blue Level

ORANGE LEVEL

Green Level

Red Level

Gold Level

Silver Level

Aqua Level

Brown Level

Plum Level

Cherry Level (K)

THE McDOUGAL, LITTELL ENGLISH PROGRAM

Building English Skills

Orange Level

McDougal, Littell & Company
Evanston, Illinois
New York   Dallas   Sacramento   Raleigh

Prepared by the Staff of
THE WRITING IMPROVEMENT PROJECT

J. A. Christensen, East High School, Salt Lake City, Utah

Stephen G. Ham, New Trier Township High School East, Winnetka, Illinois

Patricia Phelan, Chairperson, English Department, Hale Jr. High School, San Diego, California

Marcia Baldwin Whipps, East High School, Salt Lake City, Utah

The Staff wishes to thank the more than 1500 students who contributed samples of their writing for analysis.

Consultants

Beth Johnson, English Department Chair, Polk County School District, Lakeland, Florida.

Karen Kutiper, Language Arts Coordinator, Alief Independent School District, Houston, Texas.

Adrian W. McClaren, English Consultant, Memphis City Schools, Memphis, Tennessee.

Julia S. Nichols, English Department Chair, North Area II, Memphis, Tennessee.

Harry H. Raney, Teacher, Memphis School District, Memphis, Tennessee.

ISBN: 0-8123-5550-4   TE ISBN: 0-86609-302-8

Acknowledgments: Simon & Schuster: For entries from *Webster's New World Dictionary,* Student Edition; copyright ©1981 by Simon & Schuster, Inc. Macmillan Publishing Company: Chapters 1 and 6 contain, in revised form, some materials that appeared originally in *English Arts and Skills, Grade 9,* by Ronald J. Wilkins et al, copyright ©1965, 1961 by The Macmillan Company. Used by arrangement. (Acknowledgments are continued on page 725)

2 3 4 5 6 7 8 9 10 11 12 13 14 15 / 90 89 88

Contents

Chapter 13   Critical Thinking   261

Grammar, Usage, and Mechanics

Chapter 1

Building Your Vocabulary

Why does this English book begin with a chapter on building your vocabulary? It begins this way because your success in school and work will depend to a great extent on your knowledge of words. Words are tools that you use in writing, reading, speaking, and listening. They are the tools that you will use in mastering other subjects—history, science, foreign languages, and so on.

Studies have shown that the larger your vocabulary is, the greater your chances are for success in school and in later life. If you study this chapter seriously, you will indeed enlarge your vocabulary. More importantly, you will acquire the *power* to add to your supply of words.

Part 1 Learning Word Meanings from Context

From reading books or viewing television programs, you know that a detective who is called to the scene of a crime examines the surrounding territory for clues that might help to solve the case. In much the same way, you can often learn the meaning of an unfamiliar word by examining the "surrounding territory"—the context in which the word is used. The **context** of a word is the sentence or group of sentences in which the word appears. Often the context of an unfamiliar word will help you determine its meaning.

Several types of context clues can help you discover the meaning of an unfamiliar word. The most common types, all of which you should become familiar with, are these:

1. Definition and restatement
2. Example
3. Comparison
4. Contrast

Once you have learned to use these clues, you can unlock the meanings of many unfamiliar words. With a large vocabulary at your command, you will be able to master your school subjects more quickly and easily. You will also be able to express your own thoughts and feelings more precisely.

Definition and Restatement

Sometimes a writer will reveal the meaning of a word by defining it for you. At other times, the writer may restate an idea in other words. These types of clues are the easiest to detect. Study the example below. What words give you some indication as to the meaning of the italicized word?

> The long climb up the steep cliff was a *grueling* experience—one that left us utterly exhausted.

According to *Webster's New World Dictionary*, *grueling* means "very tiring, exhausting." Notice that the phrase following the dash is nearly the same as the dictionary definition.

Here is another example.

> Howard Hughes spent the last few years of his life *secluded* in hotel suites, shut off from personal contact with even his closest associates.

Even if you do not know the word *secluded*, the context of the passage points to the words "shut off from." One dictionary definition for this word is "barred or shut off from the view of or relations with others." Thus the context provides a definition of the word *secluded*.

The most obvious context clue in this category is the **appositive,** a restatement of the same idea in other words. An appositive is often set off by commas, which makes it easy to identify. Here is an example of this type of restatement.

> The directors of the Bay City Zoo have announced the purchase of a pair of *quetsals*, crested birds native to Central America.

Without the appositive phrase "crested birds native to Central America," you might not know whether *quetsals* were animals or vending machines.

Here is another example of an appositive.

> Uncle Ivan is very fond of *kohlrabi*, a vegetable related to the cabbage.

For people unfamiliar with *kohlrabi*, the appositive phrase "a vegetable related to the cabbage" provides a context clue essential to unlocking the meaning of the word.

By skillful use of the context clue of Definition or Restatement, you will be able to unlock the meanings of many unfamiliar words quickly and easily. You will also be able to use these clues in your own writing as a way to introduce a new term or phrase to your reader.

Example

Context can also help to unlock the meaning of an unfamiliar word by giving one or more examples. When several examples are cited, they achieve a "snowball" effect; that is, they pile up so that, with a little thought, you can make a guess at the meaning of the word. In this type of clue, watch for certain "key" words that will help you unlock the meaning of the unfamiliar word.

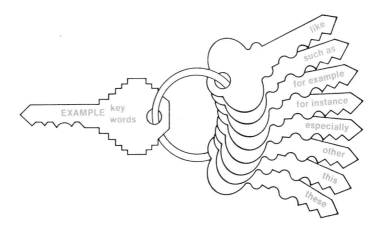

Be alert for key words in the following example.

> A small museum near Vicksburg, Mississippi, contains some excellent examples of Civil War *memorabilia,* such as flags, cannonballs, maps, guns, photographs, and Union and Confederate uniforms.

In this example, several clues help you determine the meaning of *memorabilia.* The word *examples,* the key words *such as,* and the list of examples, all help you understand the meaning of *memorabilia*—"a collection of things worth remembering."
Here is another example.

> The reading teacher must be prepared to deal with *dyslexia* and other reading problems.

The skillful reader can use the key word *other* to help unlock the meaning of *dyslexia*—"a type of reading problem."

Comparison

A third very effective type of context clue is comparison. In this type of clue, the writer compares the unfamiliar word with other, more familiar, words. By paying close attention to these comparisons, you can unlock the meanings of many unfamiliar words.

Certain key words can help you determine the meaning of an unfamiliar word when you use the comparison context clue.

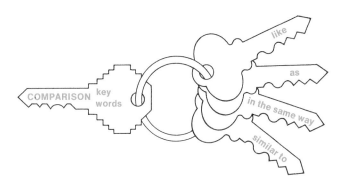

Note how the use of a key word in the following example helps you understand the meaning of the word *dromedary.*

> The *dromedary,* like all other desert animals, can go for long periods of time without drinking water.

Even though the context does not fully reveal that the dromedary is a type of camel, the word *like* helps to point out the dromedary as a type of desert animal. By comparing the unfamiliar word to something more familiar, the writer gives you a key to help unlock the meaning of the unfamiliar word.

Contrast

By contrasting an unfamiliar word with something familiar, the writer of a passage gives you a valuable context clue. Here again, certain key words will help you determine the meaning of the unknown word.

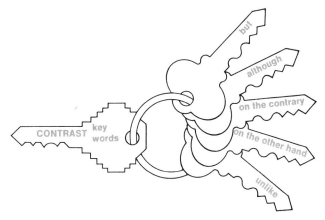

The contrast in the following example helps to clarify the meaning of the word *archaeologist*.

> The *archaeologist,* unlike many other students of ancient history, actually digs in the earth to uncover remains left by former civilizations.

Two context clues help you understand the word *archaeologist* in the example above. The word *unlike* tells you that the archaeologist is being contrasted with someone else. The word *other* tells you that the archaeologist is one student of ancient history. The rest of the sentence tells you that the archaeologist's methods are different from those of the other students of ancient history. Sometimes more than one context clue will be given in a particular sentence.

Exercises Learning Word Meanings from Context

A. The sentences on the next pages contain words with which you may be unfamiliar. Using the context clues that you have just studied, select the *best* meaning for the italicized word in each passage. Write down the letter that you think represents the correct response. After the letter, tell which context clue (or clues) you used to determine the meaning of the italicized word.

1. Several *lustrous* objects added to the brightness of the room, especially the glimmering chrome sculpture, the gleaming crystal chandelier, and the sparkling silver doorknobs.

    A. stolen   B. expensive   C. shining   D. handmade

2. I was simply *petrified* from fright; I couldn't move a muscle.

    A. panicked   B. paralyzed   C. thrilled   D. scared

3. Some nations have unwisely *exploited* their colonies, taking as much wealth out of them as they could.

    A. taken advantage of   C. destroyed
    B. enslaved   D. bought and sold

4. Of course this narrative is *fictitious;* it has no basis in fact.

    A. colorful   C. important
    B. changeable   D. imaginary

5. The story was too *somber.* I prefer something with a more cheerful setting.

    A. sleepy   B. sad   C. lengthy   D. noisy

6. Paul's *scrupulous* attention to detail, such as dotting every *i,* crossing every *t,* and forming every letter perfectly, makes his handwriting a pleasure to read.

    A. careless   C. very careful
    B. left-handed   D. occasional

7. SALT, for Strategic Arms Limitation Talks, and NATO, for North Atlantic Treaty Organization, are examples of *acronyms.*

    A. governmental agencies
    B. important business organizations
    C. words formed from the first letter of other words
    D. words borrowed from foreign languages

8. Although the cheerleaders maintained their usual *exuberance*, the fans silently mourned the team's tenth consecutive loss.

    A. high spirits   C. appearance
    B. embarrassment   D. routine

9. The works of two *prolific* authors, Agatha Christie and William Shakespeare, fill several shelves in most libraries.

    A. poor   C. respected
    B. producing many works   D. lucky

10. The sign beside the beautiful fountain in Rome contained the warning AQUA NON POTABLE. Those who failed to heed this *admonition* became sick from drinking the water.

    A. invitation   B. information   C. sign   D. warning

B. Read the following passage very carefully. Copy the underlined words on a sheet of paper. After each word, write your idea of the meaning of the word. Check your meaning with a dictionary. (You may want to review the types of context clues before you begin.)

    Shortly after the *Golden Clipper* left Pago Pago, several of the crew members became ill with enterocolitis. Since everyone who suffered from this intestinal disorder had eaten at the same cafe, the ship's doctor surmised that the crew members had contracted this disease by eating tainted fish.

    The government of the Philippines, however, fearing the spread of a contagion, refused to let the ship dock in Manila Bay. Instead, the entire crew was transferred to a lazaretto floating three miles offshore. A staff of doctors and nurses cared for those who were ill and carefully observed the other crew members for any signs of the malady. When no new cases developed after three days, the Philippine doctors ruled out any possibility of a contagion. The ailing crew members were then transferred to a hospital in Manila, and the others were permitted to return to the *Golden Clipper* and dock in Manila Bay.

C. Choose a feature article from a newspaper or a magazine. The article can be about fashion, sports, or any other subject. Read the article carefully. When you come across an unfamiliar word, copy the sentence in which it appears. Using the skills you have learned for unlocking the meanings of new words, write the definition you have determined from the context clue. Be ready to point out the context clue that helped you unlock the meaning of the word.

Part 2   Inferring Word Meanings

The context in which an unfamiliar word appears does not always provide clues as obvious as the ones in the examples you have just seen. Instead of directly stating the meaning of the word, the writer may just imply certain things. The reader must read between the lines to pick up clues. This process of reading between the lines to reach some conclusion is called **inference.** Most of the context clues you used in Part 1 were found in the same sentence with the unfamiliar word. When you are trying to **infer** the meaning of a word, you will frequently have to look elsewhere in the paragraph, or at the paragraph as a whole.

There are five common types of inferences used to determine word meaning from context. These are inferences based on main ideas, stated details, cause and effect relationships, implied comparison, and implied contrast. Each one requires a slightly different approach.

Inference Based on the Main Idea

The main idea of the paragraph that follows concerns the meaning of the term *planned obsolescence.* No doubt, you already know the meaning of *planned,* but you may not know the meaning of *obsolescence.*

> Much of the American economy is based on the principle of *planned obsolescence.* Consumer groups have criticized manufacturers for turning out products that are designed to wear out in a short time, although the technology exists to make longer-lasting products. Criticism has also been directed at the automobile industry for "brainwashing" the consumer into believing that a year-old car is outdated as soon as the new models go on sale.

From the main idea of this paragraph, you can infer that *obsolescence* means one of the following:

A. investment   C. high prices
B. uselessness or outdatedness   D. patriotism

Inference Based on Stated Details

The various details in the following paragraph help you infer the meaning of *impromptu.*

> It was an intensely hot summer Sunday. Most of the neighbors were indoors with air conditioners and color TVs going full blast. Suddenly, there was a power failure. After about a half hour, most houses had lost their pleasing coolness, and people began to drift outdoors in search of a gentle breeze. Before long, everyone was sharing soda, lemonade, and iced tea. Food began to appear, someone fetched picnic tables, and an *impromptu* block party developed. All around me, people were getting acquainted, and no one seemed to care that the power was still off. Nor did the spirit of the party die with the end of the evening. We have since organized a block softball team and a number of charity projects. Ever since that power failure, our neighborhood has been a more pleasant place to live.—PETER PAGE

From the details stated in this paragraph, you can infer that *impromptu* means one of the following:

A. done without previous preparation
B. carefully planned and organized
C. exciting and lively
D. wooden and uninteresting

Inference Based on Cause and Effect Relationship

You read the following passage in Part 1 to determine by context the meaning of *admonition.* As you read the passage this time, note that the effect, or outcome, of an action is stated in the paragraph. See if you can correctly infer the meaning of the Italian phrase AQUA NON POTABLE.

> The sign beside the beautiful fountain in Rome carried the warning AQUA NON POTABLE. Those who failed to heed this admonition became sick from drinking the water.

The cause and effect relationship in this passage leads you to infer that the Italian phrase means one of the following:

A. keep off the grass
B. no swimming
C. water for horses only
D. undrinkable water

Inference Based on Implied Comparison

From the implied comparisons in the following passage, try to infer the meaning of *amalgam*.

> Sonia's pleasing personality is an *amalgam* of the most desirable traits of the other members of her family. She has her father's cheerfulness, her mother's sense of humor, and her grandfather's calmness.

From the comparisons in this passage, you can infer that *amalgam* means one of the following:

A. combination
B. denial
C. mockery
D. delight

Inference Based on Implied Contrast

The contrasts in the following passage should enable you to infer the meaning of *transformation*.

> Sophia took a hard look at him; an astounding *transformation* had taken place. No longer did he appear lackluster or even middle-aged. His expression sparkled, his clean-shaven face was flooded with color; he had shifted his shoulders about until his coat fitted him the way the tailor had meant it to; he bristled with a youthful zest and energy. . . . But most important for her were his eyes, now bright, clear, knowledgeable, the lids opened wide to let in all the sights the world had to bestow upon an eager and penetrating mind—IRVING STONE

What is the best meaning for *transformation* in this passage?

A. accident
B. change
C. movement
D. sin

Exercise Inferring Word Meanings

Read each of the following passages in its entirety. Then reread each passage, paying particular attention to the italicized word or words. Based on your understanding of the passage, try to infer the meaning of each of the italicized words. Write your inference and check it in a dictionary.

1   Many politicians are masters at the art of *circumlocution*. This fact is often best illustrated in press conferences. In response to a controversial question posed by a reporter, some politicians can talk for several minutes without ever really answering the question.

2   Most Americans would find it difficult to adapt to the *ascetic* lifestyle of a monk. Garage door openers, dishwashers, garbage disposers, stereos, and color televisions—the luxuries that many pampered Americans consider necessities—are missing from the life of a Franciscan monk.

3   The sudden collapse of the Brennan Dam sent a *torrent* of devastation into the St. Thomas Valley. Within a matter of hours, however, numerous organizations and individuals met the *exigency* of the situation with food, clothing, shelter, and medical help.

4   A true *gastronome* like Julia Child is probably unimpressed by the billions of hamburgers sold by fast food, carry-out restaurants. Better known as "The French Chef," Mrs. Child is the author of a number of books on French cooking. For her, the measure of cooking rests more in the quality than in the quantity of the final product.

5   The immediate destruction caused by the earthquake was much less than the destruction caused by the *ensuing holocaust*. The earthquake ruptured gas and water lines throughout the city. Without a water supply the firefighters were unable to combat the fires fueled by the broken gas lines.

6   The Better Business Bureau is investigating a new product that claims to cure practically every type of human ailment. It

claims to bring immediate relief for arthritis, headaches, colds, vitamin deficiency, low vitality, backache, and sleeplessness. Because of the *preposterous* claims of the new medicine, the suspicions of the medical profession have been aroused.

Part 3   Analyzing Word Parts To Determine Meaning

In the preceding two chapter parts, you learned to determine the meaning of a word by examining the sentence or paragraph in which it appears. Sometimes, however, the word itself contains all of the information you need to figure out its meaning.

Many large English words are composed of smaller units, called **word parts.** Each word part carries its own specific meaning. If you combine the meanings of the individual parts, you can often determine the meaning of the entire word.

In order to complete this type of analysis, you must first be able to recognize the smaller units that can make up a word. You can begin by learning about three basic types of word parts: base words, prefixes, and suffixes.

Base Words

Base words are shorter English words that lie at the heart of longer words. Other word parts may be added to a base to create new words. What base word was used to make all of the words in the following list?

distrust   trustful
mistrust   distrustful

The word, of course, is *trust.* The beginnings *dis-* and *mis-* were added to it. The ending *-ful* was also added. You can see that adding these parts resulted in new words, each with its own distinct meaning. However, you also know that all of the words still have something to do with the idea of "belief in the reliability of some person or thing." This gives you a starting point for determining the meaning of the longer word. You can complete the process if you understand the meaning of the other word parts, prefixes and suffixes.

Prefixes

A **prefix** is one or more syllables placed at the beginning of a base word to change the meaning of the base word. Many new words can be made simply by adding a prefix to a base word. For example:

PREFIX	+	BASE WORD	=	NEW WORD
in-	+	correct	=	incorrect
extra-	+	ordinary	=	extraordinary
mis-	+	manage	=	mismanage

Every prefix has one or more meanings. If you can identify the prefix and the base word, you can often determine the meaning of the longer word. You need only know the meaning of both parts.

The prefixes in the following chart mean "not" or "the opposite of." For example, *appropriate* means "fitting" or "suitable." The word *inappropriate* means "not suitable."

Prefixes That Mean "Not" or "the Opposite of"

PREFIX	EXAMPLE	WORD MEANING
in-	inconsiderate	not considerate
ir-	irregular	not regular
im-	immobile	not mobile
il-	illegible	not legible
dis-	disclaim	opposite of claim
un-	unknown	not known
non-	nonpoisonous	not poisonous

The following prefixes show relationships in time or space. For example, *subsoil* means "the *lower* layer of soil."

Prefixes That Show Relationships in Time or Space

PREFIX	PREFIX MEANING	EXAMPLE	WORD MEANING
sub-	beneath, under, lower	subcommittee	a committee under the control of another committee
pre-	before	prepaid	paid ahead of time
post-	after	postdated	dated after a certain date
super-	over, above, beyond	superstructure	structure built above another
extra-	outside, beyond	extralegal	outside the law

The following prefixes show judgment. For example, *malpractice* means "improper practice."

Prefixes That Show Judgment

PREFIX	PREFIX MEANING	EXAMPLE	WORD MEANING
pro-	in favor of	probusiness	in favor of business
anti-	against	antimissile	a device that acts against a missile
mis-	wrong	misplace	put in the wrong place
mal-	bad or badly, wrong	malnourished	not properly nourished

When you analyze words, be careful not to confuse words that have prefixes with words that contain letters that only resemble prefixes. For example, *prepaid* is a base word with a prefix. *Pressure* is simply a word that contains the letters *p, r,* and *e.*

Suffixes

A **suffix** is one or more syllables placed at the end of a base word to form a new word. Each suffix has its own meaning or meanings. When you can recognize suffixes and attach meanings to them, you can use them to determine the meanings of longer words. See how suffixes have been added to the following base words to form new words.

BASE WORD	+	SUFFIX	=	NEW WORD
compose	+	-er	=	composer
friend	+	-ship	=	friendship
fury	+	-ous	=	furious

Notice that the spelling of a base word may change when a suffix is added. In the examples above, the silent *e* was dropped from *compose*, when *-er* was added. The final *y* in *fury* was changed to *i* when *-ous* was added.

Noun Suffixes

Noun suffixes are those suffixes that make nouns out of the base words they are added to. The suffixes in the following chart all change their base words into a particular type of noun.

Noun Suffixes That Mean "One Who Does Something" or "That Which Does Something"

SUFFIX	EXAMPLE	WORD MEANING
-eer	puppeteer	one who operates puppets
-er,-or	computer conductor	that which computes one who conducts
-ist	physicist	one who studies or is experienced in physics
-ian	electrician	one who works with electric devices

The words that you find listed in the following chart are all **abstract words.** That is, they describe a state of being or a quality. For example, *boredom* is the state of being bored. *Cleverness* is the quality that makes a person clever. Remember that the spelling of a base word may change when a suffix is added to it. The *e* in the word *wise,* for instance, is dropped when the suffix *-dom* is added.

Noun Suffixes That Make Abstract Words

SUFFIX	EXAMPLES
-dom	boredom, wisdom
-hood	statehood, womanhood
-ism	patriotism, realism
-ment	settlement, encouragement
-ness	cleverness, kindness
-ship	leadership, friendship
-ty	certainty, frailty
-ity	sanity, rapidity

Adjective Suffixes

Adjective suffixes change base words to adjectives — words that describe or modify other words. Study the following charts to learn about different types of adjective suffixes.

Adjective Suffixes That Mean "Full of"

SUFFIX	EXAMPLE	WORD MEANING
-ous	glorious	full of glory
-ful	graceful	full of grace

The adjective suffixes listed in the chart on the next page mean "relating to" or "pertaining to."

Adjective Suffixes That Mean "Relating to" or "Pertaining to"

SUFFIX	EXAMPLE	WORD MEANING
-al	regional	relating to a region
-ic	angelic	like an angel
-ical	historical	pertaining to history
-ish	stylish	relating to style

The adjective suffixes in the following chart mean exactly what they say.

Adjective Suffixes That Mean What They Say

SUFFIX	EXAMPLE	WORD MEANING
-able, -ible	imaginable	something that one is able to imagine
	digestible	something that is able to be digested
-most	foremost	being at the very fore (front)
-less	blameless	without blame
-like	catlike	like a cat

Exercises Examining Word Parts

A. Determine the meaning of the prefix in each of the following words. Then write the meaning of the prefix next to the meaning of the base word to find the meaning of each complete word.

1. imprecise
2. nonbinding
3. superstar
4. antifreeze
5. inaccurate
6. disallow
7. substructure
8. postwar
9. misquote
10. irregular
11. unbound
12. prearrange
13. extraordinary
14. malpractice
15. impractical

B. Determine the meaning of the suffix in each word on the next page. Then write the meaning of the base word next to the meaning of the suffix to find the meaning of each complete word.

1. auctioneer	6. calculator	11. violinist
2. statistician	7. knighthood	12. consumerism
3. agreement	8. likeness	13. authorship
4. humanity	9. outrageous	14. tactful
5. global	10. curable	15. matchless

C. Determine the meanings of the prefixes and suffixes in each of the following words. Then write the meaning of each complete word by adding the meanings of the prefix and suffix to the meaning of the base word.

1. inexcusable	6. irregularity
2. impracticality	7. disadvantageous
3. nonconformist	8. precolonial
4. mismanagement	9. malodorous
5. uncontrollable	10. extraterritorial

Part 4 Applying Your Skills

You now have several useful tools for unlocking the meanings of words. The following exercises will allow you to practice using these tools. The exercises are much like those you will encounter in the vocabulary sections of standardized tests. Use the skills you have learned in this chapter to unlock the meanings of the words.

Section 1: *Determining Word Meanings from Context.* Select the best meaning for the italicized word in each passage. Write the letter that represents the best answer.

1. The detective *surmised* that the man was lying. Her guess was right.

(A) knew (C) worried
(B) guessed (D) solved

2. A rainbow is an *evanescent* thing; it gradually disappears, leaving only a memory.

(A) temporary (C) even; balanced
(B) shaped like an arch (D) beautiful

3. Like any other beginner, a *novice* in the kitchen will make mistakes.

    (A) cook   (C) helper
    (B) young person   (D) someone new to an activity

4. Places of *egress,* such as the plane's doors and removable windows, must be clearly labeled.

    (A) public transportation   (C) exit
    (B) mistake   (D) first-aid stations

5. Tell me the *gist* of the movie. I don't have time for a long description right now.

    (A) rating   (C) complete explanation
    (B) characters   (D) main idea

6. The child was *precocious.* She could read before she started nursery school.

    (A) hard to manage   (C) likely to brag
    (B) ahead in development (D) very young

7. *Avarice* is different from other kinds of greed in that its sole object is money.

    (A) wealth   (C) greed for food
    (B) a sickness (D) strong desire for money

8. The coach had strict rules for the team. New players had trouble obeying such *stringent* orders.

    (A) athletic   (C) rigorous
    (B) unfair   (D) limp, like string

9. I like a *succinct* sports announcement, not one that rambles.

    (A) brief; clear   (C) wise; well-informed
    (B) witty; joking   (D) wordy; repetitious

10. A guinea pig is *vulnerable.* It can't fight well, it can't run fast, and it has no tough hide nor bad scent to protect it.

    (A) hopeless   (C) popular pet
    (B) lovable   (D) easily hurt

11. Although he isn't handsome, he has a *winsome* manner. Everyone considers him charming and likeable.

(A) ugly   (C) talkative
(B) pleasing   (D) conceited

12. Tom Sawyer didn't *cajole* his friends into painting the fence. He made the job look like so much fun that his friends paid him to let them do it.

(A) lead   (C) coax
(B) teach   (D) worry

13. Such *heinous* crimes as murder or kidnapping usually receive the harshest punishments.

(A) rare   (C) very wicked
(B) against the law   (D) improper

14. The agency's activities were *covert*. No outsiders knew anything about them.

(A) illegal   (C) dangerous
(B) secret   (D) governmental

15. Backstage, the rock star sulked, complained, and growled at the band. His *petulant* manner, however, disappeared on stage.

(A) nervous and shy   (C) irritable and bad-tempered
(B) annoying   (D) too confident

Section 2: *Inferring Word Meanings.* Read each passage. Write the letter that represents the best definition of the italicized word.

1.   The Battle of Antietam was the bloodiest twelve hours of the Civil War; 22,719 soldiers were killed or wounded. Yet Clara Barton did not turn back in horror from the *carnage* of the battlefield. She had taken upon herself the duty of nursing the injured. She did not flinch from stepping across corpses to tend to the mangled survivors.

carnage

(A) combat   (C) filth
(B) enemy   (D) mass killing

2. When news broke that a tanker had spilled tons of oil off-shore, students from the local high school rushed to the beach. There they bathed oil from the feathers of helpless seabirds so that the birds could fly again. The students had *mitigated* at least some of the damage caused by the spill.

mitigated

(A) made worse (C) caused
(B) made milder or less serious (D) ignored

3. The letter from home had a *salutary* influence on Ginger. Its effect was like that of a swim on a hot day or a thermos of lemonade during a long hike.

salutary

(A) favorable; good (C) warming
(B) honorable (D) unpleasant; uncomfortable

4. Kevin's new *lassitude* worried his family. He no longer dashed cheerfully from task to task or from one pleasure to another. He seemed to have lost his enthusiasm for whatever the day might bring.

lassitude

(A) great tiredness (C) pep; enthusiasm
(B) a small lasso (D) loss of self-respect

5. A severe back injury had forced Eileen Gardner into a rather *sedentary* life. For months she did little more than watch television and do light chores around the house. Originally a capable athlete, her muscles were beginning to *atrophy*. Then Eileen Gardner decided to fight back.

sedentary

(A) used to sitting; getting little exercise (C) sad
(B) used to running; active (D) angry

atrophy

(A) waste away (C) strengthen
(B) develop (D) became tight

6.   The damage caused by the testing of the new insecticide has angered local residents. In an attempt to *mollify* its outraged neighbors, the Kental Corporation has offered to make *restitution* for any damage. The offer is not enough. Residents say that no amount of money can make up for the fear, worry, or loss of crops that has resulted from the testing.

mollify

(A) make fun of   (C) accuse
(B) soothe   (D) mislead

restitution

(A) a place of rest   (C) the act of paying or
(B) refusal to be responsible   making up for damage
                               (D) apologies

7.   Friday was the *antithesis* of the rest of that whole, miserable week. The sun shone for the first time, the air was warm, and the pools of water began slowly to evaporate. Although the pleasant weather could not really make up for the damage caused by the storm, it could at least *alleviate* the depression of those who had lived through it.

antithesis

(A) cause   (C) last day
(B) opposite   (D) best

alleviate

(A) give a reason for   (C) increase
(B) prepare for   (D) relieve

Section 3: *Examining Word Parts.* Write the letter that represents the best definition for each italicized word.

1. *antislavery*
   (A) after slavery   (C) opposed to, or against, slavery
   (B) before slavery   (D) in favor of, or for, slavery

2. *postdate*
   (A) to occur after   (C) a special occasion
   (B) to occur before   (D) in favor of dating

3. *disquiet*
   - (A) a quiet mood
   - (B) the lack of mental peace; uneasiness
   - (C) anger; disgust
   - (D) sudden

4. *illimitable*
   - (A) not legal
   - (B) one who places limits
   - (C) able to be confined
   - (D) without limit; infinite

5. *pro-American*
   - (A) not an American
   - (B) a professional athlete
   - (C) opposed to America
   - (D) in favor of America

6. *nonmetallic*
   - (A) not made of metal
   - (B) like metal
   - (C) an unknown metal
   - (D) a metalworker

7. *supernatural*
   - (A) frightening
   - (B) fiction
   - (C) related to things beyond the natural world
   - (D) less than natural

8. *inglorious*
   - (A) full of glory
   - (B) dishonorable
   - (C) beautiful; magnificent
   - (D) someone who wins an honor

9. *mischance*
   - (A) luck; fortune
   - (B) misconduct
   - (C) another chance; second try
   - (D) bad luck; unlucky incident

10. *impracticality*
    - (A) that which is impossible to practice
    - (B) perfectly possible
    - (C) involvement in some sort of preparation
    - (D) a condition of not being practical

SUMMARY AND APPLICATIONS CHAPTER 1

1. One way to determine the meaning of an unfamiliar word is to look at its context. The **context** of a word is the sentence or group of sentences in which the word appears. Context clues include definition or restatement, example, comparison, and contrast.

2. Another method of determining word meaning is **inference**. To infer meaning, the reader must "read between the lines" to reach a conclusion about the word.

3. The meanings of **prefixes** and **suffixes** can help unlock word meanings. Prefixes and suffixes are word parts added to a base word to form new words.

4. These word-attack techniques may be used whenever you come across unfamiliar words. They may also be used in the vocabulary sections of standardized tests. The expanded vocabulary you acquire will help you to speak and write more precisely.

Applications in Other Subject Areas

Science / **Math** / **English.** Start a vocabulary notebook. Label several pages with the names of your courses. You may use classes other than those listed above. In this notebook, record the new words and definitions that you learn in your classes. Note with symbols which meanings you were able to determine from context (C), which meanings from the word parts (WP), and which meanings from dictionaries or other formal sources of definitions (D).

Biology
1. antibody— a substance that works against harmful elements (WP)
2. gene — a unit on the chromosome by which hereditary characteristics are passed on (D)
3. catalyst— something that causes a process to happen or to be speeded up (C)

Chapter 2

The Dictionary as a Key to Word Power

If you were trying to improve your skill in some sport, you would know where to look for help. You could ask your coach to evaluate your skills. You could study the techniques of another player. You could read a book or an article about the subject. You might even study a film or videotape of yourself in action.

As you work to improve your vocabulary skills, you also have several sources to which you can turn. Often, you can ask a friend or teacher to define an unfamiliar word. Sometimes the words themselves or the contexts in which they appear provide helpful information. Your best source, however, is a book that you have used for years, but with which you might not be very familiar even now. This book is the dictionary.

This chapter will teach you how to read and use a dictionary. It will provide the key with which you can unlock this amazing treasure chest of information.

Part 1 Finding Information in a Dictionary

Abridged and Unabridged Dictionaries

There are two main types of dictionaries that you should learn to use—unabridged and abridged. An **unabridged dictionary** is as complete as its writers and editors can make it. It is a huge volume containing information about hundreds of thousands of words. You can find an unabridged dictionary in the reference section of your school or public library. Occasionally you will need to use an unabridged dictionary, but many of the words in an unabridged dictionary are words that people rarely use.

For most of your work, you will use an **abridged dictionary.** The word *abridged* simply means "shortened." The smaller size of an abridged dictionary makes it easier to use. In addition to being aware of these two main classifications of dictionaries, you should also familiarize yourself with the many specialized dictionaries that are available. See Chapter 14, "Using the Library," for a list of dictionaries that you are likely to find useful.

As you examine the different types of dictionaries, remember that no two dictionaries are quite the same. Dictionaries may be organized differently, and they may use different symbols and abbreviations. Try to work with and become familiar with one dictionary. If you work with one dictionary consistently, you will soon find it easy to use and understand.

What You Will Find on a Dictionary Page

Although some aspects of a dictionary vary from book to book, certain elements are standard. Among these are the general design of a dictionary page and the types of information presented. We will begin by looking at the dictionary page as a whole.

On pages 32 and 33, you will find a reproduction of a dictionary page. As you study the information that follows, refer to that reproduced page.

1. Guide Words. At the top of each dictionary page are two words in large type. These **guide words** tell you the first and last words that you will find on that page. Beneath the guide words are the words that fall between the guide words. They are listed in alphabetical order. The guide words help speed up the process of locating a word.

Not all dictionaries alphabetize words in the same way. The introduction to your dictionary will explain how words are alphabetized in that dictionary. (This information will help you decide, for example, whether to look for *Mt. Rushmore* under *mt-* or *mo-*.)

2. Entry. An **entry** is the information given about a word. Different dictionaries give different types of information, and may list the information in different orders.

3. Key. In most dictionaries, a **key to pronunciation** is printed on the bottom of each right-hand page. This key explains the symbols used to show how words are pronounced. A fuller set of symbols and abbreviations is printed at the front or back of the dictionary.

What You Will Find in a Dictionary Entry

Different dictionaries may contain different types of information. However, there are certain elements of a dictionary entry that are somewhat standard. These elements are listed below. Refer to the reproduced dictionary page as you study each item. Each entry on that page follows this general pattern:

1. entry word
2. pronunciation (or pronunciations)
3. part of speech
4. etymology
5. definition (or definitions)
6. synonymy
7. words derived from the entry word
8. cross-reference

Not every item is included in every entry.

1. Entry Words. Each **entry word** is printed in dark type and divided into syllables. Sometimes, when you are writing or typing a paper, you may have to divide a long word at the end of a line. The divisions in the entry words show how to divide the word correctly.

Occasionally you will see what appears to be the same entry word listed twice. Each entry is followed by a small, raised number. Such words are **homographs**—words with the same spelling but with totally unrelated meanings. See the entries for *pale* for examples of homographs.

2. Pronunciation. The **pronunciation** of each word is given in parentheses, directly following the entry word. By using the pronunciation key at the bottom of the page, you can determine the pronunciations. If a word has more than one acceptable pronunciation, or if the word is pronounced in different ways at different times (for example, *address*), those differences will be shown and explained. Like the entry word itself, the pronunciations are also divided to show syllables. It is important to notice that pronunciation divisions and end-of-line divisions are not always the same.

3. Part of Speech. Following the pronunciation of the word *palate* is the letter *n*. It indicates that *palate* is a noun. Often a word can function as more than one part of speech. If so, other part-of-speech abbreviations will be found somewhere in the entry. A key to these abbreviations can be found in the front or back of the dictionary. If the plural of a noun is not formed by simply adding -*s* or -*es*, the correct spelling of the plural will also be given at this point.

4. Etymology. Some words are quite new, and others are ancient. However, every word has a history. Many words have been borrowed from other languages. Some were derived from the names of people or places. Still others were invented only this year to describe new ideas or inventions. (See Chapter 3, "Using Language for Different Purposes," for a discussion of how words are created.)

The history of a word is told in its **etymology**, which traces the word back to its origins. In the entry for *palette*, you will find that *palette* comes from a French word spelled the same way, which in turn came from the Latin word *pala*, meaning "a shovel." The symbols and abbreviations used in etymologies will be explained in the front or back of your dictionary.

5. Definition. Following the etymology, you will find the **definition** of the word. For most words, you will find more than one meaning listed in the definition. It is a good idea to read *all* the listed meanings, even if you think you have found the one you want at once. You may find another that is more specific, or more suitable to the context in which it is used.

6. Synonymy. A **synonymy** is a list of words that are similar in meaning to the entry word. Notice the abbreviation **SYN.** after the definition of *pale*[1]. Here you find a discussion of words that are similar in meaning to *pale*. This synonymy points out the slight differences in the meanings of *pale, pallid, wan, ashen,* and *livid*. The abbreviation **ANT.** at the end of the synonymy introduces antonyms for *pale*, words with the opposite meaning. The synonymy can be an invaluable aid when you write. Use it to help you choose the most precise synonym for a term or idea.

7. Derived Words. Following some dictionary entries, you will notice additional words, printed in bold type and divided. These are words that are **derived** from the entry word. These words are so closely related to the entry word that the editors of the dictionary did not feel it necessary to list them as separate entries. See the entry for *paleontology* for an example.

8. Cross-Reference. A **cross-reference** directs you to another entry for more information. At the end of the etymology for *palaver*, the word PARABLE in small capital letters tells you that additional information about the etymology can be found in the entry for *parable*. If you look closely, you will find additional cross-references on this page.

Other Information. Certain abbreviations and symbols provide you with additional information about a word. For example, a star ☆ sometimes marks a usage that first appeared in our country. Check the front or back of your dictionary for a key to other abbreviations and symbols.

Exercises Learning How To Use the Dictionary

A. Answer the questions below. They will help you decide how well you understand what information you can get from a dictionary.

1. What is an etymology?
2. What is a synonymy?
3. What is a derived word?
4. What is a cross-reference?
5. What is a key?

B. The following questions refer to the sample dictionary page reproduced on pages 32 and 33. Some answers will be found in the pronunciation key.

1. What is the etymology of the word *palliate*?

2. Which synonym for *pale* suggests the paleness resulting from a serious illness?

3. Would you expect a person who was interested in paleography to be interested in ancient Egyptian hieroglyphics?

4. Which of the words below is a palindrome?

          clip   loop   lap   deed

5. What derived form of *Palestine* is listed?

6. Where would you find information about the etymology of the word *palatial*?

7. Which definition of *palisade* is an Americanism?

8. List two familiar words that have the same vowel sound as the vowels in *Palawan*.

C. Use your own dictionary to answer the following questions.

1. List the abbreviations used in the etymologies for these languages: Latin, Greek, French, Middle English, Hungarian.
2. What words are synonyms for *humble*?
3. Copy the pronunciation for *narwhal*.
4. How many meanings are given for *paradox*?
5. Where could you divide the word *consonant* at the end of a line of writing?

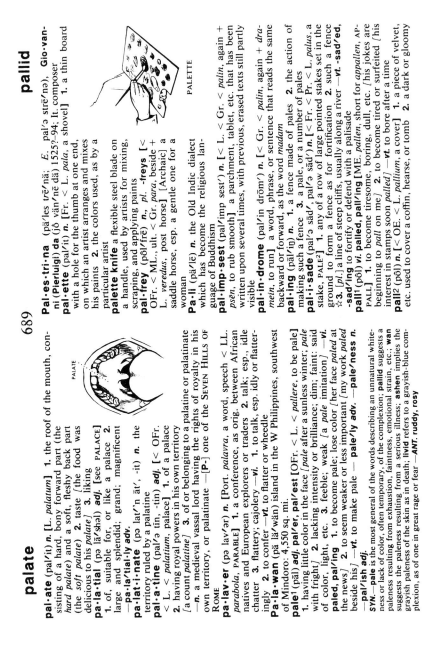

pal·ate (pal′it) *n.* [L. *palatum*] **1.** the roof of the mouth, consisting of a hard, bony forward part (the *hard palate*) and a soft, fleshy back part (the *soft palate*) **2.** taste [the food was delicious to his *palate*] **3.** liking

pa·la·tial (pə lā′shəl) *adj.* [see PALACE] **1.** of, suitable for, or like a palace **2.** large and splendid; grand; magnificent —**pa·la′tial·ly** *adv.*

pal·at·i·nate (pə lat′′n āt′, -it) *n.* the territory ruled by a palatine

pal·a·tine (pal′ə tin, -tin) *adj.* [< OFr. < L. < *palatium*, palace] **1.** of a palace **2.** having royal powers in his own territory [a count *palatine*] **3.** of or belonging to a palatinate or palatinate —*n.* **a** medieval vassal lord having the rights of royalty in his own territory, or palatinate —[**P-**] one of the SEVEN HILLS OF ROME

pa·la·ver (pə lav′ər) *n.* [Port. *palavra*, a word, speech < LL. *parabola*, PARABLE] **1.** a conference, as orig. between African natives and European explorers or traders **2.** talk; esp., idle chatter **3.** flattery; cajolery —*vi.* **1.** to talk, esp. idly or flatteringly **2.** to confer —*vt.* to flatter or wheedle

Pa·la·wan (pä lä′wän) island in the W Philippines, southwest of Mindoro: 4,550 sq. mi.

pale[1] (pāl) *adj.* **pal′er, pal′est** [OFr. < L. < *pallere*, to be pale] **1.** having little color in the face [*pale* after a sunless winter; *pale* with fright] **2.** lacking intensity or brilliance; dim; faint: said of color, light, etc. **3.** feeble; weak [a *pale* imitation] —*vi.* **1.** to become pale; lose color [her face *paled* at the news] **2.** to seem weaker or less important [my work *paled* beside his] —*vt.* to make pale —**pale′ly** *adv.* —**pale′ness** *n.* —**pal′ish** *adj.*

SYN.—**pale** is the most general of the words describing an unnatural whiteness or lack of color, often temporary, of the complexion; **pallid** suggests a paleness resulting from exhaustion, faintness, emotional strain, etc.; **wan** suggests the paleness resulting from a serious illness; **ashen** implies the grayish paleness of the skin as in death; **livid** refers to a grayish-blue complexion, as of one in great rage or fear —**ANT.** ruddy, rosy

PALETTE

Pal·es·tri·na (pä′les trē′nä; *E.* pal′ə strē′nə), **Gio·van·ni** (**Pierluigi**) **da** (jō vän′nē dä) 1525?-94; It. composer

pal·ette (pal′it) *n.* [Fr. < L. *pala*, a shovel] **1.** a thin board with a hole for the thumb at one end, on which an artist arranges and mixes his paints **2.** the colors used, as by a particular artist

palette knife a flexible steel blade on a handle, used by artists for mixing, scraping, and applying paints

pal·frey (pôl′frē) *n., pl.* **-freys** [< OFr. < ML., ult. < Gr. *para*, beside + L. *veredus*, post horse] [Archaic] a saddle horse, esp. a gentle one for a woman

Pa·li (pä′lē) *n.* the Old Indic dialect which has become the religious language of Buddhism

pal·imp·sest (pal′imp sest′) *n.* [< L. < Gr. < *palin*, again + *psēn*, to rub smooth] a parchment, tablet, etc. that has been written upon several times, with previous, erased texts still partly visible

pal·in·drome (pal′in drōm′) *n.* [< Gr. < *palin*, again + *dramein*, to run] a word, phrase, or sentence that reads the same backward or forward, as the word *madam*

pal·ing (pāl′iŋ) *n.* **1.** a fence made of pales **2.** the action of making such a fence **3.** a pale, or a number of pales

pal·i·sade (pal′ə sād′, pal′ə sād′) *n.* [< Fr. < Pr. < L. *palus*, a stake, PALE[2]] **1.** any of a row of large pointed stakes set in the ground to form a fence as for fortification **2.** such a fence ☆**3.** [*pl.*] a line of steep cliffs, usually along a river —*vt.* **-sad′ed, -sad′ing** to fortify or defend with a palisade

pall[1] (pôl) *vi.* **palled, pall′ing** [ME. *pallen*, short for *appallen*, APPALL] **1.** to become tiresome, boring, dull, etc. [his jokes are beginning to *pall* on me] **2.** to become tired or surfeited [his interest in stamps soon *palled*] —*vt.* to bore after a time

pall[2] (pôl) *n.* [< OE. < L. *pallium*, a cover] **1.** a piece of velvet, etc. used to cover a coffin, hearse, or tomb **2.** a dark or gloomy

pale² (pāl) n. [< MFr. < L. palus, a stake: for IE. base see PEACE] 1. a narrow, pointed stake used in fences; picket 2. a fence; enclosure; boundary: now chiefly figurative [outside the pale of the law] 3. a district enclosed within bounds ☆ pale·face (pāl′fās′) n. a white person: a term said to be first used by N. American Indians

Pa·lem·bang (pä′lem bäŋ′) seaport in SE Sumatra, Indonesia: pop. 723,000

pa·le·o- [< Gr. palaios, ancient] a combining form meaning ancient, prehistoric, primitive, etc. [Paleozoic, paleolithic]: also, before a vowel, pa·le-

Pa·le·o·cene (pā′lē ə sēn′, pal′ē-) adj. [< PALEO- + Gr. kainos, recent] designating or of the first epoch of the Tertiary Period —the Paleocene the Paleocene Epoch or its rocks: see GEOLOGIC TIME CHART

pa·le·og·ra·phy (pā′lē äg′rə fē, pal′ē-) n. 1. ancient writing or forms of writing 2. the science of identifying or translating ancient writings —pa·le·og′ra·pher n. —pa·le·o·graph′ic (-ə graf′ik), pa·le·o·graph′i·cal adj.

pa·le·o·lith·ic (pā′lē ə lith′ik, pal′ē-) adj. [PALEO- + -LITHIC] designating or of the middle part of the early Stone Age, during which stone and bone tools were used

pa·le·on·tol·o·gy (ān täl′ə jē) n. [< Fr.: see PALE(O)- & ONTO- & -LOGY] the branch of geology that deals with prehistoric life through the study of fossils —pa·le·on′to·log′i·cal (-tə läj′i k'l), pa·le·on·tol′o·gist n.

Pa·le·o·zo·ic (-ə zō′ik) adj. [PALEO- + ZO- + -IC] designating or of the era between the Precambrian and the Mesozoic —the Paleozoic the Paleozoic Era or its rocks: see GEOLOGIC TIME CHART

Pa·ler·mo (pə lur′mō; It. pä ler′mō) seaport on the N coast of Sicily: pop. 659,000

Pal·es·tine (pal′əs tīn′) 1. region on the E coast of the Mediterranean, the country of the Jews in Biblical times 2. territory in this region, west of the Jordan River, held by the British as a mandate from 1923 until the establishment of the state of Israel in 1948 —Pal·es·tin′i·an (-tin′ē ən) adj., n.

covering [a pall of smoke] 3. a cloth, or cardboard covered with cloth, used to cover the chalice in some Christian churches —vt. palled, pall′ing to cover as with a pall

Pal·la·dio (päl lä′dyō), An·dre·a (än dre′ä) (born Andrea di Pietro) 1518-80; It. architect —Pal·la·di·an (pə lā′dē ən, -lä′-) adj.

Pal·la·di·um (pə lā′dē əm) n., pl. -di·a (-ə) 1. the legendary statue of Pallas Athena in Troy on which the safety of the city was supposed to depend 2. [p-] anything supposed to ensure the safety of something; safeguard

pal·la·di·um (pə lā′dē əm) n. [ModL., ult. < Gr. Pallas, the goddess] a rare, silvery-white, metallic chemical element: it is used as a catalyst, or in alloys with gold, silver, etc.: symbol, Pd; at. wt., 106.4; at. no., 46

Pal·las (pal′əs) Gr. Myth. Athena, goddess of wisdom: also Pallas Athena —Pal·la·di·an (pə lā′dē ən) adj.

pall·bear·er (pôl′ber′ər) n. [PALL² + BEARER] one of the persons who bear the coffin at a funeral

pal·let¹ (pal′it) n. [< MFr.: see PALETTE] 1. a wooden tool consisting of a flat blade with a handle; esp., such a tool for smoothing pottery 2. same as PALETTE (sense 1) 3. a low, portable platform for storing goods in warehouses, etc. 4. any of the clicks or pawls in the escapement of a clock, etc. which engage the teeth of a ratchet wheel to regulate the speed: see illustration at PAWL

pal·let² (pal′it) n. [< MFr. < OFr. paille, straw < L. palea, chaff] a small, crude bed or a mattress filled as with straw and used on the floor

pal·li·ate (pal′ē āt′) vt. -at′ed, -at′ing [< LL. pp. of palliare, to conceal < pallium, a cloak] 1. to lessen the pain or severity of without curing; alleviate [aspirin palliates a fever] 2. to make appear less serious or offensive; excuse [to palliate an error] —pal′li·a′tion n. —pal′li·a′tor n.

pal·li·a·tive (pal′ē ā′tiv, -ə tiv) adj. that palliates, eases, or excuses —n. something that palliates, as a drug

pal·lid (pal′id) adj. [L. pallidus, PALE¹] lacking in normal or natural color or brightness [a pallid face] —see SYN. at PALE¹ —pal′lid·ly adv. —pal′lid·ness n.

fat, āpe, cär; ten, ēven; is, bīte; gō, hôrn, tōōl, look; oil, out; up, fur; get; joy; yet; chin; she; thin, then; zh, leisure; ŋ, ring; ə for a in ago, e in agent, i in sanity, o in comply, u in focus; ' as in able (ā′b'l); Fr. bäl; ë, Fr. coeur; ö, Fr. feu; Fr. mon; ö, Fr. coq; ü, Fr. duc; r, Fr. cri; H, G. ich; kh, G. doch; ‡ foreign; ☆ Americanism; < derived from. See inside front cover.

Part 2 The Multiple Meanings of Words

Most of your vocabulary development in school has probably involved learning one meaning and spelling for each new word. For some words, this plan is acceptable. For many other words, however, it does not go far enough. Most words have more than one meaning. By assigning just one meaning to a word you ignore the additional meanings of that word.

Before you read the following sentences, write a definition for the word *court*. Now compare your definition with the uses of that word in these sentences.

1. Helen and Alice are going to the tennis *court* for a game this afternoon at three.
2. The strolling players set up their stage in the inner *court* of the castle.
3. The Queen and her entire *court* attended the gala New Year's Ball.
4. The judge asked the *court* to consider the evidence carefully and impartially.
5. Some politicians *court* the favor of those people who have powerful positions.
6. The King usually held *court* on the first day of the month, to receive the petitions of his subjects.
7. In some areas, a man must still ask permission of a woman's parents to *court* her.
8. Some people are foolish enough to *court* danger.
9. Our home is on a very short street known as Canterbury *Court*.
10. If you feel the ticket is unfair, you can plead your case in traffic *court*.

Did your definition of *court* fit any of the sentences? If not, share with the class a sentence using *court* to fit your definition. The excerpt from *Webster's New World Dictionary* shown on the following page, lists thirteen different meanings for the word *court*.

Dictionary Entry for *court*

court (kort) **n.** [OFr. < LL. < L. *cohors:* see COHORT] **1.** an uncovered space wholly or partly surrounded by buildings or walls **2.** a short street, often closed at one end **3.** *a*) an area for playing any of several ball games [a tennis *court*] *b*) a part of such an area ☆**4.** a motel: in full, **motor court 5.** *a*) the palace of a soverign *b*) the family, advisers, etc. of a sovereign, as a group *c*) a sovereign and his councilors as a governing body *d*) any formal gathering held by a sovereign **6.** attention paid to someone in order to get something **7.** courtship; wooing **8.** *a*) a person or persons appointed to examine and decide law cases, make investigations, etc.; judge or judges *b*) a place where trials are held, investigations made, etc. *c*) an assembly or meeting of the judge or judges, the lawyers, and the jury in a law court **—vt. 1.** to pay attention to (a person) in order to get something **2.** to try to get the love of; woo **3.** to try to get; seek [to *court* favor] **4.** to make oneself open to [to *court* insults] **—vi.** to woo **—adj.** of or fit for a court **—out of court** without a trial **—pay court to** to court, as for favor or love **—court′er n.**

From these examples, you can see the need for being aware of multiple meanings. The dictionary is your best tool for learning about all the possibilities of meaning in a single word.

Exercises Words with Multiple Meanings

A. Each of the four words below has more than one meaning. Write at least five sentences for each word. Each sentence should illustrate a different meaning for the word. Use a dictionary.

> note   light   round   ring

B. The word *key* may be used differently by each of the people named below. Look up the meanings in a dictionary and show the use of each in an original sentence.

1. a locksmith
2. a typist
3. a singing teacher
4. a person solving a puzzle
5. a piano teacher
6. a composer of songs
7. a student of the geography of Florida
8. a student studying pronunciations in a dictionary
9. a mathematics teacher

C. Give the meaning of the word *square* in each of the following sentences. Check with a dictionary in cases where you are not sure.

1. A concert will be held in the village *square* tonight after the fireworks display.
2. On Monday we can *square* our accounts.
3. Carpenters use *squares* to test right angles.
4. The *square* of 2 is 4.
5. He *squared* the surface with a straightedge.
6. The sergeant told the recruits to *square* their shoulders and stand at attention.
7. What is the formula for the area of a *square*?

D. The following sentences contain phrases using forms of the word *book*. Explain the meaning of each italicized phrase. Use the dictionary if necessary.

1. Even though her team had lost the final game, the coach admitted that the referees had called the fouls *by the book*.
2. Ms. Carr has *kept books* for our neighborhood food cooperative for many years.
3. The officer *booked the man* for suspicion of burglary.
4. The candidate said he wanted to *make an open book* of his family finances.

Part 3 Gaining Precision in the Use of Words

The concert singer who is exactly on pitch, the archer who hits the bull's-eye, the sky diver who lands directly on target—all display a precision that marks superior skill. Similarly, speakers and writers who display precision in their choice of words show themselves to be skillful users of language.

Precision in the use of words is essential to achieving word power. Precise use of synonyms and antonyms distinguishes the person with a powerful vocabulary from the person with an ordinary vocabulary.

Using Synonyms

Synonyms are words that have similar meanings. They do not usually mean *exactly* the same thing. Each one has a meaning that is slightly different from the others. It is important to have many synonyms in your vocabulary so that you can say exactly what you want to say and understand exactly what you read and hear.

Let's see how synonyms work. If a neighbor asked you if you were a *pupil* in East High School, would you say "Yes"? If she suggested that your ten-year-old brother was *student* at Jefferson Elementary School, would she be right? If she called you a *scholar*, would she be using the correct word?

Here is how one dictionary explains the differences in meaning among these three synonyms.

1. The word *pupil* applies to a child in school, or to someone studying privately with a teacher.

   EXAMPLES: Ruthmarie is a *pupil* of the famous singer Carlo Amato.

   Bobby is a *pupil* at Jefferson Elementary School.

2. The word *student* applies to someone attending a junior high school, a high school, a college, or university.

   EXAMPLES: Several hundred college *students* attended the rally.

   I am a first-year *student* at East High.

3. The word *scholar* is reserved for a learned person who is an authority in some field, or to a student who has earned a scholarship.

   EXAMPLES: Uncle Andrew is a Biblical *scholar.*

   Charlotte is a Rhodes *scholar.*

You can see from these examples that you might feel somewhat insulted if someone said you were a *pupil* at East High. You would probably prefer to be called a *student*. At the same time, you will realize that you probably should not be called a *scholar*. This is exactly what is meant by precision in the use of words. The more careful you are in the choice of synonyms, the more effective your use of the language will be.

A good dictionary is a valuable tool for developing precision in the use of synonyms. As you learned in Part 1 of this chapter, most dictionaries contain **synonymies,** listings of synonyms explaining their differences or shades of meaning. Use the synonymy sections of your dictionary carefully, since there are few absolute synonyms in English.

Examine the synonymy entered in *Webster's New World Dictionary* following the word *brave.*

Dictionary Entry for *brave*

brave (brav) **adj.** [Fr. < It. *bravo*, brave, fine, orig., wild, savage < L. *barbarus*, BARBAROUS] **1.** not afraid; having courage; valiant **2.** fine; splendid [a *brave* new world] —**n.** **1.** any brave man **2.** a N. American Indian warrior —**vt. braved, brav′ing 1.** to face with courage [they *braved* the storm] **2.** to defy; dare —**brave′ly adv.** —**brave′ness n.**

synonymy **SYN.**—brave is the general term that implies fearlessness in meeting danger or difficulty; **courageous** suggests readiness to deal firmly with any dangerous situation because of self-discipline and strong convictions; **bold** stresses a daring nature, whether shown by courage, insolence, or defiance; **audacious** suggests reckless boldness; **valiant** emphasizes a heroic quality in the courage shown; **intrepid** implies absolute fearlessness in facing something new or unknown; **plucky** is usually used of someone who continues fighting even though at a disadvantage —**ANT. craven, cowardly**

To the casual user of the language, the words *brave, courageous, bold, audacious, valiant, intrepid,* and *plucky* are interchangeable. To the precise user of the language, they are not. A precise user of the language might speak of a *brave* or *valiant* warrior or a *bold* or *audacious* robber, but is not likely to describe the robber as either *brave* or *valiant.* Each synonym carries a meaning not present in the other six words.

Synonyms add variety and color to our language. They also help us to avoid boring repetition of the same word. Certain words, particularly colloquial expressions, are overused to such an extent in daily conversation that they lose much of their impact. In your speaking and writing, make a conscious effort to avoid such repetition.

The Thesaurus. A thesaurus is a reference book that can be an invaluable help to a writer. It is a storehouse of synonyms and advice on word usage. Clarity and effectiveness in writing are dependent upon accurate word choice, and a thesaurus can help you find the exact word you need. However, when you use a thesaurus, remember that the differences in meaning among synonyms are of critical importance. Before you use a synonym that you find in a thesaurus, check its full meaning in a dictionary. Be sure that it is the correct word for the use you have in mind.

Here is an entry from *Roget's Thesaurus.*

DANGER.—I. *Nouns.* **danger,** chance, hazard, insecurity, jeopardy, peril, unsafety, risk, pitfall, endangerment; storm brewing, clouds gathering, clouds on the horizon; crisis.
dangerousness, riskiness, touch and go, unsafety, treachery; venturousness, etc. (see *Adjectives*).
[*dangerous person*] **menace,** threat, serpent, viper; dangerous woman, *femme fatale* (*F.*).
II. *Verbs.* **endanger,** expose to danger, hazard, jeopardize, peril, imperil, risk, speculate with, venture, compromise.
[*accept danger*] **risk,** hazard, venture, adventure. dare, stake, set at hazard, speculate.
III. *Adjectives.* **dangerous,** chancy, risky, ticklish, touch-and-go, venturous, venturesome, adventurous, adventuresome, speculative; hazardous, perilous, parlous, precarious, insecure, jeopardous, critical, queasy, unsafe, ugly, treacherous, serpentine, viperous.
See also CHANCE, FEAR, THREAT, WARNING.
Antonyms—See PROTECTION.

Using Antonyms

Antonyms are words with meanings that are the opposite of each other. *Summer—winter, night—day, near—far, happy—sad* are examples of antonyms. Knowing how to use antonyms well will help to make your speech and writing more colorful and more precise. Antonyms are also useful when you need to present a contrast.

You have already seen that antonyms can be found at the end of dictionary entries. A thesaurus may also provide you with antonyms.

Exercises Gaining Precision in the Use of Words

A. Read the following paragraph. Note the monotonous effect of the overuse of the word *fantastic.*

> The Homecoming dance was a *fantastic* affair. The decorations committee did a *fantastic* job. The band, James and Company, was really *fantastic.* The students consumed all of the *fantastic* refreshments. Everyone agreed that this was the most *fantastic* dance ever held at Jefferson High School.

Rewrite this paragraph, substituting other words for the overused word *fantastic.* The rewritten paragraph should give the reader a more precise picture of what the dance was actually like. After you have rewritten the paragraph, check your words in a dictionary.

B. Study the following synonymy for the word *estimate* from *Webster's New World Dictionary.* Write a sentence for each of these four words—*estimate, appraise, evaluate,* and *rate*—to illustrate the different shades of meaning of each word.

> **SYN.**—**estimate** refers generally to the forming of a personal opinion or judgment; **appraise** implies the intention of giving an accurate or expert judgment, as of value or worth [to *appraise* a new house]; **evaluate** also connotes an attempt at an exact judgment, but rarely with reference to value in terms of money [let us *evaluate* the evidence]; **rate** implies the comparing of one person or thing with another or others as to value, quality, etc. [he is *rated* the best in his field]—see also **SYN.** at CALCULATE

C. Answer the following. Use your dictionary for help.

1. Could the same person be *uninterested* and *disinterested* in the same project at the same time?

2. Could a person be *healthy* in an *unhealthful* climate? Explain.

3. If someone said you were a *bore*, would you be happy about it? If the same person said you were a *boor*, would you feel better or worse?

4. Explain the difference between *flash, glitter,* and *sparkle.* Use each in an original sentence.

5. A person with an *irritable* disposition is easily annoyed. A person with an *irascible* disposition has what trouble?

6. Can you be *happy* without being *cheerful?* Could you be *cheerful* without being *happy?*

7. *Neat, tidy,* and *trim* are often used interchangeably, but each word implies something different from the others. Use each in an original sentence that will make the distinctions clear.

8. Could you be *eager* without being *anxious?* Explain.

D. Answer the following. Use your dictionary if necessary.

1. Would you deal with a person who is *unscrupulous?* What word would you use to designate the opposite trait?

2. *Parsimonious* people have few friends. What quality would they have to cultivate to change the situation?

3. Would an *illiterate* person necessarily have to be *uncultured?* Explain.

4. You attend a student meeting; nothing much is accomplished. A classmate says the meeting was *unorganized;* another says it was *disorganized.* Is there a difference? Explain.

5. You find the word *abridged* on the cover of a novel you are about to read. Would you expect a complete telling of the story as the author wrote it?

6. If you found a package of corn seeds marked "atypical," what type of corn would you expect to grow from them?

7. If you were told that doing a certain thing would be a *disservice* to you, would you do it? Give a reason for your answer.

8. What type of person is a *malcontent?*

9. What is the difference between *asocial* and *antisocial?*

10. Would you describe a secret code as being *indecipherable* or *illegible?* Use each word in a sentence.

E. Write down two synonyms for each of the words given below. Use a dictionary or thesaurus if necessary. Then use each synonym in an original sentence that clearly shows the difference in meaning.

1. fear	6. hesitate	11. oblivious
2. lazy	7. spite	12. deplore
3. guard	8. injure	13. observe
4. scoff	9. scanty	14. noticeable
5. scold	10. hateful	15. error

1. The dictionary is an excellent source for increasing and strengthening your vocabulary. It can also be used as a reference text for many different subject areas.

2. There are two main types of dictionaries—unabridged dictionaries and abridged dictionaries. You will use the shorter, abridged dictionaries in most of your work.

3. All standard dictionaries contain the following information:

    Guide words   Entry words   Etymologies
    Entries   Part of speech   Synonymies
    Pronunciation   abbreviations   Derived words
      keys and respellings Definitions

    Check your dictionary for additional elements and for symbols and abbreviations.

4. Use a dictionary to discover the precise meaning of a word in a particular context. Also use dictionary synonymies or a thesaurus to choose precise words as you write.

Applications in Other Subject Areas

Foreign Language.   Look through your classroom dictionary. Identify the symbol that indicates foreign words and·phrases. Then find at least twenty foreign words and phrases. Write them, along with their pronunciations and definitions.

Speech / **Math** / **Science** / **Social Studies.**   Most dictionaries have special charts at the front or back containing different types of information. Some contain tables of weights and measures, metric conversion tables, lists of colleges and universities, terms and symbols from areas of specialization, and even maps. Find a dictionary that contains such graphic aids. Summarize or list the aids found in one of these. Prepare a brief report for oral presentation to your class.

Chapter 3

Using Language for Different Purposes

Would you be upset if someone accused you of *brangling* too much? Would you be disturbed if you were offered a *nuncheon*? You probably would have no idea how to react. However, an American colonist who lived in the 1700's would understand that you had been accused of quarreling in the first instance, and had been offered a snack in the second. The same colonist, though, would be perplexed by such words as *Skylab*, *plastic*, and *laser*.

A changing vocabulary is just one example of the adaptability of our language. Sometimes we must change the way we speak or write simply to suit the situation or company in which we find ourselves. We can do this by using different kinds, or **levels**, of language.

This chapter will examine these two aspects of our rich and fascinating language. You will learn how language changes with time. You will also learn how individual speakers and writers adapt language to suit particular situations.

Part 1 Borrowed Words

America has been called a melting pot because it is made up of people from many different countries and cultures. In the same way, the English language can be called a melting pot of other languages. Since its beginnings over 1,500 years ago, English has grown to be the largest language in the world, containing over 790,000 individual words. Most of this enormous vocabulary has been borrowed from other languages, especially from Latin, French, German, and Greek.

When another language has a word for which we have no term of our own, we borrow it as it is, or we change it to fit into our language. In colonial America, for example, the colonists did not want to use the monetary terms of the British. Instead, they borrowed the Dutch word *daler*, which meant "coined in the valley," and this became our term *dollar*. When the Texas cowboys of the Old West were learning how to handle angry herds of longhorned cattle, they adopted the Spanish word *estampeda* and changed it to *stampede*. These are but two of the hundreds of thousands of borrowed words that help make up our language.

Refer to the list on pages 45 and 46 for other borrowed words that have enriched our language.

Exercises Recognizing Borrowed Words

A. Use a dictionary to discover the language from which each of the following words was borrowed. You will have to refer to the abbreviations key in your dictionary. Copy the definitions of any words that you do not already know.

1. piano	5. tycoon	8. opossum
2. ensemble	6. khaki	9. veldt
3. tea	7. mosquito	10. gusto
4. jaguar		

B. Using a dictionary, encyclopedia, or other source, find fifteen words that came into English from other languages. Note whether these words were changed or left as they were when adopted.

Words Borrowed from Other Languages

AFRICAN

| tote | gumbo | jazz | canary |

AMERICAN INDIAN

moccasin	wigwam	hominy	squash
chipmunk	skunk	raccoon	moose
powwow	pecan		

ARABIC

| algebra | mosque | almanac | magazine |
| zero | mattress | | |

AUSTRALIAN

| boomerang | kangaroo | outback |

CHINESE

| yen | typhoon | silk | catsup |

DUTCH

ahoy	boom	deck	hoist
pickle	wagon	boss	landscape
sketch	yacht		

ESKIMO

| igloo | kayak |

FRENCH

machine	fiancé(e)	chic	religion
seige	ballad	literature	courage
gentle	liberty	virtue	parliament
charity	bureau		

Words Borrowed from Other Languages

GERMAN

frankfurter	delicatessen	kindergarten	stein
zinc	cobalt	poltergeist	spiel

HEBREW

amen	sabbath	cinnamon	hallelujah

ITALIAN

spaghetti	soprano	violin	cello
volcano	studio	sonata	fresco
balcony	trombone		

JAPANESE

soybean	kimono	judo	haiku

PERSIAN

kiosk	chess	jasmine	lemon
lilac	paradise	jackal	azure
bazaar	spinach		

SCANDINAVIAN

ski	fiord	geyser	viking
smorgasbord	sauna		

SLAVIC

gherkin	babushka	polka	vampire

SPANISH

canyon	cigar	desperado	renegade
comrade	vanilla	alligator	bronco
rodeo	siesta		

Part 2 Created Words

> The new circumstances under which we are placed call for new words, [for] new phrases, and for the transfer of old words to new objects. — THOMAS JEFFERSON

New ideas need new words. Because new concepts and inventions are continually being developed, our language must grow in order to communicate these ideas. In this section we will briefly look at several ways in which new words are created.

Compounds and Blends

A **compound word** is made by combining two existing words to form a new word.

night + shirt = nightshirt   foot + ball = football

People develop compound words to describe new ideas or things while still using familiar terms. With a little thought, you should be able to explain how and why such new words as *superstar, spacewalk,* and *drive-in* were created.

If two words are combined, but some of the letters are dropped, the resulting word is called a **blend**. For example, *walrus* is a blend made from the animal's original name, *whale horse*. The word *laundromat* was made from *laundry* and *automatic*. More recently, *situation comedy* has become the familiar term *sitcom*.

Clipped Words

Sometimes, one or more parts of a word are dropped and the remaining part is used alone as a word. Such words are called **clipped words**. They are commonly used in less formal speaking and writing.

The following are some common clipped words:

gymnasium-*gym*   examination-*exam*   gasoline-*gas*
advertisement-*ad*   teenagers-*teens*   photograph-*photo*

Recognizing Compounds, Blends, and Clipped Words

A. Using a dictionary, find the clipped form of each of the following words. Check the definition of any word that you do not know.

1. cabriolet
2. laboratory
3. fanatic
4. omnibus
5. airplane
6. zoological gardens
7. pianoforte
8. pantaloons
9. chimpanzee
10. delicatessen

B. Using a dictionary, determine whether each of the following terms is a compound, a blend, or a clipped word. Then write the word or words from which each one was made.

1. dorm
2. splashdown
3. splurge
4. typewriter
5. brunch
6. marketplace
7. chortle
8. fence
9. phone
10. gasohol
11. wristwatch
12. smog
13. sub
14. bookkeeper
15. moped

Acronyms

Sometimes a new word is created from the first letters of a group of words. This new word is called an **acronym**. *Scuba,* for instance, is an acronym for "self-contained underwater breathing apparatus." *Radar* means "radio detection and ranging." The computer industry has created the word *Cobol,* which is a specific computer language, from "common business oriented language."

People and Place Names

Many proper names have passed into our language to form new words. The term *mesmerize,* for example, comes from the name of Dr. F. A. Mesmer, an Austrian physician who was known for his work with hypnotism. The word "tuxedo" was originally the name of a country club near Tuxedo Lake, New York. Here are some other words made from names:

Words from Names

saxophone	from Adolphe Sax, the Belgian inventor of this musical instrument
tantalize	from Tantalus, a Greek mythological king who was condemned to be forever tempted by water and food that he could not reach
sideburns	from Ambrose E. Burnside, a Union general during the Civil War who had very distinctive whiskers
bowdlerize	from Thomas Bowdler, a British editor who, in 1818, published a heavily censored edition of the works of Shakespeare
paisley	from the city of Paisley where wool shawls with colorful, intricate patterns were made
Frisbee	from "Mother Frisbie's" cookie jars, the lids of which were used for a game by Princeton students
silhouette	from Étienne de Silhouette, a French finance minister, much disliked because of his poor economic policies. His name came to be associated with pictures which were, like his abilities, incomplete.

Exercises **Using Acronyms and Words Made from Names**

A. Give the acronym for each of the following:

1. Cooperative for American Relief Everywhere
2. Zone Improvement Plan
3. Beginners All-purpose Symbolic Instruction Code

4. Housing and Urban Development
5. Volunteers in Service to America
6. North Atlantic Treaty Organization
7. Light Amplification by Stimulated Emission of Radiation
8. Wide Area Telecommunications Service
9. Health Maintenance Organization
10. World Health Organization

B. Research the following words. Do they have their origins in the names of people or of places? Explain how each term was added to our language.

1. boycott	6. Fahrenheit	11. laconic
2. calico	7. bloomers	12. diesel
3. tangerine	8. turquoise	13. derby
4. July	9. Braille	14. cardigan
5. Wednesday	10. watt	15. quisling

C. The names of things often come from the names of people, but the reverse is also true. People's names often come from the names of things or qualities. Using reference materials, look up the following names and find out what they originally meant:

1. Adam	6. Vincent
2. Deborah	7. George
3. Robert	8. Barbara
4. Thomas	9. Mary
5. Florence	10. Bonnie

Terms from Specialized Areas

When members of a profession or industry develop their own specialized vocabulary, this vocabulary is called a **jargon.** Jargon can be very useful because it helps people within a profession to communicate efficiently.

Often the terms used in jargon enter everyday speech. Notice how much of the jargon on the following chart has come to be widely used by people outside these areas of specialization:

Television/Radio		Sports	
network	commercial	grand slam	icing
channel	prime time	game plan	dribble
transistor	station break	knockout	match point

Automobiles		Music	
convertible	crankshaft	woodwind	cadence
power drive	spark plugs	motif	libretto
carburetor	shocks	counterpoint	crescendo

Computers		Space	
byte	terminal	satellite	skylab
software	input	astronaut	launching pad
disk	printout	blastoff	space shuttle

Sometimes members of different professions use the same word but attach different meanings to them. For example, an electrician *wires* a house; a newspaper reporter *wires* a story to an editor. A reporter sends in a *scoop;* a chef uses a *scoop* to cook.

Exercises Recognizing Jargon

A. Define each of the terms below as it would be used in the two listed professions. You may have to use a dictionary.

1. trace   (A) *physician*   (B) *police officer*
2. culture   (A) *biologist*   (B) *sociologist*
3. bumper   (A) *farmer*   (B) *auto mechanic*
4. fault   (A) *geologist*   (B) *tennis pro*
5. book   (A) *librarian*   (B) *talent agent*

B. Give two examples of jargon from each field listed below. You may have to consult reference works such as encyclopedias.

1. painting   4. law   7. teaching
2. religion   5. banking   8. cosmetics
3. medicine   6. carpentry   9. swimming

Part 3 The Levels of Language

"If we spoke as we write, we should find no one to listen; if we wrote as we speak, we should find no one to read."—T. S. ELIOT

No speaker or writer of English uses the language in the same way all the time. Instead, it is often necessary to vary the way one speaks or writes to suit a particular audience. For example, you probably speak one way when you are talking with your friends, another way when you are speaking in class, and perhaps a third way when you are giving a speech or oral report. The same sort of language variation also occurs in written material. The types of language that one uses on different occasions are called the **levels of usage.**

Standard English

Language that is acceptable at all times and in all places is called **standard English.** The rules and guidelines of standard English enable all speakers and writers of the language to communicate clearly and precisely without fear of misunderstanding. This textbook presents the rules and guidelines for using standard English.

Formal and Informal English. There are two accepted levels of standard English, formal and informal. **Formal English** is found primarily in writing but is appropriate in any circumstance that is serious, dignified, or ceremonial. **Informal English,** also known as colloquial English, is appropriate in most everyday situations. It is the language used in most magazines, newspapers, casual letters, and conversation. Look at these examples:

FORMAL: No written law has ever been more binding than unwritten custom supported by popular opinion.

INFORMAL: Traditions and habits are both hard to break.

Now examine the chart on the following page.

Characteristics of Formal and Informal English

	FORMAL	INFORMAL
Tone	Serious, reserved, academic, ceremonial	Personal, friendly, casual
Vocabulary and Mechanics	Sometimes uses longer or more complicated words Avoids contractions, clipped words, and slang Uses correct grammar, spelling, and punctuation	Uses simpler words Often uses contractions and clipped words Avoids slang Uses correct grammar, spelling, and punctuation
Organization	Longer, carefully constructed sentences	Sentences of a great variety of lengths Similar to conversational English
Appropriate Uses	Reports or serious essays Legal, academic, religious, or other professional documents Formal speeches, debates, or interviews	Writing intended for a general audience Conversations, letters Informal talks
Audience	Readers of scholarly material Readers of professional documents Persons in positions of authority	Friends, co-workers Most general audiences

Nonstandard English

Language that is not accepted at all times and in all places is called **nonstandard English.** This level of language includes all grammatical forms and constructions that are not widely accepted, such as *He ain't got none* or *Pass me them papers.* Also included are slang and all language containing errors in punctuation, spelling, capitalization, and manuscript form.

Slang. The term **slang** is applied to all words and phrases that are not accepted as standard English. Slang words usually lead brief but colorful lives and then drop out of common usage. For example, American youths in the 1960's developed a large vocabulary of slang that included such terms as *groovy, hip, far out, square,* and *uptight.* Most of these terms now seem quaint and dated. However, some words that originate as slang eventually do become accepted as standard. This is true of most clipped forms and of such now standard words as *hot dog* and *lengthy.*

Slang can be appropriate on occasion. However, you must be careful about when and how you use it. Slang would not be appropriate in a group discussion or in a business letter, but it might help enliven conversation with friends or dialogue in a short story.

Exercises Levels of Language

A. The following report contains several different levels of language. Rewrite the report. Eliminate all nonstandard English and replace inappropriate phrases and slang with formal language.

Gerbils belong to the scientific family *Cricetidae.* There are approximately one hundred different species of these furry, ratlike rodents, but the one most folks know is the Mongolian gerbil. As a matter of fact, all pet gerbils in the United States are descendants of twenty-two Mongolian gerbils sent to America by a Japanese laboratory in 1954. Gerbils make really neat pets because of all the interesting stuff that they do.

Pet gerbils should be fed commercial gerbil pellets or a mixture of fruits, small seeds, and raw vegetables. Watching them eat is a real blast, because they stuff a lot of food in the pouches of their cheeks. Water should be made available in their cages, though they sure don't drink much. Gerbils obtain water primarily through moisture in the food they eat. If properly cared for, a pet gerbil should live up to four years, give or take a little.

B. As you learned in the preceding section of this chapter, you should avoid slang except for a few special purposes. One such purpose is the writing of realistic, casual dialogue. The following slang expressions were popular during the 1920's. Using these expressions, write a conversation between two young people of 1925.

1. *caveman*—in boxing, a strong slugger with little skill
2. *dive*—a cheap restaurant or public place
3. *give (someone) the gate*—to jilt
4. *lam*—to leave quickly
5. *scrim*—a large dance party
6. *on the shelf*—not interested in getting married
7. *palooka*—a prizefighter
8. *pal*—any close friend; used in the 1920's to refer to women as well as men
9. *raspberry*—a sharp, harsh, scornful comment
10. *the bee's knees*—any excellent or popular thing

Part 4   Writing and Speaking Clearly

The purpose of language is to communicate. The best speakers and writers use language that is simple, direct, and appropriate to their audiences. Sometimes, however, people make their speech or writing unnecessarily difficult. This may occur as they unconsciously, or intentionally, attempt to impress or mislead others. Such writers use unnecessary jargon, complicated sentences, and long or uncommon words. This language is sometimes called **gobbledygook.**

Gobbledygook is often found in professional publications and in public statements made by professional people. Occasionally, it is the result of some writer's attempt to be too precise and thorough. For example, there are some insurance contracts that sound like this:

> This policy is issued in consideration of the application therefor, a copy of which application is attached hereto and made part hereof, and of the payment for said insurance on the life of the above-named issued.

This passage uses legal jargon and complicated sentence structure to "dress up" its simple meaning: "Here is your insurance policy."

To avoid writing gobbledygook yourself, remember to use simple, direct language. Avoid using jargon that is unfamiliar to your audience, and replace long-winded phrases with shorter, clearer ones. When writing reports avoid trying to "dress up" straightforward statements by padding your sentences or using big words when small ones will do.

Look at the "translations" of gobbledygook in the chart that follows:

GOBBLEDYGOOK	DIRECT STATEMENT
1. We need some help *in the area of budgetary planning considerations.*	1. We need some help planning our budget.
2. He *made inquiry regarding* the letter.	2. He asked about the letter.
3. He *is of the opinion that* . . .	3. He believes . . .
4. The manager hoped *to escalate in terms of* production.	4. The manager hoped to increase production.
5. These machines *have the capability of* flying.	5. These machines can fly.
6. *The accident was caused by a failure to maintain sufficient altitude to avoid neighboring terrain.*	6. The plane crashed.

Exercises **Writing Clearly**

A. Our language contains many concise, familiar expressions that are models of simple, direct prose. Some examples are "A stitch in time saves nine," and "Time and tide wait for no man." Match the following passages of gobbledygook with the corresponding familiar sayings on the right.

1. One photographic exposure merits an appraisal identical to that accorded a ten hundredfold sum of verbiage.

2. Under no circumstances and on no occasion presume to calculate the entirety of those barnyard fowl that are identified as belonging to you prior to the termination of their incubation.

3. He whom one might designate as deficient in understanding is in record time in a state of disconnectedness from his legal tender.

4. Objects that scintillate are not necessarily auric in nature.

a. A fool and his money are quickly parted.

b. All that glitters is not gold.

c. A picture is worth a thousand words.

d. Never count your chickens before they hatch.

B. Translate these gobbledygook sentences into understandable standard usage. Your dictionary will help you with unfamiliar words.

1. He gave up his employment because he came to the conclusion that the remuneration involved was not commensurate with his performance load.

2. Demand for parking does not appear to exceed significantly the supply of available parking spaces within our building's designated parking lots even during peak demand periods.

3. In the concluding montage of this cinematic debacle, the star foregoes his prior Western equestrian pursuits, accedes to the ingenue's matrimonial ambitions, and proceeds to osculation.

4. Before performance can be initiated on stage, all illumination in contingent areas must be lessened to the maximum extent.

1. As the world changes, language must change with it. Our vocabulary grows as we borrow words from other languages and create compounds, blends, clipped words, acronyms, words derived from people and place names, and jargon.

2. Whenever you speak or write, choose language that is appropriate to the occasion and to your audience.

3. Standard English is language that is acceptable to all audiences on all occasions. The two levels of Standard English are **formal English** and **informal English**.

4. Nonstandard English is language that is not acceptable to all audiences on all occasions.

5. Avoid slang except in casual conversation or in dialogue. Avoid "gobbledygook" altogether.

Applications in Other Subject Areas

Science / Math. Much of the English language is made up of scientific and technical terms. Most of these terms are borrowed from Latin and Greek. From your science and math texts, begin collecting as many examples of these terms as you can. Look them up in a dictionary to determine their meanings and origins.

All Subjects. As you go through your next day of school, notice the specialized vocabularies used in different classes. What terms are unique to your gym class? Which are heard only in science? art? music? Choose one class and make a dictionary that defines the jargon used in that subject area.

All Subjects. Listen carefully to the language you hear during class. Compare it to the type of language used during lunch or out on a playing field during gym. How does the language used in these situations differ? Is each level of language appropriate to the situation in which it is being used? Does the language a speaker uses affect your opinion of that person?

Chapter 4

Using the Senses in Writing

Imagine being a child again and experiencing the world for the first time. How strange and beautiful life would seem, how fascinating and full of wonders! As writers, we must be like children in this respect. We must be aware of the carnival of sensation all around us, and try not to take for granted the extraordinary world revealed by our senses.

Writers have to remember vividly how their subjects look, sound, taste, smell, and feel. Then they must find the right words to make these remembered sensations live in their readers' imaginations. By training yourself to use your senses fully and by learning how to translate your sensory experience into words, you can make your own writing come alive.

Part 1 The Sense of Sight

Most of our knowledge of the world comes to us through our eyes. This is why the verb *to see* means not only "to look," but also "to know" or "to understand." In the following poem, writer John Moffitt describes the kind of seeing that leads to understanding:

To Look at Any Thing

To look at anything,
If you would know that thing,
You must look at it long:
To look at this green and say
"I have seen spring in these
Woods," will not do—you must
Be the thing you see:
You must be the dark snakes of
Stems and ferny plumes of leaves,
You must enter in
To the small silences between
The leaves,
You must take your time
And touch the very peace
They issue from.

Study "To Look at Any Thing" carefully. What is Moffitt's advice? What evidence is there in the poem that he has taken his own advice? What words does he use to re-create his own visual experience?

Whenever you write, you must observe the world around you as carefully as this poet does. You must learn to "be the thing you see" so that you can become aware of even the tiniest details. You must also learn how to communicate what you see and learn.

You can begin to develop these abilities by "training" your sense of sight. The exercises that begin on the next page will give you practice in using your eyes. They will help you become more sensitive to the world of form and color.

Training in Seeing

You are already a kind of expert at observing the world with your eyes. You notice the color when you pick out your favorite shirt. You notice subtle changes in expressions on other people's faces.

Begin a journal in which you record your work for this chapter. Your first entries will be your responses to the following suggestions for training your sight to be even sharper.

1. Select a small object near you—something on your desk, on the floor, or on the wall. Study it carefully for a short time. Then move so that you can no longer see it. Write a detailed description of the object without naming it. Include specific information concerning its size, color, shape, texture, and unusual characteristics. Compare it to other objects. Is it the size of a walnut? Is it the color of lemons? When you feel you have included all possible details, turn back to see how well your description fits. Share your writing with another person by reading your description of the object without naming it. See if this person can recognize what you are describing.

2. Sit down in a familiar place in a room at home or at school, or outside if you wish. Write down everything you can see without turning or moving your circle of vision. Notice all the things you usually see in this spot; then concentrate on finding something you did not expect to see here. Describe it as specifically as you can, allowing your other senses to affect what you see. Share your experience with someone.

3. Stretch your sense of sight by careful observation on your way to or from school. Going your same familiar way, find ten things of interest that you never noticed before. Be prepared to write out this list of new "sights" to share with the rest of the class.

The lists of "sight" words on the following pages will help you make your descriptions more vivid and exact. Study the words and try to determine how each of the related words is different. Add your own words to the list and record them in your journal.

Sight Words

Red

pink
salmon
rose
coral
raspberry
strawberry
tomato
currant
cherry
crimson
cardinal
vermilion
carmine
flame
ruby
garnet
wine
blood
maroon
burgundy

Green

celery
mint
apple
lime
moss
pea
kelly
emerald
olive
pistachio
chartreuse

Blue

sky
sapphire
azure
delft
porcelain
turquoise
aqua
aquamarine
violet
peacock
teal
cobalt
royal
navy
steel
powder

Brown

sandy
almond
amber
tawny
hazel
cinnamon
nutmeg
chocolate
coffee
copper
rust
ginger
bronze
walnut
mahogany

Yellow

beige
buff
straw
peach
apricot
butter
buttercup
lemon
chartreuse
citron
canary
chrome
gold
topaz
ochre
saffron
sulphur
mustard
butterscotch
orange
tangerine
persimmon

Black

jet
ebony
licorice

Gray

ashen
dove
steel

Purple

lavender
amethyst
lilac
orchid
mauve
plum
mulberry
pansy
fuchsia
magenta

White

snow
milky
marble
cream
ivory
oyster
pearl
silver
platinum
bone
bleached

General

colorless
rainbow
drab
stark
bland
vivid
vibrant

Sight Words

Fast	careen	bounce	saunter
	rush	swoop	loiter
hurry	race	plunge	stray
run	zoom	swing	slink
scamper	zip	fly	stalk
skip	ram	sail	edge
scramble	chase		sneak
dart	hurl	**Slow**	stagger
spin	swat		lope
sprint	flick	creep	waddle
stride	whisk	crawl	drag
streak	rip	plod	sway
trot	shove	slouch	soar
gallop	swerve	lumber	lift
drive	smash	tiptoe	drift
dash	drop	bend	droop
bolt	plummet	amble	heave

flat	oval	jutting	broken
round	conical	irregular	spindly
domed	cylindrical	proportioned	skinny
curved	tubular	angular	thin
wavy	hollow	triangular	wiry
scrolled	rotund	rectangular	shapely
globular	chubby	hexagonal	winged
rolled	portly	octagonal	shapeless
scalloped	swollen	square	crooked
ruffled	lumpy	pyramidical	curved
frilled	clustered	tapering	straight
crimped	padded	branching	wide
crinkled	tufted	twiggy	narrow
flared	pendulous	split	stretched

Sight Words

dotted	cheap	muscular	expansive
freckled	ugly	sturdy	imposing
spotted	ramshackle	robust	regal
blotched	tired	stolid	stately
wrinkled	exhausted	hardy	elegant
patterned	arid	strong	statuesque
mottled	awkward	healthy	huge
striped	crooked	frail	immense
bright	loose	fragile	massive
clear	curved	pale	gigantic
shiny	straight	pasty	showy
glowing	orderly	sickly	decorative
glossy	formal	tiny	distinctive
shimmering	crisp	miniature	dazzling
fluid	pretty	timid	jeweled
sparkling	heavy	shy	lacy
iridescent	flat	fearful	lavish
glassy	stout	apprehensive	exotic
flashy	rigid	tearful	gorgeous
glazed	narrow	nervous	radiant
sheer	overloaded	frightened	vivid
transparent	congested	terrified	flushed
opaque	cluttered	hysterical	fiery
muddy	crowded	wild	blazing
grimy	jammed	bold	verdant
drab	packed	dramatic	fresh
dingy	squeezed	tantalizing	clean
dull	bruised	irresistible	tidy
dark	stretched	exuberant	handsome
dismal	erect	energetic	pleasant
rotted	lean	animated	sunny
worn	slender	perky	calm
untidy	supple	attractive	serene
shabby	lithe	arrogant	unruffled
messy	lively	flamboyant	nerveless

Exercises Using "Sight" Words in Your Writing

Here is a chance to practice using specific details in order to help your reader "see" what you are describing as clearly as you do.

A. Write a sentence describing each of these nine things.

the sidewalk   a stone   a button
the sky   a dog or a cat   a leaf
someone's hair   a slice of bread   a piece of soap

B. Here is a paragraph that re-creates a vivid sight impression.

. . . On windless summer evenings I stalk along the creek bank or straddle the sycamore log in absolute stillness, watching for muskrats. The night I stayed too late I was hunched on the log staring spellbound at spreading, reflected stains of lilac on the water. A cloud in the sky suddenly lighted as if turned on by a switch; its reflection just as suddenly materialized on the water upstream, flat and floating, so that I couldn't see the creek bottom, or life in the water under the cloud. Downstream, away from the cloud on the water, water turtles smooth as beans were gliding down with the current in a series of easy, weightless push-offs, as men bound on the moon. I didn't know whether to trace the progress of one turtle I was sure of, . . . or take a chance on seeing the carp, or scan the mudbank in hope of seeing a muskrat, or follow the last of the swallows who caught at my heart and trailed it after them like streamers.

—ANNIE DILLARD

Make a list of all the words or phrases in the paragraph that create especially strong pictures in your mind. Next, make a list of all the words or phrases that create action or movement.

C. You have stretched your sight experiences and are now ready to write your own paragraph. You may use any of the subjects from the following list. You may also use an entirely new idea of your own.

your room   outside the window   a dream
the kitchen   a puddle of water   a quiet or a busy scene

Part 2   The Sense of Hearing

Have you ever temporarily lost your sense of hearing, perhaps from an ear infection or a bad cold? Only at such times are you likely to be aware of how much you depend on this particular sense as you move through your day, from the alarm clock on waking up, to the sounds of traffic as you cross the street, to the greetings of friends at school, and conversations around the dinner table in the evening.

Notice the vivid sounds recorded by the writer of the following passage:

> I like the quiet crackling of root beer foam; the swish, then flap of the net as the basketball passes through . . . squeaky popcorn; slept-on mattress . . . moccasins treading soft sand, crisp as toasted linen; steel door weightlessly slammed shut; secret roar of sea shell; whirr of a movie reel; the ps-s-s-t of freshly opened coffee . . . whirr and buzz of the WALK signal; a Band-Aid coming off . . . creaky wicker chairs . . . .
>
> —SISTER MARY LOIS GLONEK

Training in Listening

In order to increase your sensitivity to sounds, you may sometimes need to close your eyes and concentrate only on listening, without your sense of sight to distract you. It is possible to develop more acute hearing, to notice more with your ears than you did before? Careful listening to sounds can add a rich new dimension to your life and to your writing. Here are some suggestions for training your ears to hear even more. Record your responses in your journal.

1. Take your journal to bed with you tonight. After you are comfortably settled in the dark room, listen carefully to every sound you hear. Then turn on the light long enough to write down all of the sounds you were able to hear. Take this list with you to school in the morning so that you can share what you heard with someone else. Did this careful listening affect how easy or difficult it was for you to sleep?

2. Listen to three conversations: one at school, one at a store or on the way home, and one at home. Listen to the tone of voice the speakers use and determine how this tone affects the meaning of what is said. Record your findings by re-creating one of the dialogues as well as you can remember it. In your writing, indicate changes in tone of voice and the emotion you think each person is feeling as shown below.

> *Customer*   (loudly and angrily): That item is marked a dollar and nine cents.
>
> *Cashier*   (bewildered): Isn't that what I charged you? It's right here on the sales slip.

3. List the sounds that you are so used to at home that you do not ordinarily notice them.

4. List five sounds that you like to hear and five that you do not like to hear.

Following are lists of "hearing" words to study. As you read each word, try to hear the sound each one conveys. Add more words to the list and record them in your journal.

Hearing Words

LOUD SOUNDS

crash	yell	clap	brawl
thud	whistle	stomp	bedlam
bump	whine	stamp	pandemonium
thump	squawk	noise	hubbub
boom	bark	discord	blatant
thunder	bawl	jangle	deafening
bang	bray	rasp	raucous
smash	bluster	clash	earsplitting
explode	rage	caterwaul	piercing
roar	blare	clamor	rowdy
scream	rumble	tumult	blast
screech	grate	riot	yowl
shout	slam	racket	shatter

SOFT SOUNDS

sigh	mutter	gurgle	speechless
murmur	snap	swish	mute
whisper	hiss	rush	faint
whir	crackle	chime	inaudible
rustle	bleat	tinkle	melody
twitter	peep	clink	resonance
patter	buzz	hush	harmony
hum	zing	still	musical

SPEECH SOUNDS

stutter	sing	bellow	whimper
stammer	yell	growl	talk
giggle	scream	chatter	speak
guffaw	screech	murmur	drawl
laugh	snort	whisper	hiss

Exercises Using "Hearing" Words in Your Writing

A. Here are fifteen sounds you are familiar with. Spend a few minutes "hearing" the sounds in your mind. Write a sentence about each sound that describes it as vividly as you would want your reader to hear it. Record the sentences in your journal.

the wind	a fire
feet walking	the rain
a car starting	a door opening
opening a can of soda	turning on a faucet
a police car siren	a lawn mower
sawing a board	a garbage truck
an ice cream wagon	someone roller skating
a train	a washing machine

B. Read the following passage carefully. List all of the words that are used to describe the terrifying sounds of a city threatened by an erupting volcano. What other sense is appealed to in these paragraphs?

> Then he began to hear sounds. Peculiar sounds, like animals under the earth. Hissings and groanings and muffled cries that a dying creature might make dislodging the stones of his underground cave. There was no doubt about it now. The noises came from underneath . . . .
>
> It was then the crashing began. First a sharp crackling, like a monstrous snapping of twigs; then a roar like the fall of a whole forest of trees; then an explosion that tore earth and sky. The heavens, though Tito could not see them, were shot through with continual flickerings of fire. Lightnings above were answered by thunders beneath. A house fell. Then another. By a miracle the two companions had escaped the dangerous side streets and were in a more open space. It was the Forum. They rested here awhile—how long he did not know.
>
> —LOUIS UNTERMEYER

C. Now put all of your hearing experiences and practice together to write a paragraph in which sound plays an important part. Use an idea from your journal or from the following list:

1. I adjusted the ear plugs to protect my ears, dove into the water, and all of a sudden . . .

2. As I was listening to the radio with my headset on, the strangest thing happened.

3. Without warning, all sound suddenly disappeared. It had become a strange new world in which I did not fit.

4. The elevator dropped swiftly, and the quick descent seemed to plug up my ears.

5. Suddenly, the band leaped on stage and the packed auditorium exploded with noise.

6. Take an ordinary sound that is familiar to you. Exaggerate this single sound in your writing until it takes on a new meaning. It might, for example, become sinister or exciting.

7. Contrast two completely different sounds, or a particular sound and quiet.

8. Describe an event by sound words only. Do not give your reader the final clue as to what you are describing until the last sentence of the paragraph.

9. Go to a place where there is a great deal of noise and activity, such as a store, airport, or carnival. Shut your eyes for a moment and listen. Take notes on what you hear. Now go home and write a paragraph about the place you visited, using as many sound words as possible.

10. Imagine a new invention and the sound it might make. Briefly describe it so that someone else could "see" and "hear" it.

Part 3 The Sense of Touch

Touch is the one sense we can't turn off. We can close our eyes to shut out sight. We can move away from sounds or smells. No matter what we do, however, we will still be touching something.

The things we feel are usually physical objects of some kind. We must make a conscious effort to touch them. Sometimes, however, sensation comes from emotions within us. Read the following passage for an example of this type of feeling.

> He was freezing; he couldn't lie there all night. Inch by inch he crawled away. Silent as a shadow he went back across the lake. There was danger everywhere now, every time he moved a muscle. He could feel it all around him, feel a prickling in his scalp and a supernatural certainty that as he was stalking Mathieu, Mathieu was stalking him. Cautiously, with long waits, he approached his camp. The fire was out. His fingers touched the game-bag and drew back. Something was there, something that shouldn't be! *Something was wrong.* Chills went up and down his spine. He whirled toward a deeper patch of shadow, knowing with the certainty of panic that gunfire would belch from that shadow and blind him. His eyes roamed round in his head in the darkness and he waited, turned to stone.
>
> —ELLIOT MERRICK

Training in Touching

To gain a wider appreciation of your sense of touch, follow the directions given below and record your responses in your journal.

1. List all of the objects you can touch while you are seated in your chair right now.

2. Describe your physical sensations now. Are you cold, hot, warm, cool, comfortable? How do you know?

3. List rough objects in the classroom, then smooth ones.

4. List some things that are cold to the touch, hot to the touch, rough, smooth, wet.

5. List some things you do not feel with your hands, such as the wind or the touch of your clothes.

6. Describe the type of ride you get on different forms of transportation.

7. Imagine that you are sitting in your classroom on a hot summer day. How do you feel? Now imagine you are in the same room on a bitter winter day. How do you feel now?

Below is a list of touch words. Study it and write down an object that you think belongs with each word.

Touch Words

cool	slippery	silky	gritty
cold	spongy	satiny	sandy
icy	mushy	velvety	rough
lukewarm	oily	smooth	sharp
tepid	waxy	soft	thick
warm	fleshy	woolly	pulpy
hot	rubbery	furry	dry
steamy	tough	feathery	dull
sticky	crisp	fuzzy	thin
damp	elastic	hairy	fragile
wet	leathery	prickly	tender

Exercises Using "Touch" Words in Your Writing

A. Write sentences describing how each of these things or activities feels. Record your sentences in your journal.

a piece of cotton   an ice cube   the bark of a tree
an apple   a warm bath   roller skating
a dry leaf   a sunburn   a spring shower

Read what you have written, checking for the use of vivid and precise words. Would another person know what you were describing if the name of it were left out?

B. Read the passage below. Then, answer the questions.

As he tried to make his inept way, the pain was with him, because every time he tried to inhale, the night air hit the holes in his teeth and attacked the open nerves. The street was hard and filled with sharp dark things and he didn't have shoes on to protect him. He was still in his pajamas, a helpless creep just like the stoop gang always said, staggering along . . . Something jammed into his foot then, something that hurt enough to penetrate into his brain deeper than the air against the nerves. Babe hoped it wasn't the broken glass but only maybe a rock that would hurt like crazy but not lay his foot open to even more serious pain. — WILLIAM GOLDMAN

What particular feelings does Babe have? What particular words are used to describe objects of touch? What particular words are used to describe Babe's internal reactions to these objects of touch?

C. This paragraph will give you an entirely new feeling about rain.

There were things that crawled on his skin. Things grew upon him in layers. Drops fell and touched other drops and they became streams that trickled over his body, and while these moved down his flesh, the small growths of the forest took root in his clothing. He felt the ivy cling and make a second garment over him; he felt the small flowers bud and open and petal away, and still the rain pattered on his body and on his head. In the luminous night — for the vegetation glowed in the darkness —he could see the other two men outlined, like logs that had fallen and taken upon themselves velvet coverings of grass and flowers. The rain hit his face. He covered his face with his hands. The rain hit his neck. He turned over on his stomach in the mud, on the rubbery plants, and the rain hit his back and hit his legs. — RAY BRADBURY

This is not a soft and gentle spring rain. What is it? Where do you imagine these men to be? What specific words and phrases associated with touch are used in the paragraph? What is the overall effect of these words and phrases?

  D. Look over your notes and the material in your journal. Choose a topic from these sources or choose one of the topics listed below. Write a paragraph emphasizing touch.

diving into the water of a lake or pool	trudging through the snow on a cold day
walking along a beach or a road on a hot day	playing a sport

Part 4   The Sense of Taste

  Unlike your other senses, the sense of taste does not operate well alone. Much of what we experience as taste is a reaction to the way foods look and smell, or the way they feel against the mouth and tongue. Therefore, when describing tastes, it is a good idea to include references to other senses as well.

  On Sunday morning Momma served a breakfast that was geared to hold us quiet from 9:30 A.M. to 3 P.M. She fried thick pink slabs of home-cured ham and poured the grease over sliced red tomatoes. Eggs over easy, fried potatoes and onions, yellow hominy, and crisp perch fried so hard we would pop them into our mouths and chew bones, fins, and all. Her cathead biscuits were at least three inches in diameter and two inches thick. The trick to eating catheads was to get the butter on them before they got cold — then they were delicious. When, unluckily, they were allowed to get cold, they tended to a gooeyness not unlike a wad of tired gum. — MAYA ANGELOU

Training in Tasting

Record the following in your journal.

1. At dinner tonight concentrate on your sense of taste. Sort out the flavor of each thing you eat. After dinner make a list of the foods you had. Beside each food write a short phrase that describes the flavor. Make some notes about your tastes in general. Do you like strong or mild flavors? Are there some foods you would eat hot but not cold, and vice versa?

2. Think of one taste you like or don't like. Describe what happened when you last experienced this taste.

3. Make a list of some things you have tasted and their quality of taste. For example: lemons — sour, candy — sweet.

4. Survey your family or some of your friends to see what tastes they like and don't like. Compare your results with those of a classmate.

Here is a list of taste words. As you think about each taste, try to recall your own experience. What things would you relate to each taste? Add more words and record them in your journal.

Taste Words

oily	sugary	tangy	gingery
buttery	crisp	unripe	hot
salty	ripe	raw	burnt
bitter	bland	alkaline	overripe
bittersweet	tasteless	medicinal	spoiled
sweet	sour	fishy	rotten
hearty	vinegary	spicy	
mellow	fruity	peppery	

Exercises Using "Taste" Words in Your Writing

A. The sense of taste differs in each person. Here are some things you may have tasted. Write a sentence for each one, trying to use exact words to describe how it tastes to you. Record the sentences in your journal.

peanut butter	an orange	a pencil
a piece of toast	gum	medicine
a blade of grass	an egg	cola
ice cream		

Reread your sentences. Would every member of your family agree with your descriptions? Compare your sentences with those of someone sitting next to you. Where do you agree and disagree?

B. Read the following passage and notice all of the words that appeal to the sense of taste.

> To me, the memories of the circus will always remain tied to the tastes of the food upon which I gorged myself. My parents warned me about eating too much, and even I knew that these treats were the worst things in the world for a child's stomach. Still . . . I loved the feeling of smooth, rich ice cream coating my lips and sliding down my throat. I crunched happily on bags of popcorn that was usually too salty and always slightly stale. I treasured the flavored ice-crystals of snow cones as they melted into sweet streams of cherry-flavored syrup, and I could chew on a sticky rope of licorice for hours. But my favorite, my absolute favorite, was the cotton candy. What could be better than biting into a huge pink cloud of spun cotton and then feeling the mouthful of gossamer dissolve into little wisps of sugar on your tongue? I was always sick and remorseful for at least a day afterwards, but, after all, wasn't that part of the fun?

What foods are mentioned in the paragraph? What words are used to describe them? How many specifically relate to the sense of taste? What other senses are employed to describe the food? Make lists to record your answers.

C. Do you think your tastes change with time? Are there some things you like now that you didn't like before? After concentrating on tastes, you are ready to write a paragraph of your own in which you appeal to the sense of taste. Look over the ideas in your journal or try some of the following ideas.

1. Ask someone at home to give you something that is all right to eat, but not to tell you what it is. Close your eyes so that you can concentrate only on the taste. In a paragraph, describe the experience and the taste. Keep the events in the order they happen.

2. What is your favorite taste? Can you remember the first time you tasted it? What was happening at the time? Where were you? Who was with you? In a paragraph, re-create the moment or create a brand new situation in which you might be tasting the same thing.

Part 5   The Sense of Smell

Human beings do not have a highly developed sense of smell. Smells must be particularly strong or near for us to notice them. Even then, we quickly become used to most smells and soon can no longer smell them.

Nonetheless, smells are all around us, and many evoke strong memories, emotions, and moods. What moods are evoked by the sense of smell in the following passage?

There were all the smells of salt and seaweed, of fish and water and wind. There were all the human smells too of the hundreds of people who filled the boardwalk: ladies in print dresses smelling like passing gardens; swimmers with their scents of sun-tan oils and skin lotions; there were the smells of the eating places: of mustard and onions, of hamburgers frying; and the sudden sharp smell of stacks of dill pickles, as brisk in the nose as a sudden unintended inhalation of sea water. There was the smell of frying fish from the many fish grottos. And outside these places, in the middle of the boardwalk like miniature, land-locked seas, the glass tanks, where passers-by might admire the grace and color of their dinners before eating them. It was hard to say who did the most looking; fish outward from these sidewalk aquariums, at the strange pale gill-less pedestrians, or pedestrians inward at the finny swimmers. — JESSAMYN WEST

Training in Smelling

Record the following in your journal:

1. List your favorite smells; then list the smells you dislike.
2. Starting when you leave this room, begin to list everything you can smell. Be aware of how the smells change with place, time of day, temperature, or other variables.
3. Choose a room at home or at school and describe all the different smells that are there when you walk in.
4. Think of an outdoor place you like. List all the smells you can recall that are there. If you can go to this place on your way home, check to see how well your nose "remembers."
5. Think of a past experience you have had that has a particular smell connected with it. List what you can remember about the place, such as the time of day, what happened, and the smells you remember.

Below is a list of words related to smell. As you study these words, try to recall vivid experiences with each smell. Add your own words to the list and record them in your journal.

Smell Words

sweet	piney	briny	rancid
scented	minty	acidic	sickly
fragrant	odorous	acrid	stagnant
aromatic	pungent	burnt	moldy
perfumed	tempting	gaseous	musty
flowery	spicy	reeking	mildewed
heady	savory	putrid	damp
fresh	sharp	rotten	dank
balmy	gamey	spoiled	stench
earthy	fishy	sour	stale

Using the Sense of Smell in Writing

A. Write a sentence describing the smell of each of the things listed below. Record your sentences in your journal.

a fire   perfume
a flower   toothpaste
food cooking   cookies
wet coats   chalk
rain   popcorn

If the thing you are talking about were not named in the sentence, would your reader still know what you were describing?

B. Read the following paragraph. Then, list all of the smells recorded in the paragraph.

The wolf wrinkled its nose in disgust, its wary expression contorting into a grimace of distaste. The scent of the man was strong here, much more so than at any time in the past several hours. The acrid odor of the clothing alerted the wolf first — the musty smell of an ancient wool coat saturated with a disagreeable, sickly-sweet stench of sweat and fear. And then there was the oppressive odor of the man himself, the heavy musky smell of warm skin and racing blood. The wolf lowered its head and cast about. Finally it located faint, cow-like traces of thin, grease-caked boots. Hurriedly, nose to the ground, the wolf darted along the trail.

C. Concentrating especially on the sense of smell, write a paragraph using smell as a central idea. Use ideas from your journal, something from the suggestions below, or a new idea.

1. Write the first paragraph of a story that opens with a particular smell. It could be any kind of story, even a mystery, in which the smell plays an important part.

2. Smells often trigger memories. Write a paragraph that begins with a character in the present who is experiencing a smell. Then, describe the character's memories associated with this smell.

Part 6   All of the Senses Working Together

You have spent a lot of time practicing the use of your five senses, concentrating on one at a time and sharpening each one. Now it's time for you to pull together all you have learned. Look over the work you have done thus far on your senses — your lists, notes, and all of the material in your journal. Find the writing that you most enjoyed doing, or the activities that were most satisfying to you. Before you write, study this example of sensory writing in which all of the senses are working together to achieve a unifed effect.

> The evening is lovely.
>
> True, it is not raining but still is lovely. The puriri stands at the window motionless and shadowy, the forest mysterious and still, and between them the clearing, without the foxgloves which have died down in the winter. Water voices drift up from the river, the tui lets fall an occasional note, his signature to the evening, while from the forest emanates an odor made up of all the winter decomposition and all the summer blooming; exotic, pungent…heady.
>
> It is the enchanted moment when day faces night, a magic time which holds in itself a capacity for improbability unlikely in the daytime. The fire is still going in the stove with one overlong arm of wood beckoning from the firebox, while moths and other night-winged creatures make a freeway of the window. — SYLVIA ASHTON-WARNER

List the senses used in these paragraphs, with the words and phrases related to them. What one sense is missing? The writer speaks of enchantment, "magic," "improbability." What senses are involved here? What kind of mood does this passage create in the reader?

In the paragraph on the next page, the effect is quite different. Notice, again, the senses to which the writer appeals.

Above me the clouds roll in, unfurling and smoking billows in malignant violet, dense as wool. Most of the sky is lidded over but the sun remains clear, halfway down the west, shining beneath the storm. Over my head the clouds thicken, then crack and split with a roar like that of cannon balls tumbling down a marble staircase; their bellies open—too late to run now!—and suddenly the rain comes down.

Comes down: not softly, but gently, with no quality of mercy, but like heavy water in buckets, raindrops like lead pellets smashing and splattering on the flat rock, knocking the berries off the juniper, plastering my shirt to my back, drumming on my hat like hailstones, running like a waterfall off the brim.

— EDWARD ABBEY

Exercise All of the Senses Working Together

You are now ready to write about all of the senses working together. Reread John Moffitt's poem "To Look at Any Thing" on page 60. To experience any thing fully, the poet says, you must "Be the thing." If you are a fish, for example, you live in a watery world. Light and dark are shadowy; color is muted. You are cold blooded. You have scales, fins, a tail. Your eyes are on the sides of your head. You have to search for food. Dangers are of a different order. Time doesn't exist as humans know it.

Write a short composition in which you are something other than yourself. Put all your senses to work in your particular world. *Be the thing.*

Here are some suggestions to stir your imagination, but you can be anything else you wish.

a motorcycle	a pillow
a snake	a bird
a bee	an animal
a stone	a window
a rug	a fence
a tooth	a weed

SUMMARY AND APPLICATIONS

1. Good writers make their work come alive by vividly describing how things look, taste, sound, feel, and smell.

2. Skillful use of the senses can make you a better writer. It will also strengthen your powers of observation in all subjects and situations.

3. Train yourself to be more aware of your senses by concentrating on one sense at a time. Record your sensory experiences in a journal.

4. When you write descriptions, use strong sensory words such as the ones included in this chapter.

5. Depending upon the purpose and the subject of your writing, you may concentrate on one sense or use several senses in combination with one another.

Applications in Other Subject Areas

History. Historians depend upon many sources to learn about the past. Among these, first-hand accounts are extremely important. These accounts often contain vivid sensory details that re-create the atmosphere surrounding an historical event. Find a first-hand account of an historical event in a history text, an autobiography, a journal, or a magazine article. Then list the important sensory details in the account.

Science. A scientist must have the ability to make detailed observations and to record them accurately. Select one of the following subjects or choose one of your own. Observe the subject carefully for at least fifteen minutes, jotting down notes on sensory details. Use as many of the senses as possible.

a. an ant hill

b. any animal at a zoo

c. a constellation

d. a mixture of oil and water

e. a spider and its web

f. any science experiment

Chapter 5

Sentence Combining

An important part of good writing is learning how to write sentences that express your ideas clearly and directly. This skill also involves creating sentences that are interesting to your reader. For example, compare the following two ways of expressing the same ideas.

> Andrea sat at the computer. She sat there for hours. She hunted for the mistake in the program. The mistake had baffled the rest of us.
>
> Andrea sat at the computer for hours, hunting for the mistake in the program that had baffled the rest of us.

The second example contains the same information as the first, but presents it in a much more interesting and efficient way. The first example is a set of short, choppy sentences. The second is a combined sentence that flows smoothly and shows how the ideas are related.

This chapter will give you practice in combining short, related sentences. The skills you learn will be useful as you revise your writing.

Part 1   Joining Sentences

Two sentences that state related ideas of equal importance can usually be combined into a single statement by a comma and the word *and.*

> The storm will pass tonight. Tomorrow will be fair.
> The storm will pass tonight, and tomorrow will be fair.

The sentences could also be joined by a semicolon.

> The storm will pass tonight; tomorrow will be fair.

Two sentences that state contrasting ideas of equal importance can usually be joined by a comma and the word *but.*

> Tomorrow will be fair. Another storm is on its way.
> Tomorrow will be fair, but another storm is on its way.

Two sentences that express a choice between ideas of equal importance usually can be joined by a comma and the word *or.*

> Will the weekend be sunny? Is another storm coming?
> Will the weekend be sunny, or is another storm coming?

Exercises   Joining Sentences

A. Join each pair of sentences by following the directions.

1. The car was locked. The keys were inside. (Join with **,and**.)
2. The race was stopped. No one knew why. (Join with **,but**.)
3. Can you meet me at the library? Do you have to go directly home? (Join with **,or**.)
4. Lightning struck. All our lights went out. (Join with **,and**.)
5. The promoters of the concert advertised widely. Attendance was excellent. (Join with ;.)

B. Join sentence pairs using **,and**, **,but**,or **,or**.

1. Many people believe in UFO's. Few have ever seen one.
2. Do I have to wear glasses? Can I wear contact lenses?

3. The legendary Red Baron flunked his first flying tests. He became one of the most notorious pilots of World War I.

4. The force of the blizzard increased. The city was paralyzed.

5. The team's record must improve. The coach might be fired.

Part 2   Joining Sentence Parts

Two sentences may express ideas that are so closely related that words are repeated in the sentences. It is usually best to combine such sentences and eliminate the repeated words.

Sentence parts with similar ideas of equal importance can often be joined by *and*. (Italicized words are eliminated.)

> Louise stepped onstage. *Louise* walked to the podium.
> Louise stepped onstage and walked to the podium.

> The papers ignored the election. TV stations *ignored it, too.*
> The papers and TV stations ignored the election.

Sentence parts that express contrasting ideas usually can be joined by *but*.

> I arrived late. *I* worked harder than anyone else.
> I arrived late but worked harder than anyone else.

Sentence parts that express a choice between ideas usually can be joined by *or*.

> Is the Shuttle launch scheduled for Thursday? *Is the Shuttle launch scheduled for* Friday?
> Is the Shuttle launch scheduled for Thursday or Friday?

Exercises   Joining Sentence Parts

A. Join the related parts in each pair of sentences by following the directions in parentheses. Eliminate the italicized words.

1. Natalie called. Andy *called.* (Join related parts with **and**.)

2. The software for this system is excellent. *It is* expensive, *though.* (Join related parts with **but**.)

3. The missing hikers may have followed Hurricane Trail. *The missing hikers may have* left the trail system completely. (Join related parts with **or**.)

4. Jensen took a quick look toward first base. Then *Jensen* went into his windup. (Join related parts with **and**.)

5. Most of the popular musical groups are from England. *Many are from* Australia. (Join related parts with **or**.)

B. Combine each of the following pairs of sentences by joining related sentence parts. You decide which parts to join.

1. Computers fascinate some people. They terrify others.

2. Searchers never found the plane's tail section. They never found the plane's "black box," either.

3. A Rubic's Cube is fascinating. It is also frustrating.

4. Richard Pryor may be approached for that role. Eddie Murphy may also be asked.

5. The bobsled whipped around the curve. Then it plummeted down a big hill.

Part 3   Adding Single Words

Sometimes the ideas in two sentences are not equally important. However, there may be one word in the second sentence that could add a great deal of meaning to the main idea. The one important word can be added to the first sentence to create a tighter and more effective way of expressing the idea.

> Williston was a little town. *It was a* quiet *place.*
> Williston was a quiet little town.

Notice that the italicized words were eliminated.

You may be able to combine more than two sentences in this manner. You can do so if one of the sentences states a main idea and each of the other sentences adds only one important detail.

> A cloud passed in front of the moon. *The cloud was* dark. *The moon was* silvery.
> A dark cloud passed in front of the silvery moon.

Be careful to choose the right location in the main sentence for each word that you add.

You may have to use a comma when you add more than one word to a sentence.

> Below the falls was a pool of water. *The water was* cool. *The water was* bubbling.
> Below the falls was a pool of cool, bubbling water.

See Section 14 for further discussion on the uses of the comma.

Occasionally, a word does not quite fit into a sentence because of the form it is in. In this case, you may have to change the form of the word slightly. Sometimes you will have to add *-ing* or *-ed.*

> We sang folk songs around a fire. *The fire* blazed.
> We sang folk songs around a blazing fire.

> Pour the batter into a baking dish. Butter *the baking dish.*
> Pour the batter into a buttered baking dish.

At other times you will have to add *-ly.* Often, the word ending in *-ly* can be placed in any of several positions in the sentence.

> Insulation increases fuel economy. *The increase is* great.
> Insulation increases fuel economy greatly.
> Insulation greatly increases fuel economy.

Exercises Adding Single Words

A. Combine these sentences by adding the important word. Eliminate italicized words and follow any special directions.

1. Scott wore a watch. *The watch was* waterproof.

2. The laser cuts through steel. *The steel is* hardened. *The laser cuts* smoothly.

3. The ending made the movie worth seeing. *The ending was* thrilling. *The ending was a* surprise. (Do not use a comma.)

4. Two pairs of eyelashes protect a camel's eyes from the desert sand. *The sand* stings. (End the important word with **-ing**.)

5. The program was interrupted for storm warnings. *The interruptions were* repeated *several times.* (End the important word with **-ly**.)

B. Combine the following sentence pairs by adding important words to the first sentence. You decide how to join the sentences. You may have to change the form of a word before adding it.

1. The boat was caught in a storm. The storm was sudden.
2. Mary oiled the hinges. The hinges squeaked.
3. I saw the light of a TV screen. The light flickered.
4. Matsuko visits the art galleries. Her visits are frequent.
5. The framework of the building is steel. The steel is welded to make the framework.

Part 4   Adding Groups of Words

One sentence may contain a group of words that can add important information to another sentence.

Ken stacked the cartons. They are in the basement.
Ken stacked the cartons in the basement.

If you can learn to recognize these word groups, you will be able to create stronger, more precise sentences.

Adding Groups of Words Without Changes

Sometimes you can add a group of words without changing it. When the words give more information about someone or something, add them near the name of the person or thing.

The clouds were alarming. *The clouds were* on the horizon.
The clouds on the horizon were alarming.

When the words describe an action, add them near the words that name the action.

Geraldo was waiting. *He was* at the corner.
Geraldo was waiting at the corner.

When the words add more information to the entire main idea, you may add them at the beginning or the end.

We hold a family reunion. *It happens* every summer.
Every summer, we hold a family reunion.
We hold a family reunion every summer.

Sometimes you will have to separate the group of words from the rest of the sentence with a comma or a pair of commas.

The robot is controlled by a microprocessor. *A microprocessor is* an electronic device smaller than a postage stamp.
The robot is controlled by a microprocessor, an electronic device smaller than a postage stamp.

Adding Groups of Words with *-ing*

When you add words to a sentence, you may have to change the form of one of the words. The new word will often end with *-ing*.

Helicopters began arriving in the morning. *They* carried food.
Helicopters carrying food began arriving in the morning.

More than one group of words can be added to a sentence. You may have to use a variety of techniques to combine them.

We saw a ferry. *It* carried hundreds of passengers.
It was just off the coast of Ontario.
We saw a ferry carrying hundreds of passengers just off the coast of Ontario.

Exercises Adding Groups of Words

A. Combine each of the following pairs of sentences by adding a group of words to the first sentence. Eliminate the italicized words. Follow any special instructions given in parentheses.

1. The gray door leads to the main office. *The door is* at the end of this hall.
2. The call was from Anthony Metrakas. *He is* a newspaper reporter. (Use a comma.)
3. The flight is from Tampa. *The flight is* arriving at Gate 16.

4. The Chesapeake and Ohio Canal was completed in 1850. *The canal* linked Washington, D.C., and Cumberland, Maryland. (Use **-ing** and a pair of commas.)

5. Rescuers plunged out of the burning school. *They* carried children in their arms. (Add **-ing** to one of the words.)

B. Combine each group of sentences.

1. The Pioneer Days celebration will begin with a flapjack breakfast. The breakfast will start at 8:00.

2. Cairo was founded in A.D. 969. Cairo is the capital of Egypt.

3. Brass was first produced in ancient Rome. Brass is an alloy of copper and zinc.

4. Ted will write a column. The column will list plays. He will write the column for the Hinsdale *News.*

5. The historic park contains houses and shops. The houses and shops date back to the 18th century.

Part 5 Combining with *who, which,* or *that*

When you add a group of words to a sentence, you may sometimes find it necessary to add an introductory word to that group. The words *who, which,* and *that* are used for this purpose.

Use *who* to add information about a person or group of persons. If the information is absolutely necessary to the meaning of the sentence, simply add the words as near as possible to the word they refer to. If the information is not absolutely necessary to the meaning, it should be set off with commas.

The newscaster won the award. *She* covered the fire.
The newscaster who covered the fire won the award. (The added information is necessary. It tells *which* reporter.)

The newscaster won an award. *She* is popular with viewers.
The newscaster, who is popular with viewers, won an award. (The added information is not necessary to the meaning.)

Which and *that* are also used to add groups of words. When the added information is necessary to the meaning of the sentence, use *that*. When the information is not necessary to the sentence, use *which* and set off the word group with commas.

Here are the guitar strings. You asked me for *them* last week.
Here are the guitar strings that you asked me for last week.

The existence of the Loch Ness monster has yet to be proven. *The monster's existence* has been debated for decades.
The existence of the Loch Ness monster, which has been debated for decades, has yet to be proven.

Exercises Combining with *who, which,* and *that*

A. Combine each of the following pairs of sentences.

1. Tim Hutton has starred in several movies recently. *He* first became known in *Ordinary People.*(Combine with **,who**.)
2. This type of bicycle weighs less than ten pounds. *The bicycle* is used for racing. (Combine with **,which**.)
3. This is the book. I told you about *it* yesterday. (Join with **that**.)
4. The wrench is in the bottom drawer of the tool chest. I need *the wrench* to loosen this tight pipe. (Combine with **that**.)
5. The committee member was Terri. *Terri* suggested the project. (Combine with **who**.)

B. Combine each of the following pairs of sentences. Decide on your own whether to use **,who**, **,which**, or **that**.

1. The whale had beached itself on the coast of the tiny fishing village. The whale had been caught by the tide.
2. The computer company has just gone out of business. The company designed one of the first home computers.
3. The eighty-five-year-old comedian was honored with a banquet. He is loved by everyone in the entertainment field.
4. The trolley has finally been replaced. It ran on this avenue since the early 1900's.
5. The astronomer had the new comet named for him. The astronomer made the discovery.

SUMMARY AND APPLICATIONS

1. Related ideas may often be combined into a single sentence that clearly shows how the ideas are related.

2. Sentences and sentence parts that state ideas of equal importance can usually be joined by a comma and the word *and, or,* or *but*.

3. You may be able to combine two or more sentences by adding individual words or groups of words from one sentence to another.

4. Sometimes when you add words to a sentence, you will have to change the form of one of them. In its new form, the word will often end with *-ing* or *-ly*.

5. When you add a group of words, you may need to add the word *who, which,* or *that* at the beginning of the word group.

6. Use these sentence combining techniques when you are writing reports or compositions for your classes. Also use them to make talks and speeches more interesting.

Applications in Other Subject Areas

Literature. The writing styles of many authors are easily identifiable by the types of sentences that are used. Find one short story or novel by Ernest Hemingway and another by John Steinbeck. Which writer tends to use short, simple sentences? Which uses more complex sentences? Copy several typical sentences from each writer's work. See if you can identify any sentence combining techniques. You and your classmates may wish to discuss the effects these different styles have on the reader.

All Subjects. A textbook definition often combines a great many ideas into a single sentence. Find four such single-sentence definitions in your health, science, history, or mathematics texts. Break these statements down into the individual ideas that were combined to produce the definitions.

Chapter 6

Improving Your Sentences

A contractor would never construct a building using weak or unsound materials. Timbers might buckle, walls could crumble, and the whole structure might collapse. Similarly, a conscientious writer must be concerned with the building blocks of a piece of writing — sentences. If individual sentences are awkward, wordy, or repetitive, the writing as a whole will lose its impact and have little appeal to the reader.

To avoid producing ineffective materials, a good writer carefully examines and evaluates every sentence he or she produces and revises whenever necessary. This chapter will help you understand how to do such revisions. It gives examples of unsatisfactory sentences and shows you how to go about improving them. It then supplies additional sentences for you to revise on your own.

Almost all of the sentences you will work with in this chapter were written by high school students. They did not have a chance to revise what they had written. You will be doing the revising for them. You will also be training yourself to think and write clearly.

Part 1 Avoiding Empty Sentences

The purpose of a sentence is to say something. Unfortunately, words may be put into sentence form and still not say anything. Such a sentence is called an **empty sentence.**
There are two kinds of empty sentences.

1. Those that repeat an idea and end up where they started.
2. Those that make statements but fail to support them with a fact, a reason, or an example.

Sentences That Repeat an Idea

Notice the repetition of an idea in the following sentences.

FAULTY   He had no friends, and so he was always alone.
(Omit the second clause. It merely repeats the idea
He had no friends.)

REVISED   He had no friends.

FAULTY   I have a minor *crisis* in my life, and to me it presents
a *problem.*
(Since *crisis* and *problem* are similar, use only one.
Omit the second clause entirely.)

REVISED   I have a minor crisis in my life.

Sometimes a whole sentence is repeated. This repetitious style is boring and monotonous to read.

FAULTY   My father *complains* that I'm always on the phone,
no matter what the time of day. His *complaint* is that
I don't give anyone else a chance to use it.

REVISED   My father complains that no one else has a chance
to use the phone because I'm on it all day.
(Expressing the idea of *complaint* once is sufficient. The father's complaint has two parts: (1) *I'm
always on the phone,* and (2) *I don't give anyone
else a chance to use it.* Combine these ideas.)

FAULTY   From my earliest days I have been an avid reader. I suppose I inherited this love of books from my mother. *She also loves to read.*

REVISED   From my earliest days I have been an avid reader. I suppose I inherited this love of books from my mother. (The second sentence indicates the mother's love of reading in her love of books. *She also loves to read* is unnecessary repetition.)

FAULTY   I asked Tom to stop at my house *for a snack* and *to meet my mother.* After he *met my mother,* we went into the kitchen and *had a snack.*

REVISED   Tom accepted my invitation to stop at my house for a snack and to meet my mother.

Two suggestions will help you avoid this writing fault: (1) read aloud what you have written, and (2) revise.

Exercise Revising Sentences That Repeat an Idea

Revise the following sentences.

Suggestions

1—Look for repeated words in the same sentence.
2—Look for repeated ideas in the same sentence.
3—Look for sentences that repeat an idea already expressed.
4—Omit the repetitions wherever possible.
5—Combine two sentences into one, if necessary.
6—Realize that there is more than one way to revise these sentences.

1. Many people are interested in chess because it is a very interesting game.

2. The movie was boring, and I found it very dull.

3. Of course, you can't go on a hike without food. Who would ever dream of going on a hike without food?

4. Dad can't understand why I have to call my friends when I get home from school. He claims that I see my friends all day long in school, so I don't have to phone them as soon as I reach home.

5. At this point I usually burst into a torrent of tears. Mom and Dad usually know the right words to comfort me, however, for I soon feel better and begin to be a little more cheerful.

6. Have you ever watched television in a crowd? If you haven't watched it in a crowd, you can't imagine what it is like to watch television with three hundred people.

7. On Sunday we are going on a trip for the day. I am sure we will have a good time if the weather permits. There are seven of us going on the trip, and everyone is praying that we will have a wonderful day for our trip.

8. When I was small, I was spoiled. It wasn't because I was an only child, because I had two brothers. It was because I was the only girl and the only granddaughter. You see, all my cousins were boys.

9. In our high school, at every lunch period, there is a long cafeteria line. In the cafeteria we can buy yogurt, salad, fruit, hot food, and so on. To buy these items, we must stand in a line.

10. If you have ever been to the zoo, you know what a great time you can have there. The zoo is a place to visit again and again. At the zoo there is always something new, wonderful, and educational.

Sentences That Contain Unsupported Statements

A kind of emptiness in writing results from statements that are not supported by reasons, facts, or examples. The question "Why?" is left in the reader's mind.

Try to find the unsupported statement in this group:

> Not only does chess provide players with a challenging and enjoyable pastime, but it also sharpens thinking skills as players plan and carry out strategies.
>
> Chess is becoming popular with people of all ages. Even young children play it. I think it would be good for everyone to learn the game.

The unsupported statement is not difficult to find. Look for the sentence that involves an opinion. *Why* would it be good for everyone to learn chess? The writer should add one or more reasons that support the opinion.

Exercise **Revising Unsupported Statements**

Revise the following selections. They contain statements that need more support.

Suggestions

1—Locate the statement or statements that need support.
2—Ask "Why?" Then add whatever reasons or facts you think are necessary.

1. You can get a good laugh from practical jokes played in school. They can relieve the monotony of lessons. However, school is not the place for practical jokes.

2. There are more good job opportunities for minorities now because more good jobs are opening up.

3. Detroit is making a lot of small cars now. I think that is very good. I like these small cars and hope to save enough money to own one in a few years.

4. Some people are talking about making the school year longer. This would be a mistake. I think that the school year is long enough as it is.

5. I want to get a part-time job this year. I could work at least two hours after school each day. My parents do not approve of the idea.

6. Parents and teachers often complain about how much time young people spend watching television. However, many television shows are good for us to watch.

7. According to the state law, you have to be eighteen before you can get a decent job. I think this is very bad. I think the law should be changed.

8. Every year a million Americans travel to Europe. I wonder how many of those people have traveled around this country. It seems to me that people should see their own country before traveling to Europe.

9. When I watch a football game on television, I always cheer for the Steelers (or Bears or Jets or Cowboys) because they are my favorite football team.

10. The movie rating system ought to be changed because it isn't effective the way it is.

Part 2   Avoiding Padded Sentences

A padded sentence is one that contains unnecessary words or phrases. Some sentences contain padding such as *the fact that* and *the reason is.* Others contain clauses that could be reduced to phrases without any damage to the thought. Although such padding may not always be considered incorrect, it often clutters the sentences and prevents writers from expressing their ideas clearly and concisely.

Taking Out the Padding

Phrases that puff up a sentence with unnecessary words get in the way of the meaning of the sentence. Getting to the meaning can be like trying to find a path that is overgrown with weeds.

The following expressions usually add little to a sentence and should be avoided:

"FACT" EXPRESSIONS	"WHAT" EXPRESSIONS
because of the fact that	what I mean is
owing to the fact that	what I believe is
due to the fact that	what I want is
on account of the fact that	what I want to say is
the fact of the matter is that	

OTHER EXPRESSIONS TO AVOID

the point is	the thing is
the reason is	being that

Sentences are smoother and simpler when unnecessary words are omitted.

PADDED   My family did not go to the shore *on account of the fact that* there was a storm.

REVISED   My family did not go to the shore *because* there was a storm.

PADDED	*What I mean is* that his ideas of summer camp are not realistic.
REVISED	His ideas of summer camp are not realistic.
PADDED	*The reason* I washed my father's car *was* that he hinted that it was dirty.
REVISED	I washed my father's car *because* he hinted that it was dirty.
PADDED	*What I want* is to go to Baltimore to see my grandparents if I don't get a job.
REVISED	I want to go to Baltimore to see my grandparents if I don't get a job.
PADDED	I know *that* if I study hard *that* I can get a scholarship.
REVISED	I know that if I study hard I can get a scholarship.

Reducing Clauses to Phrases

Clauses that begin with *who is* and *which is* can sometimes be simplified to phrases.

LENGTHY	We admired the lights at the airport, *which is across the bay.*
REVISED	We admired the lights at the airport *across the bay.*
LENGTHY	Her latest movie, *which is a modern Western,* has been nominated for an Oscar.
REVISED	Her latest movie, *a modern Western,* has been nominated for an Oscar.
LENGTHY	The swimming meet, *which was the most exciting event of the year,* attracted crowds of students.
REVISED	The swimming meet, *the most exciting event of the year,* attracted crowds of students.

or

The swimming meet was *the most exciting event of the year* and attracted crowds of students.

Revising Padded Sentences

A. Revise these sentences by reducing and simplifying them.

Suggestions

1—Look for "fact" expressions, "what" expressions, and other padding.
2—Look for *who* or *which* clauses that can be simplified.
3—Eliminate as many unnecessary words as possible.
4—Realize that there is more than one way to revise these sentences.

1. What Sarah wants is to be a baseball coach.
2. The thing that nobody could understand was Ann's fear.
3. You must admit that even if you don't admire him that he plays well.
4. The Eiffel Tower, which is located in Paris, is a symbol of France.
5. On account of the fact that she had learned to bowl during the summer, Debbie wanted to join the school team.
6. We immediately called Mrs. Vincent, who is our lawyer, to ask for advice.
7. Due to the fact that the fog was dense, the two huge tankers collided.
8. What I believe is that you succeed largely because of your own efforts.
9. The point is that the study of French has many values.
10. Howie, who will do anything for a laugh, wore a T-shirt that had a formal black tie and ruffles printed on it.

B. Revise these sentences.

1. The reason that we took the car through the car wash was that it was covered with tree spray.
2. The rocks that extend out into the bay are dangerous.
3. The reason that Venice is fascinating is that many of its streets are all water.
4. Whenever it happens to rain hard, our cellar fills up with water and becomes a lake.

5. Many ruins in Rome are visible to tourists on account of the fact that much excavating has been done.

6. What I couldn't help hearing all night was the drone of the planes.

7. I knew that if I had to change the typewriter ribbon that I would create a hopeless tangle.

8. The fountain of Trevi, which is in Rome, is connected with a legend about coins.

9. What we finally did about our rehearsals was hold them in Mr. Steiner's garage.

10. I bought this ring in Harper's novelty store, which is on Walnut Street.

Part 3   Avoiding Overloaded Sentences

Long sentences containing a number of ideas, usually connected loosely by *and*'s, are confusing and ineffective. They give the reader a whole series of ideas to sort out without any clue to their relationship. Such sentences violate the principle that a sentence usually contains *one* central thought.

LENGTHY   I went into the building, *and* I waited for the elevator in the lobby, *and* when it didn't come I had to walk up eight flights of stairs.

REVISED   I went into the lobby of the building and waited for the elevator. When it didn't come, I had to walk up eight flights of stairs.

LENGTHY   Horrible faces glared at me from the shelves in the costume shop. All of them were contorted, *and* most of them were scarred, *and* they were a deathly gray with a greenish cast.

REVISED   Horrible faces glared at me from the shelves in the costume shop. All of them were contorted, and most of them were scarred. The faces were a deathly gray with a greenish cast.

Exercise **Revising Overloaded Sentences**

Revise the following sentences.

Suggestions

1. Separate each sentence into two or three shorter ones.
2. Reduce the number of *and*'s.

1. Debbie got a white bike for her birthday, and it is a ten-speed model and it has a suede saddle.

2. Dad lost his wallet last Saturday with all his credit cards in it, but, luckily for him, it was returned yesterday by a neighbor who found it in the street outside our house.

3. For the Halloween party Luis dressed as Rocky Balboa, and Anna dressed as the Cookie Monster, and several people came as Darth Vader, but the Wizard of Oz won the costume contest.

4. My family picked apples at an orchard, and we learned how to tell which apples were ripe and how to keep from bruising the fruit and how to climb ladders to reach the top branches, and the biggest bonus was the juicy apple pies we made.

5. Some children learn to read at age three or four, and others learn in school, and experts disagree about the value of very early training in reading.

6. Different styles of furniture change the mood of a room. Early American furniture has a comfortable look, and contemporary furniture has a sleek look, and traditional furniture has a formal look, and there are also ethnic styles, like Mediterranean.

7. One tree in our town is six hundred years old, and it has a hole in the trunk, and twenty people can stand inside it, and Indians used the tree long ago as a meeting place.

8. The art department offers classes in ceramics and photography, and this year there will be a printmaking class, and many students are eager to learn about etching and lithography.

9. Hurricanes are tropical cyclones, and they start over oceans, especially near the equator, and the winds can reach 150 miles per hour, and the most destructive hurricane occurred in 1972.

10. The Olympic Games are patterned after an ancient Greek festival, and the first modern games were held in 1896, and since then the number of sports and participants has greatly increased.

Part 4   Writing Sentences That Make Sense

   Sometimes students write sentences that do not make complete sense because they shift from what they started to say to something else. In between, the main idea has become confused or lost. They may also write quickly and carelessly and fail to check what they have written. The result is a hodgepodge, and situations like these occur:

1. A verb has no subject or a subject has no verb.
2. A prepositional phrase is used as a subject.
3. A faulty comparison is made.
4. Single words, necessary to complete the meaning of the sentence, are left out.

Making Sure That the Verb Has a Subject

   Study the following examples.

FAULTY   If you constantly practice is a help in becoming a better dancer.
   (There is no subject for the verb *is*.)

REVISED   Constant practice helps you to become a better dancer.

FAULTY   His character was very weak and never did the right thing.
   (There is no subject for the verb *did*.)

REVISED   His character was very weak, and *he* never did the right thing.

FAULTY   The speech was long and were bored.
   (There is no subject for the verb *were*.)

REVISED   The speech was long, and *we* were bored.

   You can eliminate this problem by rereading and revising what you have written.

Avoiding the Use of a Prepositional Phrase as the Subject

A preposition is a short word used to show a relationship in time or space. Common prepositions include *to, at, on, with, by, from, of, for, after, until,* and *around.* Prepositional phrases, groups of words that begin with prepositions, should never be used as subjects of verbs.

Study the following examples.

FAULTY   By setting up observation posts near volcanoes and detecting eruptions early can save many lives.
(A prepositional phrase is used incorrectly as the subject of *can save.*)

REVISED   *Setting* up observation posts near volcanoes and *detecting* eruptions early can save many lives.
(The italicized words are acceptable subjects for *can save.*)

Avoiding Faulty Comparisons

A special kind of senseless sentence is one in which there is a faulty comparison or one in which two things are treated as though they were similar when they are not.

FAULTY   *Studying biology* in high school is very different from *college.*
(*Studying biology* should not be compared with *college.*)

REVISED   *Studying biology* in high school is very different from *studying it* in college.

FAULTY   The requirements for the job are an engineer and at least one year of experience.
(An *engineer* is a person and does not equal the word *requirements.*)

REVISED   The requirements for the job are an engineering degree and at least one year of experience.

Making Sure That Necessary Words Are Included

The omission of a single word can make a sentence meaningless. This kind of carelessness can be avoided by rereading and revising your work.

FAULTY   The little Swiss family find themselves comfortably situated as conditions will permit.
(The word *as* has been left out.)

REVISED   The little Swiss family find themselves *as* comfortably situated as conditions will permit.

FAULTY   Elizabeth Barrett, an invalid for many years, knew what she wanted to do but was afraid of her father to attempt it.

REVISED   Elizabeth Barrett, an invalid for many years, knew what she wanted to do but was *too* afraid of her father to attempt it.

Exercises Revising Sentences That Do Not Make Sense

A. Revise the following ten sentences.

Suggestions

1. Make sure that every verb has a subject.
2. Make sure that a prepositional phrase is not used as a subject.
3. Correct the faulty comparisons.
4. Make sure that necessary words have been included.

1. The cost of running a small car is less than a big car.
2. The real test of Donna's personality was her older sister.
3. The easier a subject is and the higher marks you can get with little work does not mean you should choose it.
4. To anyone who observes life and the game of football will soon detect many similarities.
5. The only real problem I find I wear out the rug by dancing.
6. Paula's fever has broken and is now feeling much better.

7. You could tell by the expression on my face the anguish I was through.

8. Andy's explanation of scuba diving is clearer than high-diving.

9. By applying for a summer job early is the best way for a student to be hired.

10. The faster the car goes is not the most important reason for buying it.

B. Revise the following sentences.

1. Playing football in college is much different from high school.

2. The way I check a person is how he or she acts.

3. The more you have to do and the less time makes you work harder.

4. Some hobbies are so that you can make money out of them.

5. Going to college or a job is a question every student must face before he or she graduates.

6. I burned the hamburgers is why we finally went to McDonald's.

7. Because it's a white dog with black spots all over it is why I'm sure it's a Dalmatian.

8. Any fad that Jerry hears about, he follows it.

9. Radio commercials don't bother me as much as TV.

10. You tell a good friend what he or she wants to hear is not always the kindest thing to do.

Part 5   Varying Your Sentence Beginnings

You want people to enjoy reading what you have to say. You are therefore interested in making your writing lively and effective. One way to achieve this is to vary the beginnings of your sentences, to give them a new look by inverting the order of their parts. You must be careful not to overwork this technique, but it can effectively be used to intensify a situation or an idea, or momentarily to slow down the pace of your writing.

Ways To Vary Your Sentence Beginnings

1. Put an adverb before the subject.

USUAL ORDER   Butch inched his way *cautiously*.
                               (adverb)

INVERTED   *Cautiously*, Butch inched his way.

USUAL ORDER   She stopped *abruptly* and stared at him.
                               (adverb)

INVERTED   *Abruptly*, she stopped and stared at him.

2. Put the verb or direct object before the subject.

USUAL ORDER   The *torrents* of rain *poured* down.
                          (verb)   **(subject)**

INVERTED   Down *poured* the *torrents* of rain.

USUAL ORDER   *Anchorage was* twenty miles ahead of us.
                                (verb)   **(subject)**

INVERTED   Twenty miles ahead of us *was Anchorage*.

USUAL ORDER   *I* could not tolerate an *insult* like that.
                         (object)   **(subject)**

INVERTED   An *insult* like that *I* could not tolerate.

USUAL ORDER   *I* can recall certain *songs* without difficulty.
                          (object) (subject)

INVERTED   Certain *songs I* can recall without difficulty.

3. Begin the sentence with a prepositional phrase, a participial phrase, or an infinitive phrase. Be sure the phrase modifies the proper word.

USUAL ORDER   I waited alone *for ten minutes.*
                      (prepositional phrase)

INVERTED   *For ten minutes* I waited alone.

USUAL ORDER	Nothing is more beautiful *to me* than a snow-storm.
	(prepositional phrase)
INVERTED	*To me*, nothing is more beautiful than a snow-storm.
USUAL ORDER	James led her into the hall, *taking her gently by the hand*.
	(participial phrase)
INVERTED	*Taking her gently by the hand*, James led her into the hall.
USUAL ORDER	We headed for the dude ranch, *excited about our unusual vacation*.
	(participial phrase)
INVERTED	*Excited about our unusual vacation*, we headed for the dude ranch.
USUAL ORDER	Sharon went to the library *to get information about satellites*.
	(infinitive phrase)
INVERTED	*To get information about satellites*, Sharon went to the library.
USUAL ORDER	Dick must pass a physical examination *to be eligible for the team*.
	(infinitive phrase)
INVERTED	*To be eligible for the team*, Dick must pass a physical examination.

4. Begin the sentence with a subordinate clause.

USUAL ORDER	Paula's mother was at the airport to meet the girls *when they got off the plane*.
	(subordinate clause)
INVERTED	*When the girls got off the plane*, Paula's mother was there to meet them.

USUAL ORDER   I felt like a millionaire *as I boarded the ship for France.*

(subordinate clause)

INVERTED   *As I boarded the ship for France*, I felt like a millionaire.

Exercises Varying Your Sentence Beginnings

A. Rewrite the following sentences, varying the positions of the words or word groups in italics.

1. We tried not to shake *as we walked onto the stage.*
2. The clock *finally* struck ten.
3. He looked stiff and unhappy, *dressed in his best suit.*
4. The plow was tossing up huge mounds of snow *in the corners of the parking lot.*
5. Nothing will happen *unless I make the first move.*
6. The driver was *suddenly* blinded by a flash of light.
7. The frightened people hurried *out into the rain.*
8. I lost my interest in snowmobiling *after the accident.*
9. Paul buried himself in his work *to fight against his fear.*
10. One of the instruments Leona plays is *the tenor sax.*

B. Rewrite each sentence below. Change the positions of words so that you have an effective variation of the sentence.

1. My pen ran dry in the middle of the test.
2. The swirling, muddy torrent came down, dragging tents and equipment with it.
3. Peter sold his stamp collection reluctantly.
4. My dad gave me my first driving lesson after I reminded him that the car was insured.
5. She went off to the fitting room, carrying three new dresses.
6. Joe's problem grew heavier as he shuffled down Main Street.
7. The police questioned the suspect for eight hours.
8. Diana hurried to her locker as soon as the game was over.
9. Andy kept on eating pizza even though he knew he was gaining too much weight.
10. Dad climbs the walls when our kitten climbs the curtains.

Revising Sentences with Various Problems

Revise the following sentences. They contain various problems you have dealt with in this chapter.

1. I know that if I try that I can get into college.
2. The pen that has the red felt tip leaks.
3. Each time, I went through a routine that was different.
4. Television lets you sit back and let a machine think for you. You don't do any of the thinking yourself.
5. My speech did not go over well due to the fact that I was extremely nervous.
6. What I sometimes wish is people wouldn't behave like sheep.
7. Mr. Russo is completely bald is probably the reason he always wears a cap.
8. The photos of the surface of Mars look just like the Painted Desert of Arizona.
9. I got sick on account of the fact that I ate too many tacos.
10. Disc jockeys at many radio stations are given a "play list" of songs that have been selected by a computer, and these songs are either popular now or expected to be popular soon, and the disc jockey has to play the songs on the list.
11. The reception on my parents' stereo is better than my radio.
12. When you think about it, you realize that death is something that happens to everyone, but most of the time you think it will happen only to other people and that it will never happen to you.
13. In Switzerland, skiing is a popular sport. Many Swiss ski regularly.
14. Make my bed, clean up my room, but put away my barbell is the only thing I forget to do.
15. How to load an Instamatic camera is the thing I have trouble doing.
16. My brother says that microcomputers are going to be the hottest home entertainment industry since television, and he says people are just starting to see how much fun these little gadgets can be, and he predicts that people will soon be bored by television.

1. A good writer reviews his or her work carefully and revises awkward, repetitious, or wordy sentences.

2. Some sentences lack meaning because they either make unsupported statements or repeat the same idea in different words.

3. Padded sentences contain unnecessary phrases and clauses that obscure meaning and decrease readability.

4. Overloaded sentences contain too many different ideas. These sentences should be divided into several shorter statements.

5. Some sentences are illogical because of grammatical errors, faulty comparisons, or missing parts.

6. One way to make writing more interesting is to vary sentence beginnings.

7. Mastery of these techniques will help you write, think, and speak clearly. Try to be aware of them whenever you express your ideas.

Applications in Other Subject Areas

Industrial Arts / Home Economics. Instructions for completing projects, operating tools and machinery, and repairing or checking different items must be extremely clear and precise. Poor sentence construction can weaken such directions. Find an example in which poor sentences have led to muddled instructions. Then revise the instructions on your own.

Speech / Social Studies. Effective speakers, like effective writers, must avoid empty, padded, or overloaded sentences. Listen to speakers in any two of the situations given below. Write down any examples of poor sentences that weaken their speeches. Then revise the sentences so that they express the ideas more clearly.

    a. a class speech or lecture   c. a televised speech
    b. a city or town council meeting   d. an interview

Chapter 7

The Process of Writing

As you bite into a piece of cake, look at a painting, or read a book, you usually give little thought to the processes that were involved in creating each product. For instance, the artist whose painting you are admiring may have considered and rejected several possible subjects. He or she may then have drawn dozens of sketches. Even while actually painting, the artist may have blotted out sections and begun over.

There is another process to which you may never have given much thought. This is the **process of writing**. No matter what you compose, you should follow certain steps of preparation and development. Like the artist in the example above, you plan what you want to do, try out ideas, and then modify or rework those ideas. These are the three stages of the process of writing: prewriting, writing the first draft, and revising. The better you understand this process, the more satisfying and successful your writing will be.

Part 1   Pre-Writing

The pre-writing stage is one of the most valuable parts of the writing process. It is at this planning stage that you decide exactly what you will be writing about and how you can most effectively present your ideas. Careful attention to the pre-writing stage makes the writing that follows much easier. Complete each of the following steps as part of the planning process.

1. Select and limit your topic.

Choosing a topic. Often you will be writing in response to a specific assignment or requirement. Sometimes, however, you will be given the chance to select your own topic. To produce a list of possible writing topics, begin by asking yourself questions such as these:

> What do I know about?
> What would I like to learn more about?
>
> What do I remember from my reading and past experience?
>
> What is happening to me or around me that I could observe or record?

The answers to these questions may provide you with possible topics for your paper.

The techniques listed in the chart on page 113 may also help you find interesting and enjoyable subjects for writing. Begin a "writing file" with the ideas you gather from these methods. Write interesting facts, headlines, quotations, and other bits of information on note cards. Cut out intriguing stories or articles. Keep all of these topic possibilities in a file box or folder. Refer to this file whenever you need a writing idea.

Limiting a topic. Topics may need to be limited, or narrowed, so that they fit the length of paper you want to write. Your topic is the right size if it can be fully developed in the specified length. If you are writing a long paper, make sure your topic is large enough to provide you with enough information and details so that you do not have to stretch your information or pad your sentences.

Pre-Writing Techniques

Journal Writing. Keep a spiral notebook in which you record interesting ideas, thoughts, feelings, impressions, and experiences. Write in your journal on a regular basis. Such a book can become a treasure-chest of writing ideas.

Reading. Skim magazines, books, and newspapers for intriguing topics, or for stories that trigger your imagination. Keep a list of possible subjects.

Discussions and Interviews. Other people are often a source of fascinating ideas. Listen carefully for the opinions and stories that emerge in conversation. Be aware that everyone has special experiences to share.

Brainstorming. This technique may be done individually or with others. It simply means starting with one idea and then building on it or branching out from it. The topic "railroads," for example, could eventually lead to topics as varied and interesting as "how a train yard works," "building the transcontinental railroad," or "work songs."

Clustering. Clustering is actually a type of brainstorming. Begin by writing a word or phrase on a piece of paper. Circle it. Now, outside that circle, write down any word or idea that you associate with the "nucleus" word. Put each in its own circle and connect it with a line to the nucleus word. Branch out from the new ideas in the same way. When a completely new train of thought strikes you, begin again from your nucleus idea.

2. Decide on your purpose.

Once you have a topic, you can limit it further by deciding exactly what you want to say about your subject. Do you want to analyze it? describe it? explain it? criticize it? defend it?

You must also decide what effect you want your writing to have. Do you want to inform? entertain? persuade? In longer pieces of writing, you may wish to include a statement of your topic and controlling purpose. This is sometimes called a **thesis statement.**

3. Identify your audience.

Not only should you determine the effect you wish to create on your readers, you must also pinpoint who those readers are. Your audience will determine whether you write formally or informally. It will also indicate the type of vocabulary and level of language you should use. (See Chapter 3, "Using Language for Different Purposes," for a discussion of the levels of language.) Finally, the audience determines, to some extent, how you will develop your topic. Consider these questions:

> What do my readers already know?
> How familiar are they with my topic?
> What are their attitudes or opinions toward it?

Choose your supporting details accordingly.

4. Gather your supporting information.

There are many ways to gather additional material once you have a specific audience, purpose, and topic in mind. You can generate details through brainstorming, discussing, reading, and observing. Make use of your own personal knowledge and experiences, or use outside sources such as the library. Finally, take notes on your ideas so that you can evaluate them.

5. Evaluate and organize your information.

Looking at your lists and notes, evaluate their content. Are there any unrelated details that should be deleted? Are there any gaps in your information? Should other details be added for clarity? Next, decide how your material can most effectively be organized. What would be a clear order for this particular type of information? What would make the most sense to your readers? The details of a simple story, for example, would probably be organized in the order in which they occurred. The arguments of a persuasive piece would be arranged to build up to the most powerful argument.

Remember that all of these pre-writing steps are designed simply to help you begin writing in a thoughtful, organized way. None of the decisions that you make at this stage are final. Any of them could be adjusted, changed, or completely discarded.

Study this example of pre-writing notes:

1. Possible topics
   my surprise party   Mammoth Cave
   the class dance   roller skating *

2. Narrowed topic
   my five minutes at the roller rink

3. Purpose
   to describe my feelings, thoughts and
   actions as I began to skate

4. Audience
   my classmates

5. Specific details
   ~~new, different skates~~
   ~~blue canvas, size 7~~
   (4) rubberized wheels
   (3) Royal Sport skates
   ~~$3.00 for 2 hours~~
   (7) falling
   (8) badly sprained ankle
   ~~emergency room~~
   ~~crutches for two weeks~~
   (5) no control over arms or legs
   (6) earth seemed to tilt
   (1) nervous before I began
   (9) embarrassed—blushing
   (2) worried—add the thoughts going
                through my head?

6. Order of details
   chronological--time order

Exercises Completing Pre-Writing Notes

A. Copy this section of a writer's pre-writing notes. Delete any unrelated details. Add details that you think would make the notes more complete. What might be a good order for presenting the details? Number the details in the order you would present them in a paper.

NARROWED TOPIC

the sand sculpture calamity

SPECIFIC DETAILS

Ted and I arrived at beach
go to beach several times a month
sand sculpture competition going on
entered competition
later, I wanted to throw Ted into lake
couldn't decide on a design
fought as we built
built it too close to the water
people of all ages were competing
gathered supplies from all over the beach
creation began to collapse
waves began to eat at it
Ted tripped and fell into it

ORDER OF DETAILS?

B. Make a pre-writing plan like the one on page 115. You might begin by brainstorming for possible topics for a general category such as those listed below. Save your notes for use later in this chapter.

1. Ten Years From Today
2. Favorite Places/Activities
3. My Most Embarrassing Experience
4. Special People
5. The Best of Days
6. The Real Me

Part 2   Writing a First Draft

Careful attention to the pre-writing steps makes writing a first draft much easier. At this point in the process, simply write to get the ideas from your pre-writing notes in paragraph form. Do not worry about details such as spelling and punctuation. This would only interrupt your flow of ideas and break your concentration. You will have the opportunity to correct these errors later, during revision.

In a first draft, you are exploring to see whether your writing plan is workable. You are also experimenting with your ideas. You will find that many of your best ideas come to you *after* you begin to write. Add these new details, and delete others that you no longer think are interesting or relevant. Change your organization if it becomes necessary. You may even want to start over as a more exciting idea occurs to you. As you continue working, keep your main idea, purpose, and audience in mind.

To write your first draft, choose a writing tool that is most comfortable for you. It may be a pencil, pen, typewriter, or word processor. Changes are easy to make on a word processor and can be made at any stage in the writing process.

Remember, a first draft is *not* the final product. Professional writers often complete several drafts before they are satisfied. You should be prepared to spend time on your writing.

Sample Rough Draft

On the next page is the first draft of a paragraph written from the pre-writing notes on page 115. Read it carefully.

Notice that the writer has expanded the detail of being worried by including the thoughts that were running through his head. The writer has eliminated some details describing the skates and some relating to the consequences of the skating episode. Despite these improvements, however, the paragraph needs a great deal more work before it will seem completely developed and interesting to a reader.

As I tightened the laces of the sleek, rented roller skates, I felt nervous. I had not been on skates since I was eight years old. These were Royal Sport skates with rubberized wheels. Could I manage to roll along with my freinds? Would I fall? Would everyone laugh at me? As I took my first steps I lost my ballance. I fell backwards. I had no control. I was so flustered, I felt like an awkward kid. The earth tilted as I hit the floor. The pain in my ankle told me I wouldn't be skating for awhile and my embarrasment told me I didn't want to be.

Exercise **Writing a Rough Draft**

Using your pre-writing notes from Exercise B in Part 1, write a rough draft of a paragraph. Remember that changes and revisions in your plan are not only possible, but probably necessary at this point.
Ask yourself the following questions:

Are there any unrelated details that interfere with the flow of ideas?

Could I add any details that would make my writing clearer or more interesting?

As I write, am I keeping my topic, audience, and purpose in mind?

Part 3   Revising

Revision is a continuous part of the writing process. Although it is listed as the last stage, it occurs from the moment you begin your pre-writing steps. For instance, you changed and refined your ideas as you worked on your pre-writing notes and as you wrote the rough draft. Now examine your work thoughtfully. Begin by asking yourself these questions:

1. Did I stick to my topic?
2. Did I include everything I wanted to?
3. Are there any unrelated or unnecessary details?
4. Could any details be added to clarify or improve my writing?
5. Have I accomplished my purpose?

Now read aloud what you have written. Often your ears will catch what your eyes do not. Listen to the rhythm of your writing. Is there variety in the type and structure of your sentences?

Check your arrangement of details. Is your writing organized logically? Is there a beginning, a middle, and an end to the development of your main idea? Do the details flow well? You may want to have a conference with your teacher or to have a friend read your work. Are your ideas clear to them?

Finally, polish your writing. Concentrate on every word. Are your ideas expressed in an interesting manner? Did you clearly express to your reader what you wanted to say? Is each word the most precise or vivid word for the situation?

Proofreading

At some time after you have finished your content revisions, perhaps in a second draft, proofread your paper. This is primarily an opportunity to correct mistakes in spelling, capitalization, and punctuation. You will find that many of these types of errors will have been corrected as you worked through your drafts. Use reference texts as well as the sections on grammar, usage, and mechanics in this book to correct any errors that remain. You may also use the proofreading symbols on page 124.

As I tightened the laces of the sleek, rented
roller skates, I felt nervous. I had not been
(was terrified) *(What was I doing at*
the Wacky Wheels Roller Rink?)
on skates since I was eight years old. *Skating*
been easy then, but I was worried now. I knew I wouldn't be *had*
These were Royal Sport skates with rubberized
trying anything fancy. I'd settle for just staying on my feet.
wheels. Could I manage to roll along with
or
my freinds? Would I fall? Would everyone
halting
laugh at me? As I took my first steps I
and then lurched
lost my ballance. I fell backwards. I had
forward with my arms moving like windmills
no control. I was so flustered, I felt like an
whole rink seemed to
awkward kid. The earth tilted as I hit the
hard *sharp* *after*
floor. The pain in my ankle told me I
The stifled
wouldn't be skating for awhile, and my
snickers of my friends and the tingling blush creeping up
embarrasment, told me I didn't want to be.
my neck, *that I was just as glad!*

Exercises   Revising the Rough Draft

A. Look at the rewritten, or revised, paragraph on this page. Compare it with the first draft. What content changes have been made? Why were they made? Several errors in spelling and mechanics have been corrected. Can you find two more mistakes that need correction?

B. Revise the rough draft of the paragraph you wrote for the Exercise in Part 2. Then proofread your paper for errors in spelling and mechanics.

Part 4　Preparing the Final Copy

Finally, when you are satisfied that your writing is clear and correct, you are ready to prepare your final copy. Write carefully. Make your work as neat as possible. Be sure to follow the manuscript form that your teacher requires. When you have completed your final copy, proofread your work again.

FINAL COPY

I was terrified as I tightened the laces of the rented roller skates. What was I doing at the Wacky Wheels Roller Rink? I had not been on skates since I was eight years old. Skating had been easy then, but I was worried now. I knew I wouldn't be trying anything fancy. I'd settle for just staying on my feet! As I took my first halting steps, I lost my balance. I fell backwards and then lurched forward with my arms moving like windmills. The whole rink seemed to tilt. After I hit the hard floor, the sharp pain in my ankle told me I wouldn't be skating for a while. The stifled snickers of my friends and the tingling blush creeping up my neck told me that I was just as glad!

Exercise　Making the Final Copy

Prepare the final copy of the paragraph that you revised for Part 3, Exercise B.

Guidelines for the Process of Writing

Pre-Writing

1. Select a topic that interests you.
2. Narrow the topic until it can be thoroughly developed in a specified length.
3. Decide on your purpose.
4. Use your understanding of purpose and audience to determine your type of language and choice of details.
5. Gather and list details that you could use to develop your topic.
6. Evaluate and organize your list of details. Delete unrelated ideas. Add new ones. Put your details into a logical order.

Writing the First Draft

1. Keeping your audience and purpose in mind, begin to write.
2. Let your thoughts flow freely. Modify your initial plans for content and organization, if necessary. Do not be too concerned with grammar and mechanics at this point.

Revising

Read what you have written. Answer the following questions:

1. Did you stick to your topic?
2. Did you include everything you wanted to?
3. Are there any unnecessary or unrelated details?
4. Is each main idea clearly expressed and thoroughly developed?
5. Do your ideas flow smoothly?
6. Is your writing organized logically, with a beginning, a middle, and an end? Are the ideas presented in an order that makes sense?
7. Is your writing interesting and lively? Is there variety in the type and structure of your sentences?
8. Is each word vivid and precise?
9. Do the language and content suit your audience?
10. Have you accomplished your purpose?

Revise as necessary. Then proofread your work, using the checklist on page 123.

Proofreading Checklist

Proofread your paper, by answering the questions below. Additional instruction on each concept may be found in the indicated Sections.

Grammar and Usage

Are there any sentence fragments or run-ons? (Sect. 1, 2)
Have you used the correct form of each pronoun? (Sect. 4)
Have you used verb tenses correctly? (Sect. 5)
Have you used adjectives and adverbs correctly? (Sect. 6)
Do all verbs agree with their subjects? (Sect. 10)
Are compound and complex sentences written and punctuated
    correctly? (Sect. 11)

Capitalization

Did you capitalize first words and all proper nouns and adjectives?
    (Sect. 13)
Are titles capitalized correctly? (Sect. 13)

Punctuation

Does each sentence have the proper end mark? (Sect. 14)
Are end marks, such as colons, semicolons, apostrophes, hyphens,
    and quotation marks, used correctly? (Sect. 14)

Spelling

Did you check all unfamiliar words in the dictionary? (Sect. 15)
Are plurals and possessive forms spelled correctly? (Sect. 3, 15)

Form

Were corrections made neatly? (Sect. 16)
In your final copy, is the writing legible?
Have you used the proper heading and margins?
Did you follow all points of good manuscript form?

Proofreading Symbols

SYMBOL	MEANING	EXAMPLE
$\wedge$	insert	would gone *have*
$\equiv$	capitalize	United states
/	make lower case	our club President
$\sim$	transpose	t h i e r
$\mathcal{e}$	delete	finished the (the) race
$\P$	make new paragraph	....be complete. $\P$ Another reason
$\cup$	close up space	head line
$\odot$	period	....and stop Before going...
$\wedge$	add comma	However few people

124

1. All types of writing—from compositions in English to reports in science or history—become easier and more satisfying when a writer is aware of the stages involved in the process of writing.

2. Careful pre-writing efforts make actual writing much less difficult. This advance work includes choosing and narrowing a topic, deciding on the audience and purpose for the writing, and gathering and organizing ideas.

3. The first draft is simply the writer's initial attempt to get the ideas down on paper. Mechanical details are not important at this time.

4. Revising and proofreading are the final stages of the process of writing. The writer completes one or more drafts of a paper, checking for complete coverage, a precise vocabulary, and sound organization. Finally, the writer proofreads for errors in grammar, capitalization, punctuation, and spelling.

5. Careful attention to the writing process will help train you to think through problems clearly and logically.

Applications in Other Subject Areas

Science. Like writing, scientific research and experimentation is a process involving very specific stages. Look up "Science" or "Scientific Method" in a good encyclopedia. Write a short paper describing the stages in the process of conducting an experiment.

Computer Science. For a good example of careful planning, interview an expert on computer programming. Ask him or her to explain the process of developing the step-by-step instructions that are fed into a computer. Notice especially the care that is taken to include every detail and to organize those details in a logical order.

Chapter 8

Writing Effective Paragraphs

Have you ever tried to squeeze an important message into a twenty-second recording on an answering machine? If you have, you know how frustrating the experience can be. When you have a complex idea to communicate, you need enough time to express it correctly.

A sentence often has the same sort of limitations. If you want to relate an incident or describe a scene, a single sentence simply may not be adequate. Several sentences together, however, might do the job. When sentences are grouped together for such a purpose, they result in the unit of writing called the **paragraph**.

In this chapter, you will learn to express your ideas in paragraphs. You will also learn to write paragraphs that communicate your ideas clearly and in a variety of ways.

Part 1   What Is a Paragraph?

A paragraph is a group of sentences dealing with a single topic or idea. Usually, one sentence, called the **topic sentence**, states the main idea of the paragraph. All the other sentences are related to this topic sentence. They further explain or support the main idea.

Example 1

Study the following paragraph.

> My father was a master storyteller. He could tell a fine old story that made me hold my sides with rolling laughter and sent happy tears down my cheeks. He could tell a story of stark reality that made me shiver and be grateful for my own warm, secure surroundings. He could tell stories of beauty and grace, stories of gentle dreams, and paint them as vividly as any picture with splashes of character and dialogue. His memory detailed every event of ten or forty years or more before, just as if it had happened yesterday.—MILDRED D. TAYLOR

This is a well organized, well written paragraph. In the first sentence, the writer states, "My father was a master storyteller." In the remaining sentences, she supports that idea by describing the many kinds of stories that her father told.

Example 2

The following is also a well written paragraph.

> The wolverine may well be nature's most fearsome fighter. In battle with an enemy, he is a twisting, slashing blur of sheer fury that bewilders and terrifies an adversary. He has been known to attack a 1,200-pound moose—an animal more than forty times his weight—and is capable of defending himself against an entire pack of wolves.—REED MILLARD

The writer begins with the sentence, "The wolverine may well be nature's most fearsome fighter." In the sentences that follow, he describes the wolverine's fighting abilities. By doing so, he supports the main idea stated in the topic sentence.

In this example, and also in Example 1, all the sentences relate to one idea. They are tied together by that idea.

Example 3

Study the following example.

> Native Americans cultivated and developed many plants. Among them were white potatoes, sweet potatoes, corn, beans, tobacco, chocolate, peanuts, cotton, rubber, and gum. Native Americans were also expert builders and tanners. Plants were used for dyes, medicines, soap, clothes, shelter, and baskets.

The first sentence indicates that the paragraph will be about the cultivation and development of plants by Native Americans. However, sentence 3 refers to non-agricultural skills. This idea is not related to the main idea of the paragraph.

The problem is easily solved by removing the third sentence:

> Native Americans cultivated and developed many plants. Among them were white potatoes, sweet potatoes, corn, beans, tobacco, chocolate, peanuts, cotton, rubber, and gum. Plants were used for dyes, medicines, soap, clothes, shelter, and baskets.

Example 4

The following example has a different problem.

> Almost anyone would have treated me better than Uncle Eldon did. From the first day, he worked me like his slave.

This paragraph is incomplete. The reader is left with the question, "Exactly what did Uncle Eldon do to the writer?"

Sometimes a writer fails to explain thoroughly the idea stated in the topic sentence. The reader, therefore, does not get all the information needed to understand the idea completely.

The paragraph above needs specific detail, as in the revision on the next page.

Almost anyone would have treated me better than Uncle Eldon did. From the first day, he worked me like his slave. I cut down trees. I sawed the fallen trees into logs. I dragged the logs to the house and cut them into kindling. Whenever the kindling pile was high, I was sent to clean the drafty old barn.

By expanding the number of sentences, the writer has developed the topic into an interesting paragraph that explains the topic sentence and satisfies the reader. Every good paragraph must be developed just as thoroughly, with equal attention to detail.

Exercise Analyzing Paragraphs

Read each paragraph carefully. Some are good paragraphs; others are not. Some of the weak paragraphs contain sentences that are unrelated to the topic. Other paragraphs are not adequately developed. Identify the poor paragraphs. Be ready to discuss which sentences should be dropped, or the types of details that should be added.

1   Paula Murphy is known as the fastest woman in the world. She has raced over Ontario Speedway and Bonneville Salt Flats fast enough to leave her competition far behind in the dust. She is slim, soft-spoken, and friendly. She has broken through speed records, broken down sex barriers, and broken her neck for racing. She is a female drag-strip racer.

2   Your grandmother could probably tell you what it was like to run a house on coal. Back then, she had a ton or so delivered down a chute into the basement.

3   I have never known a hotter July. There was a soft, hazy, constant heat that hung over everything and never let up—only seemed to turn dark with evening. In our garden the black earth dried and crumbled brown, shrinking away till the twisted tomato roots showed above the ground. Out in the country the fields were a parched patchwork and only the trees were still green against the dust-yellow roll of the hills.

4   The main advantage of the metric system is its simplicity. It uses three basic units of measurement.

5   I felt good. I think the park had something to do with it. Trees, grass, bushes—everything appeared in brand-new togs of shining green. The warm yellow sunlight sifted down through the trees, making my face feel alive and healthy and casting shadows on the paved walks and the unpaved walks and the wooden benches. Slight breezes tickled my nostrils, caressed my face, bringing with them a good, clean odor of things new and live and dripping with greenness.

Part 2   Paragraph Unity and Coherence

You have just learned that each sentence in a paragraph must relate to a single idea. The sentences either state the idea or contribute in some way to its development. When the sentences work together in this way, a paragraph is said to have **unity**.

Unity

The topic sentence of a paragraph plays a key role in establishing paragraph unity. The sentence is like a contract between writer and reader. The writer is saying, in effect, "I have an idea I want to explain to you." The reader is answering, "All right, explain it to me." For the writer to hold to the contract, he or she must explain the idea stated in the topic sentence.

Look at these three examples of topic sentences.

1. *The shell in my hand is deserted.*
2. *The King was a quiet man who did not like to speak overmuch.*
3. *The dodo was a very odd-looking bird.*

Writer 1 says she is going to explain something about a deserted shell. Writer 2 says she wants to explain something about the king's quietness. Writer 3 says he wants to explain something about the appearance of the dodo bird. Let's see how well each honors the contract implied by the topic sentence.

1   *The shell in my hand is deserted.* It once housed a whelk, a snail-like creature. Then, after the death of the first occupant, it sheltered a little hermit crab, who has run away, leaving his tracks behind him like a delicate vine on the sand. He ran away and left me his shell. It was once a protection to him. I turn the shell in my hand, gazing into the wide open door from which he made his exit. Had it become a burden? Why did he run away? Did he hope to find a better home, a better mode of living?

The paragraph does give an explanation of the writer's opening statement, so the contract is complete.

2   *The King was a quiet man who did not like to speak overmuch.* This was partly, no doubt, because he had a serious speech defect. He had inherited the long, heavy, out-of-balance jaw of the Hapsburg line, together with their round high forehead, golden hair, and blue eyes. Due to the configuration of his jaw, the King's teeth did not meet squarely; and when he spoke it was with a curious lisp. Besides, I believe that he was shy and that he had learned, in his years at court, that it was fatal to trust anyone with all your heart.

The remainder of the paragraph explains why the king was a quiet man. Again, the contract is complete.

3   *The dodo was a very odd-looking bird.* It was related to the solitaire and lived on the island of Mauritius in the Indian Ocean. Jacob Corneliszoon van Neck, a Dutch admiral, discovered the bird in 1598. Dutch settlers to the island, as well as the animals they brought, ate the dodo birds. The last dodo on Mauritius was eaten in 1681. By 1800, scientists were beginning to doubt whether the dodo bird had ever existed.

In this paragraph, the writer has not held to the contract. In his topic sentence, Writer 3 has promised to describe the dodo's appearance. By the end of the paragraph, you know other facts about the dodo, but you do not know a single specific detail concerning the dodo's unusual physical characteristics.

Coherence

Not only must all the sentences in a paragraph relate to one idea, but they must also logically relate to each other. When all of the sentences in a paragraph follow one another naturally, the paragraph has **coherence**.

The following paragraph has a problem with coherence.

Example

A whale, one of the largest animals in the world, is killed by Soviet and Japanese whale hunters every seventeen minutes. This makes some people angry. Someday, whales might be like the dinosaur and disappear forever. People are showing their anger in many ways. One Japanese businessman says, "Many Japanese could not live without whale meat." Some people are writing letters to the Japanese Prime Minister, and others are asking people not to buy Japanese products. If this hurts Japanese business enough, the Japanese government may stop the whale hunting.

Analysis

At first glance, all the sentences in the paragraph seem to relate to the killing of whales. However, it is hard to tell for sure because the ideas are so disorganized. They must be rearranged so that they relate to each other in a logical way.

If you were asked to revise this paragraph, you might begin by listing all the sentences that refer to whales.

1. A whale, one of the largest animals in the world, is killed by Soviet and Japanese whale hunters every seventeen minutes.
2. Someday, whales might be like the dinosaur and disappear forever.
3. One Japanese businessman says, "Many Japanese could not live without whale meat."

Next, list sentences that refer to the attitude of the people.

1. This makes some people angry.
2. People are showing their anger in many ways.

3. Some people are writing letters to the Japanese Prime Minister, and others are asking people not to buy Japanese products.
4. If this hurts Japanese business enough, the Japanese government may stop the whale hunting.

The first two sentences about whales are closely related. Sentence 1 is about the killing of whales. Sentence 2 suggests that if the killings continue, whales might someday disappear. The two sentences could be tied together even more closely with the addition of the clause "if this killing continues" to sentence 2.

> A whale, one of the largest animals in the world, is killed by Soviet and Japanese whale hunters every seventeen minutes. Someday, if this killing continues, whales might be like the dinosaur and disappear forever.

The third sentence, about the Japanese businessman, does not relate to sentences 1 and 2. That sentence should be removed. Then the four sentences about the attitude of the people should be added, making the following six-sentence paragraph.

> A whale, one of the largest animals in the world, is killed by Soviet and Japanese whale hunters every seventeen minutes. Someday, if this killing continues, whales might be like the dinosaur and disappear forever. This makes some people angry. People are showing their anger in several ways. Some people are writing letters to the Japanese Prime Minister, and others are asking people not to buy Japanese products. If this hurts Japanese business enough, the Japanese government may stop the whale hunting.

All the ideas in the paragraph are now presented in a logical way. Two sentences, however, contain a weak repetition of ideas.

1. This makes some people angry.
2. People are showing their anger in several ways.

The sentences can be combined.

> This makes some people angry, and they are showing their anger in several ways.

Exercise Checking for Unity and Coherence in Paragraphs

Study the following groups of sentences. Some are good paragraphs. Others lack either unity or coherence in their presentation. Identify the groups of sentences that are not good paragraphs. Revise them by dropping sentences, by rearranging sentences, or by making other changes.

1   There lived in the Land of Oz two men who were the best of friends. One was a Scarecrow. That means he was a suit of blue Munchkin clothes, stuffed with straw, on top of which was fastened a round cloth head, filled with bran to hold it in shape. On the head were painted two eyes, two ears, a nose, and a mouth. The Scarecrow had never been much of a success in scaring crows; but he prided himself on being a superior man because he could feel no pain, was never tired, and did not have to eat or drink. His brains were sharp, for the Wizard of Oz had put pins and needles in the Scarecrow's brains. The other man was made all of tin, and his arms and legs and head were cleverly jointed so that he could move them freely. He was known as the Tin Woodman, having at one time been a woodchopper. Everyone loved him because the Wizard had given him an excellent heart of red plush.

2   If parents show an interest in the programs their teenagers watch on television, useful discussions will often result. Few things are more important to fourteen-year-olds than having their opinions listened to and respected. The types of things teenagers watch on television will change with age. Values and situations shown on television can be the basis for lively exchanges of ideas.

3   My father has a peculiar habit. He is fond of sitting in the dark, alone. Sometimes I come home very late. The house is dark. I let myself in quietly because I do not want to disturb my mother. She is a light sleeper and has to get up early to go to work. I tiptoe into my room and undress in the dark. I go downstairs to the kitchen for a drink of water. My bare feet make no noise.

4   The rainy season came to the forest, as it must come every year. At night the water fell with a roar like thunder. In the morning it beat against the branches of the trees and tore their leaves from them. It pounded against the thatched roofs of the villages and rushed about the footpaths. Little girls set pots under the sky to catch the water, and ran back slipping and sliding. The small, friendly rivers became deep and wide, and covered the sides of their banks. During the darkness the people fastened their doors and did not even look outside, for they could hear nothing but rain, rain, rain.

5   When my little dog died, I was very sad. It happened on Valentine's Day. My birthday is on February 22, eight days after Valentine's Day. I cried a lot, but it didn't bring my dog back. My Dad and I buried him in a vacant lot, and put a tombstone on the grave. On my birthday, I got new roller skates.

6   People have trouble identifying my heritage. Indians mistake me for one of their own. In Chinatown they give me a menu written in Chinese, and once a Japanese boy asked me if I was Korean. My ancestors are full-blooded Japanese, but I have had to get used to people thinking I'm something else.

7   The needs of our country have changed since its beginnings. The first settlers had to work very hard. Now the majority of American workers do not do hard physical labor. The Pilgrims were able to increase their food supply and build shelters from the cold. In Japan, too, industry is highly mechanized.

8   I grew up on the island of Puerto Rico in an atmosphere of natural story-tellers. I had a father whose occupation took him all over the island; a grandmother whose stories always ended with a nonsense rhyme or song, setting feet to jump, skip or dance; elder sisters who still remembered tales told by a mother; and finally, a stepmother whose literary taste was universal. I never ever went to bed without a round of stories told. The characters of my favorite ones became part of my everyday life: I traveled to strange lands of shepherds, princesses and princes, Kings and Queens; I laughed at the cunning of the animals and suffered with the punished ones.

Part 3   Pre-Writing:
Deciding on a Topic

You are now ready to begin writing effective paragraphs of your own. The first step, of course, is to choose a topic. Remember that you yourself are a good source for interesting topics. Survey your own interests, knowledge, and concerns. Choose a subject that appeals to you, and limit it to a size suitable for a paragraph. A little background reading or observation might help you in this task. Determining your audience and purpose will also provide some guidelines.

Careful attention to this part of the process can result in many interesting topic possibilities. Describing the crucial play of a football game for someone who did not see the game, giving reasons why soccer is a better sport than football to someone who is deciding which sport to play, and explaining the history of the National Football League to someone who is very familiar with the game are three possible paragraph topics involving football. Yet, each would include very different material based on considerations of purpose and audience.

Once you have decided on a topic, audience, and purpose, writing a topic sentence will help you to clarify what you want to accomplish with your paragraph. The topic sentence provides an "umbrella statement" that helps to shape the rest of your paragraph.

The Topic Sentence

A topic sentence makes a general statement that is wider in its scope than the rest of the sentences in the paragraph. A good topic sentence is broad enough to be developed by specific details.

To clarify this point, let's look at two good topic sentences:

1. *The English language spoken in the United States owes much to Spanish importation.*

2. *A person must be quite courageous to be an individual.*

These sentences contain very little specific information. They are well written and interesting, but the information contained in them is only enough to arouse curiosity. After reading them, you might find yourself saying "Don't stop there. How did the Spanish language influence English? Why does it take courage for one to be an individual? Tell me more."

A good writer will satisfy your curiosity by giving specific details in the rest of the paragraph. The details will explain the general statement in the topic sentence.

Let's see how the writers of the two topic sentences explained their general statements.

1   *The English language spoken in the United States owes much to Spanish importation.*

The English language spoken in the United States owes much to Spanish importation. Such Spanish words as *desperado, sombrero, mesa, sierra, arroyo, cañon, chaparral, mesquite, adobe, ramada, cabaña, hacienda, patio, plaza, coyote, jaguar, serape, machete, mañana* are used all the time. Also, a long list of Spanish words has become so thoroughly "naturalized" that people have forgotten they were ever Spanish — words like *vigilante, filibuster, barbecue, corral, tobacco, vanilla, hammock, tornado, cigar,* and *banana.* More than two thousand cities and towns in the United States have Spanish names. At least four hundred of them are in California, with two hundred and fifty each in Texas and New Mexico, and more than a hundred in both Colorado and Arizona. Spanish place names can be found all over the West and, in fact, in every state in the Union.—JOHN TEBBEL AND RAMÓN EDUARDO RUIZ

The writers of this paragraph first make the general statement, "The English language spoken in the United States owes much to Spanish importation." Then, to develop this idea, they give three supporting details for their statement: Spanish words are used often; Spanish words have been "naturalized" into English; and the United States has thousands of Spanish place names. Notice that each of the three supporting details is further developed through the use of specific examples.

2   *A person must be quite courageous to be an individual.*

A person must be quite courageous to be an individual. How much easier it is to blend in with a crowd, to accept generally held beliefs and adopt the popular lifestyles. How difficult it is, though, to listen to sneers when your ideas differ. How frustrating and frightening it can be when a unique action leads to suspicion from others. Yet a person of courage knows that daring to be an individual is the only way to achieve a truly good life, and that is worth the struggle.

This writer also makes a general statement, "A person must be quite courageous to be an individual." However, instead of giving supporting details, he develops, or expands, his idea. He explains *why* being an individual takes courage: one must listen to the criticisms of others. Then he states why having courage is important: it is the only true means of having a satisfying life.

Exercises Pre-Writing: Composing Topic Sentences

A. In the following paragraphs, the topic sentences have been removed, leaving only the specific details. Read the paragraphs. Study the hint given after each. Then write an interesting topic sentence for each paragraph. Be sure your topic sentence is broader than the details in the rest of the paragraph.

1   It was already hot, and the grasshoppers began to fill the air. Still, it was early in the morning, and the birds sang out of the shadows. The long, yellow grass on the mountain shone in the bright light, and a scissortail hied above the land.

Hint: The topic sentence might include the idea of a person waking up on a summer morning.

2   Take a lesson from the cat, who so well represents potential energy. As he moves, stretches, relaxes, he looks almost lazy. He wastes no energy. Let a mouse run by, though, and the cat pounces with one swift, forceful movement.

Hint: The topic sentence should present the idea that human beings can learn from animals about the conservation of energy.

3   At first his feet slipped but then they took hold. He charged low and hard with mouth opened up like a steam shovel. The lower jaw and the big teeth flashed as he crossed the pit bottom. The wildcat fell back from the heavy charge and rolled under the dog. In that second he raked his claws into the dog's stomach.

Hint: The topic sentence should describe the start of the attack.

4   One group of Indians caught big Southern catfish by diving into the water with any available red object for bait. They grabbed the fish as it approached and dragged it to shore. Inspired by their example, the explorers in Lewis and Clark's party invented new ways to catch fish. Once, using only bayonets, they caught enough salmon to feed themselves. Another time, an explorer killed a sturgeon with an ax.

Hint: The topic sentence should include the information that long ago, people fished without having what is now called "fishing equipment."

5   The largest complexes, like Vail and Aspen, have plenty of rooms, and also plenty of people to fill them. Christmas week and much of February and March are especially hectic there and at all resorts. Many lodges take reservations for these periods as early as July. Most resorts advise that, no matter the time of year, visitors should call ahead for reservations well in advance of their intended trips.

Hint: The topic sentence should indicate that reservations at ski resorts can be a problem.

6   According to folklore experts, *light elves* are masters at shape-changing and can travel through four dimensions. They are good-natured but seldom seen by humans. *Dark elves* make their homes in the earth and their skin reflects its colors: grey, brown, red, and black. These elves prefer to roam late at night. *Dusky elves* are the most numerous. They are bound by laws of time, space, and place, and are easily recognized by humans.

Hint: The topic sentence should introduce the idea that there are three classifications of the old folklore creatures, elves.

B. Following is a list of topic sentences, each of which makes a general statement. Choose at least two of these sentences. For each, make a list of three or four specific details that support or develop the topic sentence.

1. Autumn was advancing, and the sky was full of luminous clouds.
2. The Rolling Stones are a successful rock group.
3. Mr. Nolan's grocery store had closed for the last time.
4. Sometimes I feel as though I'm a half-dozen different people.
5. A TV addict is a person who can't turn off a television set.
6. Today people talk about "the good old days."
7. Television advertisers are masters of persuasion.
8. Why does my tongue always freeze at the wrong time?
9. The car wheezed, coughed, and sputtered, fouling the air with dirty black smoke.
10. In the world of make-believe, I can be anything I wish.
11. Shabbiness and neglect marked the apartment building.
12. Pets-a-Plenty is the noisiest store in the shopping center.

The Function of the Topic Sentence

In your earlier study of the paragraph, you saw how the topic sentence operates as a type of contract. With it, you promise your audience that you are going to explain something about your topic. The topic sentence states the main idea, and *all the other sentences must be related to this topic sentence.* Therefore, the topic sentence, written with a specific audience and purpose in mind, *controls* the content of the paragraph.

In *limiting* what can be discussed in the paragraph, the topic sentence functions in a slightly different way.

The topic sentence makes a general statement, a statement that is broader in scope than the rest of the paragraph. However, if the topic sentence is too general, the remainder of the paragraph will have to be either extremely long in order to give an adequate explanation of the idea, or it will have to contain nothing but more general statements.

The following is an example of a paragraph with a topic sentence that is too general.

> Winter is a cold season, but it is also beautiful. The white, glistening snow on the ground, trees, and houses is an eye-catching scene.

"Winter is a cold season, but it is also beautiful" is much too broad a topic sentence to be adequately supported in a paragraph. You could write an entire composition on that subject. Because it is so broad, all the writer can do is give another general statement about the snow.

To limit the topic sentence so that the idea can be developed in a paragraph, the writer first had to narrow the subject. She narrowed it to a specific winter's morning and wrote the following topic sentence: "The winter morning was cold and still." Then she added specific details to develop the idea, as follows:

> The winter morning was cold and still. The crust of the snow was like fragile glass and shattered with a loud noise as my feet broke through it. The icy air froze my nostrils and numbed my hands. Except for my footsteps, the world was silent, frozen to attention by winter's command.

The writer now has described a cold, still winter morning, using many specific details that help the reader to visualize the scene.

Exercises Working with Topic Sentences

A. Below is a series of sentence pairs. In each pair, one topic sentence is too general; the other is limited in its scope. Decide which one is too broad and which one has been sufficiently limited to be covered in a paragraph.

1. a. Basketball is an interesting game.
   b. Basketball demands quick thinking and split-second timing.
2. a. James failed history because he spent too much time in dramatics.
   b. Extra-curricular activities are time-consuming.

3. a. Several old buildings on Mason Street should be torn down because of their bad condition.
   b. Old buildings should be torn down.
4. a. Mountains are beautiful.
   b. The Blue Ridge Mountains stretched before us like a scene from a movie.
5. a. Pets can be a nuisance.
   b. My cat, Siggy, is constantly getting into mischief.
6. a. Because he bought the cheapest one he could find, Joe's bicycle didn't last very long.
   b. Economy doesn't always pay.
7. a. Graduation from high school is very important.
   b. Without a high school diploma, it is almost impossible to get a good job.
8. a. People of all ages read comic books.
   b. My grandmother likes to read my *Super Comics*.
9. a. Reckless driving is a serious problem.
   b. Statistics show that most automobile accidents are caused by reckless driving.
10. a. Works of art are difficult to create.
    b. Oil painting takes time, effort, and patience.

B. Following is a list of broad topic sentences. Rewrite each one, limiting its scope.

1. Automobiles are not as safe as they could be.
2. Travel is becoming faster—and noisier—all the time.
3. Pedestrians should be careful.
4. The Presidency of the United States is a difficult job.
5. You couldn't find a more interesting neighborhood than the one I live in.
6. Smoking is dangerous to a person's health.
7. Cats are interesting animals.
8. Growing vegetables is educational.
9. Most television programs are alike.
10. I wear different clothes for different occasions.

C. Study the following list of subjects. Write a limited topic sentence for each subject.

1. Things I Fear
2. Radio Shows
3. Human Rights
4. Cities
5. The Future
6. Unpleasant People
7. Photography
8. Television Commentators
9. Popular Dances
10. Lonely Feelings
11. Records
12. The Game of Monopoly
13. Vacations
14. School Sports
15. Unfinished Projects

Part 4 Pre-Writing: Gathering Ideas

Once you have decided upon your topic and topic sentence, the next step is to develop your main idea into a well-organized paragraph. Remember that you have many resources available for gathering information. Use the pre-writing techniques discussed in Chapter 7, and keep these points in mind as you plan your paragraph.

1. Don't overlook yourself. What information do you know about the topic? What ideas do you have? What can you observe about it?

2. Use other people as sources. What information can be obtained through discussion with others? through interviewing others? through observing others?

3. Use printed material to develop your idea. What books, articles, and pamphlets are available on your topic?

The types of details you gather about your topic can be classified in four ways.

1. Sensory details
2. Facts or statistics
3. Specific examples
4. Incidents and anecdotes

Using Sensory Details

Vivid, descriptive words are essential to the development of an effective paragraph. They can make the difference between dull writing and lively, precise ideas. Through careful observation and the skillful use of your senses, you can find details that will help you re-create a scene or experience on paper.

Sensory details give your reader a feeling of participation, the opportunity to experience what you felt. They allow the reader to picture a scene and "hear" the sounds. Sensory details can even communicate ideas of touch, taste, and smell. Let's look at the following example.

> Biting my pencil eraser, staring at my paper, and trying to think of a topic on which to write, I sit here in the library and listen to the sounds of silence. Soft whispers come from a table across the room. Someone giggles and I stop thinking for a moment. I glance up from my work, and the sudden shift in my concentration changes the people and their clothes into a blur of color. Now someone clumps along the floor, stops, and then whirrs the pencil sharpener over his pencil. Satisfied, he walks away. I hear a jingle and I turn around to see the janitor with a huge ring of keys fastened to his belt. Picking up papers as he goes along, he adds a rustle to the silence. Now I hear the sound, somewhat like a zipper, of someone tearing a sheet of paper from her spiral notebook. The background buzz of the flourescent lights overhead ties the other sounds together. The hum of the bell reminds me that I must leave. Study period is over.

The writer has chosen to appeal primarily to the sense of hearing in this paragraph because she has been struck by all of the noises she can identify in the "silence" of the school library. How many separate sounds has she identified? Notice the vivid, specific words she has used to help re-create the sounds she has heard. The boy doesn't "walk" along the floor; he "clumps." This writer has also used a comparison. To what does she compare the sound of tearing spiral paper from a notebook? Why is this comparison effective?

Pre-Writing: Developing a Paragraph with Sensory Details

Go to a specific place in your school, such as one of the areas listed below. Spend at least five minutes there and jot down exactly what you see, feel, hear, and smell. What vivid, specific words best describe these sensory details? Write a topic sentence for a paragraph that would describe this place. Then list your sensory details below the sentence. Save your work for use later in this chapter.

1. the hall during passing period
2. the hall after school
3. study hall
4. a locker room
5. homeroom before school
6. the auditorium
7. the front entrance
8. the cafeteria
9. your locker
10. the gymnasium

Using Facts or Statistics

To understand how topic sentences may be developed by the use of facts or statistics, let's look at the following example.

> The abacus, probably the earliest calculating tool, was invented by the Chinese so long ago that no one even knows for certain when it was. It is a framework of wires with beads mounted on them. Each bead on the bottom part of the frame, below the crossbar, represents one unit; each bead above the bar represents five. The beads that touch the bar are counted to make up a number, and by moving the beads on different rows, or places, any number can be recorded. The beads can be manipulated to do addition, subtraction, multiplication, or division. Using an abacus, an expert can do addition or subtraction even faster than an electric calculator can. It was many centuries before any other civilization invented a calculating tool so fast and efficient.—LINDA O'BRIEN

The writer begins with a topic sentence that identifies the abacus as an early calculating tool. She next gives facts about the abacus, facts related to its construction and use. Then in her final two sentences, she gives facts about the speed and efficiency of the abacus.

**Pre-Writing: Developing a Paragraph
with Facts or Statistics**

A. Following is a series of paragraphs that were developed with facts or statistics. For each paragraph, list the facts or statistics given.

1   By 1963, almost 130,000 Czechs had migrated to this country. They had settled on rural homesteads and in farming communities. They also had formed enclaves in cities, principally in Chicago, Cleveland, and New York.

2   There are sixty million homes in the United States and over ninety-five percent of them are equipped with a television set. In the average home, the set is turned on for five hours and forty-five minutes a day. Average viewers watch television for a total of over 3,000 entire days — roughly nine full years.

3   Oysters provide valuable products. In addition to providing food, oysters can be induced to grow pearls inside their shells. The process is begun when workers place single grains of sand inside the shells of young oysters. Pearls grow around these grains.

4   The Great Wall of China is the largest fortification ever built. It meanders for 1,500 miles across northern China. At its base, the Great Wall is from 15 to 20 feet thick. At the top, 25 feet above the base, the wall narrows to 15 feet. Every 200 to 300 yards, towers project from 35 to 40 feet into the air.

B. Following is a list of general topics, that lend themselves to paragraph development through the use of facts or statistics. Choose two topics or make up two of your own. Research the topics; then write a limited topic sentence that can be developed in a paragraph. List the facts and/or statistics you would use to develop your topic sentence. Save your work for future use.

1. Television violence	6. Ocean pollution
2. Cable television	7. Mass transportation
3. Computers	8. Microsurgery
4. Solar heating	9. Cars
5. U.S. agriculture	10. Breeds of dogs

Using Specific Examples

Sometimes a topic sentence will be a general idea that is best supported with specific examples. Look at this paragraph.

Life was hard for young Stevie Wonder. No matter how developed his sense of touch became, there were some things he could never understand through touch. He could never touch the sun, or the horizon. He could never touch a mountain. Some things were too fragile, like snowflakes and live butterflies. It would be too dangerous to try to understand burning or boiling through touch. No matter how developed his ability to measure "sound shadows" became, he would only be able to measure the width and bulk of a large building, not its height. He could learn that the sky is blue and the grass green, but he would never *see* blue or green. He could not *watch* television. —JAMES HASKINS

The writer begins with a general statement: "Life was hard for young Stevie Wonder." He goes on to explain that there were many things the boy couldn't understand through touch. In the next seven sentences he gives specific examples of these things.

The following paragraph uses a similar technique.

Enterprising inventors have made American life richer, safer, and more comfortable. Gail Borden invented condensed milk, a healthy, safe product, in a time (1859) when fresh milk was often dangerous. In 1902 Willis Carrier invented something he called "air conditioning." Clarence Birdseye developed frozen foods, and Aaron Montgomery Ward brought the department store to the most isolated farm through the distribution of a mail order catalog. —K.S. KNODT

This writer also states a general idea: "Enterprising inventors have made American life richer, safer, and more comfortable." He then supports that statement with examples.

1. Gail Borden's invention of condensed milk
2. Willis Carrier's invention of air conditioning
3. Clarence Birdseye's development of frozen foods
4. Ward's distribution of a mail order catalog

Pre-Writing: Developing a Paragraph with Specific Examples

Here is a list of general topic sentences. Choose three of them or write your own. Then list at least three specific examples for each of them. Save your work for use later in the chapter.

1. Yesterday's science fiction is today's reality.
2. Even great leaders can fail in something.
3. Animals are often surprisingly intelligent.
4. Some comic strips are more serious than funny.
5. Winners have sometimes overcome severe handicaps.
6. Some common houseplants are poisonous.
7. Disaster movies are popular entertainment.
8. Fast food restaurants line the main street of our town.
9. Some people are experts at everything.
10. Americans are a generous people.

Using an Incident or an Anecdote

The incident or anecdote can add a personal touch to almost any form of writing. In this type of development, the writer explains or clarifies a general idea by relating an amusing story or describing an interesting event. The selection may be from personal experience or from the experiences of others. The strength of this type of development lies in the fact that an incident or anecdote, if well chosen, can imprint an idea clearly on the reader's mind. Read the following example.

> Children have taught me much of what I know about love. To them love is nothing fancy, but very real—a feeling to be taken seriously. "If you love somebody," a six-year-old boy named Charlie once told me, "you help him put his boots on when they get stuck."—LESLIE KENTON

The writer could have developed the topic sentence with the addition of several more impersonal statements, but instead she includes a simple personal experience that makes the paragraph "come alive." Notice how the writer of the following paragraph has used a wonderful childhood experience to explain an idea.

I think that one of the reasons I became a writer was because once, when I was driving home with my parents, they let me keep a date with a rainbow. There had been a heavy summer storm, when suddenly I screamed, "Stop the car! I must write a poem about that beautiful rainbow!" My father pulled up at the side of the road and off I went into the drizzle and the sunshine, while they waited. It was one of those special moments that change you, make you more than you've been. It is an experience in saying "Yes!" to life — and that's really what spontaneity and joy are all about. —EDA LeSHAN

Here again, the writer could have explained her topic sentence with facts or examples. Instead, she used one simple anecdote to clarify her reasons for becoming a writer.

Exercise **Pre-Writing: Developing a Paragraph with an Incident or an Anecdote**

Here is a list of topic sentences, each one of which may be developed by an incident or an anecdote. Choose two of the sentences or write sentences of your own. For each, make a list of details related to a specific incident or anecdote that develops the topic. Save your work for use later in this chapter.

1. A kind friend can help you forget your troubles.
2. Sometimes a bad experience can turn out to be funny.
3. An angry word can ruin your day.
4. It usually pays to be on time.
5. Experience is sometimes a tough teacher.
6. You don't have to travel to find adventure.
7. Sometimes you have to learn to say "No!"
8. Baby-sitting is not the world's easiest job.
9. There are some things you can't learn from books.
10. A good laugh can sometimes be "good medicine."
11. A pet can teach you how to love.
12. You don't have to join a team to learn sportsmanship.
13. Repairing a _____ can teach you patience.
14. Hero-worship sometimes pays off.
15. There are times when you have to forgive.

Part 5   Pre-Writing: Organizing Ideas

Once you have gathered information and ideas for your paragraph, it is important to decide on a good order for presenting them. An orderly and logical presentation is helpful to your readers. It enables them to understand how your ideas are related to each other.

In selecting a method of organization, consider both the purpose and type of development you have decided on for your paragraph. Then ask yourself questions such as the following:

1. How does this idea relate to my other details?
2. Does one piece of information logically precede another in time or in degree of importance?
3. Is one idea more familiar to my readers than another?

When you make decisions based on these questions, you are taking the first steps toward coherence in your writing.

There are five main methods of organization:

1. Chronological order, or time sequence
2. Spatial order
3. Order of importance
4. Order of familiarity
5. Order by comparison and contrast

Chronological Order

When you use chronological order, or time sequence, you arrange your details in the order in which they happened. This method of organization is particularly useful for paragraphs developed by anecdote or incident, as in the following example.

> Over the years, a number of major league baseball players have developed odd mental blocks. Mike Ivie, an outstanding catching prospect, was signed as a teenager by the San Diego Padres in 1970. In his first workout with the Padres, Ivie threw the ball too low to the pitcher and hit the screen used to pro-

tect pitchers during batting practice. A fellow catcher joked about it, and Ivie developed a block about throwing the ball back to the pitcher. Ivie switched to first base and, after a mediocre career with two other teams, is now a journeyman player for the Detroit Tigers. —TIME

The topic sentence in this paragraph promises to tell about the mental blocks that some baseball players develop. The incident that develops this promise begins with information about a promising rookie, Mike Ivie. The paragraph continues by describing, in the order in which they occurred, the problems that led to this player's mental block. The paragraph ends with a statement about Ivie's situation today.

Spatial Order

With spatial order, details are presented in a sequence that duplicates the order in which a viewer might notice them. Such an organization might proceed from side to side, from top to bottom (or the reverse), or from near to far (or the reverse). This method is useful in organizing sensory details, primarily visual ones. Read the following description of a canyon. Be aware of how the writer shares his impression of the scene by presenting the details in the order he himself probably noticed them.

On one side, beginning at the very lip of the pool, was a tiny meadow, a cool surface of green that extended to the base of the frowning wall. Beyond the pool a gentle slope of earth ran up and up to meet the opposing wall. Fine grass covered the slope—grass that was spangled with flowers, with here and there patches of color, orange and purple and golden. Below, the canyon was shut in. There was no view. The walls leaned together abruptly and the canyon ended in a chaos of rocks, moss-covered and hidden by a green screen of vines and creepers and boughs of trees. Up the canyon rose far hills and peaks, the big foothills, pine-covered and remote. And far beyond, like clouds upon the border of the sky, towered minarets of white, where the Sierra's eternal snows flashed austerely the blazes of the sun.—JACK LONDON

Order of Importance

This method of organization is appropriate for organizing facts and statistics, or for arranging specific examples. Judge the specific statements you wish to use according to the impact you think that they will have on your readers. Then organize them, beginning with the least important idea and ending with the strongest.

> Space has been called the last frontier, and eager adventurers are already seeking to tame it. Yet, unlike the Old West, space is one unknown that we can never hope to explore or understand completely. Where once an explorer could muster an expedition with several thousand dollars and a few volunteers, now billions must be spent to develop equipment and armies of personnel are required. Despite these numbers, each journey results in only a small increase in our understanding of the stars and planets that whirl around us. Most daunting, however, is the fact that no matter how much of the universe we explore, an infinite amount will remain unknown.

The writer began with the general idea that space is an unconquerable frontier. The first reasons he gave concerned basic restrictions of money and distance. The final, most powerful statement notes the impossibility of exploring the endless regions of space.

Order of Familiarity

This is another good method for organizing facts and statistics or specific examples. You move from ideas that are familiar to your reader to those that are not. In this way, you can prepare your reader for new concepts by providing familiar background.

> There may be a revolution going on in the audio industry. Despite improvements in quality, the basic technology of sound reproduction—the needle and groove—hasn't changed since Thomas Edison's phonograph in 1877. Now, however, the audio industry has come up with something that may turn the stereo turntable and record albums into quaint antiques. It is the compact digital audio disk player. Known as the CD player,

this stereo sound system is considered revolutionary because music is represented by a digital code that is embedded under the surface of a 4.5-inch disk. When it is played, the information is "read" by a low-power laser beam, which erases background noise and the hiss found on conventional records.

Here the writer begins with the familiar historical beginnings of the phonograph. She introduces the basic technology, and then mentions a new technological concept, the CD player.

Comparisons or Contrasts

This approach can be used to organize facts, examples, and incidents. This method helps to highlight the similarities or differences between two or more things.

A paragraph that compares persons, things, or events emphasizes the similarities between the subjects.

> A five-speed bike combines the worst of a three-speed and a ten-speed. The typical five-speed is built on the same heavy frame as the three-speed, often has the same wide saddle and upright handlebars, but has the five-speed gear cluster and changer bolted on in back. For two extra gears of questionable value, you pay almost as much as you would for a low-priced ten-speed.—S. MARSHALL

By comparing the five-speed bike with three-speed and ten-speed bikes, the writer is able to bring out the disadvantages of the five-speed. He has noted the similarities that illustrate his purpose and left out all irrelevant points of comparison.

A paragraph that contrasts persons, things, or events emphasizes differences. The following paragraph is an example.

> Although Henry Chatillon and Tête Rouge were the same age, that is, about thirty, they were very different. Henry was twice as large, and fully six times as strong as Tête Rouge. Henry's face was roughened by winds and storms; Tête Rouge's was softened by idle living. Henry had led a life of hardship and privation; Tête Rouge never had a whim which he did not gratify the first moment he was able.—FRANCIS PARKMAN

When an idea is presented side-by-side with its opposite, both become more striking because of the contrast. The personalities of the two men in the paragraph on the preceding page become clearer and more vivid because of this method of organization.

Exercise Pre-Writing: Organizing Details

Select one of the sets of pre-writing notes that you developed in the earlier exercises on paragraph development. Decide what method of organization would best fit your purpose. Then, number your specific details in the order in which you would present them. Delete or add details if necessary.

Part 6 First Draft and Revision

After carefully following all the steps of the pre-writing stage, you are ready to write your first draft. Remember that the first draft is simply your initial attempt to get your ideas on paper. Do not worry about spelling and punctuation at this point. You are still in the process of discovering, expanding, and refining.

At the revision stage, however, you must work thoughtfully. Review the discussion of revision in Chapter 7, "The Process of Writing." Refresh your memory about what you should be considering and asking yourself at this point.

All good writers go through this stage, as the example on the next page illustrates. This is a revised rough draft of the paragraph on page 144 which is developed through sensory details.

Notice the many different types of revisions this writer made. Of course, there are some corrections of errors in grammar, usage, and mechanics. The writer has also improved her word choice and expanded some of her ideas. Problems of coherence were solved when the writer moved sentences from the middle of her paragraph to the beginning. She has also reorganized details so that the details that broke her concentration are grouped together at the beginning. Finally, she omitted the statement, "I'll never get my homework done!" While this might be a real concern, it interrupts the unity of her development.

[handwritten: Biting my pencil eraser, staring at my paper, and on which]

As I sit here trying to think of a topic to write, I can hear *[handwritten: sit here in the library and]* ~~the sounds of the library. I can hear the sounds of whisper-~~ *[handwritten: listen to silence. Soft whispers come from a table across the room.]*

~~ing people. I look up and~~ I can see many colors of clothes. *[handwritten: glance from my work, and the sudden shift in my concentration changes the people and their clothes into a blur of color.]*

Now someone *[handwritten: clumps]* walks along the floor, then that ~~same person~~ *[handwritten: and]* ~~turns~~ *[handwritten: whirrs]* the pencil sharpener over his pencil. Satisfied, he walks

away. I hear a noise *[handwritten: jingle]* and I turn around to see the janitor be- *[handwritten: with a huge ring of keys fastened to his belt.]* ~~hind me picking up papers as he goes along.~~ *[handwritten: he adds a rustle to the silence.]* Someone gig-

gels and I stop thinking for a moment. The buzzing sound *[handwritten: The background buzz of the fluorescent lights overhead ties the other sounds together.]*

~~above is bugging me. I'll never get my homework done!~~ Now

I hear the sound, somewhat like a zipper, of someone tear-

ing a sheet of paper from their spiral notebook. The hum of

the bell reminds me *[handwritten: that]* I must leave. ~~I rush up the stairs and~~

study period is over.

Exercises Writing and Revising the Rough Draft

A. Use the pre-writing notes that you developed in the previous parts to write a rough draft of a paragrah.

B. Revise the rough draft of the paragraph that you wrote for Exercise A. Work on improvements in unity, coherence, and word choice.

1. A paragraph is a group of sentences dealing with a single topic.

2. The topic sentence of a paragraph is a general statement of what the paragraph will be about.

3. When all of the sentences in a paragraph develop the topic sentence and relate logically to each other, the paragraph has **unity** and **coherence**. Remember that unity and coherence are important to any clear expression of ideas.

4. Paragraphs can be developed with sensory details, facts, statistics, examples, incidents, or anecdotes.

5. Ways of organizing paragraphs include the following five methods: chronological order, spatial order, order of importance, order of familiarity, and comparison-contrast. Whenever you are given a writing assignment in one of your classes, choose the most appropriate organizational method for your presentation.

Applications in Other Subject Areas

History. Using news magazines or a United States history textbook, choose one recent event (since 1960) that you believe greatly affects life today. Write a paragraph that supports your view. Your topic sentence should tell which event you have chosen and how it affects people now. The remainder of the paragraph should support your idea with specific evidence.

History / Science. In your history or science textbook, find examples of each of the following:

   a. a paragraph developed with facts or statistics
   b. a paragraph developed with specific examples
   c. a paragraph organized in chronological order

Copy the topic sentence in each paragraph. List the supporting details and any connective words or transitions.

Chapter 9

Types of Paragraphs

You have studied four different ways of developing paragraphs—with sensory details, with facts or statistics, with specific examples, or with an incident or anecdote. You have also learned several different methods of organizing your ideas. You are now ready to apply what you have learned to composing specific types of paragraphs:

> Narrative paragraphs
> Descriptive paragraphs
> Explanatory paragraphs

Each type of paragraph has special characteristics and is used for a particular purpose. Your strategies for the development and organization of each kind will vary. The wide range of options available to you will help you develop paragraphs that are uniquely suited to the ideas you want to express.

Part 1 The Narrative Paragraph

The purpose of the narrative paragraph is to relate an event. "Once upon a time…"; "Last night while I was watching television…" are phrases that signal the beginning of a narrative.

The narrative paragraph is a simple, natural form of writing with many variations. It may be based on fact, on imagination, or on a combination of both. The narrowed topic of a narrative paragraph may recall a personal experience or an event observed by, told to, or thought up by the writer. Narrative paragraphs may be written in the first or in the third person.

FIRST PERSON

When I woke, the sun was low. Looking down from where I lay, I saw a dog sitting on his haunches. His tongue was hanging out of his mouth; he looked as if he were laughing. He was a big dog, with a gray-brown coat, as big as a wolf. I sprang up and shouted at him but he did not move—he just sat there. I did not like that. When I reached for a stone to throw, he moved swiftly out of the way of the stone. He was not afraid of me; he looked at me as if I were meat. No doubt I could have killed him with an arrow, but I did not know if there were others. Moreover, night was falling.—STEPHEN VINCENT BENÉT

THIRD PERSON

Leaning on his cane, Mr. Mendelsohn stood up and walked out of the kitchen and down the long hallway into the living room. It was empty. He went over to a large armchair by the window. The sun shone through the window, covering the entire armchair and Mr. Mendelsohn. A canary cage was also by the window, and two tiny yellow birds chirped and hopped back and forth energetically. Mr. Mendelsohn felt drowsy; he shut his eyes. So many aches and pains, he thought. It was hard to sleep at night, but here, well…the birds began to chirp in unison and the old man opened one eye, glancing at them, and smiled. Then he shut his eyes once more and fell fast asleep.

—NICHOLASA MOHR

Pre-Writing Steps

Selecting Details for a Narrative Paragraph. It is not difficult to gather the information needed for a narrative paragraph. This simply consists of recalling or developing all of the details needed to re-create the story for the reader. A writer should, however, be careful not to stray from the main story line or include details that interrupt the flow of the narrative. The writer should also attempt to make the story as interesting as possible by choosing sharp, precise words to develop the ideas. This will help the resulting story to be vivid and extremely effective.

Organizing a Narrative Paragraph. The events or actions described in a narrative paragraph are usually told in **chronological order**, the order in which they occurred in time. In some paragraphs, such as the following narrative about a fisherman, the chronological order is clear and direct from beginning to end.

> A fisherman walked along a beach on a moonlit night, searching for firewood. Above the reaches of the high tide, he saw a gnarled branch, polished by the rough sand and entwined in seaweed. In the eerie silver light and sudden shadows, the branch seemed almost alive. The fisherman lifted it cautiously and shook off the sand. As he turned it in his hand and the moonlight gleamed on its polished surface, he saw the subtle outline that had caused him to mistake the branch for a living creature. The fisherman took his knife from his pocket and quickly cut away the protruding twigs. Then he carefully cut, shaped, and smoothed the ancient wood. Finally he held in his hand a graceful wood sculpture—the perfect, almost living form of an undersea serpent!—BARBARA BRUNO

Many narrative paragraphs indicate the order of time and the passing of time by using words and phrases such as those listed in the chart on the following page. These words and phrases are called **transitional devices.** They help to unify your paragraph by providing signals to your reader about how your details are related to each other.

Time Words and Phrases

A POINT IN TIME

one month	next year	at midnight
two days	yesterday	tonight
tomorrow	last week	at this moment

ORDER OF TIME

next	soon	immediately
then	instantly	the next day
later	finally	the following Friday

PERIODS OF TIME

for a moment	during the day	for a long time
for an hour	after a week	during the winter

ACTIONS REPEATED IN TIME

seldom	occasionally	once
sometimes	frequently	twice

A BREAK IN TIME

meanwhile	before this	at the same time

When chronological order is clear as in the paragraph about the fisherman, time words merely reinforce the flow of the narrative. However, in paragraphs where the passage of time is uneven, time words are essential to understanding the events.

> *Soon* the biggest of the boys poised himself, shot down into the water, and did not come up. The others stood about, watching. *After a long time* the boy came up on the other side of a big, dark rock, letting the air out of his lungs in a sputtering gasp and a shout of triumph. *Immediately,* the rest of them dived in. *One moment,* the morning seemed full of chattering boys; *the next,* the air and the surface of the water were empty, but through the heavy blue, dark shapes could be seen moving and groping.—DORIS LESSING

The Topic Sentence

Because narrative paragraphs tell a story rather than develop a single idea, they do not always have a topic sentence. In the following paragraph, for example, the writer begins telling her story without making a preliminary controlling statement.

> Paul was cutting trees one morning up in Minnesota. He had to get them to the sawmill which was in New Orleans, and he decided that the best way to do it would be by river—but there was no river. So Paul had a light lunch of 19 pounds of sausage, 6 hams, 8 loaves of bread, and 231 flapjacks, and each flapjack was slathered with a pound of butter and a quart of maple syrup. It was a skimpy lunch for Paul, but he figured on eating a hearty supper to make up for it. Paul dug his river that afternoon and he called it the Mississippi, which as far as I know, is what it is called to this day.—BARBARA EMBERLEY

Although this type of paragraph is common, you should practice writing narrative paragraphs *with* topic sentences:

1   *I spent the day wandering aimlessly through the bright streets.* The noisy penny arcades with the gaggle-giggle of sailors and children and the games of chance were tempting. After walking through one of them, though, it was obvious that I could only win more chances and no money. I went to the library and used a part of my day reading science fiction.—MAYA ANGELOU

2   *One day a strange thing happened.* It was spring, and for some reason I had been hot and irritable all morning. It was a beautiful spring. I could feel it as I played barefoot in the backyard. Blossoms hung up from the thorny, black locust trees like clusters of fragrant, white grapes. Butterflies flickered in the sunlight above the short, new dew-wet grass. I had gone into the house for bread and butter, and coming out I heard a steady, unfamiliar drone. It was unlike anything I had ever heard before. I tried to place the sound. It was no use. It was like a sensation I had when searching for my father's watch, heard ticking unseen in a room. It made me feel as though I had forgotten to perform some task that my mother had ordered. Then I lo-

cated it, overhead. In the sky, flying quite low and about a hundred yards off was a plane! It was a little plane, flying no higher than the eaves of our roof. Seeing it come steadily forward, I felt the world grow warm with promise. I would catch the plane as it came over and swing down fast and run into the house before anyone could see me. Then no one could come to claim the plane. It droned nearer. Then, when it hung like a silver cross in the blue directly above me, I stretched out my hand and grabbed. It was like sticking my finger through a soap bubble. The plane flew on, as though I had simply blown my breath after it.—RALPH ELLISON

Exercise Writing Narrative Paragraphs

Choose an interesting incident to write about. The incident may be real or imaginary. Write a narrative paragraph about this incident. Complete the following steps.

Pre-Writing: After selecting your general topic, narrow it by identifying the peak point or points of the experience. Decide how the experience made you or your main character feel. Also decide on the impression you want your readers to have when they have finished reading.

Write a topic sentence that identifies your narrowed topic and the impression you want to give your readers. Select details that help re-create the experience as vividly as possible. Organize the details, using chronological order.

First Draft: Referring to your pre-writing notes, get your ideas down on paper. Remember to use transitional words and phrases to help you re-create the flow of events.

Revision: Go over your rough draft several times. Are the details organized logically? Do any details need to be added or deleted? Have you included vivid words and details that will make your story come alive for your readers? Refer to the Guidelines for the Process of Writing on page 122 for further help with revision. When you are satisfied with your content, use the Checklist on page 123 to help you check sentence structure, spelling, capitalization, and punctuation.

Part 2   The Descriptive Paragraph

A descriptive paragraph paints a word picture that appeals to a reader's senses. The clarity of the word picture depends on carefully selected words and precise details. The writer's purpose and the impression he or she wants to create for an audience guide the selection of those words and details.

Pre-Writing Steps

Selecting Details for a Descriptive Paragraph. In the following example, the writer selected details that appeal to the reader's visual sense.

> The village was a fairly typical one. It consisted of small shacks with walls built out of the jagged offcuts from the sawmill, and whitewashed. Each stood in its own little patch of ground, surrounded by a bamboo fence. The gardens around the shacks were sometimes filled with a strange variety of old tins, kettles, and broken barrels, each brimming over with flowers. Wide ditches full of muddy water separated these "gardens" from the road. The ditches were spanned at each front gate by a small, rickety bridge of roughly nailed branches.—GERALD DURRELL

The writer's purpose was to describe the village so that his audience could clearly visualize it. During the pre-writing stage, he had to decide exactly what he wanted his readers to see. By focusing on the houses and gardens, he narrowed his topic. Then he carefully selected precise details that helped to create a vivid impression of the scene. Follow a similar line of thought as you plan your own paragraphs.

Organizing a Descriptive Paragraph. The details, particularly in visual descriptions, are usually organized in **spatial order.** You will recall that in spatial order, the writer presents details from top to bottom, from side to side, or from near to far. Other methods of organization are possible, however, provided that the order is clear to the readers.

When a writer needs to clarify the order, he or she uses the types of transitional devices shown in the chart below. These space words and phrases follow the description from one place or thing to another.

Transitions relating to space fall into three general categories: those indicating direction, those specifying distance, and those identifying area.

Space Words and Phrases

DIRECTIONS

left	through	around
right	into	between
above	ahead	among
below	behind	in front of
center	across	in back of
up	toward	forward
down	away from	backward
past	against	parallel

DISTANCE

foreground	on the edge of	close to
background	in the center of	next to
first	approximately	leading to
last	twenty feet	far
halfway	about ten miles	near
beyond	twenty kilometers	long
distant	remote	short

AREA OF SPACE

outside	field	hall
inside	plain	stairway
interior	hillside	stage
exterior	acre	alley
lawn	hut	street
garden	villa	road
courtyard	mansion	narrow
park	closet	wide

Following are four descriptive paragraphs. Three have common methods of organization. In the fourth, the writer has followed a unique order. As you read the paragraphs, notice how space words lead you from one place or thing to another.

1. FROM SIDE TO SIDE

The set is magnificent. The left half of the stage depicts a hillside in cherryblossom time with, in the foreground, a garden and thatched entrance gateway. The gateway is freestanding—the fence omitted as superfluous. On the right-hand side is a villa raised off the ground.—WIM SWANN

Notice the use of the space words *left, foreground,* and *right*— all of which lead the reader from one side of the stage to the other. Notice also the many space words that indicate area.

2. FROM TOP TO BOTTOM (OR THE REVERSE)

Ruiz had come to our town about a month before from Seville, in Spain. He was tall, and his shoulders were so wide and powerful that they seemed to be armored in steel instead of muscle. His hair, which was gold-colored, grew thick on his head like a helmet. He had blue eyes, so blue and handsome that anyone would have envied them. His face was handsome, too, except that around his mouth there always lurked the shadow of a sneer.—SCOTT O'DELL

After introducing Ruiz, the writer makes a general statement about his size, emphasizing the man's shoulders. He then leads you down from hair, to eyes, to face, to mouth. This writer does not need to use space words, as the order is clear without them.

3. FROM NEAR TO FAR (OR THE REVERSE)

We drove past a barbed-wire fence, through a gate, and into an open space. There, trunks and sacks and packages had been dumped from the baggage trucks that drove out ahead of us. I could see a few tents set up, the first rows of black barracks, and beyond them, blurred by sand, rows of barracks that seemed to spread for miles across this plain.

—JEANNE WAKATSUKI HOUSTON AND JAMES D. HOUSTON

The writers begin with a description of the scene nearest them. They then draw your attention to "a few tents," to "the first rows of black barracks," to "rows of barracks that seemed to spread for miles across this plain," using space words such as *past, through, into, first,* and *beyond.*

4. UNIQUE ORDER

Our first camp in Glen Canyon is almost unimaginably beautiful. The site is a sandstone ledge below two arched caves. Clear cliffs soar up behind the caves. Just below the camp is the masked entrance of Hidden Passage Canyon. Its outthrust masking wall throws a strong shadow against the cliffs. Beyond this masking wall is the kind of canyon that is almost commonplace here, but that anywhere else would be a wonder.

—WALLACE STEGNER

The writer first explains that the camp is located below two caves, behind which are cliffs. He next describes the scene below the camp. His description moves back to the cliffs, then down again to the scene below. The writer uses space words and phrases to eliminate any confusion from these changes in direction.

Describing a Person

Describing a person is different from describing a place or a thing. The writer's purpose is to capture the essence of a person by going beyond physical characteristics.

Example 1

The writer of the following description, for example, selects words and details that reveal much about the inner reality of the woman being described.

She was a big, awkward woman, with big bones and hard, rubbery flesh. Her short arms ended in ham hands, and her neck was a squat roll of fat that protruded behind her head as a big bump. Her skin was rough and puffy, with plump, mole-like freckles down her cheeks. Her eyes glowered from under the mountain of her brow and were circled with expensive mauve shadow. They were nervous and quick when she was flustered and darted about at nothing in particular while she was dressing hair or talking to people.—ALICE WALKER

With phrases such as "rubbery flesh," "ham hands," and "squat roll," the writer creates an overall impression of ugliness. She notes the woman's "expensive mauve shadow," which hints at vanity. She uses words such as *glowered, nervous, quick,* and *darted* to imply suspicion and insecurity.

The writer makes the woman come alive for the reader. She paints a picture of an interesting, complex human being.

Example 2

Here is another description, this time of a young boy. Try to determine how the writer has made his description so colorful.

> When Wheldon first arrived at our school, he was carrying a natty little briefcase and wore a pink spotted tie and short trousers. His long, thin face was as white as a sheet in a TV ad, and his eyes were so watery behind his huge spectacles that gazing into them was like looking out of the portholes of a sinking ship. He had collapsed shoulders almost meeting under his chin, and his hair looked as if each separate strand had been carefully glued into place, ready for church. He reminded me of a cheerful but undernourished sheep.
>
> —PETER JONES

The writer has used descriptive words such as *natty, pink spotted, watery,* and *collapsed.* He has also incorporated several direct and indirect comparisons into the description:

> He compares the color of the boy's face to a sheet in a TV ad.
> He equates gazing into the boy's eyes with looking out of the portholes of a sinking ship.
> He compares the boy to an undernourished sheep.

Like the writer of the previous description, this writer has presented a physical description that reveals inner qualities as well. Can you describe in your own words some of these qualities?

Exercises Writing Descriptive Paragraphs

A. Choose a topic from the box or make up one of your own. Write a descriptive paragraph. Complete each of the steps below.

Possible Topics
1. An interesting building in your home town
2. The waiting area in an airport or train station
3. A machine shop or car repair garage
4. The check-out counter of a store
5. A doctor's or dentist's office
6. An interesting piece of art

Pre-Writing: Narrow your topic by selecting a specific place or thing to describe. What impression do you want to create? What details will reinforce this impression? What organization will you use?

First Draft: Use your pre-writing notes to get your ideas down on paper. Use vivid words that will help your reader "see" your subject.

Revision: Go over your rough draft several times. Can you add space words and phrases to help with unity? Can you add more precise words and phrases to make your description more vivid? When you are satisfied with the content, check sentence structure, spelling, and mechanics. Refer to the Guidelines on pages 122 and 180.

B. Choose a topic from the box or make one up. Write a paragraph describing a person. Complete the steps on the next page.

Possible Topics
1. An interesting person you have known
2. A character in a movie
3. A grandparent
4. An unusual individual you noticed on the street
5. A singer
6. The host on a TV game show

Pre-Writing: Narrow the topic by selecting a *specific* person. Decide exactly what qualities you wish to reveal about the person. What details will help communicate these qualities? What would be the best organization for these details?

First Draft: Use your pre-writing notes to get your ideas down on paper.

Revision: Go over your rough draft several times. Does every detail reinforce what you wish to reveal about the character? Can you add other details that will tell even more about the physical appearance or personality of the character? Check for spelling, punctuation, and capitalization errors. Refer to the Guidelines on pages 122 and 180.

Appealing to the Senses

Thus far, the examples of description have appealed only to the sense of sight. Descriptive paragraphs may also appeal to the other senses, either individually or in combination. Following are five paragraphs, four of which appeal to a single sense and one of which appeals to two senses. As you read, pay particular attention to the vivid language each writer uses.

SOUND

Through the window next to her chair she heard the household noises as sounds on a distant stage. There was Father's pipe clacking against the ashtray, and the rustle of his newspaper. There was a small boy throwing books onto a chair, and the cookie jar thudding onto tile.—ROSEMARIE BODENHEIMER

TASTE

Gradually the peat glowed, the water boiled, and an hour later Miyax had a pot of caribou stew. On it floated great chunks of golden grease, more delicious than the butter from the gussak store. She put a savory bite into her mouth, sucked the juices, then chewed a long time before she swallowed.

—JEAN CRAIGHEAD GEORGE

TOUCH

A few months ago, on her sixteenth birthday, Mr. Dale had given Muffin a new, wide suede watchband. Lately, she found herself rubbing the velvety leather, letting her fingers smooth the fine, sleek texture, but then suddenly dragging her fingers backward against the grain, feeling the bits of leather recoil.

—SHARON BELL MATHIS

SMELL

The filthy streets are seldom cleaned. The inaccessible alleys and rear yards are never touched, and in the hot summer months the stench of rotting things will mark these places. Here and there an unwitting newcomer tries the disastrous experiment of keeping a goat, adding thereby to the distinctive flavor of the neighborhood.

COMBINATION

Early morning is a time of magic in Cannery Row. In the gray time after the light has come and before the sun has risen, the Row seems to hang suspended out of time in a silvery light. The street lights go out, and the weeds are a brilliant green. The corrugated iron of the canneries glows with the pearly lucence of platinum or old pewter. No automobiles are running then. The street is silent of progress and business. The rush and drag of the waves can be heard as they splash in among the piles of the canneries. It is a time of great peace, a deserted time, a little era of rest. —JOHN STEINBECK

Exercises Using the Senses in Describing

A. Write a paragraph describing the *sound* of an item below. (For all the exercises in this section, remember to follow all of the steps of the process of writing.)

1. A jet landing
2. Eating potato chips
3. A cricket
4. A police siren
5. A ticking clock
6. A crying baby
7. Traffic on a city street
8. A musical group

B. Write a paragraph describing the *taste* of an item below.

1. A hot pepper 5. A pickle
2. Root beer   6. Peanut butter
3. An apple   7. Fresh mushrooms
4. A lemon   8. Vanilla ice cream

C. Write a paragraph describing the *feeling* of an item below.

1. Walking barefoot   5. An electric shock
2. Snow down your back   6. Burning your finger
3. Sandpaper   7. Petting a dog or cat
4. A foot falling asleep 8. Drinking ice water

D. Write a paragraph describing the *smell* of an item below.

1. A barbecue   5. Frying hamburgers
2. A bouquet   6. A school gymnasium
3. A dentist's office   7. A laundromat
4. A stale garbage can   8. A crowded room

E. Write a paragraph in which you use a *combination of senses* to describe an item below.

1. A cut finger   5. A classroom
2. Eating a raw carrot   6. A child crying
3. A rainy afternoon   7. Riding a bicycle
4. A football game   8. A forest trail

F. Select one of the following statements as the topic sentence for a paragraph. Write a short description in which you create a single sensory impression.

1. The scene before me was one of total dreariness.
2. The room was bright with color.
3. The street was a carnival of activity.
4. The delicious smells made my mouth water.
5. The outfit was as crazy as the wearer.
6. I had never seen him so angry.
7. He was trying to make lunch for the children.
8. The room was an absolute mess.

Part 3   The Explanatory Paragraph

A friend asks how to write up a science experiment, and you give instructions. A foreign exchange student wants to know what Thanksgiving is, and you define it. Your parents want to know why you want to join the soccer team, and you give them reasons. Although your purposes are somewhat different, in each of these situations you are being asked to do the same thing—explain something.

Explanations are often oral. However, they can also be written. When a written explanation takes the form of a paragraph, it is called an explanatory, or expository, paragraph. There are three main types of explanatory paragraphs:

> those that explain a process
> those that define
> those that give reasons

The Paragraph That Explains a Process

In its simplest form, the explanatory paragraph is used to explain a process. It may tell how something is done or how something works. The following paragraph, for example, gives clear, accurate instructions on how to grow bean sprouts.

> Here's a quick and easy way to grow bean sprouts. Put about two tablespoons of bean seeds into a wide-mouthed jar and cover with at least three-quarters of a cup of warm water. Let the seeds soak overnight. In the morning, drain the water off the swollen seeds and rinse them with warm water. Drain well and return to the jar. Cover the jar with two layers of cheesecloth held in place with a rubber band. Keep the jar in a dark place. Rinse the seeds with warm water morning and night. The sprouts will be about one inch long in two to three days. When they are one to two inches long, place them in the refrigerator to stop growth. You can eat the entire sprout — root, seed, and if there are some, the tiny leaves. —BARBARA AND D.X. FENTEN

When you are composing a paragraph that explains a process, your pre-writing notes should list all of the facts necessary for the successful completion or understanding of the process. Since most paragraphs that explain a process are organized in chronological order, the next pre-writing step would be to number your facts using this method. As you write the first draft, include transitional words and phrases to make the order of the ideas even more definite. Notice the clear order of the following two paragraphs.

1   During a fire, opening a hallway door to attempt an escape can be dangerous. To minimize the risks, take these simple precautions. First, touch the door. A hot door means danger. Do not open it. If the door is not hot, brace your foot against the bottom and carefully open the door about an inch. If you feel pressure against the door or an in-rush of heat and fire, close the door at once. If there is no pressure or heat, open the door wide enough to look into the hall. An absence of fire and extreme heat means that the hallway is safe. You can proceed rapidly through it to the outside.

2   Video cassette recorders are becoming increasingly popular in American homes, yet few people understand how they work. Actually, the basic principles are quite simple. A television program is made up of sound and light patterns. These patterns are transmitted by converting them into electric waves. The waves can then be channeled into the video recorder. There, they magnetize the recording head of the machine which, in turn, transfers the pattern to a special magnetic tape. This tape, a thin plastic ribbon coated on one side with iron oxide or some other easily magnetized material, records the magnetic pattern from the recording head. When the process is reversed, the patterns are converted back into electric waves. The electric waves are then turned back into the sound and light of the television program.

In these paragraphs, the steps of the process are presented in the order in which they should be followed or the order in which they occur.

Writing To Explain a Process

Choose a topic from the box or make up your own. Write a paragraph explaining a process. Complete each of the steps below.

Possible Topics

1. Explain how to find information in the Yellow Pages of the telephone directory.
2. Tell how to adjust a television set.
3. Explain how to repair a flat bicycle tire.
4. Describe how a pencil sharpener or some other simple machine works.
5. Choose a park, a building, a shopping center, or an historical site in your area. Write a paragraph telling how to get there from your house.
6. Explain how a three-speed bicycle works.

Pre-Writing: Narrow your subject and write a topic sentence that indicates your specific topic, purpose, and audience. What are the steps of the process? In what order should they be presented?

First Draft: Use your pre-writing notes to get your ideas down on paper. Include all the details your reader would need to understand the process completely.

Revision: Go over your rough draft several times. Are your instructions or descriptions clear? Has anything been left out? Are there any errors in spelling, usage, or mechanics?

The Paragraph That Defines

Clear definitions help a person to understand new words, things, and ideas. Expanding upon the short "dictionary definition," a paragraph of definition first places the term to be defined in a general category, and then identifies several distinguishing characteristics of the term. These characteristics help to separate the term being defined from others closely related to it.

To explain Thanksgiving to a foreign exchange student, for example, you might begin by identifying it as an American holiday. Next you would give identifying characteristics of this holiday, such as its origin, its traditions, its purpose, and its date of observance. These details would differentiate Thanksgiving from other holidays such as Labor Day or Independence Day.

Generally, the details in a paragraph of definition are organized from most general to most specific:

> Jai alai is a fast-paced game that closely resembles handball. It is popular in many parts of Latin America and in Florida. Jai alai is played with a small, hard ball, called a *pelota*, and a basketlike container, called a *cesta*, which is strapped to the player's arm. The game is played on a court that has high walls on three sides. The server hits the ball against the wall by hurling it from the curved end of the *cesta*. The opponent must catch the ball in his or her *cesta* either before it hits the floor or on the first bounce. The opponent then hurls the ball back against the wall, and the server must try to catch it. Play continues until one player misses the ball.

This paragraph begins by placing jai alai in a larger category, games. The sentences that follow give specific characteristics that distinguish jai alai from other games. Often, defining paragraphs include a physical description as well as an explanation of the term's function, purpose, or use.

Exercise Writing a Definition

Choose a topic from the box or make up your own. Write a paragraph of definition. Complete each of the steps on the next page.

Possible Topics

1. An unusual animal   5. Jazz
2. A grandparent   6. A dirt bike
3. A good friend   7. A hologram
4. A sand dune   8. A board game

Pre-Writing: Decide whether the term to be defined is specific enough to be explained in one paragraph, or whether it needs to be narrowed further. To what general class does your subject belong? What are its identifying features? What is the best method of organization?

First Draft: Use your pre-writing notes to get your ideas on paper. Use precise words to present your subject's characteristics clearly.

Revision: Go over your rough draft several times. Did you state a general category for your term? Do the characteristics you chose help to distinguish your term from closely related ones? Do your facts or examples illustrate your characteristics? When your definition is complete, carefully check your paper for mechanical correctness.

The Paragraph That Gives Reasons

Whenever you try to explain why something is, or why something should be, you are composing an explanatory paragraph that gives reasons. You say that something happens *because* something else occurred first, or that an action or idea is right *because* certain facts or reasons logically support it.

For this type of writing, it is especially important to design a good topic sentence that clearly states your topic and reflects your purpose. Often, the topic sentence of this type of paragraph is a statement of opinion: It presents your personal view on a subject. Such a statement needs strong reasons to support it.

Many types of details can be used to develop a paragraph that gives reasons. You may use facts, statistics, examples, or anecdotes. Choose these details carefully. They should provide logical support for your topic sentence. They then become evidence of the truth of your topic sentence.

In a paragraph that gives reasons, organization is closely related to both the purpose and the type of development.

In spite of claims of a "fitness boom," most Americans do not get enough exercise to be considered physically fit. A recent U.S. Department of Health and Human Services study supports this claim. It reports that nearly two-thirds of American adults did not engage in enough regular exercise to achieve fitness. Our lifestyle is a major cause of this lack of physical activity. Given a choice, we often prefer to watch television rather than play an active sport, and we are more likely to take an elevator than to climb the stairs. Secondly, a majority of American adults are only "weekend exercisers." They engage in physical activity only when it does not conflict with the daily routine of work or school. Finally, even those Americans who do participate in sports may achieve only partial fitness. For instance, sports such as bowling or softball are more for socializing than they are for fitness. Even conditioning sports such as basketball and tennis are stop-and-go activities. They are less helpful in achieving overall fitness than sustained aerobic exercises such as swimming or jogging.

In the topic sentence, the writer states that most Americans are physically unfit. She then gives three reasons which support this statement. Her last reason is her strongest because it explains how even people who participate in sports may not be totally fit.

Exercise Giving Reasons

Choose a topic from the box or make up your own. Write a paragraph giving reasons. Complete each step on the next page.

Possible Topics

1. A new wrist watch you have had for only a few days has already stopped running three times. You have decided to send the watch back to the company for a refund. Write a one-paragraph letter to the company, explaining why you are returning the watch.

2. You have just read a help-wanted ad for a job that interests you. Write a one-paragraph letter to the company, explaining why you are qualified for the job.

3. In a paragraph, explain something you like or don't like.

4. Think of a book, movie, or song that you enjoyed. Write a "review," telling why you thought it was good.

Pre-Writing: Write a topic sentence that states an idea or opinion that needs to be supported by reasons. The sentence should also reflect your narrowed topic, your purpose, and your audience. What reasons could be used to support your topic? What details can help develop these reasons? What method of organization would be most effective?

First Draft: Using your pre-writing notes, get your ideas down on paper. You may think of better supporting reasons as you write. Include them.

Revision: Go over your rough draft several times. Check for coherence by imagining a "because" in front of every piece of evidence you use. If you can logically link each piece of evidence to your topic sentence with a "because," your paragraph has coherence. Then check further. Are your reasons fully explained? Are your reasons organized to have the best effect on the reader? Remember to do a final check for errors in grammar, usage, and mechanics.

The Paragraph That Persuades

A paragraph of persuasion is a special type of paragraph that gives reasons. A paragraph of persuasion usually contains a signal of its purpose in the topic sentence. The sentence will be worded so that a definite opinion is given on an issue that has two or more sides. It may also contain words such as *should* or *ought to*, or words that express a judgment about a thing or idea.

The reasons in a persuasive paragraph must be chosen and organized carefully because your purpose is to persuade others who may not agree with the idea you are expressing. Facts and statistics provide strong support, but examples and incidents may also be used effectively. The reasons in a persuasive paragraph are often organized from the least important to the most important. This helps to build strong support for the opinion, and leaves your reader with your strongest reason freshly in mind.

When you write a persuasive paragraph, use reasonable language. Do not make unfair remarks or use harsh, slanted language. Let your reasons make your point. See Chapter 13, "Critical Thinking," for a discussion on logical argument.

"The first black mayor." "The first woman astronaut." Such phrases are common on TV, in newspapers and magazines, and in casual conversation. It is time we made them obsolete. First of all, a person's race, sex, or religion has nothing to do with whether he or she is qualified for a certain position. What does matter is whether the individual has mastered the skills and knowledge necessary to perform the job well. If this is the case, labels such as the ones mentioned only make the qualifications seem less important. Moreover, our society should be beyond the point where such distinctions are something that we even notice. If a police chief is a Latino, or a senator a Jew, these facts should be as unimportant as hair color or height. Only when we stop pointing out these characteristics will we be close to the time when we are no longer aware of them.

Exercise Writing To Persuade

Choose one of the topics from the box or make up one of your own. Write a persuasive paragraph. Complete the steps below.

Possible Topics
1. _____ music is _____.
2. TV has a beneficial/harmful effect on young children.
3. _____ is a good/bad book because _____.
4. The news media are/are not effective in reporting events.
5. The driving age should be raised/lowered.
6. Air pollution is/is not a serious issue.

Pre-Writing: Narrow your topic to a specific issue and write a topic sentence that identifies your opinion. What reasons support your opinion? Which of these are most effective?

First Draft: Use your pre-writing notes to get your ideas down on paper. Use well thought-out reasons and reasonable language.

Revision: Go over your rough draft several times. Is your opinion clearly stated? Do all your reasons logically support your opinion? Have you included specific details to support your claims? Have you arranged your reasons in the most effective order?

Guidelines for Writing and Revising Paragraphs

These Guidelines will help to remind you of the qualities necessary for good paragraphs. However, your writing procedure should also include the steps in Guidelines for the Process of Writing on page 122.

1. Does the paragraph deal with only one main idea?

2. Does the topic sentence state the main idea?

3. Does the topic sentence control and limit the ideas that are discussed in the rest of the paragraph?

4. Does the paragraph have unity and coherence?

5. Are there enough details — facts, statistics, examples, incidents, or anecdotes — to develop the paragraph fully?

6. If it is a narrative paragraph, is it developed in chronological order? Does it use time words and phrases?

7. If it is a descriptive paragraph, does it use vivid sensory details? Does it present these details in a logical order? Does it use space words and phrases? If the paragraph describes a person, does it try to capture the essence of the person? Does it appeal to the senses?

8. If it is an explanatory paragraph, does it clearly explain a process? give reasons? define? Is the supporting material presented in an effective order? Is the purpose of the paragraph clear to the reader?

1. There are three main types of paragraphs: narrative, descriptive, and explanatory.

2. Narrative paragraphs relate events. They can be written in the first or third person, and are generally organized in chronological order.

3. Descriptive paragraphs create word pictures through the use of sensory details. These details are usually organized in spatial order.

4. Explanatory, or expository, paragraphs can explain a process, give definitions, or offer reasons to support an idea. The most common methods of organization for this type of writing are most familiar to least familiar idea, and least important to most important idea.

5. Different topics require different types of paragraphs. Whenever you are writing for any of your classes, choose types of paragraphs that are appropriate to your material.

Applications in Other Subject Areas

Science. Explanatory paragraphs are extremely common in scientific writing. Using a science textbook or an encyclopedia, collect information on one of the following terms. Then, write a paragraph that explains or defines it.

> Photosynthesis   The Doppler Effect   Oxidation

Fine Arts. Choose an area of the fine arts—drama, music, dance, or art—and write three paragraphs about that general topic, as follows:

    a. Describe an exciting or embarrassing incident connected with the subject (your first recital, for example).

    b. Describe an effective example of that art (a striking sculpture, a haunting melody).

    c. Explain how to perform an activity in that area (a dance step, a dramatic monologue).

Math. Choose a difficult problem in your math book. Write a paragraph explaining how the problem could be solved.

Chapter 10

Writing a Composition

From your work in Chapters 8 and 9, you know that paragraphs may be developed in several ways. Despite these variations, you may have felt limited as to what you could accomplish in the space of a single paragraph. For this reason, the different types of paragraphs are seldom used alone. Instead, they are usually combined in larger pieces of writing called **compositions**.

A composition provides you with the opportunity to explore many different aspects of an idea. Before you can do so, however, you must have a good understanding of how a composition works. In this chapter, you will study the different parts of a composition. You will also learn how you can apply your knowledge of the writing process to take advantage of the possibilities this type of writing offers.

Part 1   Defining a Composition

The definition of a composition is only slightly different from that of a paragraph.

> A paragraph is a group of sentences dealing with a single topic or idea. Usually, one sentence, called the topic sentence, states the main idea. All the other sentences are related to this topic sentence. They further explain or support the main idea.

A **composition** is a group of paragraphs dealing with a single topic or idea. Usually, one paragraph, called the introductory paragraph, states the main idea of the composition. All the other paragraphs are related to the introductory paragraph. They further explain or support the main idea.

A composition has three main parts: the introductory paragraph, the body, and the conclusion.

The **introductory paragraph** is similar to the topic sentence of a paragraph. It presents the main idea of the composition.

The **body**, or middle paragraphs, support the main idea.

The **conclusion**, or final paragraph, may perform one or more of the following tasks: It may restate the main idea. It may summarize the information that has been presented in the preceding paragraphs. It may also make a final comment on the information that has been given. The three parts all work together to develop a single topic or idea, the subject of the composition.

Here is an example of a composition.

Television

We sometimes find it difficult to think of our television sets as mere pieces of machinery. They greet us with news and music in the morning, entertain us in the evening, and soothe us to sleep at night. They are an important part of the world in which we live.

Television has had great influence on the feelings and beliefs of contemporary Americans. It has affected our feelings about politics by bringing us face to face with the candidates. It has affected our feelings about violence in our cities by giving us close-up views of the disorders. Finally, it has affected our feelings about war by bringing the ugliness and the pain of the battlefields into our living rooms.

Television has increased our general level of education through news coverage, special reports, and talk shows, as well as with educational programming. Teachers, acknowledging the importance of television, have brought both public and closed circuit broadcasts into many classrooms.

Television has greatly affected the popular arts. Despite some of its poor drama, television has actually encouraged the production of several good plays. By offering entertainment that competes with movie theaters and by showing movies, television has stimulated the movie industry to produce films that are destined for the home screen. Television has also affected the book publishing industry. By raising the general level of public knowledge, TV encourages people to buy books. On the other hand, it lures some people away from books by providing a competitive source of entertainment and escape.

The inferiority of so many television programs stems from the economic forces that control the industry. Most broadcasting in this country is commercial; it is paid for by advertisers. Programs are selected and retained, not for their quality but for the number of viewers they can reach and convert into customers. This practice of programming for immediate financial advantage has, thus far, prevented television from realizing its full educational and cultural potential.

—RISSOVER AND BIRCH

The introductory paragraph tells you that the composition is going to be about television in our lives. The next three paragraphs explain this idea by giving the following information.

1. The political and social influence of television
2. The impact of television on education
3. The effect of television on the popular arts

The final paragraph comments on the economic factors that have limited television's potential influence on the political, social, educational, and artistic aspects of American life. Each paragraph develops in some way the main idea of the composition.

Part 2   Pre-Writing: Deciding on a Subject

The first step in writing a composition is to choose a subject. When you are doing so, keep these three guidelines in mind:

1. *Choose a subject that interests you.* This is important. Without interest on your part, you will have a difficult time creating interest on the part of your readers.
2. *Choose a subject that is familiar to you.* You will then be able to write with confidence about your subject.
3. *Choose a subject that has value for you.* You will then communicate something of value to your readers.

Your best source of subjects that are interesting, familiar, and valuable is your own feelings, ideas, knowledge, and memories. Your journal is a good source for this type of subject. Brainstorming is another way to search your mind for ideas. Of course, you should not overlook other people as a source of subjects for writing. Discussion and interviews with others can yield a rich store of subject ideas for your composition. In general, these personal subjects fall into two groups.

1. Subjects based on first-hand experiences and knowledge
2. Subjects based on imagination

Subjects Based on First-Hand Experiences

You are an individual. No one else in the world is exactly like you. No one has lived the same life as you. No one has had the same experiences or the same feelings. Your experiences, therefore, are a good source for unique composition subjects. They can also lead to many different types of writing.

Subjects based on things that have happened to you are likely to meet the three guidelines for choosing subjects. They are interesting because they are drawn from your own life. They are familiar because they are part of you. They are valuable because your experiences and feelings help to make you the person you are, and thus may help others understand you better.

The writer of the following composition has drawn from his personal experiences to communicate his thoughts and feelings about his upbringing and its importance to his career as a pilot and astronaut.

Words To Grow on

So far as I can remember, my training to become a command pilot of the space shuttle *Columbia* began when I was an eight-year-old boy writing a letter to my favorite aunt.

After finishing the letter, I showed it to my parents, expecting a pat on the back. To my surprise, they were not enthusiastic. "I see you've misspelled a few words and scratched out some things, Jack," my father said. "Better make a clean copy." My mother nodded in firm assent and told me to *"Do it right or not at all."* That was the first time I'd heard that old cliché, but it sure wasn't the last. Those words were a caution to take the time and care to do a job correctly — and my parents applied them to everything I did.

In March 1982, I had special reason to be grateful that my parents insisted on excellence in performance. After I'd spent six years as an astronaut and 1,000 hours training in a computerized flight simulator, I rocketed into space with my co-pilot, Colonel C. Gordon Fullerton. It was the *Columbia's* third mission, an eight-day marathon of tests and experiments.

But nothing we did in outer space was more crucial than the last moments of the mission: setting the ship safely down on planet Earth. Our instructions were to take over the 110-ton Columbia from the automatic system and land it manually. Our airspeed would be 230 miles an hour. Our target for landing at this blinding speed: a scant three miles of runway. Talk about putting a camel through the eye of a needle!

In a fraction of a minute, all the hours I'd put into doing the job right in the simulator came into play — for real. So, when our wheels kissed the ground and *Columbia* was home, I paused for a moment of thanks. And I thanked my mother and father for setting the standard that helped me react to pressure with confidence.—COLONEL JACK R. LOUSMA

Subjects Based on Imagination

Some of the most interesting subjects are drawn from imagination. These subjects often are developed into narrative compositions. However, they can also be developed into other types of compositions, as illustrated in the following description.

A Fable for Tomorrow

There was once a town in the heart of America where all life seemed to live in harmony with its surroundings. The town lay in the midst of a checkerboard of prosperous farms, with fields of grain and hillsides of orchards where, in spring, white clouds of bloom drifted above the green fields. In autumn, oak and maple and birch set up a blaze of color that flamed and flickered across a backdrop of pines. Foxes barked in the hills and deer silently crossed the fields, half hidden in the mists of the fall mornings.

Then a strange blight crept over the area and everything began to change. Some evil spell had settled on the community: mysterious maladies swept the flocks of chickens; the cattle and sheep sickened and died. Everywhere was a shadow of death. The farmers spoke of much illness among their families. In the town the doctors had become more and more puzzled by new kinds of sickness appearing among their patients. There had been several sudden and unexplained deaths, not only among adults but even among children, who would be stricken suddenly while at play and die within a few hours.

There was a strange stillness. The birds, for example—where had they gone? Many people spoke of them, puzzled and disturbed. The feeding stations in the backyards were deserted. The few birds seen anywhere were moribund. They trembled violently and could not fly. It was a spring without voices. On the mornings that had once throbbed with the dawn chorus of robins, catbirds, doves, jays, wrens, and scores of other bird voices there was now no sound. Only silence lay over the fields and woods and marsh.

On the farms the hens brooded, but no chickens hatched.

The farmers complained that they were unable to raise any pigs—the litters were small and the young survived only a few days. The apple trees were coming into bloom, but no bees droned among the blossoms, so there was no pollination and there would be no fruit. The fields browned and withered as though swept by fire. These, too, were silent, deserted by all living things.

No witchcraft, no enemy action had silenced the rebirth of new life in this stricken world. The people had done it themselves.—RACHEL CARSON

Exercises Pre-Writing: Choosing a Subject

A. The following subjects are meant to stimulate your thinking about possible topics for compositions. Study them. Then, begin to brainstorm. Drawing from your own experiences, knowledge, and imagination, make a list of at least ten subjects. If any of the subjects listed here interest you, add them to your list.

1. I Am Owned by a Cat/Dog
2. Violent Storms
3. Growing Up Bilingual
4. A Strange Noise in the Night
5. Being a Friend
6. Thank Goodness, No Bones Were Broken
7. Getting in Shape for _____
8. I Shouldn't Have Said It
9. The Day I Grew Up
10. Rural Life
11. The Uniqueness of My Parents
12. I Wish I Were _____
13. The Art of Following Directions
14. How I Have Changed in the Past Year
15. Family Rituals

B. Study your list of subjects carefully. Select the one that interests you the most. This will be the first pre-writing step in the Process of Writing.

Part 3 Pre-Writing: Narrowing the Subject

In your study of the paragraph, you learned that an idea must be narrow enough to be developed adequately within the limits of the paragraph. The same holds true for the composition. The topic must be narrow enough to be covered in a few paragraphs.

Sometimes a subject based on first-hand experience does not need to be narrowed if a writer has a specific incident in mind. On the other hand, a subject in which you have a general interest or knowledge may be too broad for a composition. Your hobby may be collecting butterflies, but, unfocused, this subject would be too broad for a short composition. Brainstorming might help you to identify possible composition topics within this subject:

Identifying Butterflies
Capturing and Mounting Butterflies
Catching a Monarch
The Joys of Butterfly Collecting

The subject "Video Games" is also too broad for a composition. Again, the writer must decide on a specific topic. Some possibilities include the time spent on video games, the money spent on video games, the types of video games, or the writer's favorite video game. By choosing one of these specific topics, you could cover the material in a few paragraphs, as did the writer of the following composition.

Too Much Money!

Almost anyone could use an extra $100. This is the amount a person would spend in a year by playing video games at the rate of $2.00 a week. If the player regularly spends more than that amount, as many do, the total can skyrocket. Although many people like the games, some are also worried that they are spending too much money on them. They also wonder *why* they spend so much. Actually, there are several simple reasons why players spend more than they should on video games.

First of all, most players think the games are entertaining and exciting. The games are not only fun, they are also challenging and stimulating to players' imaginations. This sense of excitement can cause problems. Because players are having so much fun, they don't realize how much they're spending.

Second, a single game is fairly inexpensive. Each time a person plays, he or she thinks, "It's only a quarter." Yet all those quarters add up, and it is easy to overspend. If people had to pay for all their games *before* entering a game room, they might think twice about whether an hour in front of some machines is worth the price.

A third reason people spend more than they should is that video games are addictive. Many people have admitted, "Once I start, I can't stop." There is always the challenge of beating your own score, or of reaching the highest score ever achieved on a particular machine. People play over and over and put in dozens of quarters with the hope of achieving that elusive top score. They always think it will be "next time!"

Just imagine a one-hundred-dollar bill disappearing like an enemy spaceship on a video screen. Video games may be exciting, challenging, and inexpensive, but the money certainly does add up!

Notice how thoroughly the writer of this composition was able to develop the main idea after the subject was narrowed. Three reasons for video "addiction" were identified, and each one was solidly supported with different types of details. If, on the other hand, the writer had not narrowed the subject, the composition would have been merely a collection of unsupported and uninteresting generalizations. Careful limitation of the topic, therefore, can make the difference between a strong and a weak composition.

Exercise Pre-Writing: Narrowing the Subject

In your last assignment, you chose a subject for a composition. Think about that subject and decide whether it is narrow enough to be covered in a five-paragraph composition. If it is not, list several specific topics within the general subject and choose one as the topic for your composition.

Part 4 Pre-Writing: Deciding on the Audience and the Purpose

Before you begin to develop a plan for your composition, you must answer two questions.

1. For whom are you writing the composition?
2. What is your purpose for writing?

Your Audience. You should know two things about your readers. First, you should know their approximate age. The need for this information is clear. If, for example, your readers will be very young, you must use simple words, avoid difficult ideas, and explain your ideas very carefully.

Second, you should know the readers' familiarity with your subject. This will influence the amount and difficulty of the information you can include. It will also determine the number and types of explanations and definitions that you must give.

Your Purpose. Before developing a plan for your composition, decide whether you want to tell a story; to describe an object, place, or person; or to explain something. You must decide whether you want your readers to laugh, to cry, or to think seriously about an idea.

A one-sentence **statement of purpose** might help you to clarify your topic and goal. This statement is for your own guidance only. It will not be included in your composition. Here are three examples of such statements:

1. In my composition I will *explain* why it is important to take part in extracurricular activities.
2. In my composition I will *describe* the three most beautiful areas of Yellowstone Park.
3. In my composition I will *tell a story about* a humorous incident that happened on my first day of high school.

Later, when you write the introduction for your composition, you may wish to include a more formal version of this statement. It will then become the **thesis statement** of your composition.

Sample Paragraphs. The two paragraphs that follow are both written on the same general subject, sickness. However, they are written with different audiences and purposes in mind.

1   Finding the cause of a sore throat calls for some detective work. Your doctor will ask you questions, give you an examination, and maybe do some tests. Doctors do this to get clues. The doctor will ask how you feel, how long you have been sick, and if anything else hurts. When you tell the doctor how you feel, you are telling your symptoms. The doctor will examine you to look for other clues, called signs. Some signs that doctors look for are fever, rash, swollen tonsils, and swollen lymph nodes, small lumps under the skin on the sides of the neck.

—DONAHUE AND CAPELLARO

2   Snooks, under a pile of faded quilts, made a small, gravelike mound in the bed. His head was like a ball of black putty wedged between the thin covers and the dingy yellow pillow. His little eyes were partly open, as if he were peeping out of his hard, wasted skull at the chilly room. The forceful pulse of his breathing caused a faint rustling in the sheets near his mouth, like the wind pushing damp papers in a shallow ditch.

—ALICE WALKER

Paragraph 1 is explanatory. It explains the detective work needed to find the cause of a sore throat. Most of the words are simple; two of the harder words, *symptoms* and *lymph nodes*, are defined within the paragraph. The writer presents simple information, easily understood by most young readers.

Paragraph 2 is a narrative paragraph. It paints a grim picture of a very sick child. In contrast to Paragraph 1, it contains difficult words; longer, more complicated sentences; and complex language. The writer of this paragraph had a much older, more experienced audience in mind than the writer of Paragraph 1.

Exercise Pre-Writing: Deciding on the Audience and the Purpose

Decide on the audience for your composition. Then write a one-sentence statement of purpose.

Part 5 Pre-Writing:
Planning the Composition

Before you begin writing, you will need to develop a writing plan. This will allow you to work with your ideas before you write your first draft. A writing plan has two main steps:

1. Putting down ideas
2. Organizing the ideas.

Putting Down Ideas

As you begin to plan your composition, you probably have ideas about what you want to include. Write these ideas on a sheet of paper or on 3″ x 5″ cards, keeping in mind your audience and your purpose for writing. As you think more about your topic, additional ideas will come to you. Jot them down also. Make no attempt at this time to write the ideas in any particular order.

One writer chose the universal appeal of music as her topic. Her purpose was to give several reasons why everyone seems to enjoy music. She made the following list of ideas.

Music: The Universal Language

everyone involved —⟨ touches our feelings
different age groups respond to
everyone can create

cultural exchanges	blues
Mendelssohn	popular artists
Bach	Latin music
Handel	elation of boogie
high school choirs, bands	jam sessions
festivals	rhythm bands
ethnic music	campfire sing-alongs
concerts	toddlers dancing, responding
jazz	everyone has contributed

The purpose of this first step is to get down as many ideas as possible. Many of these will become details in the writer's composition, but the list is not final. As the writer works through the writing process, she will continue to delete unrelated ideas and to add better ones. Note that the list has no real organization. The sorting and organizing take place in the next step.

Exercise Pre-Writing: Writing Down Ideas

Make a list of ideas related to your composition topic. Keep in mind your audience and your purpose for writing.

Organizing the Ideas

Your next step in planning is to organize your ideas in relation to each other; that is, to group similar ideas together.

The writer of "Music: The Universal Language" studied her list of ideas. She decided that they fell into three groups. She then listed the related ideas under each heading.

1. People of many times and cultures have contributed to music.
    –Bach
    –Handel } old masters
    –jazz
    –blues } Black America
    –Latin music
    –folk tunes

2. All ages respond to music.
    –rhythm bands
    –triggers memories in older people
    –toddlers
    –work companion
    –campfire sing-alongs
    –jam sessions

3. People respond emotionally to music.
    –Mendelssohn—sadness
    –Jump Shout Boogie—elation
    –popular artists—love

After grouping your ideas, you may have a few "extra" ideas that do not seem to fit under any of your headings. The writer of the sample composition had several such ideas. These were deleted so that they would not disturb the unity of the individual paragraphs. On the other hand, the writer added other details so that the three general groups became more focused. For instance, under the group, "All ages respond to music," the writer decided that all age groups should be mentioned. Many of her original ideas related only to teenagers. She deleted some of those so she could include details pertaining to other age groups, too. Can you find additional details that were added?

Exercises Pre-Writing: Grouping Ideas

A. Following is a list of ideas related to the topic "Camping in a Cabin." They can be grouped under two general headings.

   I. Six A.M.
  II. Midnight

Write each idea under the appropriate heading.

1. Sounds: a scratching, a rustling, then silence
2. Sights: sunlight in the cabin
3. Sights: stars, blackness
4. Sights: moonlight through the window
5. Smells: coffee, bacon
6. Sounds: friends laughing and talking
7. Sounds: fire crackling, bacon sizzling
8. Smells: lingering trace of smoke

B. Two of the following ideas can be used as general headings. Find them. Then group the remaining ideas under the appropriate headings.

1. provide adequate street lighting
2. pedestrians injure themselves
3. they cross streets diagonally
4. they cross streets in the middle of the block
5. they walk with their backs to traffic on the highway

6. pedestrian lives can be saved
7. they step into traffic from parked cars
8. provide traffic lights for pedestrians
9. they step from behind parked cars
10. give traffic tickets to pedestrians
11. they cross against lights
12. they don't watch for traffic

C. Study the ideas for your own composition. Decide on three general headings that seem to cover most of them. Then list each idea under the appropriate heading.

Completing Your Writing Plan

After gathering and grouping your ideas, you are ready to organize them into a final writing plan. This involves two steps:

1. Arranging groups of related ideas into logical order
2. Organizing the ideas within each group.

Logical Order. Logical order is an order that is appropriate to the content of the composition and is, therefore, easy for a reader to follow. Just as paragraphs use different orders, so do compositions. As a writer, you must find the order that best suits the ideas you want to express.

Some compositions are organized in **chronological order**; that is, in the order of time. Most narratives and some explanatory compositions are developed in this way.

Some compositions are organized in **order of importance**; that is, from the least important to the most important, according to the writer's way of thinking. When order of importance cannot be established, a writer might arrange groups of ideas in **order of familiarity**, from the most familiar to the least familiar.

A fourth way to organize compositions is in **spatial order**; that is, in the order in which a writer wishes the reader to picture a place, object, or person. For example, a writer might decide to describe a room from near to far. The group of details that describes the nearest part of the room would be first. The group of details that describes the farthest part of the room would be last.

Comparison and contrast organization is a useful method of organization when the writer is explaining the similarities or differences between two or more things. In this type of organization, the writer first discusses a characteristic of one subject. He or she then presents the corresponding detail of the other subject, pointing out how the two are alike or different. Another way of handling this type of organization is to discuss all the characteristics of one subject before going on to the characteristics of the other.

Look at the following writing plan for the composition on music. Notice the order in which the writer has organized both the main ideas of the composition and the details that support those main ideas.

Music: The Universal Language

1. All ages respond to music.
   –toddlers dancing
   –rhythm bands in elementary school
   –campfire sing-alongs
   –jam sessions (teenagers)
   –companion for work (teenagers/adults)
   –triggers memories in older people

2. People respond emotionally to music.
   –Mendelssohn causes sorrow.
   –Jump Shout Boogie causes a feeling of elation.
   –Other music strengthens feelings of love.

3. People of many times and cultures have contributed to
       music.
   –folk music
   –old masters like Bach and Handel
   –Latin music
   –jazz and blues of Black America

The writer rearranged not only her groups of ideas, but also the ideas within each group. The main groups of ideas were organized in order of familiarity. Within paragraphs, other methods of organization were used. Can you identify the order for each paragraph?

Pre-Writing: Making a Writing Plan

Make a writing plan by organizing the three groups of ideas for your own composition in a logical order. If necessary, rearrange the ideas within each group so that they are presented more effectively.

Part 6 First Draft: Writing the Composition

Your pre-writing stage is now finished. Your topic has been selected, your audience and purpose identified, and your ideas organized into an outline. You are now ready to write the first draft of your composition.

The Introductory Paragraph

The introductory paragraph of a composition serves two important functions.

1. It gives the main idea of the composition.
2. It catches the reader's attention.

The opening sentence of an introductory paragraph sets the tone for the entire paragraph. A good writer, therefore, avoids dull and uninteresting opening sentences such as these.

1. In this paper, I am going to describe someone who died.
2. Families can be fun.
3. I am going to explain something about being an American.
4. Music is enjoyed by everyone.

Each of these sentences indicates, in a general way, the main idea of the composition. However, the sentences lack the specific details that would catch the interest of a reader.

The four introductory paragraphs on the next page begin with good opening sentences. The paragraphs are based on the same subjects as the poor topic sentences above. Notice how each paragraph now gives the main idea of a composition in a way that makes you want to read further.

1   Charley Lockjaw died last summer on the reservation. He was very old — a hundred years, he had claimed. He still wore his hair in braids, as only the older men do in his tribe, and the braids were thin and white. His fierce old face was like a withered apple. He was bent and frail and trembling, and his voice was like a wailing of the wind across the prairie grass.

                                                                     —DOROTHY JOHNSON

2   There were seldom fewer than fifteen men, women, and children at our Sunday get-together. On the Sundays when it rained, there would be as many as thirty. It was obvious that no one else in Mount Allegro had as many relatives as I did. It was also true that no one else's relatives seemed to seek one another's company as much as mine did. Sundays or weekdays, they were as gregarious as ants but had a far more pleasant time. There were always relatives and friends present or about to arrive. When they finally left for the night, they occasionally came back for a surprise visit which they called a *sirinata*. —JERRE MANGIONE

3   "We, the people" is an eloquent beginning. However, when the Constitution of the United States was completed on the seventeenth of September in 1787, I was not included in that "We, the people." I felt for many years that somehow George Washington and Alexander Hamilton just left me out by mistake. Through the process of amendment, interpretation, and court decisions I have finally been included in "We, the people." —BARBARA JORDAN

4   Every person is a unique collection of opinions, tastes, ideas, and beliefs. No two people like exactly the same things or feel precisely the same way about an issue. Yet there is one thing that all people enjoy, and which is an important part of almost everyone's life — music. Music is a universal art that ignores boundaries of age, culture, and time.

    The last paragraph is the final version of the introduction for "Music: The Universal Language." Read it again and decide whether it has the requirements necessary for a good opening paragraph.

Exercises Writing the Introductory Paragraph

A. Read the following opening sentences for introductory paragraphs. Decide which ones have definite reader appeal. Be ready to explain why the others do not catch your attention.

1. By the time the saber-toothed tiger had slunk into oblivion, and the mastodon was only a memory, the human being had developed two brains.
2. In skiing and skating and riding a bicycle, the beginner is faced with one overwhelming problem.
3. This composition is about learning to meditate.
4. My horse is a good animal.
5. As I rounded the curve of the mountain, I saw the tiny village far below me.
6. I spent a nice week at the Mardi Gras in New Orleans.
7. First of all, I want to introduce myself.
8. I'm glad I'm a woman!
9. I'm glad I'm a man!
10. Once we lived in my grandfather's house.
11. Well, this young girl I'm going to tell you about was named Angela.
12. The strange young boy had the type of otherwordly appearance that made you notice him immediately.
13. My mother had a happy childhood.
14. Most zoos are old.
15. My teacher has asked me to write a paper about mythology.
16. I was prepared to dislike Max even before I knew him.
17. Imagine, if you can, a small room, hexagonal in shape, like the cell of a bee.
18. The little fellow was lying on the bare hospital cot, arms rigidly straight and teeth clenched tightly together.
19. I remember my first pet.
20. His name was Frank X. Farrell and I guess the X stood for "Excuse me."

B. Write the introductory paragraph for your composition. Be sure that it gives the main idea of your composition and that it will catch your readers' attention.

The Body

The body is the second major part of a composition. In the body paragraphs, the main idea of the composition, which was presented in the introductory paragraph, is supported or explained.

The writer of "Music: The Universal Language" used her writing plan to get her ideas down in a first draft of her body paragraph. In doing so, she not only recorded the details she had already thought of, but she also discovered some new ideas. These were included where they were appropriate and where they did not upset the unity of a paragraph.

Even if you're not a famous composer, and even if you don't like orchestra concerts, music is still a part of you. Almost as soon as they are steady on their feet, toddlers begin "dancing" by moving in time to the rhythm of music. As these babys get older, there will be rhythm bands in school campfire sing-alongs or jam sessions with friends. Music on the radio or stereo will become a companion for work around the house or for travel. Finally, for old folks, the strains of certain tunes will recall memories of times gone by.

Music touches us all because it evokes a lot of feeling. One person may be touched by a sorrowful selection of mendelssohn. Another person may get the same feeling when Barry Manilow sings This Song's for you. Music can also bring joy. Who can resist feeling good when a rythmic tune like Jump Shout Boogie bounces across the air waves? And of course, music can affect love. Music edifies the soul!

Not only do we all like music, we all take part in it's creation. Some of us can do no more than hum off key, but we have still made a contribution. So have other poeple. Folk melodies remain with us from a long time ago. Back and Handel sent us music from Europe. South Americans gave us the tango and rhumba. Black Americans gave us jazz and the blues.

The writer has already made some changes and additions from her writing plan to her rough draft. Remember that changes at this stage are still likely, and usually desirable. You need only keep your audience, purpose, and main idea in mind as you work.

Achieving Unity and Coherence

Unity. When writing a first draft, a good writer tries to keep the ideas unified. As you write, check to see that each body paragraph directly relates to the introductory paragraph. Then make sure that the supporting details in each paragraph relate directly to the topic sentence. If you keep these things in mind, your composition will be unified by the main idea that is presented in the opening paragraph.

Coherence. To reinforce the unity of idea, a writer may repeat key words and phrases throughout a composition. For example, the writer of the sample composition repeated the word *music* in the introductory paragraph and in each body paragraph.

A writer may also make use of transitional devices. These words and phrases tie the paragraphs of a composition together by referring both to the idea that precedes and the idea that follows.

There are six basic transitional devices.

1. **Using a Word That Indicates Time.** These words include:

first	before	meanwhile
next	after	until
then	afterwards	later
finally	today	hundreds of years ago

EXAMPLE

A special type of Japanese wrestling is called *sumo.* Sumo is probably Japan's oldest sport. It began hundreds of years ago as part of a Shinto religious ceremony. Some Shinto shrines had special buildings built for sumo matches, held to honor the gods. In the year 858, it is said, the two sons of the emperor wrestled to see who would succeed to the throne.

Today sumo is so popular that tournaments are held every year in the large cities. Thousands go to the huge stadiums to watch the matches. Others view them on television. The sumo wrestlers are tall and heavy, sometimes weighing 300 pounds. Each wrestler wears only a ring about his waist and a loincloth. The place where they perform is a circle that measures fifteen feet across. —LEE W. FARNSWORTH

2. Using a Word That Shows the Relationship Between Ideas. Such words include the following:

and	because	therefore	moreover	unless
also	since	besides	similarly	

EXAMPLE

For the individual American, the main advantage of the metric system is its simplicity. Instead of the fifty-five measurement units of the English system, the metric system has only three: meters, grams, and liters. They all are made up of units of ten.

Because all multiples are powers of ten, calculations are simpler. To multiply, you simply move the decimal point.

3. Using a Word That Shows an Opposite Point of View. Such words include the following:

but	while	on the other hand
however	although	in contrast

EXAMPLE

Over the years, oil and natural gas gradually replaced coal as the major fuels for homes and industry. Gas and oil were cheaper. They were also more convenient.

Today, however, America is faced with an energy dilemma. The demand for gas and oil has outstripped domestic supplies. Now, America must rely heavily on foreign imports. Gas and oil are no longer cheap or convenient.

4. Using a Word That Repeats a Word Used Earlier.

EXAMPLE

Almost everybody daydreams. What do such dreams indicate about a person? How do one person's dreams differ from another person's?

Science is just beginning to probe the deeper meanings of daydreams, yet it has come up with some startling preliminary findings. —DOROTHY BRANT WARWICK

5. Using a Synonym for a Word Used Earlier.

A tornado blew through Arcadia, Nebraska, last week, and the next day in a town seventy-five miles east, somebody picked up a canceled check that had been in an Arcadia businessman's desk drawer. Impressed by this news, I turned to Roger Welsch, who teaches folklore at the university and keeps up with which way the Nebraska wind blows, to ask him if storms like that are common here.

Roger said that after one of these Nebraska cyclones, a sleeping man found himself still in bed, but the bed was in the kitchen. The only damage done was that his underclothes were on upside down and buttoned in the back. —CHARLES KURALT

6. Using a Pronoun That Refers to a Word Used Earlier.

Along the cool morning dew, along the cool forest floor crept a spider, a shabby little thing of a spider, looking for a place to spin a silken line or two.

Over speckled fishlike skins of leaves he crept, over earth-soft mossy pads, over turtle still adream, earth-anchored in its shell, over bogs of stones and crackling twigs he crept, crept on and on, seeking a place to spin a silken line or two.

—GEORGE MENDOZA

Exercises Studying and Writing Body Paragraphs

A. Study the following pairs of paragraphs carefully. Identify the transitional device, or devices, that each writer has used to tie the paragraphs together.

1   The coach, noting Sarah's unusual stamina and fluid motion, had convinced her that long-distance events were her best, and Sarah had trained long and hard for them.

Henry's coach on the other hand, had permitted Henry to play basketball even though he knew that he lacked peripheral vision. —*Woman's Day*

2 I was standing in the driveway, alone, stock still, but shivering. Someone had given the polyphemus moth his freedom, and he was walking away.

He heaved himself down the asphalt driveway by infinite degrees, unwavering. His hideous, crumpled wings lay glued and rucked on his back, perfectly still now, like a collapsed tent.

—ANNIE DILLARD

3 They came, silently, dark-bellied clouds drifting up from the south, and the wind, increasing, swept in the heavy scent of the approaching storm. Lightning flashed over the low, distant hills, and the clouds closed quietly around the moon. The thunder rumbled and the heavy drops began to fall, slowly at first, then irregularly, then increasing to a rhythmic rush of noise as the gusts of wind forced the rain in vertical waves across the shingled roof.

Much later, when the rain had moved ahead and the water began to drip from the roof and the countless leaves, the boy slipped out of his worn denim pants and took off his shirt and lay down. —DURANGO MENDOZA

4 Paul loved his father "like no one in all the world," although as a young man he would later regret that his childhood was so programmed. "If I had had time … that wasn't blocked out and filled in for me, I think my imagination would have been more developed. As it is, I've almost none. All my time was crowded with lessons to learn, games to play, books to read, chores to do. I never can remember having had hours in which I had nothing to do, and had actually to entertain myself out of my own mind."

Nevertheless, he always looked forward to the summer, when his sister and brothers would come home on vacations. He would play football with Ben, who would show him how to throw a pass, how to block and tackle. Bill, the brain of the family, taught him how to question what he read, how to draw his own conclusions, and how to defend them. Then there was Marion, who intended to become a teacher like her mother. Strong-willed but cheerful, she always brought laughter to the household.

—DOROTHY BUTLER GILLIAM

5   We were in the marsh now, moving, on our way to say good-bye to Bald Head Island.

Bald Head sits at the southeastern tip of North Carolina, where the Cape Fear River flows into the Atlantic Ocean, and the best access is by boat, across four miles of relatively tranquil water from the shrimp and fishing village of Southport.

—WILLIAM McILWAIN

6   They circled a square and slipped into a quiet, narrow street overlooking a park, stopping before the tallest of the apartment houses in the single commanding row.

Alighting, Miss Cynthie gave this imposing structure one sidewise, upward glance, and said, "You live like bees in a hive, don't you?" —RUDOLPH FISHER

7   I walk on past brown unpainted houses, chipped sidewalks. Home is near and I want to get there and feed my hungry stomach. I see a plain brick house and run towards its broken wooden gate. I smile at the smell of stewing beans. I enter and sit at a table made of Hunt's tomato boxes. My mother silently brings me a plate of cooked beans with sliced onions and chile and a half-dozen tortillas.

She sits next to me and watches me eat. I dip a large spoon into the beans, bring it up to my mouth and, slurping, swallow the stuff on it. A rolled tortilla follows, and munching sounds come from me. —RUDY GALLARDO

B. Write a draft for the body of your composition. Use your writing plan as a guide. Add new ideas that occur to you as you write. If necessary, change your organization as your ideas develop.

The Conclusion

After you have finished writing the body of your composition, your final step is to write the conclusion. The concluding paragraph indicates to the reader that the composition is finished. It can restate the main idea of the composition, summarize the ideas that have been presented in the body paragraphs, or make a comment about the information that has been given. The conclusion is the final idea that your readers will take from your work. Therefore, it should be as interesting as the introduction.

The writer of the following conclusion summarizes his feelings toward his subject, mountain rivers.

> By such a river it is impossible to believe that one will ever be tired or old. Every sense applauds it. Taste it, feel its chill on the teeth: it is purity absolute. Watch its racing current, its steady renewal of force. It is transient and eternal. Listen again to its symphony of sounds hiss and splash and gurgle, the small talk of side channels, the whisper of blown and scattered spray gathering itself and beginning to flow again, secret and irresistible, among the wet rocks. —WALLACE STEGNER

The following writer ends his composition with a moving statement on the death of his dog.

> That afternoon I drove Shamrock's body back to the gorge in the hills and buried him there. The bear cubs will tell the others that the little white lion has come home at last. When winter comes, the deer will step high in the snowdrifts in that green glade, over the place where lies my little friend, the one I can never forget. —FREDERICK A. BIRMINGHAM

The writer of "Music: The Universal Language" wrote this conclusion. Does it meet the requirements of a good conclusion?

> Music is a universal language. It springs from every country and affects each individual. It will exist as long as there are people to listen.

The first sentence in this conclusion restates the main idea of the composition. The conclusion also ties in to the title.

Exercises Finishing the Composition

A. Write the concluding paragraph of your composition. Be sure that it ties in well with the rest of your paper.

B. Write the title for your composition. You can take the title from your writing plan, or you can write a new one.

Part 7 Revising the Composition

This is the stage of the writing process where you are concerned with getting everything just right! At this point, you want to select the most vivid word or phrase, strengthen your organization, and check the unity and coherence.

To keep your concentration focused during this stage, you may find that the best solution is a many-part revision process. Since you will want to check and revise your ideas, word choice, unity, coherence, and level of language, try looking over your draft several times. Correct problems in just one or two areas at a time.

Chapter 7, "The Process of Writing" and the Guidelines for Writing and Revising Compositions on page 212 will help you focus your revisions and do a thorough job.

The writer of "Music: The Universal Language" made many revisions in her rough draft, as shown on the next page.

Analysis of the Revision

The changes that the writer made in her revised draft improved her composition in many ways.

1. Vivid, specific words have been added or have replaced weaker language. For instance, the writer has added "distinctive wails" to modify jazz and "torchy strains" to modify blues.

2. More formal language has replaced informal language. For instance, the writer deleted all uses of "you" in her paper. She also deleted the term "old folks" in paragraph two.

3. Unity has been strengthened. For instance, the word "universal" now appears in the title, the introduction, and the conclusion. The addition of "reflecting all time periods and cultures," to the topic sentence in the third body paragraph ties it more closely to the introduction, too.

4. Coherence is strengthened by adding transitional words and phrases such as "still later in life" in the first body paragraph.

5. Many errors in grammar and mechanics were spotted. For instance, the writer corrected the misspelling of "babies." She also inserted commas where they were needed in a series.

Music: The Universal Language

is a unique collection of

Every person has special opinions, tastes, ideas, and beliefs.
exactly ^ *precisely* *about an issue*
No two people like the same things or feel the same way. Yet

there is one thing that all people enjoy — music. Music is an
universal *boundaries of* *(and which is an*
art that ignores age, culture, and time. *important part of*
everyone is, *almost everyone's life)*

Even if you're not a famous composer, and even if you don't
or an *buff, yet* *important to each one of us, no*
like orchestra concerts, music is still a part of you. Almost as *matter*
what
soon as they are steady on their feet, toddlers begin "dancing" *our age*

ie
by moving in time to the rhythm of music. As these babys get
they take part in
older, there will be rhythm bands in school, campfire sing-
Still later in life,
alongs or jam sessions with friends. Music on the radio or ste-
It provides entertainment at parties and background for dancing.
reo will become a companion for work around the house or
as more time passes
for travel. Finally, for old folks, the strains of certain tunes

will recall memories of times gone by.
multitude *s*
Music touches us all because it evokes a lot of feeling. One
deeply affected
person may be touched by a sorrowful selection of mendels-

sohn. Another person may get that same feeling when Barry
dolefully
Manilow sings This Song's for you. Music can also bring joy.
Few people *elated* *h* *, spirited*
Who can resist feeling good when a rythmic tune like Jump

Shout Boogie bounces across the air waves? And of course,
enhance *How many times has a special song made one*
music can affect love. Music edifies the soul! *person long for another.*
can *enjoy* *but* *can also* *e*
Not only do we all like music, we all take part in it's creation.
little
Some of us can do no more than hum off key, but we have still
of all time periods and cultures
made a contribution. So have other poeple. Folk melodies re-
centuries *h The* *of simple people*
main with us from a long time ago. Back and Handel sent us
the graceful, complex *Composers such as*
music from Europe. South Americans gave us the tango and
of *contributed* *added* *enticing rhythms*
rhumba. Black Americans gave us jazz and the blues. *of the*
the distinctive wails of *torchy strains of the*

209

Proofreading

Many errors in grammar, capitalization, punctuation, and spelling will be corrected during revision. However, you must still proofread your revised draft specifically for these types of errors. Use the proofreading symbols on page 124 as the writer of the sample composition did. The following paragraph shows some of the errors the writer found during this final check.

Music touches us all because it evokes a ~~lot~~ multitude of feeling. One person may be ~~touched~~ deeply affected by a sorrowful selection of mendels-sohn. Another person may get that same feeling when Barry Manilow sings dolefully "This Song's for you." Music can also bring joy. ~~Who~~ Few people can resist feeling ~~good~~ elated when a rythmic, spirited tune like "Jump Shout Boogie" bounces across the air waves? And of course, music can ~~affect~~ enhance love. ~~Music edifies the soul.~~ How many times has a special song made one person long for another.

When you are satisfied with your composition, make a final, neat copy. Use whatever heading your teacher directs. Below is the final version of the composition on music.

Music: The Universal Language

Every person is a unique collection of opinions, tastes, ideas, and beliefs. No two people like exactly the same things or feel precisely the same way about an issue. Yet there is one thing that all people enjoy, and which is an important part of almost everyone's life—music. Music is a universal art that ignores boundaries of age, culture, and time.

Not everyone is a famous composer or an orchestra concert buff, yet music is still important to each one of us, no matter what our age. Almost as soon as they are steady on their feet, toddlers begin "dancing" by moving in time to the rhythm of the music. As these babies get older, they take part in bands in school, campfire sing-alongs, or jam sessions with friends. Still later in life, music on the radio and stereo becomes a companion for work around the house or for travel. It provides entertainment at parties and background for dancing. Finally, as more time passes, the strains of certain tunes recall memories of days gone by.

Music touches us all because it evokes a multitude of feelings, no matter what one's taste in music is. One person may be deeply affected by a sorrowful selection of Mendelssohn. Another person may get that same feeling when Barry Manilow dolefully sings "This One's For You." Music can also bring joy. Few can resist feeling elated when a spirited, rhythmic tune like "Jump Shout Boogie" bounces across the air waves. Of course, music can also enhance love. How many times has a special song made one person long for another?

Not only can we all enjoy music, but we can also take part in its creation. Some of us can do little more than hum off key, but we have still made our contribution. So have people of all time periods and cultures. The folk melodies of simple people remain with us from centuries ago. Composers such as Bach and Handel sent us the graceful, complex music of Europe. South Americans added the enticing rhythms of the tango and rhumba. Black Americans contributed the distinctive wails of jazz and the torchy strains of the blues.

Music is a universal language. It springs from every country and affects each individual. It will exist as long as there are people to listen.

Exercise Completing the Composition

Revise and proofread the rough draft of your composition. When you have completed your revision, make a neat, final copy.

Guidelines for Writing and Revising Compositions

As you write a composition, follow the steps in Guidelines for the Process of Writing on page 122. Use the following Guidelines as you revise your first draft.

1. Has the subject been narrowed to a topic that can be covered in a few paragraphs?

2. Does the composition deal with a single topic or idea?

3. Does it have an introduction, a body, and a conclusion?

4. Does the introduction present the main idea? Does it catch the reader's interest?

5. Does the body explain or support the main idea?

6. Does the conclusion restate the main idea, summarize the information, or comment upon it?

7. Do the paragraphs work together to develop a single topic or idea that is the subject of the composition?

8. Is the composition appropriate for the audience for which it is intended? Is the purpose clear?

9. Are the ideas presented in a clear, logical order?

10. Does the composition have unity? Are the supporting ideas in each paragraph related to the topic sentence? Is each paragraph directly related to the main idea in the introductory paragraph?

11. Does the composition have coherence? Are there transitional devices that tie the paragraphs together?

12. Is the title meaningful and interesting?

Additional Guidelines

If it is a narrative composition, are the events told in the order in which they happen?

If it is a descriptive composition, does it use specific sensory details to paint a word-picture? Are the sight details presented in spatial order?

If it is an explanatory composition, does it explain how something is done or why something is believed to be so? If the composition gives instructions, are the steps organized in time sequence? In a composition that supports an idea with reasons, are the reasons organized logically? Are the reasons convincing?

1. Compositions are groups of paragraphs that develop a single idea.

2. The introductory paragraph of a composition tells what the composition will be about. The body paragraphs develop this idea. The final paragraph, or conclusion, summarizes the information and says "the end" to the reader.

3. Narrow the subject of the composition to an idea that can be covered within the specified limits of the paper.

4. Organize information for a composition by taking notes, identifying main ideas, grouping details under these main ideas, and putting the material in logical order.

5. As you write rough drafts, remember that change and new ideas are expected, even desirable, at this point.

6. Revise for content, unity, and coherence. Proofread your material when the content changes are complete.

7. Follow these steps when you write compositions for all subjects and purposes.

Applications in Other Subject Areas

Literature/All Subjects. In an essay, a writer explains or analyzes something in a personal way. An essay may be humorous or serious. In your school library, find a book of essays. These may be from any subject area. Read two or three essays. Attempt to identify the purpose, audience, and main idea of each one.

All Subjects. Pretend that you are working on a student-written handbook for next year's freshman class. Write a brief composition entitled "How To Succeed in (name of a subject)." Follow the guidelines given in this chapter.

Chapter 11

Types of Compositions

Skim the pages of a magazine or newspaper. Look at the different kinds of articles you find. Each type has its own particular purpose and special characteristics. Some articles are written to inform, some to entertain, some to explain, and some to persuade. Each writer has carefully matched what he or she wanted to say and accomplish with a particular type of writing.

As you write your own compositions, you must go through a similar process. You must match your topic and purpose to the type of composition that will most effectively communicate those ideas. In this chapter you will learn how to apply the process of writing to different types of compositions.

Part 1   The Narrative Composition

Pre-Writing: Planning the Narrative

The narrative paragraph describes an event or tells a story. The narrative composition has the same purpose. In the longer narrative composition, however, elements such as character, setting, point of view, and conflict are more thoroughly developed. During the pre-writing stage of the composition, each area must be explored.

Character refers to the people (or animals) in the narrative. Each character should have a distinct personality. This personality may be described directly or revealed through the action or speech of the characters. In thinking about the characters in a narrative composition, ask these questions:Who are the characters? What are they like? What do they do? What do they want? How do they feel about themselves and their situation?

Setting refers to the time and place of the story. It tells where the action develops. To develop your setting, you might ask these questions: Where is the action taking place? What does the area look like? Does it have any effect on the characters?

Point of view refers to the "angle" from which the narrative is told. It helps determine the kind of information that the narrative includes.

Sometimes the narrator, or person telling the story, takes part in the action. Then the narrative is written from the **first-person point of view.** Stories written from the first-person point of view use pronouns such as "I" or "we." You are limited in this type of narrative to what you (or the imaginary character who is telling the story) personally know, see, observe, think, or feel.

At other times, the narrator is outside the action of the story. The narrative itself tells about what happened to others. This type of composition is written from the **third-person point of view.** Personal pronouns such as "he," "she," and "they" are used. Using the third-person point of view, the writer has two choices. He or she may present a strictly factual account, or enter the minds of various characters and tell what they think, feel, see, or hear.

Conflict refers to the struggle or problem in which the characters become involved. Conflict usually arises because of something the character wants. There are four types of conflict.

Types of Conflict

THE INDIVIDUAL AGAINST SOCIETY: the struggle against such problems as injustice, prejudice, and loss of individual freedom. This also includes the struggle of one person against another.

THE INDIVIDUAL AGAINST SELF: the struggle within the mind of an individual as he or she tries to make a personal decision.

THE INDIVIDUAL AGAINST A SUPERNATURAL FORCE: the struggle against God, or the gods (as in the ancient myths and legends). Also, the struggle against the devil or evil forces.

THE INDIVIDUAL AGAINST NATURE: the struggle to survive natural catastrophes, such as floods, earthquakes, and hurricanes. This would also include the struggle against animals, and, in some cases, against plants.

Following is an example of a narrative composition. As you read it, keep in mind the definitions of character, setting, point of view, and conflict.

Rascal

All raccoons are attracted by shining objects, and Rascal was no exception. He was fascinated by brass doorknobs, glass marbles, my broken watch, and small coins. I gave him three bright, new pennies which he hoarded with the happiness of a little miser. He felt them carefully, smelled them, tasted them, and then hid them in a dark corner with some of his other treasures.

One day Rascal decided to carry one of his pennies to the

back porch. Poe-the-Crow was perched on the porch rail teasing the cats, but keeping just beyond their reach. This raucous old bird, who cawed and cussed in crow language, was arching his wings and strutting like a poolroom bully as Rascal pushed open the screen and trundled into the sunlight, his penny shining like newly minted gold.

Poe and Rascal had taken an instant dislike to each other when first they met. Crows, like most other birds, know that raccoons steal birds' eggs and sometimes eat fledglings. In addition Poe was jealous. He had seen me petting and pampering my small raccoon. However, Rascal was large enough now to pull a few tail feathers from the big, black bird during their noisy squabbles. And Poe, who was no fool, was taking few chances.

The penny, however, was so tempting that the crow threw caution to the winds and made a dive for the bright object (for crows are as insatiably attracted by glittering trinkets as are raccoons and in addition are inveterate thieves). Rascal was carrying the penny in his mouth, and when Poe swooped to conquer, his beak closed not only on the penny but upon half a dozen of Rascal's coarse, strong whiskers. When the black thief tried to make his fast getaway he found himself attached to the raccoon, who with a high scream of fury began fighting for his property and his life. Such a tangle of shining, black feathers and furious fur you have seldom seen as Rascal and Poe wrestled and struggled. I arrived to untangle them, and both were angry with me. Rascal nipped me slightly for the first time, and Poe made several ungracious comments.

The penny, meanwhile, had rolled from the porch into the grass below, where the crow promptly spotted it, seized it once again, and took wing. I gave the incident no more thought, pacified Rascal with another penny, and resumed work on my canoe in the living room.—STERLING NORTH

There are three *characters* in this narrative. The major characters are Rascal, a pet raccoon, and Poe-the-Crow, an ill-tempered old bird. The minor character is the narrator. The *setting* is the back porch of the narrator's house. It is on the porch that the *conflict* between Rascal and Poe-the-Crow takes place, a struggle between two individuals over possession of a bright penny. In describing this struggle, the author uses the *first-person point of view*.

Unity, Coherence, and Emphasis

Like any good piece of writing, a narrative composition must show unity and coherence.

Unity is achieved when every sentence in the composition relates to one main idea. The writer of the narrative about Rascal achieves unity by developing the idea presented in the introductory paragraph: he explains what happens because of Rascal's attraction to shining objects. He makes use of two other unifying techniques as well. He uses colorful, interesting details throughout the narrative, and he ties together ideas with these transitional devices:

1. Repeating the names *Rascal* and *Poe*
2. Repeating the words *crow, raccoon,* and *penny*
3. Using synonyms for the word *shining*
4. Using the word *however* to show opposite points of view
5. Using the words *and* and *in addition* to show the relationships between ideas
6. Using *one day, now, when,* and *meanwhile* to indicate time.

Coherence is the logical arrangement of ideas. The writer achieves coherence in this narrative by organizing the ideas into chronological order. With the exception of one flashback in which he recalls the dislike between Rascal and Poe, the writer describes the incident as it happened.

Emphasis is achieved (1) by selecting a central idea, then grouping details around that idea; and (2) by stressing those details that are important in relation to the central idea. The writer of "Rascal" achieves emphasis by focusing on one central idea in the narrative—the fight between Rascal and Poe-the-Crow over the penny. All the details relate to that central idea. These details include those that he gives about Rascal's attraction to shining objects, about Poe's character, and about the animals' dislike for each other.

Writing a Narrative Composition

Check your writing journal for possible subjects for a narrative composition. They can be based on events in which you participated or on events that were observed by you. They can even be based on events that were described to you by someone else. They can be based on fact, on imagination, or on a combination of both.

List some possible subjects. Then complete the following steps:

Pre-Writing: Select and narrow your topic. Who are the characters? What is the setting? What is the conflict? Choose details to develop each of these elements. Then concentrate on some finer points. What point of view will you use? What order will be the most effective for your material?

First Draft: Use your pre-writing notes to get your ideas down on paper. Give some thought to unity and coherence. Add new details as they occur to you.

Revision: Go over your rough draft several times. Are your characters well developed? Is the conflict clear? Is the same point of view used throughout? Do you need to include other details? Refer to the Guidelines for Writing and Revising Compositions on page 212. Also review the two sets of guidelines at the end of Chapter 7.

Part 2   The Descriptive Composition

Description is seldom the basis for an entire composition. Instead, it is usually used along with other types of writing. However, there may be times when you are particularly moved by a place, a scene, or a person and want to express your feelings in writing. The descriptive composition is one way of doing so.

Before you begin a descriptive composition, you need to understand unity, coherence, and emphasis as they apply to this type of writing. You also need a better understanding of point of view, which affects the other three characteristics.

Point of View

Physical Point of View. In your study of the descriptive paragraph, you learned to put details into a logical order. You learned to describe things from side to side, from top to bottom (or the reverse), and from near to far (or the reverse). You also learned to use other methods of organization, along with key words that show a change in direction.

What you learned about organizing paragraphs also applies to compositions. You can arrange the details in a descriptive composition in any order, as long as it is logical and fits your subject. No matter what plan you choose, though, you must have a physical point of view.This is the place from which you choose to view the object of your description.

Once you have decided on a physical point of view, your description should include only those details that can be observed from that point. For example, if you choose a high cliff overlooking a mountain valley as your physical point of view, you will describe only the things that you can hear, see, touch, taste, and smell from that location. A physical point of view provides a sense of realism to your composition. Your readers will "see" in their mind only what they would see if they were actually looking at the scene you are describing.

Mood, or Mental Point of View. The mood of a piece of writing is the overall feeling the writer wishes to create. In a description, mood changes according to the individual and the situation. For example, imagine that you are looking at a mountain valley. The sky is dark; heavy, black clouds are forming on the horizon; the wind is moaning faintly through the pines; and thunder crashes over the distant peaks. The sight may make you feel sad and depressed. This is your mood at the moment, and you will want to re-create this feeling in your composition. Choose details and descriptive words that convey this mood to your reader.

Now imagine that you visit the valley on another day. The morning sun is shining; the sky is a cloudless blue; a woodpecker is clattering rhythmically in the distance; and a hint of pine scents the air. You may feel happy, carefree, even excited. This is the mood that you want to communicate in your composition.

Unity

When you write a descriptive composition, you are trying to create a single, unified impression for your reader. You can achieve this if you do the following:

1. Maintain a definite physical point of view and mood.
2. Choose details carefully.
3. Make sure that the sentences in each paragraph relate to the topic sentence. Also make certain that each paragraph relates back to the introductory paragraph.
4. Use transitional devices that tie ideas together.

Choosing Details To Achieve Unity. Choosing details carefully means selecting those details that add to the impression you wish to create. It also means describing the details with precise words that create a strong image for the reader.

For an example of precise writing, contrast the following:

1. The bird sang in the tree.
2. The mourning dove grieved in the old pine.

The first sentence is vague and imprecise. The second sentence carefully identifies the bird, the tree, and the action being performed.

Here is another example:

1. The elephant moved down the ramp.
2. The huge elephant lumbered down the wooden ramp.

The second sentence includes specific adjectives and a strong, precise verb. It creates a much clearer image than does the first sentence.

Coherence

Coherence, or clarity, is achieved through the logical arrangement of ideas. Several logical orders were mentioned in the discussion of physical point of view. Another order is chronological, or time, order. It is used occasionally in description, but more often in explanatory and narrative compositions. Whatever order you use, transitional words and phrases—such as those listed on pages 160 and 164—help to tie your ideas together and make them clear to your reader.

Emphasis

Emphasis may seem easy to achieve in a descriptive composition. After all, you have already chosen one specific scene or particular object as the subject of your description. However, an even more precise focus may help to strengthen your descriptive composition even more.

In describing a scene, for example, the writer often chooses a center of interest. This may be an unusual mountain, a unique building, or an interesting play of light or color. All other details are then grouped around this point of focus. The central image dominates the scene; the other details are described in relation to it.

Studying a Descriptive Composition

The following composition, which describes a fall afternoon, illustrates the concepts presented thus far in Part 2. As you read, try to determine the author's point of view. Also look for ways in which the writer achieves unity and coherence.

November Afternoon

It is not yet 4:30, and the sun is nearing the low ridge to the west. Soon the brightness of the late autumn afternoon will yield to twilight, to dusk, and to dark.

The sun begins to set behind the ridge. The last, long light climbs from the valley's frosted pasture grass up the gray trunks of the naked maples and seems to pause on the hilltops to the east. Then it is gone. Twilight, the glow of November evening, possesses the day.

At first there is the bright, shadowless light, a sunless daylight in which the growing moon, halfway up the eastern sky, is only a ghost. Then the glow comes, a rosy suffusion so subtle it could be a reflection of the maple leaves at the roadside or the bronze-red grass in the neglected meadow. The air seems to thin and brighten, and the chill diminishes distances. The world comes close, the familiar world of this place called home.

The glow fades. Dusk creeps in, unhurried but insistent, and the clarity of vision dims. In its place is a deceptive clarity of hearing. The farm dog barking just down the road sounds no closer than a truck shifting gears on a hill a mile away. The rustle of leathery leaves in an oak not ten feet away seems as far off as the hooting of the barred owl across the valley. And time somehow has lost its dimensions. It is evening and it is autumn, and the moon has begun to glow. The scuffle of leaves at the roadside just ahead could be a noontime cat or a midnight fox or the evening breeze.

Sunset, twilight, dusk, darkness, all by six o'clock on a mid-November evening, is late autumn's summary of serenity.

—The New York Times

The physical point of view is a spot within a valley. The mood is one of peace. The single, unified impression is that of serenity. Unity is achieved through a stable point of view and the choice of precise details. Carefully chosen words, such as "The last, long light climbs from the valley's frosted pasture grass" and "Dusk creeps in, unhurried, but insistent" strengthen the feeling of serenity.

Each paragraph relates to the introductory paragraph by telling something about the late autumn afternoon. The paragraphs, and the ideas within the paragraphs, are tied together by the use of the word *light*. The repeated use of synonyms for light— for example, *brightness, glow,* and *rosy*—also ties ideas together in the composition.

Coherence is achieved through the logical arrangement of ideas into chronological order. The writer describes sunset, twilight, dusk, and darkness in the order in which they happen.

Emphasis is achieved by grouping the details in relation to *light*. The changing light, reflecting the oncoming night, is the central image in the composition. All other objects are seen and heard through this light.

Exercise Writing a Description

Following the techniques described in Chapter 10, "Writing a Composition," write a descriptive composition of five paragraphs. Begin by choosing a subject based on personal experience. Check your journal for possibilities, or try brainstorming for ideas. Once you have a topic, complete the following steps:

Pre-Writing: Narrow your subject. Decide on your audience and your purpose. Decide on your physical point of view and mood. Gather, group, and organize your ideas in a writing plan.

First Draft: Write a rough draft, using your writing plan as a guide. Try to use vivid, precise words in your description.

Revision: Check to make sure that all ideas are related to each other and to the introductory paragraph. Does your composition have unity, coherence, and emphasis? Did you use strong verbs, precise nouns, and vivid descriptive words and phrases? Refer to the Guidelines for Writing and Revising Compositions on page 212. Also review the two charts at the end of Chapter 7.

Part 3 The Explanatory Composition

There are three main types of explanatory compositions. An explanatory composition, sometimes called an expository composition, can explain a process, define, or give reasons. Like all compositions, an explanatory composition opens with an introductory paragraph that catches the reader's attention and gives an indication of what will follow. The body paragraphs explain or support the ideas presented in the opening paragraph. A concluding paragraph signals the end of the composition.

The well written explanatory composition is characterized by unity, coherence, and emphasis. These three qualities are achieved in much the same way as they are achieved in descriptive compositions. Unity is created by a structure in which all the parts work together, by precise details, and by transitional devices. Coherence is created by the logical arrangement of ideas. In some compositions, especially those that give instructions and those that include incidents or anecdotes, logical order means chronological order. In others, logical order fits the special content of the composition. The third quality, emphasis, is achieved by selecting a central idea that dominates the other ideas presented in the composition.

The Composition That Explains a Process

A composition that explains a process tells how to do something or how something works. The writer's purpose is to explain the process so that it may be easily done or understood by the reader. Therefore, the composition is usually written in a direct, straightforward style. A composition of this type is most often developed through facts or examples that are presented in chronological order.

Following is an example of an explanatory composition that explains a process. See if you can identify the specific methods used by the writer to achieve unity, coherence, and emphasis.

How To Read Faster

When I was a kid in Philadelphia, I must have read every comic book ever published. I zipped through all of them in a couple of days, then reread the good ones until the next issues arrived. As I got older, though, my eyeballs must have slowed down. I mean, comic books started to pile up faster than my brother Russell and I could read them. It wasn't until much later, when I was getting my doctorate, that I realized it wasn't my eyeballs that were to blame. The problem is that there is too much to read these days, and too little time to read every word of it. That's when I started to look around for commonsense, practical ways to help me read faster. I found three that are especially good. And if I can learn them, so can you—and you can put them to use immediately.

The first way is previewing. It is especially useful for getting a general idea of heavy reading like long magazine or newspaper articles and nonfiction books. To preview, read the entire first two paragraphs of whatever you've chosen. Next read only the first sentence of each successive paragraph. Then read the entire last two paragraphs. This will give you a quick, overall view of the long, unfamiliar material. It will keep you from spending time on things you don't really want—or need—to read.

The second way to read faster is skimming. It is a good way to get a general idea of light reading like popular magazines or the sports and entertainment sections of the paper. It is also a good way to review material you've read before. To skim, think of your eyes as magnets. Force them to move fast. Sweep them across each and every line of type. Pick up only a few key words in each line. You will end up reading about half the words in *less* than half the time it would take to read every word.

The third way to increase your reading speed is clustering. Clustering trains you to look at groups of words rather than one at a time. For example, instead of reading a line like this: My—brother—Russell—thinks—monsters, you would read it like this:

My brother Russell   thinks monsters

For most of us, clustering takes constant practice because it's a totally different way of seeing what we read. To practice clustering, begin with something easy to read. Read it as fast as you can. Concentrate on seeing three to four words at once rather than one word at a time. Then reread the piece at your normal speed to see what you missed the first time. Practice fifteen minutes every day until you can read clusters without missing much the first time.

So now you have three ways to help you read faster: previewing to cut down on unnecessary heavy reading; skimming to get a quick, general idea of light reading; and clustering to increase your speed and comprehension. With enough practice, you'll be able to handle more reading at school and at home in less time. You should even have enough time to read your favorite comic books!—BILL COSBY

The introductory paragraph explains that the composition is about three ways to help you read faster. The three body paragraphs develop this idea. The sentences in each paragraph relate directly to the topic sentence. Following the body is a conclusion which summarizes the ideas in the composition and which relates back to the introductory paragraph. This carefully thought out structure contributes to the unity of the composition.

Another way that this composition is unified is by the repetition of the words *read* and *way* throughout the five paragraphs.

Coherence is achieved by the logical arrangement of ideas throughout the composition and within each paragraph. The opening paragraph introduces the idea of three ways to read. The next three paragraphs each explain one way. Each paragraph is structured so that it first names the way, next tells a little more about it, then gives specific directions for applying the method.

Emphasis is achieved by grouping all the ideas around the central idea of reading faster. Details about why it is important to read faster, about what kind of materials can and should be read faster, and about the ways to increase reading speed are all related to the central idea.

Exercise Writing a Composition That Explains a Process

Choose one of the topics from the box or make up one of your own. Then complete the steps that follow.

Possible Topics

1. How to get a part-time job
2. How to study for a test
3. How to tune a bicycle
4. How to train a dog

5. How to build a model
6. How a rocket works
7. How a telephone works
8. How a camera works

Pre-Writing: Narrow your topic and identify your purpose and audience. What facts and examples are necessary to explain the process clearly? What are the main steps? How should your material be organized so that the reader can follow the steps easily?

First Draft: Using your pre-writing notes, get your ideas down on paper. Concentrate on thorough explanation and clear transitions.

Revision: Go over your rough draft several times. Is your explanation broken down into simple steps? Is it easy to understand? Have any steps been left out? Refer to the Guidelines for Writing and Revising Compositions. Also review the two sets of Guidelines at the end of Chapter 7.

The Composition That Defines

A composition that defines includes the same main parts as the paragraph that defines. It states

1. the term to be defined
2. the general category to which the term belongs
3. the unique characteristics that separate the term from similar members of the general category.

The remainder of the composition builds on that basic definition. It may further explain the unique characteristics of the subject. It may also identify the term's various parts, types, or uses. The facts or examples that develop the composition are usually presented from least important to most important. Another common order is most familiar idea to least familiar idea. This order helps the reader by building on knowledge he or she already has.

The following composition defines a sophisticated term that could not be thoroughly explained in a single paragraph.

Lasers

Compared to other light forms, laser light is definitely "the new kid on the block." Lasers were developed less than twenty-five years ago, but they are already used in such widely different areas as medicine, manufacturing, and the military.

A laser is an electronic device that emits an intense, highly concentrated beam of energy in the form of light rays. It does this by amplifying an existing light. In fact, the word *laser* itself is an acronym standing for light **a**mplification by **s**timulated **e**mission of **r**adiation. Laser light differs from ordinary light forms in two ways. First, a laser light is a single, pure color. Secondly, laser light is highly directional. Where regular light travels in all directions, a laser light travels in a narrow beam and thus has high intensity.

Lasers are divided into three types based on their light-amplifying substance. The most widely used is the *solid laser*. Its light is amplified by a crystal, glass, or semi-conductor. *Gas lasers* use gas or a mixture of gases to amplify light. They produce a continuous beam of light, and are especially useful in communications and in measuring. A third type of laser is the *liquid laser* which uses a dye dissolved in a special liquid. It can produce either bursts of light or continuous light.

More and more uses are being found for lasers all the time. In manufacturing, lasers are used for a source of intense heat. They can weld a variety of metals, cut hard materials, and drill minute holes. In medicine, the laser substitutes for the surgeon's scalpel. Its heat seals off blood vessels during operations, resulting in so-called "bloodless surgery." Lasers even have a use in national defense! The military can bounce lasers off moving targets and determine their distance and speed.

Lasers produce the most powerful light beam known today. They may be new, but they've already proven their worth.

The first paragraph introduces a very general definition of a laser as a light form. It also makes a statement about the value of lasers. The second paragraph contains the full definition of the term as well as its unique characteristics. The third paragraph divides the term into various types and briefly identifies each of these. Finally, the last body paragraph presents various uses of the laser. The conclusion refers back to the introduction by restating the laser's general category and value.

This structure and the repetition of the term *laser* help create unity. Coherence is achieved by presenting the material in a logical order, least to most important. That is, although the definition and description of the laser are necessary to the reader's understanding, the most important thing for the reader to understand is how the laser is important to his or her life.

Exercise Writing a Composition That Defines

Imagine that you have been asked to write an article for your school newspaper. This article should define an organization to which you belong or a subject about which you have special knowledge. Once you have identified and narrowed a topic, complete the following steps:

Pre-Writing: Consider your audience. What do they know about your topic? What details will they need? Next consider your subject itself. To what general category does your term belong? What are its identifying characteristics? Can it be divided into types or parts? What is its function? Finally, select and organize your details. Which order would work best? Least to most important? Most to least familiar?

First Draft: Use your pre-writing plan to get your ideas down on paper. Remember to begin with a general definition. Then work toward a more specific definition.

Revision: Have you clearly explained your term? Can it easily be distinguished from other closely related terms? Are your supporting paragraphs developed with enough detail? Refer to the Guidelines for Writing and Revising Compositions on page 212. Also review the two sets of Guidelines at the end of Chapter 7.

The Composition That Gives Reasons

Compositions of this type give reasons why a fact or an opinion is so. In the introductory paragraph, you clearly state a fact or present an opinion. The paragraphs that follow give reasons that support the fact or opinion in this type of composition.

The reasons may be additional facts, statistics, examples, or anecdotes. They must be carefully chosen, though, if they are to provide good support for your initial statement or opinion. Generally, you present your reasons either in their order of importance or in order of familiarity. Make this decision based on the material itself and on your knowledge of your audience.

230

Pets Are Better Than Medicine

Pets are usually thought of as pleasant, amusing little animals that stroll through the house or patiently swim around in a bowl. Their purpose is simply to provide companionship and simple amusement for their owners. Yet animals can be much more than friendly housepets. When used by knowledgeable therapists, they can actually be powerful weapons against disease and mental illness. It is this function of pets that we must recognize and take better advantage of.

In a very basic way, animals can improve everyone's health. Recent studies show that the simple pastime of watching a tank full of fish can actually *lower* a person's blood pressure. Also, even though blood pressure will rise when people talk to other people, there is no rise in people's blood pressure when they talk to their pets. This may be because animal companionship is uncritical and non-judgmental. Whatever the reason, pets seem to provide a safe, non-threatening outlet for our emotions and concerns.

In medicine, animals are being used increasingly in physical therapy. For instance, riding horseback can have several advantages for physically disabled children. It can give them confidence and help them improve their balance. Riding also stimulates muscles that can't develop in wheelchairs. People with cerebral palsy, for example, suffer from tightness of the thigh muscles. Sitting on a horse stretches those muscles.

Pets can also be used to reach people who are withdrawn and lonely, or who are severely depressed. In several cities, the Anti-Cruelty Society takes puppies around to centers for the elderly. In one case, an elderly woman who had suffered a stroke was very withdrawn. At first she responded only to the dog, but on later visits she began to show the puppy to other patients and to interact with them. Pets are used as therapy in hospitals for the mentally ill, too. Social workers feel that animals help to establish bonds of trust and communication.

For all these reasons, the therapeutic value of animals should be recognized. Pets may be friendly, lovable, or cuddly; but they can also be powerful medicine.

In the introductory paragraph, the writer states her position that animals should be thought of as valuable aids to good health. She achieves unity by developing three reasons why this is so:

1. Animals are beneficial to general well-being.
2. Animals are used in physical therapy.
3. Animals are used in mental and emotional therapy.

Each reason ties into the initial statement about pets and is developed with specific examples. Phrases such as "for instance," "for example," and "finally" also provide unity. The reasons are organized so that the most widely understood appears first. From this familiar idea, the writer moves to the more unfamiliar uses of animal therapy. This order helps provide a coherent structure.

Exercise Writing a Composition That Gives Reasons

Choose one of the topics from the box or make up one of your own. Then complete the steps below.

Possible Topics

1. Favorite movies
2. My best quality/my worst quality
3. Why study history?
4. It is the best of times/it is the worst of times
5. The advantages of newspaper/television news

Pre-Writing: Narrow your topic and identify your purpose and audience. What idea or opinion do you want to express? What details develop these reasons? How can they best be presented?

First Draft: Use your writing plan to get your ideas down on paper. Try to present your reasons clearly and logically.

Revision: Have you stated your position clearly? Are your reasons logical? fully developed? Refer to the Guidelines for Writing and Revising Compositions on page 212. Also use the two sets of Guidelines at the end of Chapter 7.

The Composition That Persuades

A special type of composition that gives reasons is the composition that persuades. The first step in writing this type of composition is to find an issue with two or more sides. Next, you must decide which side you will take. Identifying your audience in the pre-writing stage is a crucial matter. For this type of paper, your audience will be those people who have not made up their minds about the issue, or those who disagree with your opinion. Your purpose, then, is to persuade this audience that you are right.

To persuade this audience, select the strongest and most convincing reasons possible. Also, select reasons that will have the most impact on your particular group of readers. The same reasons may not be equally effective with different age groups or types of people.

As with paragraphs of this type, your reasons and supporting details may include statistics, facts, examples, or anecdotes. The order you present your ideas in is usually from least important to most important. In this way, you build a case that leaves a strong impression in your reader's mind.

The Computer as Friend

The growing influence of computers has many people ill at ease. They fear the way these machines are creeping into businesses, homes, and even such familiar places as libraries and stores. Yet these individuals shouldn't be so concerned. Despite their forbidding aspects, computers really have a great deal going for them. Each of us must set aside our misconceptions and prejudices, and see computers for the fantastic resources they are.

Computers, if you're not afraid of them, can be marvelous companions. First of all, they are an endless source of stimulation and fun. They can tease you, play games with you, and stretch your creative powers. Also, in contrast to TV which does not interact with viewers, computers force users to keep their minds alert. In addition, computers can help you with your work (something even your best friends might be reluctant to do).

Uncomplainingly, a computer will plan your budget, reorganize a report, or draw a graph. It will do its best to make you look good.

Computers also provide their users with a sense of achievement. The day you finally understand computer techniques, you feel as you did the day you learned to ride a bicycle. You also finally realize that computers will not one day rule the world. You rule the computer. It is yours to direct.

Finally, computers provide a chance to prepare for the future. Like it or not, these devices are here to stay. In a few years, the ability to use a computer may be a standard requirement for high school graduation. Ignorance of computers will hinder an individual in all phases of his or her life. Those people who establish early friendships with computers will enjoy a head start in the race toward the twenty-first century.

Computers can be a treasure chest of wonders, if only we're not afraid to look inside. They can also be powerful friends. It's time to put aside our distrust and welcome them into our lives as wonderful new companions.

Notice that the writer has identified his audience, those who feel ill at ease with computers, in his introduction. His opinion is that computers "have a great deal going for them." His purpose is to convince his audience that it is time to put aside fears and learn what computers have to offer.

The emphasis in the composition is placed on the positive, nonthreatening aspect of computers. This mood is reinforced with words such as "marvelous," "fun," "achievement," and "friendships." The writer's reasons for championing the computer become increasingly more serious. His first reason points out the fun of computers while his last reason emphasizes the computer's link to future success. Finally, the writer achieves unity by repeating the word "computer" and by clearly stating his reasons so that they relate to his opinion.

Finally, notice the writer's use of reasonable language. He lets his reasons do his arguing for him, and he does not resort to undue criticism of others or harsh language. All good persuasive compositions follow this strategy.

Exercise **Writing a Composition That Persuades**

Consult your writing journal, look through a newspaper, or brainstorm for topics that require persuasion. Choose a topic and then complete the following steps:

Pre-Writing: Narrow your topic. What is your opinion? Who is your audience? What reasons support your opinion? What details will best develop those reasons? What would be the most effective order for presenting your reasons?

First Draft: Use your pre-writing plan to get your ideas down on paper. Use unbiased, reasonable language to present your material.

Revision: Have you clearly stated your opinion? Does the emphasis of your composition reflect your audience's concerns? Does your paper have unity and coherence? Refer to the Guidelines for Writing and Revising Compositions on page 212. Also use the two sets of Guidelines at the end of Chapter 7.

1. Narrative, descriptive, and explanatory compositions each have specific purposes and characteristics. All well-written compositions, however, incorporate unity, coherence, and emphasis.

2. Narrative compositions are used to relate events or incidents. They include the elements of character, setting, conflict, and point of view.

3. Descriptive compositions are used to "paint a word picture" of places, scenes, or people. Such compositions emphasize sensory details.

4. Explanatory, or expository, compositions can be used to explain a process, define a term or idea, or provide reasons for a statement or opinion. A special type of composition that gives reasons is the composition that persuades.

Applications in Other Subject Areas

Home Economics / Industrial Arts. Write down several projects that you have completed this year, such as making an item of clothing or tuning up an engine. Write a composition that would explain one aspect of the project to someone who has just transferred into the class. The composition should be clear enough that the student would be able to complete the project after reading the composition.

Mass Media / Social Studies. A newspaper includes many different types of items. Choose one of the following ideas and write a short article that could be turned in to an editor.

    a. A human interest story about a special moment in the life of an individual.

    b. A special feature story describing a local event such as a school carnival, art fair, concert, canoe race, or marathon.

    c. An editorial giving reasons for or against taking some action in your school or community.

Chapter 12

Writing a Report

You are asked to report on different types of painting styles for your art class. Your science teacher assigns a paper on the development of a chicken embyro. A history project is due, and you decide to write about the causes of the Industrial Revolution. In each of these cases, you may know something about the subject, but not enough to write a fully developed composition.

When the material for a composition must come from outside sources, rather than from your own knowledge or experience, the composition is called a **report.** The main purpose of writing a report is to gather information from a number of sources and then to present the material clearly and accurately. Preparing a report involves the same stages of pre-writing, development, and revision as any other composition.

Part 1 Pre-Writing: Choosing a Subject

When you are not assigned a specific topic for a report, your first step is to choose a subject. Make a list of subjects that interest you and that would be interesting to your readers. Remember that the subject you select should not have *you* as the main source of information.

Subjects based on learned information may need to be narrowed. In limiting your subject, keep two things in mind:

1. the amount of information available on the subject
2. the length of your report

At this stage, it is sometimes helpful to consult a general encyclopedia article on your subject or the index of a book dealing with your subject. Checking either of these may provide possibilities for limited subjects.

Consider, for example, the subject "Japanese Culture." It is so broad that to develop it would take an entire book at least. Even if the subject were narrowed to "Japanese Culture in the Twentieth Century," it would still be too broad for a short, five-paragraph report.

The general topic "Japanese Culture" does, however, contain a number of possible report topics. Examination of a book or article on Japan might yield the following ideas:

Japanese Family Relationships   A Japanese Garden
The Japanese New Year Celebration   Koto Music of Japan
Residential Architecture in Japan   Japanese *No* Theater

Many more topics could be added to the list. Each could be developed adequately in a short report.

Another example of a subject that is too broad for a short report is "The Rodeo." A little research, however, could provide these topic possibilities:

The Ropers   Steer Wrestling
Bronc Riding   The Bull Ride
Barrel Racing   History of the Rodeo

A. The following topics are too general to be covered in a short report. Choose ten of the topics and limit each one so that it is suitable for a five-paragraph paper. You may have to do some research.

1. famous architects	11. weather
2. Native Americans	12. pollution
3. acupuncture	13. YMCA
4. mythology	14. metric system
5. the British monarchy	15. earthquakes
6. folk music	16. space flight
7. oceanography	17. extinct species
8. early explorers	18. Franklin Roosevelt
9. photography	19. the ocean
10. railroads	20. hang gliders

B. From the list of topics you made in Exercise A, choose five topics for which you might like to gather more information. Then add five more topics of your own. Be sure to limit each one so that it is appropriate for a five-paragraph report. Keep this list.

Part 2 Pre-Writing: Preparing To Do Research

Once you have narrowed your topic, you may be tempted to check out an armload of books and begin reading. However, a little thought and preparation at this point could save you hours of unnecessary research time later.

Identifying Your Purpose

A subject can be approached in several different ways depending on the purpose of the report. Identifying the purpose will help you to focus your thinking and research.

For most reports, your purpose will be to **inform** your readers about your topic. Look for material that will give your readers the facts and details they need to understand your subject. For instance, if your topic were "Frank Lloyd Wright's Prairie Style," you would have to find facts defining this style of architecture.

On the other hand, your purpose might be to **compare and contrast** Wright's style of architecture with that of another architect. If this were your purpose, you would begin by reading about each style separately. Then, you would look for details that the two styles share or ways in which they are directly opposite.

Finally, your purpose might also be to **analyze** your topic. For example, you might decide to write on "The Effect of Wright's Prairie Style on Modern Architecture." In this case, you would need to present facts that would help your readers draw conclusions about the topic.

At this point, you may wish to clarify your topic by writing a **statement of purpose.** This statement, sometimes called a **thesis statement,** may be used in the introduction to your report.

Identifying Your Audience

Identifying your audience is an important task. The audience's knowledge of your subject will determine the amount of background material you will have to present. It will also help you to know how technical you can get in the body of your report.

Suppose, for example, that your topic is the use of home computers. Your audience is your classmates, who have just finished a home computer unit in math. In this case, you would not need to define a home computer in your report. You would, however, be able to use terms from that specialized area that a less-informed audience might not understand.

Understanding Fact and Opinion

As you begin to do your research, you should know how to identify useful information. One important skill that will help you is the ability to separate fact from opinion. A report is composed of facts. A **fact** is a piece of information that is verifiable; that is, a fact can be shown to be true. "Frank Lloyd Wright was born on June 8, 1867," is a statement of fact. To verify it, you could read a biography or an encyclopedia article about Wright. You could also go right to the source by traveling to his birth place and searching out the old birth records.

An **opinion,** on the other hand, is not verifiable. It cannot be proven true. An opinion is often signaled by judgment words, such as *best, worst, valuable,* and *terrible.* An opinion may also be signaled by such phrases as *should* or *ought to.* You may agree with an opinion, but that does not make it a fact that is appropriate for a report. "*Great Expectations* was written by Charles Dickens" is a usable fact. "*Great Expectations* is a good book" is an opinion. You may agree with it, but you should not use it for your report.

In gathering material for your report, be sure to record only facts. You must also make sure these facts are from a source that is up-to-date, reliable, and unbiased. See Chapter 13, "Critical Thinking," for more information on facts and opinions.

Exercise **Learning To Work with Facts**

Assume that you are writing a report called "Bronc Riding." The purpose is to inform people of your age who are unfamiliar with the topic. Look at the following statements. Keeping your subject, purpose, and audience in mind, find five statements that are not appropriate for your report. Write them and be ready to tell why you would not use them. Remember that opinions should not be used.

1. The broncbuster supplied ranchers, the U.S. Army Calvary, the stage lines, and Wells Fargo wagons with fresh supplies of horses.
2. Broncbusters were the toughest men in the West.
3. Bronc riding should be outlawed because it is a form of cruelty to animals.
4. The rider must keep one hand free and away from the horse.
5. Bronc riders developed from the early professional horse trainers.
6. Each animal is fitted with two belts in the chute.
7. Bronc riding is usually the opening activity at a rodeo.
8. Bronc riding is too dangerous to be enjoyable as a sport.
9. Twisting and jumping broncs bound out of the chute.
10. Bareback bronc contests are limited to eight seconds.

11. There are very specific rules for bronc riding.

12. Bronc riding has a fascinating history.

13. The bronc's strongest bucks come during the first two or three seconds.

14. Bronc riding is a more interesting event than calf roping.

15. The rider must spur the horse above the point of the shoulders during the first jump out of the chute.

Making a List of Questions

Identifying your purpose and learning to recognize facts are two ways to focus your research. Another method is to make a list of questions that you or your audience might want answered about your subject. With these questions in mind, you will be sidetracked less easily. You will also know that you have done adequate preliminary research when you have answers to all your questions.

After a little preliminary reading, a writer who decided on "Snake Venom" as a topic made a list of the following questions to guide her research:

1. How is snake bite treated?
2. Do poisonous snakes provide any benefit for people?
3. What is antivenin?
4. How is antivenin made?
5. How is venom extracted?

As you continue research for your report, other questions may occur to you, and you may find and record facts that do not fit in as answers to your original questions. It is all right to use this new information if it seems consistent with your audience and purpose.

Exercise **Preparing To Do Research**

Choose a topic from the list you made in Part 1. This will be the topic of your report. Identify your purpose and audience. Then write five to ten questions about your topic that you can use to guide your reading.

Part 3   Pre-Writing: Gathering Information

After doing some preliminary work on your topic, your time in the library will be well spent. Begin by reading a general encyclopedia article for an overview of your topic. Then use the *Readers' Guide to Periodical Literature* and the card catalog to find articles and books on your subject. You may also want to use specialized reference books. See Chapter 14 for help in using the library.

Making a Working Bibliography

As you use the *Readers' Guide* and the card catalog, record on 3″ x 5″ note cards the sources that you find. Write only one source on each card. Organize these cards in alphabetical order, and write an identifying number on the upper right-hand corner of each card. This list of sources, recorded in this manner, is your **working bibliography**. Even after you have found your sources, keep your bibliography cards; they will be useful later.

Guidelines for Bibliography Cards

1. **Books.** Give the author, last name first; the title of the book; and the year of publication. Put the library call number in the upper left-hand corner of your card.

2. **Magazines.** Give the author, last name first (unless the article is unsigned); the title of the article; the name of the magazine; the date of the magazine; and the page numbers of the article.

3. **Encyclopedias.** Give the title of the entry; the name of the encyclopedia set; and the year of the edition.

4. **Other reference works.** Give the title of the article or entry; the name of the book or set; the volume number of the entry; the page numbers of the entry; and the year of publication.

The writer of a paper on robots had the following cards in her working bibliography.

Book

1

RD
130
.B47

Berger, Melvin.
Bionics.
1978.

School Library

Magazine

2

Friedrich, Otto.
"The Robot Revolution,"
Time,
Dec. 8 1980,
pp. 72-83.

Public Library

Encyclopedia

3

"Robot."
Collier's Encyclopedia.
1984 ed.

School Library

You may not use all of the sources you record. Some may not be available, and others will not have the right information. Delete or add cards, as necessary.

Making a Working Bibliography

Make a working bibliography for your report. Use 3″ x 5″ cards to record your information. Follow the guidelines given in this lesson for recording sources. Save your cards for later use.

Taking Notes

As you find information on your topic, use 3″ x 5″ note cards to record your facts. Be sure to write only one item on each card. This will allow you to organize your information easily, either as you are doing research or later on, during the actual organization process. Also include the number of the bibliography card that identifies the source of the information, and the page numbers on which the information can be found.

Rewording Information. When you are taking notes for your report, be sure to record the information in your own words. This will ensure that your report is an original one. It will also help you avoid **plagiarism**—the uncredited use of another person's material. Notice how the writer of the note card below transferred information from her source to her notes.

> Now that robots have proved efficient and economical, the main effort is to create "smart" robots and thus give them an ability to make decisions. To become smarter, robots are learning to "see" and "touch," and report to their computer brains what their new senses tell them.

> *Robots that can "see" and "touch"*②
> *are now being designed. These*
> *new capabilities will make*
> *robots "smarter" and capable*
> *of making decisions.*
>   *page 72*

Quoting a Source Directly. Sometimes an author will say something so well that you will want to use an exact quote. In this case, accurately copy the passage you want to quote. Put quotation marks around it on your note card. Give credit for the quote in your report by mentioning the author's name.

The writer of the report on robots also had the following cards.

①

The simplest industrial robot is a mechanical arm that brings raw material to a machine to be processed and then takes the processed item away.
        page 76

④

Robots with rudimentary "vision" are able to inspect glowing diodes that light numbers in pocket calculators. Humans could do this work accurately for only a short time.   page 76

③

An android is a robot that resembles a human in both appearance and activity.

       page 114

Exercises **Taking Notes**

A. Rewrite the following information in your own words.

A fairly sure sign of possible volcanic eruption is a series of earthquakes near a volcano. These, with tilting of the ground, indicate that sections of the earth's crust are shifting. New channels may be opening up for magma, and underground pressures are perhaps increasing. Wells in the area may go dry— indicating that cracks underground are allowing the water to leak deeper into the earth. Water reaching hot rocks, far down, may turn to steam and boost the pressures that are causing the quakes. A volcanic eruption may also be hinted at by changes in the earth's magnetism. —*The Story of Geology*

B. Assume that you are writing a report on the Mohawk Indians. Write five note cards on this article from page 48 of *The Indian Book*. Assume you have assigned this book source number "2."

The Mohawk lived in what is now upper New York State and a bit of Canada. Their villages stood in clearings in the forest that covered the land. They had large houses, called long-houses, in which a number of families lived. The men hunted, fished, and made war. The women grew corn, beans, and squash outside the village.

Four other tribes, the Oneida, Onondaga, Cayuga, and Seneca, lived near the Mohawk. All five tribes spoke the same basic language and lived in much the same way. Long ago, these five tribes had joined together to form a strong group. They called their group by a name meaning, "we are of the longhouse."

Their enemies, the Algonquin Indians, called all the people of the longhouse by a name meaning "poisonous snakes." To French explorers, the Algonquin word sounded like Iroquois (IHR uh kwoy). We still know them by this name.

C. Take notes for your own report on 3″ x 5″ cards. Follow the guidelines in this lesson for recording sources and information.

Using Graphic Aids

"A picture is worth a thousand words" is an old cliché, but there is some truth in it. Often such graphic aids as pictures, illustrations, sketches, diagrams, maps, tables, and charts will accompany the text of a book or article. Don't overlook them. They contain facts that could be used in your report. Information from graphic aids can be summarized and put on your note cards, too. As with written text, you must interpret the material accurately and carefully. See Chapter 15, "Study and Research Skills," for more information on graphic aids.

Interviewing

Even though a report cannot have you as a main source of information, it could have someone else as a source. Interviewing experts or authorities is another means of gaining facts for your report. Authorities and experts are people with specialized knowledge in a field. They can often give more current information on subjects than you can find in books.

If you do ask an expert for an interview, be sure to make the most of your opportunity by following these guidelines:

Guidelines for Conducting an Interview

1. Arrange a specific time and place for the interview.
2. Do background work on your topic before the interview.
3. Prepare a list of questions to ask during the interview.
4. Leave space under each question to take notes on the answers that the interviewee gives.
5. Be prompt for the interview.
6. Be prepared with pens, paper, and/or a tape recorder.
7. Phrase your questions so that they cannot be answered with a simple "yes" or "no."
8. Ask follow-up questions.
9. Be courteous.

Exercises Using Additional Sources

A. Study the following diagram from page 471 of *A Proud Nation*, by Ernest R. May. The diagram illustrates the structure of a corporation from the stockholders, or investors, to the actual employees of the company. Make note cards summarizing the information given in the diagram.

CORPORATION STRUCTURE

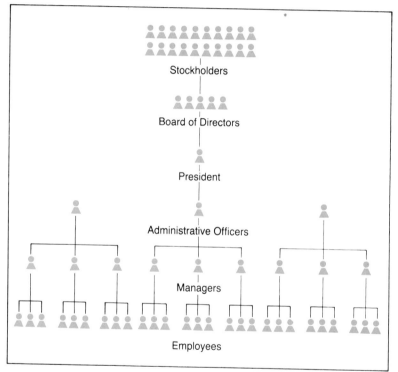

B. Consider the topic of your report. Assume that you will use an authority or expert as a source of information. Describe the credentials of the person you plan to interview. Then prepare ten precise interview questions that you could ask such an expert. Remember to phrase your questions in a manner that calls for a full answer, not merely a "yes" or "no."

Part 4   Pre-Writing: Organizing a Report

Once you have gathered all your information, you are ready to organize your notes. At this point, the reason for putting a single fact on each note card will become clear. Find a big table and begin arranging your note cards by ideas. Which facts seem to be related? What term or key idea describes each grouping? The note cards allow you to try out various groupings and to delete, rearrange, and add to your ideas as you refine them.

The writer of the report on snake venom had note cards with these facts:

–Venom cannot be extracted by machine
–Drug from Russell's viper for clotting of blood
–The large snake fangs are grooved or hollow
–Venom is stored in a freezer
–Small amount of venom injected into horses
–Blood from immune horses collected and processed
–Venom used to make snakebite serum
–Venom used in some unusual ways
–Herpetologist uses sterile container
–People with snakebite are given horse serum; lives saved
–Horses become immune gradually
–The snake bites the covering of the container
–Drug from Egyptian cobra is not perfected yet but could be used to fight organ transplant rejection
–Collections of snakes maintained for extracting venom
–*Cobroxin* from cobras is a painkilling drug; no addiction
–Death from snakebite is a rarity
–The venom collects in the vial until the snake's supply is gone

After experimenting with a few arrangements, the writer found that her notes seemed to fall into four main groups. They were:

Valuable Product
Unusual Uses
Venom Extraction
Snakebite Serum

Once the writer had determined the four main ideas, she organized her note cards under those ideas, as follows:

VALUABLE PRODUCT

1. Collections of snakes maintained for extracting venom
2. Venom used to make snakebite serum
3. Venom used in some unusual ways

UNUSUAL USES

1. *Cobroxin* from cobras is a painkilling drug; no addiction
2. Drug from Russell's viper for clotting of blood
3. Drug from Egyptian cobra is not perfected yet but could be used to fight organ transplant rejection

VENOM EXTRACTION

1. Venom cannot be extracted by machine
2. Herpetologist uses sterile container
3. The snake bites the covering of the container
4. The venom collects in the vial until the snake's supply is gone
5. Venom is stored in a freezer

SNAKEBITE SERUM

1. Small amount of venom injected into horses
2. Horses become immune gradually
3. Blood from immune horses collected and processed
4. People with snakebite are given horse serum; lives saved

Notice that the writer was not able to use two of her facts:

–Death from snakebite is a rarity
–The large snake fangs are grooved or hollow

These facts did not fit under any of her main ideas, so she deleted them from her report.

The Order of Information

As with other types of compositions, the method you use for organizing your report will depend on your subject and your purpose. Reports are often organized from least important idea to most important idea, or from most familiar concept to least familiar concept. Comparison and contrast is a useful order for a topic such as "Farming Before and After Machines." For still other subjects, spatial order and chronological order will be the best method of organization. Sometimes, the facts themselves will determine the order.

The writer of "Venom" may have had the following thoughts as she chose an order for her groups of ideas:

1. The audience is not likely to know much about snake venom or its uses. They may also find the subject unattractive. Therefore, the idea group that gives some basic information about snake venom and emphasizes its value should come first.

2. The idea groups on how venom is extracted and how serum is produced from venom are two parts of a process. They should be presented in chronological order.

3. The remaining group of ideas is on unusual uses of venom. These ideas help the audience understand just how important the products of venom may someday be in their own lives. This group works well as a final body paragraph.

Your own planning and organization should be similarly thought out. Also remember to organize the ideas within each group in a logical order.

Making an Outline

Some writers like to compose their rough drafts working directly from their organized note cards. Others prefer to prepare an outline first. An outline gives you a structured framework from which to work in writing your paper. It is easier to refer to than a stack of cards. It also formalizes the organizational work that you started with your note cards.

Each group of note cards becomes a major division in an outline. The key idea of the group becomes the division's main heading. It is labeled with a Roman numeral. The individual facts on the note cards become major points underneath the heading. They are labeled with capital letters. Refer to Section 17 for more detailed information on outlining.

The writer of "Venom"made the following outline.

Venom

I. Valuable product
   A. Obtained from snakes
   B. Used to make serum
   C. Used in unusual ways

II. Venom extraction
   A. Cannot be done by machine
   B. Must be done by herpetologist using a sterile container
      1. Forces snake to bite covering of container
      2. Pumps venom into container until snake's supply is gone
      3. Stores venom in freezer

III. Production of snakebite serum
   A. Venom injected into horses
   B. Horses develop immunity
   C. Blood collected and processed

IV. Unusual uses of venom
   A. *Cobroxin*
      1. Is obtained from cobras
      2. Is a non-addicting painkiller
   B. Drug from the Russell's viper venom
      1. Used by dentists
      2. Aids blood clotting
   C. Drug from Egyptian cobra venom
      1. Still being developed
      2. Will be used to fight organ transplant rejection

Notice that the writer used chronological order in developing her individual paragraphs on venom extraction and snakebite serum. She arranged her ideas in the last paragraph from most to least familiar or common. She mentioned the major use of venom before she mentioned some lesser known uses.

As you work, you may find that you need to return to the library to gather more facts to develop one or more divisions of your outline. You may also want to try several organizational methods in your outline before settling on the one that best fits your purpose, audience, and topic.

Exercises Organizing Your Report

A. Divide the note cards you prepared in Part 3 into three or four related groups. Put the groups and the ideas within them into a logical order.

B. Working from your note cards, prepare an outline for your report.

Part 5 The First Draft

The report, like other types of compositions, has three main divisions: the introduction, the body, and the conclusion.

The Introduction

In the introduction of a report, you want both to introduce your topic and to catch your audience's attention.

The following paragraphs are possible introductions for the report on venom.

1. I am going to report on venom. Although it is poisonous, venom can be useful.
2. The most valuable product provided by snakes comes from their greatly feared venom. Some collections of poisonous snakes are maintained for the specific purpose of extracting venom. Once removed from the snakes, venom is used in making snakebite serum and also in some surprising other ways.

The first paragraph does introduce the topic, but it is dull and lifeless. It does nothing to catch the reader's attention or to maintain the reader's interest. On the other hand, the second introductory paragraph introduces the topic in a more lively way. By stating that something valuable comes from something greatly feared, the writer suggests an irony that catches the reader's attention. Cleverly, the writer introduces some interesting factual material from her outline, but she also leaves her reader wondering, "What are these other surprising uses for snake venom?" Leaving a question planted in the reader's mind is often a good technique for sustaining interest in your report.

Some writers believe that the introduction is the hardest part of a report to produce. If you are one of those writers, you may want to work on the body of the report first. This often helps you feel more secure about your subject.

Exercise Writing an Introduction

Write an introduction for your report. Either use Section I from your outline or begin with an entirely new idea.

The Body

You are now ready to write the body paragraphs of your report. In a sense, you are filling in the details on the framework of your outline.

Each body paragraph will cover the information listed under one of your outline headings. The key idea of each heading will be used to write the topic sentence for each paragraph. The sentences that follow develop the key idea. Of course, if you have done a careful, thoughtful job in constructing your outline, your body paragraphs will take shape more easily.

The writer of "Venom" used Section I on her outline for her introduction. She then developed the remaining divisions.

> II. Venom extraction
> III. Snakebite serum
> IV. Unusual uses

As this writer worked on her rough drafts, she revised the content of her report several times. Sometimes she reorganized details. Often, she added or deleted information. Finally, she checked for precise word usage and errors in mechanics.

As you work on the drafts of your own report, remember that it is not too late to add, delete, or rearrange ideas. In fact, such work is expected since revision is a natural part of writing.

Exercise Writing the Body Paragraphs of a Report

Using your outline, write the three body paragraphs of your report. Add, delete, and rearrange your material as long as you are careful to maintain the unity of your composition.

The Conclusion

Like any composition, the report should end with a short conclusion in which you restate your main point or briefly summarize your facts. The conclusion should also leave your readers with a sense of closure, a feeling of "the end."

The writer of "Venom" dramatically underscores the main idea of her report, the value of venom, in her conclusion. In doing so, she also adds to the unity of the paper.

> Ounce for ounce, venom has a greater dollar value than gold. However, its medical value to people cannot be measured in terms of money.

Now look at the final report on "Venom." Notice how the three body paragraphs fit together to form a unified whole. Remember that this is the final copy. It is the result of several drafts.

Venom

The most valuable product provided by snakes comes from their greatly feared venom. Some collections of poisonous snakes are maintained for the specific purpose of extracting venom. Once removed from the snakes, venom is used in making snakebite serum and also in some surprising other ways.

No machines have been invented that can carry out the dangerous task of extracting venom. To obtain the precious golden fluid, a trained herpetologist carries a venomous snake to a special table to which a sterile collecting vial is fastened. As the herpetologist holds the snake, the serpent sinks its fangs into the fleshlike, rubberized covering of the container. The fluid from the snake's fangs trickles down the inside of the collecting vial until the venom supply is used up. The snake's fangs are then lifted from the collecting glass, and the poison is stored in a freezer.

To produce snakebite serum, small quantities of snake venom are injected into "donor horses." These horses are kept under special care for many months. Eventually the injections of poison cease to have an effect on the horses. As each horse becomes immune to the snake venom, a quantity of its blood is collected. In a medical laboratory the horse blood is processed into snakebite serum, which is distributed to hospitals and doctors. When a person bitten by a poisonous snake is injected with the horse serum, or antivenin, the snake poison in the victim's body is made ineffective.

Medical researchers have developed many drugs from snake venom. One is *cobroxin*, an astonishing, painkilling drug made from cobra venom that does not cause addiction as narcotic painkillers often do. Another is a blood-clotting medication containing venom from the Russell's viper. This drug is administered by dentists to stop bleeding after a tooth has been pulled. Researchers are working on a drug made from the poison of the Egyptian cobra that someday may be used to overcome the body's rejection of transplanted organs and tissues.

Ounce for ounce, venom has a greater dollar value than gold. However, its medical value to people cannot be measured in terms of money—J.M. ROEVER

Exercise **Writing Conclusions**

Write the conclusion to your report. Make sure that it ties the report together, restates your main idea, and provides the report with a definite finish.

Part 6 Revising Your Report

As with other types of compositions, revisions of your notes, outlines, and rough drafts have been an ongoing part of the writing process. After you complete your final draft, however, revision is again important. Use the Guidelines on pages 122 and 212 to improve your writing.

In a report, there is also an extra step in the revision process. This involves checking all your facts for accuracy. Check the spelling of names and terms, the accuracy of dates, and the correct relationship of the ideas and procedures mentioned.

When all your revisions are complete, make a clean copy of your report. Follow your teacher's directions for preparing the final copy.

Proofread for errors in mechanics one more time. Use the checklist on page 123 to guide your revision.

Exercise Revising a Report

Read, revise, and proofread your report. Make a final copy.

Part 7 Preparing a Bibliography

After you have completed your actual report, there is still one more part you need to prepare. This is the bibliography.

The **bibliography** is a list of the sources you consulted in gathering facts for your report. This list appears at the end of your report.

To prepare your bibliography, look back over the cards from your working bibliography. Discard any that you did not consult or use in writing your final report. Your bibliography should consist of only those references from which you directly obtained information.

Next, alphabetize your list by the author's last name, or by the title of the source if no author is given. Copy the source information from your bibliography cards.

Look at the following bibliography. The first entry is for a magazine article, the second for a book, and the third for an encyclopedia article. Use this form in your own bibliography.

Bibliography

Hecht, Annabelle. "Snake Venom — A Medicine?" *FDA Consumer*, Sept. 1981, pp. 18-20.
Minton, Sherman A., Jr. *Venomous Reptiles.* 1980.
"Snake." *World Book Encyclopedia.* 1984 ed.

Notice that periods follow the author's name and the end of the entry. In addition, a period follows a book title. Finally, if an entry runs to more than one line, all lines after the first line of an entry are indented.

Exercise **Preparing a Bibliography**

Using your bibliography cards, make a bibliography for your report. Follow the form and procedure that was discussed in the lesson. Depending on your teacher's directions, place your bibliography directly after your conclusion or on a separate sheet of paper. Now proofread the final copy of your report one last time. Correct any remaining errors.

1. A report is a piece of writing in which information is gathered from outside sources and presented clearly and accurately. Writers compose reports for school, in newspapers, in business situations, and for many other purposes.

2. Reports can inform the reader, compare or contrast subjects, or analyze a topic. The topic and purpose of the report determine the kind of research needed.

3. A working bibliography should be prepared on 3″ x 5″ note cards. Research information should also be put on 3″ x 5″ cards. Be sure to record facts, not opinions. Also record information in your own words.

4. A special part of any report is the bibliography. A bibliography is the list of outside sources used in the report.

5. When you are writing a report, be sure to complete every stage in the process of writing.

Applications in Other Subject Areas

Science. Choose one of the following subjects, research it, and write an explanatory report concerning it:

a. the stages of sleep
b. the space shuttle
c. the structure of a cell
d. the social organization of a bee, termite, or baboon colony
e. the creation of a mountain, volcano, or glacier.

Computer Science. There are hundreds of home computers on the market today. Visit a computer store, or read some issues of a computer magazine. Gather information on two of the top-selling units. Write a short report aimed at the typical confused consumer. Compare the strengths and weaknesses of the two brands.

Chapter 13

Critical Thinking

The U.S. Library of Congress contains over 535 miles of book-shelves. The U.S. Government Printing Office produces millions of books and pamphlets every year. A single big city newspaper contains more printed information than most people of two hundred years ago read in their entire lives.

You live in an age of information. Every day you read or hear hundreds of facts and opinions. Some come from television, books, newspapers, or magazines. Some come from other people. To make the best use of all this information, you must know how to analyze and evaluate it. In other words, you need to learn the principles of critical thinking.

Part 1 Facts and Opinions

Most information comes to us as statements about the people, things, and events around us. Statements can be as simple as the sentence "This is a hot day" or as complicated as a long mathematical equation. Some statements can be proven true. They are called **facts**. Other statements cannot be proven true or false. Such statements are called **opinions**.

Facts

There are two kinds of facts: **definitions** and **observations.**

Definitions. The following statements are definitions:

An *isthmus* is a narrow strip of land having water at each side and connecting two larger bodies of land.

Cytoplasm is the living matter of all animal or plant cells.

Such statements of fact do not have to be proved. They are true because people have agreed upon the meanings of the words that they contain. In other words, they are *true by definition.*

Observations. All other statements of fact are observations. Consider the following examples:

Adult blue whales are larger than adult humans.

The precise geographical center of the North American continent is in a town called Rugby, North Dakota.

There are more people in New York City than in the entire country of Ireland.

These statements are all facts because they can be shown to be true by at least one of the following methods:

1. Making personal observations
2. Asking experts who have made personal observations
3. Referring to a work in which other people have recorded their personal observations.

Opinions

An opinion is a statement that cannot be shown to be true or untrue. Consider the following statements:

STATEMENT OF FACT: The works of Beethoven are considered classical music.

STATEMENT OF OPINION: Classical music is more enjoyable than rock and roll music.

By referring to an encyclopedia or consulting a music expert, you can prove whether or not the first statement is true. Therefore, it is a statement of fact. However, no amount of observation can prove the second statement. People can and do disagree about what type of music is more enjoyable. Because the second statement cannot be proved, it is an opinion. The following statements are also opinions:

Detective fiction is more interesting than science fiction.

There is life on other planets.

The first statement is an opinion because people disagree about it and cannot settle their differences by making observations. The second statement is also an opinion because there is no way to make observations to prove whether it is true or false. If someday it becomes possible to prove the second statement, then it will become fact.

Many opinions can be recognized by their use of judgment words. These are words that tell how someone feels about a subject. The following judgment words are often found in opinions:

good, better, best   excellent, wonderful, magnificent
bad, worse, worst   terrible, awful, worthless
ugly, beautiful   stupid, clever, intelligent
valuable, worthless

Many other opinions contain words that express desires, such as *should* or *ought to: People should be more considerate; the committee ought to rethink its decision.*

Exercises Facts and Opinions

A. Tell whether the following facts are true by definition or true by observation. If the statement is true by observation, tell what observation you would have to make to prove that it is true.

1. Some horses are easily frightened.
2. Appaloosa horses have black and white markings.
3. The Greek thinker Thales believed that the world was made entirely of water.
4. Water and H_2O are the same thing.
5. An abacus is a kind of calculating machine.
6. Few people in America use the abacus for calculations.
7. A cheetah can run up to seventy miles an hour.
8. Offside plays are among the most common hockey violations.
9. The appestat is the appetite control center of the brain.
10. Origami is the Japanese art of paper folding.

B. Tell whether the following are statements of fact or statements of opinion. If the statement is an opinion, identify any judgment words that it contains.

1. This senator would make an excellent President.
2. Life was much better in the good old days.
3. Astrological forecasts are poor reasons for decisions.
4. Jupiter is the largest planet in our solar system.
5. Popsicles taste wonderful on a hot summer's day.
6. Thousands of popsicles are sold on hot summer days.
7. There are only about one hundred whooping cranes left in existence.
8. The Mississippi is the longest North American river.
9. Autumn is the best of the four seasons.
10. Today's music is not as interesting as that of the last two decades.

C. Keep a notebook of facts and opinions for three days. Every day, write down five facts and five opinions that you hear or read. Put a star beside facts that are true by definition.

Part 2   Evaluating Statements of Fact

Often, you will have to act upon information provided by some other source. Because everyone can make mistakes, some of this information will be false. To avoid accepting false statements as facts, it is important for you to learn how to evaluate factual information. As mentioned earlier, facts can be evaluated in one of three ways: by making personal observations, by asking an authority, or by consulting a reference work.

Evaluating Facts Through Personal Observation

Whenever possible, check the facts yourself. If someone tells you that there is a kangaroo in your yard, take a look. If an advertiser claims that his or her prices are cheaper than anyone else's, contact competitors and compare the results. Personal observation is not always convenient or even possible, but it is by far the most reliable method for evaluating statements of fact.

Evaluating Facts Through Reference to Authority

Much of the information that we act upon every day comes from other people. We may receive this information through direct contact or through such media as books, newspapers, or television programs. The following are some helpful guidelines for evaluating these statements:

1. Is the statement provable? Suppose that you read a statement like "Life was much more exciting in the 1920's." The first step in evaluating this statement is to decide whether it is indeed a statement of fact. Ask yourself whether observations can be made that will prove the statement true or false. If the answer is "no," the statement is not a fact. It is an opinion.

2. Is the information up-to-date? A history textbook written before 1959 will say that there are forty-eight states in the United States. Many scientific articles written before 1887 will tell you that space is filled with an invisible substance called ether. Today, both of these statements would be considered false. When you use an authoritative source, you use the most recent one available.

3. Is the statement consistent with other known facts? Suppose the clock on your wall says 12:00, but a sunrise can be seen through your window. Since the time indicated by the clock contradicts, or *is inconsistent with,* other known facts, the clock must be wrong. Whenever you evaluate a fact, check to see that it is consistent with other facts that you already know.

4. Is the source of the information reliable? If your source is a person, does this person speak from expertise or personal experience? If your source is other than a person, is the source well regarded? For example, a doctor would be a reliable source on the treatment of headaches. However, a television commercial would not be a reliable source on the same subject. Television commercials are written by people with no special training.

5. Is the source of the information unbiased? Always make sure that your source does not have any personal prejudices that would lead to inaccurate statements. For example, a salesperson for one company is unlikely to be an unbiased source on the quality of a competing company's products. Such a salesperson would be biased by loyalty to his or her company and product.

Exercises Evaluating Facts

A. None of the following statements are true. Identify each statement as out-of-date, inconsistent with other known facts, or both.

1. Most news about world events is received by word of mouth.
2. Use "he" when referring to professional people because women do not usually hold professional jobs.
3. Objects that are heavier than air always fall.
4. Ninety percent of Americans live on farms.
5. It is possible for objects to burn without oxygen.

B. List two possible kinds of sources for answers to the following questions. The sources may be specific reference works, authorities, or your own experience and knowledge. Which of your sources is the most reliable in each case? Be specific in your answers, and be prepared to defend these answers in class.

1. Who has the best batting average in the major leagues?
2. Are dogs and wolves related?
3. You discover a rash on your skin. What is its cause?
4. Where was Thomas Jefferson born?
5. How do you keep a bicycle in perfect working order?

C. Make a list of six facts that you know to be true. Two of these facts should come from personal observation. Two should come from an acknowledged expert. Two should come from a respected written source. Make sure that you gather facts, not opinions. Be prepared to defend in class the reliability of these facts and of your sources.

Part 3   Evaluating Statements of Opinion

Many people believe that "one opinion is as good as another." This is untrue. For example, in Christopher Columbus's day, only a few people believed that the earth was round. This belief was considered an opinion because people of the time had no way to prove that it was true. However, there *was* evidence to support this opinion: When a ship sailed out to sea, the top of the sails could still be seen after the rest of the ship had disappeared over the horizon. Good opinions are those that can be supported by *evidence*, which is another name for facts.

Recognizing Weak Opinions

Weak opinions are those that have few or no facts to support them. The opinions on the following page are all weak.

Women are more emotional than men.
He's hot-tempered because he's a redhead.
Very few people really care about one another.
Politicians are all dishonest.

When evaluating an opinion, apply what you have learned about evaluating statements of fact. See if observations can be made to support the opinion. Make sure that the source of the opinion is reliable, unbiased, and up-to-date. Make certain that the opinion agrees with presently known facts.

Weak opinions often contain the following errors:

1. Overstatement. Weak opinions often contain words such as *all, every, always, everyone, never, no one, none,* and *most.* Better opinions often use words such as *many, few, some, several, often, occasionally,* and *frequently.*

> WEAK OPINION: Everyone should attend college.
>
> ANALYSIS: College is important for success in many careers. It can be valuable in other ways as well. However, for some people, attending a vocational school, getting a job, or serving an apprenticeship may be better.
>
> BETTER OPINION: Some students should attend college.

2. Use of "snarl words" and "purr words." These are words that are used to create negative or positive reactions in others. They express emotion not information. Included among "snarl words" are many terms that are used in "name calling" such as *crook* or *bum.* Included among "purr words" are such expressions of approval as *lovely, good,* and *sweet.*

> WEAK OPINION: *Decent* citizens will support this program.
>
> ANALYSIS: The word *decent*, offers no facts about the program or the citizens who support it. The term merely creates a positive feeling that is then associated with the program.
>
> BETTER OPINION: This program will cause a decrease in the crime rate.

3. Use of undefined or unclear terms. Sometimes a word has no one, clear definition. Its meaning may vary depending on the speaker or the situation. Such words should be avoided unless they are clearly defined. Many snarl words and purr words fall into this category.

WEAK OPINION: Libraries should carry only the *right* kind of books.

ANALYSIS: *Right* in what sense? *Right* for whom? *Right* in what circumstance? Because the meaning of the word *right* is not clear in the context of this sentence, the statement itself has little or no meaning.

In matters of personal taste, everyone is entitled to his or her opinion. Some people like comedies; some people like dramas. Some people like solitude; some people like being in groups. When expressing personal tastes, it is permissible to use snarl words, purr words, and vague, undefined judgment words like *wonderful* or *beautiful*. However, it is important to remember that personal tastes are not facts. You cannot expect other people to share them.

Exercises Evaluating Opinions

A. All of the following statements are opinions. Identify those opinions that can never become facts and those opinions that may eventually become facts.

1. Scientists can find a cure for cancer.
2. Every home needs a computer.
3. Algebra is much easier than geometry.
4. Lilacs smell better than roses.
5. Solar energy is the most efficient and practical energy source to use.
6. Abraham Lincoln was as great a President as Thomas Jefferson.
7. Visiting New York City is more interesting than visiting Washington, D.C.
8. There is life on other planets.

B. The following statements of opinion contain overstatements, snarl words, purr words, and words that are undefined or unclear. Identify the problem or problems in each sentence.

1. At the time of Columbus's arrival, North America was populated by savages.
2. He created the most beautiful sculpture the world will ever see.
3. Nobody goes to discos anymore.
4. Only proper clothing and behavior are suitable for attending an important event.
5. Personal freedom is the most important goal for people to strive for.
6. Fabulous Zip laundry detergent cleans and brightens your clothes until they are wonderfully fresh, blindingly clean, and bursting with the fragrant scent of roses.
7. Everyone should participate in a team sport.
8. That is the most idiotic statement I've ever heard.

C. Study the following dialogue. What are the two people arguing about? Why can they never come to an agreement about the subject of their argument? Why are they failing to communicate? What overstatements, snarl words, and purr words are used by the speakers?

MONICA: Why don't we go to the *Men at Work* concert next month?

MAURICE: You're kidding.

MONICA: What do you mean, "You're kidding"? They're great.

MAURICE: Great what? Certainly not musicians. I don't know how you can listen to that noise. It gives me a headache.

MONICA: They happen to be one of the most popular groups around these days.

MAURICE: I tell you, some people enjoy every piece of garbage that comes along.

MONICA: Well, you're certainly not one of them, because I can't think of anything that *you* enjoy. You've got a negative attitude about everything.

Part 4   Discovering Errors in Reasoning

Reasoning is the process of drawing a conclusion from known information. Poor opinions often result from errors in reasoning. Such errors are called **fallacies.** The following fallacies are among the most common:

Circular Reasoning

Occasionally someone attempts to prove a statement by simply repeating that statement in other words. This is called **circular reasoning.** The statement "team sports are better than individual sports because it's better to play with a team," is an example of circular reasoning. The speaker has not provided any evidence to support the argument. Instead, the initial statement has just been repeated in different words.

The Cause and Effect Fallacy

When one event happens after another event, people sometimes assume that the first event caused the second. They make this conclusion even though there is no direct evidence proving that the two events are related. This error is a **fallacy of cause and effect.** Many superstitions are based upon just such reasoning. For example, a person who breaks a mirror and then has bad luck might conclude that breaking mirrors causes bad luck. However, the two events would actually be unrelated.

The Either/Or Fallacy

When someone claims that there are only two alternatives when there are actually more, this is called the **either/or fallacy.** One common example of this fallacy is the remark "You're either with us or against us." This remark leaves out several possibilities. The person being spoken to might not have taken any side, or perhaps the person sees good points on both sides.

Overgeneralization

A statement that refers to several people, places, things, or events is a **generalization**: *Many people study best in the afternoon.* When a generalization is so broad that it covers people, places, things, or events that it should not cover, then it is an **overgeneralization**: *All people study best in the afternoon.*

Stereotype

One type of overgeneralization is the **stereotype.** Stereotyping occurs when an entire group is said to have the characteristics of a few individual members of the group. For example, you might meet a discourteous salesperson in a local store and decide that "All salespeople in this store are discourteous." This would be an unfair stereotype of the other salespeople in the store.

Rationalizing

Sometimes a person or a group justifies an action by giving a reason that is believable, but which is not the real reason. This is called **rationalizing.** For example, suppose that a community council decides to spend money on a cable TV system rather than a little league program. The council cancels its youth program stating, "We feel that Little League creates an unhealthy, overly competitive atmosphere for our youngsters." The council has attempted to justify its action with an explanation that is believable, but which is not the real reason.

Bandwagon/Snob Appeal

When someone tells you that a particular idea is right simply because others believe that it is, this is called the **bandwagon fallacy.** If someone says that you ought to like certain things because everyone else does, you are being asked to "hop on a bandwagon." One form of the bandwagon fallacy is **snob appeal.** This is used to make people feel that taking a certain action will make them part of an elite group. Snob appeal is common in advertising: *People with style wear our styles.*

Exercises **Discovering Fallacies**

A. Identify the logical fallacies in the statements given below. Each fallacy is used only once.

a. circular reasoning
b. the cause and effect fallacy
c. the either/or fallacy
d. overgeneralization

e. stereotyping
f. rationalizing
g. bandwagon/snob appeal

1. Drinking milk is really good for a cold. I drank a quart of milk, and I was much better in just a couple of days.

2. Wear Action jeans. Or be the only one who isn't.

3. These guitars are the best made because they are so well constructed.

4. Come on, make up your mind. You liked the movie, or you didn't. It's that simple.

5. I need to watch my diet, but if I eat this one little piece of chocolate, it will give me lots of energy for my exam next period.

6. Nobody believes in palm reading anymore.

7. The people on that team are unfair. I heard one of them say he would gladly move the ball while the referee wasn't looking.

B. Write your own example of each of the logical fallacies listed above.

1. Logical thinking is necessary for clear writing and speaking. It is also essential to help you evaluate what you read and hear.

2. Facts are statements that can be proved through observation or by referring to authorities.

3. Opinions cannot be proved through observation. Sound opinions can be supported by factual evidence.

4. A factual statement must be evaluated before it can be used. Make sure that observations can be made to prove the statement. If direct observation is impossible, check your source. Be sure that the information is up-to-date, consistent with other known facts, and taken from a reliable, unbiased source.

5. To evaluate an opinion, apply the same process used for evaluating facts. Make sure the opinion is supported by factual evidence. Also check the opinion for overstatements, snarl words, purr words, and undefined or unclear terms.

6. Be alert to logical fallacies in your own writing and speaking and in the writing and speaking of others.

Applications in Other Subject Areas

Science. A scientific hypothesis is a type of opinion. Read about a scientific experiment in your science textbook or in a scientific magazine. Identify the hypothesis or opinion being evaluated. Then discover the method used by scientists to support or disprove the hypothesis.

History. Find a history textbook and identify two statements of fact and two statements of opinion. Determine what facts are used to support the two statements of opinion that you discover.

Mass Media. Listen to several commercials on TV or radio. List the fallacies and poorly supported ideas that you hear.

Chapter 14

Using the Library

Learning to use library resources efficiently and quickly will be of great practical value not only for your work in English but for all your studies. In high school you will do research in literature, history, science, and other subjects. You will find the library an indispensable tool.

Before you can make efficient use of the library, however, you will have to know how books are classified and arranged on the shelves. You will have to know how to use the card catalog to find books. You should also be familiar with a wide variety of reference works, so that you will be able to find the best available information on any subject.

Suppose, for example, that you were asked to write a brief biographical sketch of Mark Twain. Would you read a short biography, or read entries on Twain in *Twentieth Century Authors* and in a large encyclopedia? What other sources could you use? If you know what resources the library has, you will be able to answer these questions immediately.

This chapter will give you the basic information you need to make the best use of the library.

Part 1 How Books Are Classified and Arranged

It is important for you to understand the classification and arrangement of books in a library. All libraries, no matter what their size or purpose, arrange materials according to the same basic system. Understanding this system will enable you to find any book you need.

The Classification of Books

Fiction. Novels and short-story collections are usually arranged in alphabetical order by author. For example, if you want to read the American classic *The Pearl*, by John Steinbeck, you would first look for the section in the library that has shelves marked FICTION. Then you would look for books that have authors whose last names begin with S and find the book in its alphabetical position. If the book is not there, someone else has borrowed it, or a browser has carelessly returned it to the wrong position. You would be wise to check part of the shelf to see if the book has been returned out of alphabetical order. If you do not find the book and you need it soon, fill out a reserve card (a postcard mailed to you when the book has been returned to the library) that the librarian will give you.

Nonfiction. Most libraries classify nonfiction books according to the Dewey Decimal System. This system, which is named for its originator, the American librarian Melvil Dewey, classifies all books by number in ten major categories:

000–099	**General Works**	(encyclopedias, handbooks, almanacs, etc.)
100–199	**Philosophy**	(includes psychology, ethics, etc.)
200–299	**Religion**	(the Bible, theology, mythology)

300–399	**Social Science**	(sociology, economics, government, education, law, folklore)
400–499	**Language**	(languages, grammars, dictionaries)
500–599	**Science**	(mathematics, chemistry, physics, biology, etc.)
600–699	**Useful Arts**	(farming, cooking, sewing, nursing, engineering, radio, television, gardening, industries, inventions)
700–799	**Fine Arts**	(music, painting, drawing, acting, photography, games, sports, amusements)
800–899	**Literature**	(poetry, plays, essays)
900–999	**History**	(biography, travel, geography)

As you can see from the major categories of the Dewey Decimal System, each field has a classification number. For example, all science books have a number between 500 and 599, and all history books have a number between 900 and 999. The system becomes more detailed as each of these major groups is subdivided. The table below shows how the subdividing works in the literature category (800–899).

800–899 Literature	**810–819 Literature Subdivided**
810 American literature	810 American literature
820 English literature	811 Poetry
830 German literature	812 Drama
840 French literature	813 Fiction
850 Italian literature	814 Essays
860 Spanish literature	815 Speeches
870 Latin literature (classic)	816 Letters
880 Greek literature (classic)	817 Satire and Humor
890 Other literatures	818 Miscellany
	819 Canadian-English Literature

Arrangement of Books on the Shelves

You will see at a glance that books are arranged on the shelves numerically in order of classification. Most libraries mark their shelves prominently with the numbers indicating the books to be found in each particular section. Within each classification except biography, books are arranged alphabetically by authors' last names. Biographies are arranged alphabetically by the last name of the person the book is about.

Biography. The Dewey Decimal System division for Biography is 920. However, large libraries will often place biographies in a separate section because of the large number of these books. In this case they will have a "B" or a "920" on the spine of the book and on the catalog card. If you are looking for a particular biography and are unable to find it, ask the librarian for assistance.

Reference Books. Reference books of particular types or on specific subjects are also shelved together, often with the letter *R* above the classification number.

Exercises How Books Are Classified and Arranged

A. In which major division would the following information be located?

1. Plays for high school productions
2. How to plant a vegetable garden
3. A comparison of Greek and Roman gods
4. "Killer" bees
5. Motocross racing
6. Recessions and depressions in the United States
7. Macramé
8. Rules for playing lacrosse
9. How to say "no" in any country
10. Operating a CB radio

B. Using the Dewey Decimal System listed in this chapter on pages 276 and 277, assign the correct classification number to each of the following books:

1. *Voices of the Rainbow: Contemporary Poetry by American Indians,* ed. Kenneth Rosen
2. *Great Religions of the World,* ed. Merle Severy
3. *America,* by Alistair Cooke
4. *Metric Power,* by Richard Deming
5. *A History of American Painting,* by Ian Bennett
6. *Dolphins,* by Jacques Cousteau and P. Diolé
7. *Planning the Perfect Garden,* ed. *Good Housekeeping*
8. *Afro-American Folklore,* ed. Harold Courlander
9. *The Art of Printmaking,* by E. Rhein
10. *Clarence Darrow: A One-Man Play,* by David W. Rintels

Part 2   Using the Card Catalog

To determine whether the library has a book you want and where to find it, use the **card catalog**. The card catalog is a cabinet of small drawers or file trays containing alphabetically arranged cards. Each card bears the title of a book that the library has on its shelves. The card also carries the classification number, or as librarians say, **call number**, in the upper left-hand corner. (See the illustration on the next page.)

To find your book, write down the call number on a slip of paper. If it is a literature book—for example, *Selected Poems* by Langston Hughes—the call number will be in the 800 range. Specifically, American poetry will be found in 811.

Go to the section of shelves marked 811, and you will find your book alphabetically placed among those authors' last names that begin with *H*. The same call number you originally found on the catalog card will be imprinted on the spine of the book near the bottom.

There are usually three cards for the same book in the card catalog: the *author card*, the *title card*, and the *subject card*.

The Author Card. Perhaps you are writing a paper about a modern-day sports figure, or you are simply interested in reading about sports. Sports conditioning is the topic of a book by Frank O'Neill. The author card in the card catalog looks like this:

613.7
ONe
    O'Neill, Frank, 1929–

        Sports conditioning: getting in shape, playing your best, and preventing injuries; by Frank O'Neill, with Bill Libby. 1st ed. Garden City, N.Y. Doubleday, 1979.
        194 p., [16] leaves of plates; ill. Includes index.

○

Author cards for all books by one author will be filed together alphabetically according to title. Notice also that books *about* the author are filed *behind* his or her author cards.

The Title Card. Suppose you do not know the author's name, but do know the title of the book about sports conditioning. Look in the card catalog for a card bearing the title at the top as follows:

613.7
ONe
    Sports conditioning

        Sports conditioning: getting in shape, playing your best, and preventing injuries; by Frank O'Neill, with Bill Libby. 1st ed. Garden City, N.Y. Doubleday, 1979.
        194 p., [16] leaves of plates; ill. Includes index.

○

Look for the title card under the first letter of the first word in the title. (*A*, *An*, and *The* do not count as first words.)

The Subject Card. You may not know whether a book has been written about sports conditioning. To check, you examine the cards cataloged under the general subject *Sports*. There, you will find the following card:

```
613.7     SPORTS
ONe
              Sports conditioning: getting in
          shape, playing your best, and
          preventing injuries; by Frank O'Neill,
          with Bill Libby. 1st ed. Garden City,
          N.Y. Doubleday, 1979.
              194 p., [16] leaves of plates;
          ill. Includes index.

                         ◯
```

Subject cards are most useful when you want information on a specific topic from a variety of sources. Cards for all books on a particular subject are cataloged together. The subject card may also indicate whether a book has chapters on a single aspect of the topic you are interested in. The publication date on the card will help you find the most up-to-date book on your subject. Note that the heading is printed in capital letters. This will help you distinguish a subject card from an author or title card.

Card Information

Notice that all three types of catalog cards (author, title, subject) give the same information.

1. The call number
2. The title, author, publisher, and date of publication
3. The number of pages, and a notation on whether the book has illustrations, maps, tables, or other features

Often the catalog card will provide more information.

4. A brief description of the nature and scope of the book
5. A listing of other catalog cards for the book

Cross-Reference Cards

Sometimes you will find a card that reads *See* or *See also*. A "See" card refers you to another subject heading in the catalog that will give you the information you want. Look at this card for the subject "television commercials":

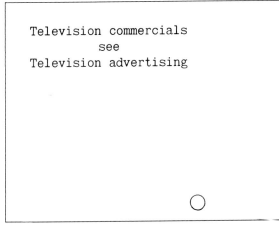

```
Television commercials
          see
Television advertising
```

This card means that the library catalogs all books on television commercials under the heading of television advertising.

The "See also" card refers you to other subjects closely related to the one you are interested in.

```
Biology

   see also
Natural history
Physiology
Psychobiology
Variation (Biology)
Vitalism
Zoology

   See also headings Biological
```

Guide Cards

Besides the catalog cards, you will find guide cards in the cabinet trays. These are blank except for the guide word on a tab that projects above the other cards. Guide cards aid you in finding other catalog cards quickly. For example, if you want books on cartooning, you will find them easily by means of alphabetically arranged guide cards such as the following:

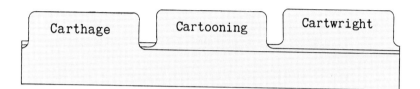

Exercises Using the Card Catalog

A. The drawing below represents the first six trays of a card catalog. The items at the right name authors, titles, and subjects that would be filed in these trays. Copy the list at the right on a separate sheet of paper, and write 1, 2, 3, 4, 5, or 6 in the blanks to show in which trays you would find the items listed. Remember that *A, An,* and *The* do not count as first words in a title.

1—	A—Boat	
2—	Bog—Cist	
3—	City—Deep	
4—	Den—Ebony	
5—	Eco—Fed	
6—	Fil—From	

___*A Doll's House*
___Charles Dickens
___*The Call of the Wild*
___*The Art of Walt Disney*
___Backgammon
___E. E. Cummings
___Frisbees
___*The Bermuda Triangle Mystery—Solved*
___Backpacking
___*A Christmas Carol*
___Nathaniel Benchley
___*Famous Ghost Stories*

B. Use the card catalog in your public library to find the title, author, call number, and publication date of the following books. Number your paper from 1 to 10 and write the answers.

1. A book by Ray Bradbury
2. A book about Harry S. Truman
3. A book on consumerism
4. A book on Renaissance art
5. A book by Agatha Christie
6. An anthology containing poems by Robert Frost, Emily Dickinson, and Carl Sandburg
7. A book with information and statistics on immigration to the United States
8. A book with plays by Eugene O'Neill, Tennessee Williams, and Thornton Wilder
9. A book by Harper Lee
10. A book about cross-country skiing

C. What subject cards would direct you to books about the following topics? Discuss your answers in class.

1. "Peanuts" cartoons
2. Repairing minibikes
3. Developing photographs
4. Stamp collecting
5. How films are made
6. The origin of the Olympics
7. The first astronauts
8. Popular music
9. Fashions of today's youth
10. The first television program

D. Using the card catalog in your school or public library, list the title, author, call number, and publication date of all books about two of the following people:

1. Eleanor Roosevelt
2. Henry Kissinger
3. Mark Twain
4. Gwendolyn Brooks
5. Pablo Picasso
6. Billie Jean King
7. James Baldwin
8. Walt Whitman
9. Beverly Sills
10. Ernest Hemingway

Part 3   Using Reference Works

One of the best ways to get information is to consult a reference work. Suppose your teacher asked you to write a brief biographical sketch of the American writer John Steinbeck. One good source would be *Twentieth Century Authors*, by Kunitz and Haycraft. It may be found in the reference room of most libraries. Know the various types of reference works and where they are kept in your school and public library.

Reference works are tools, and like tools, should be used in definite ways. Information may be arranged in any of various ways within a reference work. It may be alphabetical, chronological, or under major subject headings. Most reference works have prefaces that describe how information is arranged, show sample entries, and explain the symbols and abbreviations used in the book. Before using any reference work for the first time, you would be wise to skim the preface.

Nine basic types of reference works are described in this part.

1. Dictionaries. The most widely used reference books in the library are the general dictionaries. They may be classified in three major types. The first is the unabridged (complete) dictionary containing more than 500,000 words. Second, there are abridged (shorter) editions, commonly called "desk" or "collegiate" dictionaries. The third group are pocket-sized; they are convenient for checking the spelling of ordinary words, but too limited for high school and college use.

Here is a list of reliable dictionaries for your use.

GENERAL DICTIONARIES

The American Heritage Dictionary of the English Language
The Macmillan Dictionary
The Random House Dictionary of the English Language
Thorndike-Barnhart Dictionary
Webster's New World Dictionary of the American Language
Webster's Third New International Dictionary of the English Language

Another group of dictionaries are those dealing with certain aspects of the English language: synonyms and antonyms, rhymes, slang, Americanisms, etymology (word history), and so forth. Finally, there are special-purpose dictionaries that deal exclusively with music, medicine, biography, and many other subjects. The list below is by no means complete, but it provides good source material for you. You may check your school and community library as to the availability of specific-subject dictionaries.

DICTIONARIES ON SPECIFIC SUBJECTS

Abbreviations Dictionary (Abbreviations, Acronyms, Contractions, Signs, and Symbols Defined)
Acronyms, Initialisms, and Abbreviations Dictionary
Brewer's Dictionary of Phrase and Fable
Comprehensive Dictionary of Psychological and Psychoanalytical Terms: A Guide to Usage
Compton's Illustrated Science Dictionary
Dictionary of Biology
Dictionary of Economics
Dictionary of Literary Terms
Dictionary of Science and Technology
A Dictionary of Slang and Unconventional English
A Dictionary of Word and Phrase Origins (3 volumes)
Gregg Shorthand Dictionary
Grove's Dictionary of Music and Musicians (10 volumes)
Harper's Dictionary of Contemporary Usage
Harvard Dictionary of Music
Mathews' Dictionary of Americanisms
The New Roget's Thesaurus in Dictionary Form
The Oxford Dictionary of English Etymology
Roget's International Thesaurus
Webster's Biographical Dictionary
Wood's Unabridged Rhyming Dictionary

2. Encyclopedias. These are collections of articles, alphabetically arranged, on many subjects. Guide letters on the spine of each volume and guide words at the top of the pages aid you in finding information. It is best, however, to check the general index first when looking for information. It may list several good sources. For up-to-date information on a topic, check the yearbook that many encyclopedias issue. (A word of caution: When you write essays and reports, you must put all material taken verbatim from encyclopedias and all other sources in quotation marks or separate it from the rest of your paper by indention and single-spacing.) The following are some of the most reliable encyclopedias:

GENERAL ENCYCLOPEDIAS

Collier's Encyclopedia (24 volumes)
Compton's Encyclopedia (26 volumes)
Encyclopaedia Britannica (30 volumes)
Encyclopedia Americana (30 volumes)
World Book Encyclopedia (22 volumes)

The library has many special-purpose encyclopedias dealing with a wide variety of subjects. These encyclopedias are located in the library's reference room or area.

ENCYCLOPEDIAS ON SPECIFIC SUBJECTS

The Baseball Encyclopedia
The Concise Encyclopedia of Archaeology
The Concise Encyclopedia of English and American Poets and Poetry
The Concise Encyclopedia of Modern Drama
The Encyclopedia of American Facts and Dates
Encyclopedia of Animal Care
Encyclopedia of Auto Racing Greats
Encyclopedia of Careers and Vocational Guidance
The Encyclopedia of Chemistry
Encyclopedia of Gardening
Encyclopedia of Occultism
Encyclopedia of Religion
Encyclopedia of World Art (15 volumes)
Grzimek's Animal Life Encyclopedia (13 volumes)
The Illustrated Encyclopedia of Aviation and Space
The Illustrated Encyclopedia of World Coins
The International Encyclopedia of Cooking

International Encyclopedia of Social Sciences (17 volumes)
LaRousse Encyclopedia of Mythology
McGraw-Hill Encyclopedia of World Biography (12 volumes)
McGraw-Hill Encyclopedia of World Drama (4 volumes)
The Mammals of America
The New Columbia Encyclopedia
The Pictorial Encyclopedia of Birds
Universal Encyclopedia of Mathematics

3. Almanacs and Yearbooks. Published annually, almanacs and yearbooks are the most useful sources of facts and statistics on current events, as well as matters of historical record in government, economics, population, sports, and other fields. Some almanacs are shelved in the 000-099 category of the Dewey Decimal System, others in 300-399.

Guinness Book of World Records
Information Please Almanac, Atlas and Yearbook
Statesman's Yearbook
Women's Rights Almanac
World Almanac and Book of Facts

4. Biographical References. There are brief biographical notations in dictionaries and longer biographical articles in encyclopedias. Often, however, a better source is one of these specialized works:

American Men and Women of Science
The Book of Presidents
Current Biography
Dictionary of American Biography
The International Who's Who
Twentieth Century Authors
Who's Who
Who's Who in America
Who's Who in American Women
Who's Who in the East (and Eastern Canada)
Who's Who in the Midwest
Who's Who in the South and Southwest
Who's Who in the West

5. Books About Authors. Six good reference works are the following:

American Authors 1600–1900
British Authors of the Nineteenth Century
Contemporary Authors
Twentieth Century Authors
Twentieth Century Authors: First Supplement
Writers at Work

6. Literary Reference Books. The following are valuable reference books on the history of literature, on quotations and proverbs, for locating poems and stories, and for finding information about writers:

Bartlett's Familiar Quotations
Contemporary Poets
Cyclopedia of Literary Characters
A Dictionary of Literature in the English Language
Encyclopedia of World Drama
Granger's Index to Poetry
A Literary History of England
A Literary History of the United States
Mencken's *A New Dictionary of Quotations*
The Oxford Companion to American Literature
The Oxford Companion to English Literature
The Oxford Companion to the Theater
Poetry Handbook
Twentieth Century Authors
World Authors

7. Pamphlets, Handbooks, and Catalogs. Many libraries have pamphlets, handbooks, booklets, and clippings on a variety of subjects, including vocations, travel, census data, and program schedules. They also have a collection of college catalogs. All of these are kept in a set of file cabinets called the **vertical file.** One important feature about the vertical file is that the information in it is kept current. This file can be an invaluable source to you when writing a report on a contemporary topic, seeking current statistics, or looking for information on careers.

8. Atlases. We usually think of an atlas mainly as a book of maps, but it contains interesting data on a number of subjects. The excellent *National Geographic Atlas of the World*, for example, lists some of the following topics in its table of contents: "Great Moments in Geography," "Global Statistics," and sections on population, temperatures, oceans, and place names. Following is a list of other widely used atlases.

Atlas of World Cultures
Atlas of World History
Atlas of World Wildlife
The Britannica Atlas
Collier's World Atlas and Gazetteer
Goode's World Atlas
Grosset World Atlas
Hammond Contemporary World Atlas
Hayden's Atlas of the Classical World
The International World Atlas from Rand McNally
The Times Atlas of the World
Webster's Atlas with ZIP Code Directory

9. Magazines. When you are writing about a current topic, magazines are an important resource. They often contain the latest information on a subject. Most libraries subscribe to many magazines and journals. Recent issues are generally kept on open racks, while back issues are stored in bound volumes or on microfilm. The librarian can tell you what periodicals your library collects and how to go about requesting the issue you need for your research.

The *Readers' Guide to Periodical Literature* is an invaluable aid when you are looking for articles on a particular topic. It is an index that lists the titles of articles, stories, and poems published during the preceding month in more than one hundred leading magazines. It is issued twice a month from September through June and once a month in July and August. An entire year's issues are bound in one hardcover volume at the end of the year. Articles are listed alphabetically under *subject* and *author* (and *titles* when necessary).

The following excerpt from the *Readers' Guide* illustrates how articles are listed:

Excerpt from the *Readers' Guide*

PARISH management. See Church management — "see" cross reference
PARK CITY, Utah
    Park City Utah. C. Pepper. Trav/Holiday 151:31 F '79
PARKER, Ann, and Neal, Avon
    Molas: dazzling folk art of the Cuna Indians. il Horizon — title of article
      22:60-4 Mr '79
PARKER, Dave
    Loudmouth and his loud bat. R. Blount. il por Sports Illus — name of magazine
      50:42-5 Ap 9 '79 *
PARKER, David M.
    Thoughts on wind wanes; excerpt from Ocean voyaging.
      Motor B & S 143:60+ Ap '79
PARKER, Olivia — volume number
    Clear Yankee eye. O. Edwards. il Sat R 6:46-7 Mr 3 '79 *
PARKER, Sanford S. and others — page reference
    Business roundup. See issues of Fortune
PARKER, Stewart
    Spokesong. Reviews
      N Y 12:85 Ap 2 '79 •
      New Yorker 55:53 Mr 26 '79 • — date of magazine
PARKER, Thomas Wendell
    Topographical and marine paintings in the Bostonian Society.
      il Antiques 115:522-33 Mr '79
PARKER, Tracey
    She sets sights on the Olympics. il pors Ebony 34:47-8+ F '79 * — illustrated article
PARKER-SPARROW, Bradley
    Public monies a solution to this musician's job needs. por
      Down Beat 46:10 Mr 22 '79
PARKER Pen Company. See Pens—Manufacture
PARKES, Joseph P.
    Ireland after England leaves. America 140:210-12 Mr 17 '79
PARKING meters — subject entry
    Is it such a sin to put another nickel in? P. Carlyle-Gordge.
      il Macleans 92:4 Ja 15 '79
PARKINSON, C. Northcote — author entry
    To the tables down at Guernsey. Sat R 6:57-8 Mr 31 '79
PARKINSON'S disease
    Parkinson's disease: search for better therapies. J. L. Marx.
      il Science 203:737-8 F 23 '79
PARKS, Lillian (Rogers)
    Her tales of White House life head for TV. G. Clifford. il
      pors People 11:26-7 Ja 29 '79 *
PARKS
    See also
    National parks and reserves
    Playgrounds — "see also" cross reference

Exercises Using Reference Works

A. Find information on one of the following subjects by using the general index of three different encyclopedias available in your school or public libraries. You may need to look under more than one subject heading. Write a brief report on the topic. At the end of your report tell which of the three encyclopedias was most useful. Give reasons for your choice.

The Middle Ages	Greek Mythology
The Globe Theatre	Aberdeen Angus Cattle
Ellis Island	The Metric System
The Roaring Twenties	The Structure of a Cell
The Opera	Great American Humorists
Television Networks	The Olympic Games
Volcanoes	Impressionist Painting

B. Using the dictionaries available in your library, write answers to the following questions. After each answer, write the title of the dictionary you used. If possible, try not to use the same dictionary more than once.

1. Define the word *crepuscular* and use it in a sentence.
2. What is the origin of the American word *gerrymander*?
3. List four synonyms for the word *product*.
4. List three antonyms for the word *delightful*.
5. List fifteen words that rhyme with *kind*.
6. Define the word *antediluvian*. Discuss its origin and use it in a sentence.
7. List three synonyms for the word *devote*. Define each one.
8. Define the word *nepotism* and use it in a sentence.
9. Give three different meanings for the word *mute*.
10. What is *Bushido*? Who uses it?
11. Define the slang term *skedaddle*. During what historical period did it become popular?
12. What is a synonym for the word *vortex*?
13. Define *discophile* and tell whether or not you are one.
14. Define the word *plover* and give its origins.
15. List three synonyms for the word *banish*. Define each one.

C. Use the current *World Almanac* to answer these questions:

1. When was the Smithsonian Institution established?
2. What is the principal form of religion in Japan?
3. What happened on May 4, 1886, in Chicago?
4. What team won the Stanley Cup in hockey last year?
5. Where are the following national parks located?

Bryce Canyon   Rocky Mountain
Everglades   Mammoth Cave
Yosemite   Acadia

6. What is the capital of Ethiopia? What is the country's official language?

7. Give the name and location of the world's highest waterfall.

8. In the election of 1844, Henry Clay was a candidate of what political party? How many electoral votes did he receive?

9. Which American magazine has the largest circulation?

10. Who won the Academy Award for Best Actor in 1963?

D. Use the *Readers' Guide* to answer the following:

1. Turn to the "Key to Abbreviations" in the *Readers' Guide* and write the meaning of the following symbols:

bibliog   v   Je   Mr   pub   abr   Jl
O   il   rev   no   bi-m   ed   Ja

2. List the titles of three articles on each of three subjects of current international importance. (List titles, authors, magazines, page numbers, and dates.)

3. Following the directions above, make a list of articles about a prominent person who interests you.

E. Using the special-purpose dictionaries, encyclopedias, and biographical and literary reference works noted in this chapter, find answers to the following questions. Write the name of the reference work you used after each answer.

1. Who are the authors of the following four passages and from what works are they taken?

"Hog butcher for the world, Tool maker, stacker of wheat, Player with railroads and the nation's freighthandler;…"

"I'm Nobody! Who are you?
Are you—Nobody—Too?"

"Before I built a wall I'd ask to know
What I was walling in or walling out."

"I must go down to the seas again to the lonely sea and sky,
And all I ask is a tall ship and a star to steer her by."

2. What reference works contain information on the following?

Susan B. Anthony   William Shakespeare
Carl Sandburg   Gerald R. Ford
Helen Keller   Clarence Darrow

3. What literary reference work includes a discussion of *Tom Sawyer?*

4. What are pelagic animals?

5. Name four works by the conductor-composer Leonard Bernstein.

6. In what year did the Russian author, Alexander I. Solzhenitsyn, win the Nobel Prize?

7. Who was Crispus Attucks, and what did he do?

8. What great American President lived at Monticello, and where is it located?

9. What is the longest river in your state?

10. Name the three goddesses known as The Fates in Greek mythology.

1. Libraries contain different materials and sources of information on every subject area. Learning to use the library properly is particularly important for research. It can also provide you with many enjoyable opportunities in reading.

2. Fiction books are arranged on the library shelves in alphabetical order, according to the author's last name.

3. Nonfiction books are shelved in categories and subcategories according to the Dewey Decimal System.

4. The card catalog holds alphabetically organized cards for every book in the library. A book may be listed on author, title, and subject cards.

5. Reference books are generally marked with an "R" and kept in a special section of the library. They include dictionaries, encyclopedias, almanacs, yearbooks, biographical and literary reference works, pamphlets, atlases, and magazines.

Applications in Other Subject Areas

Math. The following is a list of famous people in the history of mathematics:

Euclid	Archimedes
Pythagoras	Sir Isaac Newton

Go to the library and find at least five sources of information on the people in this list. Only one of your sources may be an encyclopedia article.

Computer Science. Many libraries, especially city and university libraries, are being equipped with computers. These computers help the library visitor locate books and other sources quickly. They may also provide information about the local community. Write to or visit a library that has such a system. Find out what information a visitor has access to. If you can, find out something about the program the library uses to store information.

Chapter 15

Study and Research Skills

In your high school classes, you will be asked to perform many varied and complex tasks. Tests, quizzes, reports, projects, exercises, compositions, experiments, speeches, research papers—all of these and more will be required of you. In addition, you may begin to have many outside interests and responsibilities that will take up a great deal of your time.

If you are to meet the demands of your high school years, it is important that you understand how to manage your time well. This includes learning how to study efficiently and productively, how to prepare for examinations, and how to balance the demands of school and outside activities. This chapter will help you to master these and many other skills.

Part 1 Understanding and Remembering Assignments

Following Directions

Before you begin an assignment, be sure you understand exactly what needs to be done. These guidelines will help.

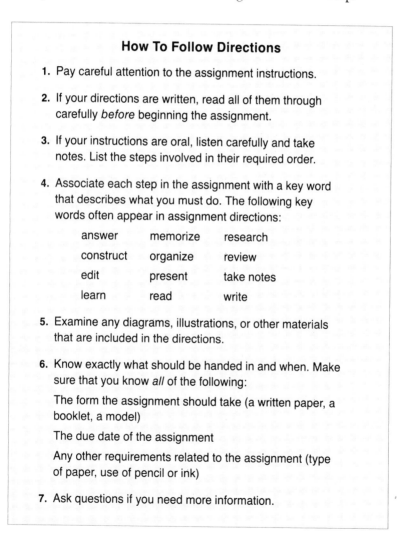

How To Follow Directions

1. Pay careful attention to the assignment instructions.

2. If your directions are written, read all of them through carefully *before* beginning the assignment.

3. If your instructions are oral, listen carefully and take notes. List the steps involved in their required order.

4. Associate each step in the assignment with a key word that describes what you must do. The following key words often appear in assignment directions:

answer	memorize	research
construct	organize	review
edit	present	take notes
learn	read	write

5. Examine any diagrams, illustrations, or other materials that are included in the directions.

6. Know exactly what should be handed in and when. Make sure that you know *all* of the following:

   The form the assignment should take (a written paper, a booklet, a model)

   The due date of the assignment

   Any other requirements related to the assignment (type of paper, use of pencil or ink)

7. Ask questions if you need more information.

Keeping an Assignment Notebook

Record each assignment in an assignment notebook. The pages of the notebook should resemble the one shown in the sample below. Include in the notebook the directions and due dates for every assignment. Make sure to copy down all oral instructions or suggestions.

	Class	Assignment	Date Assigned	Date Due
○	Algebra	1. Read chapter 9 2. Do even-numbered problems on p. 56 3. Use pencil	12/3	12/4
	English	Write personal essay a. Write controlling idea and outline b. Gather materials c. Write rough draft d. Revise rough draft e. Proofread revision	12/1 — — — — —	12/5 12/1 12/3 12/4 12/4
○				

Exercises Understanding and Remembering Assignments

A. Complete the following assignment:

1. Find an 8½″ x 11″ piece of unlined, white paper.

2. Write your name and class period in the upper left-hand corner of the paper.

3. Draw five vertical columns on the paper.

4. Choose any five-letter word.

5. Write the letters of the word at the top of your paper, one letter in each column.

6. On the left-hand side of the paper, make a list of any four categories of objects; these may be books, animals, games, or whatever you wish.

7. Think of two words that begin with each of the letters at the top of the page. The two words must also be examples of the categories listed on the left-hand side of the page. Example: *chrysanthemum* and *catnip* are the names of two plants that begin with the letter "c."

8. Write your answers in the appropriate spaces on the chart you made on your paper.

9. Do not complete steps 7 and 8.

10. Use pencil.

B. Start keeping an assignment notebook to record your school work. Follow the directions given in this chapter. Use the illustration on page 298 as a guide.

Part 2   Organizing Your Studies

Choosing a Study Area

Football should be played on a playing field. A show should be performed on a stage. Sculpting is best done in an art studio. In fact, any activity is more successful when carried out in the proper setting. Studying should also occur in an appropriate place: at school, at home, or in a public library. Whatever place you choose as your study area, make sure that it meets the following requirements:

1. It must be **quiet**. Distractions such as television, radio, or telephones should not interrupt your study sessions or interfere with your concentration.

2. It must be **well lighted**. Studying in poorly-lighted areas can strain your eyes and give you headaches.

3. It must be **cleared** and **neat**. You should have room in which to work with supplies in order. Clutter can be as much of a distraction as noise.

4. It must be **properly equipped**. Tools such as pencils, pens, paper, and a dictionary should always be close by so that you do not have to waste time searching for them.

Setting Goals

Usually you receive assignments that are due in one or two days. These are called **short-term** assignments. Other assignments may be due after several days, weeks, or even months. These are called **long-term** assignments. To complete each type of assignment by its due date, you must set goals. For a short-term assignment, simply decide at what time you will sit down and do the assignment completely. To set goals for a long-term assignment, you must first break the assignment down into manageable steps. Then plan time for completing each step. Look again at the sample page from an assignment notebook on page 298. Notice how the long-term assignment to write a personal essay has been broken down.

Keeping a Calendar

In addition to keeping an assignment notebook, it is a good idea to keep a calendar on which you record all of your outside activities and obligations. At the end of every school day, look over your assignment notebook. At this time, enter on your calendar all the work that you are required to do. Make sure that you avoid any conflicts with previously made commitments. For example, if you have a paper to revise for Friday and a family trip planned for Thursday evening, it would probably be a good idea to schedule your revision for Wednesday night. Keeping a study calendar will help you avoid conflicts and get your work done on time.

Monday	Tuesday	Wednesday	Thursday	Friday	Saturday	Sunday
Go to library Begin research	Staff meeting for yearbook	Research	Write article for yearbook	Pep rally and football game	Finish research	Organize notes
Begin rough draft	Rough draft	Study for Spanish test	Revise	Pizza at Sandburg's	Jazz fest all day	Make final copy

Here are some additional guidelines for organizing your studies:

Study Techniques

1. Try to allot two 20- to 40-minute study sessions per day, with at least a 15-minute break between sessions.
2. Set aside some study time each day for each class. If there is no homework one day, the time can be used for review or for a long-term project.
3. Tackle the hardest assignment first, while you are fresh.
4. Review all material within twenty-four hours of the time you first learn it. This will help you to remember what you've learned.
5. Try to learn even more about the material than what is required by the assignment. Know it so well that you can automatically recall and recite it.

Exercises Organizing Your Studies

A. Label each of the following as short-term or long-term assignments. Then break down each of the long-term assignments into short, manageable tasks.

1. Completing twenty problems from your math book, due for class tomorrow

2. Writing an analysis of a character in a short story, due in one week

3. Memorizing a French dialogue for tomorrow

4. Presenting a five-minute oral report on a topic of your choice, due in three days

5. Collecting a variety of local insects, displaying them, labeling them, and preparing an accompanying chart telling where each was caught. Due in two weeks.

B. Prepare an assignment notebook like the one shown on page 298. Then, enter the assignments in Exercise A in the notebook following the directions given in this chapter.

Part 3   The SQ3R Study Method

Have you ever read a chapter in a textbook, closed the book, and then forgotten most of what you'd just read? If so, you need a more effective approach to studying written material.

One way to get the most from what you read is to use the **SQ3R** method of study. This method consists of five steps: **S**urvey, **Q**uestion, **R**ead, **R**ecite, and **R**eview.

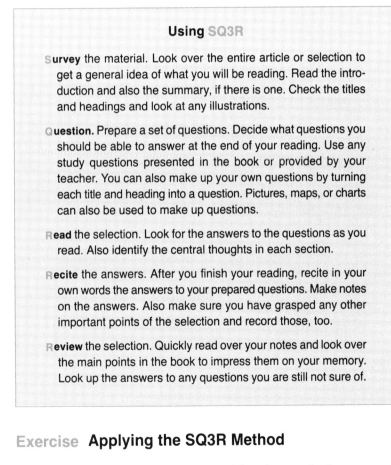

Using SQ3R

Survey the material. Look over the entire article or selection to get a general idea of what you will be reading. Read the introduction and also the summary, if there is one. Check the titles and headings and look at any illustrations.

Question. Prepare a set of questions. Decide what questions you should be able to answer at the end of your reading. Use any study questions presented in the book or provided by your teacher. You can also make up your own questions by turning each title and heading into a question. Pictures, maps, or charts can also be used to make up questions.

Read the selection. Look for the answers to the questions as you read. Also identify the central thoughts in each section.

Recite the answers. After you finish your reading, recite in your own words the answers to your prepared questions. Make notes on the answers. Also make sure you have grasped any other important points of the selection and record those, too.

Review the selection. Quickly read over your notes and look over the main points in the book to impress them on your memory. Look up the answers to any questions you are still not sure of.

Exercise   Applying the SQ3R Method

Apply the SQ3R method to Part 4 of this chapter, "Taking Notes." Be sure to complete all five steps.

Part 4   Taking Notes

Few people can remember all that they read and hear. Taking notes is one method of remedying this problem. Notes are useful as memory aids and as references or study guides for review.

When To Take Notes

Take notes on all important information that you encounter as a student. In class, take notes on material presented by the teacher, on useful comments or presentations made by other students, and on lab work or in-class reading. Do not try to copy down every word that is said in class. Instead, record only essential information. Note main ideas and important details such as definitions, dates, and the names of people, places, and events.

Listen for clues that indicate which points are most important. Such clues include key words and phrases such as *most importantly, for these reasons, first, for example,* and *to review.* Vocal signals, such as slowing down, repetition, or pausing for emphasis can also be indicators. Finally, the speaker's use of a blackboard or transparency almost always signals an important concept.

Outside of class, take notes on reading for all classes, and on all special projects, including interviews and other research work. Before taking notes on written material, skim the selection so that you will know which points are the most important and why. Take notes on these important points. Also record the answers to any questions that you prepared during SQ3R.

How To Take Notes

Use a separate notebook for each class, or a single, large notebook divided into class sections. Make sure that your name, the subject, and the date appear on each page.

When you take notes, do not worry about writing in complete sentences. Short phrases are perfectly acceptable, as long as you can make sense of them later. You might also want to take notes using a modified outline form, as shown on the next page.

Notes in Modified Outline Form

○

                    The Middle Ages
         Time period — approximately 1,000 years
              — Began at end of Roman Empire
              — Ended in the 1500's
         Social classes
              — Clergy (priests, monks, etc.)
              — Nobility (princes, dukes, earls, etc.)
              — Peasants (common people)

Notice that main ideas are placed to the left. Supporting or related details are indented beneath the main ideas to which they refer and are introduced by dashes. As with all notes, write in phrases, not in complete sentences.

If your notes are to be complete, you must be able to record information quickly. Develop a set of abbreviations and symbols to save time. The following chart offers some possibilities:

Possible Abbreviations and Symbols for Note-Taking

w/	with	*info.*	information
w/o	without	*def.*	definition
+	and	*	important
bef.	before	*amer.*	American
tho.	though	*hist.*	history

Exercises Taking Notes

A. Make a modified outline of Part 2 of this chapter, using abbreviations where appropriate.

B. Interview a friend or family member concerning some event or experience. Use a modified outline form and abbreviations.

Part 5 Adjusting Your Reading To Suit Your Purpose

You don't walk at the same pace all of the time. Sometimes you run, sometimes you walk briskly, and sometimes you stroll. Reading has similar paces. The way you read changes with the type of material and with your purpose for reading.

In-Depth Reading

When you need to absorb all of the material in a book, read it slowly and carefully, following the SQ3R method. It isn't enough to read every word; you must also understand what you read and be able to relate details to main ideas. Do this by looking for definitions, key words, headings or subheadings, and topic sentences. These are all sources for main ideas. Once you have identified a main idea, look for supporting details in the text.

Fast Reading

There are two kinds of fast reading, each with its own method and purpose. These are **skimming** and **scanning**.

Skimming involves moving your eyes quickly over a whole page or selection. Note titles, topic sentences, chapter headings, and highlighted words or phrases. Also examine the table of contents, the index, and any pictures or other graphic aids. Skim whenever you want to get a general idea of a book's content. For example, skim to decide whether a book might be a useful reference source. Also skim when you begin the SQ3R method.

Scanning involves moving your eyes quickly across a line or down a page to locate particular information. To train yourself to scan, choose a textbook that you use in one of your classes, place a folded paper or a card over the first line, and move the paper quickly down the page. Look for key words and phrases that indicate you are close to the information you need. When you locate such a clue, stop scanning and read slowly.

Exercise Adjusting Your Reading Rate

Follow these directions, one at a time. Do not read all of the directions first.

1. Skim the paragraph below to see what the topic is.
2. Read the paragraph in depth.
3. Scan to find the answers to the following questions:

> According to the ancients, what human activities were guided by Mars?
>
> In what country was Mars originally worshiped?
>
> Who were Romulus and Remus?
>
> Who was the Greek god of war?
>
> What is the meaning of the word *martial*?

The Roman God Mars

Mars was the god of war in Roman mythology. The ancient Romans gave Mars special importance because they considered him the father of Romulus and Remus, the legendary founders of Rome.

Origin. Originally, Mars was a god of farmland and fertility. The month of March, the beginning of the Roman growing season, was named for him. Since ancient times, the area enclosed by a bend in the Tiber River in Rome has been called the Field of Mars. The early Romans dedicated this section of land to Mars because of its fertility.

Mars, God of War. Mars became the god of war after the Romans came into contact with Greek culture. They gave him many characteristics of the Greek god of war, **Ares**. In time, the Romans associated Mars principally with war. Before going into battle, Roman troops offered sacrifices to him. After a victory, they gave Mars a share of their spoils. The word *martial*, which means *warlike*, is based on his name. The planet Mars is named for him.

—*World Book Encyclopedia*

Part 6 Using Graphic Aids

Sometimes information is presented in the form of pictures, charts, tables, diagrams, maps, and graphs. Such materials are called **graphic aids**. The following chart lists the most common graphic aids and presents guidelines for studying them.

Common Graphic Aids		
Type	**Purpose**	**Study Tips**
Pictures **Sketches** **Diagrams**	To illustrate text To show the parts or functions of the subject	Read caption or title Relate picture, sketch, or diagram to text Pay attention to labels of parts
Maps	To display geographical areas or geographical distribution	Read caption or title to determine the purpose of the map Look for the *legend* or *key* (list of symbols and abbreviations; indication of *scale*)
Tables **Charts**	To list information To compare information	Read caption or title Check key, if there is one, to determine how information is organized
Graphs	To show relationships between groups or sets To show development over time	Read caption or title Read all labels of parts of the graph Determine what relationship is being shown between what groups or sets

Reading Tables and Charts

Tables and **charts** provide a simple way of presenting large amounts of information. Most tables present information in numerical form and are called **statistical tables**. Study the chart shown below. What information does it provide?

American College Graduates 1900 — 1980

Year	Total (in thousands)	Male (in thousands)	Female (in thousands)
1980	999	526	473
1970	827	484	343
1960	389	253	136
1950	432	329	103
1940	187	110	77
1930	122	74	49
1920	49	32	17
1910	37	29	8
1900	27	22	5

(Figures include bachelor's and first professional degrees. Because of rounding, details may not add up to totals. Source: U.S. Department of Education.)

Every table presents information about one or more subjects called **variables**. These subjects are called variables because the numbers associated with them vary. The variables in the above table include *year, total, male,* and *female*. Whenever you read a table, make sure that you identify the variables presented. Then, determine what information is being presented about them.

Reading Graphs

Graphs are used to show relationships between sets of variables. To understand a graph, read the title and the key to symbols and abbreviations. Then, determine what variables are being presented by the graph and how these are related.

There are four major types of graphs: circle graphs, bar graphs, picture graphs, and line graphs.

Circle graphs use the circle shape to show relationships. The circle itself represents 100%, or the whole, of something. The sections within the circle graph represent parts of the whole.

A Circle Graph

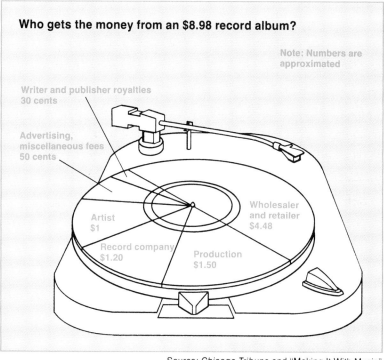

Who gets the money from an $8.98 record album?

Note: Numbers are approximated

Writer and publisher royalties 30 cents

Advertising, miscellaneous fees 50 cents

Artist $1

Record company $1.20

Production $1.50

Wholesaler and retailer $4.48

Source: *Chicago Tribune* and "Making It With Music" by Kenny Rogers and Len Epand

Bar graphs show a relationship between two variables. One variable is usually expressed in numbers. The other variable is usually expressed in words. One of the variables is listed horizontally, and the other is listed vertically. A bar extends from the variable that is expressed in words. By drawing an imaginary line along the side of the bar, you can determine the amount of the variable that is expressed in words. Look at the bar graph example at the top of the next page.

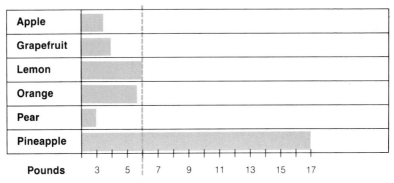

Largest Recorded Fruits

Apple	
Grapefruit	
Lemon	
Orange	
Pear	
Pineapple	

Pounds 3 5 7 9 11 13 15 17

Picture graphs are similar to bar graphs except that they use symbols to represent information instead of bars. Normally, the key explains the meaning of the pictured symbols.

Population Density of the Continents*

Estimated number of persons on each continent in 1983

= 10 people per square mile

Asia
166 per sq. mi. (64 per km²)

Europe
166 per sq. mi. (64 per km²)

Africa
44 per sq. mi. (17 per km²)

North America
41 per sq. mi. (16 per km²)

South America
36 per sq. mi. (14 per km²)

Australia
5 per sq. mi. (2 per km²)

*Antarctica has no permanent population.

Source: UN Statistical Office.

Line graphs are also used to show how two variables are related. Such graphs show a relationship over a period of time or a trend in a certain direction. By following the direction of the

line, you can determine a pattern of change. By drawing imaginary lines horizontally and vertically from a particular point on
the line, you can find out specific information.

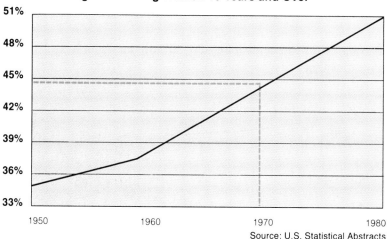

Percentage of Working Women 16 Years and Over

Source: U.S. Statistical Abstracts

Exercises Using Graphic Aids

Answer the following questions by referring to the preceding
graphic aids.

1. How many women graduated from college in America in the
year 1980?
2. Between what two dates did the number of college graduates *decrease*?
3. How much of the cost of an average album is earned by the
recording artist?
4. Who gets the most money from the sale of a record album?
5. Approximately how heavy was the heaviest lemon ever
grown?
6. What are the two variables shown on the bar graph?
7. What does the symbol ▪ represent in the picture graph?
8. Which continents have the most people per square mile?
What continent has the fewest?

9. What was the approximate increase in the percentage of working women between the years 1960 and 1970?

10. What decade showed the slowest rise in the percentage of working women?

B. Study the weather map given below. It provides a summary of the present weather situation and allows the reader to make predictions. After you familiarize yourself with the symbols, answer the questions that follow.

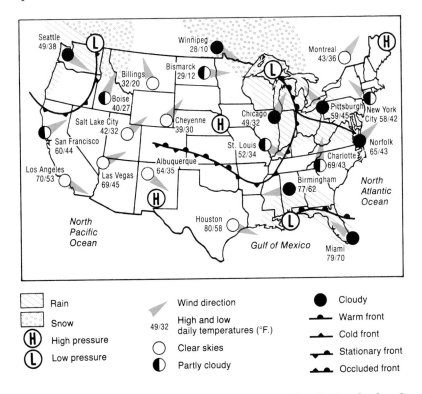

1. What western city is experiencing completely cloudy skies?

2. Is Birmingham, Alabama, likely to become warmer or colder in the next day or two?

3. In what direction is the wind blowing in Bismarck, North Dakota?

4. What American cities on the map are experiencing rain?

5. In what Canadian city shown on the map is it snowing?

C. Construct a graph to display the following information. You may choose any type of graph you wish.

Of the eight major religions of the world, Christianity is the largest, with approximately 950,000,000 members. Islam has approximately 538,000,000 adherents, followed closely by Hinduism, with 519,000,000. In addition, the following religions all have members numbering in the millions: Buddhism (245,000,000), Confucianism (176,000,000), Shinto (61,000,000), Taoism (29,000,000) and Judaism (15,000,000). These numbers are rounded to the nearest million.

Part 7   Taking Tests

Because tests are one of the primary tools employed by teachers for evaluation and grading, students are often nervous about taking them. To combat this nervousness and to increase your test scores, adopt the attitude that tests are really just another type of assignment that you can learn to prepare yourself for. Then complete the following three steps:

1. Learn how to prepare yourself mentally and physically for taking tests.
2. Learn how to study for tests.
3. Learn strategies for taking tests.

Preparing Yourself for Tests

Always get a good night's sleep and eat properly before tests. Your study plans should allow sufficient time for review so that you can avoid last-minute, late-night cramming. Just prior to taking a test, put yourself in a confident and relaxed state of mind. Remember that once you actually begin taking a test, it is no longer possible for you to prepare more thoroughly or do more studying. Worry about insufficient preparation will only detract from your concentration on the test questions and decrease your chances of doing well.

Studying for Tests

The following guidelines will help you study for tests:

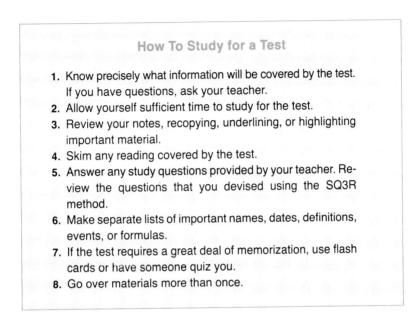

How To Study for a Test

1. Know precisely what information will be covered by the test. If you have questions, ask your teacher.
2. Allow yourself sufficient time to study for the test.
3. Review your notes, recopying, underlining, or highlighting important material.
4. Skim any reading covered by the test.
5. Answer any study questions provided by your teacher. Review the questions that you devised using the SQ3R method.
6. Make separate lists of important names, dates, definitions, events, or formulas.
7. If the test requires a great deal of memorization, use flash cards or have someone quiz you.
8. Go over materials more than once.

Taking the Test

How you take a test is just as important as how you prepare for it. The following techniques will help you use your time wisely.

1. Survey the test. Look it over completely to see what types of questions are included and how long the test is.

2. Plan your time. Read all of the directions and decide in what order you will begin answering questions. Also decide how much time you will need for each portion of the test. Allow more time for sections that require planning, such as essay questions.

3. Read each test item carefully. Make sure you understand the questions and directions completely. If there are several essay questions, read all of them before you begin so that you don't repeat yourself in several answers. Also make sure you are following the directions. For example, are you supposed to answer only one of the essay questions or all of them? Where answers are provided, read through all the choices before deciding on the correct one.

4. Save time at the end to review the test. Scan to make sure you have not accidentally omitted any answers. Try to answer those questions you skipped. Reread any answers you are unsure of. Do not change answers too often, however. Your first ideas are usually the correct ones.

The following pages contain more specific strategies for different types of test questions.

Applying Test-Taking Strategies

There are two main types of tests. One type requires you to identify correct answers or fill in blanks in statements that are given on the test. Tests of this type are called **objective examinations** and may consist of true/false, multiple choice, matching, or completion questions. The second type requires answers in complete sentences. Such tests include short answer and essay tests.

Objective Examinations

When taking objective tests, begin by answering all of the questions that you know readily. Mark difficult questions and return to them when you have finished the rest of the test. Watch for information supplied in one question that suggests the answer to another. If a question is very difficult, restate it in your own words before answering. If you cannot determine the correct answer, go ahead and guess. If you have already eliminated most of the answers provided, your chances of guessing the correct answer are greatly increased.

The following chart describes some specific types of objective tests. Read each description and study the guidelines for approaching each type.

Objective Examinations

Description	Strategies
TRUE/FALSE The student is given a statement and asked to tell whether the statement is true or false.	1. Remember that, if any part of a statement is false, the whole statement is false. 2. Words like *all, always, only,* and *never,* often appear in false statements. 3. Words like *generally, probably, some, usually, often,* and *most* often appear in true statements.
MATCHING The student is asked to match items in one column with corresponding items in a second column.	1. Check the directions to see if each item is used only once and if some are not used. 2. Read all items in both columns before starting. 3. Match those you know first. 4. Cross out items as you use them.
MULTIPLE CHOICE The student is asked to choose the *best* answer among a group of answers provided on the test.	1. Read all choices before answering. 2. Eliminate incorrect answers first. 3. Choose the answer that is most complete or accurate. 4. Pay particular attention to choices such as *none of the above* or *all of the above.*
COMPLETION The student is asked to fill in a gap in a statement provided on the exam.	1. Make sure that your answer fits grammatically into the space provided. 2. If several words are needed to make logical sense, write in all of them. 3. Write legibly, using proper spelling, grammar, punctuation, and capitalization.
ANALOGIES The student is given a related pair of words and is asked to select a second pair of words that expresses a similar relationship.	1. Determine the exact relationship between the first two words. 2. State this relationship as clearly as you can to yourself. 3. Create a sentence, using the first two words, that shows the relationship between these words. 4. Insert the paired answers into your sentence. 5. Choose the paired answer that best fits your sentence.

Amphibians live only in water. _____*false*_____

Newts are amphibians. _____*true*_____

1. simile _____
2. personification _____
3. metaphor _____
4. paradox _____

A. I'm so happy I could cry.
B. I'm as hungry as a horse.
C. The sun smiled down on us all.
D. The road was a ribbon of moonlight.

Mark Twain was born
  a. on the banks of the Mississippi
  b. in Hannibal, Missouri
  c. in Florida, Missouri
  d. none of the above

INCORRECT: When a ball is hit parallel to the ground, this hit is called _____*Line Drive*_____.

CORRECT: When a ball is hit parallel to the ground, this hit is called _____*a line drive*_____.

COLT: HORSE : : **(a)** dachshund : dog
(b) herd : buffalo   **(c)** fawn : deer

A *dachshund* is a young *dog* .

A *herd* is a young *buffalo* .

✳ A *fawn* is a young *deer* .

Short Answer Examinations

Always respond to short answer questions in complete sentences. Write legibly, paying close attention to grammar, spelling, punctuation, and capitalization.

> When, where, and by whom was paper invented?
>
> *Paper was invented in China by Ts'ai Lun in A.D. 105.*

Essay Examinations

Whenever you write an essay follow these guidelines:

Writing Essay Tests

Pre-Writing

1. Read the question carefully. Circle informational verbs such as *compare, prove, explain, interpret,* or *summarize.*
2. Know precisely what information the essay should cover.
3. If the essay question is divided into parts, organize your essay into corresponding sections.
4. Make an outline of major points and supporting details.
5. Write a statement of the main idea that includes a brief restatement of the essay question, and place this in the first paragraph.

Writing

Pay attention to all aspects of good writing, including topic sentences, transitions, and concluding sentences.

Revision

Normally, one does not have time to do complete revisions of essay exams. However, make sure that you leave yourself enough time to proofread thoroughly.

Exercises **Taking Tests**

A. Answer the following questions:

1. In addition to studying and applying test strategies, students who prepare well for tests _____ and _____ properly before tests.

2. Which of the following is not a type of objective test?
   a. multiple choice
   b. matching
   c. completion
   d. true/false
   e. none of the above

3. Match the following types of objective tests with their corresponding strategies:

   A. True/False   1. Make sure your answer fits grammatically into the space provided.

   B. Multiple Choice   2. Read all items in both columns before starting.

   C. Completion   3. Remember that, if any part of a statement is not true, the entire statement is not true.

   D. Matching   4. Choose the most complete or accurate of the answers provided.

B. Write a one-paragraph essay explaining the importance of providing wheelchair ramps in all public buildings. Be sure to use your own words, give reasons or examples to support your topic sentence, and follow the strategies outlined in this section. Allow yourself exactly 20 minutes to write this paragraph.

1. Learning good study techniques can help you approach any type of task in a logical, organized manner.

2. When you are given an assignment, record directions and other important information carefully. Schedule a time to complete the assignment and follow directions precisely.

3. When studying printed materials, use the SQ3R Method of study (**S**urvey, **Q**uestion, **R**ead, **R**ecite, **R**eview). Take notes using short phrases or a modified outline.

4. Adjust your reading speed to the materials you are studying and to the purpose for which you are reading.

5. Graphic aids include pictures, sketches, diagrams, maps, tables, charts, and graphs. Know how to interpret them.

6. Prepare yourself physically and mentally for every test. Always review the test-taking strategies described in this chapter.

Applications in Other Subject Areas

Speech / All Subjects. Collect three graphs from textbooks in other classes. Attach each one to a separate piece of lined notebook paper. Under each graph, state the following:

   a. The variables that are listed by the graph.

   b. A generalization or trend illustrated by the graph.

Prepare a short talk explaining the graph to your class.

All Subjects. Pick a class you are now taking in which you must regularly take notes. Open your notebook from that class to the most recent unit of study and skim over the last two or three pages of notes. Copy these over, using a modified outline form. Use abbreviations for commonly occurring words.

Chapter 16

Letters, Forms, and Applications

Every day, over two hundred million pieces of first-class mail are handled by the post office. People are mailing friendly notes, invitations, cards, business letters, and many other kinds of communication. In addition, they are reading and filling out hundreds of thousands of forms as they apply for jobs, request library cards, complete questionnaires, and order from catalogs. Clearly, writing has its uses outside of reports and homework assignments!

Because writing letters and completing forms are such common, everyday tasks, you probably give them little thought. Yet each requires special skills and knowledge that are important to understand. Such skills may even determine whether or not you get a particular job or are accepted at a college. This chapter will provide you with some guidelines for these special types of writing, and will show you how to apply your skills in getting a part-time job.

Part 1 Addressing the Envelope

Let's start with the simplest part of letter-writing first—the envelope. Probably the worst thing that could happen to a letter you have painstakingly written is that it is not delivered. Hundreds of thousands of letters end up in the Dead Letter Office in Washington, D.C. The usual problem is an incorrect address, which can be easily avoided. Double-check to be certain you have not transposed any numbers in the address. Do not forget the ZIP code. This is a five-digit code that identifies a small area within a city or state, and enables the post office to sort mail much more efficiently and rapidly. The ZIP should immediately follow the state in addresses. If you do not know the ZIP, and cannot find it in your telephone directory, call your post office. They have a complete ZIP code listing for every community in the United States and will be happy to help you.

Always put your return address on the envelope.

Ms. Betty Sergeant
1429 Oakridge Road
Ft. Worth TX 76135

                    Mr. Larry Spenser
                    341 Queen Avenue
                    Yakima WA 98902

Envelopes come in many different sizes and colors. The two most-used sizes are 9½″ x 4″ and 6½″ x 3½″. When sending a business letter, you should always use a white 9½″ x 4″ envelope.

If you are writing a specific person or department within a large company, you will use four lines for the address.

Ms. Betty Sergeant
1429 Oakridge Road
Ft. Worth TX 76135

Mr. Larry Spenser
A + G Electronics Company.
341 Queen Avenue
Yakima WA 98902

When addressing the small, square envelope that is usually included with invitations or note cards, you may put your return address on the flap on the back of the envelope, with the receiver's name and address centered on the front.

Mr. Larry Spenser
341 Queen Avenue
Yakima WA 98902

Ms. Betty Sergeant
1429 Oakridge Road
Ft. Worth TX
76135

Caution: Be sure to check the back on any envelope before addressing it. You may have it upside down.

Did you notice the abbreviations of the names of states on the examples? These may be used in addressing envelopes, but you *must* use the ZIP code with them. When you use these abbreviations, you do not need to separate the city and state with a comma. However, if you do not use these abbreviations, you must place a comma between the city and state.

Mr. Larry Spenser
341 Queen Avenue
Yakima WA 98902

Mr. Larry Spenser
341 Queen Avenue
Yakima, Washington 98902

Abbreviations of State Names

Alabama	AL	Montana	MT
Alaska	AK	Nebraska	NE
Arizona	AZ	Nevada	NV
Arkansas	AR	New Hampshire	NH
American Samoa	AS	New Jersey	NJ
California	CA	New Mexico	NM
Canal Zone	CZ	New York	NY
Colorado	CO	North Carolina	NC
Connecticut	CT	North Dakota	ND
Delaware	DE	Ohio	OH
District of Columbia	DC	Oklahoma	OK
Florida	FL	Oregon	OR
Georgia	GA	Pennsylvania	PA
Guam	GU	Puerto Rico	PR
Hawaii	HI	Rhode Island	RI
Idaho	ID	South Carolina	SC
Illinois	IL	South Dakota	SD
Indiana	IN	Tennessee	TN
Iowa	IA	Trust Territories	TT
Kansas	KS	Texas	TX
Kentucky	KY	Utah	UT
Louisiana	LA	Vermont	VT
Maine	ME	Virginia	VA
Maryland	MD	Virgin Islands	VI
Massachusetts	MA	Washington	WA
Michigan	MI	West Virginia	WV
Minnesota	MN	Wisconsin	WI
Mississippi	MS	Wyoming	WY
Missouri	MO		

Addressing Envelopes

A. Put each of the addresses below in proper three or four-line form as it should appear on an envelope. Capitalize, abbreviate, and punctuate correctly.

1. 462 zane avenue philadelphia pennsylvania 19111 mrs. jill erikson

2. washington d c 20013 national geographic society melvin m payne post office box 2895

3. 111 west washington street chicago illinois 60602 chicago title insurance company

4. salt lake city utah 84104 appliance department 1133 glendale drive gibson's discount center

5. mr. john johnson oklahoma city oklahoma 1462 longridge road 73115

B. Draw four "envelopes" on plain paper. Three of the envelopes should measure 9½″ × 4″, and one should measure 5″ × 5″. Now pick three of the choices below and with the aid of a telephone directory, write the addresses correctly on the envelopes. Address the 5″ × 5″ envelope to your best friend. Do not forget to include your return address.

1. Anyone whose last name is Smith

2. The service department of an automobile agency

3. Your favorite disc jockey

4. An employment agency

5. The sportswear department of a department store

6. A television station

Now that you are familiar with addressing envelopes, you are ready to study the different types of letters to put inside them. The form for an envelope does not change; it is the same for any letter.

Part 2   Writing Informal Notes

Whenever you have written a short letter thanking a relative for a gift or expressing your appreciation for a weekend visit, you have used a form of letter known as an **informal note**.

These notes all have one thing in common. They are short. They could be referred to as "people-pleasers" because they definitely impress the receiver. You might have been less than completely delighted with the complete dental-care kit your aunt and uncle sent you for Christmas, but they will be pleased to receive your letter of thanks.

Informal notes have a definite form:

Dear Uncle Fred and Aunt Fran,

You never told me you had ESP—how else could you have known I've been craving that particular album? It's great! I've played it at least twenty times, and Mom says that next time you send an album to me, she'd appreciate your enclosing a pair of earplugs for her.

Thanks so much for the perfect gift. I hope you can visit sometime and hear it for yourselves—before I wear it out!

Love,
Jennie

Labels: Date — August 30, 1985; Salutation; Body; Closing; Signature

The first part of the form of an informal note is the **date**. Remember to leave a margin between the end of the date and the right side of the paper.

The second item is the **salutation**. This simply addresses the person to whom you are writing. Always use a comma after the salutation. Next is the **body** of the letter, or the message. The **closing** can be one of many, depending on the relationship. *Sincerely, Affectionately, Lovingly, Happily*, or *Good luck* are some of the choices. If the closing is more than one word, capitalize only the first word. Always use a comma after the closing.

As you can see, a casual language style is fine. Write naturally, the way you would normally speak to the person to whom you are writing.

There are other varieties of the informal note. Apologies, congratulations, invitations, and R.S.V.P.'s are the most common. Of these, only the R.S.V.P. might require some explanation.

July 27, 1985

Dear Jim,
  You are invited to attend my birthday dinner on August 16. It will be held at the Sundance Room of the Hotel Towers at 7:30 p.m.
    I'm looking forward to seeing you.
            Sincerely,
            Mary Barnes
R.S.V.P.

R.S.V.P. is an abbreviation for a French phrase meaning "please respond." It is necessary for the sender to have an exact count of the attending guests before the party. Unless you want to appear "uninformed," you must reply. You write a brief note stating your intention to attend or not.

August 1, 1985

Dear Mary,
    I would love to attend your birthday dinner, but will be unable to as we are planning a vacation and will be out of town on August 16.
    Have a very happy birthday!

Sincerely,
Jim Harris

August 1, 1985

Dear Mary,
    Thank you so much for the invitation to your birthday dinner. I'd be delighted to attend.

Sincerely,
Jim Harris

Writing Informal Notes

Choose two of the following and write the appropriate notes on plain paper. On the back draw an envelope for each and address it correctly.

1. Write a note thanking a friend for the fantastic party he gave last Saturday.

2. Write to your friend's parents, apologizing for dropping a full bowl of punch on their new white carpet.

3. Write a note of congratulation to a friend who has moved from your neighborhood. You have just learned that he or she has won a cash prize in a contest. You determine the contest.

4. Write a note thanking a relative for something. The only problem is that you have no idea what the item is.

5. Write an invitation to a party, using R.S.V.P. Exchange your invitation with another student and write a reply.

6. Write a note to a friend's mother or father for something very nice the person did for you. You decide the reason.

7. Write a note to a cheerleader at your school, apologizing for tackling her during the last game.

8. Write a note congratulating your dog for passing obedience school.

Part 3 Writing Friendly Letters

These letters seem to be going down in popularity while long-distance telephone bills are going up. Haven't you tearfully said goodbye to a friend, promising to write, and then put it off until you didn't know what to write or where to start? It happens to everyone, and it's too bad. Through this type of letter, friendships endure over many years and more miles. This should be an easy letter to write, as you're communicating with someone you know very well—someone who has shared many experiences with you. Just keep sharing experiences—only now through letters. The language is informal, just as you would speak to the person.

There is a little more involved in the form of a friendly letter than in informal notes. Below is an example. Once you learn the parts of a friendly letter, you'll have to concentrate only on writing the body of the letter itself.

Heading

162 New Road
Raleigh, North Carolina 27608
July 16, 1985

Salutation

Dear Jess,

Body

Love, Closing

Jill Signature

The **heading** is written in three lines. The first line consists of your street address. The second line contains the city, state and ZIP. The third line is the date of the letter. Don't abbreviate on the date line.

The **salutation** can be casual in a friendly letter. The only two rules are to capitalize the first word and any proper nouns, and to use a comma following the salutation.

Dear Sue,   *Hi Slim,*
Howdy Pete,   *Hello Mark,*

The **closing** is usually kept simple: *Love, Sincerely, Always,* etc. The first word is the only one capitalized. You can use your originality and the closeness of the friendship for something more appropriate for the particular person to whom you are writing.

Lovingly yours,   *Still waiting,*
Always here,   *Frustrated,*

The most important part of any letter is the **body**. Let's hope you haven't received or been guilty of sending such an empty letter as the following:

---

162 New Road
Raleigh NC 27608
July 16, 1985

Dear Jess,

    Your letter arrived yesterday and I'm happy to hear about all the great things you've been doing.
    As usual, things around here aren't very exciting. The weather's been hot for so long I can't remember what "cool" means.
    Everyone here says to say "hi."
    There's not much more to write. Wish you were here so we could have a good talk. Write soon.

Love,

Jill

All that is needed to turn dull paragraphs into interesting ones is detail. If the person to whom you are writing were with you, what would you say? Here are a few points to remember when writing a friendly letter:

1. Make comments on the letter you have received.
2. Avoid the constant use of *I*.
3. Write one or two detailed paragraphs regarding events and people. They will be much more interesting than a series of one-sentence statements.
4. Ask questions. Then the person has something to write to you about.

With a little more time and thought, Jill might have written two opening paragraphs like this:

Maybe this letter should be written in special ink so you can read it underwater—don't you ever get waterlogged? From the sound of things you're either in training for the Olympics or trying to get a role in the next "Jaws." You're way out of my class now—unless they've started giving medals for floating in a tube. Couldn't you manage to compete in a meet around here?

Things here are not too exciting—and that's an understatement! It's been so hot for so long that everyone's dragging. I've been lying around the yard or the house most of the time. But you know my Mom—if I'm not "doing something," I can't possibly be happy. So she keeps finding things for me to "do." Clean out your closet. Water the lawn. Straighten your dresser. Water the lawn! Run to the store. Water the lawn! I'm beginning to feel as if I've got a hose growing out of my right arm! The lawn's so soaked now we could grow rice! Next summer a job is a necessity—only with my luck it would probably be watering lawns.

Detail, along with conversational writing, can make a letter come to life. Choose one of the statements in Jill's letter on page 331 and rewrite it in a detailed paragraph. Make it interesting. Be prepared to exchange your paragraph with a classmate, or read it aloud to the class.

Writing Friendly Letters

One of your best friends has moved out of the city. Write a friendly letter detailing three events that have taken place since he or she left. You can use events that have actually happened or choose from the list below.

1. Your school team lost a close game for the state basketball championship.

2. A good friend gave you a surprise birthday party.

3. You are certain that someone tried to break into your house when your parents were out.

4. Your new puppy is methodically eating his way through the house—couch, chairs, carpets, shoes.

5. You tried waterskiing (or another sport) for the first time. The results were hilarious.

6. Your class wants to go to Washington, D.C. You are on a committee to raise funds for the trip.

Part 4   Writing Business Letters

Over ten thousand business letters are processed for each friendly letter or informal note that is written. With odds like that, the business letter has to be an important letter to master. The term *business* means that the letters have a definite purpose to accomplish, not that they are written only by and for business firms.

There are two main skills you need to master in order to write an effective business letter: (1) Use the proper form. (2) Be brief and specific.

Using the Proper Form

There are two basic forms for business letters: **block form** and **modified block form**.

Heading

416 Paxton Road
Rochester, New York 14617
April 23, 1985

Inside Address

Sales Department
Stereophonics, Inc.
231 Garrison
Boston, Massachusetts 02116

Salutation

Ladies and Gentlemen:

_____
_____
_____   Body
_____
_____
_____

Sincerely,   Closing

José Martinez

José Martinez   Signature

Note: Always use plain white 8½″ x 11″ paper for business letters, whether you handwrite or type them.

Heading

416 Paxton Road
Rochester, New York 14617
April 23, 1985

Inside Address

Sales Department
Stereophonics, Inc.
231 Garrison
Boston, Massachusetts 02116

Salutation

Dear Sir or Madam:

_____

_____

_____ Body

_____

_____

_____

Sincerely,   Closing

José Martinez

José Martinez   Signature

You are already familiar with the heading of a letter. It is the same as that used for writing friendly letters.

The one section that has been added is the **inside address**. It is important to have the name and address of the person or department to whom you are writing on the face of the letter. Occasionally a letter is opened by mistake and the envelope misplaced; if this happens, the name and address are still clearly visible. The inside address is usually four lines on a business letter, as you will be writing to a specific person or department within a company. Leave a space between the inside address and the salutation.

The salutation varies, depending upon the first line of the inside address. If you are writing to a company or department within a company, use one of the following:

```
Dear Sir or Madam:
Ladies and Gentlemen:
```

If you are writing to a particular person, but do not know his or her name (such as the Personnel Manager, president, or General Manager), you should use *Dear Sir or Madam*:

The form for someone whose name you know is quite simple:

```
Dear Mr. Brown:
Dear Ms. Allred:
Dear Miss Allred:
Dear Mrs. Allred:
```

Capitalize only the first word and any proper nouns in the salutation, and always follow the salutation with a colon. Leave a space between the salutation and the body of the letter and between the body of the letter and the closing. Capitalize only the first word of the closing, and always follow the closing with a comma.

```
Sincerely,
Very truly yours,
Respectfully yours,
```

Type or print your name four spaces below the closing, and write your signature in the space between. Typing or printing your name makes it legible if you have a fancy but illegible signature.

Make a Copy. Whenever you write a business letter, make a carbon copy or photocopy for yourself. Then you will know just what you wrote or ordered in case you do not receive an immediate reply. If you use carbon paper, first place a piece of plain paper on your desk. Then place a sheet of carbon paper on top of it. The "shiny" or carbon side of the paper should be face down. Now place another piece of plain paper on top and you are ready to write. To avoid slippage, you can use a paper clip to hold the three pieces together. When you write, be certain you use the type of carbon paper that is made for pen or pencil. Typewriter keys exert much more pressure on the carbon paper than a person's hand.

Fold the Letter Correctly. Folding a business letter correctly is sometimes a problem. You want only two folds in your paper when using a standard 9½″ x 4″ envelope. Starting at the bottom of the paper, fold it into thirds toward the top. Usually you will find that after the first fold is completed, only the inside address and heading will be visible to you. When properly folded, the letter will easily fit into the envelope, and can readily be taken out by the receiver.

First Fold	Second Fold	Complete

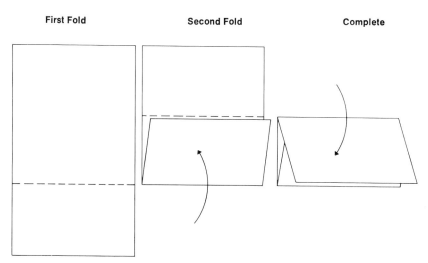

A. Below is an example of a business letter in modified block form. There are errors in capitalization, punctuation, and spacing. Correct the errors by rewriting the letter on a plain sheet of paper.

Jan. 14, 1985
1452 Balboa Drive
Pensacola Florida, 32506

General supply Company
sales mgr.
462 acacia avenue
Palo Alto Calif. 94306

Dear Sir or Madam,

    Regarding the order I placed with you on
December 15, ———————————————————————
——————————————————————————————————
——————————————————————————————————
——————————————————————————————————
——————————————————————————————————
——————————————————————————————————

Very Truly Yours

Thomas A. O'Leary
Thomas A. O'Leary

B. Using correct form, write a letter of your own with a local company as the addressee. You do not have to write the body of the letter.

Being Brief and Specific

When you write a business letter you include only what is absolutely necessary. State the purpose of the letter and then stop. Use only those details that are vital to accomplish your purpose.

1942 Griffin Road
Indianapolis, Indiana 46227
June 14, 1985

West Hills Pro Shop
571 Moon Clinton Road
Coraopolis, Pennsylvania 15108

Dear Sir or Madam:

Please send me the following items which appeared in your advertisement in the June issue of Travel and Leisure.

1 pr.	Foot-Joy Golf Shoes	Size 11D	Black	$ 48.00
2	Canvas Sunday Bags		@$19.00	38.00
1	Model M-20 Lynx Putter			25.00
			Total	$111.00

Enclosed is a money order for $111.00. The advertisement states that prices include postage and insurance.

Yours truly,

Scott Andersen

Scott Andersen

Whenever you place an order, be sure you have a complete description or a model number. Include sizes, colors, and the number of items desired. Check the charge for postage. In some instances the buyer will pay for postage and this amount must be included with the order. Also check instructions about sales tax. Any errors on your part will result in a delay in delivery, or in receiving unwanted merchandise. It is much easier to double-check an order than to return merchandise. Keep a carbon copy in case any mix-ups occur.

Exercise Being Brief and Specific

Clip an advertisement from a magazine, or choose one of the groups below and write an order letter. Total the order and add any postage that is necessary. On the back of the order draw an envelope and address it correctly.

1. Columbia House, 1400 North Fruitridge Ave., Terre Haute, Indiana 47808

> 1 8-track cartridge No. JCA34860 *Chicago XI* $7.98
> 1 record No. RS-2-4200 *BeeGees Greatest* $6.98
> 1 two-record set No. 2HS3350 *Tusk* $15.98
> Postage $.75

2. Walter Drake & Sons, 4085 Drake Building, Colorado Springs, Colorado 80940—Advertisement in August issue of *Better Homes and Gardens*

> No. S717—two sets of 1,000 name labels @ $1.00 per set
> No. S854—one set of personalized pencils @ $.89 per set
> No. S6066—two full-page magnifiers @ $1.98 each
> Postage and handling—$.40

3. Sea Horses, Box 342096, Coral Gables, Florida 33134—Advertisement in July issue of *Boy's Life*

> 3 live sea horse kits @ $ 2.98
> 2 custom aquariums @ $ 5.98
> 1 deluxe aquarium $10.95

Air mail postage paid by advertiser—live delivery guaranteed

Types of Business Letters

1. Requests for Information. Perhaps you have been thinking about buying some stereo equipment. You could write a business letter requesting information regarding additional speakers.

2. Letters of Order. You would order your stereo equipment through a business letter if you were unable to purchase it locally. See the sample letter on page 339.

3. Letters of Complaint. If your speaker did not operate when you received it, you would write a business letter to complain. The ability to write this type of letter is invaluable.

Requests for Information. Letters that request information must be as specific as possible. They should also be polite.

1315 Summer Road
Trenton, New Jersey 08618
May 15, 1985

Chamber of Commerce
Zuni
New Mexico 87327

Dear Sir or Madam:

As a class assignment, I am working on a paper dealing with the Indians of New Mexico, and particularly the Zuni tribe. Any information or addresses you could provide would be appreciated.

I am particularly interested in the culture of the Zuni Indians today as compared with the culture of the 1800's.

Very truly yours,
Susan Campbell

Special Note for Typists: If any of your business letters are extremely short, you may double-space for the sake of appearance. If you do double-space, be consistent with the prescribed form.

Exercises Writing a Request for Information

A. Write a letter to a chamber of commerce asking for information about their city. Be specific as to why you need this information: you are planning to move to that city; you are interested in vacationing there; or you have been given that particular area to research as a class assignment.

B. Write to a college or university requesting information regarding tuition costs. State your major field of interest: law, medicine, computer science, etc.

C. Write to a company in your area asking for information about summer employment. Let them know your age, qualifications, and previous experience.

D. In groups, plan the "ideal" vacation to an exotic spot. Write the various letters necessary for transportation, hotels, and tours. Then plan the vacation with the information you receive.

Letters of Complaint. Have you ever purchased something that fell apart, did not work, or was a disappointment? Write a letter of complaint. This is not a "gripe" letter; it is written to let a store or company know that there is a problem and you would like to have it taken care of. Most companies are interested in hearing from you. If you are not happy with a purchase, you probably will not buy that brand again, or maybe you will shop at a different store. This is of great concern to the seller. After all, he or she wants you to keep buying that particular product or coming to the store. Do not merely sit around and tell your friends how upset you are; let the proper people know you are unhappy. You will be surprised at their response.

Avoid the temptation to be sarcastic, angry, or vulgar. This will not accomplish your purpose; it will merely make you look bad. Let the store or company know when and where you purchased the item and exactly what is wrong with it. Volunteer to mail the item if they would like to inspect it. Manufacturers can rapidly tell if the problem was their fault or yours.

631 Inca Lane
St. Paul, Minnesota 55112
October 6, 1985

Public Relations Department
Woolcraft, Inc.
1300 West Fremont Place
St. Louis, Missouri 63142

Gentlemen:

In September I purchased one of your new "Ski-Sno" sweaters from a local department store. After wearing it twice, I washed it according to the directions on the label. While it is still soft and the colors are as bright as when it was brand-new, it is now several sizes smaller. Needless to say, I am very disappointed.

I would be happy to send the sweater directly to you, as there has obviously been some oversight in your washing instructions. I would appreciate an explanation.

Sincerely,
Elsa Johnson

Perhaps your problem is closer to home than Elsa's. After many futile phone calls to a local company, you might find it easier to state your problem in a letter.

123 La Clede Avenue
Memphis, Tennessee 38126
August 31, 1985

General Manager
Sutton's Department Store
432 Oak Street
Memphis, Tennessee 38142

Dear Sir:

In June I purchased a pair of water skis in your Sporting Goods Department. These skis are model no. 143 and the price was $26.95, on sale. I used my parents' charge account, number 47727, for this purchase. Enclosed is a copy of the sales receipt.

The July statement which we received shows a charge in the amount of $269.50. Upon calling the Billing Department, I was informed that this was a computer error and would be corrected. The August statement has a past-due charge of $2,695.00. Is there some way you can communicate with the computer and correct this error?

Your earliest attention to this problem would be greatly appreciated.

Very truly yours,
Benjamin Erickson

Exercise Writing a Letter of Complaint

Write a letter of complaint regarding one of the following problems:

1. The new jeans you purchased fell apart after three wearings. (Write to the manufacturing company.)

2. You ordered a CB antenna through the mail, but received an aquarium. (Write to a hobby shop.)

3. The records you ordered from your club were warped when delivered. (Write to a record club.)

4. The live sea horses you ordered through the mail weren't. (Write to a pet shop.)

5. Four weeks ago you ordered $28.70 in supplies for a science project. You have not received them, and it is now too late to complete your project. Explain the problem and ask for a refund. (Write to a hobby shop.)

Knowing Where and to Whom To Write

You can spend a great deal of time writing the "perfect" letter, addressing it correctly, and still not receive a response. It is frustrating, but curable. The usual problem is that you have not directed the letter to a specific person or department. There are many different departments within each large company which have different purposes. A request for employment would go one place and a complaint another. There are special sections to handle orders, service calls, parts, etc. If the address on your letter is simply to the company, it might take a week or more for it to find its way to the person qualified to respond.

If your particular problem is one that originated with the manufacturer and not the store where you made the purchase, you should write directly to the manufacturer. The address is usually on the label attached to the product. If not, you can obtain the necessary information through your local store. There is a special department that will pay particular attention to your letter and is interested in hearing from you. This department is referred to as Public Relations. They would like to hear from you because they want to keep you happy. One important thing to bear in mind is that you do not have to have a complaint to write a business letter. If you have been thoroughly happy with one particular product, let the manufacturer know. After all, we all appreciate a nice comment now and then.

Exercises Knowing Where and to Whom To Write

A. Using the list provided, where would you send a letter dealing with each of the numbered problems below?

Personnel Department   Sportswear Department
Accounting Department   Service Department
Parts Department

1. Employment information
2. Ordering parts
3. Requesting information regarding the operation of a product
4. Asking if a store carries a specific brand of swimwear
5. Being charged twice for the same item

B. How many different departments does a large store in your area contain? Can you list the different departments within a large corporation such as the telephone company? Write down as many as you can; then look in a telephone directory to see how close you are.

Part 5 Filling Out Forms

Forms fulfill many needs and perform many different functions. Their primary purpose is to obtain specific information in a particular order. An employer reads an application form to determine your qualifications for a job. A bank teller uses a savings account deposit form to keep a record of your money.

You probably have been faced with filling out at least one form in your lifetime. Most likely, you will fill out hundreds more of them as you continue through school and begin looking for employment.

The following guidelines may be helpful to you as you complete various types of forms:

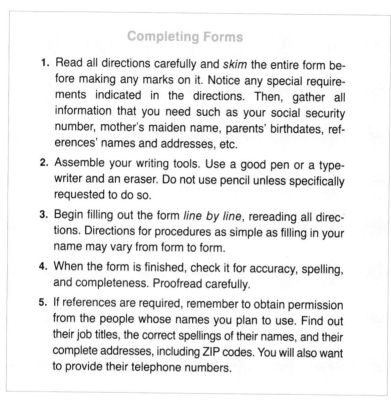

Completing Forms

1. Read all directions carefully and *skim* the entire form before making any marks on it. Notice any special requirements indicated in the directions. Then, gather all information that you need such as your social security number, mother's maiden name, parents' birthdates, references' names and addresses, etc.

2. Assemble your writing tools. Use a good pen or a typewriter and an eraser. Do not use pencil unless specifically requested to do so.

3. Begin filling out the form *line by line*, rereading all directions. Directions for procedures as simple as filling in your name may vary from form to form.

4. When the form is finished, check it for accuracy, spelling, and completeness. Proofread carefully.

5. If references are required, remember to obtain permission from the people whose names you plan to use. Find out their job titles, the correct spellings of their names, and their complete addresses, including ZIP codes. You will also want to provide their telephone numbers.

Keep in mind that you usually will have only one copy of a form. Take time to complete this copy correctly.

Exercises Completing Forms

A. You are organizing a school newspaper staff. Design a form for students who want to apply for a position on the newspaper. Be sure that the form provides you with any information that you might need, such as the student's year in school, the position the applicant is interested in, previous experience, grade point average, and how the student can be contacted.

B. Below is a sample order form from a catalog house. Examine it carefully. Then tell whether each of the following statements is true or false.

1. Information may be printed or cursive.
2. Charge cards are not acceptable for payment.
3. Sporting goods should be listed on the same form as other items being purchased.
4. Items may be returned within two weeks after purchase.
5. The narrow column after the catalog number should not be completed by the customer.

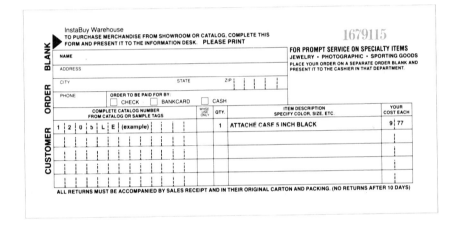

Part 6   Using Your Skills To Find a Part-Time Job

Roughly nine million teenagers, approximately half of America's teenage population, work in part-time jobs. Teenagers work for many reasons: to help with family expenses, to earn money for college, or simply to gain job experience that will be useful in later life. If you decide to look for a part-time job yourself, there are some particular guidelines that you can follow to make your job search successful.

Making an Activities Schedule

School is your full-time job, and nothing should interfere with it. Before beginning a job hunt, ask yourself, "Can I work part-time and also fulfill my school, family, and other obligations?" If the answer is yes, design an **activities schedule** by recording your daily activities, hour by hour, for one week. Examine this weekly activities schedule and determine how many hours you can realistically devote to a part-time job. Discuss this schedule with a parent or with your guidance counselor.

Activities Schedule	Mon.	Tues.	Wed.	Thurs.	Fri.	Sat.	Sun.
3:00 - 4:00	Speech team		Speech team			Mowed lawn	
4:00 - 5:00						Revised English paper	Youth group meeting
5:00 - 6:00	←		Band practice		→		
6:00 - 7:00	←		Dinner		→		
7:00 - 8:00	Homework	Wrote English paper	←	Homework	→	Movie	
8:00 - 9:00							
9:00 - 10:00							
10:00 -							

Note: Federal and state laws protect teens from overwork and dangerous working conditions. Under Federal law, if you are fourteen or fifteen years old, you may work a maximum of three hours on a school day and up to eighteen hours per week. (Hours are extended during the summer.) State laws vary and supersede Federal laws. Check with your guidance counselor about your state's child labor laws.

Assessing Your Skills

Take a good look at yourself, at the things you like to do and do well. Do you enjoy helping people? repairing bikes or small appliances? training pets? working outside? Interests often translate into job skills. For example, a talent for fixing appliances could lead to a job in a repair shop. Learning to type in school could result in an office job.

The following chart will give you some idea of the opportunities that exist for part-time employment:

Common Occupations Among Teenagers	
Self-Employment	**Employment by Others**
washing and waxing cars	newspaper route
pet sitting	clerical jobs (typist, filer, receptionist)
child care	
delivery	shoeshine stand
answering service	cashier
housework/cleaning garages or basements	retail sales (grocery stores, departments stores, etc.)
handicrafts	sales clerk
repairs	food service (waiter/waitress/cook/dishwasher)
mowing lawns/gardening	
farm work	

Exercises Preparing To Look for a Job

A. Make up an activities schedule that includes all of your commitments for a week. From this schedule, determine how many days and hours you could realistically devote to a part-time job.

B. Choose at least five words from the following list that describe activities you have done. Then, add details telling what you have done, when, and where.

> EXAMPLE: *Organized* a baseball team in my neighborhood during the summer of 1983.

performed	repaired	assisted	won
operated	cared for	participated in	scheduled
handcrafted	taught/trained	organized	served
supervised	prepared	sold	designed
typed	wrote	earned	built

Contacting Employers

How do you actually find a job? If you are going to be self-employed, speak to friends and neighbors whom you think might be interested in your services. Make up flyers and distribute them in your neighborhood. Post notices in supermarkets. You might even consider placing an ad in your local paper.

If you are looking for outside employment, the procedure becomes more complex. First, ask your school guidance counselor if he or she knows of job openings. Then, check the want ads section of your local newspaper for part-time positions. Job ads are usually carefully written to indicate requirements for the job. Look for jobs that match your skills, age, and experience.

You may also want to contact businesses in your area that hire teens. Avoid dropping in unannounced. Call, or write a letter, requesting a job application and an interview. When you call a prospective employer, give your name and ask if the business has any openings. Be sure to identify the type of job you are looking for, and briefly state the qualifications you have. Speak clearly and politely and obtain the information quickly. Keep in mind that you may be disrupting a busy work day for the person on the other end of the line.

Remember the following points when speaking with a prospective employer:

Speaking to Prospective Employers

1. Be polite. Use *please* and *thank you*.

2. Learn the employer's last name and use it along with *Mr.*, *Ms.*, or *Mrs.* Write down the employer's name for future reference.

3. Briefly provide all information requested.

4. Briefly present your qualifications, skills, and experience.

5. Write down any essential information that you learn during the call, such as the employer's address or the time that he or she wants you to come for an interview.

Job Application Forms

The next step in getting a job is obtaining and completing application forms. You may obtain application forms either by asking prospective employers to send them to you or by asking permission to drop by the place of business to pick one up.

Remember that the job application form is the first sample of your work that an employer sees. A neat, accurate, legible application will greatly increase your chances of being hired.

Read over the entire job application before filling in any spaces. This will tell you what kind of information must be provided and in what order.

Most application forms require the following information:

Job Application Forms	
Personal Data	name, address, phone, date of birth, social security number
Schools Attended	names, cities and states, dates of attendance, subjects studied, activities
Employment History	names, places, supervisors, dates, job titles, duties
Skills and Achievements	job-related skills, honors or awards, volunteer positions (Examples: *type 60 wpm, speak Spanish fluently, science lab assistant*)
References	names, titles, addresses, relationship to you

It is a good idea to prepare a list of such information that you can carry with you for easy reference.

Complete the application neatly and legibly, using a typewriter or a pen. Follow all of the guidelines given in Part 5 for completing forms.

Interviewing for a Job

The interview is the final and most crucial step in getting a job. Employers will ask about your skills and background to get a complete picture of you as a prospective employee. In an interview, employers usually observe and consider the following:

What an Employer Looks for in an Interview	
Appearance	neatness, cleanliness, posture, good grooming
Courtesy	tact, politeness, maturity of manner, friendliness
Communication Skills	listening skills, ability to answer questions, articulation of words, correct grammar, vocal quality
Job Qualifications	experience, abilities, skills, enthusiasm, eagerness to learn
Availability	other commitments, such as hours at school or special activities

A polite handshake and "Hello, my name is _____ " will begin the interview on a positive note. Listen carefully and answer all questions completely. Speak in a more formal manner than you might use in more casual conversation. Sloppy language might indicate to the employer that you would not present a good image to his or her customers.

As you answer questions, be honest about your skills and availability. Ask the interviewer about the duties you will be expected to perform. Do not accept a job you will be unable to do well.

When the interview is ended, thank the interviewer.

OPENING: Hello, Ms. White. I'm glad to meet you.

CLOSING: Thank you, Ms. White, for your time. I hope to hear from you soon.

Obtaining Other Job-Related Forms

Once you have accepted a job, there are several forms that you will have to present to your employer. The following forms are commonly required:

Work Permits. Most states require that teens obtain work permits and present these to their employers before beginning to work. To obtain an application for a permit, see your employer or your school guidance counselor. To apply for the permit, you will need a birth certificate and, in some states, a physician's statement of health.

A Sample Work Permit

```
                          STATE OF ILLINOIS                    BILLIE ANN PILLING
                        DEPARTMENT OF LABOR                        SUPERINTENDENT
STATE OF_____      DIVISION OF LABOR STANDARDS     DUPLICATE—FOR DEPT. OF LABOR
                      910 SO. MICHIGAN AVE., CHICAGO, ILLINOIS 60605
COUNTY OF_____     Certificate of Age for Minors 16 yrs. of Age and Over
                         (ACCEPTED AS PROOF OF AGE UNDER THE       CERTIFICATE NO._____
CITY OF_____       U.S. FAIR LABOR STANDARDS ACT OF 1938)   DATE OF ISSUE_____

    ISSUED FOR_____ 2. _____ 3.  AGE_____
            (NAME OF MINOR)                          (SEX)           (YEARS)    (MONTHS)
 4. THIS IS TO CERTIFY THAT THE FOLLOWING EVIDENCE OF AGE OR A TRANSCRIPT THEREOF HAS BEEN FILED IN THIS OFFICE FOR
    THE ABOVE-NAMED MINOR. CHECK EVIDENCE ACCEPTED.
 5. DATE OF BIRTH_____     EVIDENCE OF AGE:
            MONTH       DAY            YEAR           1.  BIRTH CERTIFICATE
 6. PLACE OF BIRTH _____                   OR TRANSCRIPT THEREOF_____
                       TOWN
                                                     2.  OTHER DOCUMENTARY EVIDENCE, SUCH AS:
                                                         BAPTISMAL CERTIFICATE_____
    _____    _____           PASSPORT_____
         COUNTY                  STATE                    BIBLE RECORD_____
 7.  PARENT OR                                            INSURANCE POLICY_____
     GUARDIAN_____         OTHER (SPECIFY)_____
                NAME              ADDRESS
 8.  THE ABOVE-NAMED MINOR IS TO BE EMPLOYED BY:      3.  PHYSICIAN'S CERTIFICATE OF AGE
    _____                  ACCOMPANIED BY SCHOOL RECORD
                 FIRM'S NAME                             OF AGE, AND PARENT'S AFFIDAVIT
    _____                  OF AGE _____
                FIRM'S ADDRESS

    _____                             OCCUPATION
         INDUSTRY
 9.  SIGNATURE OF MINOR _____

10.  ADDRESS OF MINOR _____

11. _____ 12. _____ 13. _____
    SIGNATURE OF ISSUING OFFICER    TITLE                      NAME OF SCHOOL
NOTE: IN CASE OF A MINOR UNDER 18 YEARS OF AGE THIS CERTIFICATE IS TO BE RETURNED BY THE EMPLOYER TO THE ISSUING
      OFFICER UPON THE TERMINATION OF THE MINOR'S EMPLOYMENT. (SEE OTHER SIDE).
```

W-4 Forms. These are used for tax purposes. Obtain one of these from your employer after accepting a position.

Health Permits. For certain jobs, especially jobs in food service, you must have a permit certifying your state of health. If your employer does not have the appropriate application form, he or she will be able to tell you where to obtain one.

Social Security Cards. Workers in jobs covered by social security (about 90 percent of the U.S. work force) must have a social security card. You apply for a card by filling out an application form. These forms are available at any social security office.

A Sample Social Security Application Form

DEPARTMENT OF HEALTH AND HUMAN SERVICES SOCIAL SECURITY ADMINISTRATION	Form Approved OMB No. 0960-0066

FORM SS-5 – APPLICATION FOR A
SOCIAL SECURITY NUMBER CARD
(Original, Replacement or Correction)

MICROFILM REF. NO. (SSA USE ONLY)

Unless the requested information is provided, we may not be able to issue a Social Security Number (20 CFR 422. 103(b))

INSTRUCTIONS TO APPLICANT	Before completing this form, please read the instructions on the opposite page. You can type or print, using pen with dark blue or black ink. Do not use pencil

		First	Middle	Last
NAA NAB	NAME TO BE SHOWN ON CARD			
1	FULL NAME AT BIRTH (IF OTHER THAN ABOVE)	First	Middle	Last
ONA	OTHER NAME(S) USED			

STT **2**	MAILING ADDRESS	(Street Apt. No. : P.O. Box, Rural Route No.)
CTY STE ZIP	CITY	STATE	ZIP CODE

CSP **3**	CITIZENSHIP (Check only one)			SEX **4**	SEX
	☐ a U.S. citizen	☐ c. Legal alien not allowed to work		☐ Male
	☐ b. Legal alien allowed to work	☐ d. Other (See instructions on Page 2)		☐ Female

DOS **5**	DATE OF BIRTH	MONTH	DAY	YEAR	AGE **6** PRESENT AGE	PLB **7** PLACE OF BIRTH	CITY	STATE OR FOREIGN COUNTRY

		First	Middle	Last (her maiden name)
MNA **8**	MOTHER'S NAME AT HER BIRTH			
FNA	FATHER'S NAME	First	Middle	Last

PNO **9**	a. Have you or someone on your behalf applied for a social security number before? If you checked "yes", complete items "b" through "e" below; otherwise go to item 11.	☐ No	☐ Don't Know	☐ Yes
SSN PNS PNY	b. Enter social security number		c. In what State did you apply?	What year?
NLC	d. Enter the name shown on your most recent social security card		e. If the birth date you used was different from the date shown in item 5, enter it here	MONTH	DAY	YEAR

DON **10**	TODAY'S DATE	MONTH	DAY	YEAR	**11**	Telephone number where we can reach you during the day	HOME	OTHER

ASD **WARNING: Deliberately providing false information on this application is punishable by a fine of $1,000 or one year in jail, or both.**

12	YOUR SIGNATURE	**13**	YOUR RELATIONSHIP TO PERSON IN ITEM 1
			☐ Self ☐ Other _____ (Specify)
	WITNESS (Needed only if signed by mark "X")		WITNESS (Needed only if signed by mark "X")

DO NOT WRITE BELOW THIS LINE (FOR SSA USE ONLY)		DTC SSA RECEIPT DATE _____
☐ SUPPORTING DOCUMENT- ☐ EXPEDITE CASE ☐ DUP ISSUED	SSN ASSIGNED OR VERIFIED SSN	NPN
		BIC
DOC	NTC	CAN
TYPE(S) OF EVIDENCE SUBMITTED		SIGNATURE AND TITLE OF EMPLOYEE(S) REVIEWING EVIDENCE AND/OR CONDUCTING INTERVIEW
	☐ MANDATORY IN PERSON INTERVIEW CONDUCTED	DATE
		DATE
	IDN ITV	DCL

Form **SS-5** (2-81)

Exercises Finding a Part-Time Job

A. Select a business in your area that employs teens. Write a letter to the owner or manager expressing interest in employment opportunities and requesting a job application. Remember to give some background about yourself and your skills.

B. Look at the social security form on page 355. Write out the information you would provide for sections 1, 2, 8, and 9. What would you write in the box at the bottom of the form labeled "Types of Evidence Submitted"?

Be sure to read the application carefully.

1. Proper form in writing is important to all forms of written communication. Your letters can make as strong an impression as your style of dress or manner of speaking.

2. The form of any letter includes the date, salutation, body, closing, and signature. Formal letters also include a heading and an inside address.

3. Business letters should be brief and specific. Types of business letters include letters of order, letters of complaint, letters of application, and requests for information.

4. When completing forms and applications, read all directions before beginning. Fill out the form carefully.

5. To find a job, begin by evaluating your time commitments and assessing your skills.

6. Possible employers should first be contacted by phone or letter.

7. Remember that the way you complete an application form and the way you present yourself during an interview may determine whether or not you are hired.

Applications in Other Subject Areas

Current Events. Write a letter to your state representative. Express your opinions on some important current issues. Remember to keep the tone of the letter polite.

All Subjects. Choose your favorite from among the following subject areas. Do some research to find out what careers are open to people who are interested in this area. Your guidance counselor may be able to provide you with sources of information or addresses to which you can write.

History	Mathematics	Home Economics
English	Fine Arts	Industrial Arts
Science	Physical Education	

Chapter 17

Giving a Talk

There is one assignment that strikes fear into the hearts of most students, turning the biggest and bravest into a mass of quivering bones and quavering voices. That assignment is, "Next week you will present an oral report to the class." Fear of speaking before groups can be overwhelming, but it can also be overcome. By acquiring the skills needed to deliver an effective speech, you can learn to speak knowledgeably and confidently to any group. You may still shake inside, but, with a little practice, no one else will even notice.

Part 1 Informal Talks

Often during your school years, you will be required to make some sort of informal oral presentation. You might be asked to introduce the speaker at an all-school assembly, to make an announcement for your club, or to issue directions at an athletic event. Your informal presentations might also include demonstrations. This part of the chapter will prepare you for giving such informal speeches.

Preparing an Informal Talk

While the amount of preparation involved in an informal talk is not great, you must do some background work. Know what you are going to say, and be sure your information is accurate and complete.

In most instances, you will not be speaking for more than a minute or two, so it is easy to write out the talk. For brief announcements, you will find that notes are adequate, but make sure that you practice reading aloud from the notes. Practicing aloud helps you to realize that what looks good on paper is sometimes difficult to read aloud.

Types of Informal Talks

Making Introductions

The chances are good that at some time you will be asked to introduce someone to a class, a club, an organization, or other group with which you are involved. Such an introduction will require more than, "This is Anita Rivera, president of the ninth grade." First, you must get some background information on the person to give to the audience. Who is she? What has she done? Why is she here? If possible, try to find some interesting or amusing anecdote to lighten your introduction. Be careful, though. While everyone should be amused, no one must ever be embarrassed.

Exercises Making Introductions

A. You are the host of a nationally syndicated talk show and will be introducing a well known author, actor, or public figure. Write an introduction that could have been used at some time in his or her life, or one that could be used today.

B. Choose a character from a book, movie, or television series and introduce him or her to the class.

C. Introduce one of your classmates. You will need to find out some information beforehand. Interview him or her, asking about hobbies, favorite subjects, jobs, favorite reading material, taste in music, and what he or she does after school.

D. Choose a famous historical figure, perhaps someone you have studied this year. Introduce this person to your class. You decide on the occasion and the circumstances for the introduction. Be sure to include any important historical facts.

Making Announcements

"Today is October 16, and here are today's announcements." You may listen to words just like these every day over your school's public address system. This is the simplest kind of informal talk, but even when delivering a speech as short and simple as a daily announcement, you must remember to include answers to the following questions:

> *What* is happening?
> *Where* is it happening?
> *When* is it happening?
> *Why* should the listeners be interested?

Always repeat *where* and *when*. Your audience may have a short attention span or may not even realize that they are interested in the announcement until you are about halfway through. They will need to hear *where* and *when* repeated at the conclusion of the speech. Speak distinctly and clearly. Do not rush. Emphasize the important information. Above all, keep the announcement short and simple.

Exercises Making Announcements

A. Pretend that you are organizing a new club, one that your school does not have. Name your club and make an announcement to the class that (1) tells the name and functions of the club, (2) tells where and when the first meeting will take place, and (3) will attract members.

B. Make an announcement to the class regarding one of the events below, or announce something else that is going on at your school or in your community. After three or four announcements have been given, see how many *what*'s, *where*'s, *when*'s, and *why*'s the class can remember.

an athletic event	an awards assembly
school elections	tryouts for cheerleaders
a field trip	college representative visits

Giving Directions

Have you ever stopped someone on the first day of school to ask the location of a classroom? If so, you know how few people can really help. The reply is usually similar to the one below.

> Just go down this hall and then turn by the water fountain (there are three) and then keep going past the typing room (you have no idea where the typing room is) and then turn at the next corner (which way?) and you'll find it.

Think your directions through before presenting them. Use accurate details, give the directions step by step, and be as clear as possible. Never back up to correct yourself. Instead, start over again, and be sure that your listener understands.

> Go down this hall towards the front of the building. Turn right at the second water fountain. At the next corner turn left, and the room will be the third one on your left.

This is still complicated for a new student, but at least the directions are accurate. Of course, if you ask for directions, you have to be a good listener.

Exercises Giving Directions

A. Choose a specific place with which your classmates are familiar. It can be in the school building or in your community. Without identifying the place, give specific directions for getting there from your classroom. Then see who can identify the exact place.

B. Give your classmates directions on how to draw some object. You may not name the actual subject of the drawing. You may only use words for geometrical shapes such as *line, circle, square,* or *triangle;* words for drawing utensils such as *pen, paper,* or *pencil;* words for relationships such as *inside, below, next to,* or *between;* and commands such as *Place, Move, Draw,* or *Sketch.*

The other students cannot ask questions as they try to follow the directions you are giving. You will know if they understand by the expressions on their faces. When you have finished, see how many students actually drew the figure. Was the problem in the directions? Was it that those who did not draw the correct figure were not listening closely? Try to analyze the problem.

Giving a Demonstration Talk

Have you ever tried to teach a child how to catch a ball without demonstrating the procedure with your hands? It seems impossible to do. Try sitting on your hands and telling a friend how to make a paper airplane or how to do a simple physical exercise. Doing one of these things makes one realize that there are some instances when it is absolutely necessary to demonstrate what you mean. In a demonstration talk, you tell how something is done while demonstrating the action at the same time.

A demonstration talk must be extremely well organized. Begin by gathering all the materials that you will need for your demonstration. Then, write your speech, making sure that you cover every part of the procedure, explaining each step precisely and thoroughly. Carefully coordinate the physical aspects of the demonstration with your speech and practice using your props. When you deliver the speech, stop occasionally to see if your listeners have understood you up to that point. Remember, what seems easy to you can be sheer frustration to someone else.

Exercise Giving a Demonstration Talk

Give a demonstration talk to the class. Remember to come pre-pared with all necessary props. You might show how to do one of the following:

swing a golf club	bake a cake or pie
repot a plant	groom a dog
work with macrame	change a bicycle tire
plant a terrarium	build a bird house
hook a rug	handle a rod and reel
make a candle	arrange flowers
make a collage	throw a Frisbee
catch a football	prepare a special salad
strum a guitar	build a campfire

Persuading an Audience

Does a future as a salesperson appeal to you? Whether you know it or not, you are a salesperson and will be one for the rest of your life. You may not have any experience selling products to the public, but you probably have a great deal of experience "selling" your ideas to teachers, friends, and employers. Many occasions arise for this kind of persuasive speaking. You might want to per-suade your parents to take a particular family vacation, or con-vince the school administration to allow a particular field trip for your club or organization. Whatever the occasion for persuasion may be, to win your point you must be well prepared, sincere, and, above all, enthusiastic.

Organize a persuasive talk much as you would any piece of persuasive writing. First, be sure you understand your purpose. Know exactly what it is you want to accomplish. Next, consider the audience to whom you will be speaking and select several good reasons or arguments that you think will persuade them to ac-cept your ideas. Finally, organize those reasons so that you build up to your strongest point. Present your reasons to your audi-ence using a sincere, pleasant tone and reasonable language. Re-member, a positive attitude and a genuine interest in your subject may be your strongest assets.

Persuading an Audience

A. Find a commercial on TV that appeals to you and list at least three things that made you like it. Do the same for a commercial that did not appeal to you, listing three things that made you dislike it. Do you think everyone would respond to these commercials as you did?

B. Ads use hidden appeals to persuade consumers, such as humor or the association of products with patriotic feelings, happy families, or famous people. Using one of these appeals, sell a fictitious or real product to your class in a one-minute commercial. Time yourself to keep your remarks brief and to-the-point.

C. Prepare a persuasive talk in which you try to convince your audience to make some sort of change. The audience may be your classmates, a school board, or your parents.

Part 2 Formal Speeches

You don't have to be the President of the United States addressing the nation or an athlete accepting a place in the hall of fame to need to know how to speak formally in front of a group. As a student, you may find yourself giving a formal talk or report in biology class, presenting a project to a committee, or making a speech at an assembly.

A formal speech is one delivered on a specific topic to a specific audience, for a specific purpose. It is lengthier than an informal talk and requires more thought, time, and preparation. Formal talks should be organized completely on paper, in a manner similar to that used to organize a composition. However, unlike compositions, speeches must be rehearsed out loud after they are written. Effective speakers do not just "read" their notes or papers. They also add expression and gestures and use good eye contact. To do this, however, they must be thoroughly familiar with their material. Practice will provide you with this familiarity. It will also help you to spot sections of your speech that seem fine on paper but become dry or dull when read aloud.

The steps required before the actual writing of a formal speech are identical to the pre-writing stage of the process of writing.

Formal Speeches: Pre-Writing

DEVELOPING YOUR TOPIC AND MAIN IDEA

1. Select and narrow your topic.
2. Define your purpose.
3. Identify your audience.
4. Develop a statement of your main idea.

RESEARCHING YOUR TOPIC

1. Gather information.
   a. from personal experience
   b. from other people (interviews)
   c. from reference materials
2. Take notes.

ORGANIZING YOUR MATERIAL

1. Group similar ideas.
2. Arrange ideas in a logical order.

Selecting a Topic

Choose a topic that will interest both you and your audience. Be aware of the following:

Unusual subjects appeal to everyone.

The familiar topic has value, but be sure to provide a fresh angle or new point of view or your speech will be dull.

Remember one thing: if you are really interested in the topic, your interest will be contagious.

As you choose your topic, remember that most speeches have time limitations. Narrow the scope of your subject to fit whatever time has been allotted, but be careful not to limit your topic too much. There is nothing worse than running out of material.

Exercise **Selecting and Narrowing a Topic**

Choose three of the following occasions and decide on one appropriate topic for each. Assume that your speech is to be between ten and fifteen minutes long. Remember to keep your audience in mind as you select and narrow your topic.

1. You are a class officer and must prepare a talk for the opening assembly.
2. Your teen group (scout troop, 4-H Club, church group) has asked you to deliver a talk at the awards banquet.
3. You have been chosen by your classmates to deliver a talk to a group of senior citizens.
4. You are giving a talk to the school board concerning an issue of importance to the students.
5. You are to give a talk to your social science class about some other part of the United States.
6. You have been asked to talk about a custom associated with some particular holiday.
7. You are the captain of a team and have to give a talk after your final game.
8. You have been asked to talk to a group of eighth graders about high school.
9. You have been asked to give a campaign speech in support of a classmate who is running for student council president.
10. You are an exhibitor at a hobby fair. The fair organizers have asked you to explain your hobby to a group of reporters.

Defining Your Purpose

Almost any speech that you will be asked to give will have one of the following purposes: *to inform, to persuade,* or *to entertain.* You must decide which of these three your speech involves.

The **informative speech** is the type you are most often asked to give. Most class reports are informative. You simply want your audience to understand or to appreciate what you are telling them. Speeches that inform might describe the advantages of belonging to a school club, explain the brake system of a car, or report on a book.

The **persuasive speech** attempts to lead to some change in the listener's point of view, attitude, or course of action. Speeches that appeal for the election of a candidate, encourage support for a school or charitable activity, or argue against an unwise course of action are all examples of persuasion.

In the **entertainment speech** you simply want your audience to enjoy what you say. A speech meant to entertain might be an after-dinner speech or a between-the-acts speech by a master of ceremonies.

Of course, any one of these speeches does not exclude aspects of the others. An informative speech, for example, should also be interesting and entertaining. A persuasive speech should also contain information to support its points.

Exercises Defining Your Purpose

A. Decide whether the purpose of each of the following speeches would be primarily to inform, to persuade, or to entertain. Explain your choice.

1. How to register to vote.
2. The voting age should be raised to age 21.
3. How to get hired for a summer job.
4. Machines are out to get me.
5. The minimum wage should be raised.
6. Cats are people, too!
7. Every household needs a computer.
8. My winter vacation, or how to do absolutely nothing for two glorious weeks.
9. Our town could benefit from a public swimming pool.
10. Magic tricks that everyone can do.
11. How to survive life with an older sister.
12. Students should attend high school all year.

B. How many formal talks have you listened to recently? Write down the occasions, the topics, the audience, and the purposes of the talks. Were they effective? If not, briefly state why you think the speaker failed in his or her purpose. You may limit yourself to five different talks.

Identifying Your Audience

Before you begin to deal with preparation of the actual talk, you must be aware of the audience. Consider your audience's average age, background, economic level, and education. Determine the amount of knowledge or background they have on the material you will be presenting. Be aware of what brings them together to listen to a speech. All of these factors can contribute to the way you develop and present your material.

Remember that your audience must be able to relate to what you are saying on an individual level. You will adjust your tone and level of language to suit the people to whom you are speaking. For example, a talk given to young children would differ considerably from a speech given to the school faculty.

Exercise Identifying Your Audience

What would you title each of the following talks if you were asked to present it to (1) your class, (2) a group of parents, (3) a sixth-grade class, and (4) a club or organization to which you belong?

robotics	a fourth of July celebration
teenage drivers	summer camp
school drop-outs	making compromises

Determining Your Main Idea

Begin the actual preparation of a speech by developing a statement of the main idea that you want to communicate to your audience. This idea can usually be stated in one sentence. It may express an opinion or a general fact about your topic.

> Violent crimes are increasing rapidly in our community.
> LucasFilms is one of the world's most successful companies.
> Unless we act now, the panda will soon perish.

The statement of your main idea is the key to your entire speech. It communicates the point of your speech to your audience, and helps you to keep your ideas unified.

Determining Your Main Idea

A. Choose three of the following topics and write a sentence that could be used to state the main idea of a speech.

the movie rating system   Halloween
year-round school   fantasy games
rumors   computer technology

B. Using your class as an audience, select a topic for a speech that you will prepare and give. Decide on the purpose and state the main idea. Do no more with it at the present time.

Researching Your Topic

In gathering material for a speech, look for ideas, details, illustrations, facts, figures, and quotations related to your topic. Possible sources include personal experience, interviews, and reference materials.

Personal experience can add a great deal of interest to a speech. It is much more fascinating to listen to someone who has actually been on a survival trip than to someone who has merely researched it. You can expand on your personal experience through reading and talking to others, but your speech will bear more weight if you can speak from actual observation and experiences.

Gathering material through interviews involves finding and questioning people who have personal experience or knowledge of your topic. When you go to an interview, be prepared. Have questions written ahead of time. Avoid any questions that can be answered "yes" or "no." Be a good listener. The person you are interviewing should do most of the talking.

When you obtain information from books or other reference materials, you must be careful. Here are some guidelines:

1. Read for specific purposes. Gather only those facts, details, and illustrations that develop your main idea.

2. Read for the main points. Do not get lost in the forest of words. Use the skimming and scanning methods studied in Chapter 15.

369

3. Evaluate the material. Do not accept ideas just because they are in print. Is the material up-to-date? authoritative? Is a particular piece of information a fact or an opinion? (See Chapter 13 for further discussion of fact and opinion.)

4. Make the material your own. Except for direct quotations, summarize what you want to use. Remember: put all information in your own words. Word-for-word copying is plagiarism, for which you could be penalized.

5. Make use of a variety of reference works. Your library will be an indispensable asset in gathering your material. In addition to encyclopedias and books, remember to refer to the vertical files and the *Readers' Guide to Periodical Literature.*

6. Take notes. Notes are the backbone of any good talk, so take notes on all research that you do, including interviews.

Notes should be taken on 3″ x 5″ cards. Write only one idea per card and write only on one side. In the top left corner of each card, write a one or two word summary of what the card contains. This will be helpful when you organize your notes. In the top right corner, indicate the source of the information and, if appropriate, the page number.

Sample Note Card

Capabilities of New
Telescope

Max Behring
Interview

"With this new telescope, we should be able to see to the edge of the known universe and — because it takes time for light to travel — almost to the beginning of time."

Using 3″ x 5″ cards, take notes on everything you might include in your speech on the topic you have chosen. Remember to write only one note per card.

Organizing and Writing Your Speech

Organizing Note Cards

The first step in preparing to write your speech is the organization of your material. Do this according to the following guidelines:

Organizing Your Notes

1. Scan the subject headings of your note cards.
2. Based upon these subject headings, make a separate list of main ideas.
3. Divide your note cards into separate groups, one group for each main idea.
4. You should have several notes providing supporting details for each main idea. If you do not, you may have to eliminate some of your main idea groups or do further research.

After you have organized your notes, make a modified outline of your speech. This outline should include, in shortened form, the material you will include in the three major parts of the speech: the **introduction, body,** and **conclusion**. In order to proceed with this organization, it will help you to know what the purpose of each main part is.

The Introduction. The introduction is used to gain your audience's attention. It should be forceful and interesting. It must set the tone of the speech and be appropriate for the occasion. Somewhere in the introduction, usually at the beginning or end of it, you must state your topic or controlling idea.

The chart below lists some ways to start introductions:

TYPE OF INTRODUCTION	EXAMPLE
An anecdote is an interesting short story that involves your audience in your talk.	A 29-year-old mother, with the help of paramedics, gave birth to a son on a moving subway train during rush hour last week. It was the woman's fifth child, but the subway system's first.
A quotation is simply a repetition of someone else's words. A humorous or inspiring quotation can be an effective introduction.	Abraham Lincoln said, "Wanting to work is so rare a merit, it should be encouraged." This statement holds true today for those teenagers who hope to find part-time employment.
A thought-provoking question or series of questions can be an excellent way to get your audience thinking about your subject.	What if you came to school one day, and everyone but you was wearing animal hides and speaking Tibetan?
An analogy is a comparison of a difficult idea or a complicated process to an idea or process your listener already knows.	If you can teach a youngster to tie a shoe, then you can program many of the "user-friendly" computers on the market today.
Startling or interesting facts surprise your audience or make them curious. Such statements can be effective attention-getters.	In the middle of the recent recession, it was revealed that six *million* U.S. homes already had video recorders. That seems to demonstrate that no matter what the situation, television and its related accessories are a high priority in the lives of most Americans.

The Body. The body of the speech is the longest and most important part. In the body, you must inform, entertain, or persuade your audience, giving them facts and information to support your main idea. The body of your speech should take at least twice as much time as the introduction and conclusion combined.

Here are some guidelines for organizing the body of your talk:

1. **Determine your major points.** Choose main ideas from the list that you made based upon the topic headings of your note cards. These main ideas will become the major headings in your outline.

2. **Arrange your main ideas in a logical order.** Your talk should build toward a climax. Sometimes, you will want to present your ideas in order of their importance. In other cases, you will have to present your ideas in a time sequence.

3. **Develop your main ideas.** After you have decided exactly what main ideas you are going to cover, use the information from your notes as supporting details listed under each main idea in your outline.

The Conclusion. The conclusion is a summary of the main points of your speech or a strong statement that signals the end of the presentation to the listener. In a persuasive speech, you might conclude with an appeal or challenge to the audience. An informative speech might end with an appropriate quotation or illustration. At some point during the conclusion of your speech, you should draw attention once again to your main idea. Remember that your conclusion may determine the final impression an audience carries away from your talk. Make sure it is as strong and interesting as the introduction.

Exercise Organizing Your Material

Organize the note cards that you made for the exercise on page 371. Follow the guidelines on the same page. Then make a list of main ideas, using the subject headings of your note cards. Based upon this list of main ideas, make a modified outline with an introduction, body, and conclusion.

Writing Your Speech

Once the outline has been written, the next step is to write the speech itself, developing the introduction, body, and conclusion so that they are both thorough and interesting. Any broad statements or opinions that are made in the speech should be backed up by specific details or references to recognized authorities. The written speech should follow all of the rules of good writing, including directness, unity, and clarity. A good speech, like any good piece of writing, requires thoughtful revision.

Exercise Writing Your Speech

Following your outline, write your speech as you expect to deliver it. You may want to refer to the Guidelines for Writing and Revising Compositions on page 212.

Part 3 Delivering a Speech

The effective presentation of any speech, whether formal or informal, is no easy task. It is possible, however, to appear relaxed and experienced if you are aware of the following three guidelines:

1. **Rehearse your speech aloud many times.** Try practicing in front of a mirror or for a friend or relative. Try to develop variety in facial and vocal expression. Don't be afraid to make corrections as you rehearse. Ask your listeners for suggestions. Eventually, the speech will flow easily.

2. **Take advantage of a tape recorder to listen to your delivery.** Be critical. If something does not sound right, try it again with emphasis on a different word or phrase. Rework your ideas into smoother sentences. If a point seems unclear or awkward, revise your sentences so that they say exactly what you want them to say. If some ideas seem out of place, do not hesitate to rearrange them so that each idea logically follows the one preceding it.

3. **Choose a method of delivery that is comfortable for you.** If you prefer to memorize the entire talk, do so. If you feel more comfortable referring to notes, practice using them. You may even wish to have the entire talk written out in front of you. In either of the last two cases, however, do not merely read the speech. If you do, you will be so engrossed in your notes that an essential part of your presentation, personal contact with the audience, will be lost.

Creating an Effective Impression

Whenever you talk to other people, you should be aware of both nonverbal and verbal communication. The following guidelines will help you:

Keys to Effective Speaking

NONVERBAL COMMUNICATION
Dress and Grooming. Dress and groom yourself in a way that will not draw attention away from your speech. Make sure that your clothing is appropriate to the audience and to the occasion.
Eye Contact. Eye contact with your audience will make them more receptive and attentive. Scan the entire audience with your eyes. Do not look solely at any one person. If you find it difficult to look your audience in the eyes, try looking at the tops of their heads.
Poise and Posture. Do not pose; just stand comfortably. Try to appear relaxed and confident. Putting one foot slightly ahead of the other or adopting a wider stance than usual will help you to maintain your balance. Move about, if possible. Do not lean on a lectern or desk except to emphasize a point. Do not slouch.
Gestures and Facial Expressions. These can be very effective to emphasize particular points. A look of concern, for example, can communicate the seriousness of an idea. Avoid planned gestures and expressions. Instead, let these develop naturally from the emotions that you feel with regard to your subject.

Volume. Speak loudly enough for your audience to hear you without difficulty, but not so loudly that they become uncomfortable. Vary your volume for emphasis.

Articulation. Speak a little more precisely than you do in ordinary conversation. Pronounce every syllable of your words clearly and distinctly. Be careful to pronounce final consonants. Do not clip vowel sounds or hold *s* sounds.

Pace. Speak a little more slowly than is common in ordinary conversation. Speak at a steady rate, with some variation for emphasis.

Pitch. Avoid speech that is too high and thin or that is artificially low. Avoid monotony by varying your pitch, slightly exaggerating the natural pitch variations that occur in ordinary conversation.

Pauses. Pause before important points for dramatic effect.

Exercises **Delivering a Speech**

A. Pronounce the following sentences, articulating every sylla-ble. Be careful to pronounce final consonant sounds. Avoid clipping vowel sounds or holding *s* sounds.

1. In the mists and fiercest frosts we went in winter weather.
2. Which width, thick or thin, best suits the situation?
3. Naturally, I couldn't, wouldn't, and didn't do it.
4. Earl heard his bird's nervous words.
5. Manny insisted that Otto utter many mutters and murmurs.

B. Listen to a newscast. List two things about the anchorperson's appearance, volume, articulation, pace, pitch, and use of pauses.

C. Deliver a speech to friends or relatives, or tape a practice ses-sion and play it for them. Ask for suggestions for improvement in your volume, pitch, rate, and articulation.

Part 4 Listening to and Evaluating Speeches

There are many occasions in which you will find it necessary or important to listen to speeches by other people. Some of these speeches will be informal such as lectures or instructions from a coach or employer. Some may be formal such as campaign speeches or church sermons. Whatever the occasion there are a few guidelines for good listening that you should always follow:

Listening Courteously

1. Do not speak when someone else is speaking.
2. Sit upright and direct your attention to the speaker.
3. Give the speaker positive feedback by using appropriate facial expressions and maintaining eye contact.
4. Take notes if appropriate.

Listening for Content

In order to get the most out of a speech, you must learn to recognize important points that a speaker is making. Listen for key words or phrases that signal the introduction of a major idea. Such signals are often similar to the transitional words used in a composition:

> first   another   most importantly
> next   similarly   in addition

If you are taking notes on the speech, jot down these main points. Then focus on how the speaker supports or develops each idea. This may help you to draw certain conclusions about the material. A strong, well-documented development, for example, may indicate a valid point or an idea worth accepting. A weak development that uses poor methods of argument or support may indicate that you should examine the ideas much more closely.

Listening To Evaluate

In some classes, you may be asked to help another student improve his or her communications skills. To do this, you must be able to point out the strong and weak points of a speech. When you are asked to make such comments on another student's speech, avoid brief, useless generalizations such as "It was good" or "I didn't like it." You will find the following guidelines helpful:

Evaluating Speeches

Be constructive, not destructive.
Always offer suggestions for improvement with your criticism. This way you will be building the confidence as well as the communication skills of a classmate.

Never criticize people, only behavior.
"You're fun" and "You're unclear" do not help the speaker to improve. Be more specific and relate your comments directly to the speech. Statements such as "The opening joke warmed your audience" or "The third example was hard to follow" are clearer and more to the point.

Limit your criticisms.
Be selective in the points you wish to criticize. Too many will confuse or exasperate the speaker and do little to improve the speech.

Comment on specific aspects of content or delivery.
Mention specific instances or examples of good or poor eye contact, poise, posture, gestures, facial expression, volume, articulation, pace, pitch, or pausing. Look for instances or examples of particularly strong or weak organization, word choice, or support of main ideas.

Use a checklist similar to the one on the following page to help you in evaluating speeches. For points not covered on the list, you may want to add a section labeled "Other Comments."

Checklist for Evaluating Speeches

	CONTENT
Introduction	___ gets audience's attention ___ is brief and to the point ___ is appropriate to the topic
Body	___ supports the main idea ___ contains no irrelevant material ___ states supporting ideas clearly ___ develops supporting ideas completely
Conclusion	___ is brief ___ provides a summary of major points or ___ draws attention back to main idea

	PRESENTATION
Nonverbal	___ speaker has good posture ___ speaker is relaxed and confident ___ speaker has good eye contact ___ gestures and facial expressions are natural and appropriate
Verbal	___ speaker is not too quiet or too loud ___ speaker's articulation is clear ___ speaker's pace is not too slow or too rapid ___ speaker's pitch is not too high or too low ___ speaker varies volume, pace, and pitch ___ speaker uses pauses effectively

Exercise Evaluating Speeches

Use the checklist above to critique a round of speeches in your class. Be sure your comments are specific and constructive.

1. All speeches, formal or informal, require preparation and should be rehearsed.

2. Informal talks include introductions, announcements, demonstration talks, and persuasive talks.

3. Formal speeches are delivered on specific topics, to specific audiences, for specific purposes. A formal speech may inform, persuade, or entertain.

4. In preparing a formal speech, follow these pre-writing steps:
   a. Select and narrow a topic.
   b. Identify your audience.
   c. Define your purpose.
   d. Research and organize supporting material.

5. Whenever you speak to others, be aware of the following elements. They can influence how well others accept what you say.

   proper dress and grooming   eye contact
   poise and posture   gestures and facial expressions
   volume and articulation   pace, pitch, and pauses.

6. Always listen courteously to other speakers and be specific in your responses or evaluations. Learn to recognize the key points of the material that is presented.

Applications in Other Subject Areas

Social Studies / Mass Media. Watch a TV editorial, the next Presidential address, or a lecture on an educational channel. Evaluate the speaker's presentation. What aspects of the speech are effective? Which are distracting or irritating to you as a viewer?

Speech / Drama. Prepare a dramatic reading of a poem, short story, or play to deliver to your class. What different or additional points concerning voice and gestures must you consider for this type of presentation?

Grammar and Usage

The Mechanics of Writing

A detailed Table of Contents appears in the front of this book.

Grammar, Usage, and Mechanics

The following seventeen sections of this text deal with grammar, usage, and the mechanics of writing (capitalization, punctuation, spelling, the correct form for writing, and outlining).

Each of the sections is divided into parts. Each part explains a topic or concept fully and gives specific examples. Definitions appear in boldface type. There are numerous exercises in each part to test your understanding of the concepts explained. There is also a variety of additional exercises provided at the end of each Section.

As you study each section, try to apply what you have learned to your own writing and speaking.

Section 1

The Sentence and Its Parts

You may not think of yourself as a mechanic. However, speaking and writing English is somewhat like building an engine. Like a mechanic working on an engine, a good writer carefully combines parts to build the driving force of English, the sentence.

An engine is composed of pistons, shafts, and cylinders. In a similar way, a sentence is made from its separate parts—subjects, verbs, modifiers, and complements. When the parts of a motor are put together properly, it runs smoothly. A well put-together sentence is also smooth and efficient.

This section will introduce the parts of a sentence and how they work together. Following sections will teach you about each sentence part in detail.

Part 1 The Complete Sentence

Sometimes in conversation we use only parts of sentences. For example, we might reply to a question with a word or two, or with a few words that do not make a complete sentence.

> Not now.   That one.   Yes.   Over that hill.

In standard written English, however, complete sentences are important. With them, we can express our ideas more clearly.

A sentence is a group of words that expresses a complete thought.

The following groups of words are sentences:

> Tom agreed to the plan.
> That red car is blocking the alley.
> The alarm at the bank sounded late last night.

When part of an idea is missing from a sentence, the group of words is a sentence fragment. A **sentence fragment** is a group of words that does not express a complete thought.

> Agreed to the plan. (Who agreed?)
> That red car. (What about the car?)
> Late last night. (What happened?)

Exercise A: Number your paper from 1 to 10. For each group of words that is a sentence, write **S.** For each sentence fragment, write **F.**

1. Lost fifteen pounds in three months.
2. A giant towered above the trees.
3. The final score of the tennis match.
4. On the river bluff near Dubuque.
5. A photo of the family reunion last August.
6. This gas station is open twenty-four hours a day.
7. Val planned the route.
8. The hot dog vendors at the ballpark.
9. Where was your cousin's wedding held?
10. A monster named Nessie lives in Loch Ness.

Exercise B: Writing For each group of words that is a sentence, write **S.** Rewrite each fragment to express a complete thought.

1. There were only sand and sagebrush for miles.
2. Who is this disc jockey?
3. Used to live in Iowa.
4. A downpour stalled the game.
5. Appeared on the video screen.
6. Our coach, Mr. Esposito.
7. The data processor made a mistake.
8. A possible new source of energy.
9. Kim raised tomatoes and pumpkins last summer.
10. Thick black smoke from the blaze.

Part 2   Kinds of Sentences

Sentences can be grouped into a few basic categories, depending on their purpose. No matter what you want to say or write, there is a particular kind of sentence to communicate your ideas. Using these different kinds of sentences, you can ask questions, issue commands, or express strong feelings.

A **declarative sentence** is used to make a statement. It ends with a period (.).

A float plane landed in the harbor.
One day Charles will be King of England.

An **interrogative sentence** asks a question. It ends with a question mark (?).

Do you enjoy volleyball?   What time is it?

An **imperative sentence** gives a command. It usually ends with a period.

Wait for the signal.   Save me a seat, please.

An **exclamatory sentence** expresses strong emotion. It ends with an exclamation point (!).

> I won first prize!   What a day this has been!

Exercise A: For each of the following sentences, write *Declarative, Interrogative, Imperative,* or *Exclamatory* to show what kind each is. Add the proper punctuation mark.

1. Are you taking the subway or a bus
2. Turn off the lights when you leave the lab
3. My friend Antonio lives on the thirteenth floor of our apartment building
4. Do the elevators work
5. All his life, Gary wanted to be an Olympic competitor in gymnastics
6. Watch out
7. Come out and see all the fireflies
8. Did Mrs. Henderson cover any new material in algebra class today
9. Pick a card
10. Thomas Jefferson enjoyed science more than his involvement in politics

Exercise B: Writing Identify each sentence by its type. Add the correct punctuation mark. Then write a sentence of your own that is the same type. Try to make your sentences interesting.

1. When is the next game
2. Try this potato salad
3. I was born in Mobile, Alabama
4. Are you and Gretchen on the same team
5. What a view this is
6. Tell Pedro to meet us here
7. Where do you go to school
8. That's fantastic
9. Which is larger, Iceland or Greenland
10. I read a book about the Vikings

Part 3 The Subject and the Predicate

Every complete sentence is made up of two basic parts: the subject and the predicate. The **subject** tells *who* or *what* the sentence is about. The **predicate** is the idea expressed about the subject. It usually tells what the subject *is*, what the subject *did*, or *what happened to* the subject.

SUBJECT	PREDICATE
(Who or what)	*(The idea expressed about the subject)*
The volcano	erupted again.
A reporter from the paper	relayed the news.
My cousin	became a graphic artist.
The subway riders	raced for the doors.

Each of these sentences expresses a complete thought about a person, place, or thing. There is a simple method of identifying the parts of a sentence. Think of the sentence as telling who did something or what happened. The subject tells *who* or *what*. The predicate tells *is, did,* or *happened.*

WHO OR WHAT	IS, DID, OR HAPPENED
The soft mud under my feet	cushioned my toes.
Our lead-off hitter	got a stand-up double.
All four tires	need air.
The first contestant	is confident.

The subject of the sentence tells *who* or *what* the sentence is about.

The predicate of the sentence is the idea expressed about the subject.

Exercise A: Head two columns *Subject* and *Predicate*. Write the proper words from each sentence in the columns.

EXAMPLE: My cousin needs a part-time job.

SUBJECT   PREDICATE

My cousin   needs a part-time job.

1. A line of motorcycles zoomed down the freeway.
2. Charlene won the bike-a-thon this year.
3. Ron carried his radio to the beach.
4. The long silver train streaked by us.
5. Our career counselor has a great deal of information on summer jobs.
6. The new P.E. wing contains two gyms.
7. This year's harvest of soybeans is the biggest ever.
8. Those jeans have been washed many times.
9. I need fifty cents for the bus.
10. Tickets for the Men at Work concert sold out after only two hours.

Exercise B: Writing Add a subject or predicate to each word group to make it into a sentence. Tell which part you are adding.

EXAMPLE: goes to the day care center

My younger sister goes to the day care center. (Subject)

1. Cara's three brothers
2. shrieked all night
3. the lean timber wolf
4. our basketball team
5. careened off the edge of the cliff
6. a bank of dark cumulus clouds
7. the ancient, bearded wizard
8. is going to take a ceramics class
9. is Rob's favorite pastime
10. suddenly emerged from the cave

Part 4   Simple Subjects and Verbs

In every sentence certain words are more important than others. These essential words are the basic framework of the sentence. Look at these examples:

SUBJECT	PREDICATE
The **volcano**	**erupted** again.
A **reporter** from the paper	**relayed** the news.
My **cousin**	**became** a graphic artist.
The subway **riders**	**raced** for the doors.

All the words in the subject part of the sentence are called the **complete subject.** Within the complete subject is a key word, the **simple subject.** In the last example above, *the subway riders* is the complete subject. *Riders* is the simple subject. Hereafter we will refer to this key word as the **subject.**

The **complete predicate** is all the words that express an idea about the subject. The key word within the complete predicate is called the **simple predicate,** or **verb.** In the sentence about the subway riders, the complete predicate is *raced for the doors.* The key word, or verb, is *raced.*

The key word in the subject of a sentence is called the simple subject. We refer to it as the **subject.**

The key word in the predicate is the simple predicate. Hereafter we will refer to the simple predicate as the **verb.**

Types of Verbs

You can more easily identify verbs if you realize that verbs can be grouped into two basic types. One type expresses action, so it is called an **action verb.** The following sentences contain action verbs:

We *skated* on Dreamland Lake.
Uncle Joe *built* a cabin last summer.

The other main type of verb expresses the existence or condition of something. It is called a **state-of-being verb**. These sentences contain state-of-being verbs.

Ramon *is* an expert swimmer.
The frog *became* a prince.

Finding the Verb and the Subject

In any sentence, the verb and the subject are the most important words. The other words only tell more about these key words.

To find these key words in any sentence, first find the verb. Remember that it expresses action or a state of being. Once you find the verb, form a question by placing *who* or *what* in front of the verb. The answer will give you the subject of the verb.

An attendant at the station checked the oil.

Verb: checked
Who checked? attendant
The subject is *attendant*.

The plane is on the runway.

Verb: is
What is? plane
The subject is *plane*.

Diagraming Subjects and Verbs

A sentence diagram is a drawing of the parts of a sentence. It is a visual representation of how the parts fit together.

A sentence diagram demonstrates the importance of the subject and the verb. These key parts are placed on a horizontal main line. They are separated by a vertical line that crosses the main line. No matter where the subject appears in the sentence, in a diagram it always appears before the verb. Later you will learn how every other word in the sentence has a particular position in the diagram, too.

In diagraming, only words capitalized in the sentence are capitalized in the diagram. No punctuation is used.

Adam spoke quietly.

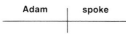

Janelle writes poetry.

Janelle	writes

Exercise A: Label two columns *Verb* and *Subject*. Number your paper from 1 to 10. For each sentence, write the verb and its subject.

1. Jack works at the hospital each Saturday.
2. Ten students are in the play.
3. This map of the city indicates bus routes.
4. The huge trawler fished the rough, stormy Antarctic.
5. The network canceled that show after only two episodes.
6. Dana's sister sets high goals for herself.
7. Six different ingredients topped the pizza.
8. A professional stunt man performed the fall.
9. The annual carnival attracted large crowds.
10. An emu is a flightless bird.

Exercise B: Writing Complete these sentences by adding subjects, predicates, or both. Tell which part you are adding. Then identify the verb in each sentence as an *action* verb or a *state-of-being* verb.

1. many of the best songs today
2. arrived in four days by pony express
3. Spielberg's latest movie
4. the vast expanse of desert
5. revved their powerful engines
6. two strange beings, with three eyes apiece
7. Marty and Jack
8. is on this side of the river
9. an elephant with a broken tusk
10. our upstairs neighbor

Part 5 The Parts of a Verb

A verb may consist of one word, or of several words. It may be composed of a **main verb** and one or more **helping verbs**, also called **auxiliary verbs**.

HELPING VERBS $+$ MAIN VERB $=$ VERB

will	return	will return
would	expect	would expect
is	leaving	is leaving
must have	shown	must have shown

To name the verb in any sentence, you must include all the words that make up the verb.

These words are frequently used as helping verbs:

am	are	have	will	may
is	be	do	would	might
was	has	does	can	shall
were	had	did	could	should

Most of these words can also be used as main verbs.

Mike *has played* guitar for years (helping verb)
Mike *has* a new guitar. (main verb)

Separated Parts of a Verb

At times you will find words inserted between the parts of a verb. These words are not included in the verb. Study the following sentences. The parts of the verb are in bold print.

Cassie **had** never **driven** a tractor.
My friends **could** not **offer** any advice.
The artist **will** gladly **show** you her work.

Some verbs are joined with other words to make contractions. In naming verbs that appear in contractions, pick out only the verb. The word *not* and its contraction *n't* are adverbs. They are never verb parts.

> Vernon **did**n't **notice** the car. (*Did notice* is the verb.)
>
> The carpenter **had**n't **measured** exactly. (*Had measured* is the verb.)

In Section 5 you will learn more about verbs and verb usage.

Exercise A: Number your paper from 1 to 10. List the verbs in the following sentences.

1. Bluegrass musicians were gathering for the festival.
2. You haven't ever needed any help before.
3. We could often read his mood.
4. David has never seen an ice hockey game.
5. You should try that new roller coaster.
6. The umpire didn't respond to the catcalls.
7. The conservation bill hasn't passed yet.
8. This year I will probably get a paper route.
9. The price does not include delivery.
10. We have never called ourselves experts.

Exercise B: On your paper make two columns headed *Helping Verbs* and *Main Verbs.* Write the verbs in each sentence in the appropriate columns. Not all sentences contain helping verbs.

1. Summer vacation doesn't begin until Tuesday.
2. A relief pitcher will sometimes finish the game.
3. My sister has already taken her driver's test.
4. A good job will usually require two coats of paint.
5. Michelle wrapped her father's present in glossy red plaid paper.
6. Someone must have cut the telephone line.
7. Your ideas will certainly help.
8. Lincoln's ghost doesn't walk until midnight.
9. The new clinic on Long Street will soon open.
10. Most of the team's new players have already signed their contracts.

Part 6   Subjects in Unusual Positions

The subject of a sentence usually comes before the verb. Sometimes, however, the structure of the sentence departs from this order. This may happen when the sentence is written to perform a special function. It may also occur if the writer is trying to add variety to his or her sentences. In these sentences, part or all of the verb may come before the subject.

To find the subject in any sentence, first find the verb. Then form a question by putting *who* or *what* in front of the verb. The answer will be the subject.

Sentences Beginning with *There*

In sentences beginning with *There*, the verb often comes before the subject.

There is used in two different ways. It may be used to modify the verb by telling *where* something is or happens.

> There are the Petersons. (*Petersons* is the subject; *are* is the verb. *There* tells where the Petersons are.)
>
> There is the exit. (*Exit* is the subject; *is* is the verb. *There* tells where the exit is.)

Sometimes *There* is used simply as an introductory word to help get the sentence started.

> There is a statue of Twain in the park. (*Statue* is the subject; *is* is the verb.)
>
> There are two drummers in the band. (*Drummers* is the subject; *are* is the verb.)

To diagram sentences beginning with *There*, you must determine whether *There* tells *where* or is an introductory word. If *There* tells *where*, it belongs on a slanted line below the verb. If *There* is an introductory word, it belongs on a horizontal line above the subject.

There stood the manager of the store.

There has been a mistake.

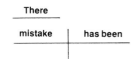

Exercise: Write the subject and the verb in each sentence. Tell whether *there* is used to tell *where* or as an introductory word.

1. There is our canoe.
2. There will be a Halloween party on Saturday.
3. There were some questions about the new schedule.
4. There is no ferry after ten o'clock.
5. There is the exchange student from Finland.
6. There has been a change of plans.
7. There is the city's civic center.
8. There are the boxes of job applications.
9. There is the kazoo marching band.
10. There have been many advances in computer technology.

Sentences Beginning with *Here*

In sentences beginning with *Here,* the subject often follows the verb.

Here comes the parade. Here is your wallet.

Unlike *there*, the word *here* always tells *where* about the verb. On a diagram it is placed on a slanted line below the verb.

Questions

In questions, subjects usually come between parts of the verb.

Have you finished? (*You* is the subject; *have finished* is the verb.)
Will Kate join us? (*Kate* is the subject; *will join* is the verb.)

Sentences Starting with Phrases or Other Words

Phrases are groups of words that do not make a complete sentence. Phrases are often used to modify other words in a sentence. When a sentence begins with a phrase or a single word modifier, the subject may come after the verb.

> Around the curve raced the runners. (*Runners* is the subject; *raced* is the verb.)
> Slowly came her reply. (*Reply* is the subject; *came* is the verb.)

To find the subject in any sentence with unusual word order, first find the verb. Then place *who* or *what* before the verb to form a question.

> Here are the scripts.
>
> *Verb:* are
> *Who or what are?* scripts
> *Subject:* scripts

Unusual word order in a sentence does not change the sentence diagram. The verb and the subject are still placed on the horizontal main line with the subject first and then the verb.

> Under the rock slithered the snake.

Imperative Sentences

You remember that imperative sentences give commands or state requests. In imperative sentences, the subject is usually not stated. Since commands are always given to the person spoken to, the subject is *you*. Because *you* is not stated, we say that it is *understood*.

> Draw a straight line. (*You* is the subject of *draw*.)
> Please repeat the question. (*You* is the subject of *repeat*.)

To diagram a sentence giving a command, place the subject *you* in parentheses.

Try again.

Exercise A: Label two columns *Subject* and *Verb*. Number your paper from 1 to 10. Write the subject and verb for each sentence.

1. Tell another joke.
2. Here is clear evidence of his guilt.
3. Have the plants been watered?
4. Quickly came his curt reply.
5. See Mammoth Cave on your trip to Kentucky.
6. Will you save a seat for me?
7. Enter through the side door.
8. Into the spotlight danced Marisa.
9. Did the psychic use tarot cards?
10. Underneath my foot lay a dollar bill.

Exercise B: Writing Rewrite these sentences using the directions in parentheses. Label the subject and verb in each new sentence.

1. A pod of whales swam in the distance.
   (Begin sentence with *In the distance*.)
2. Another space mission is planned for the near future.
   (Change this to a question.)
3. The brutal gales swept across the island.
   (Begin the sentence with *Across the island*.)
4. Snow is always on Mount Rainier.
   (Begin the sentence with *There*.)
5. The location of the buried treasure is here.
   (Begin the sentence with *Here*.)
6. You can try this one for size.
   (Make the sentence imperative.)
7. I need a flashlight and compass for the campout.
   (Change the sentence to a question.)

8. A solitary blue heron stood on one leg in the marsh.
   (Begin the sentence with *In the marsh.*)
9. The new micro-computer is here.
   (Begin the sentence with *Here.*)
10. You should take a patch kit along on your bike trip.
    (Make the sentence imperative.)

Part 7   Objects of Verbs

Some verbs do not need other words to complete their meaning in a sentence. The action they describe is complete.

The players *rested*.   The rain finally *stopped*.
Nathan *was worrying*.   The T-shirt *will fade*.

Some verbs, though, do not express a complete meaning by themselves. They need other words to complete the meaning of a sentence. We call words that complete the meaning of a sentence **complements**.

Tony reserved _____ . (Reserved what?)
The campers brought _____ . (Brought what?)

Two kinds of complements are **direct objects** and **indirect objects**.

Direct Objects

One kind of verb complement is called the **direct object**. A direct object receives the action of the verb. In the sentences below, *space* receives or tells the result of the action of *reserved*. *Firewood* receives the action of *brought*.

Tony reserved a *space*.
The campers brought *firewood*.

To find the direct object, first find the verb. Then place *whom* or *what* after the verb to form a question. *Note*: other words may follow the direct object, as in the second example on the following page.

Steve invited six friends.

> *Verb*: invited
> *Invited whom?*: friends
> *Direct object*: friends

Ann repaired the motorcycle yesterday.

> *Verb*: repaired
> *Repaired what?*: motorcycle
> *Direct object*: motorcycle

Once you understand what a direct object is, you can learn to distinguish between two types of action verbs. A verb that has a direct object is called a **transitive verb**. A verb that does not have a direct object is called an **intransitive verb**. Notice the difference in these sentences:

> Our teacher *gave* a lecture. (*Gave* is transitive.
> It has a direct object, *lecture*.)
> The sun *was shining*. (*Was shining* is intransitive.
> It has no direct object.)

Some verbs may be transitive in one sentence and intransitive in another. Look at the way the verb *called* is used in the following examples.

> INTRANSITIVE: Your sister called.
> TRANSITIVE: Your sister called a taxi.

Transitive or Intransitive?

Look at the following sentences. Are the verbs transitive or intransitive?

> Louise *left* quickly.
> Louise *left* in the afternoon.
> Louise *left* the room.

In the first two examples, the verb *left* has no direct object. In those sentences, *left* is intransitive. However, in the third sentence, if you place *whom* or *what* after the verb to form a question, you find that *room* is the direct object. In that sentence, *left* is a transitive verb.

> Louise left the room.
>
> > *Verb*: left
> > *Left what?*: room
> > *Direct object*: room

Remember, if the words following the verb tell *when, how,* or *where* the action took place, they are not direct objects.

Exercise A: Number your paper from 1 to 10. For each sentence, write the direct object of the verb.

1. The actors studied their lines.
2. Mr. Mendez has opened a new business.
3. The ship finally reached Malaysia.
4. In the morning, the workers will finish the project.
5. Please return my notebook.
6. We picked blackberries at Aunt Mae's.
7. The Canadian Prime Minister wore a red rose in his lapel.
8. Sara quickly smothered the flames.
9. The bus driver had nearly missed the exit to Tucson.
10. On Saturdays, Keith washes cars at his uncle's car wash.

Exercise B: Find the verb in each sentence. Tell whether it is *Transitive* or *Intransitive*.

1. My cousins visited yesterday.
2. She visited her friends.
3. Amy's dad leads tours for the National Park Service.
4. The general led with courage and decisiveness.
5. Some hedges grow quickly.
6. Constantine grows herbs in a window box.
7. A new worker joined the crew.
8. Some members joined late.
9. The supervisor issued several orders at once.
10. This blood donor gives frequently.

Indirect Objects

Another type of complement is an **indirect object**. Indirect objects sometimes tell *to whom* or *to what* about the verb. At other times they tell *for whom* or *for what* about the verb. The words *to* and *for* are not used in the actual sentences, however.

Jeff told **Marla** the *news*. (told *to* Marla)
The clerk sold **us** the wrong *battery*. (sold *to* us)
Carlos made **us** a Mexican *dinner*. (made *for* us)

In the sentences above, the words in bold type are the indirect objects. The words in italics are the direct objects. Indirect objects appear only in sentences with direct objects. Indirect objects are found between the verb and direct object.

Andrew handed the *teller* his deposit. (*Teller* is the indirect object of *handed*.)
Andrew handed his deposit to the *teller*. (*Teller* is not an indirect object.)

In a diagram, place a direct object on the main line after the verb. The vertical line between the verb and object does not extend below the main line.

Lana bought a poster.

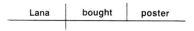

The indirect object belongs on a horizontal line attached below the verb.

Lana bought her brother a poster.

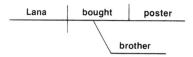

Exercise A: Number your paper from 1 to 10. Label three columns *Verb, Indirect Object,* and *Direct Object.* For each sentence below, write down those parts. Not all sentences will have all three parts.

EXAMPLE: We brought Wendy a gift.

VERB	INDIRECT OBJECT	DIRECT OBJECT
brought	Wendy	gift

1. Jonah hurriedly handed Sarah her ticket.
2. The florist arranged the roses in a blue vase.
3. A survivor told the reporters her story.
4. Does this store give customers a discount?
5. Jim passed Willie the ball.
6. The neighbors are repairing their porch this weekend.
7. Joe left the genial waitress a tip.
8. Many waitresses earn generous tips.
9. This restaurant serves terrific chili.
10. Our gym teacher taught us a new dance today.

Exercise B: Writing Some of the following sentences contain direct objects. If a sentence has no direct object, add one. If a sentence has a direct object already, add an indirect object.

EXAMPLE: Austin typed on the word processor. (Sentence without direct object.)

Austin typed his report on the word processor. (Direct object added to sentence.)

1. The glee club sang.
2. Michelle told the history of Valentine's Day.
3. General MacArthur gave the orders.
4. Southern restaurants serve grits for breakfast.
5. Don't shove.
6. My grandparents left this afternoon.
7. Our neighbor bought a piano.
8. Ken finally called last night.
9. After football practice we ate.
10. Mrs. Graziano brought a beautiful basket of fresh blueberries and strawberries.

Part 8 Linking Verbs and Predicate Words

You learned earlier that some verbs do not express action. Instead, they tell that something *is* or *exists*. Such verbs are called **state-of-being** verbs.

Often, this type of verb links the subject of a sentence with a word or group of words in the predicate. When this occurs, we call the verb a **linking verb**.

Jessica *is* a soprano.   Thomas *must be* angry.
We *are* the winners.   The typists *were* busy.

The verb *to be* is the most commonly used linking verb. *To be* can have many forms. This list will help you to become familiar with them:

be   been   is   was
being   am   are   were

The verbs *be, being,* and *been* can also be used with helping verbs. These are examples:

should be   were being   had been
may be   was being   could have been
will be   is being   might have been

The word linked to the subject by a linking verb is called a **predicate word**. The three kinds of predicate words are **predicate nouns, predicate pronouns,** and **predicate adjectives**. All of them tell something about the subject.

Brad is a *plumber*. (predicate noun)

That was *he*. (predicate pronoun)

Carlotta is *tall*. (predicate adjective)

In the above sentences, the subjects and predicate words are joined by the linking verbs *is* and *was*.

Here are some other common linking verbs.

appear	seem	sound	grow
feel	look	taste	become

Like *be*, these linking verbs have various forms (*grow, grew,* or *grown,* for instance). They can be used with helping verbs, as in *will become, can seem,* or *might have sounded.*

The lake *looked* choppy.

Bruce *has become* an excellent gymnast.

In a sentence diagram, place the predicate word on the main line after the verb. A slanted line above the main line separates the verb from the predicate word. That line, like the predicate word, points back toward the subject.

Ms. Freeman is the new advisor.

```
  Ms. Freeman  |  is  \  advisor
               |
```

That tire looks flat.

```
  tire  |  looks  \  flat
        |
```

Direct Object or Predicate Word?

A verb may be completed in one of two ways. It may have a direct object, or it may have a predicate word. How can you tell whether a complement is a predicate word or a direct object?

The verb is the key word. If the verb is an action verb, the word following it that tells *whom* or *what* is a direct object.

The nurse comforted the patient. (*Comforted* is an action verb. *Patient* is its direct object.)

The ambulance rounded the corner. (*Rounded* is an action verb. *Corner* is its direct object.)

If the verb is a linking verb, the word following it that tells about the subject is a predicate word.

> David Brenner is a *comedian.* (*Is* is a linking verb. *Comedian* is a predicate word linked to *David Brenner.*)
> These French fries seem *soggy.* (*Seem* is a linking verb. *Soggy* is a predicate word linked to *fries.*)

Sometimes, however, it is difficult to tell whether the verb is an action verb or a linking verb. When you are not sure, ask yourself how the complement is functioning in the sentence. Is it *describing or renaming the subject*, or is it *receiving the action* of the verb? Look at the following sentences:

> Jenny tasted the *sherbet.*
> The sherbet tasted *tart.*

In the first sentence, *sherbet* receives the action of the verb. Therefore it is a direct object. In the second sentence, *tart* describes the subject. Therefore, it is a predicate word.

Exercise A: Label three columns *Subject, Linking Verb,* and *Predicate Word.* Find these parts and place them in the proper columns.

1. My uncle is a zookeeper.
2. The band sounded great.
3. One endangered species is the Siberian tiger.
4. John looked upset by the news.
5. This curry smells delicious.
6. The sky appeared pink at sunset.
7. Kim must feel miserable.
8. The producer is she.
9. Jesse will become an architect.
10. Roller skates are once again popular.

Exercise B: Label four columns *Subject, Verb, Direct Object,* and *Predicate Word.* Put these parts in the right columns. Remember, no sentence can contain a direct object *and* a predicate word.

1. Sally Ride was the first female astronaut in the U.S.
2. Her home is California.

3. In her childhood, Sally played football.
4. Sally earned a doctorate in astrophysics.
5. She married another astronaut.
6. Sally flew her own plane to their wedding.
7. Ride shared her assignment with Fabian, Crippen, Hauck, and Thagard.
8. She gave the press many interviews before and after her famous ride.
9. Sally Ride became a heroine to many young women.
10. Can you tell me the name of her spaceship?

Exercise C: Writing Write ten sentences about a famous person, past or present. Label each subject *S*, each verb *V*, each direct object *DO*, and each predicate word *PW*.

Part 9 Compound Parts of a Sentence

The word *compound* means "having two or more parts."

Each of the sentence parts described so far in this section can be compound—subjects, verbs, and complements.

Two parts in a compound construction are joined by a conjunction (*and, or, but*). In a compound construction of three or more parts, the conjunction usually comes between the last two parts.

The rival leaders were Jack *and* Ralph.
The boys swam, explored, *or* ate berries most of the day.

Diagraming Compound Subjects

To diagram compound subjects, split the subject line into as many levels as there are subjects. Place the conjunction on a dotted line connecting the subjects.

Sheep, goats, and wild horses roam the foothills.

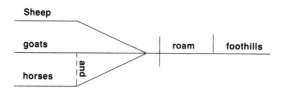

Diagraming Compound Verbs

To diagram compound verbs, split the verb line.

The freighter tossed, pitched, and rolled.

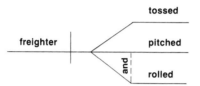

Diagraming Compound Objects

To diagram compound direct objects or indirect objects, split the object line.

Gonzales hit a homer and two singles. (compound direct object)

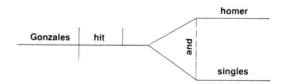

The director gave Brendon and Sandra lead roles. (compound indirect object)

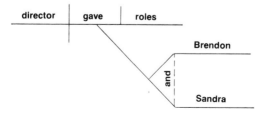

Diagraming Compound Predicate Words

To diagram compound predicate words, split the predicate word line.

> The new coaches are Brock and Rudolph. (compound predicate word)

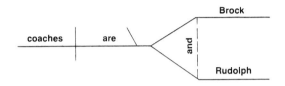

Exercise A: As your teacher directs, show the compound parts in the following sentences. Tell whether they are compound subjects, verbs, objects, or predicate words.

1. The Soviet Union and the United States produce most of the world's coal.
2. Coal is plentiful and relatively inexpensive.
3. In strip mines, machines remove earth and rock.
4. In other mines, workers and equipment dig coal underground.
5. Miners cut, drill, and blast through the rock.
6. Cars or belts carry the coal to the surface.
7. Machines wash and sort the coal at a plant.
8. Two dangerous problems in mines are ventilation and support.
9. Gases and dust in coal mines may be explosive.
10. Safety features are costly but essential.

Exercise B: Writing For each of the sentences, make the part noted in parentheses compound. Write the new sentences.

> EXAMPLE: The baby scooted across the floor. (*verb*)
> The baby scooted and wriggled across the floor.

1. At the clambake we devoured lobster. (*direct object*)
2. The audience watched carefully. (*verb*)

3. The pie had been eaten. (*subject*)
4. The Coast Guard patrols the lakes. (*direct object*)
5. The alert camera crew ran to the scene of the burning building. (*subject*)
6. Our car sputtered down the driveway. (*verb*)
7. Their creative Halloween costumes were colorful. (*predicate word*)
8. The music told a story about growing up in Harlem. (*subject*)
9. Mr. Boehm showed our class a great movie about stop-action animation. (*indirect object*)
10. The picnickers brought a barbecue grill to the beach. (*direct object*)

Part 10   Basic Sentence Patterns

You have seen that words can be organized into sentences in an endless number of ways. However, most sentences follow certain basic **sentence patterns**. The five patterns that follow are the most common ones.

Study each sentence pattern carefully. Try to think of an example of your own for each pattern.

Pattern One

This is the most basic type of sentence. It has a subject and a verb. The subject is usually a noun or pronoun. In this chart, N stands for the noun (or pronoun) in the complete subject. V stands for the verb in the complete predicate. Either the noun or the verb can be compound in a Pattern One sentence.

N	V
Fashions	change.
We	worked hard.
The goose and goslings	wandered down the path.
The white cat	yawned and stretched.

Pattern Two

In this pattern, the noun (or pronoun) that follows the verb is a *direct object*.

N	V	N
The manager	opened	the store.
Police	have named	a suspect.
Our coach	helped	us after school.

Pattern Three

Two nouns follow the verb in this pattern. The first is an *indirect object*. The second is a *direct object*.

N	V	N	N
Steve	slipped	me	a note.
Nobody	could give	Pat and Ann	directions.
The mayor	told	reporters	his latest plans.

Pattern Four

The verb in this pattern is a *linking verb* (LV). The noun that follows it is a *predicate noun* (or predicate pronoun).

N	LV	N
The experiment	was	a success.
Nashville	is	the home of country music.
The mysterious caller	is	I.

Pattern Five

Here, a linking verb is followed by a *predicate adjective*.

N	LV	Adj.
The gears	seem	stiff.
Ice hockey	is	rough and fast.
This route to Omaha	should be	direct.

Exercise A: Tell which sentence pattern is the basis of each sentence.

1. Jobs were scarce during the recession.
2. The steelworkers called a strike on Monday.
3. Juan Lopez was the star of our show.
4. These salmon from Alaska are fresh.
5. David and Amy work in their dad's store on Saturdays.
6. Rhoda finally gave Leslie and me a hint.
7. Eric photographed the skyline of San Francisco.
8. Greylock is the highest mountain in this area.
9. That request seems unfair.
10. A blizzard hit suddenly, without warning.

Exercise B: Writing Identify the pattern of each of the following sentences. Then change each sentence to match the pattern indicated in parentheses. You will have to add or change words. Try to make your sentences interesting.

1. The game ended early.   (N LV Adj)
2. That dessert looks rich.   (N V N)
3. Meredith delivers pizzas.   (N LV N)
4. Ramon sold us his tickets.   (N V N)
5. Beth told Jim her worries. (N LV Adj)
6. The computers had the answer in less than a minute. (N V N N)
7. Erica studied in the afternoon. (N V N)
8. Please give this note to the inspector. (N V N N)
9. The doctor taped Jason's ankle. (N LV N)
10. Dense fog is a hazard. (N V)

REINFORCEMENT EXERCISES

The Sentence and Its Parts

A. Identify sentences and sentence fragments. Number your paper from 1 to 10. Then tell whether each group of words is a *Sentence* or a *Fragment*.

1. Musicians entered the studio
2. Whistling in the dark
3. Harinder grew up in New Delhi
4. Doesn't she have any sense of humor
5. Arranged them in alphabetical order
6. A jigsaw puzzle with hundreds of pieces
7. Sent postcards to her friends
8. Don't just follow the crowd
9. The top album on the stack
10. On the parallel bars

B. Identify kinds of sentences. Decide whether the following sentences are *Declarative, Interrogative, Imperative,* or *Exclamatory*. Write your answer on your paper. Also write what punctuation mark should be used.

1. Show us the pictures from the party
2. Did you get a haircut
3. Yesterday Canada and the United States signed a three-year fishing treaty
4. How vicious that piranha looks
5. Who won the tournament
6. Call your brother to dinner
7. What does this code mean
8. Look out
9. Send to the Egyptian embassy for more information about the pyramids
10. Americans spend more than 350 million dollars a year on useless cold remedies

C. Find the complete subjects and complete predicates. Head two columns *Complete Subject* and *Complete Predicate*. Write the proper words from each sentence in the columns.

1. The stunt man leaped from the horse.
2. Some gardeners grow plants without soil.
3. The helicopter hovered over the small field.
4. The downhill skiers zipped through the course.
5. A large yellow van pulled into the driveway.
6. Cranberries grow best in peat bogs.
7. Truckers from all over gathered at Mel's.
8. Jeffrey led the scavenger hunt at Bonnie's birthday party.
9. Two debaters from our school won district trophies.
10. Many celebrities appear in commercials.

D. Find the verb and its simple subject. Label two columns *Subject* and *Verb*. Write the proper words from each sentence in the columns.

1. Paxton scored the first goal.
2. The nervous actors prepared for the first act of the play.
3. Bright banners in the school colors decorated the homecoming floats.
4. Beth's cousin appeared on TV.
5. Talented students from the drama club make the elaborate sets for our shows.
6. Donna asked for a map of China and Southeast Asia.
7. Few stations in this city play music all night.
8. A local store always sponsors the annual marathon.
9. Most of the music at the outdoor concert was too loud for Jody.
10. Each new student at our school sees a counselor.

E. Find the verb parts. Number your paper from 1 to 10. Write all parts of the verb in each sentence. Then write the simple subject. Watch for unusual kinds of sentences.

1. This bus is seldom late in the morning.
2. The pilot has already radioed the control tower for instructions.

3. There is a special about Antarctic penguins on TV tonight.
4. We drifted on rubber rafts down the Merced River.
5. Here is a secret compartment.
6. On the sidelines stood a man in a chicken costume.
7. We should have reported the incident to one of the officers.
8. Some streets have not been plowed yet.
9. Layer the lasagna noodles with sauce and cheese.
10. Does Randi write for the school newspaper?

F. Recognize objects. Number your paper from 1 to 10. Label three columns *Verb, Indirect Object*, and *Direct Object*. For each sentence, write the words in the proper columns. Not every sentence will have an indirect object.

1. Neil composes songs on his guitar.
2. Linda sewed me a skirt in home economics class.
3. The union finally settled its contract.
4. Every spring the theater department produces a musical.
5. Barry scheduled another appointment with his orthodontist.
6. This Japanese restaurant offers its guests sushi.
7. In the moonlight Elliot saw a strange little creature.
8. Nicholas wrote the editor a letter about the festival.
9. Snoopy told Woodstock a story.
10. The audience gave the singer a standing ovation.

G. Find predicate words and objects. Label four columns *Subject, Verb, Direct Object*, and *Predicate Word*. When these parts appear in the sentences below, write them in the columns. Remember, no sentence can contain both a direct object *and* a predicate word.

1. The blueberries will be ripe next month.
2. Su Ling tightened the spokes on her bicycle.
3. The history department has added two new courses.
4. These brownies seem very chewy.
5. Tony recently sold his trombone to Lisa.
6. The cathedral in Coventry, England, is a memorial to World War II.

7. Mindy read a newspaper on microfilm.
8. Terry is a volunteer at the hospital.
9. The musicians were playing Dixieland jazz.
10. That wax statue is a perfect likeness of Winston Churchill.

H. Find compound parts in a sentence. Write the compound parts in the following sentences. Tell whether they are compound subjects, verbs, objects, or predicate words.

1. Ted and Janeen are figure-skating partners.
2. Roald Dahl has written many novels, plays, and stories.
3. The pavement buckled and broke in the heat.
4. Down jackets look soft and warm.
5. The parachutist waited and then jumped.
6. The king cobra spread its hood and hissed.
7. This gum is sweet but sugarless.
8. Vicky and her friends threw a farewell party for Roger.
9. What main product do Argentina and Uruguay export?
10. The rowboat bounced and splashed through the waves.

MIXED REVIEW

The Sentence and Its Parts

A. Copy each sentence. Tell whether it is *Declarative, Interrogative, Imperative,* or *Exclamatory.* Then add the correct end mark. Underline the subject once and the verb twice in each sentence. If the subject is *you* understood, write *you* in parentheses.

1. Please take the dog for a walk after dinner
2. There were at least fifteen pinball machines at the auction
3. When will Coach Mendez announce next year's team
4. Karen could have joined the Navy or the Army
5. Watch out for that car
6. That may have been the best play of the season
7. Have you ever been in a hot air balloon
8. Here are the parts for Tom's bike
9. Come and play *Trivial Pursuit* with us
10. How long can you hold your breath underwater
11. The first American football game was played in 1869
12. The house is on fire
13. Joan and Gina were there when the hurricane hit
14. Tell me the name of one President from Virginia
15. Native Americans introduced popcorn to the Pilgrims
16. Who could have predicted that avalanche

B. Draw five columns on your paper. Label them *Subject, Verb, Indirect Object, Direct Object,* and *Predicate Word.* Write the parts of each of the following sentences in the correct column. Some parts may be compound.

1. The concert was a complete sellout.
2. The coach and the owner had different strategies.
3. Most critics gave the film bad reviews.
4. Bob served his family tacos and enchiladas.
5. We played volleyball and soccer.
6. Lynn and Suzanne were close friends.

7. Is your masterpiece complete?
8. Tim ordered bacon and eggs.
9. We sent Mom and Dad some flowers.
10. There is my missing album!
11. The two cats soon became gentle.
12. Larry became a cameraman.
13. Nora's aunt loaned me a calculator.
14. I replaced the turntable, the receiver, and the speakers.
15. The Bermuda Triangle is a mysterious area between Florida and Puerto Rico.

C. Identify the pattern of each of the following sentences as *N V*, *N V N*, *N V N N*, *N LV N*, or *N LV Adj*. Then rewrite each sentence to match the pattern shown in parentheses. The meaning of the sentence may change.

> EXAMPLE: I sent my sister a telegram. (N V N)
> — Pattern is now (N V N N).
> *New Pattern:* I sent a telegram last week.

1. Julio was the class president. (N LV Adj.)
2. The doctor felt helpless. (N V N)
3. The winning pitcher flashed a smile. (N V N N)
4. Bands play only original music at this club. (N V)
5. The odd animal was extremely rare. (N LV N)
6. The ranger looked at the burned campsite. (N LV Adj.)
7. Elvis Presley was The King of Rock and Roll. (N LV Adj.)
8. Jill is a jazz musician. (N V N)
9. Joe studied architecture. (N V)
10. Marlene remained friendly. (N LV N)

USING GRAMMAR IN WRITING

The Sentence and Its Parts

A. Imagine that a friend has written you a note. Before you have a chance to read it, however, your dog takes several bites out of it. You have only the piece shown below. Write what you think the note originally said. Use only complete sentences.

```
Hi!
The concert last night was
gave everyone who was there a free
together again
Saturday night? She is
party for her
going to meet
terrific!
```

B. "Urban belief tales" are a popular form of modern folklore. One well-known urban tale concerns alligators lurking in city sewers. Another tells about a hitchhiker who eerily appears on the road every twenty miles. Write the complete version of one of these tales, as you have heard it, or relate or invent some other similar story. In your narrative use all four kinds of sentences: declarative, imperative, interrogative, and exclamatory. Also try to vary the subject-verb order by using sentences that begin with phrases or other words.

C. Some people say that a dog is a person's best friend. Do you agree, or do you think that dogs are appealing only when they are attached to strong chains? Write a paragraph defending your opinion. Use sentences that include both predicate nouns and predicate adjectives. Also, try to use each of the five basic sentence patterns at least once. Underline the predicate words, and label each sentence according to its pattern type.

Section 2

Writing Complete Sentences

You now have a better understanding of the variety of fascinating ways sentences can be put together to express your thoughts. When sentences are written well, they communicate ideas clearly. If sentences are incorrectly written, however, they can cause confusion and misunderstandings.

Sometimes confusion is caused by leaving out part of a sentence. The remaining group of words is a **sentence fragment**. Another problem is created when two or more sentences are incorrectly written as one. Such a group of words is called a **run-on sentence**.

Both of these writing errors weaken communication. In this section you will learn how to avoid them.

Part 1   What Is a Sentence Fragment?

A group of words that is only part of a sentence is called a **sentence fragment**. A sentence fragment does not express a complete thought.

A fragment is confusing because something is missing from the sentence. Sometimes the subject is left out, and the reader wonders *who* or *what* the sentence is about. At other times the verb is omitted. Then the reader wonders *what happened?* or *what about it?*

FRAGMENT: Shifted into a lower gear. (Who shifted? The subject is missing.)

SENTENCE: The trucker shifted into a lower gear.

FRAGMENT: The quarterback near the ten-yard line. (What happened? The verb is missing.)

SENTENCE: The quarterback fumbled near the ten-yard line.

Sometimes both the subject and verb are missing.

FRAGMENT: In the middle of the lake. (Who or what is in the middle of the lake? What is happening there?)

SENTENCE: A canoe tipped over in the middle of the lake.

Fragments Due to Incomplete Thoughts

When a writer is in a hurry, he or she sometimes jots down only bits of ideas. The writer's pen doesn't keep up with the flow of thoughts.

Often the writer understands these fragments of ideas. However, they will probably seem unclear to a reader because at least part of the subject or the predicate is missing.

Here is an example of a series of fragments:

Went to British Columbia. Canada's Pacific Province. Spectacular mountains! The ocean, too. Hiking and fishing the best.

These complete sentences show what the writer meant:

> I went with my parents and brother to British Columbia. It is called Canada's Pacific Province. We saw spectacular mountains! We spent time along the ocean, too. For me, hiking and fishing were the best parts of our trip.

Fragments Due to Incorrect Punctuation

All sentences end with punctuation marks. The mark may be a period, a question mark, or an exclamation point. Sometimes a writer uses one of these punctuation marks too soon. Because the idea is incomplete, a sentence fragment results.

FRAGMENT: Cars with brake problems. Were recalled by the manufacturer.

SENTENCE: Cars with brake problems were recalled by the manufacturer.

FRAGMENT: Are you going? To the State Fair?

SENTENCE: Are you going to the State Fair?

FRAGMENT: A diver freed a baby whale. From a fishing net.

SENTENCE: A diver freed a baby whale from a fishing net.

Exercise A: For each group of words that is a sentence, write S on your paper. For each sentence fragment, write F. Then add words to change the fragments into sentences.

1. A new series will begin this season
2. A TV show about police work
3. Will be seen on Monday evenings at 7 P.M.
4. Several young actors
5. The director offers advice
6. Scenery, props, and sound effects
7. In each episode a chase scene
8. A stunt person jumps from a building
9. Each scene is filmed several times
10. Usually ends with an arrest

We usually think of mazes as no more than amusing puzzles. Found in magazines or amusement parks. In the past, however, mazes were considered an art form. Also a means of protection or imprisonment. Palaces in Greece and Egypt were designed as mazes. Protected the royal families. In Greek legend, a maze was built to house a horrible monster. The Minotaur. This maze was called the Labyrinth. In the 1700's, formal gardens were designed to include hedge mazes. Very intricate. The walls of these mazes are tall. Thick bushes. A person who wandered in could become lost for hours. With no idea how to get out.

Part 2   What Is a Run-on Sentence?

A **run-on sentence** is two or more sentences written incorrectly as one.

A run-on confuses the reader because it does not show where the first idea ends and the second one begins. The reader needs a period or other end punctuation mark to signal the end of each complete thought. Here are some examples:

RUN-ON:	A motorcycle turned into the alley it skidded on the gravel.
CORRECT:	A motorcycle turned into the alley. It skidded on the gravel.
RUN-ON:	Tom likes country and western music does Carla like New Wave?
CORRECT:	Tom likes country and western music. Does Carla like New Wave?

Sometimes writers make the mistake of using a comma instead of a period. Again, the result is a run-on. Look at the examples on the next page.

RUN-ON: The rookie running back carried the ball, he made a touchdown.

CORRECT: The rookie running back carried the ball. He made a touchdown.

RUN-ON: The floats were ready, the parade could begin.

CORRECT: The floats were ready. The parade could begin.

Exercise A: Correct the following run-on sentences.

1. Some radio stations have powerful signals, they can be heard in nearby states.
2. One disc jockey reads letters he also jokes with callers.
3. Several stations hold contests, prizes are often albums.
4. Tanya won one contest she named a song correctly.
5. The sound system is complex, few people could operate it.
6. The Reds won the pennant they will play in the World Series.
7. Last summer we camped it was the best vacation ever.
8. Tony has a set of barbells he lifts weights every day.
9. We saw an old Hitchcock film, it was a classic thriller.
10. A raccoon visits our back porch every evening we call him The Lone Ranger.

Exercise B: Writing Identify the run-on sentences in the following paragraph. Rewrite the paragraph correctly.

Glass is a common, inexpensive material that we take for granted. Yet long ago it was so rare and costly that it was used with gold and semi-precious stones in jewelry only wealthy women of ancient Egypt stored cosmetics and ointments in glass bottles. For centuries glass was used chiefly for ornaments, vases, mosaics, and tableware some glass was used to make stained-glass church windows and to let light into houses. Glass was used for these relatively few purposes until the twelfth or thirteenth century. Even then glass was for the wealthy. When people moved, they took their valuable glass windows with them, they even handed them down to their children as heirlooms. In England a special luxury tax was imposed on owners of houses with more than ten windows.

REINFORCEMENT EXERCISES
Writing Complete Sentences

A. Recognize sentences and sentence fragments. Tell whether each group of words is a *Sentence* or a *Fragment*. Then add words to make each fragment into a complete sentence.

1. In our neighborhood
2. A nationally known cartoonist
3. Scampered up the oak tree in the front yard
4. The horoscope in the daily paper
5. A subway train sped past
6. The overturned truck blocked traffic
7. The inventor of the telephone
8. The totem pole was gray and weathered
9. Experience is a hard teacher
10. Draws with charcoal or ink

B. Recognize sentences and run-on sentences. For each group of words that is a sentence, write *S*. For each run-on sentence, write *R*. Then rewrite each run-on sentence correctly.

1. Ray was a back-up singer now he sings lead.
2. Tony tried to skate backwards, he ended up with a badly sprained arm.
3. Burnett noticed the leaves of the bush, he realized it was a man-eating plant.
4. The peacock's tail feathers were iridescent in the early morning sunlight.
5. The German neighborhood celebrated Oktoberfest.
6. Larry was trained as a carpenter he learned quickly.
7. A pipe burst water flooded the basement.
8. Eskimos prefer to be called *Inuit,* it means *native people.*
9. The school sponsors adult classes, many people attend.
10. Many of our impressions of the Civil War come from photographs by Mathew Brady.

MIXED REVIEW
Writing Complete Sentences

A. The following paragraphs contain both fragments and run-on sentences. Rewrite the paragraphs and correct these errors. Be sure to use proper capitalization and punctuation.

You may be familiar with Scotland Yard. From watching British mystery movies. However, it isn't in Scotland and it isn't a yard, it is a nickname. For the Metropolitan Police Force of London.

Scotland Yard got its name from a short street in London. This street was the site of a palace where visiting Scottish kings stayed. Between the 900's and the 1100's. In 1829, it became London's police center. In 1890, the Metropolitan Police moved into offices on the Thames Embankment, these offices were named New Scotland Yard. They retain this name to this day.

The force is now made up of beat policemen. And detectives. These detectives are part of the Criminal Investigation Department. That started with only eight officers. Part of their job was investigating the criminal underworld, it was very dangerous work. Today the department consists of hundreds of detectives it is one of the most successful in the world. At solving crimes.

B. Use the following phrases to write a short paragraph. Avoid any sentence fragments or run-on sentences.

1. Pluto, planet ninth in distance from the sun
2. Discovered in 1930 by Clyde W. Tombaugh
3. Revolves around the sun once in about 248 years
4. Rotates every 6.4 earth days
5. Thought by some astronomers to have once been a satellite of Neptune.

USING GRAMMAR IN WRITING
Writing Complete Sentences

A. Write a twelve-month horoscope for one of the astrological signs by choosing adjectives, nouns, and verbs from the columns below. For example, the horoscope for one month might read: "Aquarius: A new relationship will bring unexpected information. Determination will bring about a valuable change." Use only complete sentences.

ADJECTIVES	NOUNS	VERBS
new	goal	gain
social	change	emphasize
creative	communications	increase
unexpected	vacation	focus
special	romance	win
valuable	sports	express
personal	response	attempt
probable	home	restore
immediate	environment	play
important	appearance	bring
sudden	information	select
foreign	problems	request
necessary	future	improve
reliable	popularity	detect
long-term	friend	realize
unusual	action	stress
secret	demands	share
financial	plans	expect
attractive	relationship	discuss
romantic	diet	join
favorable	opportunity	discover

B. Advertisers often use sentence fragments and run-ons to catch the attention of their readers. Find at least two examples of such ads in magazines or newspapers. Rewrite each one correctly.

Section 3

Using Nouns

Good, clear sentences are not accidents. They result from an understanding of how words work together.

The words used in sentences fall into certain classes, called the **parts of speech**. There are eight parts of speech:

nouns	verbs	adverbs	conjunctions
pronouns	adjectives	prepositions	interjections

You can speak and write without knowing these labels. However, skilled writers and speakers understand the different classes of words and the functions of each one.

In the next six Sections you will gain a greater understanding of the parts of speech. The first part of speech you will study is one of the most important: nouns.

Part 1   What Are Nouns?

We use words to name the people, places, and things around us. We also have names for ideas, beliefs, and feelings — things we cannot see. Words that name are called **nouns**.

A noun is a word used to name a person, place, thing, or idea.

PERSONS: landlord, Greg, Anne Murray, baby
PLACES: kitchen, Savannah, hotel, West Virginia
THINGS: blanket, mirror, lightning, *Challenger*
IDEAS: freedom, joy, sincerity, democracy

Exercise: Make three columns on a sheet of paper. Label them *Names of Persons, Names of Places, Names of Things and Ideas*. Find the nouns in the following paragraph. List each one in the proper column.

Frisbees have been part of our recreation for over thirty years. The first Frisbees were plates made of tin that were tossed back and forth by workers at the Frisbee Baking Company in Connecticut. This game inspired one of the players with an idea. Soon, discs called Frisbees were being manufactured. Their popularity with both children and adults grew very quickly. The game has now become a competitive sport, with an international championship determined each year in Pasadena.

Proper Nouns and Common Nouns

How do these two italicized nouns differ?

One *sailor, George Ruiz,* jumped from the ship.

The word *sailor* is a general term that may refer to many people. This type of noun is called a **common noun**. A common noun is a general name.

The noun *George Ruiz*, on the other hand, refers to only one person. This type of noun is called a **proper noun**. A proper noun is a specific name.

A common noun is the name of a whole group of persons, places, things, or ideas.

A proper noun is the name of a particular person, place, thing, or idea.

Look at the following examples of common nouns and proper nouns. As you can see, some nouns are made up of more than one word. Note that proper nouns are always capitalized.

COMMON NOUNS	PROPER NOUNS
magazine	*Sports Illustrated*
mountain	Mount Everest
cartoonist	Jim Davis
game	Super Bowl
city	Burlington
mayor	Mayor Anderson
religion	Buddhism
author	Mark Twain

Exercise A: Make two columns on your paper. Label one column *Common Nouns* and the other *Proper Nouns*. Place each of the following nouns in the correct column. Capitalize all proper nouns.

1. holiday inn, motel, seabreeze motel, shores hotel
2. restaurant, diner, golden bear, cafeteria
3. singer, lou rawls, album, willie nelson, ballad
4. allentown, village, asheville, town, honolulu
5. court, judge, judge ellen rodriguez, jury
6. nation, new zealand, spain, country, canada
7. airlines, trans world airlines, airport, quantas airlines
8. los angeles county hospital, clinic, sheridan dental clinic
9. first national bank, bank, banker, mr. james black, continental bank
10. team, dallas cowboys, manager, cheerleader

Exercise B: Writing Write five sentences of your own, using at least one proper noun in each sentence. Then underline every noun in each sentence.

Part 2   How Are Nouns Used?

Nouns can perform many different functions in a sentence. A noun may act as a subject, direct object, indirect object, or predicate word. Study the following examples:

> *Scientists* can predict earthquakes. (The noun *scientists* is the subject of the verb *can predict*.)
>
> The magician amazed the *audience*. (The noun *audience* is the direct object. It receives the action of the verb *amazed*.)
>
> The coach showed the *quarterback* a new play. (The noun quarterback is the indirect object. It tells *to whom* about the verb *showed*.)
>
> Gary became a carpenter's *assistant*. (The noun *assistant* is a predicate noun. It follows the linking verb *became*.)

Remember that any part of a sentence may be compound.

Exercise A: Tell whether the italicized noun in each sentence is functioning as a subject, direct object, indirect object, or predicate word.

1. A chemical *factory* dumps wastes into this river.
2. The shilling is a British *coin*.
3. The Prime Minister solemnly addressed *Parliament*.
4. Our catcher flashed the *pitcher* a secret signal.
5. The first contestant in the rodeo competition roped her *steer* in under thirty seconds.
6. Were Laurel and Hardy *actors* in silent films, too?
7. That *legend* has been told for centuries.
8. Into the hollow log slipped the frightened *fox*.
9. Dad and I made *pickles* from cucumbers.
10. The bored waiter handed each *diner* a menu.

Exercise B: Make four columns on your paper. Label them subject, indirect object, direct object, and predicate word. Write each of the nouns in the following sentences in the correct column.

1. The Olympic marathon covers twenty-six miles.
2. Police read the sullen suspect his rights.

3. The great "Satchmo" was Louis Armstrong.
4. Even small businesses can use computers.
5. Did all three movies feature Mark Hamill, Carrie Fisher, and Harrison Ford?
6. The old fisherman showed Ricardo his handmade nets and hooks.
7. The Steelers are tough defensive players.
8. The persistent interviewer asked the President a complex question.
9. Leonardo da Vinci was both a scientist and an artist.
10. Television reporters and photographers recorded the devastating flood.

Exercise C: Writing Complete each sentence by adding nouns. Make the sentences as interesting as possible. Then tell whether you have used your noun as a subject, indirect object, direct object, or predicate word.

1. _____ emerged slowly from the spacecraft.
2. King Kong knocked the _____ and _____ from the sky.
3. The animal trainer gave her _____ a _____ .
4. _____ and _____ are fascinating _____ .
5. That house has a _____ in the basement.
6. Many dancers are also excellent _____ .
7. _____ tape-recorded the _____ .
8. The wealthy woman left her _____ only an old _____ .
9. In the tree sat a _____ .
10. The _____ wore a _____ on its head.

Part 3   The Plurals of Nouns

When a noun names one thing, it is singular. When a noun names more than one thing, it is plural.

Here are some rules for forming the plurals of nouns.

1. To form the plural of most nouns, just add -s:

prizes   dreams   circles   stations

2. When the singular noun ends in s, sh, ch, x, or z, add -es:

waitresses   brushes   ditches   axes   buzzes

3. When the singular noun ends in o, add -s:

solos   halos   studios   photos   pianos

For a few words ending in *o*, add *-es:*

heroes   tomatoes   potatoes   echoes   cargoes

4. When a singular noun ends in y with a consonant before it, change the y to i and add -es:

army—armies   candy—candies   baby—babies

When a vowel (*a, e, i, o, u*) comes before the *y*, do not change the *y* to *i*. Just add *-s:*

boy—boys   way—ways   jockey—jockeys

5. For some nouns ending in f, add -s to make the plural:

roofs   chiefs   reefs   beliefs

For many nouns ending in *f* or *fe*, change the *f* to *v* and add *-s* or *-es*. Since there is no rule to follow, you will have to memorize such words. Here are some examples:

life—lives   calf—calves   knife—knives
thief—thieves   shelf—shelves   loaf—loaves

6. Some nouns have the same form for both singular and plural. They must be memorized.

deer   sheep   moose   salmon   trout

7. Some nouns form their plurals in special ways. They, too, must be memorized.

man—men   tooth—teeth   ox—oxen
woman—women   mouse—mice   foot—feet
goose—geese   child—children   louse—lice

Dictionaries show the plural of a word if it is formed in an unusual way. Here is a dictionary entry for the noun *duty*. The entry shows the plural, *duties*.

du·ty (do͞ot′ē, dyo͞ot′ē) **n.,** *pl.* **-ties [**< **Anglo-Fr.** *dueté*, what is due: see DUE & -TY¹] **1.** obedience or respect that is due to parents, older people, etc. **2.** something that one ought to do because it is thought to be morally right or necessary *[the duty of a citizen to vote]* **3.** any action required by one's occupation or position *[her duties* include writing the reports*]* **4.** a sense of obligation *[duty* calls*]* **5.** service, esp. military service **6.** a payment due to the government, esp. a tax on imports, exports, etc. **7.** service or use: see HEAVY-DUTY — **on** (or **off**) **duty** at (or having time off from) one's work or duty

Use the dictionary if you have a question about plurals.

Exercise A: Number your paper from 1 to 20. Write the plural form of each of these nouns. Then use your dictionary to see if you have formed the plural correctly.

1. leaf	6. sky	11. echo	16. spy
2. year	7. knife	12. tomato	17. goose
3. deer	8. tooth	13. bunch	18. hoof
4. holiday	9. radio	14. window	19. wish
5. coach	10. fox	15. moose	20. copy

Exercise B: Write each sentence. Correct any errors in plural forms of nouns.

1. The childs were told not to play ball in the alleys or ride their bikes in the street.
2. The donkeys carried pouchs of gold.
3. Several tooths from sharks were found on the beachs near the hotel.
4. These forks and knifes are scratched.
5. Basketball hoops are ten foots from the floor.
6. Both armies crawled forward by inchs.
7. The sheeps and calfs are kept in separate halfs of the pasture.
8. There are many types of passs and shots in the game.
9. Red tile rooves are common in the small towns and villages of southern Italy.
10. Terry Fox is one of my heros.

Part 4   The Possessives of Nouns

Nouns can indicate possession or ownership.

Mr. Lowe's car   a farmer's land   the lion's roar

Nouns can show that something is part of a person.

Meg's sense of humor   Harold's concern

Ownership is indicated by adding *'s* to a noun. Words like *farmer's*, *Meg's*, and *Harold's* are called **possessive nouns.**

Usually, only people and animals are considered able to possess items or qualities. Sometimes, however, things can also show possession. We speak of a *week's wages*, a *day's work*, or a *city's growth*.

Forming Possessives

There are three rules for forming the possessive of nouns.

1. If a noun is singular, add an apostrophe (') and s.

Amanda—Amanda's arm
Ross—Ross's desk

2. If a noun is plural and ends in s, add just the apostrophe.

artists—artists' studios   Spencers—Spencers' home

3. If a noun is plural but does not end in s, add an apostrophe and s.

women—women's discussion   people—people's choice

Exercise A: Write the possessive form of each of these singular nouns.

1. mayor	6. ranch	11. car	16. admiral
2. Meg	7. child	12. Charles	17. Jenny
3. country	8. player	13. runner	18. salesperson
4. senator	9. Penny	14. store	19. boss
5. today	10. host	15. secretary	20. Linda

Exercise B: Write the possessive form of each of these plural nouns.

1. people	6. guests	11. mice	16. families
2. fans	7. friends	12. wives	17. men
3. brothers	8. women	13. workers	18. clerks
4. hours	9. doctors	14. sheep	19. islands
5. experts	10. teachers	15. Jacksons	20. bodies

Exercise C: Write the possessive form for each italicized word.

1. The *Bears* lineup looks strong.
2. *Jerry* car needs new shock absorbers.
3. *Tuesday* game pits the Steelers against the Cowboys.
4. The *voters* choice is Ms. Marie Tonelli.
5. Reynolds beat the other *racers* times.
6. *Louis* favorite class is computer science.
7. The assistant *state* attorney met with the reporters.
8. The *children* zoo has baby animals.
9. A doctor measured the *astronauts* pulses.
10. *Donna* neighborhood has a big barbecue every Fourth of July.

Exercise D: Writing List ten unusual items that might be collected for a rummage sale. Tell who donated each item by using the possessive form. Five items were donated by single individuals; five were given by groups of people. For example: Cecily's sequined ski boots, the babies' buggy bumpers.

REINFORCEMENT EXERCISES
Using Nouns

A. Distinguish common and proper nouns. Head two columns *Common Nouns* and *Proper Nouns*. Place each noun in the proper column. Capitalize the proper nouns.

You don't have to visit antarctica to stroll past penguins and observe the icy blasts of winter. Instead you can go to sea world in san diego, california. On may 28, 1983, the popular park opened a new exhibit. Named penguin encounter by its proud creators, the display re-creates the frigid habitat of the comical birds. A separate exhibit features a tropical species of penguin—the humboldt—and other birds from the coasts of chile and peru. Travelers unable to join an expedition to south america or the antarctic will be delighted by this marvelous new world on the coast of the pacific ocean.

B. Find common and proper nouns. List the nouns in each of the following sentences. Be sure to capitalize each proper noun. Remember that proper nouns may contain more than one word.

1. A strong wind blew the lamppost to the ground.
2. A ferry takes passengers to nantucket.
3. Charlene brought sandwiches and chips.
4. We ate lunch by the fountain at the metropolitan museum of art.
5. On tuesday our class visited the lincoln memorial and the washington monument.
6. The hurricane tore through cuba and haiti.
7. After we toured lake michigan, our ship docked in milwaukee.
8. Mr. rodriguez identified the thief from a photograph.
9. Our pet rabbit, named bugs, surprised us with a litter of five babies.
10. The firefighters and police went on strike last august.

C. Recognize nouns used in sentences. Decide how each italicized noun is used in these sentences. Write the word and label it *Subject, Direct Object, Indirect Object,* or *Predicate Noun.*

1. My first *attempt* at water skiing was a joke.
2. Indians inhabited *New Mexico* thousands of years before the Europeans.
3. The difficult climb was a *challenge* to even the experienced campers.
4. The challenge of climbing Mount McKinley captured Tom's *imagination.*
5. Did Erin give *Elliot* my message?
6. Which artist painted *Starry Night?*
7. The end of the movie was a *surprise.*
8. Jessica showed *Kate* the shortcut.
9. The president assigned each *person* on the committee a task.
10. The *Pope* gave his annual Christmas greeting from the Vatican.

D. Form singular and plural nouns. Rewrite the following sentences, changing every singular noun to a plural noun and every plural noun to singular.

1. The woman carried the box and package onto the bus.
2. The athletes placed the trophies on the shelves of the display cases.
3. The child loved the ox, the moose, the sheep, and the fox in the petting zoo.
4. The spies and thieves dreaded the arrival of the hero.
5. The man repaired the pier at the beach.
6. The cowboy crossed the county to reach the rodeo.
7. Will the waitress serve the potato with our steak?
8. The clown smashed the old piano with the ax.
9. The chefs carefully placed the glazed strawberries on the pastries.
10. The echo bounced off the side of the mountain and resounded through the valley.

E. Form the possessives of nouns. Write the possessive form for each italicized noun.

1. *Nicholas* shirt doesn't match his pants.
2. *Jenny* family left for Cape Cod.
3. Someone misplaced the *painters* ladder.
4. Sarah carried *Josh* backpack after he twisted his ankle.
5. The emcee asked for the *contestant* answer.
6. *James* heroic act made the headlines.
7. The *Student Council* funds come from special projects.
8. The *Johnsons* dog is a collie.
9. We saw slides of *Ms. Marsh* trip to the Galapagos Islands.
10. The *children* theater produced a lively musical.
11. We heard the *gulls* cries as they whirled above us.
12. Socrates questioned his *students* answers.
13. *Men* clothing styles don't change much.
14. The newspapers printed the *President* speech.
15. My *dad boss* house overlooks the lake.

MIXED REVIEW
Using Nouns

A. Make four columns on your paper and label them *Singular Noun, Plural Noun, Singular Possessive,* and *Plural Possessive.* Next write each of the twenty-five nouns below in the correct column. Then complete the chart by writing the other forms of the noun in their proper columns.

EXAMPLE:	*Sing. Noun*	*Pl. Noun*	*Sing. Poss.*	*Pl. Poss.*
	hero	heroes	hero's	heroes'

1. boxes
2. city's
3. pianos'
4. bouquet
5. fish's
6. groups
7. fact
8. women's
9. flies
10. valleys
11. instructor's
12. deer
13. lioness
14. tomatoes
15. tax's
16. stereo
17. software
18. angles
19. masses
20. athlete
21. workmen
22. thieves
23. fox's
24. child
25. sea

B. Number your paper from 1 to 15. Tell whether the italicized nouns in the following paragraph are used as *Subjects, Direct Objects, Indirect Objects,* or *Predicate Nouns.* Then make a list of all of the other nouns in the paragraph. Remember to capitalize any proper nouns you find.

The last *concert* at poplar stadium was the most popular musical *event* of the summer. There was a terrific *performance* by stevie wonder. I invited *nina,* my cousin, to come from washington. She is a devoted *fan* of stevie. My *brother* is a *promoter* for the stadium. He got our *tickets.* He also gave *nina money* for a souvenir. We packed a picnic *dinner,* took the *bus* to the stadium, gave the *usher* our *tickets,* and enjoyed a great *evening!*

C. Find the nouns in the following sentences. Then make two columns labeled *Common Nouns* and *Proper Nouns*. Write each of the nouns from the following sentences in the correct column. Capitalize each proper noun. Remember that proper nouns often contain more than one word.

1. Her sister barbara drove the children to michigan.
2. Our family went to canada for christmas.
3. The most popular program on sunday is *60 minutes*.
4. My favorite class is math, but mark prefers german.
5. The massachusetts transit authority provides transportation in boston.
6. Mayor marino promised that main street would be repaired next march.
7. My cousin and my brother fished on lake erie.
8. Mary always carries gum, change, keys, and a comb.
9. The world series is a major event in baseball.
10. My parents subscribe to several magazines, including *time* and *newsweek*.

USING GRAMMAR IN WRITING
Using Nouns

A. Look at the following excerpt from an old mail order catalog:

Write at least four descriptions of your own that could be included in this catalog. You might write about an article of clothing, a miracle cure, a new gadget that no household should be without, or some other item of your own choosing. Be sure to tell what each product does, and for whom it is intended. Include several plural nouns in your descriptions and at least two possessive nouns. When you have finished your descriptions, underline all nouns.

B. While on a dangerous expedition through a treacherous mountain range, you discover a valley that is unknown to the rest of the world. In the valley are a highly sophisticated civilization, a huge lake, and many previously undiscovered plants and animals. Write a report describing your discoveries. Include the names of the valley, the lake, the people, their language, and several of the plants and animals. When you have finished, circle all proper nouns and underline all common nouns. Then, label each noun according to its use in the sentence: *S* = Subject, *DO* = Direct Object, *IO* = Indirect Object, and *PW* = Predicate Word.

Section 4

Using Pronouns

If you had only nouns to refer to people, places, and things, you would have to express an idea like this:

> Andy strummed Andy's guitar and sang the lyrics that Andy had written.

Fortunately, you can avoid such awkward sentences. Instead of repeating some of the nouns, you can use **pronouns**. Then you can say:

> Andy strummed *his* guitar and sang the lyrics that *he* had written.

Notice how the words *his* and *he* take the place of the noun *Andy*. These pronouns refer directly to the noun and convey the same meaning in a different way. Pronouns can be used to help sentences flow smoothly and to show clear relationships between words. In this section, you will learn how to use pronouns correctly.

Part 1   Personal Pronouns

A pronoun is a word used in place of a noun.

Pronouns help a speaker or writer present ideas clearly and efficiently. First of all, they help prevent unnecessary repetition. They can also be used as transitional devices to tie sentences or paragraphs together. In general, pronouns may be used in three ways:

1. They may refer to the person speaking. Such pronouns are called *first-person* pronouns.

   I pole-vault.   *We* played cards.
   That jacket is *mine*.   *Our* train leaves soon.

2. They may refer to the person spoken to. These words are called *second-person* pronouns.

   Did *you* bring *your* calculator?

3. They may refer to other people, places, or things. These pronouns are called *third-person* pronouns.

   She asked *him* a question.   *They* opened *their* mail.
   The horse tossed *its* mane.

The examples above show that a pronoun usually refers to a person. For that reason, the largest group of pronouns is called **personal pronouns**.

There are many variations of personal pronouns. Like nouns, personal pronouns may be singular or plural. In the following chart, see how personal pronouns change from the singular form to the plural form.

	FIRST PERSON	SECOND PERSON	THIRD PERSON
SINGULAR:	I, me	you, your	he, she, it
	my, mine	yours	him, her, its
PLURAL:	we, us	you, your	they, them
	our, ours	yours	their, theirs

Pronouns can also be classified according to gender. Pronouns that refer to females are said to be in the *feminine gender*. Pronouns that refer to males are said to be in the *masculine gender*. Pronouns that refer to things (and often to animals) are in the *neuter gender*.

Exercise A: Number your paper from 1 to 10. Write the pronouns used in place of nouns in these sentences. After each pronoun, write the noun or nouns it stands for.

1. A crane lifted the boulder and loaded it onto a truck.
2. Beth and George brought their own ice skates to the rink.
3. The tiny hailstones bounced as they landed.
4. Itzak Perlman dazzled the audience with his violin playing.
5. "I was born in Vienna," Joanna said.
6. Marietta uses her hands when she talks.
7. Our language got many of its words from the ancient Greeks and Romans.
8. The paramedics finally arrived. They immediately took charge.
9. The mirror shattered when it dropped.
10. Susan, did you use the microwave oven earlier today?

Exercise B: Writing Rewrite the following paragraph, replacing italicized words and phrases with the appropriate pronouns.

New York students with an interest in music, dance, or acting may attend the famous High School of the Performing Arts. At this school, *students* take both academic classes and classes designed to improve *the students'* performing talents. One girl, Shana, begins *Shana's* day with a pre-school warm-up in the dance room. *Shana* then studies math, English, and history, as well as classes in *Shana's* chosen major of dance. Says Shana, "The school is difficult, but *Shana* love *the school*. The teachers work hard to help *Shana* reach *Shana's* goal of becoming a dancer. *My friends and I* all are grateful to the school, even when each of *my friends and me* is exhausted from the work. *My friends and I* feel that the school is truly *a school that belongs to each of us*."

Part 2 Pronouns and Antecedents

A pronoun is defined as a word used in place of a noun. This noun is called the pronoun's **antecedent**. A pronoun refers to its antecedent.

> Anna lost one of *her* contact lenses. (*Her* takes the place of the noun *Anna. Anna* is the antecedent.)
>
> The shop closed *its* doors. (*Its* refers to the noun *shop. Shop* is the antecedent.)

The antecedent usually appears before the pronoun. The antecedent may appear in the same sentence or in the preceding sentence, as in this example:

> The tractor pushed the stones and bricks. *It* cleared a path. (*It* stands for the antecedent *tractor.*)

Pronouns may be the antecedents of other pronouns.

> You missed *your* bus. (*You* is the antecedent of *your.*)

A pronoun must be like its antecedent in one important way. A pronoun must have the same *number* as its antecedent. If the antecedent is singular, the pronoun must be singular. If the antecedent is plural, then the pronoun must be plural.

A pronoun must agree with its antecedent in number.

> The photographers grabbed *their* cameras.
> (*Photographers* is plural; *their* is plural.)
>
> Roberto erased *his* error.
> (*Roberto* is singular; *his* is singular.)
>
> Five famous chefs prepared *their* favorite dinners.
> (*Chefs* is plural; *their* is plural.)

One important point should be made about the use of pronouns. In writing or speaking, the antecedent of a pronoun should always be very clear. There must be no confusion about what a pronoun refers to. Sometimes a pronoun must be replaced with a noun if there is no other way of making its meaning clear.

| CONFUSING: | Melt the butter and chocolate, and let *it* cool. (Does *it* refer to the butter, the chocolate, or both?) |

| CLEAR: | Melt the butter and chocolate, and let *the mixture* cool. |

Exercise A: In these sentences the personal pronouns are italicized. Write each pronoun and its antecedent.

1. The window washers dangled from the harnesses that supported *them*.
2. Princess Diana looks stunning in *her* gown.
3. Jim looked at the shape of the package and knew *it* was an album.
4. Don't wear those boots if *they* hurt.
5. Tony left the computer on so Jenny could use *it*.
6. John Travolta grinned at *his* fans outside the theater.
7. The Petrakis family went to Phoenix, Arizona for *their* summer vacation.
8. Frieda and Joe studied *their* menus in confusion.
9. The gymnast awkwardly regained *his* balance.
10. The trainer placed *her* hand on the killer whale's snout.

Exercise B: Writing Rewrite each sentence, adding an appropriate pronoun. Underline the antecedent of each pronoun that you add. Be sure each pronoun agrees with its antecedent.

1. Some people hide _____ feelings.
2. The ship veered from _____ course.
3. I have decided on _____ future career.
4. Peter played _____ new Menudo album for me.
5. Gayle took off her backpack and placed _____ on the ground.
6. The team members took the mascot with _____ .
7. Lynne bought a flea collar for _____ cat.
8. Rod and I split the cheesecake between the two of _____ .
9. Would you lend us _____ toboggan, please?
10. Adam didn't see the car behind _____ .

Part 3 The Forms of Pronouns

Pronouns can perform all of the same functions that nouns can. Personal pronouns can be subjects, objects, predicate words, and possessives. Unlike a noun, however, a personal pronoun changes forms as its use in a sentence changes. Look at these sentences:

> *He* pitched. (*He* is the subject.)
> Riley tagged *him*. (*Him* is the direct object.)
> *His* pitch was wild. (*His* shows possession.)

The three pronouns in these examples all refer to the same person. The forms, though, are different in each sentence.

The three forms of a personal pronoun are **subject form, object form,** and **possessive form**. Here are the three forms for all the personal pronouns:

	SUBJECT	OBJECT	POSSESSIVE
SINGULAR:	I	me	my, mine
	you	you	your, yours
	he, she, it	her, him, it	his, her, hers, its
PLURAL:	we	us	our, ours
	you	you	your, yours
	they	them	their, theirs

Exercise: The following sentences use different forms of pronouns correctly. Label each italicized word *subject form, object form,* or *possessive form.*

1. *We* reported the accident to the sheriff.
2. A sudden, blinding blizzard halted *us* in *our* tracks.
3. Did *she* bring *hers* or borrow *yours*?
4. Wendy and *she* showed Tony *their* costumes for the skit.
5. The excellent editorial finally convinced *me* that a new community center is needed.
6. That was *he* in the plaid flannel shirt.
7. *They* sent *us* a post card from Michigan.

8. The camping gear and hiking boots are *his*.
9. *She* went fishing with Joe and *me*.
10. The space shuttle underwent a repair of *its* mechanical arm.
11. The Vice-President and *his* wife entertained the ambassador at *their* home.
12. Sandy makes candles and sells *them*.
13. Are the ice skates *yours* or *his*?
14. The calico cat with a bell on *its* collar is *mine*.
15. Anthony sold *him* a book of raffle tickets.

The Subject Form of Pronouns

SUBJECT PRONOUNS

I	we
you	you
he, she, it	they

When a personal pronoun is used as the subject of a sentence, the subject form is used.

They laughed and sang.   *He* punted the ball.
She carried the boxes.   *I* drew a map.

Pronouns used as subjects usually cause few problems. Predicate pronouns, though, can be more troublesome. A predicate pronoun, you recall, is a pronoun that is linked with the subject. It follows a linking verb, just as a predicate noun does.

Look at these examples of predicate pronouns:

That must be *she*. (*she* is a predicate pronoun used after the linking verb *must be*.)
The caller was *he*. (*he* is a predicate pronoun used after the linking verb *was*.)

As you see, the subject forms of pronouns are also used for predicate pronouns. That form may not sound natural at first. If you are in doubt, try reversing the subject and the predicate pronoun. The sentence should still sound correct.

The singer was *she*.   *She* was the singer.

Here are more examples of the correct use of the subject form for predicate pronouns:

> That was *he* on the phone. The winner was *she*.
> Was it *she* at the door?

Always use the subject form of a pronoun for subjects and predicate pronouns.

The Object Form of Pronouns

OBJECT PRONOUNS

me	us
you	you
him, her, it	them

When personal pronouns are used as objects, the object form is correct. Any pronoun that is not being used as a subject or a predicate pronoun is functioning as an object.

There are three kinds of objects: direct objects, indirect objects, and objects of prepositions.

In the following sentences, the object form of the pronoun is being used for direct objects.

> Dennis introduced *them*. The manager trained *me*.
> Carla followed *us*. The visitors surprised *her*.

These sentences use the object form for indirect objects:

> Terry loaned *me* his pen. Carol sent *them* gifts.
> The height made *us* dizzy. Mr. Lyle gave *her* some advice.

The third kind of object is the object of a preposition. **Prepositions** are short connecting words like *to, for, of, into,* and *with.* The pronouns that follow such words are the objects of the prepositions. For more explanation of prepositions, see Section 7.

These sentences use the object form for objects of prepositions:

> We practiced with *him*.
> My friends threw a party for *me*.
> The director showed the costume designs to *us*.

The Possessive Form of Pronouns

POSSESSIVE PRONOUNS

my, mine	our, ours
your, yours	your, yours
his, her, hers, its	their, theirs

Possessive pronouns show belonging or ownership. Unlike possessive nouns, they are not formed with an apostrophe:

Her tape of the interview
Their version of the incident

Many times possessive pronouns are used by themselves: The suitcase is *his*. At other times, possessive pronouns are used with the nouns they refer to. Look at these sentences:

Phil trained *his* macaw to talk.
Each ethnic group has *its* customs.
The mountaineers celebrated *their* success.
Will you read *your* lines?

In such cases, the pronoun is functioning as a *modifier* of the noun.

Many times, however, possessive pronouns are used by themselves. Then, like a noun, a possessive pronoun functions as a subject, object, or predicate word. Look at these examples:

That suitcase is *his*. (predicate pronoun)
Hers is much heavier. (subject)
Paul and Maria are carrying *theirs*. (direct object)
Steve gave *his* a shove. (indirect object)
Put your suitcase with *mine*. (object of preposition)

Exercise A: The personal pronouns in the following sentences are in italics. Write each pronoun and label it *Subject Form, Object Form,* or *Possessive Form.*

1. Laura rehearsed the scene with *him*.
2. *She* loaded the film into the camera.
3. The movie kept *us* on the edge of *our* seats for two hours.
4. It is *they* who won the English sheep dog.

5. Curt's older sister gave *him* a haircut.
6. Last week *I* got *my* first paycheck.
7. Jean and *her* dad went clam digging.
8. The best portrait is *his.*
9. In July *we* will leave for camp.
10. Beth loaned *me* a sweatshirt.

Exercise B: Write the correct pronoun from the two given in parentheses. Then read the sentence to yourself.

1. The news shocked (he, him).
2. The waiter spilled spaghetti on (I, me).
3. (They, Them) moved to our neighborhood.
4. The artist sold (her, hers) work at a fair.
5. Was that (he, him) or his twin?
6. All of (we, us) are taller than our parents.
7. The idea was (my, mine).
8. The cashier gave (she, her) incorrect change.
9. The announcer is (she, her).
10. All of those novels were written by (he, him).

Exercise C: Follow the directions for Exercise B.

1. A pro team drafted (he, him).
2. Is (he, him) going to the game?
3. The center forward is (she, her).
4. (He, Him) cuts lawns in the summer.
5. Next year, (we, us) will be able to drive.
6. Wasn't it (he, him) at the door?
7. Garbage surrounded (they, them).
8. Aaron handed the earphones to (I, me).
9. King Arthur made (he, him) a knight.
10. Who is that sitting by (he, him)?

Exercise D: Writing Write a paragraph describing a classmate or relative. Do not use any personal pronouns. Then, rewrite the paragraph using personal pronouns wherever they seem appropriate. Notice how the use of pronouns helps to clarify your writing and make it flow more smoothly.

Part 4   Pronouns in Compound Constructions

You have already learned that any part of a sentence may be a compound construction. These compound sentence parts are usually joined by *and, or,* or *nor,* as in *Ben and me.* A pronoun may be one or both of these parts.

It is sometimes difficult to determine which pronoun form to use in a compound construction. Here are sentences with pronouns used correctly in compound parts:

> *Laura* and *I* learned a form of self-defense. (*Laura* and *I* are both subjects. The subject form of *I* is used.)

> Mr. Kim taught *her* and *me* judo. (*Her* and *me* are both indirect objects. The object forms are used.)

> Just between *you* and *me,* I'm tired. (*You* and *me* are objects of the preposition *between.* The object forms are used.)

The examples above demonstrate that compound constructions still must use the proper subject or object form. You can easily tell which form is correct if you think of each part separately. For instance, in the first example above, omit the words *Laura and.* Should the sentence read *I learned a form of self-defense* or *Me learned a form of self-defense*? The pronoun *I* is the correct choice.

Here is another example:

> Gail gave Dennis and (I, me) more watermelon.
> Gail gave *me* more watermelon.

Exercise A: Choose the right pronoun from the two given.

1. Tim and (she, her) have entered the dance contest.
2. Judy made banana milkshakes for Lori and (I, me).
3. The Lees invited Mom and (we, us) to their cabin.
4. The strange package was addressed to Miguel and (he, him).
5. The argument was between Jamie and (they, them).
6. The kitten was a Christmas present for Angela and (she, her).

7. The fastest runners are Chris and (he, him).
8. The electrical storm made the other campers and (we, us) nervous.
9. My dog Skipper runs along the beach with (she, her) and (I, me).
10. Just between you and (I, me), I'm scared.

Exercise B: Writing Rewrite each sentence. Replace the italicized word or words with a suitable pronoun. Be sure to use the correct subject or object form.

1. The shopkeeper ignored Meg and *Carol*.
2. Katy and *David* met on a bus.
3. That speeding car headed directly at John and *Elly*.
4. It was *Marcia and her sister* who designed the maze.
5. A child with a water pistol squirted Rick and *Mario*.
6. Someone yelled at *Peter and Jim* and *Paula and me*.
7. The Bogan team and *our team* will be riding on the same school bus.
8. Tony and *Bill* may sign up for soccer.
9. The best dancers are Marshall and *Judy*.
10. Leave some chili for Marla and *Ted*.

Part 5   Compound Personal Pronouns

A **compound personal pronoun** is a pronoun with -*self* or -*selves* added.

myself	ourselves
yourself	yourselves
himself, herself, itself	themselves

When a compound personal pronoun is used for emphasis, it is being used *intensively*.

Maggie *herself* opened the vault.
They called the police *themselves*.

When a compound personal pronoun is used to indicate that the subject is acting on itself, it is being used *reflexively*.

Ella bought *herself* a digital watch.
We gave *ourselves* an hour to pack.

It is incorrect to use compound personal pronouns without antecedents.

INCORRECT: *Myself* knitted this sweater.
CORRECT: *I* knitted this sweater *myself*.

INCORRECT: You can come with Ann and *myself*.
CORRECT: You can come with Ann and *me*.

Exercise A: Number your paper from 1 to 10. Beside each number write the correct compound personal pronoun for each of the following sentences. After it, write its antecedent.

EXAMPLE: The actor thinks of (pronoun) as a star.
himself, actor

1. Dana and I wrote the lyrics (pronoun).
2. Amy gave (pronoun) a permanent.
3. The workers (pronoun) choose their hours.
4. The governor (pronoun) pardoned the prisoner.
5. The members (pronoun) set the club rules.
6. I cooked this meal by (pronoun).
7. The cheerleaders yelled (pronoun) hoarse during the last few minutes of the game.
8. The special effects were good, but the movie (pronoun) was dull.
9. Are you going to Cheyenne by (pronoun), Emily?
10. We watched (pronoun) on TV.

Exercise B: Follow the directions for Exercise A.

1. Sissy Spacek (pronoun) answered the letter.
2. Brian and Bob found (pronoun) in serious trouble.
3. The doctor (pronoun) became very sick during the epidemic.

4. We built the canoes (pronoun).
5. Give (pronoun) enough time, Debbie.
6. JoAnn tuned the engine (pronoun).
7. Carlos went camping by (pronoun).
8. The problem will work (pronoun) out.
9. I (pronoun) have never tried water-skiing.
10. Vic and Tim made (pronoun) sick by eating too
    much candy.

Part 6   Demonstrative Pronouns

The pronouns *this, that, these,* and *those* point out people or things. They are called **demonstrative pronouns.**

This and *these* point to people or things that are near in space or time. *That* or *those* point to people or things that are farther away in space or time.

This makes a good dessert.	*These* are leather boots.
That was our first date.	*Those* were great times.

Exercise: Number your paper from 1 to 10. Write the correct demonstrative pronoun for the blank space in each of the following sentences.

1. _____ are your gloves, not these.
2. _____ are spicier tacos than those Mom makes.
3. _____ is a clearer tape than the one that Alexis recorded
   yesterday.
4. _____ was a good concert last night.
5. _____ is my bike, and that blue one in the garage is my
   brother's.
6. _____ must be our bus over there.
7. _____ are the new computers, over there.
8. _____ is the most humid day we've had.
9. _____ is the edge of the canyon, just beyond those
   tall cacti.
10. _____ were Michelle's cousins from Rhode Island.

Part 7   Interrogative Pronouns

Certain pronouns are used to ask questions. They are called **interrogative pronouns**. The interrogative pronouns are *who, whom, whose, which,* and *what*.

Who won an Emmy award?   *Which* is your favorite?
Whom did Gloria call?   *What* started the fire?
Whose is this parka?

Exercise: Number your paper from 1 to 10. Write all the pronouns in these sentences. After each pronoun, write *Demonstrative* or *Interrogative* to show what kind it is.

> EXAMPLE: Is that the law?
>   *that*—demonstrative pronoun

1. Who knows how to determine the age of a tree?
2. That makes sense.
3. Which is Carlos's suitcase?
4. These must arrive in Houston by tomorrow.
5. Is that Rob's handwriting?
6. Whom does Cal trust with the money?
7. Please store these in the equipment room.
8. Are those the Green Mountains?
9. What makes Ramona so lucky?
10. Whose are these?

Part 8   Indefinite Pronouns

Some pronouns do not refer to a definite person or thing. Such pronouns are called **indefinite pronouns.**
The following are indefinite pronouns. They are singular.

another	each	everything	one
anybody	either	neither	somebody
anyone	everybody	nobody	someone
anything	everyone	no one	

Since a pronoun must agree in number with its antecedent, the above singular pronouns are used with the singular possessive pronouns *his, her,* and *its.*

> *Each* of the stores has *its* own hours.
> *Somebody* forgot *his* ski cap.
> *Somebody* forgot *his or her* ski cap.

The final example uses the phrase *his or her* instead of simply *his.* That phrase may be used to show that the indefinite pronoun may refer to a male or female.

Although most indefinite pronouns are singular, some are plural. They refer to more than one person or thing, and are used with the plural possessive *their.* Study these examples.

> both   many   few   several

> *Both* of the swimmers timed *their* sprints.
> *Few* of the passengers left *their* seats.
> *Many* of our neighbors grow *their* own vegetables.
> *Several* of the racers overturned *their* cars.

A few indefinite pronouns can be either singular or plural, depending on their meaning in a sentence. Read these examples:

> all   none   some

> *All* of the water has chemicals in *it.*
> *All* of the drivers loaded *their* trucks.
> *None* of the medicine has lost *its* strength.
> *None* of these comedians use *their* own material.
> *Some* of the fire burned *itself* out.
> *Some* of the workers took *their* breaks.

Do not be confused by phrases that appear between the indefinite pronoun and the possessive pronoun. The two pronouns should always agree.

> INCORRECT: One of the musicians left *their* instrument behind. (The possessive pronoun should agree with One, not *musicians.*)
> CORRECT: One of the musicians left *her* instrument behind.

Exercise A: For each sentence write the indefinite pronoun.

1. None of us caught a fish during that whole, frustrating trip.
2. Did someone reserve a picnic table for us?
3. Anyone can win the sweepstakes.
4. What is everybody waiting for?
5. Only one of the headlights on that old car works.
6. Several of the soccer players signed long-term contracts.
7. Many of the leaves had already fallen.
8. I read both of the Agatha Christie mysteries.
9. Why is everyone cheering?
10. We have to learn all of the state capitals.

Exercise B: Write the indefinite pronoun in each sentence. Then choose the right pronoun from those given in parentheses.

1. One of the actresses missed (her, their) cue.
2. Many of the stores have lowered (its, their) prices.
3. Somebody left (his or her, their) checkbook here.
4. Some of the runners wore out (her, their) shoes.
5. If anyone calls, tell (him or her, them) I'll be right back.
6. Neither of our wrestlers pinned (his, their) opponent.
7. Everyone listed (his or her, their) address.
8. Each of these sundaes has (its, their) own special sauce.
9. All of the passengers in the boat wore (his or her, their) lifejackets.
10. Did anybody bring (his or her, their) own paintbrushes?

Exercise C: Follow the directions for Exercise B.

1. Nobody has received (his or her, their) tickets yet.
2. Has everyone checked (his, their) equipment?
3. Few of the actors needed (his or her, their) scripts.
4. Neither of the girls remembered (her, their) music.
5. One of the trees lost all of (its, their) leaves.
6. All of the candidates approved (his or her, their) staffs.
7. Each of the horses had (its, their) mane braided.
8. Some of the artists displayed (his or her, their) work.
9. Many of the winners wrote (his or her, their) own speeches.
10. Some of the food has lost (its, their) flavor.

Exercise D: Writing Write ten sentences of your own, using these indefinite pronouns as subjects. Each sentence should also have a possessive pronoun that agrees with its antecedent.

EXAMPLE: everything
Everything is in *its* place.

nobody	one	some
everyone	neither	many
few	each	both

Part 9 Special Problems with Pronouns

Possessive Pronouns and Contractions

Certain possessive pronouns are sometimes confused with contractions that sound the same. For example, *it's* and *its* are often confused in a sentence such as the following:

The seal balanced on (its, it's) flippers.

In this sentence, the possessive pronoun *its* is correct.
Contractions are formed by joining two words and omitting one or more letters. An apostrophe shows where letters are left out.

it's = it + is *or* it + has   they're = they + are
you're = you + are   who's = who + is *or* who + has

The above contractions are sometimes confused with the possessive pronouns *its, your, their,* and *whose.* The words sound alike but are spelled differently. Remember, the possessive pronouns do not use an apostrophe.

INCORRECT: The plant lost *it's* leaves.
CORRECT: The plant lost *its* leaves.

INCORRECT: Is this *you're* radio?
CORRECT: Is this *your* radio?

To decide which word is correct in a particular sentence, substitute the words the contraction stands for. If the sentence sounds right, then the contraction is correct. If it doesn't, a possessive pronoun is required.

INCORRECT: *Who's* (who is) skates are these?
CORRECT: *Whose* skates are these?

Exercise A: Choose the right word from the two in parentheses.

1. The movers parked (their, they're) van in front of the building.
2. (Your, You're) expecting a call, aren't you?
3. Someone forgot to replace the telephone receiver on (its, it's) hook.
4. (Whose, Who's) signature is this on the voucher?
5. Is that (your, you're) camera?
6. (Their, They're) trapped in the collapsed mine!
7. (Whose, Who's) taking the ball out of bounds?
8. When (its, it's) ten o'clock in Albuquerque, people are eating (they're, their) lunch in New York.
9. (Whose, Who's) the woman with the microphone?
10. (Your, You're) friends are waiting at the station.

Exercise B: If a sentence is incorrect, rewrite it correctly. Write *Correct* if a sentence does not contain an error.

1. They're going white water rafting in Colorado.
2. Ask if its too late to buy a ticket for the incline railway.
3. Who's house shall we meet at?
4. Your subscription to *Seventeen* just expired.
5. The sign indicates that it's dangerous to travel through the mountains at night.
6. They're Dalmatian won a blue ribbon in the dog show.
7. Take you're time on the essay portion of the test.
8. Do you know whose starring in the movie?
9. The troops grew concerned as their water supply diminished.
10. The bear scratched it's back on a tree.

Who and *Whom*

Many people have trouble knowing when to use *who* and *whom*. *Who* is the subject form of the pronoun. It is used as the subject of a sentence.

> *Who* tuned the piano?   *Who* is there?

Whom is the object form of the pronoun. Although it doesn't sound as natural as *who*, it should be used when the sentence requires an object.

> *Whom* did the Regans adopt?
> (direct object of the verb *did adopt*)
> With *whom* will you go to the party?
> (object of the preposition *with*)

Be especially alert to sentences that begin with the interrogative pronoun and end with a preposition. Such sentences also use *whom*.

> *Whom* was the message directed **to**?
> (object of the preposition *to*)
> *Whom* did the pianist play **for**?
> (object of the preposition *for*)

Exercise A: Choose the right pronoun from the two given in parentheses.

1. (Who, Whom) could possibly eat a whole pecan pie?
2. (Who, Whom) insulted your friend?
3. To (who, whom) should these roses be delivered?
4. (Who, Whom) were you watching on TV?
5. (Who, Whom) is the sportscaster that reports on high school games?
6. (Who, Whom) is our Secretary of State?
7. (Who, Whom) runs the drill press?
8. With (who, whom) will you stay in Tallahassee?
9. (Who, Whom) do these running shorts belong to?
10. When you went to St. Louis, (who, whom) did you visit?

Exercise B: Follow the directions for Exercise A.

1. (Who, Whom) works the new, computerized switchboard at the hospital?
2. (Who, Whom) did the lifeguard call the ambulance for?
3. (Who, Whom) did the detective suspect?
4. (Who, Whom) is the telegram addressed to?
5. (Who, Whom) did your mother hire to do the filing?
6. (Who, Whom) used up all the hot water?
7. For (who, whom) was the school named?
8. (Who, Whom) founded Salt Lake City?
9. (Who, Whom) do you compete with at next week's swimming meet?
10. (Who, Whom) needs a yearly physical exam?

We and Us with Nouns

The pronouns *we* and *us* are often used with nouns, as in the phrases *we boys* or *us students*. Sometimes it is difficult to tell whether to use the subject form *we* or the object form *us*.

To decide whether to use *we* or *us*, omit the noun. Say the sentence with *we* and then with *us*. You will then probably be able to choose the correct pronoun.

PROBLEM: (We, Us) linemen do the blocking.
CORRECT: We do the blocking.
CORRECT: We linemen do the blocking.

PROBLEM: Nothing stops (we, us) campers.
CORRECT: Nothing stops us.
CORRECT: Nothing stops us campers.

Them and Those

Them and *Those* are sometimes confused. To use the words correctly, remember that *them* is always used as a pronoun. It is never used to modify a noun. *Those,* on the other hand, can be used as either a pronoun or a modifier. Look at the examples on the following page.

INCORRECT:	A search party found *them* hikers.
CORRECT:	A search party found *them*.
CORRECT:	A search party found *those* hikers.
CORRECT:	Hand me *those* tickets, please.
CORRECT:	Hand me *those*, please.

Exercise A: Choose the correct pronoun from the two given in parentheses.

1. (We, Us) girls hooked up the antenna.
2. (Them, Those) are the sweetest grapes I've ever tasted.
3. The foul ball nearly hit (we, us) spectators.
4. Can you take advantage of (them, those) new air fares?
5. (Them, Those) greeting cards are funny.
6. The Sunday paper ran a story about (we, us) Scouts.
7. (We, Us) athletes are often tense before games.
8. Micki King tried one of (them, those) difficult back dives.
9. When will (we, us) Americans host the Olympics again?
10. Did you see (them, those) state troopers?

Exercise B: Writing Pronouns are used incorrectly in some of the sentences below. Rewrite these sentences, correcting any errors. If there is no error, write *Correct*.

1. Fishing rights are important to us Native Americans.
2. Will them additives improve gas mileage?
3. Us boys pushed the stalled car.
4. Can any of them computers translate languages?
5. Special facilities were provided for we handicapped students.
6. There is a new club for us backgammon players.
7. Did you eat all of those blueberries?
8. Yesterday we campers hiked up Mount LeConte.
9. The hospital treats we patients well.
10. Those stakes hold the tent in place.

Exercise C: Writing Write ten sentences. Use either *we, us, them,* or *those* at least once in each sentence.

REINFORCEMENT EXERCISES
Using Pronouns

A. Find the pronouns. Number your paper from 1 to 10. Write the pronouns you find in each of the following sentences.

1. He and I streaked down the toboggan slide on his new sled.
2. She held her breath for seventy seconds.
3. May I take it to him?
4. Luke Skywalker leaped onto his speeder bike and raced through the forest.
5. Ms. Duncan gave them an unusual project.
6. They turned off their TV for a month.
7. The dog retrieved your Frisbee from the lake, didn't he?
8. My uncle restored a Victorian house for a family on his street.
9. Jeff saved her a seat next to him.
10. Do you or your sister have allergies?

B. Find the antecedents of pronouns. Write each pronoun and its antecedent.

1. Cheryl rode her horse into the meadow.
2. The archer kept his left arm steady and took aim at the distant target.
3. Alison and Kate had their lunch in Thornwood Park.
4. The sky divers released their parachutes at the last moment.
5. Laura had just hung up the telephone when it suddenly rang again.
6. Yolanda is usually a guard, but today she is playing forward.
7. The heartbeat and breathing of certain mammals and amphibians slow when they hibernate.
8. Mike, have you and Lee finished your tennis game?
9. The Greeks built a huge wooden horse to fool their enemy. They hid soldiers inside.
10. Will you sing the solo, Stephanie?

C. Use subject and object forms of pronouns. Choose the correct pronoun from the two given in parentheses.

1. (She, Her) and Luther took the photos during the ceremony.
2. The reports about (they, them) and the new board members were biased.
3. The coach asked Suzanne and (I, me) for help.
4. Todd and (she, her) work in a sporting goods shop.
5. (Him, He) and (me, I) watched the gymnasts work out.
6. Greg and (he, him) learned a new dive.
7. It was (he, him), believe it or not, in the Rolls Royce.
8. Alec took Nancy and (I, me) to a roller derby.
9. Did Jill and (she, her) take archery in gym class?
10. Bill has sold the winning raffle ticket to (he, him) or (I, me).

D. Recognize different kinds of pronouns. Number your paper from 1 to 10. Write the pronouns in these sentences. After each pronoun, write *Demonstrative*, *Interrogative*, or *Indefinite* to tell what kind it is.

1. A computer could do this in a split-second.
2. Which of the cars finished the race?
3. This is a replica of a clipper ship.
4. Are those Sue's cousins from Nova Scotia?
5. Anyone can learn to play a recorder.
6. Whom did the President assign to the task force?
7. What is the capital city of Belgium?
8. Nora had never heard that before.
9. Everyone sensed a sudden change in the atmosphere.
10. Many of the witnesses refused to answer the district attorney's question.

E. Use indefinite pronouns correctly. Choose the pronoun that agrees with the indefinite pronoun in each sentence.

1. Neither of the runners slowed (her, their) pace.
2. Only one of the karate students had earned (his, their) black belt.

3. All of the teams brought (its, their) mascots to the state meet.
4. Both of the boys wore (his, their) hockey skates to the ice rink.
5. Every boat in the marina has (its, their) own name.
6. Most of the stores advertise (its, their) sales a week ahead of time.
7. Everyone should take (his or her, their) own camera.
8. Has anyone had (his or her, their) fortune told?
9. Some of the actors apply (her, their) make-up.
10. Each of the parking lots has (its, their) own rates.

F. Solve special pronoun problems. Choose the correct word from the two in parentheses.

1. Have (your, you're) friends been waiting all this time?
2. (Who, Whom) did Mary Lou go to the concert with?
3. The president thanked (we, us) committee members.
4. (Who, Whom) received this year's Nobel Peace Prize?
5. (Them, Those) are Australia's hottest new singers.
6. (We, Us) students who ride the bus to school have to get up earlier.
7. (Whose, Who's) starring in that new comedy?
8. Have you tried one of (them, those) egg rolls?
9. The guide was very polite to (we, us) tourists.
10. The bikers loaded (their, they're) backpacks with food for the trip.

MIXED REVIEW
Using Pronouns

A. Complete each of the following sentences, using the type of pronoun given in parentheses.

1. The actors _____ were distracted by some of the special effects. (compound personal)
2. _____ are the kinds of nails I need. (demonstrative)
3. _____ won the Academy Award for best actor? (interrogative)
4. _____ was the best pizza I have ever tasted. (demonstrative)
5. In any friendship between two people, _____ should be able to trust the other. (indefinite)
6. Is that _____ bicycle or mine? (possessive)
7. Randy planned and prepared the entire dinner _____ . (compound personal)
8. I cannot seem to get _____ out of my mind. (demonstrative)
9. _____ of the students asked that the test be postponed. (indefinite)
10. With _____ were you planning to play racquetball? (interrogative)

B. Number your paper from 1 to 15. Choose the correct pronoun from the two given in parentheses.

1. (Who's, Whose) idea was it to tape this concert?
2. All of the orchestra members tuned (their, it's) instruments.
3. My friend told me that (your, you're) going sailing this weekend.
4. Tara could hardly wait to see the picture of (she, her) and (he, him).
5. (Who, Whom) did the class elect as representative to the student council?

6. (Who, Whom) won the Heisman Trophy last year?
7. The cooking instructor wondered (who's, whose) homemade bread would win the contest.
8. Have you ever seen one of (them, those) windsurfers?
9. (We, Us) citizens requested a better selection of books in the library.
10. The electrician demonstrated to (us, we) students how to repair a lamp.
11. The Johnsons found (themselves, theirselves) anxious to begin a new business after retirement.
12. Jim invited Mike and (he, him) to spend the weekend camping.
13. My grandfather and (she, her) taught (I, me) how to tune a piano.
14. Many people in the audience expressed (their, they're) appreciation by applauding.
15. Mrs. Lopez and (she, her) run a travel agency for senior citizens.

C. Rewrite the following sentences, changing all of the italicized words to personal pronouns. Then label each pronoun **S** for *Subject*, **O** for *Object*, or **P** for *Possessive*.

EXAMPLE: *Jane* bought *Jane's* silver bracelet in Mexico.
           S   **P**
        She bought her silver bracelet in Mexico.

1. *Mary* read *Mary's* computer printout.
2. *Juan* admired the boxer for *the boxer's* agility.
3. Why isn't *Joan* wearing *Joan's* favorite dress to the homecoming dance?
4. Give *the dog* *the dog's* dinner.
5. *Mickey Rooney* and *Ann Miller* starred in the hit Broadway show.
6. *Kim and I* watched *Pat, Bill and Mario* swim the final laps.
7. *The mechanic* lost *the mechanic's* wrench under the hood.
8. *Supreme Court Justice Sandra Day O'Connor* is highly respected by the other members of the High Court.
9. *The reporter* refused to reveal *the reporter's* source.
10. The winter took *the winter's* toll on the crops.

D. Rewrite the following sentences correcting all pronoun errors. If there are no errors, write *Correct*.

1. Us band students decided that them green band uniforms were more attractive.
2. Who does Nancy want for a homeroom teacher?
3. Somebody turned in their homework late.
4. A snake usually sheds it's skin once a year.
5. We players have great respect for our coach.
6. Were them boys at the hockey game?
7. No one knew where their shoes had been hidden.
8. Who did you skate with this afternoon?
9. Both the Japanese and the Americans make reliable cars.
10. The plot of that movie doesn't make sense to me.
11. I listened to she and him on the radio.
12. Someone left their ticket in this envelope.
13. Its time for the zookeepers to feed them water buffaloes.
14. Whom did you say was playing center at the next game?
15. Your definitely the best reporter on the paper.

USING GRAMMAR IN WRITING
Using Pronouns

A. Imagine that you are a millionaire writing your will. You have some friends and relatives that you would like to reward for their kindness toward you. There are also a few strangers and some favorite pets that you would like to remember. Tell which of the objects from your great wealth you intend to give to particular individuals. Explain why each person is receiving his or her reward. Use as many different types of pronouns as possible. Underline them. Be ready to tell what type of pronoun each one is.

B. Sometimes a pronoun in one sentence refers to a noun in a preceding sentence:

> Antoine Becquerel discovered radioactivity.
> For *this*, *he* received a Nobel Prize.

The pronouns *this* and *he* help tie the two sentences together. Words that are used to tie sentences together in this way are called **transitional devices.** Write the following sentences in paragraph form. Substitute pronouns for some of the nouns in order to provide transitions.

> The miller was America's first industrial inventor.
>
> People of today might consider the miller just another merchant.
>
> People don't realize that the miller was banker, businessman, and host to the countryside.
>
> The miller also had a strenuous and dangerous job.
>
> The early mill that the miller worked in was massive and powerful.
>
> A mill had huge wheels and massive gears that could easily crush a person.
>
> "Killed in his mill" was a frequent epitaph of two hundred years ago.

Section 5

Using Verbs

An ancient jalopy *lurched* down the road.
The grass snake *slithered* through the weeds.

Look at the two sentences above. Each one creates a vivid image for the reader. The words *lurched* and *slithered*, in particular, bring the sentences to life. These two words are verbs. Skillful writers and speakers know that the verb is the key word in any sentence. Without a verb, no idea can be complete. In addition, the correct choice of verbs can make the difference between dull and lively writing.

You have already learned to identify this type of word. In this Section you will learn more about how verbs are used. You will also learn how the use of just the right verb can help make your writing more effective.

Part 1   What Is a Verb?

A verb expresses an action or a state of being.

Action Verbs

One kind of verb indicates action. The action may be visible or unseen.

The storm *raged.*   Bill *expects* a raise.
A plane *landed.*   Maria *has* great ambition.

An **action verb** tells that something is happening, has happened, or will happen.

Linking Verbs

Some verbs simply tell that something exists. Such verbs express a state of being rather than action.

The election *is* Tuesday.   Spencer *was* our captain.
Rita *seems* happy.   The cake *tastes* moist.

Most state-of-being verbs link the subject with a word or words in the predicate. These verbs are called **linking verbs.**

Here are the most common linking verbs:

be (am, are, is, was,   look   smell   seem
    were, been, being)   appear   taste   sound
become   feel   grow

Some linking verbs can also be used as action verbs.

LINKING VERB   ACTION VERB
The T-shirt *looked* dirty.   Kim *looked* at the painting.
The meal *grew* cold.   The gardener *grew* zinnias.

When you look at the verb in a sentence, notice how it is used. Decide whether it expresses action or simply links the subject with a word in the predicate.

Transitive and Intransitive Verbs

In many sentences an action verb expresses an idea by itself. In other sentences a direct object completes the action of the verb. The direct object, as you have learned, tells *who* or *what* receives the action of the verb.

Verbs that have direct objects are **transitive verbs.**

> Dave *met* the mayor.
> (The direct object *mayor* completes the meaning of the verb *met.*)
>
> The officer *wore* several medals.
> (The direct object *medals* completes the meaning of the verb *wore.*)

Verbs that do not have direct objects are called **intransitive verbs.**

> The winners *rejoiced.*
> Steve *rested* under a tree.

Notice that in the second sentence, the words following the verb modify it. They do not receive the action of the verb and are therefore not objects of the verb.

Some action verbs are always transitive or always intransitive. Other verbs may be transitive in one sentence and intransitive in another. Compare these examples. Direct objects are shown in boldface type.

TRANSITIVE VERB	INTRANSITIVE VERB
The girls *swam* a **mile.**	The girls *swam.*
The artist *sketched* the **model.**	The artist *sketched* by the sea.
Ella *sings* the **lead.**	Ella *sings* tonight.

Exercise A: Write the verb in each sentence. After each verb write *Action* or *Linking* to show what kind it is.

1. Jennifer and Marcia portaged the canoe.
2. Who won this year's Nobel Prize in medicine?
3. The Senator campaigned for reelection.
4. That abandoned building looks spooky.

5. Diane programmed the computer.
6. The flight to Cleveland seemed very smooth.
7. The ranch overlooks the Rockies.
8. Water became scarce during the summer.
9. We saw an old-fashioned rodeo in Bishop, California.
10. Juan likes books about the American Civil War.

Exercise B: Follow the directions for Exercise A.

1. Judge Leonard Suchanek amazes most people.
2. At birth, Suchanek had only forty percent hearing.
3. At age five he became totally blind from an accident.
4. He studied Braille for several years at a special school.
5. The young boy soon developed an important, positive attitude toward life.
6. From childhood, Suchanek constantly challenged the limits of his handicaps.
7. He was an excellent student in both high school and college.
8. Eventually this man became a successful lawyer.
9. Today Suchanek lives with his wife and son in our nation's capital, Washington, D.C.
10. He is a federal judge.

Exercise C: Write the action verb in each sentence. After it write *Transitive* or *Intransitive* to show what kind it is. If a verb is transitive, write its object.

1. Those trucks have diesel engines.
2. The herd of elephants suddenly charged the hyenas.
3. Neon signs flashed in the dark.
4. The spacecraft explored Saturn.
5. Mrs. LaPorte videotaped the final performance of our class play.
6. The train from Washington finally arrived.
7. During the storm the airport closed.
8. Tom often swims before school.
9. Sarah reads horror stories and fantasies.
10. Through the tangle of branches we saw luminous eyes.

Part 2 The Parts of a Verb

Many verbs are made up of a **main verb** plus one or more **helping verbs**. Another name for helping verbs is **auxiliary verbs**.

The most common helping verbs are forms of *be, have,* and *do.* They may also be used as main verbs. Here are their forms:

BE—am, is, be, are, was, were, been
HAVE—has, have, had
DO—does, do, did

USED AS MAIN VERB	USED AS HELPING VERB
I *was* lucky.	I *was eating* lunch.
Jill *has* a cold.	Jill *has finished* her report.
We *did* our chores.	We *did like* the movie.

Here are other frequently used helping verbs:

can	will	shall	may	must
could	would	should	might	

Helping verbs combine with the main verb to become parts of the verb.

HELPING VERB(S) + MAIN VERB = VERB

am	going	am going
are	watching	are watching
will	stay	will stay
had	stayed	had stayed
should have	stayed	should have stayed
must	join	must join
has	joined	has joined

Sometimes the parts of the verb are separated. The words that come between them are not part of the verb. Study these examples.

Chinese food *has* always *seemed* tasty.
The team *was* barely *paying* attention.
When *will* the President *hold* a press conference?
Did the press secretary *speak?*

Exercise A: Make two columns. Label them *Helping Verb* and *Main Verb*. Find the parts of the verb in each sentence. Write them in the proper columns.

1. A new snack shop has opened.
2. The glider was soaring above the valley.
3. The express train does not stop at Webster Avenue.
4. A computer will prepare the class lists.
5. Has Bob been diving for scallops?
6. No fuel should be wasted.
7. The roan stallion must have escaped from the corral.
8. No one had ever climbed that mountain.
9. Construction workers on a job site must always wear hardhats.
10. A smoke alarm would have alerted us to the fire.

Exercise B: The helping verbs have been omitted from the following sentences. Number your paper from 1 to 10. Write each sentence adding helping verbs to complete each one.

1. The ice rink _____ _____ closed for repairs.
2. Greg _____ expecting a call from Dad.
3. The lifeguard _____ warned us several times.
4. _____ the Buckeyes receive the kickoff?
5. Jonas _____ _____ tried these clams.
6. _____ Melissa run for office?
7. The temperature _____ _____ climbed to 98°.
8. _____ the snowplows cleared the mountain pass?
9. Diaz _____ surely pitch in Thursday's game.
10. Pilots of commercial jets _____ pass rigorous requirements.

Exercise C: Writing Use the following helping verbs and main verbs to write sentences of your own.

1. may complete
2. would have followed
3. will record
4. might remember
5. must have meant
6. has believed
7. had been told
8. were nominated
9. should have brought
10. did agree

Part 3   Verb Tenses

In addition to expressing action or state of being, a verb can also tell *when* that action or state of being occurs. By changing form, verbs can indicate past time, present time, or future time.

These changes in form to indicate time are called **tenses.** The changes are usually made in one of these two ways:

1. Change in spelling

    run→ran   try→tried   close→closed

2. Use of helping verbs

    eat→had eaten   survive→will survive   climb→has climbed

In English there are three **simple tenses** and three **perfect tenses.** This list shows examples of the six main tenses for the verbs *paint* and *watch.*

PRESENT TENSE:	I paint.	She watches.
PAST TENSE:	I painted.	She watched.
FUTURE TENSE:	I will paint.	She will watch.
PRESENT PERFECT TENSE:	I have painted.	She has watched.
PAST PERFECT TENSE:	I had painted.	She had watched.
FUTURE PERFECT TENSE:	I will have painted.	She will have watched.

Simple Tenses

The **present tense** indicates time in the present. The present tense form is usually the same as the name of the verb. When verbs are used with most singular subjects, an *-s* is added to the end of verb.

I *know.*   Cathy *knows.*   My mother *knows.*

The **past tense** shows past time. Most verbs form the past tense by adding *-d* or *-ed.*

Ben *raced.*   Yvonne *called.*   I *laughed.*

479

Some verbs form the past tense in irregular ways.

They *rode.*   Sue *went* to the game.   Adam *swam.*

The **future tense** shows time in the future. In this tense, *shall* or *will* is used with the verb.

Keith *will start.*   Donna *will guess.*   I *shall return.*

The three tenses just described are called the **simple tenses.**

Perfect Tenses

The **perfect tenses** are used when we have to speak of two different times, one earlier than the other. The perfect tenses are formed by using the helping verbs *has, have,* and *had.*

The **present perfect tense** tells of an action or state of being in some indefinite time before the present. The helping verb *has* or *have* is used.

They *have arrived.*   The class *has elected*
Dean *has sold* his stereo.   its officers.

The **past perfect tense** tells of an action or state of being that preceded some other past action or state of being. The helping verb *had* is used.

They *had been* lonely until we *came.*
Marie *had waited* for the bus for hours, but it never *arrived.*
We *had* just *gone* into the house when the storm *hit.*

The **future perfect tense** tells of an action or state of being that will occur *before* some other future action or state of being.

By this time tomorrow, *you will have met* the Governor.
When the hike is over, *we will have walked* ten miles.

Exercise A: Write the verbs in the following sentences. Tell the tense of each.

1. Thunder rumbled in the distance.
2. We have lived in Fort Collins for three years.

3. The Packers had already accepted the penalty.
4. Bernstein kicks most of the field goals.
5. An overtime will decide the game.
6. Helmets protect motorcycle riders.
7. Each suspect will take a lie detector test.
8. By noon the hikers will have reached the Alpine Meadows.
9. Police thoroughly searched the hideout.
10. The mobsters had already fled through a hole in the roof.

Exercise B: Writing Write a sentence for each of the verbs below. Use the tense indicated.

1. judge (past)
2. deny (present perfect)
3. notice (past perfect)
4. live (present)
5. flip (past)

6. drive (present)
7. explode (future)
8. prepare (future perfect)
9. work (present perfect)
10. dance (future)

Part 4   The Progressive Forms

There is another way that a verb can show time. The **progressive form** of a verb indicates action which is ongoing. That action can be in the past, the present, or the future. Progressive forms are made by using the forms of *be* with the present participle:

Rosemary *is taking* mandolin lessons.
Craig *was thinking* about it.
We *will be marching* in the Labor Day parade.
Before you called, I *had been sleeping.*

Exercise: Identify the progressive forms in the following sentences. Write them on your paper.

1. They will be considering your application later this afternoon.
2. As the fog was rolling in, we were crossing the famous Golden Gate Bridge.
3. Will we be going to the movie with Jeremy?
4. The snow was piling up in huge drifts against the doors and windows.

5. The band will soon be looking for a new lead singer.
6. After the storm, the clouds were moving slowly.
7. Marco will be waiting for you at the soccer field.
8. Mozart was already composing complicated music as a child.
9. Michael was telling the story about the haunted van.
10. We will be reading play scripts all evening.

Part 5 The Principal Parts of a Verb

The **principal parts** of a verb are its basic forms. The principal parts of a verb are the **present,** the **past,** and the **past participle.** By combining these forms with helping verbs, you can make all of the six main tenses.

Most verbs form the past and past participle by adding -*d* or -*ed* to the present form. These verbs are called **regular verbs** because they form the past and past participle by following a regular pattern.

PRESENT	PAST	PAST PARTICIPLE
trust	trusted	(have) trusted
want	wanted	(have) wanted
move	moved	(have) moved
change	changed	(have) changed

Note: Some regular verbs change their spelling when the -*d* or -*ed* is added. Study the examples that follow.

PRESENT	PAST	PAST PARTICIPLE
try	tried	(have) tried
trot	trotted	(have) trotted
say	said	(have) said
slip	slipped	(have) slipped

The past participle is used for all perfect tenses. It must be used with a helping verb.

They have changed.   We had tried.
Mark must have known.   Beth has slipped.

Exercise: Make three columns on your paper. Label them *Present, Past,* and *Past Participle.* List the principal parts of these regular verbs in the proper columns.

1. cook	6. copy	11. follow
2. marry	7. happen	12. open
3. seem	8. lift	13. claim
4. belong	9. act	14. trip
5. pull	10. toss	15. drag

Part 6　Irregular Verbs

You have learned the principal parts for regular verbs. Many verbs, though, do not follow the regular pattern. That is, they do not add *-d* or *-ed* to form the past tense and past participle. Such verbs are called irregular verbs. Note the following examples.

PRESENT	PAST	PAST PARTICIPLE
throw	threw	(have) thrown
feel	felt	(have) felt
spring	sprang	(have) sprung
tell	told	(have) told
cut	cut	(have) cut

You will notice that some of the verbs have one or two different forms. Others, like the verbs *throw* and *spring*, have three different forms.

If you do not know the principal parts of a verb, look up the verb in a dictionary. If no parts are listed, the verb is regular. If the verb is irregular, the dictionary will list the irregular forms. It will give two forms if both the past and past participle are the same, as in *catch, caught.* It will give three forms if all principal parts are different, as in *ring, rang, rung.*

Some dictionaries will list a fourth principal part. It is called the **present participle.** The present participle of a verb is formed by adding *-ing* to the present form: *cook—cooking.* This participle is used to make the progressive forms of a verb.

Using Irregular Verbs

There are two ways to be sure of the forms of irregular verbs. One way is to look up the verbs in the dictionary. The other way is to learn the principal parts of commonly used irregular verbs.

Once you know the principal parts, keep the following ideas in mind. The past participle is always used with *have* or *be* helping verbs. The past participle is used for present perfect and past perfect tenses. The past form is not used with helping verbs.

The principal parts of irregular verbs can be confusing. They may seem simpler if you learn the following five patterns.

Group 1 Some irregular verbs keep the same form for all three principal parts. These are easy to remember.

PRESENT	PAST	PAST PARTICIPLE
burst	burst	(have) burst
cost	cost	(have) cost
cut	cut	(have) cut
let	let	(have) let
put	put	(have) put
set	set	(have) set

Here are some sentences using verbs from this group:

Those video games *cost* too much. (present)
I *put* my signature on the contract. (past)
Matt *has set* up the scenery. (past participle)

Group 2 Another group of irregular verbs changes form only once. The past and the past participle are the same.

PRESENT	PAST	PAST PARTICIPLE
bring	brought	(have) brought
catch	caught	(have) caught
lead	led	(have) led
lend	lent	(have) lent
lose	lost	(have) lost
say	said	(have) said
sit	sat	(have) sat

These sentences use irregular verbs from Group 2:

I *sit* in the lifeguard station. (present)
Tyrone *led* the league in R.B.I.'s. (past)
Garrett and Lynn *have caught* three salmon. (past participle)

Exercise A: Choose the correct form of the verb.

1. The convention (brang, brought) five thousand delegates to San Diego.
2. The infielder has (catched, caught) the foul ball.
3. These ice skates (costed, cost) twice as much as my old ones.
4. Estelle (put, putted) a videotape on the player.
5. Lauren (lent, lended) me a special wrench.
6. The stage crew (set, setted) up the props and scenery.
7. No one has ever (sayed, said) that before.
8. A hose in the engine (burst, bursted).
9. Duncan has (sat, sitted) on the bench all season.
10. Kris (leaded, led) in scoring for the Wildcats.

Exercise B: Follow the directions for Exercise A.

1. Somehow I (lost, losed) track of the time.
2. The reward for any helpful information was (setted, set) at $1,000.
3. Suddenly, Jane (burst, bursted) into the room.
4. Jim has (put, putted) more kerosene in the lamp.
5. Deena (caught, catched) the flu.
6. The fishermen had not (brang, brought) enough bait.
7. In 1978 gas (cost, costed) less than a dollar a gallon.
8. The exhausted soldiers (sat, sitted) wearily in their barracks.
9. Porter (led, leaded) by only a few thousand votes in the primary election.
10. The lawyer has (said, sayed) very little about the complicated case.

Exercise C: Writing Compose a paragraph that uses the present, past, and past participle forms of some of the Group 1 and 2 verbs.

Group 3 Verbs in this group add -*n* or -*en* to the past tense to form the past participle.

PRESENT	PAST	PAST PARTICIPLE
break	broke	(have) broken
choose	chose	(have) chosen
freeze	froze	(have) frozen
speak	spoke	(have) spoken
steal	stole	(have) stolen
wear	wore	(have) worn

Here are three sentences using Group 3 verbs:

Speak into the microphone. (present)
Everyone *wore* strange costumes. (past)
Joan and Bill *have chosen* their teams. (past participle)

Exercise A: Choose the correct form of the verb from the two forms given.

1. Ms. Gomez has (chose, chosen) a blue interior for her car.
2. The environmental group has (spoke, spoken) to the governor.
3. Money had been (stole, stolen) from the cash register.
4. The rock group (wore, worn) gold and glitter.
5. Evans (broke, broken) a land-speed record.
6. Tires squealed as the cars (tore, torn) around the track.
7. After an afternoon of ice skating, my feet were nearly (froze, frozen).
8. A rock has (broke, broken) the display window.
9. The country has (chose, chosen) a new leader.
10. Have you (wore, worn) the sweater your aunt bought you in Denmark?

Exercise B: Follow the directions for Exercise A.

1. A pickpocket (stole, stolen) Ken's wallet during the rally.
2. The sign read, "Spanish is (spoke, spoken) here."
3. The sailors (wore, worn) their dress uniforms.
4. The bickering lawyers have finally (chose, chosen) a jury.

5. Rain (froze, frozen) on the windshield.
6. Lori accidentally (tore, torn) up a dollar bill.
7. The relay team has (broke, broken) a world record.
8. The mourners have (wore, worn) black clothing.
9. Some top-secret papers have been (stole, stolen).
10. The social worker (spoke, spoken) about conflicts.

Group 4 The irregular verbs in this group change their final vowels. The vowel changes from *i* in the present tense to *a* in the past tense and *u* in the past participle.

PRESENT	PAST	PAST PARTICIPLE
begin	began	(have) begun
drink	drank	(have) drunk
ring	rang	(have) rung
sing	sang	(have) sung
swim	swam	(have) swum

Here are examples of irregular verbs from Group 4:

I usually *sing* off-key. (present)
The chimes *rang* softly. (past)
The police *have begun* a crackdown. (past participle)

Exercise A: Choose the correct verb form from the two given in parentheses.

1. Emily (began, begun) babysitting last year and now has many clients.
2. Someone must have (drank, drunk) all the lemonade.
3. Bill (rang, rung) for the flight attendant.
4. I wonder how many times the Beach Boys have (sang, sung) "California Girls."
5. The telephone had (rang, rung) all day.
6. When Paul Robeson (sang, sung) "Old Man River," the audience sat spellbound.
7. Our husky has (began, begun) his obedience school course.
8. Count Dracula (drank, drunk) the blood of his victims.
9. The hospital has (began, begun) a blood drive.
10. Stevie Wonder (sang, sung) his latest hit single.

Exercise B: Follow the directions for Exercise A.

1. The loud noises (rang, rung) in my ears.
2. Leslie (swam, swum) for an hour in the icy water of Lake Superior.
3. The team (began, begun) to rally in the fourth quarter.
4. Jeff (drank, drunk) a quart of milk at lunch.
5. A piranha (swam, swum) alone in the huge tank.
6. The candidates have (began, begun) to campaign.
7. After the wedding, bells (rang, rung).
8. Have you (drank, drunk) all the grape juice?
9. Many operas are (sang, sung) in Italian.
10. Had they (swam, swum) in the ocean before?

Exercise C: Writing Using Exercises A and B as a pattern, write ten of your own exercise sentences. Use verbs from Groups 3 and 4. Make a separate answer key for your exercise or, if possible, exchange exercises with a classmate.

Group 5 For some irregular verbs the past participle is formed from the present tense. The past participle looks more like the present tense than the past tense.

PRESENT	PAST	PAST PARTICIPLE
come	came	(have) come
do	did	(have) done
eat	ate	(have) eaten
fall	fell	(have) fallen
give	gave	(have) given
go	went	(have) gone
grow	grew	(have) grown
know	knew	(have) known
ride	rode	(have) ridden
rise	rose	(have) risen
run	ran	(have) run
see	saw	(have) seen
take	took	(have) taken
throw	threw	(have) thrown
write	wrote	(have) written

Here are sentences using Group 5 verbs:

I usually *eat* in the cafeteria.
Bob *ate* three helpings of spaghetti.
My dog *has eaten* my homework.

Marcy *knows* two movie stars.
I once *knew* all the state capitals.
Have you *known* him very long?

Exercise A: Choose the correct verb form from the two given.

1. Mr. Torres has (ran, run) his store for twenty years.
2. Cary (threw, thrown) a terrific party.
3. A passenger has (fell, fallen) overboard!
4. Vera (ate, eaten) raw fish at a Japanese restaurant.
5. Ken (grew, grown) four inches last year.
6. Charles Kuralt has (went, gone) to all corners of America.
7. Jory had (saw, seen) more horror films than any of us.
8. Paris is (knew, known) for its high fashion.
9. Sterling and Darrell (took, taken) a Greyhound bus to Flagstaff, Arizona.
10. Samantha has (rode, ridden) a bike across Nebraska and South Dakota.

Exercise B: Follow the directions for Exercise A.

1. The dictator has (fell, fallen) from power.
2. The job had (came, come) along just in time.
3. A gymnast (did, done) handsprings and back flips across the mat.
4. Since the 1930's, George Gallup has (took, taken) polls of public opinion.
5. Dennis (saw, seen) a strange object flying in the night sky.
6. Has everyone (gave, given) up on this project?
7. Anne (went, gone) to City Hall to see the mayor.
8. The candidate has (ran, run) her campaign honestly.
9. *The Outsiders* and *Rumble Fish* were (wrote, written) by S. E. Hinton.
10. The escaped prisoners were last (saw, seen) in an Oklahoma town.

Part 7 Active and Passive Verbs

Study the following two sentences:

The committee proposed several possible solutions.
Several possible solutions were proposed.

In the first sentence, the subject tells who performed the action. When the subject performs the action, the verb is said to be in the **active voice**.

In the second sentence, the subject tells what received the action of the verb. When the subject is the receiver or the result of the action, the verb is said to be in the **passive voice**. The word *passive* means "acted upon."

The use of active and passive voice can add variety to writing. However, a passive verb is usually not as strong as an active one. Most writers, therefore, prefer to use active verbs whenever possible to help make their writing more interesting and lively.

Forming the Passive

The passive voice is formed by using some form of *be* with the past participle. The receiver of the action precedes the verb.

ACTIVE	PASSIVE
Max *washed* the floor.	The floor *was washed* by Max.
Meg *has finished* the project.	The project *has been finished* by Meg.
The store *will add* the tax.	The tax *will be added* by the store.

Find the direct objects in the sentences in the first column above. In the sentences in the second column, the direct objects have become the subjects. Only verbs that have objects (transitive verbs) can be changed from active to passive.

A verb is active when its subject performs the action of the verb.

A verb is passive when its subject names the receiver or result of the action stated by the verb.

490

Exercise A: Write the verb in each sentence. After each, write *Active* or *Passive* to tell what kind it is.

1. One of the twins prefers country music.
2. The weather service predicted a record snowfall.
3. A meeting had been planned by the workers' union.
4. The local merchants held a street fair.
5. Ms. O'Brien read the class an interesting article.
6. A citizens' group patrolled the streets at night.
7. Several sites were considered by the builder.
8. The Potter's Wheel also sells ceramic supplies.
9. The S.W.A.T. unit was called to the scene.
10. Liz's plans were affected by inflation.

Exercise B: Writing Change the verbs in the following sentences from passive to active. Rewrite the sentences. You may have to add subjects.

1. The rug was cleaned by Mr. Harvey.
2. The scores are given by the sportscaster.
3. A new comedian was introduced by Johnny Carson.
4. New paintings were delivered to the museum.
5. The trophy had been won by our team once before.
6. Five buildings were destroyed by the fire.
7. Mr. Walters is known by everybody on our block.
8. The African safari was led by Ms. Bernstein.
9. The judge's decision will be appealed by the lawyer.
10. Letters had been sent to the President.

Exercise C: Writing Write a paragraph that describes your favorite sport or activity. Use only the passive voice. Then, rewrite the paragraph changing the passive verbs to active verbs. Note the differences between the two paragraphs. Which is more effective?

REINFORCEMENT EXERCISES
Using Verbs

A. Identify action and linking verbs. Write the verb in each sentence. After it, write *Action* or *Linking* to tell what kind it is.

1. Michelangelo painted the ceiling of the Sistine Chapel.
2. The sky appeared almost green before the storm.
3. The lineman ran out for the pass.
4. That photo of the Grand Canyon is stunning.
5. Those stunt performers are real daredevils.
6. As a library aide, Susan shelves books.
7. The evil troll gloated at the hero's dismay.
8. Was Amy Russell the pinch hitter?
9. The sleepy cat folded his paws neatly under him.
10. In the lobby, Superman looked for a phone booth.

B. Recognize transitive and intransitive verbs. Write the verb in each sentence. After it, write *Transitive* or *Intransitive* to show what kind it is.

1. Nicole pounded the last nail into the bookcase.
2. My little brother and his friends pelted us with snowballs.
3. I gasped at the news.
4. Keith's Frisbee landed on the telephone wires.
5. The timekeeper reset the clock for the next race.
6. Lee calls Jessica almost every night.
7. After a day on his cousin's sailboat, Anthony's skin glowed bright red.
8. Doug tightened the brakes on his bike.
9. Which candidate won in that primary election?
10. The Mosses have lived in New Mexico and Wyoming.

C. Recognize verbs. Find the parts of the verb in each sentence. Put them in two columns labeled *Helping Verb* and *Main Verb*.

1. The carolers were singing "O Holy Night."
2. Lindbergh must be the most famous aviator in history.

3. My jeans have finally faded.
4. Won't you donate a can of food for the Thanksgiving baskets?
5. We will organize a softball league.
6. Jody's uncle has often ridden in rodeos.
7. The passenger train will be passing through the tunnel in a few minutes.
8. Will the parade start on time?
9. Nancy should be practicing for the talent show.
10. The pilot of the small plane could not see through the fog.

D. Identify verb tenses. Write the verb in each sentence. Tell its tense: present, past, future, present perfect, past perfect, or future perfect tense.

1. Lana is our camp counselor this summer.
2. The actors' makeup will look strange.
3. Tony has sold many of his paintings at art fairs.
4. We climbed over the rocks and driftwood along the shore.
5. Are mouthpieces a necessary part of the football uniform?
6. The monsoons will soon arrive in full force.
7. Poisonous gases from that chemical factory had leaked into the air.
8. By tomorrow the fog will have cleared.
9. The divers have thoroughly searched the river.
10. Budapest was once two cities, Buda and Pest.

E. Use progressive tenses of verbs. Rewrite each sentence, changing each verb to its progressive form. Present tense verbs should become present progressive. Future tense verbs should become future progressive. Past tense verbs should become past progressive. Remember to use appropriate helping verbs.

1. The quail crouched invisibly in the tall grass.
2. The sailors slept soundly before the storm.
3. My parakeet mimics the sounds my cat makes.
4. The ushers will arrange the chairs for the recital.
5. The bamboo grows very rapidly in the hothouse.
6. You walked too fast for me, Sarah.

7. We will make all the necessary travel arrangements.
8. A bright comet streaks across the sky.
9. I will fly to Boston Friday to visit Dad.
10. The Haida chief carved a totem pole from a cedar tree.

F. Use irregular verbs correctly. Write the correct verb form from the two given.

1. Jon had (put, putted) the maps into the car.
2. Medical care has never (costed, cost) more.
3. The raft (brang, brought) us safely to the island.
4. The Celtics (lost, losed) by one point.
5. Someone (tore, torn) down the notice about the auction.
6. Has anyone (spoke, spoken) to the career counselor?
7. Stephanie has (broke, broken) her glasses again.
8. The actress had (began, begun) with only bit parts.
9. The hikers (drank, drunk) thirstily from the cool brook.
10. Eliza (saw, seen) the filming of a movie during her trip to San Antonio.

G. Recognize active and passive verb forms. Find the verb in each of the following sentences. Then tell whether it is *Active* or *Passive*.

1. The Coast Guard patrols the shore.
2. Lyle was removed from the game for the last four innings.
3. The koala eats only eucalyptus leaves.
4. Residents have been informed of the danger.
5. The flight to Miami has been canceled.
6. The cast is holding its dress rehearsal.
7. Inspector Grimm has searched every inch of the property.
8. The pilot should have informed the crew.
9. My allowance was spent too hastily on this album.
10. The rickety cart was reluctantly pulled by Dan's mule, Flossie.

MIXED REVIEW
Using Verbs

A. Find the verb in each sentence and tell whether it is *Action* or *Linking*. Then tell whether each action verb is *Transitive* or *Intransitive*.

1. Jogging can be good for you.
2. Earthquakes are common in California.
3. Underground movements cause earthquakes.
4. *The Hound of the Baskervilles* may be the best of the Sherlock Holmes stories.
5. Colored grains of sand formed the picture.
6. The term "doozy" comes from the Duesenberg auto.
7. Light travels at the rate of 186,282 miles per second.
8. The founder of the Islamic religion was Muhammad.
9. Earth is about four and one-half billion years old.
10. The children will sleep in their tent tonight.

B. Find the verb in each sentence. Identify the tense as *Present*, *Past*, *Future*, *Present Perfect*, *Past Perfect*, or *Future Perfect*. Then, rewrite each sentence, changing the verb to the tense or voice indicated in parentheses.

1. Chris made clocks in shop class.(present perfect tense)
2. Mary has chosen Jill for a running mate.(passive voice)
3. Some dinosaurs may have been intelligent.(past tense)
4. Susan went to law school.(present tense)
5. Aaron and Eva study modern dance.(past tense)
6. Mahavira founded Jainism, an Indian religion.(passive voice)
7. We have been waiting for hours.(future perfect tense)
8. John Creasey wrote twenty-two novels in one year.(passive voice)
9. Jerry Lewis devotes extraordinary amounts of time to the campaign.(present perfect tense)
10. After a brief introduction, Leontyne Price sang an aria.(future tense)

C. Draw three columns on your paper. Label them *Present, Past,* and *Past Participle.* Write down the principal parts for the following twenty verbs in the proper columns. Then choose three of the verbs and write them in each of the six main tenses.

1. sing	6. cheat	11. start	16. eat
2. jog	7. allow	12. dress	17. love
3. camp	8. describe	13. ride	18. create
4. play	9. write	14. live	19. coach
5. act	10. worship	15. catch	20. dance

D. Choose the correct verb from the two given.

1. My father (freezed, froze) the leftovers.
2. Her hair was (cut, cutted) by a stylist at "Combing Attractions."
3. The balloon (burst, busted) in midair.
4. Alicia (set, sit) the keys on the table.
5. Larry (brang, brought) the records for the party.
6. We (lost, losed) the game by twenty points.
7. Gary was (chose, chosen) by the scholarship committee.
8. A coat was (lended, lent) to the older man.
9. Two twelve-year-old girls have (swam, swum) the English Channel.
10. Mystery writer Agatha Christie has (wrote, written) eighty-seven novels.

E. The following paragraph is weak because all of the verbs are in the passive voice. Replace the italicized passive verbs with active ones, changing the sentences as necessary.

During the Middle Ages (A.D. 400-1500), many folktales *were composed* by European peasants. These stories *were written* down by no one. Instead, they *were circulated* by word of mouth by traveling minstrels and by common people. In the mid-1800's, many of these folktales *were* still *being told* by common people throughout Europe. To the delight of children everywhere, most of the surviving stories, which include "Cinderella" and the legends of Robin Hood, *have been collected* and *published* by modern scholars.

USING GRAMMAR IN WRITING
Using Verbs

A. Imagine that you are a character in an old silent comedy. You are dangling from a flagpole that projects from the twentieth floor of a building. How did you get in this situation? How are you feeling now? How will you get down safely? Write down the thoughts that would be racing through your character's mind. Notice how the verbs change form as you switch from the past tense to present and future tenses.

B. Write out a humorous story that you have heard recently. First, write it in the past tense. Then, write it again in the present tense. Decide which version is funnier.

C. Lively verbs make lively writing. Rewrite the following ad for an amusement park. Make it come alive for the reader by replacing dull verbs with precise, vivid ones, and by changing passive verbs to active verbs. Some of the words that you might consider replacing or reworking are in italics.

Spend a day at Adventure World. The park *can be visited* seven days a week, from 9:00 A.M. to midnight. *Ride* our new roller coaster, The Snake. It *will take* you to the top of a five-story hill, then *send* you down again. *Go* from The Snake to the Paratrooper. Your chair *will be lifted* high above the park and then *dropped*. A free fall *will be experienced* for several seconds before you *are stopped*. After you *get over* your ride on the Paratrooper, *walk* over to the Rapids. You *will sit* in a giant inner tube as it *goes* down a man-made river of churning waves and whirlpools. Finally, *go* to our Musical Review. There, our troupe of talented performers *will sing* and *dance* for you. *Come* out and *visit* us soon! Adventure World is an experience that *won't* soon *be forgotten*.

Section 6

Using Modifiers

How would you describe yourself so that someone could single you out in a crowd? How would you compare the ways two people walk, or describe the taste of pickles or popcorn?

If you had only nouns and verbs to communicate your thoughts, you would have difficulty describing anything clearly. You need other words to make your descriptions more specific. Such words are called **modifiers**.

Modifiers are words that change or limit the meaning of other words.

Notice the difference modifiers make in these two sentences:

A girl sat on a suitcase.
A slender girl with a large straw hat sat restlessly on
her tattered suitcase.

Without modifiers, most writing and speech would be unclear and dull. Modifiers help you express your thoughts more precisely and vividly. In this section you will learn to identify and use modifiers.

Part 1   Using Adjectives

One kind of modifier is an **adjective**.

An adjective is a word that modifies a noun or pronoun.

Adjectives can tell three different kinds of things about nouns or pronouns.

WHICH ONE OR ONES?

this step, *that* hill, *these* fish, *those* cars

WHAT KIND?

purple line, *shiny* boots, *hilarious* mood, *narrow* alley

HOW MANY OR HOW MUCH?

three months, *several* visitors, *less* pain, *little* snow

Notice that in the first set of examples, demonstrative pronouns are being used as modifiers. Possessive nouns and pronouns can also be modifiers: the *dog's* leash, a *book's* pages, *her* comb, *their* boat.

Proper Adjectives

One special kind of adjective is the proper adjective.

A **proper adjective** is formed from a proper noun, and therefore refers to a specific person, place, or thing. This kind of adjective is always capitalized. Here are some examples:

Jan's skates	an Olympic medal
a British accent	a Pacific island
a Japanese car	Paul Newman's eyes
Mexican food	Victorian furniture

Predicate Adjectives

Another special kind of adjective is the **predicate adjective**. Although most adjectives come before the words they describe, the predicate adjective follows the word it modifies. A **predicate adjective** follows a linking verb and modifies the subject of the sentence.

Nothing seemed *clear* anymore.
(*Clear* modifies the subject, *Nothing*.)

Her hair was *auburn*.
(*Auburn* modifies the subject, *hair*.)

As you can see, *clear* and *auburn* are predicate adjectives. They follow the linking verbs *seemed* and *was*. Each one also modifies the subject of the sentence.

A predicate adjective can be compound, as can modifiers in any other part of the sentence. Look at the two examples that follow.

The car was *rusty* and *dilapidated*.

Angelo looked *tired* but *happy*.

Articles

The adjectives *a*, *an*, and *the* are called **articles**.

The is the **definite article**. It points out a specific person, place, or thing.

Keep *the* ball in play. (a particular ball)

A and *an* are **indefinite articles**.

Did you find *a* ball? (not a specific ball)
I would like *an* ice cream cone. (no specific ice cream cone)

Notice that the indefinite article *a* is used before a consonant sound as in *a* rest, *a* school, *a* trip. The indefinite article *an* is used before a vowel sound, for example *an* elbow, *an* oboe, *an* urge.

Pay attention to the sound of the word, not the spelling. We say *a* helper, but *an* honor, for instance, since the *h* in *honor* is silent.

Diagraming Adjectives

In a sentence diagram, an adjective appears below the word it modifies. It is placed on a slanted line.

This team has a quick backfield.

Predicate adjectives are diagramed differently. Like predicate nouns and predicate pronouns, they are placed on the main line. A slanted line separates the verb and the predicate adjective.

These opponents are tough.

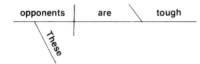

A compound predicate adjective appears on a split line.

The stereo sounds rich and full.

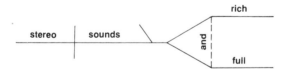

Exercise A: Write the adjectives in each sentence. After each adjective, write the word it modifies. Do not include articles.

1. The tiny shop sells old books and unusual games.
2. The new suspension bridge is long and wide.
3. Ellie spilled blue paint on her new white shirt.
4. The massive stalagmites in the cave felt cool and moist.
5. Several foreign leaders had a private meeting with the President.
6. Many soldiers were hot and tired after the long march.

7. Ten people rode in the back of the dirty, rusty truck.
8. The baby giraffe has long, gangly legs.
9. Janice drank several glasses of cold water with the salty fish.
10. Even his marvelous voice sounded harsh and tinny through the defective microphone.

Exercise B: Writing Complete these sentences by adding adjectives. Underline each predicate adjective that you use.

1. The _____ coach seems _____ .
2. _____ cars are becoming _____ .
3. The _____ team feels _____ about the game.
4. The taste of the _____ _____ chicken was _____ .
5. The gash looked _____ and _____ .
6. The _____ Ocean is _____ and _____ .
7. The sky appears _____ in the evening.
8. A _____ bear lumbered toward our _____ campsite.
9. Sue Ann is a _____ and _____ musician.
10. The video screen displayed _____ images.

Part 2   Adjectives in Comparisons

You often learn about new things by comparing them with things you already know. You might describe a restaurant's food, for example, as "*better than* homemade food." Or you might explain that a cello is *larger than* a violin.

Adjectives can help you to make such comparisons.

The Comparative

Adjectives have special forms for making comparisons. When you compare or contrast one person or thing with another, you use the **comparative** form of an adjective. Here are some examples:

> Evans is a *stronger* pitcher than Richardson.
> Venus appears *brighter* than Saturn.
> Loretta is *less patient* than I am.

The comparative form is made in two ways:

1. Add -er to short adjectives like *big* and *bright*.

   big + er = bigger   fancy + er = fancier
   wide + er = wider   young + er = younger

Notice that the spelling of some adjectives changes in the comparative form.

2. Use *more* to compare longer adjectives like *unusual*.

   more energetic   more sensitive

Most adjectives ending in *-ful* or *-ous* form the comparative with *more*.

   more powerful   more courageous

The Superlative

When you compare a person or thing with more than two others in its class, you use the **superlative** form of the adjective. Here are some examples:

   Kevin has the *smallest* part in the play.
   Carmen is the *friendliest* person I know.
   He is the *most talented* drummer in the band.
   Of the three computers, this one is *fastest*.

The superlative form of an adjective is made by adding *-est* or by using *most*. If an adjective adds *-er* for the comparative, it adds *-est* for the superlative. If an adjective uses *more* for the comparative, it uses *most* for the superlative.

ADJECTIVE	COMPARATIVE	SUPERLATIVE
green	greener	greenest
smooth	smoother	smoothest
bright	brighter	brightest
helpful	more helpful	most helpful
difficult	more difficult	most difficult
capable	more capable	most capable

Remember these points about adjectives in comparison:

1. To compare two people or things, use the comparative. To compare more than two, use the superlative.

This old coin is *more valuable* than that one.
This coin is the *most valuable* one in the collection.

2. Use the word *other* when you compare something with everything else of its kind.

WRONG: Tim is faster than any runner.
        (This sentence says that Tim is not a runner.)
RIGHT: Tim is faster than any *other* runner.

WRONG: This chair is more solid than any piece of furniture.
        (This sentence implies that the chair is not a piece of furniture.)
RIGHT: This chair is more solid than any *other* piece of furniture.

3. Do not use -er with *more*, or -est with *most*.

WRONG: Sue is much more taller than her sister.
RIGHT: Sue is much *taller* than her sister.

WRONG: Newfoundlands are the most largest breed of dog.
RIGHT: Newfoundlands are the *largest* breed of dog.

Irregular Comparisons

Some comparatives and superlatives are formed in irregular ways. Study this list and learn to use each form correctly.

ADJECTIVE	COMPARATIVE	SUPERLATIVE
good	better	best
well	better	best
bad	worse	worst
little	less or lesser	least
much	more	most
many	more	most
far	farther	farthest

Exercise A: Writing Number your paper from 1 to 10. Only two of the following comparisons are correct. If a sentence is correct, write *Correct*. If it contains an error, rewrite the sentence correctly.

1. Knowledge about computers has become importanter to high school students.
2. Snow blowers are more expensive at this store than at our local store.
3. That sailboat is the most biggest in the harbor.
4. A basketball is more big than a soccer ball.
5. The Flying Karamazov Brothers are the most best jugglers I've seen.
6. Bill swims more faster than any other boy on the team.
7. Chopsticks are difficulter for me to use than silverware.
8. Anna has the highest soprano voice of anyone in chorus.
9. The state of Maine is more farther from here than the state of North Dakota is.
10. Of the three tapes, this one is the cheaper.

Exercise B: Writing Follow the directions for Exercise A. Three of the comparisons are correct.

1. Which river is longest, the Amazon or the Volga?
2. Jack is taller than any boy at camp.
3. The raspberries this year are bigger than the ones we picked last year.
4. Who is the most popular cartoon animal, Snoopy or Garfield?
5. This science fiction novel is the most fantastic book I have ever read.
6. Which of these six snakes is the more deadlier?
7. Who scored the most touchdowns during the first half, Sam or Nick?
8. That television special on Sunday was the dullest program I have ever seen!
9. My sister says calculus is difficulter than geometry or trigonometry.
10. All of the performers in the piano recital were good, but Carol was better.

Part 3   Using Adverbs

An **adverb** is another kind of modifier. Like adjectives, adverbs help you to express your ideas clearly and vividly. They tell *how, when, where*, or *to what extent* something is true.

Using Adverbs with Verbs

Adverbs frequently modify verbs. An adverb may appear either before or after the word it modifies.

Adverbs may be used with verbs to tell *how*:

Pat *proudly* displayed her sculpture.

This computer works *accurately*.

Adverbs can also tell *when* about verbs:

Small car sales have soared *recently*.

That old desk will collapse *soon*.

Adverbs can tell *where* about verbs:

Nearby was a white picket fence.

We sat *there* on the river bank for hours.

In addition, adverbs can tell *to what extent*:

Vanessa *nearly* choked on the soup.

The earthquake was *not* destructive.

Study the following list of adverbs:

HOW?	WHEN?	WHERE?	TO WHAT EXTENT?
quickly	now	here	never
furiously	then	there	often
quietly	yesterday	upstairs	not

Try using several adverbs in the following sentence to see how different adverbs can change or modify meaning:

Jimmy Connors responded to the reporter's questions.

Using Adverbs with Adjectives and Other Adverbs

Besides modifying verbs, adverbs also modify adjectives and other adverbs. Look at these sentences:

Our pet dog is *partially* blind.
(*Partially* tells to what extent. It is an adverb modifying the adjective *blind*.)

The assembly line moved *very* quickly.
(*Very* tells to what extent. It is an adverb modifying the adverb *quickly*.)

Here are other adverbs that often modify adjectives or other adverbs:

| too | quite | rather | most | more | extremely |
| just | nearly | so | really | truly | somewhat |

Adverbs that modify adjectives and other adverbs tell *to what extent* something is true.

Forming Adverbs

Many adverbs are formed by adding *-ly* to an adjective.

weak + ly = weakly   formal + ly = formally
obvious + ly = obviously   slight + ly = slightly

At times, the addition of *-ly* causes a spelling change in the adjective.

possible + ly = possibly   dull + ly = dully
happy + ly = happily

Some adverbs are not formed from adjectives. *Quite, so, rather,* and *somewhat* are examples.

The switchboard had never been *so* busy before.
Suzanne did *rather* well on the Latin test.

Some words can be either adverbs or adjectives. *Late* and *high* are examples of such words.

The doctor arrived too *late*. (adverb)

Tony took a *late* bus. (adjective)

The glider soared *high* above the hills. (adverb)

The crew worked on a *high* tower. (adjective)

Diagraming Adverbs

In a diagram, an adverb is placed on a slanted line attached to the word it modifies. This diagram shows an adverb modifying a verb.

The fire spread rapidly.

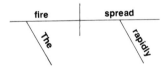

Adverbs that modify adjectives or other adverbs are diagramed like this:

Too many jobs pay very poorly.

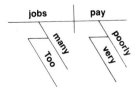

Exercise A: Number your paper from 1 to 10. Write the adverbs in these sentences. After each adverb write the word it modifies. Be ready to explain what the adverb tells about the word. A sentence may contain more than one adverb.

> EXAMPLE: A new family moved here recently.
>
> *recently* modifies *moved* (tells when)
> *here* modifies *moved* (tells where)

1. We left early for the concert.
2. Laura stood dangerously close to the fire.
3. The tornado tore fiendishly across the town.
4. The glider floated gently and silently over the airshow spectators.
5. The pilot very skillfully controlled the fall.
6. Some spectators had become extremely nervous.
7. Unfortunately, you spoke too soon.
8. A white angora cat sprawled luxuriously on the old Oriental rug.
9. Today the great bell pealed loudly.
10. The music stopped quite unexpectedly.

Exercise B: Add appropriate adverbs that answer the questions in parentheses.

1. That Steven Spielberg movie was _____ advertised on TV. (when?)
2. The movie ads sounded _____ eerie. (to what extent?)
3. The movie itself was _____ scary. (how?)
4. We went to the theater _____ . (when?)
5. The film began _____ but soon improved. (how?)
6. _____ the action moved _____ _____ . (when, how?)
7. Stunt people _____ _____ replace the real actors. (to what extent, when?)
8. This theater _____ charges _____ low prices for tickets. (to what extent?)
9. Do you _____ go to movies? (how *or* to what extent?)
10. Adventure films _____ play _____ . (when, where?)

Exercise C: Writing Change these adjectives into adverbs by adding -*ly*. Then use each word in a sentence.

careless	forceful	natural	mischievous
hungry	joyful	noisy	terrible
proper	immediate	serious	tragic

Part 4　Adverbs in Comparisons

You can use adverbs to compare actions. For example, you might say, "This team wins often but that team wins *more often*." Or you might say, "Of all the players, Erica practices *hardest*." Such comparisons help you to convey ideas clearly. Like adjectives, adverbs have special forms for making comparisons.

The Comparative

The **comparative** form of an adverb compares one action with another. Look at this example:

This thunderstorm hit the town *harder* than the last one.

The comparative is made in two ways:

1. Add -*er* to short adverbs like *long* and *fast*.

   A computer does the job *faster* than a person could.

2. Use *more* with most adverbs ending in -*ly*.

   Some blockers tackle *more roughly* than is necessary.

The Superlative

The **superlative** form of an adverb compares one action with two or more others. Notice these examples.

This flight takes off *earliest* of all.
Of the three boys, Larry spoke the *most bitterly*.

To form the superlative, either add *-est* or use *most*. If an adverb adds *-er* for the comparative, it adds *-est* to form the superlative. If an adverb uses *more* for the comparative, it uses *most* to form the superlative.

ADVERB	COMPARATIVE	SUPERLATIVE
fast	faster	fastest
tightly	more tightly	most tightly

Remember these points about adverbs in comparisons:

1. To compare two actions, use the comparative. To compare more than two actions, use the superlative.

Air mail will arrive *sooner* than surface mail.
Special delivery mail will arrive *soonest* of all.

2. Use the word *other* when you compare with every other action of the same kind.

WRONG: A queen termite lives longer than any insect.
RIGHT: A queen termite lives longer than any *other* insect.

3. Do not use *-er* with *more*, or *-est* with *most*.

WRONG: Stars appear more brighter in the countryside.
RIGHT: Stars appear brighter in the countryside.

Irregular Comparisons

Some adverbs change completely in the comparative and superlative forms. These are examples:

ADVERB	COMPARATIVE	SUPERLATIVE
well	better	best
much	more	most
little	less	least
far	farther	farthest

This saw works well.
That new saw works better.
A table saw would work best of all.

Exercise A: Writing If a sentence is correct, write *Correct*. If there is an error in the comparison of adverbs, write the sentence correctly.

1. The gymnast performed smoothlier after practice.
2. Foods cook more faster over an open fire.
3. We ate fish more often when we lived in Maine.
4. Some cars run better on unleaded gas.
5. Of all my friends, Helena speaks more openly.
6. I awaken cheerfullest on Saturdays.
7. Gardner competes more vigorously than Reese.
8. These bananas ripened the most fastest.
9. Of the four pitchers, James pitches more accurately.
10. Epoxy glue holds bestest of all.

Exercise B: Writing Use the comparative and superlative forms of the following adverbs in sentences.

1. wildly	3. gradually	5. soon	7. generously
2. loosely	4. deeply	6. intelligently	8. early

Part 5   Adjective or Adverb?

It is not always easy to know when to use an adjective and when to use an adverb. Which of the following sentences is correct?

The blast came *sudden.*   The blast came *suddenly.*

Sometimes you may have trouble deciding whether to use an adjective or an adverb. To decide, ask yourself:

1. *What kind of word does the modifier describe?*
If the word is an action verb, adjective, or adverb, use the adverb. If the word is a noun or pronoun, use the adjective.

2. *What does the modifier tell about the word it describes?*
If it tells *how, when, where,* or *to what extent,* use the adverb. If it tells *which one, what kind,* or *how many,* use the adjective.

If you applied both tests to the two sentences at the beginning of this part, you would determine that *came* requires an adverb.

An ADJECTIVE tells	An ADVERB tells
which one what kind how many **about a noun or pronoun**	how when where to what extent **about a verb, adjective or** **adverb**

Exercise A: Label two columns *Adjective* and *Adverb*. Put the modifiers you find in the appropriate column. After each adjective or adverb, write the word it modifies. Do not include articles.

1. The three motorcycles swerved sharply.
2. Heavy tractors slowly pushed the deep snow aside.
3. Open that broken window very carefully.
4. Today Lauren walked her neighbor's two large dogs.
5. Most of these shows are too predictable.
6. Two of my favorite books are *Call of the Wild* and *My Side of the Mountain.*
7. Several series have somewhat similar plots.
8. The screen glows brightly in the dark room.
9. Julio spoke very patiently to his little sister.
10. The Swiss hikers walked rather quickly and sang folk songs.

Exercise B: Choose the correct modifier from the two in parentheses. Tell whether it is an adjective or an adverb.

1. We worked (furious, furiously) to halt the flooding.
2. We'll make it to Milwaukee (easy, easily) by tonight.
3. It was (terrible, terribly) hot driving across the desert.
4. You look particularly (nice, nicely) this morning.
5. The truckers drove (slow, slowly) down the steep grade.
6. The new car gleamed (bright, brightly) in the sun.
7. The team felt (awful, awfully) about the loss.
8. An (extreme, extremely) upset man burst into the office.
9. The two teams battled (fierce, fiercely) at the game.
10. Beth's decision was very (quick, quickly).

Adverb or Predicate Adjective?

You have learned that a predicate adjective follows a linking verb and modifies the subject. Besides forms of *be*, other linking verbs are *become, seem, appear, look, sound, feel, taste, smell* and *grow*.

This melon smells sweet. (*Sweet* modifies *melon*.)

The parking lot looks full. (*Full* modifies *lot*.)

The thunder grew louder. (*Louder* modifies *thunder*.)

Alex felt cold. (*Cold* modifies *Alex*.)

In the previous sentences, the verbs *smells, looks*, and *grew* function as linking verbs. Therefore, the words that follow them are adjectives. However, these same verbs can also be action verbs. So can *sound, appear, feel*, and *taste*. When these verbs are action verbs, they are followed by adverbs instead of predicate adjectives. As you recall, adverbs tell *how, when, where*, or *to what extent* about the action verbs.

Here are sentences using the same words as linking verbs and as action verbs.

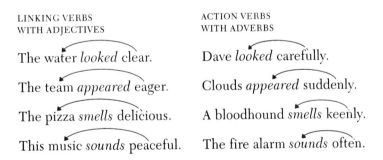

LINKING VERBS WITH ADJECTIVES	ACTION VERBS WITH ADVERBS
The water *looked* clear.	Dave *looked* carefully.
The team *appeared* eager.	Clouds *appeared* suddenly.
The pizza *smells* delicious.	A bloodhound *smells* keenly.
This music *sounds* peaceful.	The fire alarm *sounds* often.

If you have trouble deciding whether to use an adverb or an adjective, ask yourself the following questions:

1. Can you substitute *is* or *was* for the verb? If so, the modifier is probably an adjective.
2. Does the modifier tell *how, when, where*, or *to what extent*? If so, the modifier is probably an adverb.

Exercise: Choose the right modifier for the following sentences.

1. Adam looked (angry, angrily) at Bill.
2. The trumpet sounded (loud, loudly) and shrill.
3. Stained glass looks (brilliant, brilliantly) in bright light.
4. A man in a cape appeared (sudden, suddenly).
5. During the overtime the crowd grew (tense, tensely).
6. The teller sounded the burglar alarm (immediate, immediately).
7. Aretha felt (nervous, nervously) before her recital.
8. The new father looked (proud, proudly) at his daughter.
9. I feel (bad, badly) about the mistake.
10. Those big dill pickles taste (sour, sourly).

Part 6   Troublesome Modifiers

Certain modifiers are frequently used incorrectly. By studying the following pages carefully, you can avoid these errors in your writing and speaking.

Those and *Them*

Those can be used as an adjective or a pronoun.

> Where are the controls for *those* power saws? (adjective)
> *Those* are the Jackson twins. (pronoun)

Them is never an adjective, and therefore cannot be used in place of *those*. *Them* should only be used as a pronoun.

> WRONG: We framed *them* photos.
> RIGHT: We framed *those* photos.
> RIGHT: We framed *them*.

Note: The pronoun *them* should only be used as an object. Never use it as a subject.

> WRONG: *Them* are the right keys.
> RIGHT: The witness didn't recall *them*.

Here and There

Sometimes people incorrectly say "this here jacket" or "that there room." "This here" and "that there" are repetitious phrases. The word *this* includes the idea of *here*. The word *that* includes the idea of *there*. Avoid "this here" and "that there."

> WRONG: This here sandwich is stale.
> RIGHT: *This* sandwich is stale.

Kind and Sort

Kind and *sort* are singular. *Kinds* and *sorts* are plural. These words are often combined with demonstrative pronouns, as in the phrases *this sort* or *those kinds*. In such phrases, the noun and pronoun must agree in number. No matter what words follow, use *this* or *that* with *kind* and *sort*. Use *these* and *those* with *kinds* and *sorts*.

> *This kind* of boot is made of cowhide. (singular)
> *Those sorts* of snacks are high in calories. (plural)

Good and Well

Good and *well* have similar meanings, but the words are not used in the same situations. You cannot always substitute one word for the other. Look at the differences in these sentences:

> That is a *good* photo of you.
> (The adjective *good* modifies the noun *photo*.)
>
> You sing *well*.
> (The adverb *well* modifies the verb *sing*.)

Good is almost always an adjective, modifying nouns and pronouns. It is never used as an adverb.

Well can be either an adjective or an adverb. In the sentence above, *well* is used as an adverb modifying an action verb. *Well* can also be used after a linking verb to mean "in good health."

Tara doesn't look *well*.
(*Well* is a predicate adjective modifying *Tara*.)

Yvonne dances *well*.
(*Well* is an adverb modifying the action verb *dances*.)

If you are describing an action or the state of someone's health, use *well*.

The Double Negative

Two negative words used together when only one is necessary is called a **double negative**. Avoid using double negatives.

WRONG: We didn't take no time-outs.
RIGHT: We did*n't* take *any* time-outs.

WRONG: My out-of-town friends never write no letters.
RIGHT: My out-of-town friends *never* write *any* letters.

WRONG: John couldn't eat nothing all day.
RIGHT: John could*n't* eat *anything* all day.

Contractions like *couldn't* contain a shortened form of the negative *not*. Do not use other negative words after them.

Some common negative words are *no, none, not, nothing,* and *never*. Instead of these words, use *any, anything,* or *ever* after negative contractions.

Rod has*n't ever* hit a grand-slam home run.
Michelle could*n't* find *any* bargains.
The new Senator did*n't* change *anything*.

Other negative words are *hardly, scarcely,* and *barely*. Don't use them with negative contractions like *hasn't* and *didn't*.

WRONG: Rick couldn't barely control the machine.
RIGHT: Rick could *barely* control the machine.

WRONG: The movers hadn't scarcely begun.
RIGHT: The movers had *scarcely* begun.

WRONG: Lightning hardly never strikes houses.
RIGHT: Lightning *hardly ever* strikes houses.

Exercise A: Choose the correct word from the two in parentheses.

1. (Them, Those) cheerleaders sound hoarse.
2. (This, This here) video recorder has remote control.
3. You did very (good, well) at the track meet, Jed.
4. These (sort, sorts) of gym shoes wear longer than those.
5. I don't care for (any, no) cheese on my hamburger.
6. The movie we saw last night was very (good, well).
7. There (is, isn't) nobody at the computer terminal now.
8. (That, That there) car is the one that ran into our fence.
9. Are (them, those) railroad cars headed for the coast?
10. (Those, That) kind of palm tree grows all over Florida.

Exercise B: Writing Rewrite the sentences that contain errors.

1. If you listen good, you can hear a whippoorwill.
2. Barbara has not yet finished none of her homework.
3. Is that there restaurant open on Mondays?
4. The pilot couldn't barely see the runway through the fog.
5. These kinds of boats are called catamarans.
6. Although he speaks good, Ed doesn't like to make speeches.
7. Have you ever gone through them caves in Kentucky?
8. These sort of problems are difficult for a jury to consider.
9. The twins don't ever try to fool their friends.
10. Ella has taught them parrots to talk.

Exercise C: Writing Rewrite all sentences that contain double negatives, correcting the errors. Two sentences are correct.

1. Jason hasn't seen no movies lately.
2. Haven't you never been to a soccer match?
3. One runner couldn't barely clear the hurdles.
4. During the test Amy couldn't remember nothing.
5. The elevator doesn't ever work.
6. This hot dog doesn't have no mustard on it.
7. Pam hardly knows nobody in her French class.
8. Ramon and Todd haven't scarcely talked to each other.
9. Chris doesn't expect any reward for finding the purse.
10. The team doesn't have no returning players.

REINFORCEMENT EXERCISES
Using Modifiers

A. Recognize adjectives. Write each adjective in these sentences. Tell which word it modifies. Do not include articles.

1. This special exhibit will travel to thirty museums.
2. That Italian sports car has a deluxe interior.
3. Dense, black smoke poured out of the rusty tailpipe.
4. Three mysterious strangers appeared at the door.
5. Several famous sculptors worked on that huge marble statue.
6. I ate one of the biggest red raspberries in the bowl.
7. Two dignified bronze lions guarded the gate.
8. Some Indian food is cooked in clay ovens.
9. The violent storm destroyed many large homes.
10. Tiny green buds dotted the forsythia branches.

B. Find predicate adjectives. Write the predicate adjective in each sentence. Tell which word it modifies.

1. Rebecca seems quiet today.
2. That odd melody somehow sounds very familiar.
3. This dead tree is hollow.
4. The bridge is usually slippery after a storm.
5. Claire is very artistic.
6. American consumers must become more aware of safety factors.
7. Your jigsaw puzzle looks difficult.
8. The paths through the swamp were treacherous.
9. Many popular children's shows are also educational.
10. This beautiful roll-top desk is very old.

C. Use adjectives in comparison. Choose the correct adjective.

1. Jori seems (more cheerful, cheerfuller) than usual.
2. These new shoestrings are (shorter, more shorter) than the ones that broke.

3. Of the three stories, which is (more factual, most factual)?
4. The budget for this film was the (most lowest, lowest) of the series.
5. The combat forces have become (stronger, more strong) in the past few years.
6. Have you ever tasted (more spicier, spicier) chili?
7. Who was the (younger, youngest) of all the Presidents?
8. This year the business was (more profitable, most profitable) than last year.
9. Jennifer looks (happier, more happier) than her friends.
10. Of all these paperbacks, this one is the (more humorous, most humorous) to read.

D. Recognize adverbs. Write each adverb and the word it modifies. Sentences may contain more than one adverb.

1. A trap door in the floor slowly opened.
2. My grandparents arrived yesterday from Tulsa.
3. Cindy Nicholas swam the English Channel twice.
4. Carrie is too busy to answer the phone now.
5. The photographer carefully focused the camera.
6. Professional skaters practice here quite frequently.
7. Phil seemed extremely proud of his brother.
8. Currently, Congress is seriously considering other energy sources.
9. The fishing fleet always returns here in the evening.
10. Two helicopters hovered loudly overhead.

E. Use adverbs in comparison. Choose the correct adverb.

1. The sun shines (more intensely, most intensely) in California than in Alaska.
2. You will play (better, more better) if you warm up.
3. Of all the joggers, Al runs (farther, farthest).
4. She sang (more better, better) tonight than last night.
5. Brian eats (littler, less) than anyone else in the family.
6. The storm hit (hardest, most hard) in the tropics.
7. Randy can repair appliances (more skillfully, most skillfully) than his brother.

8. Of our group, Amanda lives (nearer, nearest) to the park.
9. Connors played (badder, worse, worst) than usual.
10. The flood waters receded (quicklier, more quickly) than expected.

F. Use modifiers correctly. Choose the correct word.

1. The fresh bread smelled (wonderful, wonderfully).
2. Their coach looks (impatient, impatiently).
3. The winners seemed (proud, proudly).
4. Black rolling clouds appeared (sudden, suddenly).
5. The judges tasted each contestant's pie (careful, carefully).
6. Tim's voice sounded (groggy, groggily).
7. That African nation has just become (independent, independently).
8. The veterans talked (honest, honestly) about their concerns.
9. The ice-cold watermelon tasted (sweet, sweetly).
10. Nicole looked (eager, eagerly) at the swimming pool.

G. Solve modifier problems. Eleven of the sentences below contain errors in the use of modifiers. Rewrite those sentences correctly. Write *Correct* if the sentence contains no error.

1. Jeremy dances well.
2. Take this here camera to Brad.
3. You didn't put no paste on the wallpaper.
4. Kathy couldn't find any patches to use on the tire.
5. My brothers scarcely never fight.
6. Those sort of music is called reggae.
7. Please pass me them potato pancakes.
8. Can them twigs be used as kindling for the fire?
9. Mr. Viner explained the lab procedure good.
10. These kinds of motorbikes use hardly no gasoline.
11. Phil bought a pair of those argyle socks.
12. The stranded motorist couldn't get no help.
13. These sort of fish is good for frying.
14. Lemonade tastes good on a hot day.
15. The audience couldn't barely hear the actors.

MIXED REVIEW
Using Modifiers

A. List all the modifiers in the following sentences. Identify them as adjectives or adverbs. Then list the word that each adjective or adverb modifies.

1. The nervous man walked rapidly into the subway.
2. The fans screamed wildly as the talented quarterback threw a perfect pass.
3. The young violinist drew enthusiastic applause from the audience.
4. That old house stood silent and empty for years.
5. Angela's teeth chattered uncontrollably in the bitterly cold air.
6. Miners work underground under extremely dangerous conditions.
7. Sam and his friends arrived at the game too late for the first kickoff.
8. The famous technique of this artist is very unusual.
9. Expertly, he pressed the shining apples into sweet, clear cider.
10. My new bicycle was definitely my favorite gift.

B. List the modifiers in each sentence. Do not include articles. Tell whether each modifier is an adjective or an adverb. Then give the comparative and superlative forms of each modifier.

    EXAMPLE: Angie promised to write soon.
               soon-sooner-soonest (adverb)

1. Has the family saved much money?
2. The tired, old sailor slept soundly in the tiny bunk.
3. A few little children raced wildly through the park.
4. The children in the community swim well.
5. We had a long and difficult hike because of the storm.
6. The tired announcer spoke slowly, but clearly.
7. Many people believed the honest salesperson.

8. Carol was given a pleasant assignment.
9. Sergio thought that the instructor was patient.
10. The engine in the new car was quiet.

C. All but two of the following sentences contain errors in the use of modifiers. Rewrite each sentence correctly. If a sentence contains no errors, write *Correct*.

1. Benjamin has always been real interested in mathematics.
2. The team didn't have no losses after that game.
3. Terry always dresses well for interviews.
4. Jan couldn't hardly wait for the mail to come.
5. On the corner, a musician was playing sorrowfully on a tenor saxophone.
6. These kind of shoe can be extremely comfortable.
7. I see my friends oftener than I see most of my relatives.
8. Is Lake Superior more far away than Lake Michigan?
9. The Angels played worst than usual today.
10. The band's early albums were more better than its recent ones.

D. Tell whether each italicized word or phrase in the following sentences is *Correct* or *Incorrect*. Rewrite all incorrect sentences using modifiers correctly.

1. I would not cut *them* hedges if I were you.
2. My grandparents love *that sort* of music and books.
3. My ankle still feels *tenderly* from the sprain.
4. I may look fine, but I don't feel very *good.*
5. Be *carefuller* with *them* darts.
6. Even those huge elephants are *fast* when they have to be.
7. I haven't seen *any* birds in this neighborhood for weeks.
8. Many people feel that boxing is the *most dangerous* of the two sports.
9. Ted *couldn't barely* control his temper.
10. *That there* game *hadn't scarcely* started when it began to rain.

USING GRAMMAR IN WRITING
Using Modifiers

A. If you had to choose, would you rather live the life of a house cat or that of an alley cat? Contrast the advantages of each, being sure to use both adjectives and adverbs in their comparative forms. For example, "A house cat may have a *softer* bed than an alley cat, but an alley cat can run *more freely* and roam through the town *more often.*"

B. Describe the best or worst place you have ever been. Was it a building? a place you visited on a trip? a run-down town? Be sure to involve all of your senses in describing the place. How did it smell? How did it look? How did it sound? How did it feel? If you had to eat something in this place, you might even include the sense of taste in your description.

C. The use of modifiers can change a dull piece of writing into one that is much more colorful and precise. Rewrite the following movie review. Add colorful, precise adjectives and adverbs. Replace over-used or weak modifiers with strong ones.

> The best movie of this season has to be *Gold Fever,* director I. M. Speshul's box office smash. Based on a good book by Vera Bose, the movie re-creates the atmosphere of the Klondike gold rush in the 1890's. Against this background—captured well by the pretty, on-location photography of cameraman Len Shutter—an interesting story unfolds. The story tells of a couple torn between their love for each other and their love for that shiny metal. Ivan Ego, the strong and good-looking star of television's *Suds,* gives an okay performance as "Yukon Jim," but the really nice thing about the show is Hope Foran Oscar's portrayal of "Honey," Yukon's smart but unusual sidekick. This movie is certain to leave adult audiences pleased and happy and is also great entertainment for children.

Section 7

Using Prepositions and Conjunctions

Sometimes you can communicate ideas with short sentences like these:

> Beth raced.
> The class uses paints.

More often, though, you will want to provide more information to clarify your ideas. Modifiers are useful for that purpose.

> Beth raced yesterday.
> The art class uses acrylic paints.

At times, the ideas you want to express are even more complicated. Suppose you want to say where Beth raced. Suppose you want to add that the art class also uses clay. Then you will need words to show those relationships.

> Beth raced yesterday along the lake.
> The art class uses acrylic paints and clay.

Relationships dealing with people, actions, and things are expressed by words that connect other words. In this section you will learn about two kinds of connecting words: **prepositions** and **conjunctions**.

Part 1   What Are Prepositions?

Words that join other words or word groups are called **connectives.** One important kind of connective is the **preposition.** Prepositions express a relationship between different parts of a sentence. Look at the relationships expressed in the following examples. Notice how changing the preposition can affect the meaning of the sentence as a whole.

> Sara leaped *off* her bike.
> Sara leaped *onto* her bike.
> Sara leaped *over* her bike.

The prepositions *off, onto,* and *over* show the relationship between *bike* and the verb *leaped.* In each of the above sentences, *bike* is the **object of the preposition.** Like all prepositions, *off, onto,* and *over* connect their objects to another part of the sentence.

Prepositions do not show relationships all by themselves. They begin a *phrase,* a group of words that do not have a subject or verb. The **prepositional phrase** consists of the preposition, its object, and any words that come between. In the sentences above, *off her bike, onto her bike,* and *over her bike* are prepositional phrases. Here are some other sentences that contain prepositional phrases:

> Zack politely asked *for a refund.*
> *In the spring,* Darrell returned *to school.*
> The box *of books* was too heavy.

A preposition is a word used with a noun or pronoun, called its *object,* to show the relationship between the noun or pronoun and some other word in the sentence.

A prepositional phrase consists of a preposition, its object, and any modifiers of the object.

The following list presents words often used as prepositions. Many of them, like *above, over, in,* and *beside,* help to show location. Others like *until, after,* and *before,* show a relationship of time. Still others show different kinds of relationships. Study these prepositions and try to determine the relationship each one suggests.

Words Often Used as Prepositions

about	behind	during	off	to
above	below	except	on	toward
across	beneath	for	onto	under
after	beside	from	out	until
against	between	in	outside	up
along	beyond	inside	over	upon
among	but *(except)*	into	past	with
around	by	like	since	within
at	concerning	near	through	without
before	down	of	throughout	

Exercise A: Number your paper from 1 to 10. Write the prepositional phrases in the following sentences.

     EXAMPLE: Mac went to the game with Gwen.

                    to the game, with Gwen.

1. The first competitor vaulted easily over the high bar.
2. Ask the woman at the desk for an application.
3. I waited outside the office for Pam.
4. Marta works at the mall after school.
5. By all means, talk with Gene about your plans.
6. During this season, Franklin pitched three no-hitters.
7. At first, the bite of a black widow spider may not even be noticed.
8. The figures on a totem pole have special significance to the tribe.
9. Walter jumped over the fallen halfback.
10. Don't walk through that tunnel after dark.

1. The network heard nothing from its foreign correspondent for two weeks.
2. During the storm, everyone except Dee stayed inside the bus shelter.
3. Beyond a doubt, someone had been in that cellar before us.
4. There is no one else like you in the world.
5. Bright crepe paper was strung across the gym.
6. There is a pit of quicksand near the dead tree.
7. Since last week, Anthony has been under pressure.
8. Meryl Streep walked off the stage with her award.
9. With little trouble, the Cowboys broke through the Bears' defense.
10. For over a month, that rusty old car has been parked in the alley.

Preposition or Adverb?

Many words used as prepositions may also be used as adverbs. How can you tell if a word is a preposition or an adverb?

A preposition is never used alone. It is always followed by a noun or pronoun as part of a phrase. If the word is in a phrase, it is probably a preposition. If the word has no object, it is probably an adverb.

> The visitors walked *around the courtyard.* (preposition)
> The visitors walked *around.* (adverb)
> Can you jump *over that hurdle?* (preposition)
> Can you come *over* later? (adverb)

Exercise A: Decide whether the italicized words are adverbs or prepositions. Write *Adverb* or *Preposition* for each sentence.

1. Turn the water *on* now.
2. Seagulls waited *on* the pier for handouts.
3. The golf ball ricocheted *off* a tree trunk.
4. Have you turned the oven *off* yet?
5. The captives have not been seen *since* then.

6. That was the Pirates' best game *since* last fall.
7. They found a rich vein of silver *down* there.
8. I have not seen Juanita *around* here.
9. Kittle hit the ball *over* the fence.
10. An old steam locomotive rumbled *down* the track.

Exercise B: Follow the directions for Exercise A.

1. Suzy does not ride *without* headgear.
2. What is going *on* here?
3. *Without* a word, Sam handed her the letter.
4. My aunt lives *on* San Juan Island.
5. Has the boat come *in* yet?
6. Tony put a quarter *into* the slot.
7. Finally the ball fell *through* the hoop.
8. A message to the stranded travelers got *through* on Monday.
9. Do you mind if I go *along* too?
10. Caroline inched *along* the narrow ledge.

Exercise C: Writing   Make the following sentences more interesting by adding prepositional phrases where indicated.

1. A hungry panther stalked his prey (prep. phrase).
2. That map (prep. phrase) was printed over a century ago.
3. The Flying Karamazov Brothers performed (prep. phrase).
4. The bridge (prep. phrase) is closed for repairs.
5. Are you taking the ferry (prep. phrase)?
6. (Prep. phrase) there appeared a ghostly figure.
7. Tall fir trees grew (prep. phrase) (prep. phrase).
8. A girl (prep. phrase) walked slowly (prep. phrase).
9. Davis climbed (prep. phrase) (prep. phrase).
10. A pile (prep. phrase) lay (prep. phrase) (prep. phrase).

Exercise D: Writing   Write two sentences for each of the words below. In the first sentence, use the word as a preposition. In the second sentence, use the word as an adverb.

across	inside	below	out
after	near	by	past

Part 2 Prepositional Phrases as Modifiers

Modifiers, as you know, are often single words. However, groups of words may also function as modifiers. Prepositional phrases, for example, work the same way as single-word adjectives or adverbs to modify various parts of a sentence.

An adjective phrase is a prepositional phrase that modifies a noun or pronoun.

The phrase always includes the preposition, its object, and any modifiers of the object. Like adjectives, adjective phrases tell *which one* or *what kind*. Here are three examples.

The school needs a new coach *for the track team.*
> (*For the track team* is an adjective phrase, modifying the noun *coach.* It tells *what kind* of coach.)

The door *on the left* is the emergency exit.
> (*On the left* is an adjective phrase, modifying the noun *door.* It tells *which one.*)

All *of the bank tellers* wear matching uniforms.
> (*Of the bank tellers* is an adjective phrase that modifies the pronoun *all.* It tells *what kind.*)

Adverb phrases are prepositional phrases that modify verbs.

Like single-word adverbs, an adverb phrase tells *how, when, where,* or *to what extent* something occurred.

The bottles are sealed *by a huge machine.*
> (*By a huge machine* is an adverb phrase telling *how.* It modifies the verb *are sealed.*)

On Saturday the playoffs will begin.
> (*On Saturday* is an adverb phrase. It tells *when* about the verb *will begin.*)

Hendricks sat *on the bench.*
> (*On the bench* is an adverb phrase. It tells *where* about the verb *sat.*)

Sometimes one prepositional phrase follows another. Sometimes both phrases modify the same word. Frequently, however, the second phrase is an adjective phrase modifying the object in the first phrase.

Cecily decided *on a name for her new dog.*
(*On a name* is an adverb phrase modifying the verb *decided.* *For her new dog* is an adjective phrase modifying the noun *name.*)

Jim topped the salad *with bits of cheese.*
(The adverb phrase *with bits* tells *how* about the verb *topped.* *Of cheese* is an adjective phrase describing the noun *bits.*)

Diagraming Prepositional Phrases

To diagram a prepositional phrase, place it under the word it modifies.

The guests on the show talked about their new movies.

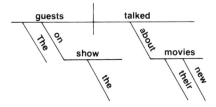

At times two or more nouns or pronouns may function as compound objects in the prepositional phrase.

On warm days we fished for trout and bass.

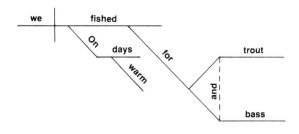

Exercise A: Copy these sentences. Underline each prepositional phrase and draw an arrow from the phrase to the word it modifies. Tell whether the phrase is an adjective phrase or an adverb phrase.

1. Nicole bought a new red jacket with a deep hood.
2. Ted walked to school with a cast on his leg.
3. Do you work for your mom after school?
4. The Navajos and Apaches were foes for hundreds of years.
5. Sacramento was a center of activity during the gold rush.
6. We spent most of the day at the zoo.
7. At the top of the hill was an abandoned farmhouse.
8. Out of nowhere rode a man with a black cape.
9. We left after lunch and arrived before dinner.
10. During the first half, four of our players fouled out.

Exercise B: Follow the directions for Exercise A.

1. A coiled black snake lay behind the rock.
2. The store down the block sells tamales.
3. The forest fire spread through the hills with incredible speed.
4. The home of Abe Lincoln is open to the public.
5. The fixture fell from the ceiling and crashed onto the floor.
6. The box under the table has sweaters for the sale.
7. After the game, shall we go to the dance?
8. Keith tripped over the rug on the stairs.
9. At low tide we saw the submerged hull of an ancient ship.
10. The beauty of the desert is overlooked by many people.

Exercise C: Writing Rewrite the following paragraph, adding an adjective (adj.) phrase or adverb (adv.) phrase as indicated.

We gave my brother a surprise party _____ (adv.). It was held _____ (adv.) _____ (adj.). You should have seen the look of shock _____ (adj.) when we yelled "Surprise!" _____ (adv.) we cooked hot dogs and ate buckets _____ (adj.). My brother sat _____ (adv.), with sixteen helium balloons tied _____ (adv.). Then came the presents. The funniest gift was made _____ (adv.) and looked _____ (adv.). The party concluded back home, where we made gigantic ice cream sundaes _____ (adj.).

Part 3 Conjunctions

A conjunction is another part of speech that shows relation-ships between parts of a sentence.

A conjunction connects words or groups of words.

Kent wrote *and* narrated the skits.
My typing is fast *but* sloppy.
We will take the train *or* the bus.
The sculptor carves *either* wood *or* stone.
Hot oatmeal is *not only* nutritious, *but also* economical.

Conjunctions connect similar words or groups of words. There are three kinds of conjunctions — coordinating conjunctions, correlative conjunctions, and subordinate conjunctions. On the following pages you will learn about the first two types of con-junctions. In Section 11 of this book you will learn about subor-dinate conjunctions.

Coordinating Conjunctions

Coordinating conjunctions are used to connect single words or groups of words of the same kind. *And, but,* and *or* are the most common coordinating conjunctions. The words connected by coordinating conjunctions are compound constructions—compound subjects, compound direct objects, and compound verbs, for example.

Cars *and* trucks often have different speed limits. (compound subject)

The skater tripped *and* fell. (compound verb)

Sue looked at the tire *but* couldn't find the leak. (compound predicate)

The candidate appeared realistic *but* hopeful. (compound predicate words)

In June *or* July we will take our vacation. (compound objects of a preposition)

Correlative Conjunctions

Like coordinating conjunctions, **correlative conjunctions** join similar words or groups of words. However, these conjunctions are always used in pairs.

both...and   not only...but (also)
either...or   whether...or
neither...nor

Both oak *and* walnut are used for furniture.
We will go to *either* Cape Cod *or* Martha's Vineyard.
I am *neither* tired *nor* hungry.
The cafeteria serves *not only* lunch *but also* breakfast.
The team discussed *whether* to kick *or* to run.

Exercise A: Write the conjunctions in the following sentences, along with words or word groups that are connected by the conjunction. Put two lines under the conjunction.

EXAMPLE: The Honda skidded and swerved.

skidded and *swerved*

1. Pigeons and sparrows pecked at the bread crumbs on the frozen ground.
2. Alice darted quickly and nervously to the telephone on the hall table.
3. The blueprints for the community center were both clear and precise.
4. Simon overslept and missed soccer practice.
5. Would you rather be a singer or a dancer?
6. Does Tokyo, Mexico City, or Los Angeles have the largest population?
7. Barbara writes humorous slogans for T-shirts and bumper stickers.
8. Todd not only notices but also remembers.
9. Do you know whether the Italians or the Chinese invented pasta?
10. The team had neither an experienced coach nor a good relief pitcher.

Exercise B: Write each compound construction with its conjunction. Then tell what kind of compound construction each one is.

1. Borg crouched and waited for the serve.
2. Dallas called time-out but couldn't decide on a new strategy.
3. Bobcats and bears prowl the back woods.
4. A piston moves up and down in its cylinder.
5. The wooden walkway was narrow, shaky, and dangerous.
6. I'll telephone either Jane's mother or her brother immediately.
7. Billie has not only a sore throat but also a bad cough.
8. In January, is New Zealand warm or cold?
9. Both the length and width of my skate blades need adjusting.
10. The restaurant specializes in salads, fruit drinks, and felafel sandwiches.

Exercise C: Writing Write two sentences for each conjunction below. After each sentence, write the word or words that are joined by the conjunctions.

and	both...and
but	either...or
or	neither...nor

REINFORCEMENT EXERCISES
Using Prepositions and Conjunctions

A. Recognize prepositional phrases. Write the prepositional phrase or phrases in each sentence.

1. During our vacation, we toured Mark Twain's home in Hartford, Connecticut.
2. Mary searched everywhere in the house for the old photograph album.
3. At the edge of the forest we saw a deer.
4. The Underground City in Montreal is the largest mall of its kind in the world.
5. Rick plays in a rock band after school, on weekends, and during the summer.
6. I have changed my mind about the party.
7. Have you looked for the article on microfilm?
8. The plane flew over the clusters of clouds.
9. At the base of the canyon is a winding stream.
10. We got off the cable car at Fisherman's Wharf in San Francisco.

B. Recognize prepositions and adverbs. Tell whether the italicized word in each sentence is a *Preposition* or an *Adverb*. If it is a preposition, write its object.

1. Carla heard someone *within* the room.
2. Did you look *behind* the couch?
3. We raced *inside* when the storm began.
4. Has Marianne stopped *by* yet?
5. Ken has never skated *before* now.
6. Utter destruction lay *in* the hurricane's wake.
7. Don't stand *near* those speakers when the band begins to play.
8. Turn the lights *off* to conserve energy.
9. One runner lagged far *behind*.
10. The restaurant is just *past* that sign.

C. Identify prepositional phrases as modifiers. Write the prepositional phrases in each sentence. Label each phrase *Adjective* or *Adverb* and tell what word it modifies.

1. The construction crew drove piles into the riverbed.
2. Are you going to camp in Wisconsin this year?
3. A movie about the Kennedys is on TV.
4. Around the castle was a moat with crocodiles in it.
5. This ski jacket is filled with down.
6. The woman with the briefcase is Dr. Sanchez.
7. A crowd of eager fans swarmed the stage after the show.
8. The young man in the green jacket is Jake Houston.
9. To everyone's surprise, the ball landed in the bleachers.
10. Nobody but Rachel understood the point of the story.

D. Recognize conjunctions. For each sentence write the conjunction. Then write the words or groups of words joined by the conjunction.

1. The Pirates and the Steelers are Pittsburgh teams.
2. Father Hildalgo of Mexico was a priest and a political leader.
3. The soldier saluted and turned to leave.
4. The speaker's voice was powerful and engaging.
5. Andrew was not only hungry but also thirsty.
6. Can you tell whether a computer or a person made the mistake?
7. Rugs, drapes, and pillows muffle the noises in a room.
8. Somebody called for you but left no message.
9. In gym class, we'll play either volleyball or softball.
10. Neither Kelley nor Rivera caught the grounder to left field.

MIXED REVIEW
Using Prepositions and Conjunctions

A. Tell whether the italicized word in each sentence is a preposition or an adverb. If it is an adverb, copy the word that it modifies. If it is a preposition, copy the object of the preposition.

1. *Outside,* a heavy rain was falling.
2. Three children ran *past,* each with a candy apple in one hand and tickets for rides in the other.
3. The Grand Old Opry is a country music hall located *in* Nashville, Tennessee.
4. The garden is beautiful, but have you seen the view *beyond?*
5. *Around* noon, a band started to play on the grandstand.
6. The ice cream truck slowed *down* and stopped *nearby.*
7. Most of the birds have migrated, but these ducks have remained *behind.*
8. Her cat goes *out* whenever it pleases.
9. The archaeologist's assistant wouldn't wait *inside* the tomb alone.
10. The country bridge was so rotten that we were afraid of falling *through* it.

B. Write the prepositional phrases in the following sentences. Then tell whether they are used as adverb phrases or adjective phrases.

1. *Star Wars,* a film by Steven Spielberg, was the first in a series of three films.
2. With a sheepish grin, the toddler removed his hand from the cookie jar.
3. The elaborate wig on the dancer's head was dyed a bright blue.
4. After the play, Jack and Diane walked to the restaurant.
5. The security guard in the supermarket looked suspiciously at the customer.
6. *Nova* is a show on PBS that deals with unusual subjects of interest.

7. The actors and actresses at the Academy Awards waited for the announcements with anticipation.
8. The bride and groom walked toward the altar and stood under an arch during the ceremony.
9. The school of fish wove through the coral of the huge reef.
10. The line outside the theater stretched around the corner and beyond the intersection.

C. Complete the following phrases or sentences, using the type of conjunction called for in parentheses.

1. _____ carrots _____ celery are vegetables often used in salads. (correlative)
2. The runner tripped over the hurdle _____ sprained his ankle. (coordinating)
3. Our new quarterback is small _____ fast. (coordinating)
4. _____ Charles _____ José went to interview the mayor. (correlative)
5. Karen designs _____ fires her own pottery and clay sculpture. (coordinating)
6. Sheila is _____ class president _____ head cheerleader. (correlative)
7. Tina could not decide whether to tell her grandmother _____ her grandfather the good news first. (coordinating)
8. Larry saw the tree, _____ could not avoid skiing directly into it. (coordinating)
9. I was told that my stereo would be repaired by Friday _____ Saturday. (coordinating)
10. Jana enjoys _____ classical music _____ reggae. (correlative)

USING GRAMMAR IN WRITING
Using Prepositions and Conjunctions

A. Describe in detail how to perform some specific athletic activity like swinging a bat, catching a football, or serving a volleyball. Circle all of the prepositions that you use in your description. Notice that prepositions often express a change in position or a relationship between two objects. For example, "Pull the string *of* the bow *toward* your chin," or "Place your hands *near* the bottom *of* the bat."

B. Write a poem in which each line begins with a preposition. It is not necessary that the lines of the poem rhyme. Here is an example:

From space a single twinkle came
Into my eye from a distant star
Through the atmosphere and endless time
Beyond my dreams and all imagining.

C. Try to write another poem in which every other line begins with the conjunction *but*. Notice that the word *but* introduces a word or an idea that is contrary to expectation.

I'd like to be swimming in moonlight,
But I'm washing the dishes instead.
I'd like to be dancing by starlight,
But it's already past time for bed.

D. Write a paragraph comparing a hot fudge sundae to a banana split. Make your descriptions so vivid that someone who has never seen or tasted these treats will feel as if he or she had just done so. Use the conjunctions *and, or, but, either/or,* and *both/and* in your comparison.

Section 8

Review
of Parts
# of Speech

Part 1   The Parts of Speech

In Section 3 you learned that there are eight **parts of speech.**
A word is classified as one of these parts of speech according to
its use in a sentence. Before continuing with this section, quickly
review the names of the eight groups:

The Parts of Speech			
nouns	verbs	adverbs	conjunctions
pronouns	adjectives	prepositions	interjections

The last part of speech, **interjections,** is the only one you have
not studied.

What Is an Interjection?

An interjection is a word or group of words used to express strong feeling.

An interjection may be either a phrase or a word. It expresses strong feeling, such as joy, anger, terror, surprise, disgust, or sadness. Because it conveys strong emotions, an interjection is followed by an exclamation mark as in the following examples.

Wow! Look at those mountains.   *Oh!* You scared me.

You now have nearly all of the terms you need to identify and classify any word in the English language. You will learn the remaining few terms in Section 9.

Exercise A: Write each italicized word and its part of speech.

1. *Fantastic!* The agent likes Vicky's demonstration record.
2. Philips *charged* frantically for the end zone.
3. Did *anybody* ever thank the Lone Ranger?
4. Anne hung a poster *inside* her locker.
5. Is Portland *or* Salem the capital of Oregon?
6. Denise will *probably* become a lawyer.
7. Your phone is always *busy.*
8. With a *tremendous* roar the volcano erupted.
9. The *stories* of O. Henry end with a surprise.
10. Lydia *remembered* the warmth of her old neighborhood.

Exercise B: Follow the directions for Exercise A.

1. The truck swerved and *avoided* a *collision.*
2. Country music *has influenced* both rock *and* soul music.
3. Many glaciers *in* Greenland are over a mile *thick.*
4. *Ugh!* I can't stand licorice.
5. The steel mills in *Gary* reddened *the* sky.
6. The explorers took a month's *supply* of food with *them.*
7. Leslie cleared the hurdles *easily.*
8. The *polite* bus driver waited *for* the limping man.
9. The zoo director *recently* returned from *Panama.*
10. Margaret Bourke-White *is* famous for her war photos.

Part 2 Using Words as Different Parts of Speech

Very often the same word can be used as different parts of speech. For example, a word might be used as a noun in one sentence and an adjective in another.

The only way to identify the part of speech of any word is to determine how that word is used in a sentence.

The artist folded *paper* into unusual shapes.
   (*Paper* is used as a noun, the direct object of the verb *folded.*)

At the picnic, we ate on *paper* plates.
   (*Paper* is used as an adjective, modifying *plates.*)

The five-dollar *bill* has a picture of Abraham Lincoln.
   (*Bill* is used as a noun, the subject of the sentence.)

The store will *bill* us for our purchases.
   (*Bill* is used as the main verb.)

What is your favorite song?
   (*What* is used as a pronoun, the subject of the sentence.)

What shows are on TV now?
   (*What* is used as an adjective, modifying the noun *shows.*)

A *low* wall surrounded the building.
   (*Low* is used as an adjective, modifying the noun *wall.*)

A plane flew *low* over the beach.
   (*Low* is used as an adverb, modifying the verb *flew.*)

After her speech, Sally sat *down.*
   (*Down* is used as an adverb, modifying the verb *sat.*)

We rowed the boat *down* the river.
   (*Down* is used as a preposition.)

Never! I won't try it again.
   (*Never* is used as an interjection.)

Mr. Bailey *never* raises his voice.
   (*Never* is used as an adverb, modifying the verb *raises.*)

Exercise A: Write the italicized word. Next to it, write what part of speech it functions as in that sentence.

1. *Really!* Do you expect me to believe that?
2. Mom *really* wants to see Paris.
3. *Name* another famous player who was with the New York Yankees at the same time as Babe Ruth.
4. One *name* given to the Conestoga wagon by pioneers was "camel of the desert."
5. *Daydreams* can serve a useful purpose.
6. Paul *daydreams* about winning an Olympic medal.
7. Who lives in *this* houseboat?
8. *This* is the corner where the accident happened.
9. *Fire* drills are scheduled every month.
10. *Fire* at the target when I signal.

Exercise B: Follow the directions for Exercise A.

1. Don't turn *on* the television during an electrical storm.
2. Her homework was lying *on* the table, under the newspaper.
3. Our mail carrier *growls* back at dogs.
4. The *growls* were getting meaner and deeper.
5. *Park* your bike in those racks.
6. This *park* provides nature walks with Braille signs.
7. The youth center keeps an up-to-date job *file*.
8. Passengers usually *file* quietly down to the subway.
9. *That* was my idea.
10. Have you already seen *that* movie?

Exercise C: Writing Write sentences using the following words as the parts of speech indicated in parentheses.

1. travel (verb)
2. travel (adjective)
3. right (noun)
4. right (adjective)
5. skate (verb)
6. guard (noun)
7. those (pronoun)
8. those (adjective)
9. fantastic (interjection)
10. fast (adverb)

REINFORCEMENT EXERCISES
Review of Parts of Speech

A. Recognize the parts of speech. Write the italicized word in each sentence and tell what part of speech it is.

1. Did the reporter quote *you* accurately?
2. *Ouch!* That antiseptic really stings.
3. *Canadians* celebrate their national independence on July first.
4. Jim talks too fast *and* too much.
5. The emergency room in Weiss Memorial Hospital is *always* crowded.
6. The art class designed and *sold* hooked rugs.
7. Robert takes his *youngest* sister to a day-care center each morning.
8. *Wow!* We got here just in time to see the kickoff!
9. A squirrel looked down at us *from* a branch of the old maple tree.
10. In North and South Dakota, winter begins *early* and ends late.
11. *This* was Norman Rockwell's studio.
12. The detective examined the skid *marks* in an effort to trace the car.
13. It can rain *for* weeks in Seattle during the winter.
14. Are you studying vertebrates in biology *now?*
15. Mr. Diaz showed us his collection of *African* masks and sculpture.
16. How did Indian summer get its *name?*
17. Did *anyone* see the No Swimming sign?
18. The oddly-shaped *leaves* of the ancient ginkgo tree look like small fans.
19. The Milwaukee Brewers won their first American League pennant *in* 1982.
20. The Navajo woman carefully *wove* bright red yarn into the blanket's design.

B. Identify words used as different parts of speech. Write the italicized word in each sentence. Tell what part of speech it is in that sentence.

1. The President tossed out the *game* ball.
2. "Facts in Fives" is my family's favorite *game*.
3. The police officers looked for *signs* of forced entry.
4. Angelo *signs* his name with a flourish.
5. My grandad was born *in* Austria.
6. We stayed *in* because of the tornado warning.
7. *That* shop specialized in exotic pets.
8. *That* was Robert Duvall's best role.
9. That man looks exactly *like* Lou Gossett, Jr.
10. We *like* to explore caves and caverns.
11. During the *rush* hour, helicopters hover above the freeways.
12. *Rush* the fallen skier to the emergency room!
13. That *picture* by Van Gogh sold for half a million dollars.
14. *Picture* yourself swimming in a cool, clear lake.
15. *This* is the third time I've run the program.
16. Can anyone read *this* message?
17. Tom trailed *behind* the other hikers.
18. We left many good friends *behind* in Indiana.
19. The hot-air balloon sailed *high* into the sky.
20. At *high* tide this area is under water.

MIXED REVIEW
Review of Parts of Speech

A. Complete this short story by inserting the parts of speech asked for in parentheses.

It (verb) a dark and (adjective) night. The (adjective) detectives, (proper noun) and (proper noun), were investigating a (noun) which took place (prepositional phrase).

"There definitely (verb) some kind (prepositional phrase) here," said (proper noun) to (proper noun). (Pronoun) crept (adverb) around the (noun) only to find (noun). Then the two detectives (verb) (prepositional phrase) and realized that (pronoun) was missing!

"(Pronoun) (verb) everything!" exclaimed (proper noun). "(Adverb) we'll have to (verb) back (prepositional phrase) (coordinating conjunction) try to (verb) this to our (noun)."

B. Write two sentences for ten of the following words. The word should be used as a different part of speech in each sentence. Tell what part of speech the word is used as in each of your sentences.

EXAMPLE: 1. Lynn and Carrie *feed* their pets each day. (verb)
2. The *feed* store closes at noon on Wednesday. (adjective)

picture	like	time	loose
rush	frame	sting	store
that	finish	throw	chase
signs	design	whistle	run
lead	wet	cut	close
watch	place	trade	open

USING GRAMMAR IN WRITING
Review of Parts of Speech

A. Try to imagine what it must feel like to go sky-diving for the first time. Record your feelings as you experience the sensation of free fall, the sudden catch of the chute in the wind, and the slow drift to earth. Use a few interjections to express your intense emotions as you plunge through the air and the ground rushes to meet you. Your paragraph should also include examples of each of the other parts of speech.

B. Imagine that you work for an advertising agency and that your supervisor has assigned you the task of writing an ad for a new means of transportation. The manufacturers of the product claim that it will make cars obsolete. Your boss says to you, "Make every word count! Give me powerful verbs! Dynamic nouns! Dazzling modifiers! Perfect pronouns and punchy interjections!" You have been given a limit of one hundred words to "Sell that product!" To top it off, you must underline ten verbs, ten nouns, five modifiers, and two interjections that you have used in the ad so that your boss can see at a glance how interesting it is.

C. Flip through a dictionary, magazine, or book and select sixteen words. Try to include two of each of the eight parts of speech. Now, try to use these words to write a story. The story must make sense, but it may be serious or humorous.

Section 9

Using
Verbals

In addition to the eight basic parts of speech, there are three other useful kinds of words. Because they are formed from verbs, these words are called **verbals.** The three verbals are **gerunds, participles,** and **infinitives.** Even though verbals are formed from verbs, they do not function as verbs in sentences. In this section you will learn to use verbals and verbal phrases.

Part 1 Gerunds

A gerund is a verb form that functions as a noun.

A gerund ends in *-ing*. It may be used in any way that a noun is used — as a subject, a direct object, an object of a preposition, or as a predicate word.

> *Drawing* is Alissa's hobby. (subject)
> Debbie tried *surfing*. (direct object)
> The best place for *jogging* is the park. (object of a preposition)
> A major industry here is *mining*. (predicate word)

The Gerund Phrase

Often a gerund has a modifier or an object or both. Together they form a **gerund phrase.** The entire gerund phrase is used like a noun.

Because a gerund is formed from a verb, it can have an object.

> We won by *scoring a touchdown* in the last minute.
> (*Scoring* is a gerund; *touchdown* is the object of *scoring*. The phrase *scoring a touchdown* is the object of the preposition *by*.)

Because a gerund is formed from a verb, it can be modified by adverbs.

> Elliot started *laughing again.*
> (*Laughing* is a gerund; *again* is an adverb modifying *laughing*. The phrase *laughing again* is the object of the verb *started*.)

Because a gerund is used as a noun, it can be modified by adjectives.

> *Quick thinking* saved us.
> (*Thinking* is a gerund; *quick* is an adjective modifying *thinking*. The phrase *quick thinking* is the subject of the verb *saved*.)

Gerunds can also be modified by prepositional phrases.

Sitting on these benches is uncomfortable.
> (*Sitting* is a gerund; *on these benches* is a prepositional phrase modifying *sitting*. The entire gerund phrase is the subject of *is*.)

In these examples *drawing, surfing, jogging, mining, scoring, laughing, thinking,* and *sitting* all look like verbs but are used as nouns. Therefore, they are gerunds. Along with the modifiers and objects that are used with them, they form gerund phrases.

Diagraming Gerunds

A gerund or gerund phrase used as a subject, direct object, or predicate word is diagramed on a line above the main line. The gerund belongs on a line drawn as a step. Its modifiers are placed on slanted lines below it. Its object is shown on the horizontal line following the gerund.

Telling jokes will cheer us up.

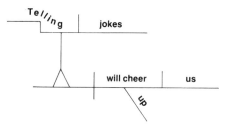

This job requires fast, accurate typing.

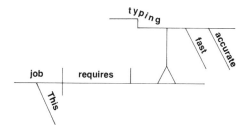

His hobby is painting miniatures.

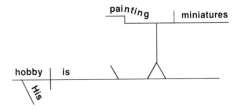

A gerund or gerund phrase used as the object of a preposition is diagramed below the main line. The preposition belongs on a slanted line going down from the word modified. Again, the gerund appears on a stepped line.

We thanked Valerie for helping us.

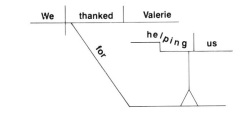

Exercise A: Write the gerunds or gerund phrases. Then tell how each one functions in the sentence.

1. Yelling at the umpire caused Joanne's laryngitis.
2. Faulty wiring started the disastrous fire in the apartment complex.
3. The big concern in this valley is flooding.
4. We were tired from running so far.
5. Our vacation plans include a day of water skiing on Lake Michigan.
6. Washing the windows of skyscrapers is hazardous.
7. Nearly everybody dislikes dieting.
8. Wind surfing is one sport I'd like to try.
9. Logical thinking can be learned.
10. One worthwhile way to spend free time is volunteering at the health clinic.

Exercise B: Follow the directions for Exercise A.

1. Sharpening her tennis game is Jean's current goal.
2. Will writing to the editor have any effect?
3. My grandmother enjoys scuba diving.
4. Moving to Boston stirred Ken's interest in history.
5. Painting a dragon on the van was Sonya's idea.
6. Mending nets took much of the old fisherman's time.
7. Winning the war cost many lives.
8. Is discus throwing an Olympic event?
9. How many calories does an hour of walking burn?
10. The fire department warns against keeping the oven on for warmth.

Part 2   Participles

A participle is a verb form that functions as an adjective.

You learned that the **past participle** is one of the principal parts of a verb. The past participle of a regular verb is formed by adding -d or -ed to the present tense, as in *dance — danced* or *dress — dressed*. The past participles of irregular verbs are formed differently and must be learned separately: *tear—torn, sing—sung*.

You also learned that there is another kind of participle besides the past participle, called the **present participle**. The present participle is always formed by adding -ing to the present tense: *dance—dancing, dress—dressing, tear—tearing, sing—singing*.

VERB	PAST PARTICIPLE	PRESENT PARTICIPLE
look	looked	looking
bring	brought	bringing
cry	cried	crying

Participles may be used as parts of verb phrases: *had danced, am going*. When used as verbals, however, both past and present participles always function as adjectives. A participle modifies either a noun or a pronoun.

Exhausted, Martina sat down with a sigh.

(*Exhausted* is a past participle modifying the noun *Martina.*)

Whistling, he made his way home through the snow.

(*Whistling* is a present participle modifying the pronoun *he.*)

A *fallen* tree blocked the street.

(*Fallen* is a past participle modifying the noun *tree.*)

The *flying* object had four headlights.

(*Flying* is a present participle modifying the noun *object.*)

The Participial Phrase

A participle is not always used alone. Often a participle has a modifier or an object or both. Together, they form a **participial phrase.** The entire participial phrase is used as an adjective.

Because a participle is formed from a verb, it may have an object.

The goat *chewing the shoe* belongs to Pete.

(*Chewing the shoe* is a participial phrase modifying *goat. Shoe* is the object of the participle *chewing.*)

Because a participle comes from a verb, it may be modified by adverbs.

Racing madly, Carla beat the throw to home plate.

(*Racing madly* is a participial phrase modifying *Carla. Madly* is an adverb modifying the participle *racing.*)

A participle may also be modified by prepositional phrases.

We heard the foghorn *moaning in the distance.*

(*Moaning in the distance* is a participial phrase modifying *foghorn. In the distance* is a prepositional phrase modifying the participle *moaning.*)

In the examples on this page, *exhausted, whistling, fallen, flying, chewing, racing,* and *moaning* all look like verbs but are used as adjectives. Therefore, they are called participles. Modifiers and objects used with them form participial phrases.

Diagraming Participles

To diagram a participle, place it on an angled line below the noun or pronoun it modifies. Put modifiers of the participle on lines slanted down from it. An object follows the participle on a horizontal line.

Reading the fine print carefully, Erin studied the contract.

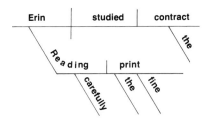

Exercise A: Write the participles or participial phrases in these sentences. Show which word the participle or phrase modifies.

> EXAMPLE: Raising her eyebrows, Regina stared at the conductor.
>
> *Raising her eyebrows* (modifies *Regina*)

1. Working hard, the firefighters controlled the blaze.
2. The glittering snow blinded him for a minute.
3. Fried chicken was heaped on the platters.
4. Cheryl scraped the peeling paint from the rocker.
5. Frightened by the odd noise, I called the police.
6. Harris slipped on the freshly waxed floor.
7. Someone wearing high heels made these footprints.
8. The pie cooling on the table is for dessert.
9. Snapping her fingers, Lynn set the rhythm.
10. The man with the hat pulled down over his eyes was once a baseball star.

Exercise B: Follow the directions for Exercise A.

1. Nodding her head, Mrs. Chang accepted the salesman's final offer.
2. That is a widely-known fact.
3. There was no hope for a seat on the packed bus.

4. Opening the door, Mark accidentally bumped Mr. Hays.
5. Bits of broken glass in the street told the story.
6. Take gloves off frostbitten hands slowly and carefully.
7. Falling softly on the roof, the rain sounded peaceful.
8. Most of our scattered relatives got together for the reunion.
9. I was trapped inside the revolving door for an hour.
10. Payton, leaping into the air, caught the ball.

Gerund or Participle?

The two kinds of verbals you have studied, gerunds and participles, often look the same. Gerunds and present participles are both formed by adding *-ing* to the present tense of verbs. How can you avoid confusing them?

To tell whether a word is a gerund or a present participle, look at how it is used. If it is used as a modifier, it is a participle. If it is used as a noun, it is a gerund.

Look at the following sentences.

> *Hiking along the nature trail* takes two hours.
> (The gerund phrase *hiking along the nature trail* is the subject of the verb *takes*.)
>
> *Hiking along the nature trail*, we saw several deer.
> (The participial phrase *hiking along the nature trail* modifies the pronoun *we*.)

Exercise: For each sentence, write the gerund or participle and say which each is. Be prepared to explain your answer.

1. Diving from the high board requires control.
2. Diving from the high board, Jeff lost control.
3. Tuning the old piano, Hank listened carefully to each tone.
4. Tuning the old piano will improve its sound.
5. We were exhausted after climbing the hill.
6. Climbing the hill, Sandy spotted a waterfall.
7. The police chief suggested dusting for fingerprints.
8. Using a newspaper, Lynn chased the bee outside.
9. The people sitting in the front row get the best view.
10. Steve calmed the dog by stroking it.

Part 3   Infinitives

An infinitive is a verb form that usually begins with the word *to*.

to write	to shout	to find	to forget
to say	to like	to join	to remind

You have learned that the word *to* is used as a preposition. *To* is a preposition when it is followed by a noun or pronoun as its object. However, when *to* is followed by a verb, it is called the **sign of the infinitive**. Compare these examples:

PREPOSITIONAL PHRASES	INFINITIVES
We went to the youth center.	We tried to remember.
Justin listened to the music.	Kristin wants to rollerskate.
A sign was nailed to the tree.	Evan wants to leave.

The Infinitive Phrase

Like gerunds and participles, infinitives are not always used alone. An infinitive can have modifiers and objects. The infinitive with its modifiers and objects forms an **infinitive phrase**.

Because an infinitive is formed from a verb, it may have an object.

Megan planned *to have a party.*
(*Party* is the direct object of the infinitive *to have.*)

The coach wanted *to give the team a good workout.*
(*Team* is the indirect object and *workout* is the direct object of the infinitive *to give.*)

Because an infinitive is formed from a verb, it may be modified by adverbs.

The choir tried *to sing together.*
(*Together* is an adverb modifying the infinitive *to sing.*)

A tape recording asked me *to call again later.*
(*Again* and *later* are adverbs modifying the infinitive *to call.*)

Infinitives may also be modified by prepositional phrases.

One customer demanded *to talk to the manager.*
(*To the manager* is a prepositional phrase modifying the infinitive *to talk.*)

Many people like *to picnic in the park.*
(*In the park* is a prepositional phrase modifying the infinitive *to picnic.*)

Uses of the Infinitive Phrase

Unlike gerunds and participles, infinitives can be used as more than one part of speech. An infinitive or infinitive phrase can be used as a noun, an adjective, or an adverb.

Infinitives and infinitive phrases can be used in ways that nouns are used. As you know, nouns may be subjects or direct objects.

SUBJECT: *To learn a new language* takes time.
(*To learn a new language* is the subject.)
DIRECT OBJECT: Diane forgot *to send the entry fee.*
(*To send the entry fee* is the direct object.)

Infinitives and infinitive phrases can also be used as adjectives or adverbs. The infinitive or infinitive phrase is used as an adjective if it modifies a noun or pronoun. It is used as an adverb if it modifies a verb, adjective, or adverb.

ADJECTIVE: These are the logs *to burn in the fireplace.*
(*To burn in the fireplace* modifies the noun *logs.*)
ADJECTIVE: Shelly needs someone *to advise her.*
(*To advise her* modifies the pronoun *someone.*)
ADVERB: Everyone came *to celebrate.*
(*To celebrate* modifies the verb *came.*)
ADVERB: Greg is afraid *to talk to Jessica.*
(*To talk to Jessica* modifies the adjective *afraid.*)
ADVERB: The ball flew too high *to catch.*
(*To catch* modifies the adverb *high.*)

You can see that infinitives look like verbs but are not used as verbs. They function as nouns, adjectives, and adverbs.

The Split Infinitive

Sometimes a modifier is placed between the word *to* and the verb of an infinitive. A modifier in that position is said to *split* the infinitive. Usually, a split infinitive sounds awkward and should be avoided.

AWKWARD: Marietta tried to *patiently* wait.
BETTER: Marietta tried to wait *patiently*.

Diagraming Infinitives

To diagram an infinitive or infinitive phrase used as a noun, place it on a platform above the main line. *To,* the sign of the infinitive, belongs on a slanted line. The infinitive is shown on a horizontal line. Modifiers appear on lines slanted down from the infinitive. An object is shown on a horizontal line following the infinitive.

Dale tried to answer the questions correctly.

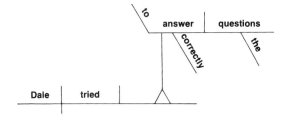

To diagram an infinitive or infinitive phrase used as a modifier, place it on a platform below the word modified. Modifiers and objects of the infinitive appear as explained above.

Sandpaper is used to smooth the wood.

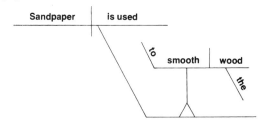

Exercise A: Write each infinitive or infinitive phrase.

1. Don neglected to mention a few important facts.
2. The coat was too expensive to buy.
3. Ruth is too intelligent to believe entirely in luck.
4. Chief Joseph had hoped to lead his people to Canada.
5. To own her own horse is Sheila's dream.
6. I want to read more about the Mayan civilization.
7. All the candidates promised to find people jobs.
8. Our youth group plans to hike the Appalachian Trail.
9. Did Cynthia manage to find her way without a map?
10. To become a West Point cadet is Brian's goal.

Exercise B: Find the infinitive or infinitive phrase in each sentence. Then tell whether it is used as a subject, direct object, adjective, or adverb.

> EXAMPLE: Deborah wants to tell her side of the story.
> *to tell her side of the story* (infinitive phrase, used as direct object)

1. I never got a chance to thank Quentin for the birthday card he sent.
2. The counselor is the person to ask about a job in the school office.
3. We learned to program computers this year.
4. Jeff tried to enter his cat in the dog show.
5. To study cello at Julliard is Angela's dream.
6. The pigeons tried to avoid the spray of water from the fountain.
7. Great tacos are not difficult to make.
8. To walk to the stadium would take at least two and a half hours.
9. The forty-niners hoped to make their fortunes in California.
10. The potter started to put glaze on the vase.

Exercise C: Writing Write five sentences that describe some things you would like to do next summer. Include an infinitive in each sentence. Underline the infinitives and tell how they are used. Try to include several different uses.

Part 4 A Review of Verbals

Although verbals are verb forms, they are always used as other parts of speech.

The three kinds of verbals are gerunds, participles, and infinitives. All three kinds of verbals may be used alone or in phrases. These phrases are called gerund phrases, participial phrases, and infinitive phrases. Because they are like verbs, all three kinds of verbals may take objects or modifiers.

Gerunds are the verb forms used as nouns. Gerunds, which end in *-ing*, may be used in all the ways nouns are used.

> *Marching* tired us out. (subject)
> The troops began *marching along*. (direct object)
> The band makes designs by *marching in formation*.
>   (object of preposition)
> The next event is *precision marching*. (predicate word)

Participles are verb forms used as adjectives. Like adjectives, participles modify nouns and pronouns. Present participles end in *-ing*. Past participles of regular verbs end in *-d* or *-ed*. Past participles of irregular verbs are formed in various ways. (See Section 5, pages 483 to 489.)

> *Turning*, Richard skated back to his friends.
> The girl *turning sideways* is Nancy.
> The *broken* calculator was useless.
> Mario crossed the finish line, *breaking the record*.

Infinitives are the verbals that begin with the word *to*. Infinitives and infinitive phrases may be used as nouns, adjectives, or adverbs.

> *To say his lines right* was a challenge for Eric.
>   (noun used as the subject)
> The president asked us *to say our names*. (noun used as the
>   direct object)
> Ms. Fields has a few words *to say*. (adjective)
> Everyone rose *to say the pledge*. (adverb)
> This tongue-twister is not easy *to say*. (adverb)

Exercise A: Write the verbal or verbal phrase in each sentence. Tell whether the verbal is a gerund, a participle, or an infinitive.

1. We were invited backstage to meet the cast.
2. The burglar entered through an unlocked window.
3. Jeans made in America are popular all over the world.
4. Where did you learn to speak Spanish?
5. Rita lugged the broken TV to the repair shop.
6. Reading the news is Dan Rather's occupation.
7. Theresa tried juggling five oranges and failed.
8. Martin woke to the smell of frying bacon.
9. The wagon master was responsible for leading the wagon train.
10. It is too early to tell the outcome of the game.

Exercise B: Follow the directions for Exercise A.

1. The defeated candidate accused the winner of vote fraud.
2. Try to understand the lyrics of the song.
3. Talking before a group is hard for many people.
4. Turning on the siren, the police officer drove her squad car through the busy intersection.
5. The wastebasket was filled with crumpled paper.
6. Separating Mexico from the United States, the Rio Grande flows to the Gulf of Mexico.
7. Reading science fiction stretches my imagination.
8. Martha has saved enough money to buy a ticket.
9. Diving for the ball, the third baseman brought the fans to their feet.
10. Playing video games can develop your coordination.

Exercise C: Writing As you can see from the examples below, many famous sayings contain verbals. Write five of your own "famous sayings" using at least one verbal in each. Underline the verbals and tell whether they are gerunds, participles, or infinitives.

> *Seeing* is *believing*.
> A *rolling* stone gathers no moss.
> A penny *saved* is a penny *earned*.
> *To be* or not *to be*, that is the question.

REINFORCEMENT EXERCISES
Using Verbals

A. Recognize gerunds. Find each gerund phrase. Tell whether it is used as a subject, direct object, or object of a preposition.

1. Jonas tried pitching with his left hand.
2. Sky diving looks like a thrilling sport.
3. A palette is used by artists for mixing paints.
4. Twenty sound tracks were used in making this record.
5. Nora suggested returning the carton of sour milk to the grocery store.
6. Rabbits survive by running away from danger.
7. Washing clothes in hot water might shrink them.
8. Gluing the pottery fragments together took several hours of tedious work.
9. There is an observation deck for viewing the city.
10. Mark tried wrestling in the 130-pound weight class.

B. Recognize participles. Write the participle or participial phrase in each sentence. Tell which word it modifies.

1. Overloaded with cargo, the freighter sank into the St. Lawrence Seaway.
2. Screaming wildly, fans stormed the stage.
3. Sue found Tommy finger painting on the wall.
4. The hikers found a deserted cabin.
5. We toasted marshmallows over the glowing embers of the campfire.
6. Hidden rocks could cut through the hull of the boat.
7. Discouraged, the artist set the sketch aside.
8. Sitting on the levee, Mary Beth watched the barges move slowly down the river.
9. The wildflowers growing in the park are goldenrod, bee balm, and goatsbeard.
10. Leaping out of the water, the dolphin sailed through the hoop.

C. Recognize Infinitives. Write the infinitive or infinitive phrase in each sentence. Tell whether it is used as a subject, direct object, adjective, or adverb.

1. The displaced passenger had to take the next flight.
2. Our environmental group has several exciting projects to complete.
3. Each carrier has a certain amount of mail to deliver.
4. Our mayor campaigned to become governor.
5. To admit mistakes takes courage.
6. Spielberg's movies are always exciting to watch.
7. I hope to see Waylon Jennings in Nashville.
8. The government tries to warn us of health hazards.
9. To hike in this heat would be foolish.
10. Laura hopes to find work picking strawberries.

D. Identify verbals. Write the verbal or verbal phrase in each sentence. Label it *Gerund, Participle,* or *Infinitive.* Tell how it is used in the sentence.

1. The diver tried to conserve his precious oxygen.
2. After baking two dozen cookies, we ate them all.
3. Josh sat on a balcony overlooking Central Park.
4. Delighted with the waterfall, Al stood under the cascade.
5. Hang gliding requires knowledge of air currents.
6. Moving West in the 1800's demanded toughness and stamina.
7. The audience persuaded the Beach Boys to sing an encore.
8. Forced out of their native country, the refugees sought protection in the United States.
9. A gymnast training for the Olympics concentrates on little else.
10. This is the golf club to use in sand traps.

MIXED REVIEW
Using Verbals

A. Write the verbal or verbal phrase in each sentence. Label it *Gerund, Participle,* or *Infinitive.*

1. Leaving home was very difficult for Carlos.
2. It was very difficult for Carlos to leave home.
3. Is that your grandmother dancing the Charleston?
4. Jim liked to sit in the first row at the theater.
5. It is foolish to ride a motorcycle without a helmet.
6. Living dangerously is normal for a stunt person.
7. Janice looked forward to picking fresh strawberries in the field.
8. She enjoyed watching the crowds on 42nd Street.
9. Collecting samples, the amateur biologists combed the beach.
10. Jogging through the park, I saw two woodchucks.

B. Each sentence below contains an italicized verbal phrase. Read the three statements that follow each sentence, and choose the one that describes the verbal correctly.

    EXAMPLE: Angela likes *to work jigsaw puzzles.*
          a. a prepositional phrase modifying *likes*
     → b. an infinitive phrase used as a direct object
          c. an infinitive phrase used as an adverb

1. *Trimming the hedges* is Sharon's least favorite chore.
   a. gerund phrase used as the subject
   b. participial phrase modifying *chore*
   c. infinitive phrase used as a subject

2. Felice likes *to design her own jewelry.*
   a. a gerund phrase used as the direct object
   b. an infinitive phrase used as the direct object
   c. a prepositional phrase modifying *likes*

3. The children *looking through the toy shop window* smiled.
   a. gerund phrase used as the subject
   b. gerund phrase used as the direct object
   c. participial phrase modifying *children*

4. Diana had wanted *to become a doctor* since her first visit to the emergency room.
   a. participial phrase modifying *Diana*
   b. infinitive phrase used as the direct object
   c. gerund phrase used as the direct object
5. His heart *thumping wildly*, Ramon ran the final ten meters.
   a. participial phrase modifying *heart*
   b. infinitive phrase used as the subject
   c. gerund phrase used as the subject
6. She called him *to explain her strange behavior.*
   a. infinitive phrase used as an adverb
   b. infinitive phrase used as an adjective
   c. infinitive phrase used as the direct object
7. Kathryn lost weight by *following her diet.*
   a. participial phrase modifying *weight*
   b. gerund phrase used as the object of a preposition
   c. gerund phrase used as the direct object
8. My grandmother bought a new suit *to wear on her first day at work.*
   a. participial phrase modifying *suit*
   b. infinitive phrase used as the direct object
   c. infinitive phrase used to modify *suit*
9. *Careful planning* is required in the selection of high school courses.
   a. participial phrase modifying *is required*
   b. gerund phrase used as the subject
   c. gerund phrase used as the predicate noun
10. Often, the best therapy for loneliness is *helping others.*
    a. participial phrase used as an adverb
    b. participial phrase used as an adjective modifying *loneliness*
    c. gerund phrase used as a predicate noun

USING GRAMMAR IN WRITING
Using Verbals

A. Imagine that, at age seventy, you have been asked by an editor of *Time* magazine to summarize the outstanding events, achievements, and successes of your distinguished career. The editor says to limit your list to seven items. Then she wants you to list three of your greatest disappointments or failures. The combined list will form the basis of an outline for the editor's "Person of the Year" cover story. The editor requests that you begin each statement with a gerund. Here is an example: *Graduating* from high school.

When your list is complete, choose the one item that you consider the most important and write a paragraph explaining it in detail.

B. What would you do if you had one year in which to do anything you pleased? Write a paragraph about your dream year (you may also assume that you have won a lottery and do not have to be concerned about money). Draw a line under each infinitive that you use. If you use a prepositional phrase that is introduced by the preposition *to*, mark it as a preposition to show that you know it is not part of an infinitive.

C. Imagine that you are a news announcer reporting on a huge outdoor concert given by your three favorite musical performers. Thousands of people have gathered to hear the concert, excitement is mounting, and you can see storm clouds and lightning approaching the concert grounds from the east. Write your moment-by-moment coverage of the event as the storm hits the assembled fans. Be sure to include participles and participial phrases in your description. If you also include any gerunds or infinitives in your report, mark them.

CUMULATIVE REVIEW
The Parts of Speech

Recognizing the Parts of Speech and Verbals. Number your paper from 1 to 25. Decide whether each italicized word or phrase in the paragraph below is being used as a *Noun, Pronoun, Verb, Adverb, Adjective, Conjunction, Preposition, Interjection, Gerund, Infinitive,* or *Participle.* Write your answer next to the corresponding number. Remember that the part of speech a word is often depends on how it is used in the sentence.

Volcanoes are *openings* in the earth's crust. From these openings, gases and lava are expelled under pressure. Lava is molten, *liquid* rock from far beneath the earth's surface. When the opening of a volcano *is blocked* by solid material, the various gases beneath the earth's surface force *themselves* up in a series of explosions. The gas and lava then erupt from the new opening.

One of *the* most famous volcanic eruptions in *history* took place in Italy *in* A.D. 79, when Mount Vesuvius, thought *to be* extinct, erupted. The explosion destroyed the towns of *Pompeii* and Herculaneum, among others. *Roman* observers wrote that there was a strong earth tremor *on* the first morning, followed by an explosion that sent a tower of ash and rock twelve miles into the sky. *Incredible!* After *this*, there was a fall of lava ash and cinders about three feet deep. *Fleeing* saved some; others took shelter inside, *thinking* that the catastrophe must *soon* be over. However, the next day there was *another* eruption that caused a rain of molten lava, pumice rock, and cinders that buried the town of Pompeii and killed more than *two* thousand citizens.

Since that time Mount Vesuvius has *never* been completely inactive. An eruption in 1631 killed eighteen thousand people. The last eruption *occurred* in 1944. Mount Vesuvius has been quiet since then, *emitting* only puffs of gas; *but* scientists do not expect it *to remain* quiet for long.

CUMULATIVE REVIEW
Usage (I)

Understanding How Words Are Used. A word or group of words can be used in different ways within a sentence. Number your paper from 1 to 20. Decide whether each italicized word or phrase in these sentences is being used as a *Subject, Verb, Adjective, Adverb, Predicate Noun, Direct Object, Indirect Object,* or *Object of a Preposition.* Write each word and your answers next to the corresponding number.

1. The curved spines of the *barrel* cactus once *were used* as fish hooks.
2. Fred *nearly* forgot to turn the stove *off.*
3. The *Tyrolean* folk costumes were *colorful.*
4. Amy *patiently* turned the handle of the old ice cream *freezer.*
5. Mr. MacBride *plays* the *bagpipes* in a highland band.
6. Juan *decided* to sign up for *soccer.*
7. What is your favorite *subject* at school *this* year?
8. The detective examined the *tire marks* left by the tires.
9. The tracks were *finally clear* after the derailing of the train.
10. Those are *black* raspberry *bushes.*
11. *Swimming* is an excellent *form* of exercise.
12. That sergeant gives the *recruits* a tough but excellent *training* session.
13. *Below* we could see the deserted *remains* of a town.
14. *Few* of the stable's horses were *thoroughbreds.*
15. *Below* the blossom hovered a *hummingbird.*
16. I did not want *to arrive early.*
17. The gawky giraffe can move *quite fast* when startled.
18. Athletes like him give *boxing* a bad *name.*
19. The young marathon *runner* was not ashamed of *finishing last.*
20. In the near future, *becoming a space colonist* will no longer be an unrealistic *dream.*

Section 10

Making Subjects and Verbs Agree

Read the following sentences. Do they sound correct to you?

McCartney and Jackson sings together on that album.
That guppy don't look healthy.

Both sentences have the same problem. In each, the verb does not agree with its subject. This is a common error in both speaking and writing. In fact, it is one of the most important things to look for whenever you are proofreading your written work.

This section will make you aware of some common problems of subject-verb agreement. Study them carefully so that you can avoid them in your own writing.

Part 1   Making Subjects and Verbs Agree in Number

The **number** of a word refers to whether the word is singular or plural. A word is **singular** when it refers to one thing and **plural** when it refers to more than one thing. If a subject and verb are the same in number, they agree.

A verb must agree in number with its subject.

If a subject is singular, its verb must be singular. If a subject is plural, then its verb must be plural.

SINGULAR	PLURAL
She *watches*.	They *watch*.
He *dances* well.	They *dance* well.
The monkey *chatters*.	The monkeys *chatter*.

You can see that in the examples, the singular form of each verb ends in -*s*. In each plural verb, there is no -*s*.

Agreement of subjects and verbs usually occurs naturally in speaking and writing. Problems arise, though, when it is not clear which word is the subject of the sentence.

The subject of the verb is never found in a prepositional phrase.

When you are trying to make subjects and verbs agree, watch out for phrases that appear between the subject and the verb.

The *tapes* on this shelf *are* mine.
That *book* of poems *is* by Robert Frost.
The *words* to that song *are* catchy.
One of the trains *is* late.

Remember that to find the subject, first find the verb. Then place *who* or *what* before the verb to form a question.

The papers in this folder are important.
  Verb: are
  What are? papers
  The subject is *papers*.

Phrases beginning with the words *with, together with, including, as well as,* and *in addition to* are not part of the subject.

A fire *truck*, in addition to the police car, *is* here.
Honesty, as well as courage, *is* a virtue.
The *meal*, including dessert, *costs* four dollars.

Exercise A: Choose the verb that agrees with the subject.

1. Even the best tennis players (try, tries) to improve their techniques.
2. The mission of those pilots (was, were) accomplished with the help of the ground personnel.
3. The radio, as well as the flashlights, (needs, need) batteries.
4. That row of the bleachers (is, are) almost empty.
5. Two of the bones in her foot (is, are) broken.
6. The oil on the waves (was, were) from the damaged tanker.
7. Homes near the river (has, have) to be evacuated before the dam breaks.
8. The woman in the red sandals (works, work) at the clinic.
9. Jane's rings, as well as her bracelet, (has, have) been stolen.
10. Those photographs, including the one of Jake, (is, are) in the album.

Exercise B: Follow the directions for Exercise A.

1. A person with third-degree burns (requires, require) immediate medical help.
2. Leslie, as well as many other students, (takes, take) the subway to school.
3. The mongrel with the brown spots (leads, lead) that pack.
4. The boats in the bay (sail, sails) every weekend in summer.
5. Some members of the committee (is, are) planning a skating party.
6. The keys on that piano (is, are) in need of dusting.
7. Only two theaters in town (shows, show) first-run movies.
8. The snow on the walks (needs, need) shoveling.
9. The pumpkins in this patch (is, are) ready to pick.
10. A doe, with her two fawns, (was, were) grazing in the meadow.

Part 2   Compound Subjects

As you have learned, a compound subject is two or more subjects used with the same verb.

A compound subject joined by *and* is plural. Therefore, it requires a plural verb.

> The *radio* and the *stereo* **are playing** the same song.
> *Steve* and *Marcella* **write** for the newspaper.

When the parts of a compound subject are joined by *or* or *nor*, the verb should agree with the subject nearer to the verb.

> Neither Jan nor her *friends* **stay** for lunch.
> Either the jugglers or the tightrope *walker* **performs** next.

Exercise A: Choose the verb that agrees with the subject.

1. Huck and Tom (was, were) creeping through the cave.
2. Janet and Beth (is, are) taking a dune buggy ride.
3. Either the seat or the handlebars (has, have) to be adjusted.
4. Boots and jeans (seems, seem) to be Mike's uniform.
5. Neither the potholes nor the curb (has, have) been repaired.
6. Neither the curb nor the potholes (have, has) been repaired.
7. Either the Smoky Mountains or Yellowstone (is, are) my choice for a vacation.
8. Ecuador and Colombia (exports, export) coffee.
9. Both Liz and Marilyn (bowls, bowl) at that alley.
10. Neither Joyce nor Pam (bowls, bowl) at that alley.

Exercise B: Writing Some of these sentences contain errors in subject-verb agreement. If a sentence contains no error, write *Correct*. If the sentence is incorrect, rewrite it correctly.

1. Neither the drugstore nor the grocery open until 8 A.M.
2. Either Ms. McGee or Mr. Baez teaches that math class.
3. Both hail and wind storms damage crops.

4. Either the Pep Club or Student Council is selling homecoming mums.
5. Neither the mother panda nor her new cubs is on view yet at the zoo.
6. Neither the parade nor the fireworks were as good as usual this year.
7. Cancer and TB attacks people of all ages and all occupations.
8. Either the piano or the singers is off-key.
9. Neither the Cabinet members nor the President are available.
10. Rockets and a mission to outer space were once only science fiction.

Part 3   Indefinite Pronouns

To make a verb agree with an indefinite pronoun used as the subject, you must determine whether the pronoun is singular or plural. As you have learned, an indefinite pronoun may be singular or plural. Some may be either, depending on the context in which they appear.

The following indefinite pronouns are **singular**:

another	each	everything	one
anybody	either	neither	somebody
anyone	everybody	nobody	someone
anything	everyone	no one	

Nobody here *knows* the answer.
Someone is clearing the creek of debris.
Each of the rooms *has* cable TV.
Everything was ready by 9:00 A.M.

The following indefinite pronouns are **plural**:

both   few   many   several

Several of the candidates *agree* on the issues.
Both of those countries *have* mild climates.

The following indefinite pronouns are **singular** if they refer to one thing and **plural** if they refer to several things.

all   any   most   none   some

All of the equipment *is* clean and new.
All of the representatives *are* in Washington.

Most of the lake *has* a mud base.
Most of the beaches *have* lifeguards.

Some of the money *is* Linda's.
Some of the boats *are* at the pier.

Exercise A: Choose the verb that agrees with the subject.

1. Most of the batteries (is, are) still good.
2. Each of the coaches (has, have) a different approach.
3. Few of the rumors (seems, seem) likely to be true.
4. (Is, Are) all of the islands inhabited?
5. Everyone here (has, have) heard that joke before.
6. Somebody upstairs (is, are) playing the piano.
7. Some of the wranglers (was, were) heading for Omaha.
8. Nobody in town (has, have) spoken to the stranger.
9. Most of the sunken treasure (is, are) still underwater.
10. Some of the spaghetti sauce usually (splatters, splatter) on the stove.

Exercise B: Follow the directions for Exercise A.

1. Most of the track (needs, need) repair.
2. Most of the roads (needs, need) repair.
3. Neither of the pens (has, have) a fine point.
4. Everybody in the band (is, are) playing at the festival.
5. All of the tribes (is, are) gathering for the ceremony.
6. Most of the raffle tickets (has, have) been sold.
7. Many of us (wants, want) to take archery.
8. One of the twins often (pretends, pretend) to be the other.
9. Everybody in the bleachers (was, were) cheering.
10. No one (know, knows) the true identity of the Lone Ranger.

Part 4   Other Problems of Agreement

Doesn't and Don't Used with Pronouns

The verb *doesn't* is singular. *Doesn't* is used with the subjects *she, he,* and *it.* All other personal pronouns are used with *don't.*

It *doesn't* matter to me.	I *don't* like jogging.
He *doesn't* live near the city.	We *don't* watch much TV.
She *doesn't* speak Spanish.	They *don't* play fairly.

Sentences Beginning with *There, Here,* or *Where*

When sentences begin with *There, Here,* or *Where,* the subject comes after the verb. You must look ahead to find the subject of the sentence. Then you must use the verb that agrees.

There *are* two *versions* of that song.
Here *is* the beach *towel.*
Here *are* an *ax* and a *saw.*
Where *are* the *peaches?*

Words of Amount and Time

Words or phrases that express periods of time, fractions, weights, measurements, and amounts of money are usually regarded as singular.

Thirty dollars *is* too much for that watch.
Three-fourths of the flour *has* been used.
Eight hours *seems* a long time to be on a plane.
Five hundred pounds of dog food *is* unnecessary.
Six yards of fabric *was* not expensive.

Sometimes a prepositional phrase with a plural object falls between the subject and the verb. When this happens, the verb remains singular if the subject is meant as a single thing. The verb is plural if the subject is meant as a plural thing.

Fifty kilograms of raspberries *is* enough.
Six of the boxes *are* in the garage.

Exercise A: Choose the verb that agrees with the subject.

1. Where (do, does) Paul Newman and Joanne Woodward live?
2. She (doesn't, don't) often lose her temper.
3. Here (is, are) some suspicious-looking pawprints.
4. Where (is, are) the Ionian Islands?
5. They (doesn't, don't) believe in ghosts.
6. (Doesn't, Don't) he look like Michael Landon?
7. (Doesn't, Don't) they go to Eagle River to camp?
8. There (is, are) some mail for you on the radiator.
9. Here (come, comes) that yellow Thunderbird with the sunroof.
10. There (doesn't, don't) seem to be a road up the mountain.

Exercise B: Follow the directions for Exercise A.

1. (Doesn't, Don't) they live near the ravine?
2. Here (is, are) cheese and mushrooms for the pizza.
3. (Isn't, Aren't) there submerged rocks along this pier?
4. Where (is, are) your backpack?
5. He (doesn't, don't) like lox and bagels.
6. Where (is, are) your new sweatshirt with the hood?
7. It (doesn't, don't) snow here at Christmas.
8. Here (is, are) the hooks and bait for your fishing trip.
9. She usually (don't, doesn't) appear with another singer.
10. There (was, were) several fire trucks heading for the wharf.

Exercise C: Writing Write two sentences that begin with each of the following words. Make sure that subjects and verbs agree.

doesn't	here	there
don't	where	

REINFORCEMENT EXERCISES
Making Subjects and Verbs Agree

A. Make verbs and subjects agree in number. Write the verb that agrees with the subject.

1. The lane for bicycles (is, are) on the west side of the road.
2. A truckload of bananas (has, have) spilled onto the highway.
3. My recipe for brownies (is, are) unbeatable.
4. Two pieces of the puzzle (is, are) missing.
5. Several people, including Marion, (has, have) never tried skiing.
6. Victor, as well as his sisters, (play, plays) in a band.
7. The sounds of a foghorn (drift, drifts) across the harbor.
8. Our chances of winning (is, are) better than the other team's.
9. A bag of peanuts (is, are) my favorite movie snack.
10. All roads leading from town (is, are) flooded.
11. The purpose of the rigorous camping trips (was, were) to develop survival skills.
12. Roger, together with his brothers, (works, work) on a ranch each summer.
13. The monkeys in that cage (seems, seem) livelier than the chimpanzees.
14. The list of grievances (grow, grows) each month.
15. The photographs on this page (looks, look) very old.

B. Make verbs agree with compound subjects. Write the verb that agrees with the subject.

1. Peanuts or popcorn (makes, make) a good snack.
2. Warm gloves and a down jacket (is, are) important for winter sports.
3. Both fog and rain (have, has) inspired painters and poets.
4. Tolerance and honesty (is, are) not always easy to practice.
5. Neither cardinals nor chicadees (fly, flies) south in winter.

6. In school, neither Thomas Edison nor Albert Einstein (was, were) considered a good student.
7. Neither white rice nor white bread (provides, provide) as much nutrition as brown rice.
8. Both salt water and chlorine (aggravate, aggravates) the infection.
9. Farming and ranching (has, have) replaced buffalo hunting for many Plains Indians.
10. Either Los Angeles or Chicago (is, are) second in size to New York City.

C. Make verbs agree with indefinite pronouns. Write the verb that agrees with the subject.

1. (Has, Have) any of the ice cream bars melted?
2. All of the snow (has, have) been blown into huge drifts.
3. All of the balloons (was, were) released at the rally.
4. Everyone in the stands (cheers, cheer) when the teams enter the stadium.
5. Each of the gondolas (carry, carries) ten passengers.
6. Both lacrosse and jai-alai (require, requires) agility.
7. None of the coaches (allow, allows) players to skip practice.
8. Some of the fudge (is, are) for the bake sale.
9. Another of those old Westerns (is, are) on tonight.
10. Either logging or forest fires (has, have) leveled these hills.

D. Solve other problems of agreement. Write the verb that agrees with the subject.

1. It (doesn't, don't) take long to learn this dance.
2. He (doesn't, don't) remember much about the accident.
3. There (is, are) a swinging bridge across Capilano Canyon.
4. There (is, are) special box seats for famous visitors.
5. Where (is, are) the rental canoes?
6. Here (is, are) a wood-burning stove and some fuel.
7. Where (is, are) my running shorts?
8. She usually (don't, doesn't) complain like this.
9. (Doesn't, Don't) they have the lead roles?
10. Here (is, are) several abandoned miners' huts.

MIXED REVIEW
Making Subjects and Verbs Agree

A. Some of the following sentences contain errors in subject-verb agreement. If there are no mistakes, write *Correct*. If there is a mistake, rewrite the sentence correctly.

1. Don't the paintings in this exhibit look familiar?
2. Either the reporters or the editor need to check the facts more thoroughly.
3. Neither of the twins have ever been out of New York.
4. A teenager with dental problems often benefit from braces.
5. High technology, including various types of computers, has revolutionized many industries.
6. The winning teams in our division is in the playoffs.
7. The vegetables in my neighbor's garden seem to grow better than mine.
8. My father and his co-workers plays racquetball during their lunch hour.
9. There is the maps of the route for the bicycle race.
10. Thousands of barrels of oil are imported into the United States every day.

B. Add words to complete each sentence. Make sure that your subjects and verbs agree. Write your sentences in the present tense.

1. Both Washington and Hawaii
2. Few in the crowded hall
3. Neither exercises nor diet
4. Each of the band members
5. The ringmaster, as well as several performers
6. Some of the caves in the Smoky Mountains
7. Lee, Ann, and Sara all
8. Swimming and jogging
9. Either my grandparents or my great-uncle
10. Several of the stray dogs

USING GRAMMAR IN WRITING

Making Subjects and Verbs Agree

A. Imagine that in order to select a group to perform at a school event, you have conducted a survey on musical tastes in your school. Your results are as follows:

	Students	**Teacher**
Do you enjoy music?	yes — 100%	yes — 100%
Do you enjoy loud music?	yes — 70% no — 30%	yes — 25% no — 75%
Would you prefer rock, new wave, or easy listening music?	Rock — 50% New Wave — 40% Easy Listening — 10%	Rock — 50% New Wave — 10% Easy Listening — 40%

Using indefinite pronouns such as *none, all, every, each, both, no one,* and *everyone,* write a paper reporting your results. Compare and contrast the results received from students and from teachers.

B. Zyxxt and Qlut are extraterrestrials who have just landed on earth. To make a good impression, Qlut has prepared a speech in English. She has, however, made some mistakes in subject-verb agreement. Rewrite the speech for her, correcting all errors.

Greetings, Earth People: We, Zyxxt and Qlut, come in peace from the planet Thorax. We doesn't want to frighten you. Zyxxt don't mean harm, and I doesn't either. Where are your leader? We want to explain our mission. Here is some gifts of fruit from our planet. There is glimps, blyds, and flizzers for you to eat. Doesn't they look delicious? We doesn't plan to stay on earth very long, but we hope you will visit our home in the future. There is many interesting things to see and do on Thorax.

CUMULATIVE REVIEW
Usage (II)

Using the Correct Form of Words. Number your paper from 1 to 10. Write the correct word from the two given in parentheses.

1. The lake had finally (froze, frozen) solid.
2. Everyone had drunk (his or her, their) water before we had hiked five miles.
3. Is it (he, him) whom everyone calls "Lightning"?
4. (Who, Whom) was the award presented to this year?
5. Of the last two governors, whom do you think was the (better, best)?
6. Did you finish painting all of (them, those) figures?
7. The stubborn camel walked very (slow, slowly).
8. It seems that (we, us) freshmen will have to plan the dance.
9. The President spoke to the press; his voice sounded sad and (hesitant, hesitantly).
10. The prize money was divided between Luis and (I, me).

Finding Errors in Usage. Eight of the following sentences contain at least one error in usage. Some are errors of agreement, and some are errors of form. Identify the errors and rewrite each incorrect sentence. Write *C* if a sentence is already correct.

1. The squirrels or that raccoon chews through that there screen door every summer.
2. The divers swam careful among the strange ocean plants.
3. Who wants to see us squad leaders about last night's game?
4. The costumes and the scenery looks well under the lights.
5. The speaker will attempt to learn us about the desert and it's strange beauty.
6. No one asked for his or her money back.
7. Was the Samurai warriors more fiercer than modern soldiers?
8. The ranger had saw the smoke before Leah.
9. Who did you tell about them cracks in the bleachers?
10. Leave me raise the sail of the boat this time.

Section 11

Using Compound and Complex Sentences

In preceding sections, you learned how the parts of a sentence work together. In this section, you will learn about four kinds of sentences that differ in their basic structure. They are called simple sentences, compound sentences, complex sentences, and compound-complex sentences.

Part 1 Review of the Sentence

The sentence is composed of two basic parts, the subject and the predicate.

SUBJECT	PREDICATE
Lights	flash.
Lights	flash a signal.
Blinking lights on the control panel	flash a signal.

The **subject** of a sentence names the person or thing about which something is said. The **predicate** is the idea that is expressed about the subject.

The **simple predicate** is the verb. The subject of the verb is called the **simple subject.**

Within the subject of the sentence are the simple subject and its modifiers. In the predicate of the sentence are the verb, objects, predicate words, and their modifiers.

Compound Parts of a Sentence

You have learned that all of the parts of the sentence may be **compound**. Each one, in other words, may have more than one part.

COMPOUND SUBJECT:	Neither sleep nor dreams are fully understood.
COMPOUND VERB:	The audience clapped, shouted, and cheered.
COMPOUND PREDICATE:	Derek cleaned the fish and then fried it on an open fire.
COMPOUND OBJECT:	Janelle designed the store decorations and window displays.
COMPOUND OBJECT OF THE PREPOSITION:	On holidays and weekends, the store is closed.
COMPOUND PREDICATE WORD:	That TV studio is large and empty.

The Simple Sentence

Even though sentences may have compound parts, they still express only one main idea. Such sentences, like all of those you have been studying, are called **simple sentences**.

A simple sentence is a sentence with only one subject and one predicate.

The subject and the predicate, along with any part of the subject or predicate, may be compound.

Now you are ready to distinguish simple sentences from other types of sentences.

Exercise A: Copy each of the following simple sentences. Then draw a line between the subject and the predicate.

1. Teresa and Nat have social security cards.
2. Theodore Roosevelt and Franklin D. Roosevelt were Presidents with strong personalities.
3. Dave found the tuxedo and the top hat in a thrift shop.
4. Stevie Wonder and Brenda Lee both began their singing careers as children.
5. China and Russia border Mongolia.
6. Mr. Mendoza's two cats are Siamese and Burmese.
7. Maria carefully measured the space for the shelf and then sawed the plywood.
8. The figure skaters were agile and daring.
9. The lifeguard wears a whistle around her neck.
10. Sharon keeps a flashlight and candles on hand for use during power failures.

Exercise B: Write the compound subjects, verbs, and objects you find in these simple sentences.

1. The crew cleared and bulldozed ten acres of wilderness.
2. Vince Evans and Doug Williams are both quarterbacks.
3. First grate and measure the cheese.
4. Fireflies blinked in the trees and bushes.
5. South American Indians have unique crafts and customs.
6. Early settlers made soap from ashes, water, and grease.

7. Scrooge and Tiny Tim are two of Dickens's characters.
8. Theo feeds, grooms, and exercises horses at the stable.
9. Julia and Sandy left an hour ago.
10. Did you and Martha take snorkeling lessons?

Part 2   The Compound Sentence

Sometimes two simple sentences express such closely related ideas that they are joined to form one sentence. The resulting sentence has more than one subject and more than one predicate. It is called a **compound sentence.**

A compound sentence consists of two or more simple sentences joined together.

The parts of the compound sentence may be joined by a coordinating conjunction (*and, or, but*) or by a semicolon (;).

The World Series is over, **and** the football season has begun.
This hill is small, **but** it's perfect for sledding.
Return your library books today, **or** you will have to pay a fine.
Special tags on the clothing can set off an alarm; they help to prevent shoplifting.

Compound sentences add variety and interest to a piece of writing. They break what might otherwise be monotonous strings of short, choppy sentences. Look at the following paragraph:

John Adams met Thomas Jefferson in 1775. Both men helped create the new government. They had opposing views about it. At first the men were close friends. Their political views drove them apart. They fought for the Presidency. They criticized each other's leadership. In their later years they began corresponding with each other. They patched up their differences. Jefferson died on July 4, 1826. Coincidentally, Adams died the same day.

The series of simple sentences, one after another, becomes dull and tiresome. Notice how much better the same paragraph sounds when some of the sentences are compound sentences.

John Adams met Thomas Jefferson in 1775. Both men helped create the new government, but they had opposing views about it. At first the men were close friends, but their political views drove them apart. They fought for the Presidency, and they criticized each other's leadership. In their later years they began corresponding with each other, and they patched up their differences. Jefferson died on July 4, 1826, and, coincidentally, Adams died the same day.

Diagraming Compound Sentences

If you can diagram simple sentences, you can diagram compound ones. The diagram simply demonstrates that a compound sentence is two or more simple sentences joined together. The simple sentences are diagramed one under the other. Then they are connected with a dotted line between the verbs. The conjunction sits on a "step" of the line.

The press secretary spoke first, and then the President held a press conference.

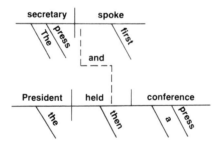

Exercise A: Label three columns *Subject/Verb, Conjunction,* and *Subject/Verb.* For each sentence, fill in the columns.

EXAMPLE: Nina sings well, but Angie and Ted sing better.

SUBJECT/VERB	CONJUNCTION	SUBJECT/VERB
Nina/sings	but	Angie, Ted/sing

1. The movie was dull, but the book was fascinating.
2. Do you have a radio, or should I bring one?

3. I have lost my pen, or else somebody has borrowed it.
4. Montana is the Treasure State, and California is the Golden State.
5. The instructions confused me, but the nurse explained them.
6. Max cleared the fence, and I scrambled after.
7. The first vehicle with a steam engine worked well for a few hours, but then its engine failed.
8. The team is very strong this year, and we are almost sure to win the city championship.
9. The cavalry had ridden into Mexico on the trail of Chief Geronimo, but he evaded them.
10. The disc jockey talks to callers first, and then she plays records.

Exercise B: Writing Rewrite this paragraph, changing the italicized simple sentences into compound sentences.

The oak tree is one of the most common trees in the United States. There is the white oak group and the black oak group. *The acorns of white oaks mature in one year. Those of the black oaks take two years.* The two trees differ, of course, in appearance. *White oaks have pale bark. Black oaks have dark bark.* Oak is used as hardwood timber for lumber and fuel. Oak is also used as timber for barrels and railroad ties.

Punctuating Compound Sentences

One of two punctuation marks is used in a compound sentence. Either a **comma** before a coordinating conjunction or a **semicolon** is needed to separate the two parts.

In a compound sentence, a comma is used before a coordinating conjunction. Notice how the comma is used in these compound sentences:

The subway car was nearly full, *but* all of us piled in anyway.

Sandra talked to her adviser, *and* he helped her with her schedule.

Note: Sometimes commas are not necessary in very short compound sentences.

s. v.   s. v.
Either we're late or you're early.

s.   v.   s.   v.
Alarms rang and everyone awoke.

Instead of a comma and a conjunction, a **semicolon** may be used alone to separate the parts of a compound sentence.

s.   v.   s.   v.
Gil climbed the palm tree; he returned with a coconut.

s.   v.
Mount McKinley is the highest point in the country;

s.   v.
Death Valley is the lowest.

A semicolon may also be used with a **conjunctive adverb**. A conjunctive adverb is an adverb like *therefore, however, moreover, consequently,* or *otherwise.* It joins the two parts of a compound sentence and shows the relationship between them.

s.   v.   s.   v.
We missed our bus; *however,* we caught a later bus.

s.   v.   s.
Heavy rains halted repairs on the highway; *therefore,* the crew

v.
is behind schedule.

As you can see, a conjunctive adverb is used after a semicolon and is followed by a comma.

Compound Sentence or Compound Predicate?

In order to punctuate sentences correctly, you must be able to recognize the difference between a compound sentence and a simple sentence with a compound predicate. A compound predicate is composed of two verbs along with their complements and modifiers. Both verbs refer to the same subject. The parts of a compound predicate are joined by a coordinating conjunction. The conjunction is *not* preceded by any punctuation.

Alana *joined the team* and *made the starting lineup.*

A compound sentence, as you have just learned, is composed of two simple sentences, each with its own subject and verb. The two sentences are almost always separated by a comma and conjunction, or by a semicolon.

Alana *joined* the team, and **she** *made* the starting lineup.

As you compose your own sentences, you must be aware of whether a sentence is a compound sentence or a simple sentence with a compound predicate. If each verb has its own subject, then the sentence is compound. If the verbs share the same subject, then only the predicate is compound. Once you have determined what kind of sentence you are writing, you will know how to punctuate it correctly.

Kyle entered a baking contest and *won* first place.
(This simple sentence has a compound predicate. Both verbs, *entered* and *won,* have the same subject, *Kyle.* The conjunction is not preceded by a comma.)

Kyle entered a baking contest, and his *cheesecake won* first place.
(This is a compound sentence. The verb *entered* has its own subject, *Kyle.* The verb *won* has its own subject, *cheesecake.* The conjunction is preceded by a comma.)

The *clerk types* letters and *files* information.
(The conjunction *and* joins the compound predicate of this simple sentence. Both verbs, *types* and *files,* have the same subject, *clerk.* The conjunction is not preceded by a comma.)

The *clerk types* letters, and the *computer files* information.
(This compound sentence is actually two simple sentences joined by a comma and the conjunction *and.*)

Exercise A: For each sentence, write the two words between which the punctuation belongs. Put in the comma or semicolon. If a sentence needs no punctuation, write *Correct.*

1. You can make delicious pies from Concord grapes however, you must remove their seeds first.
2. Dr. Jekyll was the kind doctor and Mr. Hyde was Jekyll's evil other self.
3. The clouds parted and revealed a full moon.
4. Sharon writes the newsletter Jerome distributes it.
5. I met Diana last week and liked her immediately.
6. Sal and Joy bought season tickets but they attended only the first and the last games.
7. Vanilla extract and unsweetened chocolate both smell good but they taste bitter.
8. The planet Mars has an average temperature of -45° and Martian winds can blow at 300 miles per hour.
9. Cleo caught the trout and cleaned it.
10. Basketball players must wear appropriate shoes otherwise, they risk injury to their feet and ankles.

Exercise B: Follow the directions for Exercise A.

1. My brother wrote a play and directed it.
2. Ivy hung like streamers and roses clambered up the wall.
3. Sheila signaled an S.O.S. with her flashlight however, the people on the beach did not know Morse code.
4. Sailors recognize an upside-down flag as an appeal for help and railroad engineers respond to a red flag by the track.
5. Stories about vampires and monsters are popular and have been told for many centuries.
6. The judge heard the evidence and then dismissed the case.
7. Alligators look slow nevertheless, they can move very fast.
8. Quilts and oak furniture were once used in many homes but now they are too expensive to be common.
9. Students in the work-experience program can get jobs with sponsor companies or they can find jobs themselves.
10. Mother Jones was a union organizer and an activist but earlier she had taught in a convent.

Part 3   The Complex Sentence

Now that you understand the structure of simple sentences and compound sentences, you are ready to study **complex sentences.** However, before you can understand the structure of a complex sentence, you must know what a clause is.

A clause is a group of words containing a verb and its subject.

According to this definition, a simple sentence is a clause. It contains a verb and its subject.

> s.   v.
> Keith ran in the marathon.

> s.   v.
> Many stores have clearance sales.

It will be easier to understand sentences, though, if you think of a clause as *a group of words within a sentence.* Compound sentences, for example, contain two or more clauses.

> s.   v.   s. v.
> Lara demonstrated the loom, and she wove fibers for a rug.

> s.   v.   s. v.
> Sherlock Holmes is a fictional character, but he has a large fan club.

Clause or Phrase?

Clauses differ from phrases. Like a clause, a phrase is part of a sentence. However, a clause has a subject and a verb. A phrase does not.

PHRASES: before the gold rush
                to cut the grass

CLAUSES: after the Bengals kicked off

                before you left

Subordinate Clauses

Each of the clauses of a compound sentence can stand alone. In other words, each can function by itself as a sentence. Such a clause is called a **main clause**, or **independent clause**. A main clause is a clause that can stand by itself as a sentence.

Subordinate clauses, or **dependent clauses,** are clauses that cannot stand alone. A subordinate clause is not a complete sentence. Study these examples:

s.   v.
If you sign the contract

s.   v.
Before the gates close

Both of the subordinate clauses above contain subjects and verbs. However, neither of them expresses a complete thought, and neither can stand alone. Both leave you wondering *then what?*

The words that begin subordinate clauses have an important function. Without *if* and *before,* the clauses above become sentences. Words like *if* and *before* are called **subordinating conjunctions.** We say that they *subordinate,* or make *dependent,* the words they introduce. Many, though not all, subordinate clauses begin with subordinating conjunctions.

Words often used as subordinating conjunctions are shown here:

Words Often Used as Subordinating Conjunctions			
after	because	so that	when
although	before	than	whenever
as	if	though	where
as if	in order that	till	wherever
as long as	provided	unless	while
as though	since	until	

Note: The words above are subordinating conjunctions only when they begin clauses. Many of these words can be used in other ways.

Furthermore, not all subordinate clauses begin with subordinating conjunctions. Some clauses begin with words like these:

that	who, whom, whose
what, whatever	whoever, whomever
which	why
how	

Exercise A: Copy each sentence. Find the main clause and underline it. Then find the subordinate clause in each sentence and enclose it in parentheses.

1. Carla broke her glasses when she fell off her bike.
2. The prize would go to whoever danced the longest.
3. Although I prefer peach yogurt, I like strawberry yogurt, too.
4. If the Braves lose this game, they are out of the pennant race.
5. When the smoke cleared, we saw the charred ruins of the mansion.
6. We arrived after the concert started.
7. Do you know where the Isle of Skye is located?
8. The fans in the gallery were quiet while the golfer putted.
9. Dr. Frankenstein smiled as he entered the laboratory.
10. Our basement flooded while we were on vacation.

Exercise B: Writing Using *if, because, when, after,* and *since,* make subordinate clauses out of these sentences. Then use each subordinate clause in a sentence.

1. The bus was late.
2. The platform looks shaky.
3. Diane enjoys bowling.
4. There is a pinball machine in the back.
5. The juke box played only old songs.
6. This sundial is very accurate.
7. Flies were buzzing around the table.
8. Keith's contact lens is lost.
9. Strawberries are in season.
10. The cruise ship headed for the tropics.

Definition of the Complex Sentence

Now that you know the difference between main clauses and subordinate clauses, you can understand the complex sentence.

A complex sentence is a sentence that contains one main clause and one or more subordinate clauses.

MAIN CLAUSE	SUBORDINATE CLAUSE
We'll be out of the tournament	unless we win this game.
The real funs begins	when Anthony arrives.
King Kong is a fictional ape	that attacks New York.

Exercise A: Copy the subordinate clause in these complex sentences. Underline the subject once and the verb twice.

1. Roberto asked if we liked oysters.
2. Summer was over before we knew it.
3. These clothes are on sale because they are unusual sizes.
4. The plane ticket tells when we will arrive.
5. The orchestra tuned up before the conductor appeared.
6. Claudia looks as if she knows the punchline.
7. Mattie steadied the ladder while Dawn replaced the bulb.
8. The ham will spoil unless you refrigerate it.
9. Unless it rains, we'll go to the fair Monday.
10. Although Bobbie disliked buckwheat pancakes, she politely finished hers.

Exercise B: Follow the directions for Exercise A.

1. These windows stick when the weather is humid.
2. Jill climbed onto the top of a truck so that she could see over the crowd.
3. As the Buick was turning left, the light changed.
4. When John is daydreaming, he ignores everything else.
5. Wherever there are wars, there are refugees.
6. You can paint the room any color, as long as it's not too dark.
7. Maria acted as though she had not heard the news.
8. Can't he remember where the bases are?
9. I don't know if Juanita speaks Portuguese.
10. Tina explained how the controls of the kiln should be set.

Part 4 Adverb Clauses

Complex sentences contain subordinate clauses. These clauses may be one of three kinds. One type is the **adverb clause.** An adverb clause functions as any adverb or adverb phrase.

An **adverb** modifies a verb, an adjective, or another adverb. It tells *how, when, where,* or *to what extent.*

ADVERB: Marissa watched *intently.*

An **adverb phrase** is a prepositional phrase used as an adverb.

ADVERB PHRASE: Marissa watched *on the sidelines.*

An adverb clause is a subordinate clause used as an adverb.

ADVERB CLAUSE: Ed watched *while the gymnasts practiced.*

When the voters were polled, Al was leading.

Adverb clauses, like adverbs and adverb phrases, tell *how, when, where,* and *to what extent.* They modify verbs, adjectives, and adverbs.

Note that a clause, unlike a phrase, has a subject and a verb.

Diagraming Adverb Clauses

To diagram an adverb clause, place it on a separate horizontal line below the main line. A dotted line connects the adverb clause to the word it modifies in the main clause. The subordinating conjunction is shown on the dotted line.

When Carlos was twelve, he moved to New York.

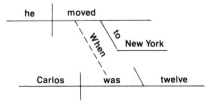

Exercise A: Copy the adverb clause from each sentence. Underline the subject of each clause once and its verb twice.

1. We waited at the airport until his plane departed.
2. If the treaty is signed, the Secretary of State will return tomorrow.
3. Although they're sisters, they are different in every way.
4. Will school close if the blizzard continues?
5. The snow was twelve inches deep before the city managers agreed upon a removal plan.
6. The council objected when the mayor proposed his plan.
7. Helmets flashed in the sun as the bikers roared past.
8. Greg stirred the chili with one hand while he answered the phone with the other.
9. Walt Disney made his cartoon animals act as though they were human.
10. Although there were storm warnings, we foolishly took the boat out.

Exercise B: Follow the directions for Exercise A.

1. Nurses can usually find jobs wherever they go.
2. Although Rita Gomez has not appeared in movies here, she is a popular movie actress in the Philippines.
3. When the President addressed the United Nations, his speech was translated into many languages.
4. The doctor had to reset Linda's broken arm because she fell on it again.
5. Before electricity became available, many people went to sleep right after sundown.
6. If the newsstand is out of papers, try the drug store.
7. Whenever Jeannie makes a winning basket, she seems amazed.
8. As Sam answered the questions, the computer recorded the answers.
9. Mom learned German when her dad was stationed near Heidelburg.
10. Because Gail had taken a first aid class, she knew immediately what to do.

Part 5   Adjective Clauses

The second kind of subordinate clause is the **adjective clause.** An adjective clause has the same function as an adjective or an adjective phrase.

An **adjective** modifies a noun or pronoun.

> ADJECTIVE: Melissa wears *big, round* sunglasses.

An **adjective phrase** is a prepositional phrase that modifies a noun or pronoun.

> ADJECTIVE PHRASE: We glanced at the list *of sandwiches.*

An adjective clause is a subordinate clause used as an adjective to modify a noun or pronoun.

> ADJECTIVE CLAUSE: A polygraph is a machine *that is used in lie detection.*
>
> Anyone *who tries hard enough* can stay awake.

Adjective clauses, like adjectives and adjective phrases, tell *what kind* or *which one.* They usually come directly after the word they modify. Unlike adjective phrases, adjective clauses have subjects and verbs.

There are several words used to introduce adjective clauses. Two of them are *where* and *when.*

> This is the studio *where recordings are made.*

> This is the time *when the moon is full.*

Relative Pronouns

Besides *when* and *where,* the words *who, whom,* and *whose* are also used to begin adjective clauses. *Who, whom,* and *whose* are called **relative pronouns.** They relate a clause, called a **relative clause,** to a noun or pronoun in the sentence. Sometimes *that* and *which* are relative pronouns.

Relative pronouns are special because they function in three different ways:

1. They introduce adjective clauses.
2. They link the clause to a word in the main clause of the sentence.
3. They have a function within the clause. They act as subject, object, or predicate pronoun of the verb within the adjective clause. They may also be the object of a preposition in the clause. *Whose* functions as an adjective.

Students *who work part-time* are dismissed early.
(The adjective clause modifies *Students*, the subject of the main clause. *Who* is the subject of *work* within the adjective clause.)

The dentist's office plays music *that is soothing.*
(The adjective clause modifies *music* in the main clause. *That* is the subject of *is* within the adjective clause.)

The person *whom we need most* is Anna.
(The adjective clause modifies the word *person* in the main clause. *Whom* functions as the direct object of *need* within the adjective clause.)

The tall, blonde girl *with whom I chatted* turned out to be my distant cousin.
(The adjective clause modifies the subject of the main clause, *girl. Whom* is the object of the preposition *with* within the adjective clause.)

Children *whose parents work here* may attend the day-care center.
(The adjective clause modifies *Children* within the main clause. *Whose* modifies *parents*, the subject of the adjective clause.)

Sometimes you may be confused about whether *who* or *whom* is the correct relative pronoun to use. To decide, see how the pronoun is used within the clause. Keep in mind that *who* is the subject form. *Whom* is the object form.

She is the artist *who* painted the mural.
(*Who* is the subject of *painted* within the clause.)

She is the artist *whom* I most admire.
(*Whom* is the direct object of *admire* within the clause.)

Diagraming Adjective Clauses

To diagram an adjective clause, use a separate line beneath the main line. A dotted line runs from the relative pronoun to the word in the main clause that the adjective clause modifies.

The people who run the space program are in Houston.

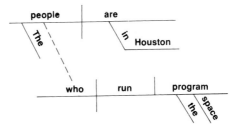

One of the players on whom we depend was injured.

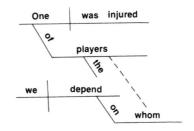

Exercise A: Copy the adjective clause from each sentence. Underline the subject once and the verb twice. Before the clause, write the word it modifies.

> EXAMPLE: She is the teacher who wrote our textbook.
>
> teacher—who wrote our textbook

1. It was the coldest winter that New Yorkers had ever experienced.
2. The maple tree that Grandad planted is over twenty feet tall.
3. Staph germs in the body head for tissue that is damaged.
4. Donna is the cheerleader who also plays baseball.
5. One American writer who lived in Paris was James Baldwin.
6. The man who is wearing a neck brace was in a car accident.
7. The mayor is the person to whom the petition should be sent.
8. Fireflies, which are really beetles, produce cold lights.
9. The milk that is in this carton smells sour.
10. This is the time of day that I like best.

Exercise B: Follow the directions for Exercise A.

1. One of the cities that produced early jazz is New Orleans.
2. The carpenter who made this cabinet is eighty years old.
3. In almost every family there is someone who cannot throw anything away.
4. Panama, which joins Central America and South America, is a small but important country.
5. The silo in which the soybeans were stored was struck by lightning.
6. The artist and her husband designed their own home, which was made of steel and glass.
7. The manager gave the reporter a list of the players whose contracts had been renewed.
8. The man whose dog bit me drove me to the hospital.
9. Sunday night is the time when television attracts the most viewers.
10. The window which was broken was repaired by a glazier.

Part 6   Noun Clauses

The noun clause is the third kind of subordinate clause.

A noun clause is a clause used as a noun in a sentence.

Like a noun, a noun clause can be used as a subject, an object of the verb, a predicate word, or an object of a preposition. It can be used in any of the ways that nouns are used in a sentence. Unlike adverb and adjective clauses, however, noun clauses do not modify.

Uses of Noun Clauses

SUBJECT: *Whoever sent the mayday alert* must need help urgently.
What concerns everyone is inflation.

DIRECT OBJECT: Scientists cannot always predict *when an earthquake will occur.*
The controller radioed *that the runway was clear.*

OBJECT OF PREPOSITION: Rod was impressed by *whatever Joyce said.*
The signs point to *where the trail begins.*

PREDICATE NOUN: City life is *what he wants.*
The fact was *that the car was missing.*

As you can see from these examples, many noun clauses begin with the words *that* and *what.* The words *whatever, who, whoever,* and *whomever* can also signal noun clauses. *Where, when, how,* and *why* are used, too.

Diagraming Noun Clauses

To diagram a noun clause, extend a bridge from the place where the clause is used in the sentence. If the word that begins the clause functions simply as an introductory word, place it on a line over the clause. Look at the three examples on the next page:

1. Noun clause used as subject

What you need is a sense of humor.

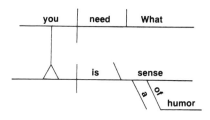

2. Noun clause used as object of the verb

Many people say that good times are ahead.

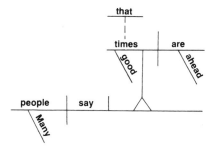

3. Noun clause used as object of a preposition

The candidate talked to whoever would listen.

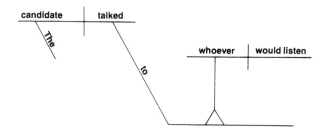

Exercise A: Copy the noun clauses in these sentences. Underline the subject once and the verb twice. Tell how the clause is used.

1. Now I understand why you left early.
2. Patrice explained how yogurt is made.
3. St. Louis is where ice cream cones were first sold.
4. The problem is that the battery is dead.
5. You can make a scarf from whatever fabric is left.
6. What the audience wanted was another encore.
7. There will be enough food for whomever you invite.
8. Whoever made that statement does not know the facts.
9. Mickie starts a conversation with whoever sits next to her.
10. We all wondered where the magician learned her tricks.

Exercise B: Follow the directions for Exercise A.

1. The manager promised that she would look for my jacket.
2. Hal asked why the game had been delayed.
3. How the pyramids were built is a fascinating story.
4. Alex said that high ozone levels give him headaches.
5. I wonder who lost this watch.
6. Whenever you must leave, just let me know.
7. Ken thinks that he has the winning ticket.
8. The only solution is that we raise the funds ourselves.
9. The minister spends her time with whoever needs it.
10. What the neighbors will think bothers him too much.

Part 7 A Review of Subordinate Clauses

You have learned about the three kinds of subordinate clauses. They are the adverb clause, the adjective clause, and the noun clause.

You can identify the kind of clause by looking at its use in the sentence. A clause used as a noun is a noun clause. A clause used as a modifier is an adverb or adjective clause, depending on the word modified.

Exercise A: Write the subordinate clause in each sentence. If the clause is used as a noun clause, write how it is used in the sentence. If the clause is used as an adjective or adverb clause, write the word it modifies.

1. Nevada is one state where wild horses still roam.
2. I wonder where I stored my backpack.
3. When the movie was over, the audience was silent.
4. Mr. Chang, who owns vegetable markets, spoke to our JA club.
5. Carol suddenly realized who was on the phone.
6. Tom always worries about what he will say next.
7. The school days that were lost during the snowstorm will be made up in June.
8. Ellie remembered that meteors would be visible in the early evening.
9. Find a seat wherever you can.
10. Trees that follow day-night cycles may be injured by bright streetlights.

Exercise B: Follow the directions for Exercise A.

1. The ring, which had belonged to her grandmother, was Celia's most cherished possession.
2. Call the clinic right away if the pain in your shoulder becomes worse.
3. Neighborhoods that have no parks are rare in Chicago.
4. The census taker who visited our block spoke Spanish and Polish.
5. I tried to sketch the scene I saw from our cabin window.
6. Who will start is the coach's decision.
7. Julio will not eat junk food while he is in training for the gymnastics team.
8. While Glenda was rehearsing a loud scene from the play, the people next door became worried about her.
9. As Rome was burning, the emperor supposedly played his fiddle.
10. The janitor said that he would replace the doorknob tonight.

Part 8 Clauses as Sentence Fragments

You have learned that a sentence fragment may lack a subject or verb or both.

Alone on the lake.   Played the jukebox.

The subordinate clause can be a sentence fragment, too. Even though it does have a subject and verb, it still does not express a complete thought. For that reason, it is a sentence fragment.

Notice the difference between these word groups:

The TV was on.   While the TV was on.

The first word group is a sentence. In the second group, the subordinating conjunction *while* creates a sentence fragment. The reader cannot tell *what was happening* while the TV was on. The subordinate clause should be used as part of a sentence.

A subordinate clause must not be written as a complete sentence. It must always be joined to a main clause.

MAIN CLAUSE   Australians are having summer.
AND FRAGMENT: When we are having winter.
SENTENCE: Australians are having summer when we are having winter.

Exercise A: Writing Number your paper from 1 to 10. Decide whether the groups of words below are sentences or fragments. Write *S* for *Sentence* and *F* for *Fragment*. Add words to make each fragment a complete sentence. Be sure to punctuate and capitalize where necessary.

1. what did the announcer say
2. when is the playoff game
3. what the fortune teller said
4. after the rain stops
5. after a while everyone returned
6. that showroom is filled with new cars

7. the book that you needed
8. before the dance started
9. why is the flag at half-mast
10. why the dogs are barking

Exercise B: Writing Find the fragments in the paragraph below. Then rewrite the paragraph, eliminating all fragments.

Although Henry Ford has been credited with inventing the assembly line. He really did not. He perfected the process, however. In 1908 the Model T could be sold for $850. While other similar cars sold for $2,000 to $3,000. Although the price of the Model T was remarkable then. Ford and his engineers were not content. When the last Model T's were produced on the assembly line in 1927. The price was $290.

Part 9   Compound-Complex Sentences

You have already been introduced to simple, compound, and complex sentences. The fourth and final kind of sentence is the **compound-complex sentence.**

A compound-complex sentence consists of two or more main clauses and one or more subordinate clauses.

It may help you to think of a compound-complex sentence as a compound sentence plus a subordinate clause. Actually, the compound-complex sentence joins two main clauses, at least one of which has a subordinate clause. The subordinate clause may be an adjective, adverb, or noun clause. The main clauses are joined by either a coordinating conjunction or a semicolon.

Main Clause   Main Clause   Subordinate Clause
Yogurt is nutritious, and some say *that it brings good health.*

Subordinate Clause   Main Clause   Main Clause
When Dan called, he was angry; however, he soon calmed down.

Exercise: Identify the two main clauses and the subordinate clause in these compound-complex sentences.

1. A bola is a rope that has weights at the end; it is used to catch cattle.
2. Larry tried the dance steps that we demonstrated, but he couldn't quite master them.
3. The instructor told us how we could revive a heart attack victim, and she demonstrated on a dummy.
4. Blair House is located across the street from the White House, and foreign leaders who visit Washington often stay there.
5. Hiawatha was the hero of a poem; moreover, he was a Mohawk chief who organized tribes into the Five Nations.
6. The election judges distribute the ballots, and then they count them after the polls close.
7. In earlier times, infants were wrapped snugly with strips of cloth; people thought that this "swaddling" made babies feel secure.
8. Al drives a snow-removal truck, and whenever a heavy snow falls, he is called to work.
9. Some television sets have tubes; however, newer models, which are usually smaller, are solid state.
10. I've just learned that Dad's vacation was changed; as a result, we'll leave earlier for Michigan.

Part 10   A Review of Sentences

There are four basic kinds of sentences.

A **simple sentence** contains one subject and one predicate. Parts of the simple sentence, however, may be compound. A simple sentence expresses one idea.

s.   v.
The tower transmits radio signals.

s.   v.   v.
Alexis was born in Alaska but grew up in the state of Texas.

A **compound sentence** is made up of two simple sentences. These simple sentences are connected by a comma and coordinating conjunction or by a semicolon. Sometimes a conjunctive adverb follows the semicolon. A compound sentence expresses two related ideas. Notice how the ideas are joined together in these sentences.

        s.   v.   s.   v.

The tower is 300 feet tall, and it transmits radio signals.

    s.   v.   s.   v.

Alexis was born in Alaska; however, she grew up in the state of Texas.

A **complex sentence** contains one main clause and one or more subordinate clauses. The subordinate clauses may be used as adverbs, adjectives, or nouns. A complex sentence expresses one main idea and one or more dependent ideas. Notice how the example sentences have changed.

            s.   v.   s. v.

Because the tower is the tallest structure in the city, it is used to transmit radio signals.

         s.   v.   s.   v.

Although Alexis was born in Alaska, she grew up in the state of Texas.

A **compound-complex sentence** contains two main clauses and one or more subordinate clauses. The subordinate clauses may be adverb, adjective, or noun clauses. A compound-complex sentence expresses two main ideas, as well as one or more dependent ideas.

       s.   v.   s.   v.

The tower is the tallest structure in the city, and it transmits

         s.   v.

radio signals *that are heard throughout the Midwest.*

     s.   v.   s.   v.

Although Alexis was born in Alaska, she grew up in the state

     s.   v.

of Texas; now she is living in New York.

Exercise A: Number your paper from 1 to 10. For each sentence, write *Simple, Compound, Complex,* or *Compound-Complex* to show what kind it is.

1. Why did the governor veto that bill?
2. Bradley asked how high the waterfall was, and the forest ranger told her.
3. The helicopter can carry thirty soldiers and some supplies.
4. The members of the Drama Club not only produce plays but they also write them.
5. When Cortez arrived in Mexico, the Aztecs mistook him for the god of the morning star, and they worshiped him.
6. What a grotesque mask that is!
7. Helena hopes that one day she will become a chef.
8. Deep in space is a cloud of comets that are made of dust, rock fragments, and frozen gases.
9. The planet Pluto is very small and very far away; it was not discovered until 1930.
10. Does the discovery of a new planet influence astrology?

Exercise B: Follow the directions for Exercise A.

1. Tracy sings while she plays the banjo.
2. The paramedics arrived as soon as they could, but it was too late.
3. The planner interviewed the neighborhood residents, and then she wrote her recommendations.
4. After I wrote the report, I proofread it.
5. After this exercise you should flex your shoulders and stretch.
6. The man in the pinstriped, three-piece suit looked odd with the wet dog in his arms.
7. Do you like the pudding, or are you just being polite?
8. Do you drink diet drinks, which might contain a harmful substance, or do you drink sugared drinks, which are fattening?
9. General MacArthur said that he would return.
10. The airlines know that some passengers will not show up; therefore, extra tickets are sold for each flight.

Exercise C: Writing Rewrite each of the following sentences or sets of sentences. Follow the directions in parentheses. Use correct punctuation.

1. People expect Peru's coast to be a jungle. The coastline is actually arid. (Combine the two sentences with *but* to make a compound sentence.)
2. The wind died. We were sailing near the cove. (Combine the two sentences with *when* to make a complex sentence.)
3. The sun set. The wind started up. The temperature dropped to 65°. (Using *when* and *and*, combine these three sentences to make a compound-complex sentence.)
4. Sara sprained her ankle. She completed the marathon. (Combine these sentences with *although* to make a complex sentence.)
5. Connie read the novel. She did not see the movie. (Combine the two sentences with *but* to make a compound sentence.)
6. Keith preferred ball point pens. He tried a fine line marker. (Combine the sentences with *until* to make a complex sentence.)
7. Karen doodles on the phone book. Jason twists the phone cord. They talk on the telephone. (Combine these sentences with *and* and *while* to make a compound-complex sentence.)
8. The hurricane hit Galveston, Texas. Many people were left homeless. (Combine the sentences using *after* to make a complex sentence.)
9. An airplane flight from Chicago to Orlando takes less than three hours. An auto trip takes about twenty-four hours. A train trip the same distance takes thirty-six hours. (Combine these sentences using *and* and *but* to make a compound sentence.)
10. School closed. The community swimming pool has been open daily. (Combine these sentences using *since* to make a complex sentence.)

REINFORCEMENT EXERCISES

Using Compound and Complex Sentences

A. Analyze simple and compound sentences. Number your paper from 1 to 10. Write *Simple* or *Compound* to show what kind each sentence is.

1. At this airport, a plane departs or lands every minute.
2. Janna loves tennis and has won many medals.
3. The map is old, but it will serve as a general guide.
4. The hubcap fell off and clattered down the road.
5. Debra applied for a job at the stables, and she got it.
6. Peter, Paul, and Mary have sung together for over twenty years.
7. Some Islamic women wear veils, but others do not.
8. This beanbag chair is extremely comfortable; I almost fell asleep in it.
9. Ernie ordered dessert, but he couldn't finish it.
10. This restaurant is always open and always full.

B. Analyze and punctuate compound sentences. Copy these compound sentences. Underline each subject once, and each verb twice. Punctuate correctly.

1. Marshmallows are candy marsh mallows are plants.
2. Many players dislike artificial turf nevertheless they must play on it.
3. We must catch that train it is the last one today.
4. Houses collapsed and trees were uprooted.
5. Ron's final dive was superb but he still didn't win the contest.
6. Will you telephone Mom or shall I call?
7. The snow has melted and soon the trees will bud.
8. The truck weighs three tons it cannot stop very fast.
9. The factory has closed however it will reopen soon.
10. Rachel seems shy and introverted but she has a wonderful sense of humor.

C. Distinguish clauses and phrases. Tell whether the italicized words in each sentence are a *Clause* or a *Phrase*.

1. The pool doesn't open *until Memorial Day.*
2. The passenger was nervous *until the plane landed.*
3. *As Jerry made a basket,* the backboard shattered.
4. *As a special reward,* John received twenty dollars.
5. The coach gave us a pep talk *before the second half.*
6. *Before we pitched the tents,* Marla chopped firewood.
7. We have lived in Juneau *since last May.*
8. *Since Joshua's braces are off,* he smiles more.
9. *After the alarm rang,* firefighters dashed to their trucks.
10. *After the concert,* fans waited by the stage door.

D. Recognize adverb clauses. Write each adverb clause. Underline its subject once and its verb twice. Then write the word modified by the clause.

1. Although we came to Boston for a weekend, we stayed there for two weeks.
2. Carolyn spilled the paint as she reached for the brush.
3. Because Ed has practice every day, he values his free time.
4. Since Ian had been benched, Cal got a chance to play.
5. Dan fixed his lunch before he left for school.
6. Our radio doesn't play well unless it is facing south.
7. The editor spliced the film after she cut a scene.
8. The courtroom artist sketched as the witness talked.
9. We will need canteens if we hike all day.
10. After her defeat, Sue trained harder than she had before.

E. Recognize adjective clauses. Write each adjective clause. Underline its subject once and its verb twice. Then write the word modified by the clause.

1. One animal that can live more than fifty years is the raven.
2. February 2 is the day when the groundhog looks for its shadow.
3. One artist whom I admire is Georgia O'Keeffe.
4. The candidate who receives the most electoral votes wins.
5. Pavarotti is the only opera singer to whom I enjoy listening.

6. The cabinet where the supplies are kept is in here.
7. The coach, who had once played professional basketball, brought the team to first place.
8. Where did Karen put the card that I brought?
9. The priest calmed the people who had been hurt.
10. Here is the telescope that I borrowed.

F. Recognize noun clauses. Write each noun clause. Underline the subject once and the verb twice. Tell whether the clause is used as a subject, direct object, object of a preposition, or predicate noun.

1. Nicole explained how glaciers create valleys.
2. Whatever was making the noise has stopped.
3. In the fog, Liz could hardly see where she was going.
4. The problem is that the boat has a leak.
5. A trophy was made for whoever won the contest.
6. The newspapers told how the crime was committed.
7. Dan commented that the Steelers had a strong defense.
8. Whoever answered the phone was rude.
9. The President listened to what the Senator said.
10. David told us only what we wanted to hear.

G. Identify sentences. For each sentence, write *Simple, Compound, Complex,* or *Compound-Complex.*

1. Paula shoveled the drive, and Megan did the walk.
2. After school Jerome has a paper route.
3. Jane steered the jeep down the muddy road to the river, and then she discovered that the bridge had collapsed.
4. The callouses on her hands are not from work; they are from climbing the rope in gym.
5. Long ago, soldiers bit on bullets while they were having surgery.
6. The young recruits lined up and listened for their orders.
7. If you place the avocado pit in water, it will soon sprout.
8. When Superman arrives, outlaws haven't a chance.
9. Eric Heiden won five Olympic gold medals, and his sister Beth won a bronze medal.
10. Our van holds more people than a station wagon does.

MIXED REVIEW
Using Compound and Complex Sentences

A. Copy each sentence, adding any necessary punctuation. Then tell whether each sentence is *Simple, Compound, Complex,* or *Compound-Complex.*

1. When Sandy came to the plate the bases were loaded and there were two outs.
2. Linda participated in the Outward Bound program and learned a great deal about herself.
3. Every Saturday Lila does her chores at home goes to dance class cooks dinner and visits friends.
4. The medical profession is always making breakthroughs in disease control.
5. How often does Halley's Comet enter the atmosphere of the earth?
6. Many people have a fear of closed places but some can overcome their fear through therapy or hypnosis.
7. After he met his graduation requirements in summer school Raymond applied to the paramedic program.
8. The control tower received the message and the pilot who sent the information waited for instructions.
9. She went on most of the really terrifying rides but she wouldn't go near the Ferris wheel.
10. Benjamin loves any game that deals with words.

B. Find the subordinate clause in each of the following sentences. Copy it onto your paper. Then, write the letter of the phrase that best describes the clause.

1. Because of the foul weather, we canceled our picnic.
   a. Adjective clause modifying *picnic*
   b. Adverb clause modifying *canceled*
   c. Noun clause used as the subject
2. The umpire ruled that the ball was out of bounds.
   a. Adjective clause modifying *umpire*
   b. Adverb clause modifying *ruled*
   c. Noun clause used as the direct object

3. If you don't tie up the bundle of food, the bears will steal it.
   a. Adjective clause modifying *bears*
   b. Noun clause used as the subject
   c. Adverb clause modifying *will steal*
4. Phil is very interested in carpentry, which is the vocation of his father and his sister.
   a. Adjective clause modifying *carpentry*
   b. Adjective clause modifying *Phil*
   c. Noun clause used as the subject
5. That we would have a hot summer was predicted by the *Farmer's Almanac.*
   a. Adverb clause modifying *was predicted*
   b. Noun clause used as the subject
   c. Adjective clause modifying *summer*
6. The person whom Elena respects most is her great-grandmother.
   a. Noun clause used as the direct object
   b. Adjective clause modifying *Elena*
   c. Adjective clause modifying *person*
7. By the time the flood waters receded, several homes had been evacuated.
   a. Adverb clause modifying *had been evacuated*
   b. Adjective clause modifying *homes*
   c. Noun clause used as the subject
8. She acted as though she had been on the stage all of her life.
   a. Adjective clause modifying *She*
   b. Adverb clause modifying *acted*
   c. Noun clause used as the object of a preposition
9. The students who volunteer at the nursing home enjoy the companionship of the residents.
   a. Noun clause used as the direct object
   b. Adjective clause modifying *students*
   c. Adjective clause modifying *home*
10. My younger brother asked me what causes sonic booms.
    a. Adjective clause modifying *brother*
    b. Adverb clause modifying *asked*
    c. Noun clause used as the direct object

C. Rewrite each sentence or group of sentences, following the directions shown in parentheses. You may have to add, rearrange, or delete words.

1. Karen enjoyed watching the Steelers' games on television, and she attended as many home games as possible. (Rewrite as a simple sentence.)
2. Tom cut three lawns. He used the money he earned to buy a birthday gift for his cousin. (Rewrite as a compound sentence using *and*.)
3. The computer breaks down. The company loses a lot of money. (Rewrite as a complex sentence using *if*.)
4. On a clear night, many of the constellations can be seen with the naked eye. (Rewrite as a complex sentence using *when*.)
5. Either we study the past, or we will repeat the mistakes of our ancestors. (Rewrite as a complex sentence using *unless*.)
6. The theme of this year's science fair is "Alternate Energy Sources"; several students are doing projects that involve solar energy. (Rewrite as a compound sentence.)
7. After we developed the pictures, we sent them to a newspaper. (Rewrite as a compound sentence.)
8. Thousands of people gathered at Cape Canaveral; they wanted to see the re-entry and landing of the space shuttle. (Rewrite as a complex sentence using *because*.)
9. The recipe called for butter. Juan did not have any. He used margarine. (Rewrite as a compound-complex sentence using *which* and *so*.)
10. Mara's family was not rich, but they were wealthy in many ways. (Rewrite as a complex sentence using *although*.)

USING GRAMMAR IN WRITING
Using Compound and Complex Sentences

A. The following article contains only simple sentences. Rewrite the article, making some of the sentences compound and some complex. You may also include simple sentences with compound predicates.

The earliest cameras were invented in the 1500's. They were difficult to use. They were very large, bulky, and awkward. Few people wanted to bother with them. Very few photographers existed. For over three hundred years after its invention, photography was almost unknown.

During the mid-1800's Mathew Brady became a well-known photographer. He captured striking scenes of the U.S. Civil War. He took many formal portraits of President Lincoln. Brady stimulated public interest in photography.

Few people had Brady's patience with large, complicated cameras. Then, in 1888, there was a great improvement. George Eastman invented the first box camera. It was much simpler than earlier cameras. It could easily be held in the hand. The camera cost $25. It had a leather case. It came with Eastman's new roll film.

By 1900 the camera was even smaller and simpler. It sold for $1. More people could now afford one. Photography became the latest rage.

Today, photography is a national hobby. We owe it all to George Eastman. Strangely enough, he was a terribly shy man. He rarely allowed his own picture to be taken.

B. Imagine that you are given the plans for an important new product to guard for a day. Spies from other companies are trying to steal these plans. What precautions would you take to be sure that they would not succeed? Write your ideas first in simple sentences only. Then go back and combine some of these sentences into compound or complex sentences for a more mature and fluid style.

CUMULATIVE REVIEW
The Sentence (I)

Kinds of Sentences. The paragraphs below contain simple sentences, compound sentences, complex sentences, and compound-complex sentences. Number your paper from 1 to 15. Next to each number, write either *S, CD, CX,* or *CD-CX* to identify the type of sentence it is. Also write *INT* next to the numbers of the interrogative sentences, and *E* next to the numbers of the exclamatory sentences.

(1) You have probably heard of the seven wonders of the ancient world. (2) Did you know, though, that only one of these seven wonders is still standing? (3) That wonder is the Egyptian Pyramids, which were originally built as tombs for kings. (4) The second wonder was the Hanging Gardens of Babylon. (5) These gardens hung about seventy-five feet above the ground, and they were irrigated by slaves who hauled up water from the Euphrates River. (6) The third wonder was the gold and ivory statue of the god Zeus at Olympia; the fourth was a temple of the goddess Artemis. (7) Archaeologists in Turkey recently found a few fragments of the temple, which was once famous for its decoration and extensive use of marble. (8) How excited they must have been when these pieces were unearthed!

(9) No traces of the other three wonders remain. (10) One was a tomb, or mausoleum, built for Mausolus, who was an official of the Persian empire. (11) There was also a colossal statue of Apollo in the harbor of Rhodes, Greece; this was said to be so huge that ships could pass between its legs. (12) Finally, there was a huge lighthouse of white marble, which stood for one thousand years and was finally toppled by an earthquake.

(13) Ancient builders contributed many marvels to the civilized world. (14) How much more awesome, though, are the events of nature that destroyed even these magnificent structures! (15) Which of our own modern wonders will survive these powerful natural forces, and which will most impress future generations?

CUMULATIVE REVIEW
The Sentence (II)

Correcting Fragments and Run-ons. On your own paper, rewrite the following passage. Correct all sentence fragments and run-on sentences. You may have to add a few words, but most of the errors can be corrected with punctuation and capitalization changes only.

Every day articles about the advantages and disadvantages of different types of energy. In newspapers, magazines, and on television. There is so much information on these subjects that we find it hard to decide what would be the best course of action.

The fuel most used in the United States and throughout the world is oil, this is the same fuel that most experts believe will be exhausted within thirty years. Natural gas and coal and other sources of fossil fuels. These are more abundant than oil, but, like oil, they will eventually be exhausted. In addition, coal produces harmful products when burned, these particles increase pollution of air and water.

Nuclear reactors currently produce about one-tenth of the energy in the United States. And could easily supply more, many people, however, feel that the dangers of radioactivity are too high a price to pay for this form of energy.

Renewable energy sources, such as solar power and wind, are used very little at present. Solar collectors and wind turbines are expensive to build. But some experts say that such sources could provide about one fourth of the United States' energy needs by the year 2000. Until the many problems of energy sources are solved. Conservation, or using less energy, seems to be the best policy for ourselves and for the world.

CUMULATIVE REVIEW
The Sentence (III)

Writing Good Sentences. Rewrite each sentence on your own paper. Follow the directions given in parentheses.

1. Sally looks like a powerful soccer player. (Change this N LV N sentence to one with an N V N pattern.)
2. Suddenly, somebody turned off all the stage lights. (Change the active verb to a passive verb.)
3. An eruption at Mount St. Helen's took place in 1980. About two thousand people were evacuated from the path of its destruction. (Change these simple sentences to one complex sentence.)
4. Repairs are needed on this highway. Accidents could occur. (Change these simple sentences to one compound sentence by adding the word "otherwise" and the proper punctuation.)
5. The slime monster was subdued by the furious chemist. (Change this passive verb to an active verb.)
6. Stephen made chili for dinner, and Sarah made a tossed green salad. (Change this compound sentence to a simple sentence with a compound subject and a compound direct object.)
7. I hope to become an oceanographer. (Add a prepositional phrase to this sentence.)
8. That omelet has a strange taste. (Change this N V N sentence to one with a N LV Adj. pattern.)
9. Maria tossed the Frisbee to Jeremy. (Change this N V N sentence to one with an N V N N pattern.)
10. Dr. Steinman treated Chuck for his broken collarbone. (Add the prepositional phrase "with the nurse's assistance.")

Section 12

The Right Word

You have studied the different parts of a sentence and how they function together to communicate ideas. The correct use of certain troublesome words is also necessary for writing clear, standard English.

Standard English is the language of educated people. It is the language that would be judged correct or appropriate in nearly all situations. **Nonstandard English**, on the other hand, is not generally considered correct or acceptable in all situations.

In this section you will study some specific words that can cause problems for writers. Learning to use these words correctly will help you write standard English.

Part 1 Words Often Confused

The words listed in this section are often misused. The words in each pair or group may look alike or have similar meanings. However, one word cannot replace another. Study the following words, and try to use the right word at the right time.

capital means "most important." It is used to refer to an upper case letter. It also names the city or town that is the official center of government for a state or country.

capitol refers to the building where a state legislature meets.

The **Capitol** is the building in Washington, D.C., where the United States Congress meets. Notice that the *c* is capitalized.

The *capital* of New York is Albany.
The state *capitol* dome can be seen for miles.
Farmers protested outside the *Capitol* in Washington.

des′ ert means "a dry, barren region."
de sert′ means "to abandon."
des sert′ (note the difference in spelling) is a sweet food at the end of a meal.

The explorers were stranded in the *desert*.
Did the soldier *desert* his company?
Our *dessert* tonight is banana cake.

hear means "to listen to" or "to receive sound by the ear."
here refers to this place.

Did you *hear* the screeching brakes?
A new record store will open *here*.

its is a possessive, meaning belonging to *it*.
it's is the contraction for *it is* or *it has*.

The band has *its* own sound system.
It's almost midnight.

loose means either "not tight" or "free and untied."
lose means "to be unable to find or keep." It is also the opposite of *win*.

623

Several snakes from the zoo are *loose*.
I *lose* my balance when I spin on skates.
Did the wrestlers *lose* the meet?

principal means "leading," "chief," or "highest in importance, rank, or degree."
principle refers to a basic truth, rule, or law.

The *principal* industry here is steel-making.
The basic *principle* of this country is a free and democratic society.

stationary means "not moving, fixed."
stationery refers to writing paper and envelopes.

The trailer can move, but right now it's *stationary*.
The drugstore sells boxes of *stationery*.

their shows possession by *them*.
there means "in that place."
they're is the contraction for *they are*.

The steelworkers have *their* own union.
The bus route ends *there*.
They're losing their courage.

to means "toward" or "as far as."
too means "also" or "extremely."

Tracy slid *to* home plate.
I read the book, and I saw the movie *too*.

weather refers to the condition of the atmosphere, such as its heat or cold, wetness or dryness.
whether indicates a choice between two things.

The *weather* in Hawaii is usually pleasant.
Ask Stacy *whether* she is going or staying.

who's is the contraction for *who is* or *who has*.
whose is the possessive form of *who*.

Who's running the computer?
Whose sandwich is this?

your shows possession by *you*.
you're is the contraction for *you are* or *you were*.

> When is *your* birthday?
> *You're* on the team, aren't you?

Exercise A: Choose the right word from the words given.

1. From the top of the Washington Monument, we looked down at the white dome of the nation's (capital, capitol, Capitol).
2. The (deserted, desserted) building was about to be demolished.
3. Sand dunes in the (desert, dessert) are always shifting due to wind and rain.
4. We could (hear, here) the alarm four blocks away.
5. The computer at our school can correct some of (its, it's) own mistakes.
6. (Its, It's) time to leave for the show.
7. Ballet slippers should be tight, not (loose, lose).
8. I don't want to (loose, lose) this match.
9. The (principals, principles) stated in the Hippocratic Oath are still important to doctors.
10. The letter was typed on official (stationary, stationery).

Exercise B: Follow the directions for Exercise A.

1. We ate (their, there) for Mom's birthday.
2. Sometimes the players get careless when (their, there, they're) ahead.
3. All the students in the speech class have heard (their, there, they're) own voices on tape.
4. The bowling ball veered (to, too) far to the left.
5. The Rosens drove (to, too) Syracuse for Thanksgiving.
6. Are you getting off at this stop, (to, too)?
7. I wonder (weather, whether) I should call her or write her a letter.
8. (Who's, Whose) responsible for that decision?
9. (Who's, Whose) story do you believe?
10. (Your, You're) too worried about how you look.

Part 2 Troublesome Verbs

These pairs of verbs are often confused. Notice how they differ.

Bring and *Take*

Bring refers to movement toward the person speaking. Example: The pipeline *brings* water here to the desert.

Take refers to motion away from the speaker. Example: Did you *take* those books back to the library?

Here are the principal parts of these verbs:

bring, brought, brought

PRESENT:	*Bring* that hammer to me, please
PAST:	We *brought* Janet with us.
PAST PARTICIPLE:	No one *has brought* enough money.

take, took, taken

PRESENT:	When you leave, *take* some cake.
PAST:	I *took* my cycle there to be fixed.
PAST PARTICIPLE:	Someone *has taken* my keys.

Learn and *Teach*

Learn means "to gain knowledge or skill." Example: Did you *learn* the words to that song?

Teach means "to help someone learn." Example: Will you *teach* me to dribble?

Here are the principal parts of these verbs:

learn, learned, learned

PRESENT:	*Learn* the metric system.
PAST:	Cal *learned* karate.
PAST PARTICIPLE:	We *have learned* Spanish.

teach, taught, taught

PRESENT:	Mrs. Rivera *teaches* music.
PAST:	Kelly *taught* me about photography.
PAST PARTICIPLE:	This course *has taught* us about carpentry.

Let and Leave

Let means "to allow or permit." Example: *Let* her go.
Leave means "to go away from" or "to allow something to remain." Example: *Leave* us alone.
The principal parts of these verbs are as follows:

let, let, let

PRESENT: *Let* the motor run for a minute.
PAST: Dad *let* the dog out.
PAST PARTICIPLE: The landlord *has let* us stay.

leave, left, left

PRESENT: *Leave* your jacket on.
PAST: Jennifer *left* in a hurry.
PAST PARTICIPLE: The robbers *had left* with the cash.

Lie and Lay

Lie means "to rest in a flat position" or "to be in a certain place." Example: *Lie* still.
Lay means "to place." Example: *Lay* the wreath here.
Here are the principal parts of these verbs:

lie, lay, lain

PRESENT: *Lie* down on this mat.
PAST: Jason *lay* in bed all day.
PAST PARTICIPLE: The patient *has lain* very still.

lay, laid, laid

PRESENT: *Lay* the baby in her crib.
PAST: The nurse *laid* a bandage on the wound.
PAST PARTICIPLE: Workers *have laid* the foundation.

May and Can

May refers to the granting of permission. *May* also refers to something that is possible. *Might* is the past tense of *may*.

May we *have* dessert?   It *may* snow.   I *might be* wrong.

Can means being physically or mentally able to do something. *Could* is the past tense of *can*.

> *Can* you *do* a push-up?   We *could* not *remember*.

May and *might* and *can* and *could* are never used alone. They are used as helping verbs.

Rise and Raise

Rise means "to go upward." Example: The sun *rises*.
Raise means "to lift" or "to make something go up." Example: *Raise* your right hand.
The principal parts of these verbs are as follows:

rise, rose, risen

PRESENT:	The steam *rises* and disappears.
PAST:	The choir *rose* from their seats.
PAST PARTICIPLE:	The drawbridge *has risen*.

raise, raised, raised

PRESENT:	Please *raise* the window shade.
PAST:	Kim *raised* the ladder to reach the roof.
PAST PARTICIPLE:	Inflation *has raised* the cost of living.

Sit and Set

Sit means "to occupy a seat." Example: *Sit* on this bench.
Set means "to place." Example: *Set* the tools there.
The principal parts of these verbs are as follows:

sit, sat, sat

PRESENT:	*Sit* near me, please.
PAST:	We *sat* in the waiting room.
PAST PARTICIPLE:	All of the passengers *have sat* down.

set, set, set

PRESENT:	*Set* your toothbrush on the sink.
PAST:	John *set* the books in his new bookcase.
PAST PARTICIPLE:	We *have set* the costumes backstage.

Exercise A: Choose the right verb from the two given.

1. We (sat, set) aside some money in a savings account.
2. The sales tax has (raised, risen) to 6 percent.
3. Litter (lay, laid) all over the park.
4. Stranded passengers (sat, set) in the airport.
5. You can't (bring, take) your bike in here.
6. The dog (learned, taught) to obey simple commands.
7. Someone (let, left) the computer turned on.
8. (May, Can) I use Dad's jigsaw?
9. The photographer (sat, set) the film in a jar to develop.
10. Mom's boss (raised, rose) her pay.

Exercise B: Follow the directions for Exercise A.

1. Leonne insists she (may not, cannot) carry a tune.
2. (Take, Bring) those books to the library, please.
3. Mr. Ross (laid, lay) a new kitchen floor today.
4. Who (learned, taught) you judo?
5. When (may, can) you cut the grass?
6. The gymsuit has (lain, laid) in that locker all year.
7. Will you (let, leave) us skate on your pond?
8. Jenny says we (may, can) have the party here.
9. Annie Sullivan (taught, learned) Helen Keller to speak.
10. The factory (raised, rose) its level of production.

Exercise C: Writing Find the errors in the following sentences. Rewrite the sentences correcting the errors. If a sentence has no errors, write *Correct*.

1. Mrs. Motosaka learned me the art of origami.
2. Can I look through your scrapbook?
3. Set the tray on the kitchen counter.
4. The cat was laying on the rug near the woodburning stove.
5. When you go to the zoo, bring your camera.
6. It took four years to lay the transcontinental railroad.
7. The curtain has raised, and the play has begun.
8. The palace guard leaved the ambassador enter the gates.
9. Aunt Lydia set down in the seat behind the bus driver.
10. May dolphins live indefinitely underwater, without surfacing?

Part 3 Usage Problems

The words in this section are often used incorrectly. Notice the standard usages for these problem words.

accept means "to agree to something" or "to receive something willingly."

except means "to leave out." *Except* also means "not including."

> "I *accept* the blame," Todd said.
> "We'll *except* you from this rule," the counselor said.
> We bought all the supplies *except* glue.

agree on means "to come to an understanding." You and others agree *on* a plan.

agree to means "to consent to." You agree *to* something, such as a plan.

agree with means "to have the same opinion as someone else." You agree *with* somebody. *Agree with* may also be used in a colloquial sense to refer to something being suitable, as when foods don't *agree with* you.

all right is the correct spelling. The spelling *alright* is nonstandard English and should not be used.

> *All right*, I'll turn off the TV.
> Ariel felt *all right* after she got off the boat.

among refers to a group of more than two people or things.
between refers to two people or things.

> We divided the food *among* the four of us.
> There is a treaty *between* the two countries.

anywhere, nowhere, somewhere, and **anyway** are standard usages. The words *anywheres, nowheres, somewheres,* and *anyways* are nonstandard. The final *s* should be dropped.

> NONSTANDARD: She wasn't anywheres in sight.
> STANDARD: She wasn't *anywhere* in sight.

> NONSTANDARD: I know that clip is here somewheres.
> STANDARD: I know that clip is here *somewhere*.

between each, followed by a singular noun, is incorrect. *Between* should not be used with a singular noun.

NONSTANDARD: Between each game, the Bears practiced hard.
STANDARD: *Between games,* the Bears practiced hard.

NONSTANDARD: The elevator stopped between every floor.
STANDARD: The elevator stopped *between floors.*

borrow means "to receive something on loan." Don't confuse it with *lend,* meaning "to give out temporarily."

NONSTANDARD: Will you borrow me your pen?
STANDARD: Will you *lend* me your pen?
STANDARD: May I *borrow* your pen?

Exercise A: Writing Look for sentences with nonstandard usage. Rewrite those sentences, using the right words.

1. Between each quarter of the game, the band plays.
2. Every block accept ours has sidewalks.
3. Will you borrow me your bicycle?
4. Do you feel all right?
5. TV time was divided equally among the three candidates.
6. Did you agree on what that columnist wrote?
7. Scott couldn't find his calculator anywheres.
8. The jury agreed on a verdict.
9. My purse has to be around here somewheres.
10. Jane found it hard to except praise.

Exercise B: Writing Follow the directions for Exercise A.

1. Bill borrowed me his new video game.
2. The shoe store has every size accept the one I need.
3. Did Jessica and David agree with the best route to take?
4. Alright, tell me what's bothering you.
5. The family chose among the two sailboats.
6. Rock walls stood between each field.
7. The vice-president agreed with the plan.
8. Anyways, I'm heading for home.
9. Ken borrowed my hat for the costume party.
10. The President excepted the resignation of his aide.

fewer refers to numbers of things that can be counted.
less refers to amount or quantity.

> Did Nicklaus win *fewer* tournaments than Snead?
> We hear *less* noise in the country.

in means "inside something."
into tells of motion from the outside to the inside of something.

> NONSTANDARD: The performers went in the studio.
> STANDARD: The performers went *into* the studio.

> NONSTANDARD: Joe hit the hockey puck in the goal.
> STANDARD: Joe hit the hockey puck *into* the goal.

kind of a and **sort of a** are nonstandard. The *a* is not necessary.

> NONSTANDARD: What kind of a radio do you have?
> STANDARD: What *kind of* radio do you have?

> NONSTANDARD: There is some sort of a problem here.
> STANDARD: There is some *sort of* problem here.

like can be a preposition. Using *like* as a conjunction before a clause is not fully accepted. Especially in writing, it is better to use *as* or *as if*.

> NONSTANDARD: *Like* I said, you can depend on Sara.
> STANDARD: *As* I said, you can depend on Sara.

> NONSTANDARD: Ramon talked *like* he had a cold.
> STANDARD: Ramon talked *as if* he had a cold.

of is sometimes incorrectly used in phrases like *could of, shouldn't of,* and *must of*. The correct word is *have* or its contraction: *could have, could've, shouldn't have, must have, might have, might've*.

> NONSTANDARD: Darryl should of locked his bike.
> STANDARD: Darryl *should have* locked his bike.

ways does not refer to distance. *Way* is correct.

> NONSTANDARD; We drove a short ways down the road.
> STANDARD: We drove a short *way* down the road.

Exercise A: Writing Rewrite the sentences that contain nonstandard usage. If a sentence is correct, write *Correct*.

1. Chris acted like the world was ending.
2. I make less phone calls than Penny.
3. Carolyn stuffed her change in her pocket.
4. A dalmatian is less nervous than a poodle.
5. Like the President says, we must conserve energy.
6. There are less new TV programs this season.
7. The center should of practiced her lay-up shots.
8. What kind of a penalty did the ref call?
9. The stadium is a ways farther south.
10. Cautiously, they stepped in the deserted house.

Exercise B: Writing Follow the directions for Exercise A.

1. Kate has less lines to memorize in this play.
2. The council must of held some sort of a meeting.
3. The movie ended just like I thought it would.
4. Lauren slipped a message in our mailbox.
5. Fewer radio stations are playing the top ten songs now.
6. The reservoir is quite a ways from here.
7. Less people go to the later show.
8. Jim looks like he needs more time.
9. What kind of sausage goes on the pizza?
10. We should of stopped at the park for our picnic.

REINFORCEMENT EXERCISES
The Right Word

A. Use confusing pairs of words correctly. Choose the correct word from the two given.

1. Did you (loose, lose) your ticket stub?
2. Have you worn (your, you're) down vest yet?
3. The fish had jumped out of (it's, its) bowl.
4. Proper nouns begin with (capitol, capital) letters.
5. The schools were closed because of severe (weather, whether) conditions.
6. When Amie moved (here, hear), she didn't know anyone.
7. (Who's, Whose) going to the Science Fair on Saturday?
8. That house has been (desserted, deserted) for years.
9. (Principles, Principals) of Modern Agriculture is my brother's favorite college class.
10. (There, They're, Their) are many people who disagree with that statement.

B. Use troublesome verbs correctly. Choose the correct word.

1. The alarm didn't go off because you (set, sat) it incorrectly.
2. Can you (learn, teach) me how to windsurf?
3. (Leave, Let) me do this by myself.
4. Please (bring, take) me the desk calendar.
5. (May, Can) you play a musical instrument?
6. Mr. Kim (learned, taught) us Tae-Kwon-Do.
7. You shouldn't (let, leave) your camera in the car.
8. The test pilot (sat, set) at the controls.
9. Meredith (lay, laid) awake and couldn't sleep.
10. The oil has (raised, risen) to the surface of the sea.

C. Use problem words correctly. Choose the correct answer.

1. Denver is a long (way, ways) from Baltimore.
2. What (kind of a, kind of) truck is this?
3. Tim jumped (in, into) the lake from the pier.

4. (All right, Alright), we'll agree (with, on, to) a rematch.
5. Will you (borrow, lend) me your Bill Cosby tape?
6. The Eskimos divided their catch (between, among) all the villagers.
7. Juan graciously (excepted, accepted) my apology.
8. Trisha looked (as if, like) she didn't feel well.
9. There is a curb (between, between each) parking spaces.
10. I should (have, of) eaten (fewer, less) pretzels.

D. Use standard English. Rewrite these sentences. Correct all nonstandard usage.

1. The·art league hear announced it's annual contest.
2. I don't know weather the conductor will except the ticket.
3. Do you get homesick when your a long ways from home?
4. You should of taken an earlier ferry.
5. Raise the cage door and leave the dog run lose.
6. In England, the driver of a car sets on the right side.
7. Is it to late too buy tickets for the concert?
8. Alright, I'll meet you somewheres if we can agree on a place.
9. My sister always carries less books than I do, but she goes to her locker between each class.
10. Before they're events, the swimmers laid on the pool deck.

MIXED REVIEW

The Right Word

A. Choose the correct answer from those given in parentheses.

1. (Whose, Who's) idea was it to display the posters (here, hear)?
2. The (capitol, capital) of Nova Scotia is Halifax.
3. Arizona is a healthy place for some people to live because of (its, it's) (desert, dessert) climate.
4. Next year we will (lose, loose) our (principle, principal) volleyball player because she is transferring to another high school.
5. For thousands of years, people thought that the earth was (stationary, stationery).
6. Since the freshmen were successful with (they're, their, there) car wash, the sophomores decided to have one (to, too, two).
7. Visitors to Hawaii report that the (whether, weather) (there, their, they're) is ideal.
8. (Your, You're) supposed to make (less, fewer) mistakes on a retest, not more!
9. (Its, It's) pleasant to (sit, set) back and watch the clouds roll overhead.
10. He asked if it would be (alright, all right) if he (laid, lay) his books on my desk.
11. Everyone (agrees on, agrees with, agrees to) the plan (except, accept) Tim.
12. If you're tired you can (lay, lie) down over (here, hear) on the sofa.
13. Evan (could have, could of) stayed on his diet if he hadn't eaten that (dessert, desert).
14. That baby is older, but it has (fewer, less) hair on (it's, its) head.
15. Vic jumped (in, into) the van and sat down (between, among) Zach and Chris.

B. Find the errors in the following sentences. Then, rewrite the sentences correctly. If a sentence has no errors, write *Correct*.

1. Jennifer asked her brother to let her alone for a few minutes.
2. We should be able to resolve this problem between the four of us.
3. It is often difficult for parents and children to agree on a curfew.
4. The shy players were reluctant to except there awards.
5. Jackie acts like she's angry at the world today.
6. May I have some extra time to finish this report?
7. Chris laid in bed until she felt all right.
8. The Mid-Atlantic Ridge, a mountain range of 10,000 miles long, raises from the floor of the Atlantic Ocean.
9. I set your shoes near the door like you asked me.
10. Beth could of made the traveling team if she hadn't broken her ankle.
11. A guard was positioned between each column of the Capitol.
12. What kind of a radio do you have?
13. Rick shouldn't of lain his wallet on the table.
14. The manager left us stay for the next show because the theater was empty.
15. Put the album I borrowed you in its jacket so it doesn't get dusty.

USING GRAMMAR IN WRITING
The Right Word

The great American tall tale is being revived these days in stories that are being told about the fast-growing vine, *kudzu*. Originally planted to prevent erosion in the South, the kudzu vines quickly spread over trees, telephone poles, houses, barns, and abandoned cars. Kudzu grows as much as a foot a day, and is now moving toward the West. Below is a typical tall tale of the kudzu, containing many incorrectly used words. Read through the story and then revise it, correcting all nonstandard English.

Like I started to tell that agriculture expert who came down hear from the Capitol, the kudzu's not a plant: Its a kind of a green monster. Anywhere you go around hear, you may see whole farms with nothing left on them but the tip of a silo raising up out of a mountain of kudzu. Their's no stopping it because these vines grow as fast in bad whether as in good, though I've heard it said that their are less leaves on them when the temperature drops under fifty below zero. Now, you may think I'm exaggerating, but you should of seen what happened to that agriculture man when he tried to learn the farmers around hear how to get rid of this pesky weed. That so-called expert took a can of weedkiller to a farm just a short ways down the road from my place, and I guess he figured that that kudzu was just going to lay their stationery while he sprayed it. However, as soon as he walked in that kudzu field, the vine saw what he was doing and grabbed him. It was a sight. That plant rose him right off the ground and sat him down in the top of a sycamore tree. We called the volunteer fire department to get him down, but when that vine hered the sirens, it grabbed him again and rose him up higher and higher until his head hit the underside of a cloud. I imagine he's still up their, to. I guess he would of starved to death if I hadn't borrowed the fire department my shotgun so they could shoot biscuits up to him. That kudzu's mean. Except my word for it. I was their.

Section 13

Capitalization

Like most other conventions of language, capital letters help make writing easier to read. They call attention to certain special words and indicate the beginnings of sentences.

There are specific rules for capitalizing words. This section will show you the rules. You can refer to this section at any time if you have questions about capitalization.

Part 1 Proper Nouns and Adjectives

Capitalize proper nouns and proper adjectives.

As you learned in Section 3, a **proper noun** is the name of a particular person, place, or thing. In contrast, a **common noun** is the name of a whole group of people, places, or things. A **proper adjective** is an adjective formed from a proper noun.

COMMON NOUN	PROPER NOUN	PROPER ADJECTIVE
queen	Victoria	Victorian
country	Ireland	Irish
government	Congress	Congressional

There are many different kinds of proper nouns. The following rules will help you to identify the types of nouns that should be capitalized.

Names of People

Capitalize people's names. Also capitalize the initials or abbreviations that stand for names.

F. D. Roosevelt   Franklin Delano Roosevelt
Susan B. Anthony   Susan Brownell Anthony

Capitalize the titles used with people's names. Also capitalize the initials or abbreviations that stand for those titles.

The titles *Miss, Ms., Mrs.,* and *Mr.* are always capitalized.

Gov. R. T. Alberg   Major Edward J. Brooks
Ms. Susan Manzano   Dr. Evelyn Santucci
Judge Ellen O'Brien   Rev. L. K. Jenkins

Do not capitalize a title that is used without a name. It is a common noun.

Barbara Sloan is president of the bank.
The judge in this courtroom is Justice Black.

Capitalize titles of very high importance, even when they are used without names.

the President of the United States
the Chief Justice of the Supreme Court
the Prime Minister of Canada
a Congresswoman
the Pope

Family Relationships

Capitalize such family words as *mother, father, aunt,* and *uncle* when they are used as names. If the noun is preceded by a possessive word or by *a, an,* or *the,* it is not capitalized.

What was Dad like when he was sixteen, Grandma?
Jessica's mother is here, Mom.
We call our aunt and uncle Uncle Hy and Aunt Lo.
My mom's car needs a new battery.
The father in the show was played by James Stewart.

The Pronoun *I*

Capitalize the pronoun *I*.

He and I saw a movie.   I work after school.

The Supreme Being
and Sacred Writings

Capitalize all words referring to God, to the Holy Family, and to religious scriptures.

the Almighty	the Bible	the Son of God
the Lord	the Talmud	the New Testament
the Blessed Virgin	Allah	the Book of Job

Capitalize personal pronouns referring to God.

They asked the Lord for His blessing.

Exercise A: Copy the following sentences. Change small letters to capital letters wherever necessary.

1. A hurricane hit the town that dad and i were visiting.
2. My mother's medical doctor is dr. herrera and her dentist is dr. alexander.
3. If you enjoy being scared, read the horror stories of h.p. lovecraft.
4. The new testament of the bible was written many years after christ died.
5. Yesterday ms. turner told me that i could now call her sgt. turner.
6. The pope visited his homeland in 1983.
7. The director of st. christopher hospital is my cousin, rowine hayes brown.
8. Some religions honor god by not speaking his name.
9. In her lecture, professor bailey explained how laws are made.
10. State sen. dawn clark netsch sponsored the bill to protect consumers against fraud.

Exercise B: Follow the directions for Exercise A.

1. Can nate tell mr. banzali the most direct route from grand rapids to memphis?
2. The best-known leader of the dakota tribes was chief sitting bull.
3. The ten commandments are recorded in the book of exodus.
4. Did lorene help with the work on your brother's bike?
5. Few people who write to the president of the united states receive a personal answer.
6. Ms. eppie lederer gives advice under the name of ann landers.
7. My cousin dale and i work at mr. j. j. vernon's downtown office.
8. Did dad make an appointment with dr. case?
9. According to the gospels, adam and eve disobeyed god.
10. Will the president meet with governor ray?

Geographic Names

In a geographical name, capitalize the first letter of each word except articles and prepositions.

If the article *the* appears before a place name, it is not part of the name and is therefore not capitalized.

CONTINENTS:	Africa, North America, Europe, Asia
BODIES OF WATER:	the Atlantic Ocean, the Ohio River, the Gulf of Mexico, the South China Sea, Hudson Bay, the Panama Canal, Lake Michigan
LAND FORMS:	Mount McKinley, Aleutian Islands, Death Valley, Cadillac Mountain, the Black Hills, Cape Lookout
POLITICAL UNITS:	Florida, Denver, Province of Ontario, Republic of Kenya, State of Israel, Thirteenth Congressional District
PUBLIC AREAS:	Glacier National Park, Fort Sumter, Badlands National Monument, Ford Theater, Dunes State Park, Fallen Timbers Battlefield
ROADS AND HIGHWAYS:	Route 66, Interstate Highway 610, Hampton Road, Thornwood Avenue, Main Street

Directions and Sections

Capitalize names of sections of the country.

The West has several old trading posts.
The South is sometimes called "Dixie."
The Sorensons moved from New England to the West Coast.

Capitalize proper adjectives that come from names of sections of the country.

a Midwestern town	Western saddle
Southern food	East Coast company

Do not capitalize directions of the compass.

Barrow, Alaska, is north of all other United States cities.
Drive east on Interstate 80 to New York.

Do not capitalize adjectives that come from words showing direction.

The parking lot is on the north side of the building.
The southerly breeze turned into a fierce wind.

Exercise A: Number your paper from 1 to 10. Find the words in the following sentences that should be capitalized. Write the words after the proper number, using the necessary capital letters.

1. The tenth congressional district is north of chicago.
2. There is an extinct volcano called mount shasta in california.
3. The yucatan channel connects the gulf of mexico with the caribbean sea.
4. The andes mountains are in south america.
5. The district of columbia's biggest park is rock creek park.
6. Some southern foods are now popular in the north.
7. Hurricanes attacked the southeast, and tornadoes hit the southwest.
8. Both interstate 90 and route 20 run from albany to buffalo, new york.
9. The north defeated the south in a key battle at gettysburg, pennsylvania.
10. In japan, the cities are extremely crowded.

Exercise B:Writing Rewrite the following paragraph, adding capital letters where necessary.

A trip to the east coast isn't complete without a visit to the boston area. The capital of massachusetts, this old new england town is rich in historical and scenic attractions. The famous freedom trail wends among such landmarks as faneuil hall, the old north church, and the old state house. A walk on beacon street will take one past boston common, the oldest park in america. Among the tourist attractions outside the city is the village of concord, on route 2. Going south of boston on route 28 will bring you to cape cod, a tourist haven in summer, with its quaint atlantic villages and its beautiful national seashore park.

Organizations and Institutions

Capitalize the names of organizations and institutions, including political parties, governmental bodies or agencies, schools, colleges, churches, hospitals, clubs, businesses, and abbreviations of these names.

Republican Party	Children's Memorial Hospital
Federal Trade Commission	American Medical Association
Stevenson High School	National Urban League
St. Joseph's Church	**AFL-CIO**

Do not capitalize such words as *school, company, church,* and *hospital* when they are not used as parts of names.

Several people from our church work at the hospital.

Events, Documents, and Periods of Time

Capitalize the names of historical events, documents, and periods of time.

Battle of Concord	Panama Canal Treaty
Vietnam War	the Middle Ages
United States Constitution	the Reformation

Months, Days, and Holidays

Capitalize names of months, days, and holidays, but not the names of seasons.

July   Thursday   Halloween   winter

Races, Languages, Nationalities, Religions

Capitalize the names of races, languages, nationalities, and religions. Also capitalize any adjectives that come from these names.

Greek	Oriental	Catholicism	Protestant
German	Hinduism	Puerto Rican	Polish

School Subjects

Do not capitalize the names of school subjects, except course titles followed by a number.

history   Reading Workshop I
industrial arts   Math 300

Remember that the names of languages are always capitalized.

French   Spanish   Japanese   English

Ships, Trains, Airplanes, Automobiles

Capitalize the names of ships, trains, airplanes, and automobiles.

U.S.S. *Constellation*   *Concorde*   Buick Skyhawk

B.C., A.D.

Capitalize the abbreviations B.C. and A.D.

The Pyramids of Egypt were begun about 300 **B.C.**
Mohammed was born in **A.D.** 570.

Exercise A: Write the words in each sentence that should be capitalized. Use the necessary capital letters.

1. The national basketball association begins its playoffs in march.
2. Every june, elizabeth seton high school holds a carnival.
3. The high school is across the street from lakeview hospital.
4. There are many different protestant religions.
5. In the middle ages, people believed that a woman would dream of her future husband on st. agnes's eve, january 20.
6. The battle of antietam was one of the fiercest in the american civil war.
7. Montezuma II, the last aztec ruler of mexico, died in a.d. 1520.

8. Amtrak's *southwest limited* travels over eighty miles per hour on some runs.
9. King tut, the egyptian ruler, was buried in 1344 b.c.
10. The marzo family spent august traveling through europe in a volkswagen van.

Exercise B: Follow the directions for Exercise A.

1. The second monday in october is celebrated as columbus day.
2. Both the french and the americans celebrate their independence in july.
3. The democratic party received contributions from many unions.
4. The united mineworkers' union is a member of the afl-cio.
5. We are reading the declaration of independence in my history class.
6. Cheryl could not sign up for german I because it conflicted with her math class.
7. The national language of the israelis is hebrew.
8. The alaskans make the most of their short summer.
9. After graduating from howard university, judy received job offers from ibm and general foods corporation.
10. After looking at many different trucks and vans, the powells bought a new datsun.

Part 2   First Words

Sentences and Poetry

Capitalize the first word of every sentence and the first word of most lines of poetry.

The disc jockey began her show. She played a new album.

Listen my children, and you shall hear
Of the midnight ride of Paul Revere,
"Paul Revere's Ride"—HENRY WADSWORTH LONGFELLOW

Sometimes, especially in modern poetry, the lines of a poem do not begin with capital letters.

Quotations

Capitalize the first word of a direct quotation.

A **direct quotation** tells the exact words of a speaker or writer.

Emerson said, "The only way to have a friend is to be one."

In a **divided quotation,** a direct quotation is broken into two parts by words like *he said* or *she explained.* Do not capitalize the first word of the second part unless it starts a new sentence.

"I agree," Tim said, "that a good friend is rare."
"I agree," Tim said. "A good friend is rare."

Letter Parts

Capitalize the first word in the greeting of a letter. Also capitalize the name of the person addressed, or words like *Sir* and *Madam* that stand for names.

Dear Ms. Valdez: Dear Mr. Nash: Dear Sir:

In the complimentary close, capitalize only the first word.

Very truly yours,   Sincerely yours,

Outlines

Capitalize the first word of each item in an outline. Also capitalize the letters before each line.

   I. Holidays
     A. Chief legal holidays
      1. National
      2. State or local
     B. Religious holidays

Titles

Capitalize the first word and all important words in the titles of chapters, magazine articles, short stories, essays, poems, television or radio episodes, and songs or short pieces of music.

CHAPTER TITLE:	Chapter 3, "Food and Health"
MAGAZINE ARTICLE:	"Today's Changing Family"
SHORT STORY:	"To Build a Fire"
ESSAY:	"The Seeing See Little"
POEM:	"The Base Stealer"
SONG:	"Oh, What a Beautiful Morning!"

Capitalize the first word and all important words in titles of books, newspapers, magazines, plays, movies, television and radio programs, works of art, and long musical compositions.

BOOK TITLE:	*Where the Lilies Bloom*
NEWSPAPER:	*Los Angeles Times*
MAGAZINE:	*Ebony*
PLAY:	*You Can't Take It with You*
MOVIE:	*Return of the Jedi*
TELEVISION PROGRAM:	*Wide World of Sports*
WORK OF ART:	*The Sunflowers*
LONG MUSICAL COMPOSITION:	*Carmen*

Exercise A: Number your paper from 1 to 10. Write the words that should be capitalized. Use the correct capital letters.

1. dear ms. kruger:
   your two tickets to a special showing of the *star wars* trilogy are enclosed. thank you for your order.
   sincerely yours,
2. television movies about athletes such as "brian's song," always seem to have popular appeal.
3. the action photography in *sports illustrated* is excellent.
4. I. finding a cure for the common cold
   A. difficulties
   1. more than 200 cold viruses
5. our school library has back issues of several newspapers, including *the washington post.*
6. rachel chose the poem "a dream deferred" to memorize.

7. "dave," joyce called, "watch while I try a half-gainer."
8. "i keep forgetting my locker combination," said adam. "maybe i should write it down."
9. mary cassatt's painting *the letter* shows a sad woman sealing an envelope.
10. john p. davis and the russian author gogol both wrote short stories titled "the overcoat."

Exercise B: Follow the directions for Exercise A.

1. the last song of the beach boys' concert was "surfin' u.s.a."
2. it was many and many a year ago,
   in a kingdom by the sea,
   that a maiden there lived whom you may know
   by the name of annabel lee;
   —edgar allan poe, "annabel lee"
3. we discussed the chapter called "two images of the future" from the book *this endangered planet.*
4. "i'm not sure," said gerard, "what we should do now."
5. i read the article "new research in dental care" in *prevention* magazine.
6. megan asked, "have you seen the latest issue of *time*?"
7. george lucas made *american graffiti* before he made *star wars.*
8. my little sister insisted that i turn to "fraggle rock."
9. the song "some enchanted evening" is from the musical *south pacific.*
10. dear sir:
    i would like two tickets to monday night's performance of *the messiah.*
    yours truly,

Exercise C: Writing Every week, your school paper includes a feature article on ten students. This week, you are one of the ten. To complete the article, the paper needs to know the titles of your favorite song, book, and movie. They would also like you to include either a quotation or a few lines of poetry that you find especially meaningful. Write the information in a letter to Alice Evans, the paper's editor. Use correct capitalization throughout.

REINFORCEMENT EXERCISES
Capitalization

A. Use capital letters with proper nouns and adjectives. Copy these sentences, adding capitals where necessary.

1. Reg dwight changed his name to elton john.
2. My brother saw harrison ford at the airport.
3. Margaret thatcher became prime minister in 1979.
4. One writer of the new testament was st. matthew.
5. Rabbi levy and father krause compared their impressions of moses.
6. How can uncle gene get to ames by noon?
7. When he was rescued, capt. john smith thanked god.
8. Last year my mother and i took an auto repair course.
9. Jean and i met state's attorney mary m. newton.
10. Who was vice-president during president ford's term?

B. Use capital letters correctly. Copy these sentences, adding capitals where necessary. Some sentences may already be correct.

1. The okefenokee swamp is in georgia and florida.
2. We drove south through brown county into kentucky.
3. Unseasonal rains drenched the southwest.
4. The northern border of poland faces the baltic sea.
5. Motocross races are held on the east side of town.
6. I've never seen the south or the west coast.
7. Our favorite spot in the west is the grand tetons.
8. The largest lake in the united states is lake superior.
9. Sanibel island is west of fort myers.
10. We waterskied on lake tahoe in california.

C. Use capital letters correctly. Copy these sentences, adding capitals where necessary.

1. Next saturday the anti-cruelty society will move to a new building.
2. Are volvos made only in sweden?

3. The republican candidate fought in world war II.
4. Students in spanish III have lab sessions on thursdays.
5. Will revell industries be closed on december 24?
6. The scanners at many food stores are made by ibm.
7. My cousin graduated from roberto clemente high school.
8. Our history class toured the united nations building.
9. Most catholic schools are closed on good friday.
10. When is the jewish holiday of yom kippur celebrated?

D. Capitalize words correctly. Write the words that should be capitalized. Use capital letters correctly.

1. my sister auditioned for a part in *annie*.
2. a TV show based on true experience is "all creatures great and small."
3. naomi said, "this is ridiculous!"
4. tom wolfe's book *the right stuff* is about astronauts.
5. hazlitt said, "no really great man ever thought himself so."
6. "hold the ladder," said mark. "it's not too steady."
7. "hopes," pindar said, "are but the dreams of those who are awake."
8. dear mr. ortega:
   your order will be shipped immediately.
                              very truly yours,
9. tammy asked, "do you subscribe to *runner's world*?"
10. dogs display reluctance and wrath
    if you try to give them a bath.
                              —ogden nash

MIXED REVIEW

Capitalization

A. Rewrite the following sentences on your paper, capitalizing words where necessary.

1. prince charles and princess diana of england are often in the news.
2. has the pope made more than one trip to his native country of poland?
3. "dad, mom's birthday is next thursday," reminded diane.
4. in iran, egypt, and several other mideastern countries, people worship allah, the supreme being in the islamic religion.
5. our band trip took us through the ohio valley, over the blue ridge mountains, and across the rolling hillsides of maryland to our destination of washington, d.c.
6. when we visited california last year, we drove south on highway 1 from san francisco to the baja peninsula.
7. at central high school, students are only permitted to enter on the south side of the building.
8. susan is a volunteer at the local branch of the a.s.p.c.a. on lincoln avenue.
9. in 1066, the normans conquered britain in the battle of hastings.
10. the u.s.f.l. has approved several new franchises, including one in tulsa, oklahoma.
11. the best-selling car produced by general motors is the chevrolet, followed in sales by the oldsmobile.
12. the united nations was founded on october 24, 1945.
13. the french celebrate their independence on bastille day, july 14.
14. freshmen at brockman college are required to take composition 101, a science course, a computer course, and a foreign language course.
15. "would you like to go to the beach?" asked gina, "or should we try the central park zoo?"

B. Proofread the following letter for incorrect capitalization. Rewrite the letter correctly.

624 Washtenaw avenue
Ypsilanti, michigan 48109
july 4, 1985

dear Lynn,

I received your letter this afternoon, and i'll be happy to accept your invitation! I've always wanted to see the southwest, and traveling with you and aunt Pat sounds like the perfect way to do it! When I asked my mom if I could go, she said, "only if I can go along, too!" She was just teasing, because she has a new job at sears and is not eligible for a vacation until next spring. My summer school classes, chemistry 2 and the math class I told you about, will be completed next thursday. After those, I'll need a vacation!

I look forward to hearing from you concerning the details of our trip. I have already made a reservation for a flight on eastern airlines that leaves detroit on saturday, july 30, at 10:00 a.m. and arrives in tulsa at 3:10 p.m. Please let me know if Aunt Pat or rev. Thomas can meet me. (Did he replace his old buick yet?)

your cousin,

Anita

USING MECHANICS IN WRITING
Capitalization

A. If you could travel across the United States, what states, historical places, recreational areas, or natural wonders would you want to visit? The Rocky Mountains? Disney World? Zion National Park? Plan and write out a route that would take you to at least five of the places you would most like to visit in the United States. If you know the particular roads you would have to take to get you there, be sure to include them in your paper. Remember that sections of the country such as the East and the Midwest are capitalized, as well as the names of towns, parks, individual land formations, and bodies of water. You may want to consult a map or an atlas.

B. Write an essay about your favorite musical group. Where are the members from? What is the best song the group has ever recorded? What is the worst? Compare the two songs. If you can, tell when the songs were written and how they reflect the group's development as performers. Don't forget to capitalize all of the important words in the titles of the songs.

C. The year is 2000. You are on a space mission and have discovered a new planet. As your reward, the government has given you the honor of naming the planet, its land forms and bodies of water, the various creatures it contains, and so on. You may create any sort of strange new world you like. Tell about it in a few paragraphs.

Section 14

Punctuation

Road signs and traffic lights guide a driver. Similarly, punctuation marks guide a reader. **Punctuation marks** show readers where to stop, slow down, or change direction.

When you write, your punctuation signals your reader. It marks groups of words that belong together and tells how a sentence should be read. Correct punctuation, above all, helps prevent the kind of confusion that can result from a sentence such as the following:

> Lee likes rock music new wave however is his
> girlfriends favorite.

Correctly punctuated, the message reads:

> Lee likes rock music; new wave, however, is his
> girlfriend's favorite.

In your own writing, be careful to punctuate sentences correctly, to prevent confusion.

Part 1 End Marks

End marks are the puncutation marks that indicate the end of a sentence. The three kinds of end marks are the **period,** the **question mark,** and the **exclamation point.**

The Period

Use a period at the end of a declarative sentence.

A **declarative sentence** is a sentence that makes a statement.

> The streets are covered with ice.

Use a period at the end of most imperative sentences.

An **imperative sentence** is a sentence that orders or requests someone to do something.

> Use the revolving door, please.

At times, imperative sentences express strong excitement or emotion. Then an exclamation point, rather than a period, is used at the end of the sentence.

> Get away!   Hurry up!

Use a period at the end of an indirect question.

An **indirect question** indicates that someone has asked a question. However, it does not give the reader the exact words of the question.

> The captain asked whether the ship was on course.

Notice how a **direct question** differs:

> The captain asked, "Is the ship on course?"

A direct question shows the exact words of the person asking the question. A direct question ends with a question mark.

Use a period at the end of an abbreviation or an initial.

An **abbreviation** is a shortened form of a word. An **initial** is a first letter that stands for a word.

Gov. James R. Thomas   4 P.M. on Aug. 4

Lt. Margaret B. Hill   6 lb., 12 oz.

Certain abbreviations do not use periods. To check whether or not to use a period with an abbreviation, look up the abbreviation in your dictionary.

CIA (*Central Intelligence Agency*)
CB (*Citizens' Band*)
UN (*United Nations*)

Use a period after each number or letter for an item in an outline or a list.

(An Outline)   (A List)
I. Sports   1. nails
    A. Contact   2. hammer
        1. Football   3. putty

Use a period between dollars and cents and before a decimal.

$13.64   3.14

The Question Mark

Use a question mark at the end of an interrogative sentence.

An **interrogative sentence** is a sentence that asks a question.

What do you want for dinner?

The Exclamation Point

Use an exclamation point at the end of an exclamatory sentence.

An **exclamatory sentence** expresses excitement or other strong emotion.

That's terrific!   How nice you look!

Use an exclamation point after an interjection.

An **interjection** is one or more words that show strong feeling. Sometimes the interjection is a sound.

Nice!   Ouch!   Not again!   Super!

Exercise A: Copy the following sentences, adding the necessary punctuation. Be prepared to tell what punctuation marks you used and why you used them.

1. Where is Lt Moseley stationed
2. Vince asked why the car had a fiberglass hood
3. Fantastic Those twenty-dollar shirts have been marked down to $999
4. Did she want to call at 8:15 A M or P M
5. Say Where have you been
6. I Foods containing calcium
      A Dairy products
         1 Milk
7. The initials WHO stand for the World Health Organization
8. Is your appointment with Dr Sam Williams, Jr or with Dr Sam Williams, Sr
9. Gena's new address is PO Box 12, Altoona, Pennsylvania
10. The *USS Pueblo* was captured by North Korea

Exercise B: Follow the directions for Exercise A.

1. Aaron asked if China bordered the USSR
2. Please send all complaints to Brown, Brooks, and Co in New York
3. Is that an AM radio
4. Darryl Fields, RN, helps his patients to keep smiling
5. Oh, no Why did you do that
6. Should I make the check out to Dr Sara Bosco or to Sara Bosco, MD
7. If the amount is $991 or more, round it off to ten dollars
8. The NEA is an educational organization
9. Does the winter sun really set by 3 PM in Alaska
10. Halt Who's there

Part 2 The Comma

A comma is used to indicate pauses and breaks in thought. In this way, commas help you to communicate clearly.

Using Commas in a Series

Use a comma after every item in a series except the last one.

A series is three or more items of the same kind. Your writing may contain a series of words, phrases, or clauses.

WORDS: Woody Allen is a writer, an actor, and a director.

PHRASES: We searched under beds, inside drawers, and in closets.

CLAUSES: The doctor explained how the blood test is made, what it tells, and why it is necessary.

Use commas after *first, second, third,* and so on, when these adverbs introduce a series.

There are four steps to any house painting job: first, scrapping; second, sanding; third, priming; and fourth, painting.

When there are two or more adjectives before a noun, use commas between them.

The vet treated the cold, wet, sick dog.

Exercise A: Number your paper from 1 to 10. Copy the following sentences and add commas where necessary.

1. January February and March are cold bitter months here.
2. Jeff plays baseball in spring tennis in summer and basketball in winter.
3. Nan wanted to know three things about the car: first its gas mileage; second its cruising speed; and third its price.
4. Tired crews of workers picked grapes in the hot dusty fields.

5. Ron groped for the alarm shut it off and went back to sleep.
6. The radio squawked out news of a fire an airplane crash and a bus strike.
7. Kerry lifted the phonograph needle removed the dust and set the needle back down.
8. Seth has had three part-time jobs: first as a newspaper carrier; second as a cook; and third as an usher.
9. His eyes widened brightened and seemed to smile.
10. A pleasant guide told the tourists where Libya is when it was founded and how it is governed.

Exercise B: Follow the directions for Exercise A.

1. The building inspector listed these problems: first falling plaster; second cracked windows; third peeling paint.
2. Lightning flashed black clouds billowed and leaves whirled.
3. To make a soda, mix syrup ice cream and soda water.
4. Baking soda and water make a cheap effective toothpaste.
5. Betty climbed the wall gripped the ledge and threw the rope.
6. Tall thin gray lockers lined the halls.
7. Hondas Yamahas and Harley-Davidsons glittered in the lot.
8. Denny looked for work at supermarkets theaters restaurants and amusement parks.
9. First I checked the plug; second I looked at the fuse box; third I fiddled with the antennas; fourth I gave up.
10. The plumber stood up stretched and flexed her fingers.

Exercise C: Writing You have just returned from a shopping mall where you visited the following stores:

> an exotic pet store
> a gourmet grocery store
> a sporting goods store

Write a sentence about each store that includes a list of three or more things you saw inside. Use commas correctly.

Then write sentences about each item you listed above. Use at least two adjectives to describe each item. Use commas correctly.

Using Commas with Introductory Words

Use a comma to separate an introductory word, long phrase, or clause from the rest of the sentence.

No, I'm not leaving yet. (introductory word)

After four rounds with the champ, Diaz was knocked down. (prepositional phrase)

Laughing wildly, Lauren threw down the necklace and ran offstage. (verbal phrase)

When you pay the toll, the gate goes up and a green light goes on. (adverb clause)

As you can see, commas are used after introductory words like *yes* and *no*. They are also used after prepositional phrases, verbal phrases, and adverb clauses that begin sentences.

Sometimes the comma may be left out. When there would be almost no pause in speaking, no comma is used.

At noon the auction will begin.

Using Commas with Interrupters

Use commas to set off one or more words that interrupt the flow of thought in a sentence.

The judge, in any event, sentenced the man.

William, moreover, made the all-state squad.

The bus lines, I think, have increased the fare.

The cost of some foods, however, has gone down.

The following words are additional examples of interrupters. Set them off with commas.

therefore	I believe	of course
for example	by the way	furthermore
I suppose	in fact	nevertheless

Exercise A: Number your paper from 1 to 10. Copy the following sentences. Add commas where necessary.

1. Yes the first ELO album was titled "No Answer."
2. After dialing Tony's number Rita had second thoughts.
3. Waiting outside the reporter overheard a startling conversation.
4. Carlos I believe deserves our support.
5. Dazed from lack of sleep the swimmer finally reached the beach.
6. No I haven't been to Williamsburg.
7. You and your brother will be at the Valentine's Day dance I suppose.
8. To tell the truth this pie could have used more time in the oven.
9. After he talked with the coach Glenn felt better about the loss.
10. As other nations get more industry they will share our pollution problems.

Exercise B: Follow the directions for Exercise A.

1. Campbell's interception was I think the high point of the game.
2. Brenda on the other hand is a computer whiz.
3. Yes that is the quickest route to Indianapolis.
4. The British however do not like iced tea or any other chilled drink.
5. On the way home from the dentist's office Fran chipped her tooth.
6. Although Marguerite seems aloof she is just shy.
7. Delighted at the prospect of a summer on the beach Carmen took the job.
8. Whenever a new mail carrier delivers the mail we get somebody else's letters.
9. The rust I am afraid has eaten completely through the hood and doors of the car.
10. Because the public pool was closed we had no place to swim.

Using Commas with Nouns of Direct Address

Use commas to set off nouns of direct address.

Sometimes when you speak or write to someone, you use the person's name. The name of someone directly spoken to is a **noun of direct address**.

Marsha, call a time-out!

In the hallway, Mark, is a package for you.

Did anybody call, Cynthia?

As in the last example, nouns of direct address may be common nouns.

Using Commas with Appositives

Use commas to set off most appositives.

An **appositive** is one or more words that explain or identify another word. The appositive directly follows the word it explains.

Art Buchwald, a humorous writer, has a column in this newspaper.

Our assistant coach, Mr. Wagner, played with the Jets.

The Superbowl, the biggest football game of the year, is held in January.

Note that an appositive may contain a prepositional phrase. Nouns used as appositives are called **nouns in apposition**. When the noun in apposition is essential to the meaning of the word it follows, it is called a **restrictive appositive**. The restrictive appositive is not set off by commas. Usually it is one word or a group of words that function as one word.

My brother David works here.
The empress Catherine the Great lived only thirty-four years.

Using Commas with Quotations

Use commas to set off the explanatory words of a direct quotation.

The explanatory words are the statements like *he said*, *Greg replied*, or *Sheila asked*. They are not part of the quotation. Explanatory words often precede the quotation. Use a comma after the explanatory words.

Rich said, "Take the expressway to the third exit."

Now look at this quotation:

"Take the expressway to the third exit," Rich said.

In the sentence above, the explanatory words come after the quotation. Notice that the comma belongs at the end of the quotation inside the quotation marks.

Sometimes a quotation is broken into two parts. The explanatory words separate the two parts. Here is an example of a *divided quotation*:

"Take the expressway," Rich said, "to the third exit."

In a divided quotation, a comma is used within the quotation marks at the end of the first part of the sentence. A comma is also used after the explanatory words.

Indirect quotations do not tell the speaker's exact words. No commas are used.

Rich said that we should take the expressway to the third exit.

Using Commas in Compound Sentences

Use a comma before the conjunction between the two main clauses of a compound sentence.

The Dodgers won the pennant, but they lost the World Series.

The comma is not necessary when the main clauses are very short and are joined by *and*.

We worked and then we relaxed.

Sometimes very short main clauses are joined by *but* or *or*. A comma is used since the words *but* and *or* mark a change in the flow of thought.

Ken works, but he isn't paid much.

Do not confuse compound sentences with compound subjects or compound predicates. There is no comma before the *and* that joins a compound subject or predicate.

Beth dove into the pool *and* retrieved her wallet.

Exercise A: Copy these sentences. Add commas as needed.

1. Lincoln Logs the building blocks for children were designed by a famous architect's son.
2. The orthodontist a kind woman always puts her patients at ease.
3. Ms. Calder that is my cousin James.
4. Here is the hockey stick you lost Cory.
5. Don's sketch a realistic drawing of the park was displayed at the library.
6. Please submit your application to Dr. Vasquez the director of the project.
7. Shawn said "The breakfast will be held in the church."
8. "I was at that show myself" said Vic.
9. "The sun" whined the pitcher "was in my eyes."
10. Martin called several times but Nathan's line was busy.

Exercise B: Follow the directions for Exercise A.

1. Is Molly still first chair in the clarinet section or is Brian?
2. Coleman built a cabinet for the stereo and then he tucked all the wires out of sight.
3. Captain William Kidd a well-known pirate buried treasure in New York.
4. Melissa found her information at the library and Ben got his from City Hall.
5. Jackie said "I need a volunteer for my experiment."
6. "You have to watch the ball and keep your elbow straight Cindy" explained Travis.

7. "These recruits already act like professionals" said Sergeant Willis.
8. Gary likes knockwurst a sausage with lots of seasoning.
9. "Your engine" said the mechanic "needs a lot of work."
10. The coach said "Keep up the good work girls."

Using Commas in Dates

In dates, use a comma between the day of the month and the year.

Feburary 22,✓1976   May 8,✓1945

When a date is part of a sentence, a comma follows the year.

The first talking picture was shown on July 6,✓1928,✓in New York.

Using Commas in Place Names

Use a comma between the name of a city or town and the name of its state or country.

Detroit,✓Michigan   Santiago,✓Chile

Athens,✓Greece   Houston,✓Texas

When an address is part of a sentence, use a comma after each item.

For more information, write to the National Wildlife Federation,✓1412 Sixteenth Street,✓Washington,✓D.C. 20005.

Do not put a comma between the state name and the ZIP code.

Using Commas in Letters

Use a comma after the salutation of a friendly letter. Use a comma after the complimentary close of a friendly letter or a business letter.

Dear Gretchen,✓   Yours truly,✓

Using Commas with Nonrestrictive Clauses

Use commas to set off nonrestrictive clauses.

A **nonrestrictive clause** is a clause that merely adds an idea to the sentence. The sentence would be complete, and the meaning would be clear without it.

A **restrictive clause** is a clause that is essential to the meaning of a sentence. The clause is needed for the sense of the sentence. If a restrictive clause is dropped out of a sentence, the meaning changes.

NONRESTRICTIVE CLAUSE: Terry Reese, *who is the center for the Wildcats,* scored the most points.

Terry Reese scored the most points. (The clause can be dropped from the sentence.)

RESTRICTIVE CLAUSE: Terry Reese is the player *who scored the most points.*

Terry Reese is the player. (The clause cannot be dropped.)

To see if a clause is nonrestrictive, read the sentence without it. If the meaning doesn't change, the clause is nonrestrictive. Use commas before and after it.

Restrictive clauses are often used to identify or to point out the person or thing they modify. Without this identification, the meaning of the sentence would not be clear. Nonrestrictive clauses, on the other hand, add no essential meaning to the sentence.

RESTRICTIVE CLAUSE: Janice is the girl *who found the money.* (The clause tells which girl.)

NONRESTRICTIVE CLAUSE: Janice, *who is very alert,* found the money.

Janice found the money. (The clause is not needed.)

RESTRICTIVE CLAUSE: This is the book *that has the map.* (The clause tells which book.)

NONRESTRICTIVE CLAUSE: This book, *which has pictures,* is my choice.

This book is my choice. (The clause is not needed.)

Using Commas To Avoid Confusion

Use a comma whenever the reader might otherwise be confused. Sometimes no rule applies, but a sentence might be misread without commas.

Without commas, the following sentences could be misunderstood:

Inside everything was a mess.
Whoever called called twice.

With commas, the sentences are clearer.

Inside, everything was a mess.

Whoever called, called twice.

Exercise A: Copy the following sentences. Add commas where necessary.

1. The walking catfish was first reported near Clearwater Florida on May 25 1968.
2. Dear Nicole
    My summer address will be 205 Linden Street Ladysmith Wisconsin 54848.
    I hope to hear from you.
                        With best wishes
                        Katy
3. On May 24 1844 the first telegraph message was sent.
4. Taconite Minnesota is one city that produces much iron ore.
5. The album was made in Nashville a city with many recording studios.
6. On November 1 1835 Texas declared its independence from Mexico.

7. Coins are made in Denver Colorado and Philadelphia Pennsylvania.
8. John Brown's raid on Harper's Ferry West Virginia began on October 16 1859 and was crushed on October 18.
9. Write to Lynn Brown at 665 California Avenue Ames Iowa 50010.
10. Outside the wind blew fiercely.

Exercise B: Follow the directions for Exercise A.

1. On December 3 1967 a doctor successfully transplanted a human heart.
2. Dear Caroline
   My Aunt Betsy's new address is Rural Route 3 Ridgeway Virginia 62321.

   Sincerely
   Michael
3. On August 27 1859 Edwin Drake struck oil near Titusville Pennsylvania.
4. The intruder you saw saw you.
5. Martin Luther King, Jr. was assassinated on April 4 1968 in Memphis Tennessee.
6. The school is located at 6900 South Stewart Avenue Chicago Illinois.
7. Do you come from Barcelona Venezuela or Barcelona Spain?
8. He seems to believe the saying, "Whatever is is right."
9. The first American automobile which was called a "gasoline buggy" by some was completed on April 19 1892.
10. Mary's grandmother who lives downstairs left Warsaw Poland in 1935.

Exercise C: Writing Write ten sentences that illustrate the correct use of commas. The following items should be included at least once.

commas in dates
commas in place names
commas in nonrestrictive clauses
commas to avoid confusion

Part 3   The Semicolon

Use a semicolon to join the parts of a compound sentence if no coordinating conjunction is used.

The operator interrupted the call; our time was up.

When there are several commas in the parts of a compound sentence, separate the clauses with a semicolon.

On this diet I can eat bread, fruits, and vegetables; but candy, soft drinks, and desserts are forbidden.

When there are commas within parts of a series, use semicolons to separate the parts.

In the Olympics the first place winner gets a gold medal; second place, a silver medal; and third place, a bronze medal.

Use a semicolon before a conjunctive adverb that joins the clauses of a compound sentence.

You have learned that the parts of a compound sentence are sometimes joined by such words as *therefore, however, so, consequently, besides, nevertheless, then, yet*, and *moreover*. These words, called **conjunctive adverbs**, are preceded by a semicolon and followed by a comma.

The Rams have a fine offense; however, their defense is weak.

Justin has a cold; therefore, he will not be able to go swimming this weekend.

Part 4   The Colon

Use a colon after the greeting of a business letter.

Dear Ms. Nolan: Dear Sir or Madam:

Use a colon between numerals indicating hours and minutes.

4:30 P.M.   8:15 A.M.

Use a colon to introduce a list of items.

The colon indicates a pause before the items that follow.

The FBI investigates the following federal crimes: spying, treason, kidnaping, and counterfeiting.

If there would be no pause in speaking, a colon is not used before a list.

The term "mass media" refers to television, radio, newspapers, magazines, and books.

Exercise A: Number your paper from 1 to 10. Copy the word before and after each missing semicolon or colon. Add the correct punctuation mark.

1. The fullback outran the ball the fans went wild.
2. Some people object to the following clothes made from animal skins leopard furs, sealskin coats, and alligator shoes.
3. Dear Madam
   The item that you ordered is out of stock consequently, we are unable to fill your order at this time.
4. Skaters, cyclists, and joggers crowded the path it was not a good place to stroll.
5. From the road, the ocean looked blue however, it was dull brown at the shore.
6. The Community Center requests the following foods dry milk, canned meat, canned soup, coffee, flour, sugar, and cereals.
7. The flight to Honolulu was scheduled to depart from Los Angeles at 7 30 however, we did not even board the airplane until 8 15.
8. There were many cars on the road consequently, the smog was thick.
9. The following cities are growing quickly Calcutta, India San Juan, Puerto Rico Sao Paulo, Brazil and Mexico City, Mexico.
10. Willie Nelson was not a typical country and western singer nevertheless, he became quite popular.

1. The two sides could not reach an agreement therefore, a third party was called in.
2. The picnic tables held bowls of thick, tangy barbecue sauce platters of warm, crisp, fried chicken and big, shiny loaves of fresh-baked bread.
3. Karen built a large, roaring fire and we roasted hot dogs, corn, and marshmallows.
4. Barbara works after school therefore, she will not be home until 6 30.
5. Some popular home remedies for colds include the following fruit juices, chicken soup, garlic cloves, and aspirin.
6. Dear Resident
   Would you like to win $500 a week for life?
7. Rafael Septein has an amazing kick besides, he thinks quickly.
8. On Labor Day at 7 30 P.M., the lifeguard closes the pool.
9. Spices are used in cooking for the following reasons they preserve food, they add variety to meals, and they are flavorful.
10. This year, a serious flu is widespread flu shots are being given at the clinic.

Part 5 The Dash

Using Dashes with Interrupters

You have learned about using commas with words or short phrases, like *however* and *I think*, that interrupt a sentence. A dash is used with a long explanation that interrupts the thought.

An electric car—its battery must be recharged every 1,000 miles—was introduced by one auto maker.

A TV crew—a noise truck, huge cameras, complex sound equipment, and eager reporters—arrived at the scene.

Using the Dash Before a Summary

Use a dash after a series to indicate that a summary statement will follow.

> Edsels, Packards, Studebakers, Hudsons—these cars are no longer made.

> Chocolate milkshakes, hamburgers, and potato chips—this is the diet of some teen-agers.

Be careful not to overuse dashes. They should not be used to replace semicolons or periods.

Exercise A: Number your paper from 1 to 10. Copy these sentences. Insert dashes as needed.

1. Layoffs a nearby factory cut 100 workers are one way to lower costs.
2. Taxi fares, school busing, and a new shopping district these issues were decided by the city council.
3. The Boston Red Sox what a great season they're having will play here next week.
4. That magazine the new one I told you about is in the library.
5. The coach talked about team work, timing, concentration the keys to any victory.
6. Trains, cars, buses, planes all of them were halted by the snowstorm.
7. The winter of 1982 there were not enough trucks to remove the snow set records for snowfall.
8. We can take the elevator unless it is broken again to the tenth floor.
9. Parks, beaches, shops, interesting sights Toronto has them all.
10. Trumpets, drums, saxophones, trombones the band has all these instruments.

Exercise B: Writing Write five of your own sentences, illustrating the correct use of dashes.

Part 6   The Hyphen

Use a hyphen if part of a word must be carried over from one line to the next.

Words are separated by hyphens only between syllables.

> The FBI has about 195,000,000 finger-
> prints on file.

Only words having two or more syllables can be broken by a hyphen. Never divide one-syllable words like *growl* or *weight*. Check your dictionary to learn the syllables of a word.

A single letter should not be left at the end of a line. For instance, this division of *election* would be wrong: *e- lection*. A single letter should not begin a line either.

Use a hyphen in compound numbers from twenty-one to ninety-nine.

forty-six chairs   sixty-five lockers

Use a hyphen in fractions.

a two-thirds majority   one-fourth of the votes.

Use a hyphen in certain compound nouns, such as *brother-in-law, drive-in,* and *great-grandmother.*

The *editor-in-chief* of the local paper is my *sister-in-law.*

Use a hyphen or hyphens between words that make up a compound adjective used before a noun.

The radio announcer gives a play-by-play account of the game.
but: The radio announcer describes the game play by play.

When compound adjectives are used after a noun, they are not usually hyphenated.

A dictionary will tell you if a word needs a hyphen. These are some examples of compound adjectives:

five-year-old boy   well-oiled machine
beat-up truck   best-selling book
little-used street   long-legged spider

Exercise: Number your paper from 1 to 15. After the proper number, write the word or words that should be hyphenated, and add the necessary hyphens. Use your dictionary if necessary.

1. This out of date map is no help.
2. Mary has a twenty year old computer.
3. That is a half baked idea.
4. Turn of the century houses lined the street.
5. The old library had built in bookcases.
6. My great grandmother sent me twenty five dollars.
7. Only one third of the students at that school have up to date health records.
8. The used paperbacks are forty five cents each, or three for one dollar and twenty five cents.
9. About fifty one out of every 100 babies born each year are boys.
10. Carl prefers his make believe world to the real one.
11. One half of those surveyed were younger than twenty two.
12. Three fourths of the students walk to school.
13. Most of my friends headed for the drive in.
14. The patient had a wild eyed look.
15. The editor in chief of that newspaper writes the editorials himself.

Part 7   The Apostrophe

The apostrophe is frequently used to form the possessive of nouns. To use the apostrophe correctly, you should know whether a noun is singular or plural.

To form the possessive of a singular noun, add an apostrophe and an -s.

> student + 's = student's   Les + 's = Les's
> baby + 's = baby's   Vanessa + 's = Vanessa's

To form the possessive of a plural noun that does not end in -s, add an apostrophe and an -s.

> women + 's = women's   frogmen + 's = frogmen's

To form the possessive of a plural noun that ends in -s, add only an apostrophe.

racers + ' = racers'   players + ' = players'
Reeses + ' = Reeses'   sponsors + ' = sponsors'

To form the possessive of indefinite pronouns, use an apostrophe and an -s.

everybody + 's = everybody's   someone + 's = someone's

Do not use an apostrophe with a personal pronoun to show possession.

hers   ours   yours   its   theirs

The team changed *its* attitude.

Use an apostrophe in a contraction.

In contractions words are joined and letters are left out. An apostrophe replaces one or more letters that are left out.

she's = she is   hasn't = has not
we'll = we will   won't = will not
they're = they are   I'm = I am
it's = it is   shouldn't = should not

Use an apostrophe to show the omission of numbers in a date.

the spring of '79 (the spring of 1979)
a '71 Ford (a 1971 Ford)

Use an apostrophe and s to form the plurals of letters, figures, and words used as words.

ABC's   two *n's*   three *4's*   *yes's* and *no's*

Exercise A: Number your paper from 1 to 10. Write the words that need apostrophes. Insert apostrophes where they are needed.

1. Experts cannot tell the difference between a mans handwriting and a womans.
2. Ive already met Russs sister.
3. Its going to rain before we reach the Carlsons porch.
4. The class of 70 is holding its reunion in the gym.

5. Thats Sandras favorite team.
6. Im sure the brakes on my bike are in good shape.
7. Anybodys guess is as good as mine.
8. Theyve admitted that the fault is theirs.
9. DeeAnnes name is spelled with three *e*s.
10. The trainer didnt at first notice the gorillas absence.

Exercise B: Follow the directions for Exercise A.

1. Is that Suzys book youre reading?
2. How would you describe the 1980s?
3. His *maybe*s arent the same as *yes*s.
4. The coachs jacket was a gift from her team.
5. Dont the Reeses dogs ever stop barking?
6. The band lost some of its best musicians when the class of 83 graduated.
7. Arent the clinics hours from 2:00 until 8:00?
8. The two scientists conclusions were the same.
9. This is everyones park, not just yours.
10. My little sister hasnt learned to tell the *d*s from the *b*s.

Part 8   Quotation Marks

Use quotation marks at the beginning and at the end of a direct quotation.

Quotation marks tell your reader that a speaker's exact words are being given. Here is an example:

Linda said, "Someone is following me."

Quotation marks are *not* used with indirect quotations. An indirect quotation does not tell the speaker's exact words.

Linda said that someone was following her.

At the beginning of a sentence there are often explanatory words. Use a comma directly after these words. Then begin the quotation with quotation marks. A period at the end of a sentence belongs *inside* the quotation marks.

The pilot said, "Fasten your seat belts."

Sometimes explanatory words end the sentence. Then the quoted statement at the beginning of the sentence is followed by a comma. The comma belongs inside the quotation marks.

"Fasten your seat belts," the pilot said.

When it is necessary to write a quote within a quote, use single quotation marks to enclose the inside quotation.

"It was Captain James Mugford who originally said, 'Don't give up the ship,'" Mr. Gomez told us.

Using Divided Quotations

Sometimes a quotation is divided by explanatory words. Then, each part of the quotation is enclosed by quotation marks.

"One very healthful food," Pamela said, "is granola."

When the divided quotation is a single sentence, the second part begins with a small letter. Look at the example above. At times, however, the second part begins a new sentence. Then a capital letter is used at the beginning of the second part.

"There is entertainment at halftime," Toby noted. "The band will play."

The first part of a divided quotation is followed by a comma. Commas always appear inside quotation marks.

"On the way," Derek said, "we will pick up Kelly."

The explanatory words in the middle of a divided quotation are followed by either a period or a comma. A period is used if the first part completes a sentence. A comma is used if the sentence continues after the explanatory words.

"At the plant," Eric said, "we work in shifts."

"First, we spread paste on the wallpaper," Ginger explained. "Then we hang the paper and cut it to size."

Exercise: Writing Write each of the following sentences three ways as a direct quotation. Try to use words other than *said* in some of your sentences.

> EXAMPLE: I need an honest answer.
>
> > a. "I need an honest answer," she stated.
> > b. She said, "I need an honest answer."
> > c. "I need," she declared, "an honest answer."

1. Don't talk to me while I'm working.
2. Yes, Stevie Wonder writes many of his own songs.
3. I'm sorry that I forgot to call you.
4. In the last two minutes, the Cowboys took the lead.
5. Finally, a wrecking crew attacked the vacant building.

Using Punctuation with Quotation Marks

Place question marks and exclamation points inside the quotation marks if they belong to the quotation itself.

> Andrew asked, "Who sent you a telegram?"
> Andrea screamed, "Move fast!"

Place question marks and exclamation points outside the quotation marks if they do not belong to the quotation.

> Did Keith say, "Meet me at school"?
> What a surprise it was when our drama coach said, "You made the lead role"!

Commas and periods, as you have seen, always appear within quotation marks.

Exercise A: Copy the following sentences. Punctuate them correctly with quotation marks, end marks, and commas. (There are three indirect quotations that need only end punctuation.)

1. Watch out for the hornet's nest yelled Pat
2. Mindy asked Do you like that yellow Datsun
3. Oh well said Angie a little glue will fix that
4. Ms. Pappas explained why copper wiring is used

5. I have finally had my ice skates sharpened Tisha said
6. Terry announced proudly I knocked down all ten pins
7. Adam said that he was on a diet
8. We locked this door when we left said Harris nervously
   Why is it open now
9. Did Dr. Korshak say that you should tape your ankle
10. Did the dentist say I think your tooth must be pulled

Exercise B: Writing Write each of the following sentences as a direct quotation. In some examples, put the quotation first. In others, put the quotation last. Also, divide some quotations.

1. Is Costa Rica part of Central America?
2. Don't say that!
3. I called the fire department from a neighbor's house.
4. There's a restaurant by the bowling alley.
5. I never know what Merle will say next.
6. By next June, I will have finished repairing the roof.
7. We swam in the quarry.
8. Stand back!
9. Was that snake a copperhead?
10. This weekend I have to help my cousin.

Using Long Quotations

When two or more sentences are spoken by the same person, do not use an end quotation mark until after the final sentence. Look at the following example:

> "When you keep accounts, there are credits and debits," Stacy explained. "Debits are amounts that you owe. Credits are amounts that are paid to you."

Using Quotation Marks for Dialogue

Dialogue is conversation between two or more people. It is punctuated in a special way. Begin a new paragraph each time the speaker changes.

"What are your favorite TV commercials?" Christy asked.
"I like the commercials for Coca-Cola," replied Ted.
"My favorites are Dr. Pepper and Pepsi commercials," Delia said. "Which ones do you like, Christy?"
"I like most of them," Christy answered. "Some of them are better than the TV programs that come in between."

If one speaker's words continue for more than a paragraph, each paragraph begins with a quotation mark. However, the closing quotation mark is not used until the end of the entire quotation.

Tony said, "The movie star who was nominated for an Academy Award more often than any other was Katharine Hepburn. She was nominated twelve times, and won four times.
"Bette Davis was the next most-nominated star. Nominated ten times, she won two Oscars."

Exercise: Writing Rewrite the following conversation. Make correct paragraph divisions, and use the right punctuation.

The interviewer, Mr. Brown, asked Stevie Wonder How did you learn to cope with your handicap? The singer-composer replied I've never seen my blindness as the handicap others do. Why is that? pursued Mr. Brown. Being blind, said Stevie Wonder, you don't judge books by their covers . . . The people I feel sorry for are those who have sight but still don't see.

Punctuating Titles

Use quotation marks to enclose the titles of magazine articles, chapters, short stories, essays, poems, television and radio episodes, songs, and short pieces of music.

MAGAZINE ARTICLE:	"Fads of the Eighties"
CHAPTER TITLE:	Chapter 2, "The New World"
SHORT STORY:	"Clothes Make the Man"
ESSAY:	"The Dog That Bit People"
POEM:	"The Raven"
TELEVISION EPISODE:	"Radar Writes Home"
SONG:	"Jingle Bells"

Underline the titles of books, newspapers, magazines, plays, movies, television series, works of art, and long musical compositions.

In writing or typing, such titles are underlined, like this: <u>The Chocolate War.</u> In print, these titles appear in italics.

BOOK TITLE:	*The Pigman*
NEWSPAPER:	*New Haven Register*
MAGAZINE:	*Field and Stream*
PLAY:	*The Miracle Worker*
MOVIE:	*Raiders of the Lost Ark*
WORK OF ART:	*Mona Lisa*
LONG MUSICAL COMPOSITION:	*The Pirates of Penzance*

Exercise A: Copy the following sentences, adding quotation marks around titles or underlining titles where necessary.

1. The story Saving the Pieces was published in Audubon magazine.
2. Old Abe Lincoln Came Out of the Wilderness was a popular marching song during the Civil War.
3. I reported on Althea Gibson's article, I Always Wanted To Be Someone.
4. The article appeared in the book Out of the Bleachers.
5. Our city was featured on the TV show 60 Minutes.
6. Of all the Frankenstein movies, I like Young Frankenstein most.
7. The Post-Dispatch is a St. Louis newspaper.
8. The musical West Side Story is a modern version of Shakespeare's play Romeo and Juliet.
9. Monet's painting Waterlilies has been reproduced on bedsheets.
10. Many people recognize the eerie notes of the ballet music The Firebird.

Exercise B: Follow the directions for Exercise A.

1. Surely you can think of a better title for your essay than What I Did During My Summer Vacation.
2. I like Langston Hughes's poem Dreams.

3. Julia Ward Howe wrote the song The Battle Hymn of the Republic.
4. Please read Chapter 10, The Last Frontier.
5. John Tenniel, who illustrated the book Alice in Wonderland, also drew cartoons for the magazine Punch.
6. The Time Machine was first a novel and then a movie.
7. The Searchers was a famous Western.
8. The first New York newspaper was called the Gazette.
9. The Devil's Dictionary is a book of humorous definitions.
10. Our school play last year was A Raisin in the Sun.

Exercise C: Writing Imagine that you are a famous writer who has published books, magazine articles, and song lyrics. You are on tour promoting your latest novel. A talk show host who is interviewing you asks about the new book as well as your earlier work. Write the conversation that takes place. Be sure to use quotation marks and underlining correctly.

REINFORCEMENT EXERCISES

Punctuation

A. Use end marks and commas. Rewrite the following sentences, adding the missing punctuation.

1. Skates are becoming more popular and skateboards have almost been forgotten
2. How thin you are
3. How thin are you
4. Should Carol bring her own pliers wrench and wire
5. Joan of Arc the French heroine was declared a saint in 1920
6. Ms Doyle Dr Antonelli and Mr McCoy are holding a meeting at 8:00 PM on Saturday September 3
7. On March 13 1852 the first newspaper cartoon of Uncle Sam appeared
8. Robin bought the tickets but then she lost them
9. Yes Mel I remembered to bring my new album
10. Georgia looked in her address book rummaged through a stack of old mail and finally found this address: 215 Main Street Carthage Illinois 62321
11. When the balloon burst my cat jumped straight into the air
12. On Tuesday by the way you'll meet Ann Archer the co-captain of the team
13. "Are you done Ron" Mike said "We want to leave"
14. Dear Tommy
    Here is the clipping that you asked for
    Sincerely
15. Renee who lived in France for two years can speak French fluently

B. Use semicolons, colons, dashes, and hyphens. Add semicolons, colons, dashes, and hyphens as you rewrite these sentences.

1. Racquetball, tennis, squash, and badminton Mark can play them all well.
2. The Cougars will need the following players pitchers, infielders, and left handed batters.

3. At eighty six, my great grandmother still has a happy go lucky view of life.
4. Deidre can remember everything she reads furthermore, she understands the material.
5. The commander in chief, the general, and the prime minister these people will arrive at 7 15 P.M.
6. Three fourths of the students listed these long term goals more education, an interesting job, and a happy family life.
7. Dear Madam
   We have received your letter it will be published in next week's column.
8. This weekend I can hardly wait we'll be leaving for the lake.
9. Seventy five people have entered the five mile race.
10. Margie had only a four week course in self defense however, she is already very good at it.

C. Use apostrophes, quotation marks, and underlining. Write each sentence, putting in necessary apostrophes, quotation marks, and underlining.

1. Rachel said, I like the TR-7 s that were made in the early 1970s.
2. The students theme for their dance will be from the play Grease.
3. The song Fire Lake reminds me of the spring of 80.
4. Did the teacher say that we would discuss Tillie Olsens story, I Stand Here Ironing?
5. Get out of the way! yelled Lee.
6. Is it true, asked Glorias brother, that the injured player is my sister?
7. Its somebodys problem, but not yours, said Ms. Kane emphatically.
8. Chriss contact lens cant be found anywhere.
9. All three teachers classes are reading the novel Ordinary People.
10. I dont see Meryl Streeps picture in this copy of People, said Beth. Maybe its in last weeks issue.

D. Use apostrophes, quotation marks, and underlining. Write each sentence, putting in necessary apostrophes, quotation marks, and underlining.

1. Walt Disneys feature cartoon films, like Cinderella and Bambi, are shown every seven years.
2. Most American families have two or more TVs, Mr. Lloyd said.
3. The freshmens lockers are on the first floor.
4. John Ciardis poem Beagles in the book Introduction to Poetry is one of my favorites.
5. Jenny asked, Isn't Jasons dog much older than yours?
6. Jodys grandpa recalls the stock market crash of 29.
7. Ken shouted, Somebodys car is rolling down the hill!
8. Didnt you see this weeks Mystery Theater on TV?
9. Eubie, Bonnie explained, is a musical about ragtime musician Eubie Blake.
10. Do most students parents help them with homework? Ms. Richardson asked.

MIXED REVIEW

Punctuation

A. Proofread the following letter for incorrect or missing punctuation. Rewrite the letter correctly.

3006 Merton Road
Palo Alto California, 94306
November 23 1985

Sales Manager
Rockinwell Corporation
680 Broadway
New York New York 10006

Dear Sir or Madam,

On April 26 I ordered twenty three songbooks from your company for my mother in law who is seventy eight years old. These songbooks were ordered from your catalog entitled Tunes from the 40s. For some reason the books that I received contained music such as the following; rock songs by the Bee Gees, the Rolling Stones, and Men at Work, Broadway show tunes from Pippin, The Wiz, and Annie, and blues songs by Muddy Waters.

Despite your companys error, my mother in laws choral group has enjoyed these books immensely. As she said to me after her last rehearsal Son these books are definitely going to liven things up around here.

Thank you, therefore for your error and please send me a copy of your new catalog.

Sincerely

Martin E. Hudnut

B. Proofread the following passage for incorrect or missing punctuation. Rewrite the passage correctly.

If Olympic games were held for birds the winners of the flight contests would be the swift the falcon and the tern. Swifts the earths fastest birds have been clocked at 106 miles per hour in level flight. However peregrine falcons which are related to eagles occasionally fly even faster. Diving for prey this bird has been known to reach the incredible speed of 217 miles per hour. The Arctic tern according to biologist David Attenborough in his book Life on Earth is another great flyer. In 1955 one Arctic tern was tracked, over 12,000 miles from the White Sea Coast of the USSR to the city of Fremantle Australia?

USING MECHANICS IN WRITING
Punctuation

A. The following passage is a dialogue between two characters, from the short story "Wheldon the Weed" by Peter Jones. Rewrite the dialogue, adding necessary punctuation and paragraph divisions.

> Don't touch me Crawley cried shrinking back in mock terror. All right laugh said Wheldon forcing the words out between clenched teeth but there's one thing you're afraid of and Im not. Crawley stopped laughing. Whats that he demanded fiercely. Spooks said Wheldon. Spooks? All of a sudden Crawley sounded as uncertain as a kid trying to recite a poem hed had to learn for homework. Yes spooks said Wheldon drawing the word out like chewing gum. I thought thatd wipe the smile off your face.

B. You are an agent for Dan D. Tripps travel agency. A client wants you to put together an itinerary for an exciting five-day vacation. For each day, include the following information:

> The date
> Starting place and destination
> Times of departure and arrival
> Places of interest
> Activities planned, including admission or ticket fees
> Names and addresses of hotels

Include in the itinerary at least one series of items; several introductory words, such as *first* and *next*; one or more compound sentences; a possessive noun; and a compound word. Your itinerary may be realistic or highly imaginative. Following is a sample entry:

> Saturday, July 1: Leave Des Moines, Iowa, at 8:40 a.m. Travel by United Airlines to Los Angeles, arriving 11:18 a.m. Take shuttle bus to Holiday Inn in Anaheim. Arrive at Disneyland at 1:00 p.m. The gate admission for Disneyland is $15.00.

CUMULATIVE REVIEW
Capitalization and Punctuation

Using Capitalization and Punctuation Correctly. Copy the following paragraphs. Change small letters to capital letters or capital letters to small letters wherever necessary. Add the correct punctuation marks. Leave out incorrect marks.

Last saturday my mothers youngest brother, uncle jack, went with me to the Museum of science and Industry. On exhibit was a collection of some artistic scientific and Technological inventions of the chinese. This exhibit had been recommended by: three of my teachers my english teacher my Industrial Arts I teacher and my Science teacher.

We saw a waterclock made in Ad 1,068 that had many gears and stood two stories high. Because I am especially interested in astronomy I most enjoyed the planetarium—in which a chinese astronomer could sit and be surrounded by a view of the stars. I was amazed to learn that this device was built (more than 1,000 years ago). We also saw irrigation machines; compasses looms fireworks printing presses and even a seismograph.

There were also demonstrations of ancient Arts and Crafts. Most of the visual arts developed during four dynasties; the han, the T'ang, the sung, and the ming. I asked one man, who was demonstrating chinese ink painting to write my name in chinese characters. He asked, "how do you pronounce your name"? When he had finished the painting he stamped it, with a red seal that showed I think his own name.

We also saw a silkworm exhibit. According to Chinese Legend, silk was discovered in 2700 b.c. in the garden of emperor huang-ti. One five-year old girl really enjoyed watching the silkworms produce silk fibers: She asked "if she could take a worm home to play with"; but she was given a sample of silk thread instead.

After viewing the exhibit we browsed through a special shop. This shop contained many products made in china. Their beauty made me sorry that I didn't have more time—and money— to spend at the exhibit.

Section 15

Spelling

Good spelling is a skill that is important in all writing, from school reports to messages, letters, and job applications. On the job, too, you will often need to write. Accurate spelling is essential to communicate clearly and to create a favorable impression on paper.

Becoming a good speller is not an easy task, though. The spelling of many English words does not seem logical, and many words are not spelled the way they sound.

Learning to spell well is not hopeless, however. There are certain patterns of spelling that many English words follow. There are general rules that make spelling easier, and there are methods of attacking spelling problems. With such tools, you can avoid many problems and improve spelling. This Section will show some solutions.

Part 1 How To Improve Your Spelling

1. **Locate and conquer your own specific spelling problems.** What spelling errors do you make over and over? Study your past written assignments and make a list of the misspelled words. Work on mastering those words.

2. **Pronounce words carefully.** Occasionally people misspell words because they don't pronounce them correctly. If you are writing *famly* for *family*, for instance, you are probably mispronouncing the word. Try to pronounce your words more precisely.

3. **Try to remember the letters in new words.** The habit of really looking at the spelling of new or difficult words can help imprint the correct spelling on your memory. After examining a word carefully, write the correct spelling several times.

4. **Always proofread your writing.** Many misspellings are actually careless mistakes. By examining your writing, you may catch such errors. Read over your work slowly, word by word.

5. **Look up difficult words in a dictionary.** Reach for the dictionary when you're unsure of a spelling. Get into the habit of letting the dictionary help you to spell well.

6. **Learn the few important spelling rules explained in this section.**

Part 2 How To Spell a Particular Word Correctly

1. **Look at the word and say it to yourself.** Make sure to pronounce the word correctly. Say it twice, looking at the syllables as you say them.

2. **Look at the letters.** Close your eyes and try to visualize the word. Then look at the word again. Notice any structural aspects of the word, such as prefixes, suffixes, and double letters, that are important to the correct spelling.

3. **Write the word without looking at your book or list.**

4. **Check to see if you spelled the word correctly.** Look back at your book or list. If you spelled the word correctly, repeat the process.

5. **If you made an error, note what it was.** Then repeat steps 3 and 4 until you have written the word correctly three times.

Part 3   Spelling Rules

Adding Prefixes

When a prefix is added to a word, the spelling of the word remains the same. When the addition of a prefix creates a doubled letter, be careful not to drop one of them.

im + perfect = imperfect	ir + rational = irrational
re + entry = reentry	mis + use = misuse
inter + action = interaction	mis + spell = misspell
dis + agree = disagree	il + legal = illegal

Suffixes with Silent e

When a suffix beginning with a vowel is added to a word ending in a silent e, the e is usually dropped.

save + ing = saving	value + able = valuable
style + ish = stylish	rate + ing = rating
grace + ious = gracious	imagine + ation = imagination

When a suffix beginning with a consonant is added to a word ending in a silent e, the e is usually retained.

time + less = timeless	strange + ly = strangely
like + ly = likely	amaze + ment = amazement
same + ness = sameness	hope + ful = hopeful

The following words are **exceptions.** Study them.

truly   argument   ninth   wholly   judgment

Exercise: Find the misspelled words. Spell them correctly.

1. Dorothy was gazeing at the graceful skaters.
2. They found the sameness of the plains boreing.
3. The missile exploded upon rentry to the atmosphere.
4. These arguements are not solveing the problem.
5. The man mistated several facts about the ilegal exports.
6. That penalty was wholly unecessary.
7. Our district relected that insincere politician.
8. Tim has trouble wakeing up on these freezeing days.
9. A fameous surgeon performed the operateion.
10. Leaving everthing to chance is imature.

Suffixes and Final *y*

When a suffix is added to a word ending in *y* preceded by a conso-nant, the *y* is usually changed to *i*.

carry + er = carrier   fury + ous = furious
worry + ed = worried   thirty + eth = thirtieth
silly + est = silliest   holy + ness = holiness

Note this exception: When *-ing* is added, *y* does not change.

hurry + ing = hurrying   study + ing = studying
rally + ing = rallying   cry + ing = crying

When a suffix is added to a word ending in *y* preceded by a vowel, the *y* usually does not change.

play + ing = playing   destroy + er = destroyer
decay + ed = decayed   annoy + ing = annoying

Exercise: Add the suffixes as shown and write the new word.

1. dizzy + ness
2. carry + ing
3. ready + ness
4. heavy + er
5. witty + est
6. marry + ing
7. marry + age
8. fifty + eth
9. employ + able
10. stay + ed
11. terrify + ing
12. creepy + est
13. relay + ed
14. glory + ous
15. cozy + er
16. history + an
17. joy + ful
18. enjoy + able
19. tiny + ness
20. fry + ed

Adding the Suffixes -*ness* and -*ly*

When the suffix -*ly* is added to a word ending in *l*, both *l*'s are kept. When -*ness* is added to a word ending in *n*, both *n*'s are kept. When any suffix creates a double consonant, keep both letters.

cruel + ly = cruelly   even + ness = evenness
general + ly = generally   lean + ness = leanness

Doubling the Final Consonant

In words of one syllable that end in one consonant preceded by one vowel, double the final consonant before adding -*ing*, -*ed*, or -*er*.

beg + ing = begging   thin + er = thinner
flap + ed = flapped   grab + ing = grabbing

Some two-syllable words follow a similar rule. If the final syllable is accented and ends in one consonant preceded by one vowel, double the final consonant before adding -*ing*, -*ed*, or -*er*.

admit + ing = admitting   regret + ed = regretted

In words of one syllable that end in one consonant preceded by two vowels, the final consonant is not doubled.

steer + ing = steering   lead + er = leader
join + ed = joined   fool + ing = fooling

Exercise A: Find the misspelled words. Spell them correctly.

1. Lana fooled everyone by speaking truthfuly.
2. Chris spoted the actress and beged for her autograph.
3. I finaly stopped the driping of the water faucet.
4. Something is cloging the bathtub drain.
5. Angela is hopping to become a space scientist.
6. The Richardsons usually go sailling on Sunday afternoons.
7. The miser Scrooge is generaly known for his meaness.
8. We were permited to use only bamboo fishing poles.
9. The openess of this building makes it especialy cool.
10. Are you realy digging a new trench?

Exercise B: Add the suffixes as shown and write the new word.

1. green + ness
2. tip + ed
3. boom + ed
4. lag + ed
5. top + ed
6. awful + ly
7. grim + est
8. playful + ly
9. brag + ing
10. plain + ness
11. cook + ed
12. sob + ed
13. run + ing
14. clip + ed
15. stern + ness
16. cheerful + ly
17. groan + ing
18. pat + ed
19. stop + ing
20. stoop + ing

Words with the "Seed" Sound

There is only one English word ending in *sede: supersede.* Three words end in *ceed: exceed, proceed, succeed.* All other words ending with the sound of *seed* are spelled *cede*:

recede   precede   concede   secede

Words with *ie* and *ei*

There is a general rule for words with the long *e* (*ē*) sound. The word is spelled *ie,* except after *c.* If the vowel combination sounds like a long *a* (*ā*) spell it *ei.*

I before *E*

piece   fierce   field   grief   chief
believe   relief   niece   reprieve   retrieve

Except after *C*

perceive   deceit   ceiling   receipt
conceive   conceit   receive   deceive

Or when sounded as ā

neighbor   weigh   reign

The following words are exceptions to the rule.

either   leisure   seize
weird   species   neither

Exercise A: Find the misspelled words in these sentences and spell them correctly.

1. This new law superceeds the old one.
2. South Carolina seceded from the Union in 1860 and siezed Fort Sumter in 1861.
3. My neice Meredith received a wierd surprise.
4. Sal beleives that he can clear that field in his liesure time.
5. The warden conceeded that the prisoner should get a reprieve.
6. Erin succeded in tying the boat to the pier.
7. Niether peice of land is big enough for an apartment building.
8. The forged reciept did not deceive the sales clerk, who proceded to call the detective.
9. In some cultures the period of grieving excedes two years.
10. That species of owl has a peircing shriek.

Exercise B: Writing Compose a poem or a set of song lyrics of at least eight lines. Use "seed" words and *ie/ei* words. Note that many of these words rhyme: exceed-secede, grief-chief, neither-either.

A List of Commonly Misspelled Words

abbreviate
accidentally
achievement
across
address
all right
altogether
always
amateur
analyze
anonymous
answer
apologize
appearance
appreciate
appropriate
argument
arrangement
associate
awkward
balance
bargain
beginning
believe
bicycle
bookkeeper
bulletin
bureau
business
cafeteria
calendar
campaign
candidate
certain
changeable
characteristic
column

committee
courageous
courteous
criticize
curiosity
cylinder
dealt
decision
definitely
despair
desperate
dictionary
dependent
description
desirable
different
disagree
disappear
disappoint
discipline
dissatisfied
efficient
eighth
eligible
eliminate
embarrass
emphasize
enthusiastic
environment
equipped
especially
exaggerate
excellent
exhaust
expense
experience
familiar

fascinating
February
financial
foreign
fourth
fragile
generally
government
grammar
guarantee
guard
gymnasium
handkerchief
height
humorous
imaginary
immediately
incredible
influence
intelligence
interesting
knowledge
laboratory
lightning
literature
loneliness
maintenance
marriage
mathematics
medicine
minimum
mischievous
missile
misspell
mortgage
municipal
necessary

nickel
ninety
noticeable
nuclear
nuisance
obstacle
occasionally
occur
opinion
opportunity
original
outrageous
parallel
particularly
permanent
permissible
persuade
picnicking
pleasant
pneumonia
politics
possess
possibility
practice
prejudice
preparation
privilege
probably
professor
pronunciation
propeller
psychology
quantity
realize
recognize
recommend
reference

referred
rehearse
repetition
representative
restaurant
rhythm
ridiculous
sandwich
schedule
scissors
secretary

separate
sergeant
similar
sincerely
sophomore
souvenir
specifically
strategy
strictly
success
surprise

syllable
sympathy
symptom
temperament
temperature
thorough
throughout
together
tomorrow
traffic
tragedy

transferred
truly
Tuesday
twelfth
undoubtedly
unnecessary
vacuum
vicinity
village
weird
writing

REINFORCEMENT EXERCISES
Spelling

A. Add prefixes and suffixes. Add the prefix or suffix as shown. Write the new word.

1. thin + ness
2. hot + er
3. dis + satisfied
4. shop + ing
5. rusty + est
6. engage + ment
7. true + ly
8. spine + less
9. stage + ing
10. move + ment
11. un + necessary
12. excite + able
13. angry + er
14. destroy + ing
15. stain + ed
16. continual + ly
17. luxury + ous
18. merry + ment
19. un + attractive
20. ninety + eth

B. Add prefixes and suffixes. Add the prefix or suffix as shown. Write the new word.

1. join + ed
2. natural + ly
3. slim + est
4. include + ing
5. early + er
6. dis + appoint
7. happy + ly
8. regulate + ory
9. copy + ing
10. like + ness
11. in + voluntary
12. hope + less
13. forty + eth
14. even + ness
15. grin + ed
16. usual + ly
17. employ + er
18. submit + ing
19. argue + ment
20. mis + judge

C. Spell words with *ie*, *ei*, or the *seed* sound. Find the misspelled words. Write them correctly on your paper.

1. Feirce winds knocked the pier into the lake.
2. The doctor conceeded that there was only one way to relieve the pain.
3. In the preceeding weeks we enjoyed our leisure time.

4. "Procede with your weird tale," Gail said.
5. She defended her cheif loyally, I beleive.
6. Niether of the advertisements is meant to decieve us.
7. Unbeleivable! Martin has finally succeeded in making that radio work.
8. Sam hurried over to his crying neice.
9. We recieved directions to the new baseball field.
10. Gus has succeded in putting the peices together.

D. Spell words correctly. Find the misspelled words in each sentence. Write them correctly on your paper.

1. The feirce cougar dissappeared into the cave.
2. Marcy's horse gracefully steped and trotted around the ring.
3. Annie is planning to send out the inviteations today.
4. The wide reciever was completly unnaware of the new plan.
5. David shouted angryly at his friends but immediatly was sorry.
6. Some taxpayers worryed that the money was mispent.
7. The uneveness of the slope makes skiing unusualy hard.
8. Police cars generaly preceed the President's car in a parade.
9. In all of the excitment we accidentaly misplaced our tickets.
10. The weight of the ship's cargo excedes ten tons.

MIXED REVIEW

Spelling

A. Copy each sentence. Add the suffixes and prefixes in parentheses to the words with which they are paired.

1. Susan said that none of her answers were (in + correct).
2. Who was the (win + er) of the masquerade contest?
3. Roger Ebert and Gene Siskel always (dis + agree) on that type of movie.
4. We found an insect (imbed + ed) in a piece of amber.
5. The explorers (final + ly) reached their destination.
6. Most of Inspector Clouseau's actions were completely (il + logical).
7. A lighthouse operator has to combat (lonely + ness).
8. A (fury + ous) storm ravaged the tiny island.
9. We raised money to pay for (bus + ing) our team to the Bears' exhibition game.
10. At the age of ten, she began (write + ing) her memoirs.
11. The plan called for more (inter + action) among members of different departments.
12. That dog will have to stop (bury + ing) its bones in my petunias.
13. Playwright George Kaufman first became known for the (witty + ness) of his newspaper columns.
14. Those thunderclouds definitely aren't (line + ed) with silver.
15. His new job may be causing his uncharacteristic (mean + ness).
16. Sheila is (plan + ing) on (study + ing) (biology + cal) science.
17. She has been (save + ing) money for college.
18. Has anyone (broke + en) Babe Ruth's home run record?
19. What was his (bat + ing) average?
20. No plants or animals relieve the (barren + ness) of the moon's surface.

B. Proofread these sentences for spelling errors. Write each mis-spelled word correctly. One sentence has no errors.

1. It was the silliest arguement we had ever had.
2. Mary Chase's play *Harvey* is truely amusing.
3. All merryment stopped when the host began braging.
4. Bill was cooking dinner, and Monica was bakeing dessert.
5. The losing candidate finaly decided to consede the election.
6. Which occurrence are you refering to?
7. To the amazment of onlookers, the feirce winds uprooted a huge tree.
8. To ensure the eveness of each coat of paint, we used a paint thiner.
9. Coach Marowitz spoke meaningfully about the need for modifying our defensive strategy.
10. The dog proceded to retrieve the Frisbee and bite a huge hole in it.

USING MECHANICS IN WRITING
Spelling

A. Pretend that you are a student in another country who has only recently learned English. You have just written the following letter to your American pen pal. One of your teachers suggests that you check your letter for spelling errors. Follow that teacher's advice and rewrite the letter correctly. There are nineteen mistakes. You may have to refer to the *List of Commonly Misspelled Words* on pages 699 and 700.

> Dear Freind,
>
> I recieved your letter of Febuary 4 and read happyly about what you have been doing. Your family happenings especialy made me smile.
>
> The story about when your brother was preparing dinner as your sister was cliping the dog in the kitchen realy was the funnyest I've read. When the dog tiped over the chair that your brother had set the spaghetti sauce on, I can imagine how he yelled! Has your brother recovered from his greif?
>
> Our weather has been so changable recently. One day it is raining, and the next day it is hot. On plesent days my brother and I go sailling. Do you like to sail? We like raceing our boat on the ocean. It is summer here now, you know, so we enjoy being in the water. In winter we will be plaing soccer.
>
> I have so many questions to ask you. What is the tempature now? What athletics do you enjoy? You said your sister is a sophmore. What is that?
>
> Please write soon, I appreciate hearing about the wonderful missadventures of your family.
>
> Yours truely,

B. Write a story in which a mad professor and his assistant, Igor, are working in a laboratory on one of their typically horrifying projects. Use at least fifteen words from the *List of Commonly Misspelled Words* in your story. You should be able to use many more.

CUMULATIVE REVIEW
Spelling

Spelling Words with *ei*, *ie*, *ede*, and *eed*. Number your paper from 1 to 15. Write each word correctly by adding the letters *ei*, *ie*, *ede*, or *eed*.

1. c __ __ ling
2. ch __ __ f
3. rec __ __ ve
4. l __ __ sure
5. prec __ __ __

6. dec __ __ ve
7. rel __ __ f
8. n __ __ ther
9. bel __ __ ve
10. __ __ ther

11. proc __ __ __
12. rec __ __ pt
13. ach __ __ vement
14. succ __ __ __
15. n __ __ ce

Adding Prefixes and Suffixes. Number your paper from 1 to 15. Write the word formed by adding the prefix or suffix.

1. de + code
2. re + entry
3. thirty + eth
4. strange + ly
5. study + ing

6. im + mature
7. value + able
8. copy + s
9. nine + th
10. general + ly

11. thin + er
12. mis + spell
13. coach + s
14. decay + ed
15. potato + s

Using the Correct Word. Number your paper from 1 to 10. Next to each number, write the correct word from those in parentheses.

1. If (your, you're) going to see Kate, say hello for me.
2. Equal opportunity is a basic (principal, principle) of a democracy.
3. An elephant uses (its, it's) trunk to dig.
4. If I'd waited ten more minutes, I (could of, could have) seen John Travolta in person.
5. Betty (set, sat) the test tubes in the rack.
6. Everyone agreed (on, to, with) pepperoni pizza.
7. In 1979, Mother Teresa (excepted, accepted) the Nobel Peace Prize for her aid to the poor of India.
8. The curtain (rose, raised) and the play began.
9. The four neighboring farmers shared several pieces of large equipment (between, among) them.
10. Is it (alright, all right) to bring my cousin to the picnic?

Section 16

The Correct Form For Writing

An effective writer needs to be as concerned with the form of his or her papers as with the content. Careless or sloppy form can muddle a writer's message, confuse and annoy the reader, and even prevent someone from making the effort to read the material at all.

Good form is careful, neat, and consistent. Some schools set their own specific rules for the correct form for written work. In this section you will learn about the kind of form that is accepted by many schools.

Part 1 Acceptable Form

Your papers must always be neat and legible. Neatness shows that you care about your work. Whether typewritten or hand-written in ink, give your papers that extra bit of attention that will make your reader *want* to read what you have to say.

Of course, the correct form for writing means more than a neat appearance. In a paper with acceptable form, the various parts are positioned correctly. Headings, titles, margins, and spacing should be in the correct form.

The Heading

A heading identifies your paper. It is usually placed in the upper right-hand corner of the first page. Place your name on the first line. Write the name of your class on the second line. Write the date on the third line. In a paper with a title page, the heading is placed in the upper right corner of that page.

Each page, except for page one, should be numbered. Beginning with page two, place the page number in the upper right-hand corner. To identify all pages, you might want to put your name under the page number.

Some teachers may require a different form for labeling your paper. Follow any special instructions you are given.

The Title

The title of a paper should appear near the top of the first page. In general, place the title two lines down from the last line of the heading. Begin the first line of your paper two lines below the title.

Correct form for a title also means proper capitalization. The first word and all important words in the title should be capitalized. Use capitals for only the first letters of words, not for every letter. Do not underline your title or place it in quotation marks.

When a paper is more than three pages long, a title page may be used. This page precedes the paper.

Margins and Spacing

Use correct margins and spacing to achieve an attractive appearance. Margins of one inch at the top, bottom, and left side of the paper look pleasing.

Try to keep the right-hand margin fairly even. Do not break too many words with hyphens, though, to keep the margin straight. Try to avoid hyphens in more than two lines in a row.

Double-spacing makes typed papers look neat and makes them much easier to read. Paragraphs are usually indented five spaces. Skip two spaces after the end of a sentence.

Part 2   Writing Numbers

The form for writing numbers should be consistent. Numbers that can be expressed in fewer than four words are usually spelled out. Larger numbers are written in figures.

These jeans cost *twenty-four* dollars.
The National League consists of *twelve* teams.
Ticket sales amounted to $2,125.

A number at the beginning of a sentence is always spelled out.

Thirty thousand people attended the game.
One thousand millimeters make up one meter.
Four hundred dollars was stolen.

Figures rather than spelled-out words are used for these numbers: dates, street and room numbers, telephone numbers, temperature, page numbers, decimals, and percentages.

The Battle of Concord took place on April *19, 1775*.
The clinic is at *66* West Schiller in Room *35*.
Matthew's phone number is *328-6610*.
Last night the temperature went down to *10* degrees.
Did you see that article about vans on page *16*?
Ann ran the hurdles in *15.8* seconds.
The new sales tax is *4* percent.

In large sums of money or large quantities, use commas to separate the figures. Commas are not used in dates, serial numbers, page numbers, addresses, or telephone numbers.

CORRECT: The Statue of Liberty cost $500,000.
CORRECT: The Milky Way has 200,000,000,000 stars.
INCORRECT: The first World Series was in 1,903.
CORRECT: The first World Series was in 1903.

Exercise: Copy these sentences, correcting any errors.

1. A movie shows fourteen hundred and thirty-five frames of film per minute.
2. The serial number of the typewriter is 20,002.
3. 1st prize is one thousand two hundred and fifty dollars.
4. About ninety percent of the patients who have this operation recover fully within 6 months.
5. Although the temperature was actually 30 degrees, the wind chill factor lowered it to two degrees.
6. The profit of twelve thousand two hundred and five dollars is ten percent higher than last year's.
7. 3 years ago the Chandlers moved to 1,682 Garfield Street.
8. 1 barrel of oil is equal to 31 gallons.
9. 1000 grams equals a little more than three pounds.
10. On March eighteenth, 1,959, Hawaii became our 50th state.

Part 3 Using Abbreviations

Abbreviations are shortened forms of words. In formal writing, abbreviations are usually not acceptable. Abbreviations, however, may be used for most titles before and after names. Abbreviations may also be used for government agencies and for time.

TITLES BEFORE PROPER NAMES: Mrs., Mr., Ms., Gen., Dr., Rev., Sgt., Fr., Sen.

TITLES AFTER PROPER NAMES: Jr., M.D., D.D.S., Ph.D.

GOVERNMENT AGENCIES: FBI, VA, EPA, FTC

DATES AND TIMES: A.M., P.M., B.C., A.D.

Notice that periods are omitted in some abbreviations, such as those for government agencies. If you are not sure whether an abbreviation should be written with or without periods, look up the abbreviation in your dictionary.

A title is abbreviated only when it is used with a person's name, as in *Dr. Lauren Sherwood.* The following, for example, would not be acceptable: The dr. found a cure for the disease.

Abbreviations are not used for certain titles. *Honorable* and *Reverend* are not abbreviated when preceded by *the: the Reverend Lee Withers.* Abbreviations are not used for the titles of the President and Vice-President of the United States.

In most writing, abbreviations are not acceptable for the following: names of countries and states, months and days of the week, addresses, and firm names.

INCORRECT: The Hon. John Evans was the guest.
CORRECT: The Honorable John Evans was the guest.

INCORRECT: Both the Pres. and the Vice-Pres. were there.
CORRECT: Both the President and the Vice-President were there.

INCORRECT: The Mayans built pyramids in Mex.
CORRECT: The Mayans built pyramids in Mexico.

INCORRECT: Detroit, Mich., is called "Motor City."
CORRECT: Detroit, Michigan, is called "Motor City."

INCORRECT: Tues., Nov. 2, is Election Day.
CORRECT: Tuesday, November 2, is Election Day.

INCORRECT: The bottling co. has a plant on Oak Ave.
CORRECT: The bottling company has a plant on Oak Avenue.

In ordinary writing, abbreviations are not acceptable for the following: names of school courses, and the words *page, chapter,* and *Christmas.* Abbreviations for measurements, like *ft., in., min., hr., oz., qt., mi.,* are also unacceptable.

INCORRECT: The story "A Xmas Memory" begins on pg. 108 of our literature book.
CORRECT: The story "A Christmas Memory" begins on pg. 108 of our literature book.

Exercise A: Correct the errors in abbreviation in these sentences.

1. The secy. of H.E.W. is usually not a medical dr.
2. The Pres. met with the Secy. of Defense at Camp David, Md.
3. The Rev. Amelia Gleason gave a sermon about the true meaning of Xmas.
4. McDonald's Corp. has its headquarters on Twenty-second Ave. in Oakbrook, Ill.
5. Mr. Frank Ransom, Jr., is applying for a govt. grant to start a center for sr. citizens.
6. Benito Juarez, a nineteenth-century pres. of Mexico, is described in Ch. 10.
7. Last Fri., our home ec. class visited Mercy Hosp.
8. I lost two lbs. in forty-eight hours on the diet Dr. Rossi gave me.
9. Cleopatra ruled Egypt in the first cent. B.C.
10. Pres. Roosevelt closed all banks in the U.S. on Mar. 6, 1933.

Exercise B: Writing Write each of the items described below. Use abbreviations correctly only where indicated.

1. Describe yourself. Include your full name, age, height, and weight.
2. Make up a guest list for an important White House dinner. Each guest has a title. You may use abbreviations.
3. Describe this textbook. Include its size, subject matter, number of pages, and number of chapters.
4. Write a party invitation. Include the time, date, and address.
5. Make up an itinerary for an around-the-world trip. Include dates, departure times, and the names of the cities and countries you plan to visit. You may use abbreviations.

REINFORCEMENT EXERCISES
The Correct Form for Writing

A. Understand proper manuscript form. Tell whether the following statements are true or false.

1. Your name, the date, and the name of your class should be placed on the first line of the first page of your paper.
2. Each page, beginning with page one, should be numbered in the top right-hand corner.
3. The title of a paper should appear near the top of the first page, two lines below the last line of the heading.
4. All words in a title should be capitalized.
5. Titles should be placed in quotation marks.
6. All written work should be accompanied by a title page.
7. Use a one inch margin at the top, bottom, and left side of your paper.
8. Hyphens may be used at the end of every line.
9. Double-spacing makes typewritten papers look neat and increases their readability.
10. Paragraphs are usually indented three spaces.

B. Correct errors in manuscript form. Rewrite the following sentences, correcting all errors.

1. The pres. flew to Peking from Washington, D C, a trip of six thousand nine hundred and sixty-five miles.
2. The Yangtze River, in China, is three thousand four hundred and thirty-four miles long.
3. The Pacific Ocean is a little over 36,000 feet deep.
4. 469 million people live on the continent of China.
5. The sun is 1 of 100 billion stars in our galaxy.
6. Ms Beth Henley won the Pulitzer Prize for her play *Crimes of the Heart* in nineteen hundred and eighty-one.
7. The Rev. Thomas McKay started a Xmas fund.
8. Does the Ewing Oil Co. have an office in Houston, Tex?
9. Last Wed. our eng. class read chpt. 12 of *Stories of the Amer. Civil War.*
10. The dr. told me to drink 8 oz. of water with every meal.

MIXED REVIEW

The Correct Form for Writing

The following short composition contains several errors in manuscript form and in the use of numbers and abbreviations. Rewrite the composition correctly.

Patricia Smith
Social Studies
Jan. 11, 1984

○ Mount Rushmore

Gutzon Borglum created his famous masterpiece on the face of mt. Rushmore in the Black Hills of S.D. On it he carved the busts of 4 great Amer. Presidents: Geo. Washington, Thos. Jefferson, Abraham Lincoln, and Theodore Roosevelt.

Borglum began this project in 1927 and cont. until his death 14 years later. The sculpture was completed
○ by his son, Lincoln, and was hailed as the world's largest sculpture, standing 60 ft. high. 1000's of sightseers visit the mt. every yr.

USING PROPER FORM IN WRITING
The Correct Form for Writing

A. Listed below are words and expressions that are frequently abbreviated. Using a dictionary, give the correct abbreviations for each. Be careful to capitalize where necessary.

sergeant	ante meridiem	incorporated
doctor	anno domini	limited
february	united states	senator
environmental protection agency	new jersey	adjective
	junior	assistant

B. According to *The Book of Firsts*, the first roller skates were worn to a costume party in 1760 by a man named Joseph Merlin. Merlin skated into the ballroom playing a violin and crashed into a mirror worth over $1,000. Write this story from the point of view of one of the other guests at the party. Revise and proofread your paper, and then rewrite it. Use your neatest handwriting and observe proper margins. When you have finished, exchange it with another student. See if your classmate can find any errors in form.

C. Imagine that you are living in prehistoric times and that the hunters from your clan have just come back to your cave with a woolly mammoth for you to prepare for dinner. Write a recipe for mammoth dinner, giving special attention to the proper form for numbers. Be sure to include the temperature at which your recipe must be cooked and how many it will serve.

Section 17

Outlining

One very common problem in longer compositions and speeches is weak organization. You may have collected a wealth of interesting information on your subject. Unless your facts, examples, and other information are carefully organized, however, your reader or listener may have difficulty understanding you.

From beginning to end, your ideas should flow smoothly. One point should lead logically to the next, rather than be presented in a random order.

One useful method of organizing your thoughts and facts into a logical order is an **outline**. After you have "brainstormed" your topic and gathered all your information, making an outline will help you sort and organize your ideas. That is why so many experienced writers use outlines to prepare for writing.

Outlining can also be used for several purposes other than in writing. You may use an outline to record important information from a lecture. You can use it to take notes when you do research. You can even use outlining as a study device to help clarify the main points and organization of a chapter.

In this section, you will learn the rules and guidelines for writing an outline. Familiarize yourself with them so that outlining can become a useful and comfortable organizational aid.

Organizing an Outline

To begin an outline, you should have a clear idea of the purpose of your composition. Then determine the main ideas that you want to develop. These main ideas will be the **main points** in your outline.

Next, consider how you can develop or explain each main point. The supporting ideas for these points will become **subpoints** in the outline. Consequently, related ideas will be grouped together.

Finally, decide which scheme to use for ordering the main points. While time sequence works well for some topics, order of importance or spatial order is better for others. The best order is the one that makes your topic clearest and easiest to understand.

When your outline is complete, you will have the skeleton for a composition. Fill in details and build paragraphs around related ideas to create a solid, well-organized composition.

Writing Topic Outlines

A **topic outline** is an informal kind of outline. Topic outlines use words or phrases instead of complete sentences. Topic outlines are effective for organizing compositions.

Study the topic outline on the following page. Notice that it does not use complete sentences. Pay particular attention to the grouping of subpoints under related main ideas.

The Arctic

I. Arctic lands
   A. The true arctic
   B. The subarctic
      1. Is not part of true arctic
      2. Has warmer summers
II. Natural resources
   A. Soil
   B. Minerals
      1. Coal
      2. Radioactive minerals
         a. Thorium
         b. Uranium
      3. Petroleum
   C. Plants
   D. Animals
III. Arctic peoples
   A. Eskimos
   B. Americanoids

Using Outline Form

Outlines use a precise form that does not vary. Here are some rules to follow:

1. Write the title of your composition at the top of the outline. The introduction and the conclusion are usually not considered parts of the outline.

2. Arrange numbers and letters of headings in the following order: first, Roman numerals for main points, then capital letters for subpoints. Next, Arabic numerals are used. Small letters are used for details under these ideas, then numbers in parentheses for details developing the details, and, finally, small letters in parentheses for subdetails. The arrangement on the next page shows clearly which ideas belong together. Note the placement of periods.

I. A.
   B.
      1.
      2.
         a.
         b.
            (1)
            (2)
               (a)
               (b)

II.

   A.
   B.
   (and so on)

3. Indent all headings in the outline. Place letters and numbers of all headings directly underneath the first word of the larger heading above.

4. Do not use a single subheading. A heading should not be broken down if it cannot be divided into at least two points.

5. Use the same kind of word or phrase for all headings of the same rank. If, for example, *A* is a verb, then *B* should be a verb, too.

6. Begin each item in the outline with a capital letter. In a topic outline, do not end headings with periods or other punctuation.

Exercise: Look at the partial outline on the next page. Copy it on your paper, leaving blank spaces as indicated. Then complete the outline by inserting the following headings after the appropriate numbers and letters.

Diet	Famous archaeological finds
Botanists	History courses
Excavating sites	Classification
Provides careers in four fields	Writing

Archaeology

I. How archaeologists gather information
   A. Surveying sites
   B.
      1. Varied methods
      2. Range of tools
   C. Recording and preserving materials

II. How archaeologists interpret finds
   A.
   B. Dating
      1. Absolute chronology
      2. Relative chronology
   C. Evaluation
      1. Can help explain lifestyles
         a.
         b. Work
         c. Social class
      2. Aided by specialists from other fields
         a. Zoologists
         b.

III.
   A. Discovery of Troy, 1870
   B. Discovery of King Tut's tomb, 1922
   C. Discovery of treasure ship off
      coast of England, 1939

IV. Futures in archaeology
   A. Require specific college preparation
      1. Languages
      2.
      3. Anthropology
      4. Biology
      5. Geology
   B.
      1. Museum work
      2. Government service
      3. Teaching
      4.

REINFORCEMENT EXERCISE
Outlining

Complete an outline. Copy the partial outline. Then insert the following headings where they belong in the outline.

Two meals eaten each day Nobles
Brought by missionaries Thor
No windows Clothing
Shipbuilding Religion
 Marriage

Viking Life

I. Ancestry and population
   A. Germanic background
   B. Three social classes
      1.
      2. Freemen
      3. Slaves

II. Economic activities
   A. Farming
   B. Fishing
   C. Trading
   D.
      1. Trading ships
      2. Warships

III. Daily life
   A.
      1. Parents arranged
      2. Several wives
   B. Food
      1.
      2. Food provided by husbands
         a. Wild game
         b. Farm produce
   C.

D. Housing
  1. Stone or wooden walls
  2. Sod or straw roofs
  3.
IV.
  A. Worshipped several gods
    1. Odin
    2.
  B. Christianity
    1.
    2. Ended Norse religion

Outlining

Revise this outline, correcting all errors in outline form.

The First Submarines

I. Description of modern submarine
    1. Can remain submerged for almost unlimited time
    2. Has underwater speeds of above 20 knots
    3. Holds large crews

II. The First Submarine
    A. Built by C.J. Drebbel
    B. In 1620
    C. Had strange design
        1. was rowboat covered with leather
        2. was propelled by twelve oarsmen
        3. had oars that went through flexible leather seals

III. The first combat submarine
    a. built by David Bushnell in 1776
    b. also had unusual design
        1. small, egg-shaped craft
        2. all wood
    c. operated by a man turning a propeller
    d. how it submerged
        1. pumped water in to submerge and pumped water out to surface

IV. Robert Fulton's submarine built in 1800.
    A. Called the Nautilus
    B. Was forerunner of the modern submarine
    C. The Nautilus could remain submerged for six hours.
    D. Pumped in air through a tube that went to the water's surface
    E. Used compressed air in later versions

USING MECHANICS IN WRITING
Outlining

Use the outline below as the basis of a short report on the impact of the horse on early Native American cultures. Add your own introduction and conclusion. Follow all of the steps of the Process of Writing.

The Arrival of the Horse

Purpose: The impact of the horse on early Native American cultures was as strong as that of the automobile on modern society.

I. Arrival of the horse
   A. Brought to America by Spanish conquistadors in 1519
   B. Left behind by these Spaniards and later explorers
   C. Gradually turned wild and formed herds
   D. Spread northward across the Great Plains
   E. Seen all over western America by late 1800's

II. Initial reaction of natives
   A. Heard accounts of "big dogs" used to the south
   B. Were wary of the huge animals
   C. Accepted horses gradually
   D. Learned to train them for many useful tasks

III. Uses of horses by Native American tribes
   A. Pulled heavy loads during tribe migration
   B. Used for transporation
   C. Used in battle
      1. Added speed
      2. Gave psychological advantage over tribes on foot
   D. Used on buffalo hunts
      1. Allowed easier tracking of herds
      2. Provided speed during a chase
      3. Were used as lures
         a. Disguised with a buffalo skin
         b. Lured herds within easy bow-and-arrow range

Sources of Quoted Materials

Cover

Index